AF663540

THE DHARMAŚĀSTRA: AN INTRODUCTORY ANALYSIS

THE DHARMAŚĀSTRA: AN INTRODUCTORY ANALYSIS

BRAJAKISHORE SWAIN

AKSHAYA PRAKASHAN
DELHI

First published: December, 2004
First Reprint : 2019
Second Reprint : 2023

ISBN: 978-81-88643-13-4

Published by Harish Chandra for
AKSHAYA PRAKASHAN
208, M.G. House, 2, Community Centre
Wazirpur Industrial Area, Delhi – 110 052
Tel.: (011) 41610957, Mob. : 9818452269
Email: harish@akshayaprakashan.com
Website: www.akshayaprakashan.com

Printed at D.K. Fine Arts Press (Pvt.) Ltd.
Delhi – 110 052

Contents

Preface

The Dharmaśāstra is one of the celebrated disciplines of Indian Sciences. It occupies a place of prominence next to the Vedas in regards to its authority. As Hinduism is known as a way of life, the Dharmaśāstra, here, is a discipline which determines this way of life. A life full of decency, discipline, serenity, etc. giving a real meaning to human existence is regarded as *dharma*. The Dharmaśāstra is a science to analyze, interpret, determine and finalize the characteristic of *dharma*.

Among traditional disciplines, the Dharmaśāstra comes under Kalpa which comprises Śrauta, Gṛhya, Dharma and Śulba in the form of sūtras. The Śrautasūtras determine the principles of *śrauta* sacrifices whereas the Gṛhyasūtras formulate the rules for domestic rituals. The Śulbasūtras form the norm of Vedic engineering whereas the Dharmaśāstra details out social activities. The way of life, to a very large extent, naturally depends on the Dharmaśāstras. Since man is a social animal and he is bound to live in a society, his activities are required to be society-oriented. As Dharmaśāstras regulate social activities, the way of life of human beings is certainly relied upon the Dharmaśāstras.

Speaking specifically upon the three disciplines, namely the Pūrvamīmāṁsā of Jaimini, the Vaiśeṣikadarśana of Kaṇāda and the Dharmaśāstra of Manu, etc. depict the concept of *dharma*. In the Pūrvamīmāṁsā *dharma* is comprehended as *yajña* or sacrifice, its performer Yajamāna. He offers something in honour of a *devatā* under a particular process to get a particular result. His offering is called sacrifice; because the article, which he dedicates to a *devatā* is definitely to be of his own. After dedication, his estate over that article is extincted and estate of the receiver deity is created. This sort of dedication in Vedic sacrifice is called *dharma* or *yajña* in the Pūrvamīmāṁsā. On the whole it is understood that dedication-oriented sacrifice is the core of *dharma* in the Pūrvamīmāṁsā. Here this sacrifice is materialized through action i.e. *karman*. Therefore, it is said: *karmeti mīmaṁsakāḥ*.

Instead of accepting *karman* as *dharma*, the Vaiśeṣikas categorize *dharma* as *guṇa* (endowment). *Guṇa* is comprehended as property that does not change in any case of human involvement because of its axiomatic nature. Water goes down and fire goes upward. These are treated to be their *dharma* respectively. This *dharma* is nothing, but *guṇa* or property. This does not change in spite of the intensity of time, space and individual. It defers from *karman* because *karman* has beginning and end also. But *guṇa,* in contrast, does not have a beginning or end i.e. *svabhāva* or nature. Nature does not change this nature is called *prakṛti* which is *guṇa*. When this *prakṛti* gets reformed, it becomes *Saṁskṛti*. This *Saṁskṛti* is *saṁskāra*. This *saṁskāra* is a refined or purified action or *karman*. This sort of *karman* is accepted as synonymous of *dharma*.

The Dharmaśāstra, in this place, determines this sort of refined *karman* or *dharma*. It recognizes dedication. It recognizes endowment as *dharma,* but it transforms the way of *dharma* from *prakṛti* to *Saṁskṛti* through *tyāga* or dedication. This *tyāga* is made in a social atmosphere. Its result may come out in this world or in the other—that does not matter. While introducing the Dharmaśāstra this concept of *dharma* is to be held important.

The Dharmaśāstra always declares that *karman* means action, but it is generally used to mean a certain definite connection between what is being done now and what will happen in the future. Things do not happen by accident, by chance in a disorderly way. They happen in regular succession; they follow each other in a regular order through a chain of actions and reactions. This brings the concept of *karmanipāka* in Dharmaśāstra. When *karman* gets the form of sacrifice, it becomes *dharma*. According to the Dharmaśāstra the idea of offering sacrifice is that every one should sacrifice himself to the good of others, and that all sacrifices of other things are meant to teach a man how he ought, at last, to sacrifice himself. This continuous process of self-purification ultimately teaches the dictum of living for society at large. It is the pouring out of life for the benefit of others.

The Dharmaśāstra prescribes a number of ceremonies, or rites, to be performed. The use of those ceremonies, speaking generally is: (1) to help the *jīva* to conquer and purify his sheaths; (2) to bring to his aid superior intelligences, such as the Devas and the Ṛṣis, (3) to improve the atmosphere around him and thereby making it easier for steadiness and contraction of his mind. To this end are used material objects, gestures, postures and sounds, all carefully arranged to bring about the results aimed at. Out of these ceremonies *śrāddha* is the name of the ceremony performed to help one who has put off his visible body in death, by those who remain in this world. The person who has put off his visible body is called a *preta*, and the part of the *śrāddha* performed to help him at this stage is called the *pretakriyā*. The visible body (the *Annamaya-kośa*), is carried to the burning ground so that it may be dissolved into its constituents as quickly as possible; the ashes are gathered together and thrown into running water, preferably into a recognised sacred stream (at Prayāga). When the *annamaya-kośa* is destroyed, the *prāṇa-maya-kośa* rapidly disperses, and this dispersal is quickened by some of the mantras used preferably in the cremation. Burning is by far the best way of destroying a dead body, and the destruction is important both for the departed and for those left behind. So long as it remains undissolved, the *prāṇa-maya-kośa* hangs round it, in consequence of the magnetic attraction between them, and the dead is thus linked to the earth which is bad for him; on the other hand, a slowly decaying body in the ground as in burial, sends out poisonous gases and this is bad for those remaining behind. The *śrāddhas* performed after the burning help in a rearrangement of the materials of the *manomaya-kośa*, partly by the magnetic influences of the objects used, and partly by the vibrations set up by the mantras. After a certain time, the *sapiṇḍikaraṇa* ceremony is performed, which helps the *jīva* to transmigrate from *preta-loka* to *pitṛ-loka*. He is then enrolled among the Pitṛs or the ancestors living in the subtler regions of *Bhuvar-loka*. Seven generations, one in *Bhū-loka* and six in *Bhuvar-loka*, can affect each other. When the *jīva* transmigrates on into *svarga,* he has no further need of the help furnished by *śrāddha*. This is in a nutshell the subject of *śrāddha* depicted in the Dharmaśāstras.

Unlike Vedic sacrifices, the Dharmaśāstra ordains numerous sacrifices of various kinds designating those great sacrifices (*mahāyajñas*) to be offered every day. These are: (1) the sacrifice to Ṛṣis or the Vedas (*brahmayajña*), (2) the sacrifice to Devas, (*deva-yajña*) (3) the sacrifice to Pitṛs (*pitṛ-yajña*), (4) sacrifice to men (*nṛ-yajña*) and (5) sacrifice to *bhūta* (*bhūta-yajña*). Each of these has an exterior form and meaning, and the latter leads the sacrificer on to the full life of sacrifice. The outer sacrifice to the Ṛṣis or the Vedas, is study and teaching. Everyday a man should study some sacred books, and thus gradually acquire the knowledge without which he cannot rightly understand himself, his position and his duties. And he should ever be ready to share this knowledge with those more ignorant than himself. The carefulness and closeness of the thought are more important than the amount read. The inner meaning is that all study should be a sacrifice, learning.

The outer meaning of the sacrifice to the devas is the recognition of all we owe to the kindly ministry and protection of these active intelligences working in nature, and the repayment of it by giving for their service a share of our possession. The inner meaning is the realization of our relations with the super physical worlds, and of the inter-dependence of the worlds. The outer meaning of the sacrifice to the Pitṛs is the offering of water (*tarpaṇa*). The inner meaning is the recognition of the great debt we owe to the past, to the generations who occupied the earth before us. No man is truly human who does not recognize what he owes to the past, his debt to the ancestors. The outer meaning of the sacrifice to men is hospitality. The inner meaning is the duty of serving and helping humanity. As a matter of fact, those who are rich are the stewards of the poor. The outer meaning of the sacrifice to creatures (*bhūtas*) is the putting of a little food on the ground. The inner meaning is the duty of caring for those who are beneath the human and in the lower kingdoms, the recognition of our debt to them for their service to us. Thus the five great daily sacrifices teach—man, his relations, with all round him, his superiors, his equals and his inferiors.

The Dharmaśāstras give in detail about stages of life i.e. *āśrama*. Each stage has its own duties and its own pleasures. It brings evolution in human beings. When the *āśramas* are disregarded his evolution is delayed. The first *āśrama* is meant for the students. The students now also strive for the virtues of industry, obedience, humanity and serviceableness. Youth is the preparation time to life and industrious study to acquire knowledge is absolutely necessary for useful manhood. The student must be chaste in thought and action, a celibate in mind and body. He must guard his thoughts. Of all the *āśramas* the *gṛhasthāśrama* is the most important for it supports all the others. The welfare of the family and of the nation depends on the householders and their happiness and prosperity are in his hands. When the householder sees his son able to bear the full burden of his duties, the time has come for him and his wife to surrender the headship of the home and to retire from active life. A quiet and somewhat secluded life given to study, to self-sacrifice for the good of others, to the counselling of the younger, such should be the third *āśrama* in our modern age. The last stage of life is the life of ascetics. A man passes his last days in meditation and worship, till he enters willingly the life beyond death, to reap the fruits of a well spent earthly life, hereafter to return for further evolution.

The Dharmaśāstras advise to lead a good family life. For this it has given a strong jurisprudential value to the family life. In the family, the grandfather decides the principle and formulates the law of the family. In this connection the family law of the great grandfather is the source of law (precedent). The grandfather collects the ideas from it and determines the case law. At the time of formulation of law, the grandfather adheres to the customs of the family. On the basis of this, he lays down the customary law. In each case he honours the psychology of the family, he frames the enacted law. When necessity arises, he keeps collaboration with others and formulates conventional law. When law is required to be laid down to keep contact with others in society, the grandfather determines specific law for it. This is as good as international law on part of the family. When any ambiguity or discrepancy arises, the grandfather interprets the family law. He gives verdict in case of complaints, that arise in family law. From grandfather to grandson one law continues. This establishes the law of the family. One family generation continues ordinarily for one hundred years.

Apart from these, the Dharmaśāstra covers *rājadharma,* civil and criminal law, pilgrimage, sins and their atonements, rebirth, etc. In this compedium; *Dharmaśāstra: An Introductory Analysis,* for encompassing the Dharmaśāstra in thirty one different dimensions the editor has collected articles by learned scholars from different walks of life. While doing so the editor is optimistic that the readers will refrain themselves from any bias or critical scrutiny since this humble work is nothing more than an introductory to the yet undiscovered storehouse of the vast field of the Dharmaśāstra.

I express my heartfelt gratitude and obeisance to those whose articles are included in it. Knowing fully well that some of them are no more, I once again bowdown, in benediction, my head to the sacred feet of those savants and seers.

I also pronounce my thankfulness to the Akshaya Prakashan of Delhi especially to Mr. Harishchandraji for whose efforts this work sees the outer ray of the Sun. Last but not the least, the editor owes entire responsibility for the mistakes if any in this edition.

Brajakishore Swain

Abbreviation

1.	A.B.	Asiatic Society of Bengal
2.	A.C.	Ancient Courts
3.	Ag. Pu.	*Agnipurāṇa*
4.	Ai. Br.	*Aitareyabrāhmaṇa*
5.	A.I.R.	Ancient Indian Religions
6.	A.M.	Ancient Migration
7.	A.N.	Asian Nativity
8.	Anuśāsanaparvan	*Mahābhārata*: the *Anuśāsanaparvan*
9.	A.P.C.	Asian Privy Council
10.	A.S.	*Arthaśāstra*
11.	A.S.C.	Asian State Council
12.	AV.	*Atharvaveda*
13.	Āp.D.S.	*Āpastamba-Dharmasūtra*
14.	Āp.G.S.	*Āpastamba-Gṛhyasūtra*
15.	Āśv.G.S.	*Āśvalāyana-Gṛhyasūtra*
16.	Āśv. Śr.S.	*Āśvalāyana-Śrautasūtra*
17.	Bdh.D.S.	*Baudhāyana-Dharmasūtra*
18.	Bdh.P.S.	*Baudhāyana-Pitṛsūtra*
19.	Bh.G.	*Bhagavadgītā*
20.	Bh.Pu.	*Bhāgavatapurāṇa*
21.	Bodl.W.	Dr. B. Weber
22.	Bom.	Bombay School of Hindu Law

23.	B.O.R.I.	Bhandarkar Oriental Research Institute, Pune
24.	Bṛh.Up.	*Bṛhadāraṇyaka-Upaniṣad*
25.	C.	Custom
26.	Cal.	Calcutta School of Hindu Law
27.	Cf.	Compare
28.	ch.	Chapter
29.	C.H.I.	Cambridge History of India
30.	Ch.Up.	*Chāndogya-Upaniṣad*
31.	C.S.S.B.	Chowkhamba Sanskrit Series Office, Benares
32.	E.I.H.	East Indian History
33.	E.S.H.	*Encyclopaedic Survey of Hinduism*
34.	E.S.S.	*Encyclopaedia of the Social Sciences*
35.	G.D.S.	*Gautama Dharmasūtra*
36.	G.G.S.	*Gautama Gṛhyasūtra*
37.	Gobh.G.S.	*Gobhila Gṛhyasūtra*
38.	H.D.	*History of Dharmaśastra*
39.	H.G.S.	*Hiraṇyakeśi Gṛhyasūtra*
40.	H.L.I.	*Hindu Law of Inheritance*
41.	H.M.I.	*History of Medieval India*
42.	H.S.	*Hārītasmṛti*
43.	I.A.	Indian Administration
44.	I.C.	Indian Custom
45.	Ind. St.	Indien Studien
46.	I.U.	*Īśopaniṣad*
47.	JAOS	Journal of Asian and Oriental Studies
48.	J.G.S.	*Jaiminīya Gṛhyasūtra*
49.	K.G.S.	*Khādira Gṛhyasūtra*
50.	Karṇaparvan	*Karṇaparvan* of the *Mahābhārata*

51.	K.S.	*Kāmasūtra*
52.	L.R.	Laws and Regulations
53.	L.T.	Legal Texts
54.	Mad.	Madras School of Hindu Law
55.	Man.	*Manusmṛti*
56.	M.I.A.	Modern Indian Administration
57.	M.L.J.	*Mitākṣarā Law Journal*
58.	MS	Manuscript
59.	Mu. Up.	*Muṇḍaka Upaniṣad*
60.	Nag.	Nagpur School of Hindu Law
61.	Nā.D.	*Nārada Dharmaśāstra*
62.	N.S.	*Nirṇayasindhu*
63.	OST	*Original Sanskrit Texts*
64.	p.	page
65.	pp	page to page
66.	Pār. Mādh.	*Pāraskara Gṛhyasūtras are ascribed to Mādhyandina Saṁhitā*
67.	P.C.	Privy Council
68.	P.G.S.	*Pāraskara Gṛhyasūtra*
69.	Rel.	*Religions*
70.	ṚV	*Ṛgveda*
71.	Śat. Br.	*Śatapatha Brāhmaṇa*
72.	Śāṅ. G.S.	*Śāṅkhāyana Gṛhyasūtra*
73.	Śāntiparvan	*Śantiparvan* of the *Mahābhārata*
74.	S.B.E.	*Ṣacred Books of the East*
75.	S.C.	Supreme Court
76.	S.C.R.	Supreme Court Rule
77.	Sec.	Section
78.	SV.	*Sāmaveda*
79.	Śvet. Up.	*Śvetāśvatara Upaniṣad*

80.	Tai. Ār.	*Taittirīya Āraṇyaka*
81.	Tai. Br.	*Taittirīya Brāhmaṇa*
82.	Tai. S.	*Taittirīya Saṁhitā*
83.	Tai. Up.	*Taittirīya Upaniṣad*
84.	T.L.L.	Tagore Law Lectures
85.	Vaikh. Sr. S.	*Vaikhānasa Śrautasūtra*
86.	Vā.S.	*Vājasaneyī Saṁhitā*
87.	V.D.S.	*Vaiṣṇava Dharmasūtra*
88.	V.M.S.	*Vāmana Mahāsaṁhitā*
89.	Vanaparvan	*Vanaparvan* of the *Mahābhārata*
90.	Vol.	Volume
91.	Vṣ.D.S.	*Viṣṇu-dharmottara - Saṁhitā*
92.	Vṣṭ.D.	*Vasiṣṭha Dharmaśāstra*
93.	V.S.	*Visṇusmṛti*
94.	Yāj.	*Yājñavalkyasmṛti*
95.	Y.S.	*Yogasūtra*
96.	YV	*Yajurveda*

Evolution of Dharmaśāstra

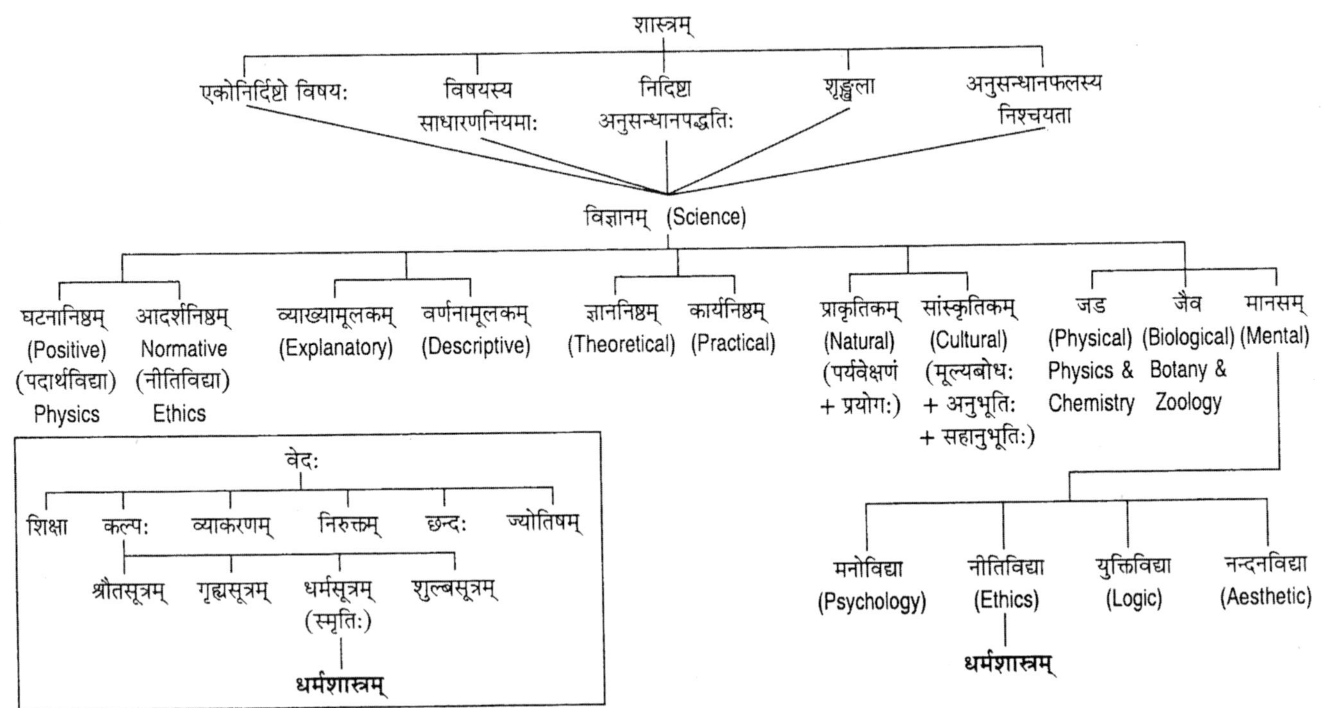

The Dharmaśāstra: An Introductory Analysis

For the first time we find mention of the eighteen kinds of sciences (*Śāstras*) in the *Viṣṇupurāṇa* (3.6.28) and the *Yājñavalkyasmṛti* (1.3). Of these two, the *Viṣṇupurāṇa* designates those sciences as *vidyā* whereas Yājñavalkya terms those as *vidyāsthāna* or *dharmasthāna*. Both the sources include Dharmaśāstra in the list of the eighteen sciences . It is an accepted view that all the orthodox sciences have their own sources in the Vedas. In this regard, the Vedas are treated as an agent which has six limbs. These limbs are termed as *ṣaḍaṅgas*. They are: Śikṣā, Kalpa, Vyākaraṇa, Nirukta, Chandas and Jyotiṣa. Of these six, Kalpa is viewed as the hands of the Vedapuruṣa. It has four divisions: *Śrauta, Gṛhya, Dharma* and *Śulba*. All are written in aphorisms being termed as Śrautasūtra, Gṛhyasūtra, Dharmasūtra and Śulbasūtra. The Śrautasūtras deal with sacrificial manuals whereas Gṛhyasūtras describe domestic rituals. The technological materials are put in the Śulbasūtras. The Dharmasūtras are different from those three literature. They deal with social codes. Having been originated from the Vedas, the Dharmasūtras are compiled both in aphorisms and metres. The metrical texts are termed as Smṛtis. By this way Dharmaśāstras comprise the Dharmasūtra and the Smṛti. The important contents of the Dharmaśāstras are: the sources of Dharma, the Vedas, the Smṛtis and time-honoured practices of the great people; the duties of the four *varṇas* and *āśramas*;

various moral *saṁskāras* of man, like *upanayana* and marriage according to the different castes, the avocation of four *varṇas* in life; the duties and responsibilities of the King, rules for taxation, ownership, guardianship, witnesses, money-lending, payment of debts and different kinds of *śrāddhas*, rules about food, duties of women and their property, *niyoga* (levirate) and its conditions; sins and their expiations and penances along with conditions. The Smṛtis deal with those topics in a more analytical and systematized form under three main heads: *ācāra* (rites), *vyavahāra* (dealings) and *prāyaścitta* (expiation).

Beginning of the Dharmaśāstra

When the Dharmaśāstras were composed is a pertinent question to be answered. But it is not possible to give a definite answer to this question. The *Nirukta* (3. 4-5) shows that long before Yāska heated controversies had raged on various questions of inheritance, such as the exclusion of daughters by sons and the rights of the appointed daughter: *putrikā*. The *Nirukta* was composed by Yāska during 600-300 B.C. Therefore, it is ascertained that the composition of the Dharmaśāstra works was started prior to this period. However, the chronology of the Dharmasūtras and the Smṛtis is still an unsettled question. It is held by a few western scholars that the Dharmaśātras are earlier than the sources of the metrical Smṛtis. But since Manu and his extant Smṛti and a few others are found cited by many Dharmasūtras, it is very difficult to maintain that all the metrical Smṛtis are evolved from the Dharmasūtras. On the other hand, it can be asserted that both kinds of texts in the form of Sūtras and verses, which were equally popular during that period have developed side by side, with the result that many Dharmasūtra texts have also incorporated the verses in *anuṣṭubh* and sometimes in other metres also.

Mention may be made here that there are certain points which distinguish the Dharmasūtras from the Smṛtis:

(a) Many Dharmasūtras are either parts of the Kalpa

belonging to each *sūtracaraṇa* or are intimately connected with the Gṛhyasūtras.

(b) The Dharmasūtras sometimes are not unique in showing their Vedic quotations for the texts of the corresponding Veda to which they belong or in the *caraṇas* of which they are studied.

(c) The authors of the older Dharmasūtras do not claim to be the inspired seers or super human beings, while the other Smṛtis such as those of Manu and Yājñavalkya are ascribed to gods like Brahmā.

(d) The Dharmasūtras are in prose or in mixed prose and verse; while the other Smṛtis are in verse.

(e) The language of Dharmasūtras is generally more archaic than that of the other Smṛtis.

(f) The Dharmasūtras do not proceed upon any orderly arrangement of topics while the other Smṛtis arrange their contents and treat of the subjects under three principal heads viz. *ācāra, vyavahāra* and *prāyaścitta*.

(g) Most of the Dharmasūtras are older than most of the other Smṛtis. Importance is given to both the *Gautamadharmasūtra* and the *Manusmṛti* as Dharmasūtra and Smṛti respectively. Those two are the oldest of all in those two lines.

In the Kalpa tradition the Dharmasūtras, as a rule, follow the Gṛhyasūtras. At present only four Gṛhyasūtras namely the *Baudhāyanagṛhyasūtra*, the *Āpastambagṛhyasūtra*, the *Hiraṇyakeśigṛhyasūtra* and the *Vaikhānasagṛhyasūtra* are found to be followed by the Dharmasūtras of their respective schools. The other Gṛhyasūtras have no Dharmasūtras to follow them. It is a moot point whether each Gṛhyasūtra possessed Dharmasūtras belonging to the same school or the Dharmasūtras were composed in a few schools of Kalpas. It is, however, undeniable fact that in distinction from the Gṛhyasūtras the Dharmasūtras cover a wider range of subjects which are by no means confined to the school of the Sūtras itself. On the otherhand, the Dharmasūtras lay down rules and regulations for the guidance of social as well as spiritual life of the community in its wider perspective. They deal with the rights and duties of different classes of society and prescribe the duties which an individual should discharge during different periods of his life. Matters relating to civil and criminal laws have also been dwelt upon in the Dharmasūtras. A few of the subjects, such as the duties of a student and those of *snātaka*, which have already been touched upon in the Gṛhyasūtras, are treated in detail by the Dharmasūtras. The Gṛhyasūtras deal with the rites and customs which are concerned with the domestic life of an Ārya, whereas the Dharmasūtras devote more attention to the social life of an Ārya. The essential difference, therefore, between the Gṛhyasūtras and the Dharmasūtras lies in the fact that the outlook of the Gṛhyasūtras is mainly limited to the customs and conventions of their respective schools, whereas the Dharmasūtras take a broader view of the whole society comprising various schools and communities.

The Dharmasūtras

The Gautamadharmasūtra

The *Gautamadharmasūtra* is believed to be the earliest among the Dharmasūtras available. Since it is specially studied by the *chandogas*, it is conjectured that it belongs to the Sāmaveda. It has twenty-eight chapters and deals with almost every topic exhaustively. Its treatment of marriage of eight kinds and of subcastes by *anuloma* and *pratiloma* marriage in which the wife is respectively of superior or inferior caste in Chap. IV is noteworthy. It allows *niyoga* under certain conditions as stated in Chap. XVIII. Like Manu, Gautama recognises twelve sons in Chap. XXVIII. Baudhāyana, Āpastamba, Vasiṣṭha and Yājñavalkya presuppose Manu. His earliest limit is decided by his Sūtras in Chap. XXVI, which is based on the *Sāmavidhāna Brāhmaṇa* and by the *Sūtra II. 28*; which is probably a reminiscence of the *Nirukta, II. 3*. Hence, this Sūtra is approximately placed between 600 and 300 B.C.

Ācārya Maskarin was the first author who has commented upon the *Gautamadharmasūtra* in a period between A.D. 900-1100. Next to him is Haradatta who wrote the *Mitākṣarā*. He was a grammarian. Most probably he has borrowed the ideas from the *Bhāṣya* of Bhartṛyajña. According to Dr. Kane it is believed that both Asahāya and Bhartṛyajña have written separate *Bhāṣyas* in different times. In the year 1989 Pandit Kulamani Mishra has written a Vṛtti named *Sūkṣmā*. It was published in 1991.

The Āpastambadharmasūtra

The *Āpastambadharmaśūtra* belongs to the Taittirīya recension of the Black Yajurveda. It forms the supplementary section of the *Āpastaṁbaśrautaśūtra* and the *Gṛhyasūtra*. It is a fulfledged Kalpa comprising Śrautasūtra, Gṛhyasūtra, Śulbasūtra and Dharmasūtra. The age of Āpastamba is settled within only approximate limits. It is later than the *Gautamadharmasūtra* and the *Baudhāyanadharmasūtra* and before A.D. 400. It is an authoritative Smṛti work acording to Śabarasvāmin. Āpastamba is enumerated by Yājñavalkya (1.5) as a writer on *dharma*. Haradatta has written a commentary called *Ujjvalā* upon it. This has been edited several times. Professor G. Buhler has translated it with an introduction which has been included in the *Sacred Books of the East*, Vol. II. This Dharmasūtra is written in a more concise and compact style than that of Baudhāyana and has more archaic and non-Pāṇinian forms than any other extant Dharmasūtra. Each of the two *praśnas* of the *Āpastambadharmasūtra* is divided into eleven *paṭalas*, there being 32 and 29 *kaṇḍikās* in the two *paṭalas* respectively. This Dharmasūtra stands in a peculiar relation to the Pūrvamīmāṁsā. It is the only extant Dharmasūtra that contains many of the technical terms and doctrines of the Mīmāṁsā.

The Baudhāyanadharmasūtra

The *Baudhāyanadharmasūtra* belongs to the Black Yajurveda. This Dharmasūtra which now comprises four *praśnas*, is regarded as part of the *Baudhāyanakalpa* ascribed to Baudhāyana. The spirit, style and language of the fourth *praśna* distinguish it from the preceding three *praśnas*. The fourth *praśna* mainly consists of verses, and some of its rules are incongruous wih those contained in the preceding *praśnas*. the *Baudhāyanadharmasūtra* is considered to be the supplementary portion of the *Baudhāyanaśrauta* and *Gṛhyasūtras*. The author of the *Baudhāyanagṛhya* and *Dharmasūtra* is known as Baudhāyana and, as such, might be a descent of this Kaṇva Baudhāyana. Govindasvāmin is known to be only commentator of this *Dharmasūtra*. He explains *Baudhāyana* in it (I.3.13) as *Kaṇvāyana*. The important chapter of the *Baudhāyanadhamasūtra* is the *Tarpaṇa* (II.5.21). In the *Tarpaṇa*, Baudhāyana mentions several appellations of Gaṇeśa, viz. Viṣṇu, Vināyaka, Sthūla, Varada, Hastimukha, Vakratuṇḍa, Ekadanta, Lambodara, etc. In the *Tarpaṇa* (II. 5.23) we have the seven planets mentioned in the order of the days of the week and also Rāhu and Ketu. Dr. Kane places the *Baudhāyanadharmasūtra* between 600 B.C. to 300 B.C. English translation of it is included in the *Sacred Books of the East*, Vol. XIV.

The Hiraṇyakeśidharmasūtra

The Hiraṇyakeśidharmasūtra (HKD) belongs to Taittirīya recension of the *Yajurveda*. It forms the 26th and 27th *Praśnas* of the *Hiraṇyakeśikalpa*. However, it is an independent work. It has been written long before A.D. 200-400. Its chapters are named as *Praśnas*. The number of *paṭalas* in the first and second *Praśna* of HKD is 31 and 20 respectively. As a matter of fact, HKD forms the 26th and 27th *Praśnas* of the *Hiraṇyakeśikalpasūtra* which has no independent existence. The contents of it are practically the same as those of the *Āpastambadharmasūtra*. It forms a *sūtracaraṇa* of the Khāṇḍikeya section of Taittirīya school.

The Vasiṣṭhadharmasūtra

The Vasiṣṭhadharmasūtra (VDS) belongs to the Ṛgveda. It has

32 chapters. Vasiṣṭha allows *niyoga* (levirate) and the remarriage of child-widows. He mentions only six forms of marriage: *brāhma, daiva, ārṣa, gāndharva, kṣātra* and *mānuṣa*. In many places his views are different from those of Gautama, Baudhāyana, etc. The *Vidvanmodinī* is known to be the oldest commentary of the VDS. The relation between the VDS and the *Manusmṛti* is most important. The VDS expressly mentions the quotations as *mānavaṁ* or *mānavaṁ ślokaṁ udāharanti*. It is assigned to a period between 300 B. C. and 100 B.C. English translation of VDS is included in *Sacred Books of the East*, Vol. XIV.

The Viṣṇudharmasūtra

The Viṣṇudharmasūtra (VIṢ. D.S.) belongs to the Kaṭha school of the Yajurveda. Nandapaṇḍita Vināyakadharmādhikāri has written a commentary named *Keśavavaijayantī* upon it. VIṢ. D.S. contains one hundred chapters. Though the number of chapters is so large, the Sūtra is not very extensive. The first chapter and last two chapters are entirely in verse. The remaining chapters are in mixed prose and verse. This work has a few chapters on *rājadharma* and punishment which are comparatively old and stand on a level with the Sūtras of Gautama and Āpastamba. It allows a Brāhmaṇa to marry from the four castes and does not envisage *niyoga* as Manu and others do. It advocates specially the worship of Vāsudeva. Indication of *suttee* is found in it. The date of its composition is fixed between 300 B.C. and 100 B.C. Dr. Julios Jolly's English translation of it is included in the *Sacred Books of the East*, Vol. XXXIII.

The Vaikhānasadharmasūtra

The *Vaikhānasadharmasūtra* by Vaikhānasa is an authority on the duties during *vānaprasthas*. Manu, Gautama, Baudhāyana and Vasiṣṭha mention Vaikhānasa. It has four *Praśnas*. It gives four kinds of Brahamacārins, four kinds of householders, *vārtā-vṛtti, śālīna, yāyāvara* and *ghoracārika*, two kinds of *vānaprasthas*; *sāpātrika* and *apātrika* with their further sub-divisions and four kinds of Sannyāsinṣ. From its style it appears to be a later production by a devotee of Nārāyaṇa. Historians speak of a *Vaikhānasagṛhyasūtra* in seven *Praśnas.*

The Auśanasadharmasūtra

The *Auśanasadharmasūtra* in seven chapters deals mainly with the duties of the four castes. It is both in prose and verse, some of the verses being found in the *Manusmṛti*. It refers to Vasiṣṭha, Hārīta, Śaunaka and Gautama. From the later *Nibandha* works like the *Smṛticandrikā* and Haradatta's commentary on the *Gautamadharmasūtra*, the *Auśanasa-dharmasūtra* is supposed to have dealt with all topics: *ācāra, vyavahāra* and *prāyaścitta*. Kauṭilya quotes it several times. He speaks of the Auśanasa method of partition in allowing one tenth as an additional share to the eldest son. The *Mahābhārata* also refers to a work on politics by Uśanas. Later works like the *Nītiprakāśikā, Mudrārākṣasa* and the commentaries on the Smṛtis of Manu and Yājñavalkya mention the Auśanasa system of politics, which is yet to be unearthed.

The Dharmasūtra of Hārīta

Baudhāyana, Āpastaṁba and Vasiṣṭha quote Hārīta as an authority. It is related to the *Maitrāyaṇīyasaṁhitā*. It mentions the Kaśmīrian word *Kaphella*. It has twofold classification of the Sūtra and its explanation. Quotations in commentaries and digests show that Hārīta dealt exhaustively with the same topics that are found in other Dharmaśāstras. Kumārila mentions Hārīta as Dharmaśāstrakāra but does not assign him to any particular *caraṇa* as he does to Āpastaṁba and others. In notable doctrines Hārīta mentions worship of Gaṇeśa. Hārīta's verses of *vyavahāra* quoted in the *Nibabdhas* are later than the Sūtra quoted by Aparārka, the *Kalpataru-brahmacāri-kāṇḍa* and the *Smṛticandrikā*. The works of *Laghu Hārīta* and *Vṛddha Hārīta-smṛtis* are also found which are later than the work of Yājñavalkya, Nārada and Kātyāyana.

The Dharmasūtra of Śaṅkhalikhita

From the *Tantravārtika* it appears that Dharmasūtra of Śaṅkhalikhita was studied by the Vājasaneyins. The *Mahābhārata* (*Śāntiparvan*.23) contains the story of brothers Śaṅkha and Likhita. The Pali story in the *Digghanikāya* seems to be based on the story in the *Mahābhārata*. Various compilations ascribed to Śaṅkha alone or Likhita alone or to both are made. The verse *Śaṅkhasmṛti* is stricter than the prose of Śaṅkhalikhita which is used in the commentaries. It speaks of twelve secondary sons, allows *niyoga*, speaks of several ordeals and defines the *Āryāvarta* as between Sindhu Sauvīra and Kāṁpilya. The probable age of the *Śaṁkhalikhitadharmasūtra* is fixed between 300 B.C.- A.D.100.

Besides the writers of Dharmasūtras mentioned above, there were many more, such as Atri, Kaṇva, Kaśyapa, Devala, Paiṭhīnasi, Gārgya, Cyavana, Jātukarṇya, Bharadvāja, Śātātapa, and Sumantu, whose works dealt with all topics of *dharma*.

The Dharmaśāstras

The term Dharmaśāstra is generally applicable to both the Dharmasūtras and the metrical codes, otherwise known as the Smṛtis. The term *smṛti* indicates that these codes are authorities on the basis of *śruti*, which is considered a revelation: *pratykṣa* from which *smṛti* (remembrance) arose.

Side by side with the comparatively late Dharmasūtras, metrical Dharmaśāstras of varied lengths came to be composed with the growing demand of society for new provisions in matters of *dharma*, religious and secular. Out of these works, which were very numerous, only those of Manu and Yājñavalkya, and a few others deserve special notice here.

The Smṛtis

The Manusmṛti

Manu is mentioned as the father of mankind in the *Ṛgveda*

and in the other Vedas. Manu is indicated in the *Śatapathabrāhmaṇa*. He is quoted in the *Nirukta* and also quoted as law-giver in *Gautama*, *Āpastaṁba* and the *Mahābhārata*. In introduction to the *Nāradasmṛti*, the *Manusmṛti* is narrated. Here four versions of Svāyaṁbhuva Sāstra according to the *Bhaviṣyapurāṇa* are also mentioned. It is almost impossible to say who composed the extant *Manusmṛti*. The *Mānavagṛhya* differs from the *Manusmṛti* in several particulars.The *Vināyakaśānti* of *Mānavagṛhya* and tests for selecting a bride are not contained in our Manu. The *Mahābhārata* distinguishes between Svāyaṁbhuva Manu and Prācetasa Manu, former promulgating the Dharmaśāstra. These two works are combined in the present Manu. Extant Manu has 12 chapters and 2694 verses. The author of the *Manusmṛti* is not the first legislator. He is recognized as an ancient writer on the Dharmaśāstra in the Dharmasūtras. They mention number and names of the Manus. Confusion is caused by the ancient texts referring to Svāyaṁbhuva Manu, Prācetasa Manu and Manu. Views of Svāyaṁbhuva are mentioned in the *Manusmṛti* VI.54, VIII.124, IX.158. The Manu Prajāpati is mentioned in I.34-36, X.78, XII.123. Among ten Prajāpatis primeval Manu is mentioned. The *Manusmṛti* says about the creation of the world by Paramātman. The fact that the *Manusmṛti* mentions human authors like Atri, Bhṛgu, etc. and refers to *dasyus* who speak *mleccha* and *Ārya* languages, etc. indicates that the extant *Manusmṛti* is not older than 200 B.C. Medhātithi is the first extant commentator on the *Manusmṛti*. Viśvarūpa quotes 200 verses from the *Manusmṛti*. Śaṁkara, Kumārila and Śabara refer to the *Manu*. Bṛhaspati had the present text of Manu before him. Aśvaghoṣa in his *Vajrasūcī* quotes several verses from the *Mānavadharma* some of which are found in our *Manusmṛti*. The *Rāmāyaṇa* (*Kiṣkindhā* 18.30-32) contains the same ideology that we see in the *Manusmṛti* VIII. 318 and 316. Manu had attained present form long before 2nd century A.D. There are earlier and later strata in the *Manusmṛti*. Contradictory statements as to Brāhmaṇa marrying a Śūdra woman, about appropriate forms of marriage, about *niyoga*, about flesh-eating, etc. are found in it. The *Manusmṛti* has not suffered several recasts. Quotations cited as Vṛddha Manu and Bṛhan Manu are later than the *Manusmṛti*. Extant Manu is older than Yājñavalkya. Manu mentions Yavanas, Kambojas, Śakas, Pahlavas and Chinese. Extant *Manusmṛti* was composed between century 2nd B.C. and 2nd century A.D. Relation of the *Mahābhārata* and Manu is noteworthy. There was a mass of floating verses ascribed to mythical Manu on which both *Manusmṛti* and the *Mahābhārata* drew attention. Manu mentions stories and names that occur in the *Mahābhārata*, but these names go into Vedic antiquities. Manu never names the *Mahābhārata*, while the latter often refers to *rājadharmas* or *śāstra* of Manu or to what Manu said. The *Anuśāsanaparvan* and *Śāntiparvan* knew a *Manusmṛti*, but earlier books, whenever they speak of Manu, refer to floating mass of popular verses. Long before 4th century B.C. there was a Dharmaśāstra in verse attributed to Svāyaṁbhuva Manu. There was another work on *rājadharma* attributed to Prācetasa Manu, that probably was one work between 200 B.C. and A.D.200. The *Manusmṛti* was a recast. Extant *Mahābhārata* was later than extant *Manusmṛti*. Vṛddha-Manu, if a separate work, must thave been composed before the 7th century A.D. Influence of Manu has been spread to Cambodia and other countries beyond India. Manu has several commentators like Medhātithi, Govindarāja, Kullūka, Nārāyaṇa, Rāghavananda, Nandana and Rāmacandra. Asahāya has commented on the *Manusmṛti*. Udayakara was another commentator and so was Dharaṇīdhara. Nārāyaṇa flourished between A.D.1100-1300. Rāghavananda was later than A.D.1400.

Contents of the Manusmṛti

It would be useful first to have an idea of the range of subjects dealt with by Manu. The opening chapter sets forth the origin of the world, creation on beings, the origin of the text as Manu taught it through Bhṛgu, the epochs of time: *yugas* and the differences in *dharmas* according to them, the four classes of men, and the differences in their respective *dharmas*. It gives also a list of the topics to be subsequently dealt with in the work.

The second chapter, with which, the main subject matter begins, speaks of the four sources and grounds or proofs of *dharma*, the person for whom this *dharma* holds good, and the area where it prevails. After dealing with these general questions, the text proceeds to describe the *dharma* as applicable to each of the four castes: Brāhmaṇa, Kṣatriya, Vaiśya and Śūdra. Of these, the first three, the twice-born: *dvijas,* are considered first; and the sacraments: *saṁskāras* are described for them in relation to the four stages of life: the *āśramas*. These are dealt with primarily with reference to the Brāhmaṇa. This chapter takes us through the *saṁskāras* beginning with birth and going up to study in the establishment of the teacher, that is up to the end of the first stage called *brahmacarya* (studentship).

In chapter III, the householder's life, which is the second stage, is taken up. Marriage and its eight different forms, married life, daily and periodical observances of a householder, the vital character and the important social role of the householder, his five daily *yajñas* or sacrifices, (viz. study and teaching of scripture, propitiation of the manes, adoration of the gods by oblations in the fire, reception of guests, gratification of other living beings and the periodic *śrāddhas* are described.

Chapter IV continues the description of the householder's life with many details, such as some are related to *dharmas* already mentioned and some are enjoining further *dharmas*, other relating to the ways of earning one's livelihood, and yet others relating to a number of personal habits and details of daily routine and principles of character and conduct.

Chapter V opens with the subject of proper food; two other topics dealt with here are the death together with obsequies and pollution and purificatory ceremonies. The last section of this chapter speaks of women (wives and widows) and their special *dharmas*.

Chapter VI is devoted to a description of the two further stages of man, the *vānaprastha* and *saṅnyāsa*, denoting life of retirement in forests and complete renunciation respectively, both having spiritual realization as their purpose. The pursuit of the spiritual aim and resignation by one who continues to be in the household life is also dealt with at the end of the chapter.

Chapters VII and VIII together form a section about rulers and their duties: *rājadharma*, which include not only their qualities and equipments, but also the art of statecraft in peace and war. Ministers and counsel, diplomacy, messengers, army, fort, wars, conquest, treatment of the conquered, administration of villages, communities, merchants, collection of revenue, punishment and clearance of anti-social elements: these are spoken of in chapter VII.

Chapter VIII deals with administration of justice and describes legal procedure in respect of the eighteen titles of civil and criminal disputes, judges, evidence, offences and punishments.

Chapter IX states the details about women, particularly from the standpoint of law, their *dharmas*, duties, expected of and towards them, their importance regarding progeny and the family, property, inheritance and partition which arise in the wake of the family. The latter part of the chapter speaks of other matters coming under the administration of justice, like debts, gambling, contracts between the employer and the employed and theft. After touching upon some of the other *rājadharmas* left over, the chapter concludes with a brief description of the *dharmas* of the Vaiśyas and the Śūdras.

In chapter X the people outside the pale of this system of *dharma* and those born by promiscuous mingling of the four classes and a system by which they could be fitted into the scheme are set forth. In the case of the four classes and their ordained duties, confusion may occur owing to extraordinary developments of private or public nature; *dharmas* permissible under such emergencies: *āpaddharmas* are, therefore, dealt with.

The main subject of chapter XI is different kinds of sins, major and minor and their expiations: the *prāyaścittas*.

The last chapter XII falls into two sections: The former section speaks of the theory of *karman*, the fruits and kinds of birth, high and low, which result from different acts, good and bad and through which the soul has to pass. The latter speaks of those *dharmas* which help of spiritual goal — the seeking of self-knowledge: the *ātmajñāna* and the attainment of the everlasting good: the *niḥśreyasa*. Incidentally, the matter of doubts on questions of *dharma* and the constitution of *pariṣad* (assemblies of the learned) for deciding such questions is also dealt with in the latter section of the last chapter.

Atri

Atri is named in the *Manusmṛti* (VII.16). The *Ātreyadharmasūtra* is found in nine *adhyayās*. The form of *Atridharmasūtra* is very systematic. Several works are styled as the *Atrismṛti*. Summary of *the Atrisaṁhitā* was printed by Jīvānanda. Atri is quoted as an authority on adoption. The *Laghu* and *Vṛddhātreyasmṛti* are also found. The *Mahābhārata* (*Anuśāsanaparvan* 65.1) quotes a verse of Atri. Aparārka quotes about a hundred verse of Atri on various topics. The *Ātreyasmṛti* was edited by K.V. R. Aiyangar.

Bṛhaspati

Bṛhaspati as an ancient teacher of the Arthaśāstra is mentioned in Kauṭilya. The *Mahābhārata* (*Śāntiparvan*. 59.80-85) credits him with compression of vast work of Brahmā on *trivarga* and mentions several of his views. The *Kāmasūtra* speaks of Bṛhaspati as a writer on *artha*; peculiar views of Bṛhaspati according to Kauṭilya are also mentioned. Bṛhaspati also wrote a prose work on *vyavahāra* and *prāyaścitta*. Probably the authors of the two works may be different. Seven hundred verses on *vyavahāra* ascribed to Bṛhaspati are quoted in the *Mitākṣarā*. This is an independent work composed between A.D. 300-500. Smaller compilations in verse ascribed to Bṛhaspati are also made. The *Brāhcspatya Arthaśāstra* edited by Dr. Thomas is a later work.

Bharadvāja

A *Śrautasūtra* and *a Gṛhya* of Bharadvāja exist at present. Viśvarūpa's work establishes existence of a Sūtra work on *dharma* of Bharadvāja. There was a Smṛti in verse also attributed to Bharadvāja. Kauṭilya shows that Bharadvāja was an ancient author on Politics. Some views of Bharadvāja are found in the *Mahābhārata*. He may be the sage of the sixth Maṇḍala of the *Ṛgveda*. He is mentioned by Pāṇini as a predecessor. The *Mahābhāṣya* mentions Bhāradvajīyas, a school of grammarians. Kauṭilya probably lumps Bharadvāja, Vyāsa and Manu and refers to them collectively as *ācāryāḥ*. Verses on *vyavahāra* attributed to Bharadvāja are found. This may probably be different from the work on politics.

Śātātapa

A Sūtra work of Śātātapa on *dharma* dealing with *prāyaścitta, śrāddha* and *ācāra* must have existed. Verses of Śātātapa are quoted in the *Mitākṣarā* work. Several verse compilations ascribed to Śātātapa, the *Vṛddha Śātātapa* and *Bṛhat Śātātapa* are also made.

Sumantu

A Sūtra work on *ācāra* and *prāyaścitta* is ascribed to Sumantu. Paiṭhīnasi includes Sumantu among thirty-six expounders of the Dharmaśāstra. Sumantu is quoted by Viśvarūpa and Aparārka. It is also quoted in the *Kalpataru*. Yājñavalkya and Parāśara do not enumerate Sumantu among expounders of *dharma*. Sumantu is mentioned in the *Mahābhārata* and the *Bhāgavata*. Verses from Sumantu on *dharma* are cited by Aparārka. It characteristically differs from the other Dharmaśāstra works with its distinct identity. There are numerous verses on *vyavahāra* quoted from Sumantu in the *Sarasvatīvilāsa*. Professor T. R. Chintamani has reconstructed the ideas of Sumantu on the basis of the *Sarasvatīvilāsa*, with a view to emphasizing the *vyavahāra* concept.

The Yājñavalkyasmṛti

Yājñavalkya as a most illustrious name among the Vedic sages is noteworthy. Stories about strained relations between Vaiśampāyana and Yājñavalkya are mentioned. Yājñavalkya and Janaka are referred in the *Śatapathabrāhmaṇa*. Yājñavalkya is specifically named as a great philosopher in the *Bṛhadāraṇyaka*. The *Yājñavalkyasmṛti* claims that the *Āraṇyaka* and the *Yogaśāstra* were composed by the author of the Smṛti. Slight variation in the number of verses is found in the *Yājñavalkyasmṛti* according to Viśvarūpa and Aparārka. Arrangement of different verses in Viśvarūpa's, *Bālakrīdā* and the *Mitākṣarā*, particularly in the *Prayaścittakāṇḍa*, is remarkable. Readings of the two commentators are also different. The *Agnipurāṇa* affords excellent check for consideration of text of Yājñavalkya.While comparing the readings of the *Agnipurāṇa* with those of Viśvarūpa and the *Mitākṣarā* show that the *Agnipurāṇa* represents a text midway between Viśvarūpa's work and that of the *Mitākṣarā*. So the *Agnipurāṇa* represents a text of Yājñavalkya current about A.D. 900. Total number of verses on *vyavahāra* in the *Agnipurāṇa* is 315, out of which the first thirty-one are not taken from the *Yājñavalkyasmṛti*. Almost all of these thirty-one are taken from the *Nāradasmṛti*. The *Garuḍapurāṇa* (ch. 93) expresses that the *dharma* promulgated by Yājñavalkya was imparted therein. It (ch. 93-106) contains the Dharmaśāstra material taken from *ācāra* and *prāyaścitta* sections of Yājñavalkya. It also deals with *ācāra* and (ch. 93-106) *prāyaścitta*. The *Garuḍapurāṇa* omits *rājadharma* section of Yājñavalkya. Only a few verses of the Yājñavalkyasmṛti are repeated word for word, while a summary only is given of several verses. Comparison of the text of the *Garuḍapurāṇa* with Viśvarūpa's text and that of the *Mitākṣarā* is required. Comparison of the *Yājñavalkyasmṛti* with the *Manusmṛti* indicates a close agreement in phraseology between the two. Yājñavalkya usually tries to compress Manu's dicta. Yājñavalkya adds the *Vināyakaśānti* and *Grahaśānti* and ordeals, while Manu omits first two and cursorily refers to two ordeals. Yājñavalkya is silent on the origin of world which we have in Manu. The style of Yājñavalkya, contents of Smṛti literature known of the *Yājñavalkyasmṛti* and nineteen authors on *dharma* are historically developed in the *Yājñavalkyasmṛti*. The *Yoga-yājñavalkya* is different. It is a small work on Yoga and has little to do with the Dharmaśāstra. There is close agreement between *VIṢ. D.S.* and Yājñavalkya and between Kauṭilya and Yājñavalkya, Manu and Yājñavalkya and difference on several points. Yājñavalkya represents a more advanced state of thought than Manu. Manu allows Brāhmaṇa to marry Śudra girl, but Yājñavalkya does not. But Manu condemns *niyoga* but Yājñavalkya does not. Same case is with gambling also. Yājñavalkya takes the *Vināyakaśānti* from the *Mānavagṛhya*. The *Yājñavalkyasmṛti* has an intimate relation to White Yajurveda. The probable date of Yājñavalkya is between 100 B.C.and A.D. 300. The *Laṅkāvatārasūtra* (*Gāthās* 814-816) refers to the *Yājñavalkyasmṛti*. Yājñavalkya shows acquaintance with Greek astrology. Dr. Jacobi's theory that naming of week days after planets was first introduced by greeks and borrowed by Indians is untenable. Yājñavalkya does not mention week days, but only the nine planets (I. 296). Yaj. does not mention the zodiacal signs. He arranges the Nakṣatras from Kṛttikā to Bharaṇī (I.268) as the *Taittirīyabrāhmaṇa* does. Yājñavalkya is explained by Viśvarūpa without reference to zodiacal signs from Vedic times. *Nakṣatras* are divided into auspicious and inauspicious. Yājñavalkya referes to *nāṇakas*. Yājñavalkya, regards the sight of yellow and robed people as an evil omen. There is a Vṛddha-Yājñavalkya, a Yoga-Yājñavalkya and a Bṛhad-Yājñavalkya and Vṛddha-Yājñavalkya. All are quoted by Mādhava and Aparārka. Bṛhad-Yājñavalkya is quoted by Jitendra and the author of the *Mitākṣarā* and as such must be earlier than A.D.1000. Bṛhadyogī-Yājñavalkya is a large work in twelve chapters and has bout 930 verses. It quotes dozens of verses from the *Manusmṛti*, the *Bhagavadgītā* and several Upaniṣadic passages without acknowledgement. We find several commentaries on the work of Yājñavalkya, by Viśvarūpa, Vijñāneśvera, Aparārka, Śūlapāṇi and Mitramiśra.

The Parāśarasmṛti

Yājñavalkya mentions Parāśara, but the extant *Parāśarasmṛti* is probably a recast of an older Smṛti.The *Garuḍapurāṇa* (Chap.107) gives a summary of thirty-nine verses of the *Parāśarasmṛti*. From Kauṭilya it appears that there was a work of Parāśara on politics in which *vyavahāra* was also dealt with. Extant Parāśara in twelve chapters and 592 verses deals with *ācāra* and *prāyaścitta* alone. Parāśara mentions ninteen Smṛti writers. Parāśara has some peculiar views on the contents of the Smṛtis. In the *Parāśarasmṛti* view of Manu is frequently cited. Several identical verses in the *Manusmṛti* and *Parāśarasmṛti* are found. Age of the *Parāśarasmṛti* is fixed between A.D. 100-500. A *Bṛhat-parāśarasaṁhitā* in twelve chapters and 3000 verses is available. It is a later work. The *Vṛddha- parāśara* is quoted by Aparārka.The *Jyotiḥ-parāśara* is quoted by Hemādri, Bhaṭṭoji and in the *Smṛticandrikā*.

The Nāradasmṛti

Two versions of the *Nāradasmṛti* on *vyavahāra*, a smaller and a larger one are available. Commentary. of Asahāya on the *Nāradasmṛti* and revised by Kalyāṇabhaṭṭa is contained in Dr. Jolly's edition. Nārada is not mentioned by Yājñavalkya or Parāśara in the list of expounders of *dharma*. He is mentioned by Manu (I.35) as one of the ten Prajāpatis. Sage Nārada is frequently figured in the *Mahābhārata*. Three introductory chapters on judicial procedure and on *sabhā*, then eighteen on *vyavahārapadas*, then an appendix on theft are included in the *Nāradasmṛti*. Some difference in the names of titles between the *Nāradasmṛti* and *Manusmṛti* is found. Printed version of the *Nāradasmṛti* contains 1028 verses. About 700 verses of the *Nāradasmṛti* are quoted in digests. Viśvarūpa's and Medhātithi's quotations from the *Nāradasmṛti* agree with printed the *Nāradasmṛti*. The *Agnipurāṇa* (ch. 253) contains thirty verses of the *Nāradasmṛti* defining the eighteen titles from *ṛṇādāna* to *prakīrṇaka* in the same order. Nārada's verses on *ācāra, śrāddha* and *prāyaścitta* are quoted in *Smṛticandrikā* and Hemādri. Probably this is a different Nārada. Form, style and metre of the *Nāradasmṛti* are systematic. About fifty verses are identical in Manu. Many more verses of the *Nāradasmṛti* closely correspond to Manu's. The *Nāradasmṛti* is based upon the *Manusmṛti*. Some verses of the *Mahābhārata* are same as in the *Nāradasmṛti*. Some verses of Kauṭilya and Nārada agree. In many points Manu and Nārada differ. Some topics are found peculiar to Nārada, viz. fourteen kinds of impotent persons, three *punarbhūs* and four *svairiṇīs*, etc. Nārada was some what later than Yājñavalkya. Nārada propounds several juristic and political principles, fixes the period of minority at sixteen. Nārada was earlier than 8th century at the latest. Nārada wrote a work on politics also. *Dināra* occurs in the *Nāradasmṛti*. *Dināras* may have been introduced into India about beginning of Christian era. Nārada flourished between A.D. 100-300. There was another *Nāradīya-manusaṁhitā*. The longer and shorter versions of the *Nāradasmṛti* were published by Jolly. Bhavasvamin, the Bhāṣyakāra of Nārada, was a Brāhmaṇa from Kerala. His date is not free from doubt. He may be placed conjecturally between A.D. 700-1000. Home of Nārada cannot be ascertained. There are many texts ascribed to Nārada viz.The *Jyotir-nārada,* the *Bṛhan-nārada and Laghu-nārada.*The *Mahābhārata* quotes Nārada's views on flesh-eating and on *utpātas* also.

The Kātyāyanasmṛti

The *vyavahāra* section of the *Kātyāyanasmṛti* has been reconstructed by P. V. Kane. It follows closely the works of Manu, Bṛhaspati, Nārada and Kauṭilya. It specially deals with *strīdhana* (dowry). Like Nārada, Yājñavalkya and Kauṭilya and some Dharmasūtrakāras like Baudhāyana and Gautama, Kātyāyana allows *niyoga* under certain conditions.

Among others mention may be made of the Smṛtis of Āṅgiras, Dakṣa, Pitāmaha, Prajāpati, Marīci, Yama, Viśvāmitra, Vyāsa, Saṅgrahakāra and Saṁvarta, who are known from citations in the later *Nibandhas* as writers on *dharma*; a few of their works, some being abridgements only, are found in the Jīvananda and Ānandāśrama collections.

Commentaries and Nibandhas

However, Dharmaśāstra literature falls into three periods, the first from 600 B.C. to A.D. 100. being the period of the Dharmasūtras and of the *Manusmṛti*, the second from A.D. 100-800 of the *Yājñavalkyasmṛti* and other Smṛtis and third from A.D. 700 to 1800 of commentators and authors of digests. First part of this last period contains commentaries and digests written from 11th century.

Asahāya

Portion of his *Bhāṣya* on the *Nāradasmṛti* (upto verse twenty-one of *Abhyupetya-śuśrūṣā*) was published. Kalyāṇabhaṭṭa has revised it. However, Kalyāṇabhaṭṭa's revision to original is not clear. Kalyāṇabhaṭṭa was encouraged by Keśavabhaṭṭa. Viśvarūpa in his commentary on the *Yājñavalkyasmṛti* (III. 263-264) mentions Asahāya by name. Asahāya's commentary on Śaṅkhalikhita is mentioned by Ānandagiri. *Hāralatā* of Aniruddha speaks of the *Bhāṣya* of Asahāya on the *Gautamasmṛti*. From a passage of the *Sarasvatīvilāsa* it appears that Asahāya commented on the *Manusmṛti* also. Medhātithi on the *Manusmṛti* 8. 156 quotes Asahāya. The *Mitāk-ṣarā* mentions the views of Asahāya. The date of Asahāya is fixed between A.D. 600-750. A few views of Asahāya has been set out, viz. definition of *dāya*, succession to *śulka* of a woman, succession to a childless Brāhmaṇa, etc.

Bhartṛyajña

Bhartṛyajña an ancient Bhāṣyakāra is mentioned by

Medhātithi (on the *Manusmṛti* 8.3). His views are cited by Trikāṇḍamaṇḍana. He wrote *Bhāṣyas* on the *Kātyāyanaśrautasūtra* as well as on the *Pāraskaragṛhyasūtra*. Probably he has commented on the *Gautamadharmasūtra*. His explanations based on the *Manusmṛti* V. 143, *Gautamasmṛti*, V. 41, XIV. 35- 40, *Vasiṣṭhasmṛti*. VIII.I are quoted in the *Kalpataru*.

Viśvarūpa

Viśvarūpa's commentary is called the *Bālakrīḍā* on the *Yājñavalkyasmṛti*. The *Mitākṣarā* refers to it in introductory verses and on *Yājñavalkyasmṛti* (I.80 and III.24). Viśvarūpa has borrowed most of the quotations from Svāyaṁbhuva Manu, but those are not ascribed to Bhṛgu. He quotes the prose passages of Bṛhaspati on *vyavahāra*. He quotes a verse of Viśālākṣa on politics and refers to the Arthaśāstras of Bṛhaspati and Uśanas. Kauṭilya has not been quoted by him, yet Viśvarūpa seems to have had his work before him. Viśvarūpa's work is saturated with the doctrines of the Pūrvamīmāṁsā. He quotes Śabara's work and the *Ślokavārtika*. Viśvarūpa was flourished between A.D. 750 and 1000.

Bhāruci

The views of Bhāruci are quoted in the *Mitākṣarā*, a commentary to the *Yājñavalkyasmṛti* I. 81 and II. 124. One Bhāruci is mentioned as an ancient teacher of Viśiṣṭa Advaita system by Rāmānujācārya in his *Vedārthasaṁgraha*. Bhāruci, the philosopher, is probably identical with another Bhāruci the jurist. From notices in the *Sarasvatīvilāsa* Bhāruci seems to have commented on the *Viṣṇudharmasūtra*. Bhāruci's work and the *Mitākṣarā* do not agree on numerous points. Bhāruci has written a commentary on the *Manusmṛti*. He is nearer to A.D.700.

Śrīkara

Views of Śrīkara have been set out as first writer to propound the view that spiritual benefit was the criterion for judging of superior rights to succession. He was a Maithila. It is difficult to say whether he wrote a commentary or an independent digest. He was flourished between A.D. 800-1050.

Medhātithi

Medhātithi wrote an extensive commentary on the *Manusmṛti*. He was a northerner and probably a Kashmirian. Literature known to Medhātithi is very extensive. He mentions Asahāya, Bhartṛyajña, Yajvan, Upādhyāya, Ṛju and Viṣnusvāmin. Medhātithi is very much saturated with the Pūrvamīmāṁsā. His *Bhāṣya* is full of the terms *vidhi* and *arthavāda*. He mentions several *nyāyas* for explaining the *Manusmṛti*. Medhātithi names only a few Dharmaśāstra writers and does not quote any Smṛtikāra with the prefix *bṛhat* or *vṛddha*. Medhātithi has written the *Smṛtiviveka* from which he quotes a few verses in his *Manubhāṣya*. He was flourished between A.D. 825-900.

Dhāreśvara

The *Mitākṣarā* while being commented on the *Yājñavalkyasmṛti* II.135 and III.24 mentions views of Dhāreśvara. Dhāreśvara is identified with King Bhojadeva of Dhārā. Works on numerous branches of knowledge were attributed to Bhoja such as on poetics, the *Rājamṛgāṅka* on astronomy. The *Mitākṣarā* and Dhāreśvara's work disagree on several points, e.g. on the question whether ownership was known from *śāstra* alone, on the meaning of *duhitaraḥ* in the *Yājñavalkyasmṛti*. The *Bhūpālapaddhati* or simply *Bhūpāla* or *Rājā* refers to a work of Bhojadeva. The *Bhujabalabhīma* of Bhojaraja is quoted in the *Tithitattva* and the *Āhnikatattva* of Raghunandana as distinct from the *Rājamārtaṇḍa*. Bhoja reigned from A.D. 1005-1054.The *Dharmapradīpa* of Bhoja is the work of another Bhoja, who was son of Bharamalla and the King of Aśapūra. It was written between A.D. 1400-1600.

Devasvāmin

Devasvāmin is the author of the *Smṛticandrikā* a digest of

Smṛtis. He is a commentator of the *Āśvalāyanagṛhya*. He has composed a digest on *ācāra, vyavahāra* and *aśauca*.The *Smṛticandrikā* quotes his views on the meaning of *yautaka*, on the meaning of *duhitaraḥ* in *Yājñavalkyasmṛti*, on Manu*smṛti* 9.141. Devasvāmin was flourished about A.D. 1000-1050.

Jitendriya

Jitendriya is frequently quoted by Jīmūtavāhana in his three works. Jitendriya held that the wives of a person whether separated or joint have the right to succeed their deceased husband. No early writer other than Jīmūtavāhana cites him. He was flourished between A.D. 1000-1050.

Bālaka

Jīmūtavāhana, Śūlapāṇi and Raghunandana have mentioned several views of Bālaka. He was flourished earlier than A.D. 100.

Śatānanda

Śatānanda Ācārya was the earliest Smṛti writer of Orissa. But he was more renowned for his notable work on astronomy called *Bhāsvatī*. It was finished in A.D. 1099 as recorded in the first and last verses of this. He was a native of Puruṣottama or Puri and was the son of Śaṁkara and Sarasvatī, his family surname being Ācārya. He did his basic astronomical calculations from the meridian of his native town Puri. But Śatānanda was also reputed as the author of two other works namely the *Śatānandaratnamālā* and the *Śatānandasaṁgraha*. Of these two the latter was definitely a work on Smṛti, as it is profusely quoted by the later Smṛti writers of Orissa and abroad. The *Śatānadasaṁgraha*, which is definitely one of the earliest Smṛti works, is now practically lost as no information about the discovery of its manuscript is found.

Śaṅkhadhara

This well-known Smṛti writer belonging to Orissa was Śaṅkhadhara, the author of the *Smṛtisamuccaya* which was accepted as an authority by the Smṛtikāras of Utkala, Gauḍa and Mithilā. Jīmūtavāhana, an earlier Smṛti-writer of Bengal has quoted twenty times from the *Smṛtisamuccaya* in his *Kālaviveka* and in another place he has criticized the views of Śaṅkhadhara and other writers. Śaṅkhadhara is cited by Śūlapāṇi, Śrīkara Ācārya, Raghunandana and other Bengali Smṛti writers. Caṇḍeśvara Ṭhakkura, the greatest Smṛti writer of Mithilā belonging to the 14th century refers to the *Smṛtismuccaya* in his *Gṛhastharatnākara*. Vidyāpati Ṭhakkura has quoted twice from this work in his *Gaṅgāvākyāvalī*, whereas this work is quoted once in each of the two works named the *Vyavahāracintāmaṇi* and the *Śuddhicintāmaṇi* by the Maithila, Vācaspati Miśra. Śaṅkhadhara who is found quoted by Caṇḍeśvara Ṭhakkura of Mithilā can definitely be placed before A.D. 1300.

Bālarūpa

The opinions expressed in the *Bālarūpa* are also cited in the *Smṛtisāra*, the *Vivādacandra* and the *Vivādacintāmaṇi*. He wrote at least on *vyavahāra* and *kāla*. The *Bālaka* and the *Bālarūpa* are probably identical. The *Bālarūpa* is certainly earlier than A.D. 1250. *Vivādacandra* once speaks of author of the *Bālarūpa*, suggesting a work named the *Bālarūpa*.

Vijñāneśvara

The *Mitākṣarā* of Vijñāneśvara has unique position on account of being esteemed as of paramount authority by British Indian courts. He quotes a host of Smṛti writers and six predecessors as authors of commentaries and digests. He mentions the views of many Smṛti writers with the prefix '*bṛhat*' or '*vṛddha*' e.g. Bṛhan-Manu, Vṛddha-Manu, Bṛhad-Vasiṣṭha, Vṛddha-Viṣṇu, etc., particularly on *āśauca* and *prāyaścitta*. He was a profound student of Pūrvamīmāṁsā. The date of Vijñāneśvara is fixed between A.D. 1100-1120.

The Kāmadhenu

It is an ancient digest but it is not discovered as yet. He is quoted in the *Kalpataru,* the *Hāralatā* and also in other works. The probable date of the *Kāmadhenu* is between A.D. 1000-1100.

Halāyudha

Several Halāyudhas are found in the medieval history. The first is the author of the *Kavirahasya* and the *Mṛtasañjīvanī*, who was flourished in the later half of the 10th century. Another Halāyudha, the author of the *Brāhmaṇasarvasva* and four other works was a Gauḍīya. He was patronized by Lakṣmaṇasena, the King of Bengal. His literary activity is assigned to the period of A.D. 1160-1200. This Halāyudha is different from one who was a jurist and composed a work on law. Another Halāyudha has composed a commentary called *Prakāśa* on Kātyāyana's *Śrāddhakalpasūtra*. He must have flourished before A.D. 1509 and later than A.D.1150. Halāyudha, the author of the *Karmopadeśinī* was earlier than 15th century.

Bhavadevabhaṭṭa

He was the author of the *Vyavahāratilaka,* the *Saṁbandhaviveka,* the *Karmānuṣṭhānapaddhati* and the *Daśakarmapaddhati*. His another work is the *Prāyaścittanirūpaṇa*. His work called the *Tautātikamatatilaka* is concerned with elucidating the Pūrvamīmāṁsā doctrines. Raghunandana criticizes Bhavadevabhaṭṭa's views several times, but also accepts his views many times. He was a great builder of temples and tanks. He was flourished between A.D. 1050-1150.

Prakāśa

It is an ancient work on *vyavahāra, dāna, śrādaha*, etc. It was a commentary on the *Yājñavalkyasmṛti* is believed to have been composed between A.D. 1000-1100.

Govindarāja

Govindarāja has written a commentary on the *Manusmṛti* and

a work called the *Smṛtimañjarī*. He is not to be indentified with the King Govindacandra of Vārāṇasī. Kullūka frequently criticizes Govindarāja. The date of Govindarāja is fixed between A.D. 1000-1110.

Kṛtyakalpataru of Lakṣmidhara

It is an extensive work which exercised great influence over early Mithilā and Bengal writers. This work is divided into fourteen *kāṇḍas*. The date of the *Kalpataru* is determined to be between A.D. 1125-1145. Passages in the *Kalpataru* on *vyavahāra* are more or less identical with those of the *Mitākṣarā*. The *Kalpataru* has an extensive size and wide range, but in quality it is, inferior to the *Mitākṣarā* and some other digests. The Passages of Devala and Aparārka have been quoted in the *Mokṣakāṇḍa* of the *Kalpataru*. It was composed in the realm of Govindacandra.

Jīmūtavāhana

Jīmūtavāhana is the first among the three great Bengal writers on the Dharmaśāstra. Only three works of Jīmūtavāhana are known such as the *Kālaviveka*, the *Vyavahāramātṛkā* and the *Dāyabhāga*. These three parts of a projected digest are called the *Dharmaratna*. The *Kālaviveka* bears profound study of Pūrvamīmāṁsā. *Dāyabhāga* the most famous of his works is a paramount authority in Bengal on the Hindu Law. This literary activity lies between A.D. 1090-1130.

Aparārka

Aparārka wrote a voluminous commentary on the *Yājñavalkyasmṛti*. History says that Aparārka or Aparāditya who belonged to a branch which ruled the North Konkan. Aparārka studiously avoids naming his predecessors who were the writers of the digests. Aparārka knew about the *Mitākṣarā*. The *Smṛticandrikā* criticizes Aparārka. Aparārka was a Śīlahara prince. His commentary on the *Yājñavalakyasmṛti* was written about A.D. 1125.

Aniruddha

He was an early as well as an eminent Bengali writer. He wrote the *Hāralatā* and the *Pitṛdayita* alias the *Karmopadeśinīpaddhati*. The contents of the *Hāralatā* and of the *Pitṛdayita* are very orthodox. Aniruddha was flourished in 3rd quarter of 12th century.

Ballālasena

Ballālasena has compiled at least four works namely: the *Ācārasāgara*, the *Adbhutasāgara*, the *Dānasāgara* and the *Pratiṣṭhāsāgara*. The subjects dealt with in the *Dānasāgara* are related to donation. The *Adbhutasāgara* was left incomplete and was finished by his son Lakṣmaṇasena. The *Dānasāgara* deals with sixteen great *dānas*, eulogy of Brāhmaṇas, etc. and contains valuable information about the *Mahābhārata* and the Purāṇas. His literary activity is marked to be in the 3rd quarter of the 11th century. Aniruddha was the guru of Ballālasena.

Harihara

Harihara was a writer on the *vyavahāra*. He was flourished before A.D. 1300. Harihara has composed a commentary on the *Pāraskaragṛhyasūtra*. This Harihara was flourished between A.D. 1150 and 1250. Harihara comments on the *Āśaucadaśaka*. Jurist Harihara might most probably be identical with Bhāṣyakāra of the *Pāraskaragṛhysūtra*.

The Smṛticandrikā

It is an extensive digest. It deals with *saṁskāra*, *ācāra*, *vyavahāra*, *śrāddha* and *āśauca*. Debaṇabhaṭṭa wrote on *prāyaścitta* also. He profusely quotes Smṛtikāra. 600 verses of Kātyāyana alone on *vyavahāra* are quoted in it. He was a southerner. His date is fixed between A.D. 1150 and 1225.

Haradatta

Haradatta is very famous as a commentator. He has authored a text, the *Anākulā* on the *Āpastaṁbagṛhya*, the *Anāvilā* on the

Āśvalāyanagṛhya, the *Mitākṣarā* on the *Gautamadharmasūtra*, the *Ujjvalā* on the *Āpastambadharmasūtra* and a commentary on the *Āpastambamantrapāṭha*. He explains the grammatical peculiarities at a great length. He was a southerner. He was also great devotee of Śiva. Haradatta was adamant on widow's right of succession. Haradatta's date was known to be between A.D. 1100-1300.

Hemādri and Mādhava

Hemādri and Mādhava were the two outstanding *dākṣiṇātya* writers on the Dharmaśāstra. Hemādri's *Caturvargacintāmaṇi* is a huge work of an encyclopaedic character. He has projected to contain five sections. Printed parts of it comprise *vrata, dāna, śrāddha* and *kāla*. Hemādri was a profound student of the Pūrvamīmāṁsā. Personal history of Hemādri was connected with Yadavas of Devagiri genealogy of the Yādavas. The *Caturvargacintāmaṇi* was composed about A.D. 1270. He has written a commentary on Śaunaka's *Praṇavakalpa*.

Kullūkabhaṭṭa

Kullūkabhaṭṭa is a famous commentator of the *Manusmṛti*. He drew largely upon Medhātithi's *Bhāśya* and Govindarāja. He wrote the *Smṛtiviveka*, of which the *Āśaucasāgara*, the *Śrāddhasāgara* and the *Vivādasāgara* were parts. The *Śrāddhasāgara* is full of the Pūrvamīmāṁsā discussions. Kullūka was flourished between A.D. 1150-1300.

Śrīdatta

Śrīdatta was one of the earliest Nibandhakāras on the Dharmaśāstra from Mithilā. He has written the *Ācārādarśa*. His the *Śrāddhakalpa* and the *Samayapradīpa* bear the testimony of his scholarship. He was flourished between A.D. 1200-1300.

Caṇḍeśvara

Caṇḍeśvara was the most prominent among Maithila Nibandhakāras. He has compiled an extensive digest called the *Smṛtiratnākara* in seven sections on *dāna, kṛtya, vyavahāra, śuddhi, pūjā, vivāda* and *gṛhastha*. He has also compiled the *Kṛtyacintāmaṇi*, the *Rājanītiratnākara*, the *Dānavākyāvalī* and the *Śivavākyāvalī*. He drew principally upon the five; viz. the *Kāmadhenu*, the *Kalpataru*, the *Pārijāta*, the *Prakāśa* and the work of Halāyudha. He was a minister of Harisiṁhadeva of Mithilā and later of Bhaveśa and weighed himself against gold in A.D. 1314. His literary activities were marked between A.D. 1314-1370.

Mādhavācārya

Mādhavācārya was the most eminent of Dākṣiṇātya writers on the Dharmaśāstra deserve special notice, viz., the *Parāśaramādhavīya* and the *Kālanirṇaya*. The *Kālanirṇaya* is known as the Kālamādhava. Mādhava has founded Vijayanagar in A.D. 1335. The *Parāśaramādhavīya* and the *Kālanirṇaya* were composed between A.D. 1340-1360. Literary activity of Mādhava Vidyāraṇya was fixed between A.D. 1330-1385.

Madanapāla

There are four Dharmaśāstra works which attributed to Madanapāla. He was a great patron of learning like Bhoja. His works include the *Madanapārijāta*, the *Smṛtimahārṇava* or the *Madana-mahārṇava*, the *Tithinirṇayasāra* and the *Smṛtikaumudī*. The *Madanapārijāta* was really composed by Viśveśvarabhaṭṭa. The *Madanapārijāta* declares the proposition with regard to *kānīna* and secondary sons. Its style is simple and lucid. All the above four works were composed by Viśveśvarabhaṭṭa. The *Subodhinī*, a commentary on the *Mitākṣarā* by Viśveśvarabhaṭṭa is a leading authority in Vārāṇasī school of the Hindu Law. The date of Madanapāla is known to be between A.D. 1300-1400. His *Madanavinodanighaṇṭu* was composed in 1431 of the Vikrama era, i.e. A.D. 1375.

The Madanaratna

The *Madanaratna* is an extensive digest on the Dharmaśāstra.

It has seven *uddyotas* on *samaya, ācāra, vyavahāra, prayaścitta, dāna, śuddhi and śānti*. The *Dānoddyota* was published by the Sanskrit Academy in 1946. Madanasiṁha has called together four learned men and entrusted composition of work to them. They were Ratnākara, Gopīnātha, Viśvanātha and Gaṅgādhara. The *Madanaratna* was composed between A.D. 1350-1500.

Vidyāpati

Vidyāpati was born in Bisapi, a village in North Bihar. He was the fourth in descent from Dhīreśvara the uncle of Caṇḍeśvara. Vidyāpati was credited with the authorship of twelve works. He was believed to be a great Vaiṣṇava, while in Mithilā he was recognized as a Śaiva. He made Queen Viśvāsadevi's work the *Gaṅgāvākyavalī* faultless and supplied textual authorities in support of her propositions. He might have flourished between A.D. 1360-1448.

The Vyavahāranirṇaya of Varadarāja

The *Vyavahāranirṇaya* bears no *Maṅgalaśloka* at the beginning. It is one of the four South Indian works on the Dharmaśāstra. In it Varadarāja's explanations are often the same as in the *Mitākṣarā*. He quotes many Smṛtis, works and authors, but nowhere refers to Bhāruci. Varadarāja was a unique a figure in the matter of the Mīmāṁsā as against the *Mitākṣarā*. He might be certainly earlier than A.D. 1515.

Śūlapāṇi

Śūlapāṇi was an eminent writer on the Dharmaśāstra from Bengal. He wrote the *Dīpakalikā* commentary on the *Yājñavalkyasmṛti*. His earliest work holds archaic views on inheritance. He has designed his fourteen treatises ending in *viveka*. The *Durgotsavaviveka* is amongst his latest work. The *Śrādddhaviveka* is his most famous work. The *Dolāyātrāviveka* of Śūlapāṇi records Dolāyātrā, the festival of swinging and when to be celebrated. His *Prāyaścittaviveka* was printed with the commentary *Tattvārthakaumudī* of

Govindananda. In the commentaries on *Śrāddhaviveka* Śūlapāṇi hardly gives any information about himself. In colophons he has styled himself as a Mahāmahopādhyāya and also a Sāhuḍīyana. He was flourished between A.D. 1365-1445.

Rudradhara

Rudradhara was a Maithila writer. He wrote the *Śrāddhaviveka*, the *Śuddhiviveka*, the *Vratapaddhati* and the *Varṣakṛtya*. The first among the works is the most famous of his works. He was flourished between A.D. 1450-1460.

Misarumiśra

Misarumiśra has written the *Vivādacandra*. This work was composed under orders of queen Lachimadevi, wife of prince Candrasiṁha of Mithilā. He was flourished about A.D. 1450.

Vācaspatimiśra

Vācaspatimiśra was the foremost Nibandhakāra of Mithilā. His *Vivādacintāmaṇi* is of paramount authority on matters of Hindu Law in Mithilā. He was a voluminous writer. Several works of his were styled as the *Cintāmani* on *ācāra*, *āhnika*, *kṛtya*, *tīrtha*, *dvaita*, *nīti*, *vivāda*, *vyavahāra*, *śuddhi*, *śauca* and *śrāddha*. A group of his works ends in *nirṇaya*, viz. the *Tithinirṇaya*, the *Dvaitanirṇaya*, the *Mahādānanirṇaya*, the *Vivādanirṇaya*, the *Śuddhinirṇaya*. He also contemplated writing seven works styled the *Maharṇava* on *kṛtya*, *ācāra*, *vivāda*, *vyavahāra*, *dāna*, *śuddhi* and *pitṛyajña*. He has also written the *Śrāddhakalpa* or the *Pitṛbhaktitaraṅgiṇī* as his last work. Vācaspati was connected with King Bhairava and his son Rāmabhadra. Vācaspati was flourished between A.D. 1425-1480.

Vardhamāna

The *Daṇḍaviveka* is the first work of Vardhamāna. This is the only extensive extant Sanskrit work on the law of crimes and punishments alone. Vardhamāna in it cites Halāyudha thirty-three times. He starts with the eulogy of *daṇḍa*. Vardhamāna wrote his *Viveka* in the reign of King Bhairava of Mithilā. His elder brothers Gaṇḍakamiśra, Śaṅkara and Vācaspati were his *gurus*. He has composed nine works. Vardhamāna must have flourished some decades before A.D. 1496.

The Nṛsiṁhaprasāda

This is an encylopaedic work. It is divided into twelve sections called *sāra*. In it the author's name is variously given as Dalapati or Dalādhiśa. The author was flourished between A.D. 1400-1510.

Pṛthvīcandrodaya

This is a large digest on Dharmaśāstra comprising several parts: *prakāśas*, perhaps sixteen as the word *Kalānidhi*, meaning moon. Its seventh part *Vyavahāraprakāśa* quotes Sūtrakāras, the Smṛtis, the Purāṇas, the *Rāmāyaṇa*, the *Mahābhārata* and digests on the Dharmaśāstra. This *Pṛthvīcandrodaya* was composed in Bundelkhand and must be placed later than about A.D. 1375.

Govindānanda

Govindānanda was the author of the *Dānakaumudī*, the *Śuddhikaumudī*, the *Śrāddhakaumudī*, the *Varṣakriyākaumudī* and a commentary called the *Arthakaumudī* on the *Śuddhidīpikā* of Śrīnivāsa and a commentary the *Tattvārthakaumudī* on the *Prāyaścittaviveka* of Śūlapāṇi. He was the son of Gaṇapatibhaṭṭa. Govindānanda was loose in giving the names of his own works. His literary activities were found between A.D. 1500-1540.

Raghunandana

Raghunandana was the last among the great writers of Bengal on the Dharmaśāstra. He wrote an encyclopaedia called the *Smṛtitattva* divided into twenty-eight sections. In it he names over 300 authors and works. Besides these twenty-eight, he wrote also a commentary on the *Dāyabhāga*. He was flourished between A.D. 1510-1580.

Nārāyaṇabhaṭṭa

Nārāyaṇabhaṭṭa was the most famous member of the Bhaṭṭa family of Vārāṇasī. He was born in A.D. 1513. Among his works are the *Antyeṣṭipaddhati*, the *Tristhalīsetu*, the *Prayogaratna* and the commentary on verses of the *Kālamādhava*. His literary activities were marked between A.D. 1540-1570.

The Toḍarānanda

This is an extensive encylopaedia of civil and religious law, astronomy and medicine by Toḍarmal. Its two parts, one on the *Sarga* and the other on the *Avatāras* were published. This work is divided into twenty-two sections called the *Saukhyas*, each *Saukhya* being subdivided into *Harṣas*. This was composed between A.D. 1572 to 1589. The *Jyotiḥsaukhya* was composed in A.D. 1572.

Nandapaṇḍita

Nandapaṇḍita was a voluminous writer on the Dharmaśāstra. He is the author of a commentary on the *Parāśarasmṛti* and on the *Mitākṣarā* of Vijñāneśvara. His *Śrāddhakalpālatā*, *Śuddhicandrikā*, a commentary on the *Ṣaḍaśīti* are the Smṛti works. His work was styled like the *Smṛtisindhu* and a summary of its style is the *Tattvamuktāvalī*. His *Vaijayantī*, a commentary on the *Viṣṇudharmasūtra* is very famous. His *Dattakamīmāṁsā* is regarded by British Indian Courts and Privy Council as a standard work on adoption. His work the *Vaijayantī* was composed in A.D. 1623. He is placed between A.D. 1580-1630.

Kamalākara

Kamalākara is the grandson of Nārāyaṇabhaṭṭa. He has composed more than twenty-two works on several śāstras– about a dozen works on the Dharmaśāstra. The *Nirṇayasindhu*, the *Śūdrakamalākara* and the *Vivādataṇḍava* are treated to be most famous. He has meant all the works on the Dharmaśāstra to be parts of a digest called the

Dharmatattva. The *Pūrtakamalākara*, the *Śāntiratna*, the *Vivādatāṇḍava*, the *Śūdrakamalākara* and the *Nirṇayasindhu* are also his works. The last one of his earliest work was composed in A.D. 1612. Therefore, his literary activities lie between A.D. 1610-1640.

Nīlakaṇṭhabhaṭṭa

Nīlakaṇṭhabhaṭṭa was the grandson of Nārāyaṇabhaṭṭa and the son of Śaṅkarabhaṭṭa. His work the *Bhagavantabhāskara* was divided into twelve *Mayūkhas* composed in honour of Bhagavantadeva, the Bundella chieftain. He has also written the *Vyavahāratattva*. His *Vyavahāramayūkha* is of paramount authority on Hindu Law in Gujarat, Bombay Island and North Konkan. He was flourished between A.D. 1610-1650.

Mitramiśra

The *Vīramitrodaya*, a vast digest was composed by Mitramiśra on all topics of the Dharmaśāstra sections called the *Prakāśas*. The *Prakāśas* on *lakṣaṇa, āhnika, vyavahāra, tīrtha, pūjā, saṁskāra, rājanīti* are highly controversial works. He generally follows Vijñāneśvara, but at times severely criticizes him. This is a work of high authority in Vārāṇasī school of modern Hindu Law. Mitramiśra also wrote a commentary on the *Yājñavalkyasmṛti*. His literary activities lie in the first half of the 17th century. He has included twenty-two *Prakāśas* in the *Vīramitrodaya*.

Anantadeva

Anantadeva has composed a vast digest called the *Smṛtikaustubha* on *saṁskāra, ācāra, rājadharma, dāna, utsarga, pratiṣṭhā, tithi* and *saṁvatsara*. The *Saṁskārakaustubha* is a most popular work. Some portion of it on adoption is called the *Dattakadīdhīti*. His *Rājadharmakaustubha* is very famous. Anantadeva has written several *Prayogas* and also a drama the *Kṛṣṇabhakticandrikā*. Anantadeva was great grandson of Ekanātha, a great Marathi poet and saint. His younger brother was Jīvadeva. His literary activities were found between A.D. 1645-1695.

Bālaṁbhaṭṭi

The *Lakṣmīvyākhyāna* or the *Bālaṁbhaṭṭi* is a commentary on the *Mitākṣarā* of Vijñāneśvara. Bālaṁbhaṭṭa favours latitudinarian views about the rights of women. He was the author of the *Bālambhaṭṭi* somewhat of an enigma. In the introductory verses he has written about the authoress Lakṣmīdevī, the real author. Bālakṛṣṇa was the son of Vidyānātha Pāyaguṇḍā, who was a pupil of Nāgojibhaṭṭa. Bālakṛṣṇa also wrote the *Upakrtitattva* and the *Dharmaśāstrasaṁgraha*. Bālambhaṭṭa was flourished between A.D. 1730-1820.

Kāśīnātha Upādhyaya

Kāśīnātha has composed an extensive work called the *Dharmasindhu*. His work in Deccan is leading now on to the religious matters. The *Dharmasindhu* was composed in A.D. 1790-91.

Jagannātha Tarkapañcānana

Jagannātha Tarkapañcānana has a digest which was got prepared by Warren Hastings. Its Persian and English renderings were made. The *Vivādasārārṇava* was compiled by Trivedi Sarvoruśarman. Among the digests compiled under the British the *Vivādabhaṅgārṇava* of Jagannātha is the most famous one. Colebrooke has translated it in 1796. Jagannātha died in A.D. 1806.

Saṁbhukara Vājapeyin and Vidyākara Vājapeyin

The two most notable Smṛti writers of Orissa who were flourished after Śaṅkhadhara were Saṁbhukara Vājapeyin and his son Vidyākara Vājapeyin. Both of them belonged to a famous Vājapeyin family, which was living in some Brāhmaṇa Śāsana or village near about the sacred town of Puri.

It is known that Saṁbhukara was a contemporary of one Nṛsiṁha, the King of Orissa. There were four Narasiṁha Devas in the Imperial Gāṅga family of Orissa who ruled between A.D. 1238-1414. But the interior and posterior limits for Saṁbhukara furnished by the above two dates, can be narrowed by the internal evidence collected from the *Nityācārapaddhati*, in which Vidyākara has referred to the *Kṛtyacintāmaṇi*, which the editor of this work has rightly taken to be work of the same name by the famous Caṇḍeśvara Ṭhākura of Mithilā. As the *Kṛtyacintāmaṇi* was compiled between A.D. 1315-1330. Vidyākara who refers to this work may be placed near about A.D. 1330. So Narasiṁha, who was a contemporary of Saṁbhukara was most likely Narasiṁha who ruled over Utkala from A.D. 1278 to 1306.

Raghunandana, the great Smṛti writer of Bengal, who makes a large number of quotations from the *Vidyākara-paddhati* states at one place in his work *Āhnikatattva* that: "thus the saying of Marīci as quoted by Vidyākara Vājapeyin." But of all his works the '*Nityācārapaddhati*' which was in course of time called the '*Vidyākarapaddhati*' maintained supreme hold in the field of Dharmaśāstra literature for about three centuries, till they were pushed to the background by the voluminous works of Gadādhara Rājaguru of Puri (A.D. 1700-1750). Narasiṁha Vājapeyin a celebrated Smṛti writer of Orissa of the second half of the 16th century refers to Vidyākara Vājapeyin twice and quotes from the *Vidyākarapaddhati* nine times in the first two parts of his *Nityācārapradīpa*. Viśvanātha Miśra, who was posterior to Narasimha refers to Vidyākara seven times and cites from the *Vidyākarapaddhati* thrice in his *Smṛtisārasaṁgraha*. Divyasiṁha Mahāpatra refers to Vidyākara Vājapeyin twice in his works. In the *Kālasarvasva* by Kṛṣṇa Miśra of the eighteenth century Vidyākara is mentioned four times and his *Paddhati* is found quoted once.

Raghunandana, the greatest Smṛti writer of Bengal refers to Vidyākara and his *Paddhati* several times in his works, a list of which was first given by late M. M. Chakravarti and has been critically examined by Sri Bhavatosh Bhattacharya. Viśveśvara Bhaṭṭa, the celebrated Smṛti writer of Northern India refers to Vidyākara Vājapeyin in his works.

A close analysis of the published volume of the *Nityācārapaddhati* shows that its author Vidyākara has made the largest number of quotations (twenty-four times) from the *Kalpataru* and referred to 'Kalpatarukāra' thrice in his works, which indicates that the *Kṛtyakalpataru* by the celebrated Lakṣmīdhara Bhaṭṭa (A.D. 1114-1154) was a great source of inspiration to him. Vidyākara Vājapeyin, who was youngest contemporary of the famous Candeśvara Ṭhākura of Mithilā and was almost of the same age as Mādhavācārya, the celebrated Smṛti writer of Southern India caused a revival of the Vedic culture in Orissa by his writing.

Bṛhaspati

Another notable Smṛti writer was Bṛhaspati, whose work called the '*Kṛtyakaumudī*' is a treatise on *ācāra*. He refers to the works of (1) Jīmūtavāhana (2) Vijñāneśvara, (3) the Rājamārtaṇḍa, (4) Lakṣmīdhara and the works named (5) the *Śatānandasaṁgraha and* (6) the *Smṛtimīmāṁsā* (7) the *Smṛtisamuccaya*, and (8) the *Smṛtisāra*. Jimūtavāhana who makes a large number of quotations from the *Smṛtisamuccaya* may be assigned to a period from A.D. 1250-1300. Bṛhaspati who mentions Jīmūtavāhana as he certainly might have flourished after A.D. 1300.

Godāvaramiśra

All branches of Sanskrit literature have developed in Orissa also under the patronage of the Emperors of the Sūryavaṁśa, that ruled over Orissa for about a century (A.D. 1435 to 1535). During this golden age of Orissan history the family of Godāvaramiśra has played an important part in the revival of Vedic tradition and culture by the performance of various Vedic sacrifices and compilation of a lot of works on Dharmaśāstra. Godāvaramiśra has written the *Harihara-caturaṅga*.

Gajapati Puruṣottamadeva

Two works on the Dharmaśāstra written by Gajapati Puruṣ-ottamadeva (1466-1497), namely the *Mukticintāmaṇi* and the *Gopālārcaṇavidhi* are so far known. This work is important as it gives the names of a lot of works dealing about the antiquity, importance and sanctity of Puruṣottama Kṣetra that were being used before the middle of the 15th century. *Gopālārcanavidhi* also called the *Nīlādrimahodayapūjāvidhi* is a work containing the procedure of worship of Lord Jagannātha at Puri that was sanctioned and promulgated by Puruṣottamadeva, the sovereign ruler of Orissa. The conception of Jagannātha as Gopāla Kṛṣṇa is recognized and proclaimed by this work, which is an important landmark in the religious history of Orissa.

Gajapati Pratāparudradeva

The authorship of the well-known *Sarasvatīvilāsa* which is recognized as an authority in the Āndhradeśa is attributed to Gajapati Pratāparudra. But the real author of this was Lolla Lakṣmīdhara Bhaṭṭa of the Āndhradeśa who remained in the court of Pratāparudra for some years prior to A.D. 1520. when he wrote a commentary on the *Saundaryalaharī*. Rāmakṛṣṇa Bhaṭṭa of Kāśī has written another Dharmaśāstra work named the *Pratāpamārtaṇḍa* in his name.

Narasiṁhamiśra Vājapeyīn

Narasiṁhamiśra Vājapeyin was the grandson of Dharādharamiśra, the cousin brother of the famous Godāvaramiśra. He was the son of Murārimiśra and received his education from Vighneśvaramiśra, the elder brother of Murāri. He was popularly known as Siṁha Vajapeyin. He has written the *Pradīpa* works: the *Nityācārapradīpa,* the *Vyavasthāpradīpa,* the *Prāyaścittapradīpa,* the *Pratiṣṭ hāpradīpa,* the *Cayanapradīpa* etc. He has been sent to the court of Akbar between A.D. 1565 and 1568.

Viśvanāthamiśra

The *Smṛtisārasaṁgraha* by Viśvanāthamiśra is very popular in Orissa. As its very name indicates that it is a small compendium of previous Smṛti works dealing on *kāla*, *ācāra* and *śrāddha*. The latest limit of the date of Viśvanātha, is

17th century. Divyasiṁha Mahāpātra, who flourished in the second half of the 17th century refers to Viśvanāthamiśra with respect as Miśra at one place of his work the *Śrāddhadīpa*. It may be mentioned in this connection that Viśvanātha does not refer to the Great Narasiṁha Vājapeyin or any of his works in his *Smṛtisārasaṁgraha* which might be due to the fact of his being almost a contemporary of Narasiṁha. But Viśvanātha being a predecessor of Divyasiṁha Mahāpātra may definitely be placed in the first half of the 17th century. Though the work is small, its author has quoted from the works of great writers like Mādhavācārya (forty times), as well as the works like the *Kṛtyakalpataru* (twenty-three times) and the Kālādarśa (twenty-seven times) and mostly refers to the important Smṛti works to make his work authoritative. The importance of this work lies in its popularity, which it did not lose inspite of compilation of voluminous works on different branches of the Dharmaśāstra by the famous Gadādhara Rājaguru (A.D. 1700-1750) of the subsequent period.

Vipramiśra

Vipramiśra is well-known for his work called the *Śrāddhapradīpa*. He begins this work after paying his respects to his preceptor Narasiṁhamiśra, who may tentatively be identified with another Nṛsiṁhamiśra. But he can definitely be placed in the first half of the 17th century as he is found quoted five times in the *Śrāddhadīpa* by Divyasiṁha Mahāpātra of the second half of same century.

Gadādhara Rājaguru

Like the great Narasiṁha Vājapeyin, Gadādhara was born in an illustrious family patronized by the ruling house of the realm. From the introductory verses of his *Kālasāra* it is known that his grandfather Śrīkṛṣṇa Mahāpātra Vājpeyin of the Kauśika Gotra got the title of Bṛhatpaṇḍita from the Rājā of Khurda for his learning and scholarship. He was the author of a Dharmaśāstra called the *Nītiratnākara* which is cited at several places in the *Kālasāra* of Gadādhara. He had three sons named Haladhara, Nīlāṁbara and Yameśvara. Haladhara, the eldest son who had performed the Śāradavājapeya sacrifice became the *guru* of the chief Queen of Rājā Harikṛṣṇadeva (1715-1718) from whom he received the grant of the Brāhmaṇa village called Vīra Hare Kṛṣṇapur near the town of Puri. His younger brother Nīlāṁbara was proficient in Vedānta, Smṛti, Jyotiṣa, Sāhitya, Vyākaraṇa, Nītiśāstra and was the author of the *Snānotsavastotra* of Lord Jagannātha. He was the founder of some *śāsanas* where many learned Brāhmaṇas well-up in sacrificial lore were settled. He won fame like Yudhiṣṭhira of the golden days by the performance of great sacrifice Caturmukha. He was the Rājaguru of Gajapati Harikṛṣṇadeva (1715-1718), who honoured his preceptor by the gift of a black umbrella bedecked with four stars and the foot-print of Kṛṣṇa made of gold; an elephant and a *cāmara*. Yameśvara, the youngest was also a Yajvā and a notable scholar. Nīlāṁbara Rājaguru and Jānakīdevi were the parents of Gadādhara Rājaguru who begins his work after paying respects to them. The same introductory verses are also found in the beginning of his work which was also published. Gadādhara is reputed as the author of eighteen works on the Smṛti each of which has got the distinguishing the term *sāra*. Besides the *Ācārasāra* the other works are referred to in his *Kālasāra,* e.g. the *Śuddhisāra, Vratasāra* etc. In his *Ācārasāra* two other new works e.g. the *Saṁskārasāra* and the *Snānasāra* are also referred to. Thus the names of the *Ācārasāra, Kālasāra, Śuddhisāra, Dānasāra, Vratasāra, Vivāhasāra, Saṁskārasāra* and *Snānasāra* are the popular eight works by Gadādhara.

The names of other works are not yet known. Gadādhara Rājaguru who was a profound scholar and had vast knowledge in different branches of the Dharmaśāstra wrote eighteen Smṛti digests called *sāra* in imitation of the celebrated Smṛti writer Narasiṁha Vājapeyin, the author of the eighteen *Pradīpas* whom he wanted to excel by his achievement. The ambition of his life was fulfilled as his three works the

Kālasāra, the *Ācārasāra* and the *Śuddhisāra* pushed the other works on the same subject to the background and are being recognized as standard works throughout Orissa since the time of their compilation till these days.

Gopinātha Vājapeyin

Another Smṛti writer of Orissa of this period is Gopinātha Vājpeyin who adorned the court of Gajapati Rāmacandradeva II (1725-1786) the Rājā of Khurda. He has written the *Paṇḍitasarvasva*. It is a standard Smṛti work, which is recognized as an authority in Orissa. This is altogether different from the *Paṇḍitasarvasva* of Halāyudha, who was a minister of the King of Gauḍa. The *Paṇḍitasarvasva*, which had circulation in Orissa was certainly much later than that of Bengal written towards the close of the twelfth century, as it cites Mādhavācārya of the 14th century. The *Paṇḍitasarvasva* is found quoted by Kṛṣṇamiśra, as such it was written prior to A.D. 1700. The interior and posterior limits for this work being A.D. 1500 and A.D. 1700 respectively, it may tentatively be assigned to the sixteenth or seventeenth century. The contents of this work are noted in its introductory portion. This work is still being used by the priests of Orissa.

Yogī Praharāja Mahāpātra

Yogī Praharāja Mahāpātra was the author of a Smṛti called the *Saṁkṣiptasmṛtidarpaṇa* a manuscript of which was first noticed by M.M. H.P. Sastri towards the close of the last century. About it he writes that the *Smṛtidarpaṇa* has been found in Orissa written by Yogī Praharāja, a scion of an influential family of Brahmins, and who for many generations were the spiritual guides of the Rājās of Orissa. They wanted to have a standard Smṛti of their own and got this work written. The writer does not seem to be old as he followed Gadādhara. The last chapter of his work contains a short history of the Raj family of Nandapur. From the last verse of his other work called the *Vaidyahṛdayānanda* it is known that Yogī was the son of Nīlakaṇṭha Praharāja who was the preceptor of the chief Queen of Vikramadeva, the King of Nandapura. At the end of each of the five *Prakāśas* to which the work is divided the author speaks of himself. It is known that Yogī Praharāja flourished in the kingdom of Nandapura when Vikramadeva was its ruler. The present district of Koraput in Orissa comprises the northern part of the old Nandapura kingdom which was very powerful and extensive during the 15th and 16th centuries. It was so called after the name of its capital town Nandapur which is now found in ruins in the Nandpur P. S. of the Koraput District. It was afterwards called Joypore State, when its capital was shifted from old Nandapur to the present town of Joypore. Vikramanṛpa is the first King of that name who ruled from A.D. 1758-1781. Thus Yogī Praharāja who was flourished in the middle of the 18th century borrowed the ideas from the works of Gadādhara Rājaguru.

Mahāmahopādhyāya Kṛṣṇamiśra

Some information about Kṛṣṇamiśra is obtained from the concluding portion of his work. It may be mentioned here that he has written the *Sudhākara*, a commentary on the *Sāhityaratnākara*. From the verse after *mangalācaraṇa* and the last verse after each section of this commentary it is known that his grandfather Rāmacandramiśra, the moon of the Kautsa family became famous in Utkala for his proficiency in different branches of learning and as performer of various sacrifices. His son Paramānandamiśra was the father of the famous Kṛṣṇamiśra. Therefore, Rāmacandra is identified with the grandfather of Kṛṣṇamiśra. M. M. Kṛṣṇamiśra has authored the *Kālasarvasva,* the *Śuddhisarvasva,* the *Vaiṣṇavasarvasva,* etc. He quotes from the works of Gadādhara and also from the work *Paṇḍitasarvasva*.

Kavibhūṣaṇa Govinda Sāmantarāya

Kavibhūṣaṇa Govinda, a famous poet and scholar of Orissa of the 18th century wrote a Smṛti work called the *Sūrisarvasva* which was very popular in Orissa. The first part of this work divided into two parts has been published by the Asiatic Society of Bengal and the second part is published by Sri Sadasiva Kendriya Sanskrit Vidyapith, Puri. The writing of this work was finished in A.D. 1778. He got the title Kavibhūṣaṇa from Gajapati Vīrakesarideva (A.D.1736-1793). His *Sūrisarvasva* which refers to a large number of works and authors is recognized as a standard work.

Manu's Dharmaśāstra in World History

Manu's *Dharmaśāstra* is the only book in the world that has made the greatest impact on the life of humanity, scattered over the largest part of the globe and over the longest stretch of time. When the Āryan tribes left their homeland in Central Asia, they scattered themselves in all directions and carried with themselves the memory of Manu's teachings. Moving towards the Pacific coast of Asia, they dropped the large groups of their populations in Central Asia, Mangolia, Japan, Formosa, Phillippine Islands, groups of Eastern Islands, along with eastern coast of Australia, ending with the Marois in New Zealand. The languages of the people of these regions, some of their religious rites and customs and other traits of culture bear resemblance to those of other countries where their Āryan brethern had settled down. In Maori mythology, for instance, the word Manu occurs.

Evidences of Manu's impact of the people of neighbouring countries are abundant and clear. Their social customs, social organization, law, etc. are founded on the basis of the *Mahābhārata* and the *Manusmṛti*. Indo-China, Vietnam, Indonesia, Bali, Malaysia, Thai and Burma have kept their permanent record of Manu's teachings. In Indonesia, for instance, the nine volumes of the *Kutra Mānava* are based on the *Manusmṛti*. The social institutions and organizations of these countries, their legal codes and their literature reveal abundant evidence of Manu's teachings.

Manu's name is a household word in India and his teachings have influenced life and thought of the people for untold millennia. His *varṇa-āśrama-dharma,* old with age and formalized, operates through the so-called caste system, while the legal institutions of the country adhere closely to Manu.

Vaivasvata Manu of India, was known as Manu Vaiwahant in ancient Iran. Manu's classification of human types, of four groups and their origin and function were based on Manu's Dharmaśāstra.

Recent investigations in the Sumerian civilization have brought to light the existence of social and cultural life that resembles closely to the one presented in Manu's Dharmaśāstra. Even the methods of dispensing justice were identical in both India and Sumeria. The word *Me* stands for the law.

In Babylon and Assyria, Manu's teachings were well-known. Manu is mentioned by name in Assurbanipals' library and some of his kith and kin are recorded. Comparison of the contents of the *Code of Lipit Ishtar* of Sumeria and Hamurabi of Assyria with that of Manu is bound to reveal some interesting and revealing results.

The great emperor Menes, of Egypt, who united the northern and southern parts of the country, claimed his descent from Manu. The ruler and law-giver of Ancient Crete was called Minos. Moses, the prophet, of the Hebrews, is also their law-giver and the social thought of these people and their customs bear close resemblance to Manu's teachings. Sir William Jones, who translated Manu's *Dharmaśāstra* in 1790 or so, emphasised the resemblance of all these words, Menes, Minos, Moses, etc., and their function as law-givers of their people and came to the conclusion that they all drew their inspiration from one source, the Manu's *Dharmaśāstra* of India.

Through the migration of Āryan tribes from Central Asia to Europe, through commercial, diplomatic and cultural relations with their ancient cousins in India, through the religion of the mysteries of Mithra, called after the Vedic God, Mitra, through presence of various Āryan tribes in this region, such as Hittites, Mittanis and others, the Āryan culture complex of India was known in, and accepted by the early seettlers in Europe. The tradition of Manu being the founder of he human race, brought over from their ancestral home, found reinforcement through subsequent contacts and Manu became Menes in ancient Greece. Plato based his Republic on Manu's teachings. The memory of Manu was kept alive by the Germanic tribes who mentioned him as the founder of their race, as Tacitus, the ancient Roman historian wrote iD. 78 in his *Germania*. Greece, like its predecessors, was under obligation to India for sciences and humanities. Rome accepted Greek culture and the knowledge of Manu's teachings was found to be very helpful by the scholars responsible for the codification of Justinian's Laws. H.G. Wells and Sir Paul Vinogradoff, former Professor of Jurisprudence in the University of London, maintain that the Roman jurisprudence is essentially oriental, both in letter and spirit. The worship of Mithra was practised extensively in Europe before the advent of Christianity. Indian and Roman emperors exchanged ambassadors during the pre-Christian era. There was an extensive export of Indian commodities, such as textiles, spices and cosmetics to Europe. It should be no wonder, then, that Roman Law drew heavily on its Hindu source, the Manu's *Dharmaśāstra*.

But the impact of Manu's teachings did not end with the Justinian Code in the sixth century A. D. Travellers moved back and forth between the European countries and India. Some Indian texts were translated into European languages. Indian commodities continued to sell in the European markets and Islam became a bridge between India and the West. To what Islam imbibed from India, she added what Greece, Unan, the land of Ionia, a point of confluence between people and cultures of Asia and Europe, had to offer. Europe continued to be a commercial and cultural outpost of India and search for direct trade routes continued to fire the navigators and sailors of Europe till Columbus set sail to find a route to India, and instead, landed in America. The story of impact of Manu on the European people and countries during the ten or twelve centuries can be reconstructed through the discovery of identity of thought between the Manu's *Dharmaśāstra* and the writings of social thinkers of Europe.

But we are on surer ground when we come to the time of the Romantist movement that took birth in Europe around 1775. A new world of thought burst upon the European thinkers when Indian texts were translated from Sanskrit into the major languages of Europe, particularly English, German and French. The translation of Manu's *Dharmaśāstra* into English by Sir William Jones in 1790 gave a great impetus to the study of this subject. The leading figures of the Romantist movement in every country became devout students of Indian thought.

The British scholars were naturally the first to come to grips with Manu's teachings. Carlyle, Coleridge and some poets, such as Shelley, Keats and Byron, became acquainted with this subject. Edmund Burke had a fascination for India and her life and thought. Southy studied the text carefully. An annotated copy of Manu's *Dharmaśāstra* was found in his library. A thorough and careful investigation into the writings of the English and Scottish social thinkers is bound to reveal some interesting results.

The leading scholars of the Romantist movement in Germany, including Hegel and Schelel, studied the text and lectured in the universities. Marx was familiar with the text, though he took a diametrically opposite view to that of Manu's *Dharmaśāstra*. But Nietzche held Manu in high esteem.

In France, Count de Masitre lectured on Manu in Moscow while serving there as representative of the King of Sardina. St. Simon imbibed a good deal of Manu's social thought, as also did his apt pupil, Auguste Comte, chauvinistically described as the father of sociology by western scholars. Mons. Louis Jacollit, who had lived in India for many years and had a fairly good knowledge of Indian point of view, maintains that the framer of the *Napoleanic Code* were greatly indebted to Manu's *Dharmaśāstra*, and he proceeds to prove this by laying side by side many provisions from both the texts, revealing, thereby, their identity of approach.

From European scene, let us turn to the American. A copy of Manu's *Dharmaśāstra* went across the Atlantic to Thoreau from one of his friends, a member of the House of Lords, in England. Thoreau studied the book very carefully, passed it on to R.W. Emerson, who also made a good study of it and reproduced it chapter by chapter in his weekly, The *Dial*. The book was passed on to Walt Whitman, a friend of Thoreau and Emerson. Josiah Royce, of Harvard and Harris of St. Louis, Mo were also keen students of Hindu thought and can be said to have got acquainted with the Manu's *Dharmaśāstra*. Many young sociologists of these times went to European universities for higher education and became leaders in sociology on their return to their country and it goes without saying that they became aware of the existence of this book and studied it to some extent.

Manu's teachings have never lost their lustre, their originality, profundity and practical usefulness in spite of their hoary age. Dealing with the totality of the social drama in all its aspects, Manu's *Dharmaśāstra* remains an unexcelled epitome of the best and the highest that the human thought has ever achieved: it has a seal of the eternal and the immortal imprinted on it. The spiritual and the intellectual elite of the contemporary world continue to pay to it their homage which it so richly deserves. We have space to mention a few names from different countries of the world who have acknowledged the supremacy of Manu's social thought over every other system devised by man in the past and the present. Among these may be mentioned H. P. Blavatsky (Russia); Dr. Annie Besant (U.K., later both of India); Swami Dayanand Saraswati, Sri Aurobindo, Ramana Maharishi, Swami Vivekananda, Rabindra Nath Tagore, Śriśaṅkarācaryas of the four Maths, Dr. Bhagawan Das, Gandhiji, Acharya Vinoba Bhave, Dr. S. Radhakrishnan, Dr. P.V. Kane, (all of India) Maurice Maeterlink (Belgium), P. D. Ouspensky (Russia) and Pitirim A. Sorokin (U.S.A.). All these teachers, philosophers and sociologists have made a profound study of Manu's *Dharmaśāstra* and paid their tribute to Manu. It would be no exaggeration to say that the next step in understanding and study of man and society lies in the direction of the teachings of Manu.

It is sometimes asked if Manu's teachings are mere abstract, intellectual formulations or have some basis in fact. Did the society, as pictured by Manu, ever exist in the past or, will it ever come into being in the future? The new discipline of sociology of knowledge affirms that there is a closer relationship between social thought and fact. Social thought cannot arise in vaccum: it is based on social situation as it exists. Social thought acquires relevance when it addresses itself to the problem of social existence. There is a close relationship between knowledge and society. This can be easily seen when we examine the contents of various utopias produced by the western thinkers. Every utopia is conceived in terms of the problems confronting the society at the time of the author's life and seeks to offer remedies for some of the social ills. Similarly, Manu's teachings depict a period of human history when the social life of man, as portrayed by him, actually existed. The Hindus have called it *Satya Yuga*, the Golden Age, the age of perfect integration, of a spiritually awakened individual and a perfect social harmony "when the Cow of Dharma stood firm and square on all its four legs." The Śruti rightly reveals that whatever Manu has said, is medicine: *yad vai kiñca manuravadat tad bheṣajam.*

Evaluation

The ethical codes are called the Dharmaśāstras or the sciences: Śāstras of right action: *dharma*. They were elaborations of what were originally called the Dharmasūtras or the aphorisms on right action, which were not the same as Jaimini's Mīmāṁsāsūtras, which also were the expositions of right action, but applications of Jaimini's concept of right action: *dharma* to the various detailed situations of social life. But the ethical codes: The Dharmaśāstras became finally the guides for social duties and the basic texts of jurisprudence for the law courts.

The first characteristic of the Dharmaśāstras is that they are the extensions and applications of the Mīmāṁsā concept of *dharma* (right action). They are not the systems of ethics or the ethical philosophies, but only applications of the idea of right action to concrete social situations. That is why they are called codes. They accept the Mīmāṁsā concept of *dharma*. But the Mīmāṁsā was interested mainly in the deeper and the trans-empirical aspects of the concept, explaining the theories underlying the workings of all action, how it produces its effects, what forms it takes for producing them and so on. And because sacrifices and their ritual also have other worldly aspects, the Mīmāṁsā sought to explain them in detail. The ethical codes accepted the Mīmāṁsā doctrine of right action: *dharma*, and explained what right action was in society, leaving out the explanation of the sacrifices and their ritual, and of salvation and its theories.

The question: "What is right action?" was answered by the Mīmāṁsā, saying: "It is action according to the injunctions of the Veda." This answer was enough for the Mīmāṁsā, because it was concerned mainly with the trans-empirical nature of actions. But there are actions which concern mainly the empirical world and society itself. Here, how are we to know what the right action is? The Dharmaśāstras gave four ways of knowing it: the Vedas, the Smṛtis (the Dharmaśāstras and the Purāṇas, etc. which are based on the Vedas, the example of good men, and what is good to oneself. Of the four, each succeeding criterion has less authority than the preceding one. That is, if there is a conflict between the two, then the preceding one prevails. So in the latter case, it holds true only when one does not get guidance from the others.

The criterion, the example of good men, made it possible for the authors of the Dharmaśāstras to observe the different communities in different places, and determine what was right action. There were people who did not accept the Vedas, there were many non-Āryan tribes with rules of conduct of their own, and even the Āryans who accepted the Vedic way of life understood the Vedas differently in different places and followed ways of life slightly different from one another. All these differences were observed and codified and rules of conduct were fixed. When once the rules were fixed, they became laws and guided not only ethical and social life, but also civil and criminal courts. Obedience and violation of the rules were considered to be as important as obedience and violation of *dharma* (righteousness) as explained by the Mīmāṁsā, because *dharma* consisted in obeying those rules.

The social rules thus became different in many respects for the different tribes. The Āryan tribes in general had one set of rules, which were different from those of the non-Āryan tribes. For instance, there was the practice of selling their children among some non-Āryan tribes. This was allowed for them; but the Āryans were punished for selling their children. There was polyandry, and divorces up to ten times among some non-Āryans. But they were illegal among the Āryans.

Besides such differences, there were different rules laid down for the castes, subcastes, and the stages of life: *āśramas*. Now all such rules are not legal. For instance, it was not legally binding on man to marry or to take to the life of the forest dweller or the monk. But if he once takes to any of these stages, he should obey the rules. But even then, some of the rules are not legally binding. For instance, a man may become a monk, then change his mind, marry and settle down as a householder. Or he may change from one sect to another. Or, although as a monk, he is forbidden to touch any money, he may become the head of a monastery, become very rich and lead a luxurious life. In such cases generally, there is only ethical censure, but no legal punishment. The ethical codes, thus, are not the mere legal codes.

But so far as the rules of the castes go, the emphasis was on the members of each caste following its own rules of conduct, and not taking to the professions of others. Even here, there was no legal punishment for violating the rules. Such punishments were very rare. There were Brāhmaṇas who took to the duties of the warrior caste and even started imperial dynasties. Some of them even took to ploughing. The Maurya dynasty, to which Aśoka the Great belonged, was of the fourth caste, the Śūdra. The Gupta dynasty, which produced equally powerful emperors and was famous for driving away the White and the Red Huns from India, belonged to the trader caste. Thus although the professions were at first determined by castes, later, in the case particularly of great men and rulers, profession began to determine the caste. But such cases were not very common. People followed their caste rules, as though by intertia. Some kind of mythological sanction was invented of the formation of the castes, and the mixing up of professions was religiously discouraged. Very few of the lower castes aspired to be Brāhmaṇas, because to become a Brāhmaṇa meant the life of priesthood, poverty, penance, purity, etc., which were difficult. Up to the profession of ruling, there was some mixing up and change of professions; but birth still conferred some prestige, not obtained by profession. The orthodox people of course resisted change, to which they had finally to reconcile themselves and invented justification.

The Dharmaśāstras prescribed legal punishments for the violation of civil and criminal laws. But whenever the violation did not come under those laws and also when the law breaker was able to escape the law, the ethical codes said that such law breakers would reap the fruit of their actions in future lives. They will not only suffer the evil fruit of their *karmans*, but also take a new birth according to the nature of the actions they have performed. That is, action, good and evil, determines future births, good and evil. The doctrine of transmigration or rebirth thus helped the ethical codes in explaining how some good action go apparently unrewarded and why some evil actions go apparently unpunished. No action goes without consquences; if they are not enjoyed in this life, they will be enjoyed in the next birth.

The causality of ethical actions helped the Indian thinkers to explain many differences between man to man. Some are born rich, or very intelligent, or healthy, or good, and so on; but others are born very poor, or very dull, or very sickly, or very evil, and so on. These differences are due to the good and evil actions performed in past lives. It should not be understood that the society was not allowed to ameliorate the needy and the sick. It is the duty of all those who are happily placed in life to help those who are not so placed. It was not supposed that not to allow the suffering to suffer was a violation of ethical law; otherwise, charity, compassion, etc., would not have been preached. Yet those who were suffering were made a warning to people against evil actions.

It is very difficult to prove the doctrine of rebirth and also to prove that the next life will be according to the nature of the actions performed in past lives. Neither it is easy to prove that the doctrine is definitely false nor, we do not have sufficient evidence for or against the doctrine. Now, we have seen, as the early Buddhism taught, birth is due to the tendency to be born, and that again due to our desires and attachments for the objects of this world. The idea of the tendency to be born explains what kind of life will be taken in the next birth. This tendency is a tendency towards a particular kind of being or living. A hardened murderer, who takes much pleasure in killing people and is quite insensitive to their agonies, has developed a tendency always to be that kind of being. He likes the life of a cruel brute, and will, therefore, be born as a tiger. Thus this tendency is a will that becomes a part and parcel of the man's being and unconsciously works through him. The Mīmāṁsakas, as it was already mentioned, maintained that every action that has not exhausted itself in its effects takes the form of a latent force: *apūrva*, enters the *ātman* of the agent, and produces for him either later in this life itself or in the other world or in some future life determining conditions for that *ātman* can enjoy the fruit. This unconscious will, not only determines the conditions of the man's character and nature, but also has a trans-empirical nature that determines the conditions of our future lives. It is the action: *karman* in its latent form and has to become kinetic or should manifest itself. And its manifestation lies in those conditions in which the *ātman* enjoys or suffers. Action can thus become a kind of unconscious will that controls the forms of the world, though not its material. This doctrine of the Mīmāṁsakas is practically accepted by the Dharmaśāstras, which introduced only one modification.

The Dharmaśāstras call themselves the Karmayogaśāstras or the sciences of the way of action, and they are all theistic, unlike the original Mīmāṁsā, which was non-theistic. The modification they introduced is theism, and all that it implies. The world is created by God, who also created the different castes (*varṇas*, lit. colours, colours of skin) and fixed their respective professions. What was originally natural and also determined and fixed by the accidents of history and convention was regarded as having been created by God. Some sub-castes and distinctions of professions were created by man himself through the intermixture of castes. People born into those castes and sub-castes had to follow their prescribed professions without the violation of God's laws.

The same God now becomes the custodian of the latent forms which our ethical actions take, and dispenses rewards and punishments for good and evil actions. Now, it is not action by itself that creates the conditions for its fructification and exhaustion, but God who supervises our actions.

Along with the idea of God, the idea of salvation or liberation from the world of action is accepted by the Dharmaśāstras. God can release an *ātman* from bondage, if the *ātman* is earnest. But man should continue to live and active life, performing actions without the attachment to their fruit. He can do this by surrendering himself and all his actions to God and remaining unattached to their fruit. And God sends his grace to those people who sincerely struggle for salvation, but find themselves weak to develop the necessary attitude.

Incidentally, the Dharmaśāstras praise the way of devotion and knowledge. But since the codes are meant to guide the life of every person, they teach primarily the way of action. Their main object is to fix the duties of every man according to his station in society, and they thought of society as primarily consisting of castes and sub-castes and of those falling outside the structure of castes and sub-castes.

We may conclude that the ethical codes are conservative, not permitting much change. It is the nature of all ethical and legal codes to be conservative, aiming to fix the social structure as they find it. But as conditions of social life change, a need is felt to reformulate the codes. Thus arose several Dharmaśāstras in India, the most important of which are Manu's Dharmaśāstra and Parāśara's Dharmaśāstra. We find difference of views among the Dharmaśāstras on certain points.

But none of the Dharmaśāstras was against the system of castes and sub-castes. One code permitted the taking back of women and girls, who were forcefully violated by Muslims, into their original castes. There was also another change, which was not so marked in its observance. The duties of the higher castes were more difficult than those of the lower, and demanded that the higher castes should be more righteous and should only follow noble professions. If a man born in the higher caste was one with evil tendencies, he was considered to be inferior to the men of the lower castes. Similarly, if one belonging to the lower caste was nobler than he was expected to be, he was considered to be higher than the men of the higher caste. But generally he was not allowed to change his caste, although respected and venerated by men of the higher castes also.

The Dharmaśāstras thus supplied the rules of social conduct for all the Indians of the time, whatever religion or philosophy they followed. Their philosophical basis is the Mīmāṁsā in its theistic forms and their social basis was the structure of castes and sub-castes, which were considered to be God-given and unalterable. We find some evidence that the ethical writers conceived of the castes in terms of the three attributes – *sattva* (clarity or purity), *rajas* (activity) and *tamas* (lethargy) – just as Plato divided his classes according to the predominance of the rational part, the spirited part, and the appetitive part of the Soul. Brāhmaṇa was one in whom purity (*sattva*) dominated; the warrior was one in whom *rajas* (activity) dominated, because his function is to acquire and accumulate wealth, which is a mixture of activity and stability; and the Śūdra was one who is a dominated by lethargy (*tamas*). But like Plato's principle of division, this principle also is not easily applicable. And besides, except in the hands of the social reformers, it did not result in the fluidity and interchange of castes according to the character indicated. And this acceptance of the castes as final prevented the ethical ideas of the codes from developing into systematic ethical and political philosophies. But all the moral ideas and virtues we find in China and the West are to be found in the Indian ethical codes i.e. in the Dharmaśāstras also.

For social ethics, though it did not develop into the systems of thought as in the West, one should turn to the Dharmaśāstras. And they are the same for all systems of philosophy– including even Jainism and Buddhism also for a long time in India– except the Cārvākas, who also could not have violated those rules that were legally enforceable. But ethics and morality are not confined to social and legal codes. Ethics is a science of self-discipline with reference to certain goals; but some of these goals transcend society. For instance, it is not a social concern that I should work for the realization of the supreme spirit or even that I should work for heaven after death. But if I have these goals, I have to go through the necessary discipline and ethics extends over, and includes this discipline also. It is transparent that the different schools of philosophy differ from one another on some points. And all disciplines meant for the realization of our ultimate being or the Buddhist Nirvāṇa are called spiritual disciplines. But we cannot separate ethical disciplines from the spiritual, because they overlap. They have many points in common. For instance, truth-speaking, charitableness and compassion are both ethical and spiritual disciplines. The two can be distinguished only from the goals they have before them. Jñānayoga (the way of knowledge) is not mere ethics, but a way of our life. Or we may express the same idea in a different language.

Ethical discipline need not be spiritual, i.e. need not have spiritual, but only social goals. But a spiritual discipline cannot be unethical. To give a similar example: politics is not the whole of ethics; but ethics covers political activity also.

Because of the above peculiarity of Indian thought one should not turn merely to the systems of salvation philosophies for studying the ethical ideas of India. One should turn to the Mīmāṁsā and the Dharmaśāstras. For ideas of spiritual discipline and their differences one should turn to those philosophies. In the light of those philosophies the same ethical ideas obtain a new perspective and a new decoration.

Conclusion

The Dharmaśāstra is a comprehensive code to regulate human conduct in accordance with the unalterable scheme of creation, and to enable every one to fulfil the purpose of his birth. The whole life of man, considered both as an individual and as a member of group (small and large) as well as man's relations to his fellow men, to the rest of animated creation, to superhuman being, to cosmos, generally and ultimately to god comes within the purview of the Dharmaśāstra. Among the duties that it lays down are both self-regarding and altruistic, those to the living and to the dead, to those who are alive and those who are yet to be born.

Bibliography

Das, Bhagavan. The *Science of Social Organisation*, Madras: Theosophical Society, 1910.

Ganguly, Jayadev. *Dharmaśāstra in Mithila*, Calcutta: Sanskrit College, 1972.

Kane, P. V. *History of Dharmaśāstra. Vol.I.* Poona: B.O.R.I. 1975.

Mahapatra, K. N. *Descriptive Catalogue of Sanskrit Manuscripts of Orissa State Museum Vol.I.* Bhubaneshwar.

The Smārtasūtras

Two classes of Sūtras *viz.* the Gṛhyas, and Sāmayācārikas—are included under the common title of *Smārtasūtra*, in contradistinction to the Śrautasūtras; the latter deriving their authority from the Śruti (the Mantras and Brāhmaṇas), the former from Smṛti, or immemorial tradition. The Gṛhya and Sāmayācārika Sūtras have frequently been confounded by European scholars; but the Brāhmaṇas distinguish strictly between the Gṛhya ceremonies, performed by the married house-holder, chiefly for the benefit of his family, and the Sāmayācārika rules, which are to be observed by the rising generation, and which regulate the various relations of every-day life. It is chiefly in the Sāmayācārika, or, as they are sometimes called, the Dharmasūtras, that we have to look for the originals of the later metrical law books, such as Manu, Yājñāvalkya, and the rest; and the statement of Megasthenes, that the Hindus at his time administered law from memory can only refer to the Smārtasūtras of the Caraṇas, and to the modern Smṛtisaṁhitās of Manu, Yājñavalkya, Parāśara, etc.

The Gṛhyasūtras, belonging to the old Yajurveda, are numerous. Quotations have been met with from Baudhāyana Bhāradvāja, Hiraṇyakeśin, the Kāṭhaka,[1] and the Maitrāyaṇīyas,[2] all names connected with the Taittirīyaveda, and proving the existence of distinct collections of the Gṛhyasūtras. The number of similar Sūtras for the bright Yajurveda seems to have been still more considerable. Every one of the fifteen Caraṇas of the Vājasaneyins is said to have

Mutwani, K. *Manudharmaśāstra: A Sociological and Historical Study*, Madras: Ganesh & Co. Pvt. Ltd. 1958.

Raju, P. T. *The Philosophical Tradition of India*, Sprinfield, U.S.A. Natraj Books, 1992.

Ramgopal. *India of Vedic Kalpasūtras,* Delhi: Motilal Banarsidass, 1983.

Swain, Brajakishore *Manusaṁhitā* (Oriya), Puri: Sadgrantha-niketan, 1997.

Swain, Brajakishore *Dharmaśastra - A Link Between Tradition and Modernity* Varanasi: Chaukhambha Sanskrit Sansthan, 2003.

been possessed of Kuladharmas, which may have been either Gṛhya or Dharma-sūtras. The only collection, however, which has come down to us is that of Pāraskara.[3] Another, ascribed to Vaijvāpin, is quoted, but has not yet been discovered in manuscript. Connected with the Sāmaveda Gṛhyasūtras of Gobhila, adopted both by the Rāṇāyaṇīyas and the Kauthumas seem to have obtained the greatest celebrity, there being but one other collection, the *Khādiragṛhya*, which is sometimes quoted as a parallel authority of the Chandogas.[4] The Gṛhyasūtras of the Ṛgveda or the Bahvṛchas were written by Śaunaka, and he is quoted as an authority on legal subject by as late a writer as the author of the *Mānavadharmaśāstra* (iii. 16). The only two collections, however, which have been preserved in MS. are those of Āśvalāyana and Śāṅkhāyana.

Various opinions are expressed by the Brāhmaṇas themselves as to the meaning of *gṛhya*. *Gṛha*, according to the commentary on Āśvalāyana, signifies not only house, but also wife. In support of the latter meaning he quotes a passage, *sagṛho gṛhaṁ āgataḥ*—"he is gone to the house with his wife." According to this derivation the *gṛhya* ceremonies would be those which are performed with the sacred fire, first lighted by a husband on the day of his marriage. This fire, or the altar on which it is kept, is called *gṛhya*, and the *gṛhya* sacrifices are all performed on that altar. But it is doubtful whether *gṛha* can ever mean wife. In the passage quoted above, it rather means house or family. Besides, as the Hindus themselves admit, this domestic fire has sometimes to be lighted by a Brāhmaṇa[5] before his marriage, in case his father should die prematurely.[6] Gṛhya, therefore, probably meant originally the house or the family hearth, from *gṛha*, house, and it was in opposition to the great sacrifices for which several hearths were required, and which were, therefore, called Vaitānika,[7] that the domestic ceremonies were called Gṛhya, as performed by means of the one domestic fire. It should be stated, however, in favour of the former interpretation, that in Gobhila's Sūtra these domestic ceremonies are not called *gṛhya,* but *gṛhya karmāṇi* and that here also the commentator admits *gṛhya* in the sense of housewife or tradition.[8]

The general name of the sacrifices performed, according to the Gṛhyasūtras, is Pākayajña, where *pāka* is not to be taken in the sense of cooking, but signifies, according to Indian authorities, either small or good. That *pāka* is used in the first sense appears from such expressions as "*yo'smat pākataraḥ*," "he who is smaller than we." But the more likely meaning is good or excellent or perfect; because, as the commentators remark, these ceremonies impart to every man that peculiar fitness without which he would be excluded from the sacrifices, and from all the benefits of his religion. As it is necessary that the marriage ceremonies should be rightly performed, that the choice of the bride should be made according to sacred rules, prescribed in the Sūtras or established by independent tradition in various families and localities, the first ceremony described in the Gṛhyasūtras is Marriage. Then follow the Saṁskāras, the rites to be performed at the conception of child, at various periods before his birth, at the time of his birth, the ceremony of naming the child, of carrying him out to see the sun, of feeding him, of cutting hair, and lastly of investing him as a student, and handing him to a Guru, under whose care he is to study the sacred writings, that is to say, to learn them by heart, and to perform all the offices of a Brahmacārin, or religious student. It is only after he has served his apprenticeship and grown up to manhood, that he is allowed to marry, to light the sacrificial fire for himself, to choose his priests, and to perform year after year the solemn sacrifices, prescribed by the Śruti and the Smṛti. The latter are described in the later books of the Gṛhyasūtras, and the last book contains a full account of the funeral ceremonies and of the sacrifices offered to the spirits of the departed.

There is certainly more of human interest in these domestic rites than in the great sacrifices described in the Śrautasūtras. The offerings themselves are generally of a simple nature, and the ceremonial is such that it does not require the assistance of a large class of professional priests. A log of wood placed on the fire of the hearth, an oblation poured out to the gods, or alms given to Brāhmaṇas, this is what constitutes a Pāka-yajña. Āśvalāyana quotes several passages from the Veda, in order to show that the gods do not despise those simple offerings, nay, that a mere prayer will secure their favour, and that a hymn of praise is as good as bulls and cows. He quotes from ṚV. viii.19.5.and 6.: "The mortal who sacrifices to Agni with a log of wood, with an oblation, with a bundle of grass[9] with a reverence, careful in his performance, his horses will press on quickly, his fame will be the brightest; nowhere will mischief, whether wrought by the gods or wrought by men reach him." Another verse is quoted from ṚV. viii.24.20., where men are called upon "to speak a mighty speech which is sweeter to Indra than milk (*ghṛta*, ghee) and honey." And lastly, reference is made to a passage (ṚV. 16. 47.), where the poet says: "With this hymn of praise, O Agni, we bring thee a sacrifice that is fashioned by the heart; may these be thy bulls, thy oxen and thy cows." All these passages are more applicable to the Gṛhya than to the Śrauta ceremonies, and though the latter may seem of greater importance to the Brāhmaṇas, to us the former will be more deeply interesting as disclosing that deep-rooted tendency in the heart of man to bring the chief events of human life in connection with a higher power, and to give to our joys and sufferings a deeper significance and a religious sanctification.[10]

The third class of the Sūtras, the Sāmayācārika or Dharmasūtras, are equally interesting on account of the light which they throw on the everyday life of the early Brāhmaṇas. According to the commentaries on these works, the existence of the Dharmasūtras is presupposed by the Śrauta and Gṛhya-sūtras. It is said, for instance, in the former, that a certain act of the sacrifice is to be performed by a man, after he has adjusted his sacrificial cord (*yajñopavīta*); but in what peculiar manner a man ought to adjust that cord is not stated, but is supposed to be known from the Dharmasūtras. The same remark is made with reference to the exact manner of rinsing the mouth (*ācamana*), and of performing the morning and evening prayers (*sandhyāvandana*). These matters are spoken of as generally known from the Sūtras, and, according to Hindu commentators, they could only be known from the Dharmasūtras. This argument, however, can hardly be considered conclusive as to the historical priority of the Dharmasūtras. On the contrary, it seems more likely that these matters, such as adjusting the sacrificial cord, etc., were supposed to be so well known at the time when the Śrauta and Gṛhyasūtras were first composed, that they required no elucidation. Instead, therefore, of considering the Dharmasūtras as earlier in time, the evidence, as far as it is known at present, would rather point in the opposite direction, and make us look upon these Dharmasūtras as the latest of the three branches of Sūtras. This impression is confirmed by other reflections. In neither of the other Sūtras is the position of the Śūdra so definitely marked as in the Dharmasūtras. Āpastamba, in his Sāmayācārikasūtras, declares distinctly that there are four Varṇas, the Brāhmaṇa, the Kṣatriya, the Vaiśya, the Śūdra, but that the initiatory rites, the Upanayana in particular, are only intended for the three first classes. The same is implied, no doubt, in the other Sūtras, which give the rules as to the proper time when a young Brāhmaṇa, a young Kṣatriya, or a young Vaiśya should be apprenticed with their spiritual tutors, but never say at what age this or similar ceremonies should be performed for one not belonging to these three Varṇas. Yet they never exclude the Śūdra expressly,[11] nor do they represent him as the born slave or client of the other castes. In the Dharmasūtras the social degradation of the Śūdra is as great as in the later Law books, and the same crime, if committed by a Brāhmaṇa and a Śūdra is visited with very different punishments. Thus, if a member of the three Varṇas commits adultery with the wife of a Śūdra, he is to be banished; if a Śūdra commits adultery with the wife of a member of the three Varṇas he is to be executed.[12] If a Śūdra abuses an honest member of the three Varṇas, his tongue is to be cut.[13] He is to be flogged for not keeping at a respectful distance. For murder, theft, and pillage the Śūdra is executed; the Brāhmaṇa, if caught in the same offences, is only deprived of his eye-sight. This is the same iniquitous law, which we find in the later Law books. But although the distinction between the Śūdras and the other Varṇas is so sharply drawn by Āpastamba, he admits that a Śūdra, if he obeys the law, may be born again as a Vaiśya, the Vaiśya as a Kṣatriya, and the Kṣatriya as a Brāhmaṇa;[14] and that a Brāhmaṇa, if he disregards the law, will be born again as a Kṣatriya, the Kṣatriya as a Vaiśya and a Vaiśya as a Śūdra.

It might be supposed that the Dharmasūtras formed merely an appendix to the Śrauta and Gṛhyasūtras, and that they should be classed with the Pariśiṣṭa literature. But such a supposition is contradicted by the fact, that the Dharmasūtras occasionally treat of the same subjects as the Gṛhyasūtras, and employ almost the same words in explaining some of the initiatory rites, the *saṁskāras*. They must, therefore, be considered as independent collections of Sūtras, later perhaps than the Śrauta and Gṛhyasūtras, but enjoying the same authority on matters belonging to Smṛti or tradition, as the Gṛhyasūtras.

We have still to mention the Ten Sūtras of the Sāmaveda.[15] Sutras[16] do not all, strictly speaking, treat of the Kalpa, or the ceremonial. Some of them are little more than lists such as we find in the Anukramaṇīs or Indices, appended to the other Vedas. Their style, however, approaches the style of the Sūtras; and, as they are quoted together as the Ten Sūtras, and, as some of them belong decidedly to the earliest productions of the Sūtra literature, it will be more convenient to place them here, than to refer them to the Pariśiṣṭa literature, with which they have little or nothing in common. They are:

I. The *Kalpasūtra*, or *Ārṣeyakalpa* of Maśaka, an index of the hymns used by the Chandoga priests, in the order in which the sacrifices are described in the *Tāṇḍyabrāhmaṇa*. Eleven *Prapāṭhakas*: 1–5, on the sacrifices called *Ekāha*; 6–9, on the sacrifices called *Ahīna*; 10–12, on the sacrifices called *Sattra*. Commentary by Varadarāja.

II. The *Anupadasūtra*, a gloss to the *Tāṇḍyabrāhmaṇa* in ten *Prapāṭhakas*,

III. The *Kalpasūtra*, already mentioned, either of Lāṭyāyana or Drāhyāyaṇa. Lāṭyāyana quotes Maśaka, and follows the order of the *Tāṇḍyabrāhmaṇa*.

IV. The *Nidānasūtra*, on Metres, in ten *Prapāṭhakas*.

V. The *Upagranthasūtra*, a treatise on the performance of some of the Sāmaveda sacrifices, commonly ascribed to Kātyāyana.[17]

VI. The *Kṣudrasūtra* or *Kṣaudra*, in three *Prapāṭhakas*, equally treating of the ceremonial of the Sāmaveda.[18]

VII. The *Taṇḍālakṣaṇasūtra*.

VIII. The *Pañcavidhasūtra*,[19] in two *Prapāṭhakas*.

IX. The *Kalpānupada* and

X. The *Anustotrasūtra*,[20] in two *Prapāṭhakas*.

We miss in this list the *Puṣpasūtra*, ascribed to Gobhila, and containing rules on the adaptation of the text of the hymns to their musical performance.

References

1. See Stenzler "*On Indian Law Books*," *Ind. St.* i. 232 and iii. 159.
2. Weber, *Vorlesungen*, p. 97.
3. Pāraskara's Gṛhyasūtras are ascribed to the *Mādhyandinīśākhā*.
4. See Āśāditya in his "*Commentary on the Karmapradīpa*," *Ind. St*. i. 58. This *Karmapradīpa*, a work ascribed to Kātyāyana, is intended as a supplement to Gobhila.
5. "भार्यादिरग्निर्दायादिर्वा तस्मिन्गृह्याणीति गौतमः" This is taken from G.D.S., v. 1.
6. गवेधुकचरुरवकीर्णिपशुश्च लौकिकेऽग्नौ भवति। तत्रावकीर्णिपशौ पुरोडाशश्रपणं भूमौ भवति न कपालेषु॥ *Kātyāyanasūtrapaddhati*.
7. वितानोऽग्नीनां विस्तारः। तत्र भवति वैतानिकानि बह्वग्निसाध्यानि कर्माणीत्यर्थः॥ Nārāyaṇa on Āśv. G.S. The three fires are the *Gārhapatya, Āhavanīya, Dakṣiṇa*; the one fire is the Āvasathya or Gṛhya.

8. अथातो गृह्यकर्माण्युपदेक्ष्यामः ॥ १ ॥ गृह्यशब्देन स्मार्ताग्निरुच्यते । तस्मिन्यानि कर्माणि तानि गृह्याकर्माणि । दीर्घत्वं छान्दसम् । अथवा गृह्या स्मृतिः । तस्यां यानि कर्माणि ॥ अथवा गृह्या पत्नी । तया सहितस्य यानि कर्माणि ॥

9. The Commentator explains *veda* as the sacred code. Such a code was not known to the authors of the hymns.

10. (Weber, "Catalogue of Sanskrit MSS." p. 33). See also Karma-pradīpa, MS. W. 465, p. 16 b.

11. Āp. D.S., i. 6. अशूद्राणामदुष्टकर्मणामुपायनं वेदाध्ययननग्न्याधेयं फलवन्ति च कर्माणि ॥ शुश्रूषा शूद्रस्येतरेषां वर्णानाम् ॥

12. MS. p. 163 नाश्य आर्यः शूद्रायां वध्यः शूद्र आर्यायाम् । (नाश्यो निर्वास्यः)

13. MS. p. 164 *b* जिह्वाछेदनं शूद्रस्यार्यं धार्मिकमाक्रोशतो वाचि पथि शय्यायामासन इति समीभवतो दण्डताडनम् ॥ पुरुषवधे स्तेये भूम्यादान इति स्वान्यादाय वध्यश्चक्षुर्निरोधस्त्वेतेषु ब्राह्मणस्य ॥

14. MS. p. 125 *b*. धर्मचर्यया जघन्यो वर्णः पूर्वं पूर्वं वर्णमापद्येत जातिपरिवृत्तौ अधर्मचर्यया पूर्वो वर्णो जघन्यं जघन्यं वर्णमापद्येत जातिपरिवृत्तौ ॥

15. The most important among them were first noticed and described by Dr. Weber, on whose authority some of our statements must rest.

16. MS. Chamb. 100.

लाठ्यायनमनुपदं निदानं कल्पमेव च ।
उपग्रन्थाश्च क्षुद्राश्च तण्डालक्षणमेव च ॥
सूत्रं पञ्चविधेयञ्च कल्पानुपदमेव च ।
अनुस्तोत्रञ्च विज्ञेयं दशसूत्रप्रकीर्त्तनम् ॥

Varadarāja in his Commentary on Kātyāyana's Pratihāra (MS. Bodl. W. 394).

17. Cf. Ind. St., i. 43, 54, 56, 58; MS. E. I. H. 121. सामवेद उपग्रन्थसूत्रम् copied Samvat, 1586 – 1530 A.D. by Paṇḍita Śrī Lakshmīdhara, son of Śrī Bhīma. इत्युपग्रन्थसूत्रे चतुर्थः प्रपाठकः ॥

18. MS. Bodl. W. 375.

19. MS. Bodl. W. 375. Begins प्रस्तावोद्गीथप्रतिहारोपद्रवनिधनानि भक्तयः तत्पाञ्चविध्यं स्मृत व्याख्यास्यामः ॥ One of these five *Bhaktis*, the *Pratihāra*, is described in the Pratihārasūtra, ascribed to Kātyāyana, and explained by Varadarāja.

20. MS. Bodl. W. 375.

Manu

1. Manu is the most powerful personality in the history of Indian civilization. Perhaps it is only the Vedic literature that exerted such a strong hold on the life: emotions and the intellect of the people as Manu. Manu was a very important personality in the Vedas and he continued to be so with added importance during the later development of the civilization of India. Even gods did not have such a persistent hold on the civilization of the country which Manu had held. In the Vedas, it is Indra who is the real hero, the leader of the people, setting an example for the life of martial heroism which the people of the Vedic age lived. But in later times, he dropped down from that position; though he was installed as the Lord of the heavens and of the gods in later mythology, he was not in the epic age the same heroic warrior which he was in the Vedic civilization. He was harassed by the demons and he had always to go to the great God Viṣṇu for protection and he even called for the help of the heroic kings on the earth in his encounters with the demons. In the Vedic age, the people and the kings looked to Indra for help and in the later times the current was reversed. In the Vedas, he had his consort, Indrāṇī; in the later epic he was more the husband of this Vedic consort than a great hero. In the Vedas, he is spoken of as the Lord of Śacī, 'Power,' in many places; Śacī became a name for his consort, Indrāṇī, in the Epics; but that did not make him any more powerful.

2. Viṣṇu was a great god even in the Vedas. But he was not in the Vedas, the great warrior with his weapons, the destroyer

of the demons and of evil in this world, the promotor of humanity against the enemies of civilized life. He had his wide strides, his all encompassing movements. His abode was the highest position in the world. In this way, his eminence in the Vedas as a great god cannot be questioned; but he did not have the position as the leader of men in the Vedas, which he became in the epics. As a matter of fact, in later times, he took the position among the people which Indra had enjoyed in the Vedas. Although a great god both in the Vedas and in the later epics, he had many changes in his nature and in his function.

3. Rudra is another great god of the Vedas, who continued in the epics as another great god along with Viṣṇu. Rudra had his weapons, and his darts were a terror to the enemies of the nation. He had a thousand remedies in his possession. Like Viṣṇu, he too came into the position of supreme eminence in the life of the people only in the epic period and he was not the same leader of the nation in the Vedas. Rudra had much of Dravidian features also added to him in his change from the Vedic Rudra to the epic Śiva.

4. In the epic period, there are three gods known as the Trinity of Gods (*Trimūrti*), namely, Viṣṇu, Śiva and Brahmā. Brahmā was not at all a god in the Vedas; in the neuter gender the name meant only the poetry of the Vedas, and in the masculine, it meant the poet. The term meant the highest truth in later times, even in the Upaniṣads, when it is in the neuter. In the Vedas, we had Viśvakarman (the maker of All) and Hiraṇyagarbha (Golden Wombed One) as the Creator of the world. It is this aspect of creatorship that was assigned to Brahmā in the epic period.

5. Manu is a great personality in the Vedas. He is the progenitor of humanity. The word Manu in the plural meant men in the Vedas and in the singular also, it meant humanity. There is the word *mānava,* related to Manu or progeny of Manu, which is one of the synonyms of man in Sanskrit. He established the religious practices along with others, in the Vedas. He is, according to later epics, the first among the kings. He is also the ruler of the world for a long period in the

history of the universe. Manu ceased to be a person and Manu became a position in the Government of the universe. In the later epics he is also the first law-giver, the person who taught the laws of moral life to humanity. From the Vedas to the epic period, Manu had only an elevation and an expansion.

6. In spite of his position as the institutor of the religious practices in the Vedas, there is no poem addressed to Manu or describing Manu, in the whole of the Vedas. That is the case with some of the leaders of Vedic civilization besides Manu; for example, there is the Aṅgiras and the Atharvan, sages who played a very prominent part in the development of the Vedic civilization. But his name appears very prominently in the Vedic literature, along with the names of the other leaders in the establishment of the Vedic civilization.

7. In a verse addressed to the gods in general, it is said that it was Manu who first performed the sacrifices, the Vedic rituals:

> (1) For whom Manu performed the first sacrifice with invocations, with the fire-kindled, on account of his mental powers, along with the seven invokers; may those sons of Aditi (the Gods), vouchsafe us freedom from fear and also happiness, may they make our path easy to traverse so that we may have eternal weal.

Manu is also spoken of as father:

> (2) The intuitive powers which Atharvan, Father Manus and Dadhyañc developed.

Here the word appears as Manus and not Manu. This is only a small difference, being two derivatives from the same root *man* (to think). But there are places where the origin of the human race is traced to other sources; thus fire is called the first to propagate the progeny of Manu and Mātariśvan, another form of fire, is mentioned as having found out the path for his son; and this Mātariśvan is also spoken of as the knower of the heaven. Such an alteration in positions and relationships and functions are met with in the Vedas; but that does not go against the basic position of Manu being the first forefather of humanity.

8. I do not know in which sense Manu is called the father of humanity. In later literature, there are fathers for a person on account of certain functions besides the father who was the cause for the birth of the person. Thus Kālidāsa says that the first King, Dilīpa, described in his *Raghuvaṁśa,* was the real father of the people because he disciplined them, protected them and maintained them. It is very likely that this notion of the function of the ruler is a Vedic belief, that the ruler of the country is also a father to the people. Nowhere is it said in the *Ṛgveda* that the whole of the human race originated in a primal pair, a man and a woman. Yama and Yamī, brother and sister, are not the originators of the human race. The whole poem in which there is a dialogue between Yama and Yamī goes against the assumption that they were the primal father and mother of humanity.

9. The most conspicuous feature of Manu is that it was he who for the first time instituted the sacrifice among the people.

(1) O fire, Manu established you as a light for the people as a whole. You have shone by the side of Kaṇva, being born from the Law and growing in size, you before whom the people bow.

(2) That form of yours which Manu, which Sumitra (the poet) has kindled, O fire, that form of yours of this nature is newer than everything. May you shine forth full of wealth, may you accept our songs; may he give us victory, may he bring us glory.

In the first of the two verses, it is certain that what is meant is that it was Manu who for the first time kindled the fire for the purposes of the sacrifices. In the same verse, Kaṇva is also joined to Manu in this act of kindling the fire. There are many places where Manu is associated with various Sages. Some of them are well-known poets who have contributed their own poems to the available collection of the *Ṛgveda,* among whom Kaṇva is one. In the second verse also, the meaning must be that Manu kindled the sacred fire for sacrifices for the first time, and in this case, he is associated with Sumitra who is the author for this poem.

(3) Just as you have performed the sacrifice for the gods with the offerings which belonged to Manu, the poet, becoming a poet among the poets, in that same way, O invoker of the gods, the most truthful, O fire, may you now perform a sacrifice with the sweet ladle.

Fire is the invoker of the gods to the sacrifice and he is also spoken of as a participant in the sacrifice, in many places. Here the position must be that Manu had formerly performed a sacrifice and in that sacrifice, the fire has taken part by invoking the gods. In the same way, the poet, Gotama Rāhūgaṇa, requests the fire to perform a similar sacrifice making use of the sweet ladle. He was making the offerings of sweet things with the ladle, and the fire is requested to invoke the gods to the sacrifice so that they may enjoy the offerings.

10. (1) By the same protections by which You both, O heroes, searched the path for the sake of Śayu, for the sake of Atri, for the sake of Manu in olden times, by which you secured for Syūmaraśmi an arrow of reed, may you both come hither with the same protections, O Aśvins.

(2) By which protections you have fully protected Manu with the arrows, may you both come hither with the same protections, O Aśvins.

Here in the first verse, the word 'in olden times' is used along with Manu. But I think that the word has to be construed with all the other names. In the second verse, there is protection given to Manu who is spoken of as a hero, Vīra. The meaning must be that the Aśvins secured weapons for Manu and not that they used the weapons against Manu's enemies and protected him. It is found that the Aśvins had secured an arrow for Syūmaraśmi, in the first verse.

11. Dadhyañc, the ancient Aṅgiras, Priyamedha, Kaṇva, Atri and Manu have known my birth; they,

> the ancients, have known my birth. They had their long association with the gods. Our navel (origin) is in them. Along their path I salute with the exalted song; Indra and fire I salute with song.

Here the poet who sings like this is Parucchepa, and it is said that the great sages herein enumerated have known his origin. The idea must be that his own ancestors were associated with the sages enumerated here and that the sages had been in association with the gods long before and that his own origin is in them, that is, he was singing the song in pursuit of the songs sung by those ancient sages.

12. Just as you have become purified for the sake of Manu, you who possess power, who destroy the enemies, who know the immense space, who possess the offerings given, in the same way, become purified, bearing wealth; abide by the side of Indra, produce the weapons.

The poet is pressing Soma and requests Soma to behave exactly in the same way in which Soma had behaved when handled by Manu. This also shows that Manu had something to do with the first institution of the sacrifice.

13. It must be on account of his prominent position in the matter of the institution of the sacrifices that Manu was supposed to be the father of men. The sacrifices contain the essence of the Moral Law. In two poems it is stated that the first sacrifice became the primal Moral Law:

> Gods performed the sacrifice and those sacrifices became the primal moral laws.

14. (1) Pardon us O Rudra and then, produce happiness for us; we worship you who are the overlord of the heroes. Since Manu the father has performed the sacrifice for happiness and bliss, may we be able to attain to that pleasure and bliss when O Rudra, you give us guidance.

(2) What pure remedies you have, O Maruts, what produce the greatest happiness, the strong, the producer of welfare, what Manu our father has

accepted, them we long for as belonging to Rudra in order that we may have happiness and freedom from suffering.

(3) That early friend of the great gods attained happiness through his intellectual powers; through his doors the father Manu sent up his thoughts to the gods.

(4) Indra has held the Soma stalk through our sons and with his strength; O Bṛhaspati, carry this person through the span of his life. This sacrifice is our father Manu of great intelligence. We ask for eternal security from danger.

In many places we are not at all certain whether it is Manu himself that is meant or only man in general, and interpreters have not agreed on the point. Thus:

15. (1) O Maruts, may he become the foremost bird among the birds, the quick flying kite among the kites; because the bird has brought for Manu (or for man) the oblation which the gods love, with his own powers, without the aid of wheels.

(2) Agni (fire) the friend quickly cooked three hundred buffaloes on account of his power. Indra drank together three lakes of Soma belonging to Manu (man) that had been pressed, so that he could kill Vṛtra.

It is mainly in the poems that are taken to be outside the genuine text of the *Ṛgveda*, the poems collected together as *Vālakhilya* (supplements) that we hear something about the parentage of Manu.

16. (1) Just as you have drunk, O Indra, the Soma from Manu the son of Saṁvaraṇa.

(2) Just as you have drunk, O Indra, the Soma from Manu the son of Vivasvat (given only as Vivasvat and not as Vaivasvata or son of Vivasvat).

In the *Atharvaveda* and in the Brāhmaṇas, he has definitely become the son of Vivasvat.

(3) Manu the son of Vivasvat became her son.

17. In the main part of the *Ṛgveda*, there is no mention of Manu as the son of Vivasvat. When it is said that Tvaṣṭṛ gave his daughter named Saraṇyū in marriage to Vivasvat, there is no mention of Manu being a son of this pair; only the name of Yama occurs there as the son of Saraṇyū, the daughter of Tvaṣṭṛ and wife of Vivasvat. But Sāyaṇa narrates a story how Vivasvat had relations with a divine woman, mistaking her to be Saraṇyū herself and how the royal Sage Manu was born. It is only in the portions outside the genuine part of the *Ṛgveda* and in the *Atharvaveda* and in the Brāhmaṇas that we find mention of Manu as the son of Vivasvat (Vaivasvata). This term Vaivasvata occurs as the name of Yama in the *Ṛgveda*. Manu Vaivasvata occurs in contrast to Yama Vaivasvata in the Brāhmaṇas.

18. It has been shown that in the portions outside the genuine part of the *Ṛgveda*, there is the name Sāṁvaraṇi (son of Saṁvaraṇa) applied to Manu. There is also the name Sāvarṇya and Sāvarṇi associated with Manu in a poem in the *Ṛgveda*. In one verse the name Manu occurs and in two others that follow, the name that appears is Sāvarṇya and Sāvarṇi respectively. Both mean "son of Savarṇa or a descendent of Savarṇa." Some interpreters do not take the word Manu as a name, but only as meaning "man". The poet is Nābhānediṣṭha, son of Manu according to the indices. Nābhānediṣṭha is the author for two poems in the *Ṛgveda*. We have to accept him as the son of Manu on the authority of the indices. In his poem appears the following reference to Manu with his two other alternative names:

(1) May this Manu become great, may he grow like a seed. Because he has dedicated thousand, hundred horses for a gift on the same day.

(2) No one can reach up to him just like the high vault of the heavens. The gifts of Sāvarṇya (son of Savarṇi) spread like an ocean.

(3) May not Manu, the leader of the villages, with gifts in thousands come to any grief. May his gift

> increase wide spreading like the Sun. May the gods carry Sāvarṇi (son of Savarṇa) through his life span. From him we hope to receive gifts without a cessation.

According to the latter-day epics, Saṁvaraṇa is a king of the lunar race who came soon after Duṣyanta and his son Bharata. Sāvarṇi is meant to become the Manu after the period of the present Manu, the son of Vivasvat (Vaivasvata Manu), and Sāvaṇ is also a son of the Sun-god.

19. I do not know how I should look at the situation. Either there is a gap between the genuine portions of the *Ṛgveda* on one side and the supplementary portions of the *Ṛgveda* and the other parts of the Vedas like the *Atharvaveda* and the Brāhmaṇas on the other side, or if there is no such break and no such gap, there is the continuity of the traditions beginning from the earliest times to the latter-day epic period. One thing is certain and that is that the latter-day epic traditions go back to some of the parts of the vast Vedic literature.

20. Manu's name occurs in the *Ṛgveda* along with the names of a large number of sages who are either poets who have contributed to the available collection or whose names are very prominent in the available collection. Some of the names that are very popular in the latter-day epics also find a place in the *Ṛgveda* along with the name of Manu. Agni is asked to visit the place of worship as he had been doing in the case of the worships conducted by Manu, Aṅgiras, and Yayāti. Yayāti figures in the *Mahābhārata* as one of the ancient heroes of the lunar dynasty; a large number of royal names that appear in the *Ṛgveda* are mentioned in the latter-day epics as coming after Yayāti in the line. Thus, Yadu and Turvaśu are the sons of Yayāti through his queen Devayānī and Druhyu, Pūru and Anu are his sons through the other queen Śarmiṣṭhā.

21. There are many places in the *Ṛgveda* where Manu is given as an example of a great person who had been worshipping the gods and who had pleased the gods through such worship:

(1) O Agni, (fire) O god, we keep you firm in our minds, you who help in the conduct of the worship, the invoker, the supremely wise, powerful, the undying messenger.

(2) The Aśvins are invoked to go to the place as to the place of worship of Manu.

(3) Agni is asked to go to them as they had done in the case of Manu; the same prayer is repeated in the next verse too.

(4) The seven rays of the fire had extended as in the case of Manu.

(5) There is reference to the worship which the fire is asked to approach, as he did in the case of Manu.

(6) Indra is asked to take delight in the Soma and to drink it as in the case of Manu.

(7) The Ṛbhus are asked to take delight in the worship as in the case of Manu, and there is a similar request to the same gods, about Soma which the poet was offering them.

(8) The poets have placed the fire firm as Manu did, have kindled the fire as Manu did and they ask the fire to worship the gods as they did in the case of Manu.

(9) There is a request to Indra and Varuṇa to go to the place as they did in the case of Manu.

(10) As Manu had done, the poet glorifies the fire for the sake of the ritual.

(11) As in the case of Manu, the fire is asked to perform the worship to the gods.

(12) The poets invoke Varuṇa after having pressed the Soma as Manu had done.

(13) The poets invoke the fire, as did Manu, Bhṛgu and Aṅgiras.

(14) People kindle the fire as Manu did.

(15) There is a prayer to the Aśvins and Indra as Manu had done.

(16) Iḷā is asked to take delight in the worship as in the case of Manu. Iḷā is again asked to take delight in the worship as in the case of Manu.

22. In this way, Manu as an example for the performance of the worship, kindling the fire and pressing the Soma, is given in the entire text of the *Ṛgveda* from the beginning to the end, practically in all the books. Again the gods gave the Fire to Manu:

(1) The Fire whom the gods gave to Manu.

(2) Mātariśvan brought the fire from the far distance for the sake of Manu.

(3) Kāvya Uśanas made the fire the invoker for the sake of Manu.

(4) Mātariśvan created the fire for the sake of Manu.

Here also it is noted that the gods gave the fire to Manu, thus meaning that Manu was the first to perform the worship which has later become the standard of the worship of the gods in the Vedas.

23. In the Brāhmaṇas there is the story of how the world was swept away in a deluge and how a fish saved Manu in a ship. Then Manu became the progenitor of humanity. The story of a deluge is found in the *Avesta* and also in the Semitic antiquities. Some say that it was borrowed by the Āryans (Vedas and Avesta) from the Semitic source; it may be the other way. It can as well be that there was a great civilization in those times in developing which both the Āryans and the Semitic people had a share.

24. Manu appears in combination with the names of other ancient poets; they are Atri, Dadhyañc, Aṅgiras, Kaṇva, Priyamedha, Śayu, Sumitra and Syūmaraśmin. But in most of the places, Manu is given alone. In all the places I have cited, I am certain that the reference is to the man named Manu and not to man in general. The word occurs in many more places in the *Ṛgveda*. There is no doubt that he was one among the most ancient of the prominent personages known to the poets of the *Ṛgveda*. Nearly all the poets speak of him as the one

person who had performed the worship which they themselves had been carrying on. There is nothing to show that the various poets of whom there is mention alongwith the name of Manu were known to the poets as contemporaries of Manu. The very fact that in nearly all the places the name of Manu appears alone shows that they knew him to be one distinct from all the others. They could have known Manu only in tradition and they knew practically nothing about his personality and his parentage and other details.

25. We have to consider the question whether in the *Ṛgveda* itself we have mention of the same Manu in all the places or whether the poets of the *Ṛgveda* knew more than one Manu. In nearly all the occurrences Manu is mentioned alone without any other names like the name of the father. It is only in the portion of the *Ṛgveda* outside the genuine parts that we find a mention of Manu being the son of Saṁvaraṇa and of Savarṇa. Then in the *Atharvaveda* and in the Brāhmaṇas there is the Manu as Vaivasvata, the son of Vivasvat. Manu the son of Vivasvat and Yama the son of Vivasvat, thus, become brothers, with the same father and, according to the traditions maintained till the time of the later commentators, with different mothers. Yama was the son of Saraṇyū, the daughter of Tvaṣṭṛ and Manu was the son of another mother, who had a divine status. In the same story it is said that the Aśvins also were the sons of the same Vivasvat.

26. The Purāṇas speak of fourteen Manus who take the position one after the other. Six Manus have already occupied the position and they have given place to later Manus. The present Manu is Manu the son of Vivasvat. Then there are seven Manus to follow. The six Manus whose time has expired, are: Svāyambhuva, Svārociṣa, Auttami, Tāmasa, Raivata and Cākṣuṣa. The seven Manus that will follow the present Manu are: Sāvarṇi, Dakṣa-sāvarṇi, Brāhma-sāvarṇi, Dharma-sāvarṇi, Rudra-sāvarṇi, Deva-sāvarṇi and Indra-sāvarṇi. Thus all the Manus who will follow are Sāvarṇi. About the next Manu, Sāvarṇi, there is a story narrated in the *Mārkaṇḍeya Purāṇa*; he was a great ruler who lived during the

time of the second of the past six Manus, the Svārociṣa Manu.

27. There must have been recollections of various civilizations that preceded the present time civilization and this present time civilization had, according to them, its origin in the Manu whom we find in the *Ṛgveda*. The Vedic literature gives us no clue to the problem of the six past Manus. But the available Vedas do not exhaust the texts relating to the civilizations of which they had some recollections in later times. The Vedic poets knew of a Manu who was the son of Vivasvat, though there is no reference to him in the *Ṛgveda*. We have to accept the whole of the Vedic literature, original texts and the Brāhmaṇas, as a unity so far as culture is concerned. From the specific mention of Manu as the son of Vivasvat in the *Atharvaveda* and from the frequent mention of a Manu in the *Ṛgveda*, we may not be far wrong from being if we assume that the Manu in the *Ṛgveda* is the same Manu who is mentioned in the *Atharvaveda* and in the Brāhmaṇas. But the problem of the Manu who is the son of Saṁvaraṇa and the Manu who is the son of Sāvarṇi remains.

28. In the case of Manu, the son of Saṁvaraṇa found in the *Ṛgveda* cannot be a mistake for son of Sāvarṇi. Now can the name Manu, son of Sāvarṇi found in the portions outside the genuine text be a mistake for Manu, the son of Saṁvaraṇa? According to the Purāṇas (the Epics), Sāvarṇi, the Manu of the immediately succeeding period after the expiry of the period of the present Manu, is a son of the Sun-God, though not mentioned as Vivasvat. He is given as the son of Sūrya. But the prominent mention of a Manu in the *Ṛgveda* and the specific mention of Manu as the son of Vivasvat in the *Atharvaveda* and in the Brāhmaṇas and the mention of the present Manu as the son of Vivasvat, make me believe that the Manu of the *Ṛgveda* is the Manu, son of Vivasvat.

29. Then, we have to fix the mutual relation of Manu, the son of Vivasvat and Yama the son of Vivasvat. According to the story narrated by Sāyaṇa, Yama and Yamī were the first children of Vivasvat and Manu was born as the son of Vivasvat later. Can it be that Manu established the system of worship

current in the Vedas, only after the time of Yama who had found the path and who had gone to the other region? From the available evidence, it is certain that Yama was a follower of the path of Vedic ritualism. Manu must have established the system of worship long before Yama found out the path. When those modes of worship were proceeding, Yama must have had a special intuition and he must have found out the path; that path was not a rival to the earlier path, not a protest against that. Yama found out the path by following the system of worship that was in vogue at that time. This makes Manu far earlier than Yama.

30. Here I must point out that the birth of Manu, according to the tradition preserved and recorded by Sāyaṇa, had some connection with the Uttara (Northern) Kurus. There is no doubt about the relation of the name Kuru with Kuruṣ in Iranian tradition; that is what we now know as Cyrus. In old Persian inscriptions, the name appears as Kuruṣ. I mention this because there is some relation between Yama and the Iranian tradition. Yama appears in the *Avesta* as Yima, who was in communion with the great God Ahura Mazda. Ahura Mazda gives instructions to Yima in the *Avesta*. But there is no Manu in the *Avesta*. The name does not occur there at all.

31. But the Yima of later Iranian tradition, known as Jamshid or Yima the King, is the exact counterpart of Manu in the Indian tradition. Both were kings and both instituted life according to the law of moral life suitable for civilized life, among humanity. Yima is not a very prominent personality in the *Avesta*. He does not appear very often in the text of the *Avesta*, not so often as the name of Yama or Manu appears in the *Ṛgveda*. The *Avesta* is a text specially related to Zarathushtra.

32. According to the Iranian tradition, Yima was the son of Vīvanhvant (Vivasvat). He ruled the country for a thousand years, when the land was happy, free from heat and cold, without diseases and death among men; but he had a rather unfortunate end and he had to spend the last days wandering about till his death. According to the *Shah Nameh* of Ferdousi,

in composing which the poet depended on the material supplied from the Palhevi literature, he was the first King to introduce civilized life among humanity. Before that, there were the kings who along with the people lived a life of wild beasts, along with wild beasts as companions. The earlier kings according to the *Shah Nameh* were Kiyūmaret, Siyāmek, Hūshang and Tahmūrat; it was then that Jamshid came to the throne, and according to the *Shah Nameh*, he ruled the country for seven hundred years. He too had a misfortune at the end of his life and he lost his life through the treachery of a tyrant, by name Sehak, who ascended the throne.

33. In spite of the difference in name between Jamshid and Manu, we cannot miss the common features, both being sons of Vivasvat (Vīvanhvant) and both having established the law of moral life among humanity, suitable for civilized life. It must also be noted that we see no sort of parallelism between Yama of the *Ṛgveda* and Yima of the *Avesta*. It must also be taken notice of that just as Manu came into great prominence in Indian tradition only at a later stage, Yima also came into great prominence only at a later stage in the Iranian tradition. In spite of the evidence of the *Avesta* we cannot ignore the fact that in the whole range of the old Persian Inscriptions, there is no mention of Yama; and for the matter of that, Zarathushtra too is not mentioned in the Inscriptions. We see only the Great God Ahura Mazda and not his Messengers on the earth, Zarathushtra and Yima. Zarathushtra, according to the Iranian tradition, gave the teaching and Yima enforced moral life. In Indian tradition, Yama gave the teaching and Manu enforced the laws of moral life.

34. Even in later stages, the Law of Moral life was traced back to Manu in India. The real authority in India for Moral Life is the Code known by the name of Manu, what is called the *Manusmṛti*. It is not really what can be called a Code of Law, meant for administration in the country; it is just a presentation of the entire field of moral life for men to know. Manu goes back to the earliest times in the history of India

and Manu remained prominent in Indian tradition through the ages, without a flicker, while Yama underwent changes. While Yama found the path to go to the other world after death, it was for Manu to find out the laws of moral life when man lived on the earth. Thus we can say that while Yama is the first teacher for religion, in the sense that religion shows the way to a life of happiness in future, Manu was the first teacher for the civilization of India, and Indian religion is nothing but a mode of civilized life. Life at a later stage after death serves only a very subordinate purpose in man's life in India. It is perhaps on account of this feature in Indian culture that Yama went out and Manu continued, gathering strength in the course of time.

35. Neither Yama nor Manu started civilized life in India; neither of them lifted humanity from a state of savage life among wild animals, into the light of civilization. Indian tradition does not know a stage in the life of humanity when there was no civilization; Indian tradition knows only a decline from the most civilized state of society to a life of sins and sufferings. Yama opened up a path for humanity to traverse after the death of man and Manu must have given a shape and form to the life of his times. Making offerings in Fire for the propitiation of the gods, the materials to be used for such offerings, the utilization of songs as an important factor in such worships, the various acts associated with the ritual of worship and such like matters might have been given a definite shape by Manu. It must have been the rituals as organized by Manu that were followed later by the people.

36. On the Iranian side, the function of Manu and the teachings of Yama got merged into each other and we have only Yama preserved in that tradition. The fact that both Manu and Yama happened to be the sons of Vivasvat might have helped in this merger. It is generally held that the *Avesta* represents an earlier phase of the civilization than what is found in the Vedas. But this is a matter that requires fresh investigation. I am of the view that it is in the Vedas that we meet with the original civilization and that in the *Avesta* we see the same culture influenced and altered by contact with

foreign cultures on the western side, the Assyrian civilization of Semitic origin. Rather than a bifurcation of the *Avestan* Yima into a Manu and a Yama in the Vedas, both being accepted as the sons of Vivasvat, the greater probability is that Yama and Manu, both sons of Vivasvat, become merged into each other to form a single teacher in the person of Yima, son of Vīvanhvant. What is really important is that both Manu and Yama played their parts in two distinct fields within the region of Indian civilization, the two fields being extensions of the same region of culture, without any mutual conflict and without any mutual rivalry.

37. In this process of mutual merging between Yama and Manu for the formation of Yima in the Iranian tradition, later known as Jamshid, it is more the Manu aspect that has become prominent. Yama who found out the path has little part in the Yima of the Iranian tradition. But there are certain features in Yama which continued in the Iranian tradition. Jamshid lost the favour of the Great God and he had to wander about, according to the *Avestan* and later traditions, and Jamshid had to meet with his death through a treachery according to other later traditions of Iran preserved in the Palhevi literature and utilized by Ferdousi in his *Shah Nameh*. In the Indian tradition too, Yama came into conflict with the Great God Śiva and had to suffer for this enmity with the God. But this common point is a very faint one.

38. Jamshid was treacherously killed by Sehak and Sehak came to the throne, according to the *Shah Nameh*. Sehak had two dragons on his shoulders. I do not know how far this can be traced to the nature of the Great God of India, Śiva, who too had serpents on his body. Ferdousi says that Sehak went to India to get cured of this deformity, and it was during this absence that a descendent of Jamshid went to him; that was Feridoon. This Sehak had two wives, a feature that we see in the Great God Śiva also in India. But the similarity ends here. The two wives of Sehak were the sisters of Jamshid whom he had managed to kill. Feridoon, after killing Sehak, married the two queens; Feridoon was born in another line and was not

a direct descendent of Jamshid. I have pointed out such matters only to show the relation between the Indian tradition and the Iranian tradition relating to Manu and Yama, and I took up the point in relation to Manu because I see more of Manu in the Iranian Yama (Jamshid) than of Yama himself.

39. In India itself, Manu had a greater hold on the mind of the people than what Yama had. Like Yama, the same Manu must have been what he acquired through his genius and it could not have been his personal name. We do not know what the original name could have been. I have indicated elsewhere that there are other teachers and philosophers who had acquired a name later, different from the original name, on account of certain associations and certain traits in character.

40. It has already been suggested that there are different Manu's in the Veda. There is a simple Manu without any appellation. Then in the *Atharvaveda* and in the Brāhmaṇas, also in later Sanskrit literature, there is Manu the son of Vivasvat (Vaivasvata). In the portions of the *Ṛgveda* outside the genuine part, there is mentioned a Manu as the son of Savarṇa and another as the son of Saṁvaraṇa. So far as the Manu is concerned who will have the name of Sāvarṇi, the story is found in the *Mārkaṇḍeya Purāṇa*, one of the eighteen epics known in Sanskrit literature; like the Vaivasvata Manu who is in the position now, this Sāvarṇi Manu too is a son of Vivasvat or the Sun-god, as is made clear in the *Mārkaṇḍeya Purāṇa*. He was originally a king in the time of the second of the Manus, the Svārociṣa Manu.

41. Each Manu lives in that position for such a long period that it is difficult to state the duration in language. There are various places in Sanskrit literature where the calculation is given. According to the *Amara Kośa*, the standard Lexicon in Sanskrit the calculation is as seventy-one divine *Yugas*. Manu says that a *Yuga* is ten thousand years and twelve thousand such *Yugas* will be a divine *Yuga*; according to the *Amara Kośa*, two thousand divine *Yugas* will form a day for the Creator (Brahmā). These are all later calculations when the conception of time had undergone great changes among the

Indians. It was when time began to be calculated in terms of such long periods that men were supposed to have been living for many thousands of years. But in the Veda itself, man lived only for a hundred years. And it is certain that the Manu and the Yama had to depart from this world after a lapse of a maximum of a hundred years. We know only his life after death in the case of Yama, and in the case of Manu, we know only about his life on the earth. Both of them must have been great teachers of very ancient times, whose fame continued even in the Vedic times; they themselves must have lived long prior to the days of the Vedas.

The Origin of Religion

I

The origin of religion is shrouded in mystery and has given rise to much difference of opinion. We may take for granted that its earliest form consists in the worship of natural powers. Man, when he first emerges from mere animal consciousness, realizes that he is almost entirely dependent upon the powerful forces of nature amidst which he is placed; and, accustomed as he is in his own experience to associate all power with voluntary effort, he ascribes these forces to sentient beings working behind them unseen. In other words, early man personifies the powers of nature which in virtue of their great strength become his gods. He cultivates a spirit of awe and reverence towards them, sings their praises and offers worship or sacrifice to them with a view either to propitiate them or to secure their favour. These deities, however, are divine only in a qualified sense, for, though called 'gods,' they are necessarily conceived in a human mould and are regarded as being actuated by the same motives and passions as the person that conceives them. They are in reality glorified human beings and are, therefore, neither wholly natural nor wholly supernatural. Though this faith looks simple and childlike, it is not altogether without a philosophic basis. It signifies a conviction that the visible world is not in itself final and that there is a reality lying hidden in it. It is also at bottom a seeking after an explanation of observed facts, implying a belief that every event has a cause; and to believe in the universality of causation is perforce to believe in the uniformity of nature. Unless primitive man had noticed the regularity with which natural phenomena recur and unless he were inwardly convinced that every event has a cause to account for it, he would not have resorted to the creation of such deities in explanation of them. It is true that he merely ascribed those phenomena to certain agencies supposed to be working behind them, and was, therefore, very far from explaining them in the proper sense of the term. Besides he was for the most part unaware that he was explaining at all. Nevertheless, there is clearly implied here a search for the causes of observed facts, however, unsuccessful or unconscious it may be. Acquiescence in any kind of accidentalism is inconsistent with the spirit of such speculation.

We are not, however, directly concerned here with this early form of belief, for Aryan religion when it appears in India has already a history behind it. As an American scholar has paradoxically put it: 'Indian religion begins before its arrival in India.'[1] It is a continuation of the primitive faith of the Indo-Europeans to which the Aryans that came to India belonged. There are to be found even now in Sanskrit old words which serve as clear indications of this fact. The word '*deva*' (*div,* 'to shine') for instance, which means 'god' in Sanskrit, is cognate with Latin '*deus*,' and points to a period when the Indo-European in his original home associated his conception of godhead with the luminous powers of nature. The spirit of veneration with which he regarded such deified powers is equally well indicated by the root *yaj,* 'to worship,' which is common to more than one Indo-European language. Again we have for example in the Vedic god Mitra the Indian counterpart of Iranian Mithra, whose cult was once in great vogue in Western Asia and Europe. These instances are sufficient to indicate what the antecedents of early Indian religion were. It had passed through the Indo-European stage as well as the Indo-Iranian in which the ancestors of the future Indians and Persians lived together and shared a common belief. The Vedic pantheon includes not only the old gods belonging to the two pre-Indian periods, but also several others whose conceptions the Aryan settlers formed in their new home, e.g. the river-deities like Sarasvatī. The number of these gods—old and new—is indefinite. Sometimes they are reckoned at thirty-three and classified into three groups of eleven each according to their abode, viz.: (i) gods of the sky, like Mitra and Varuṇa; (ii) gods of mid-air, like Indra and Maruts; and (iii) gods of the earth, like Agni and Soma—a classification which, by the way, indicates a desire to discover the interrelations of the gods and arrange them systematically. They are all of coordinate power and no supreme God as such is recognized, although some of them are more imposing than others—particularly Indra and Varuṇa, the gods respectively of the warrior and of the pious devotee.

It is not necessary to dwell here at length upon the details of Vedic mythology. We may note only such of its characteristics as have a philosophic bearing. The first point to attract our attention in it is how surprisingly close to nature the Vedic gods are. There is for instance absolutely no doubt in regard to what constitutes the basis in nature of Agni and Parjanya. They are gods and at the same time natural objects, viz. 'fire' and 'cloud.' There are other gods, it is true, like the Aśvins and Indra, whose identity is not so transparent; but what we have to remember is that, unlike Greek mythology for example, the prevailing type of Vedic gods is one of incomplete personalization. This is a remarkable feature seeing how far removed, comparatively speaking, Vedic religion is from its source. It is commonly described as 'arrested anthropomorphism'; but the expression is apt to suggest that the Vedic conception of divinity lacks a desirable feature, viz. complete personification, while in reality it points to an excellence—a frame of mind in the Vedic Aryan highly favourable to philosophic speculation. It may be that the particularly impressive features of nature in India, as has been suggested,[2] explain this 'unforgetting adherence' to it; but it is at least as much the result of the philosophic bent of the Indian mind. The fact is that the Vedic Indian did not allow his conceptions to crystallize too quickly. His interest in speculation was so deep and his sense of the mystery hiding the Ultimate was so keen that he kept before him unobscured the natural phenomena which he was trying to understand until he arrived at a satisfying solution.[3] This characteristic signifies a passion for truth and accounts not only for the profundity of Indian philosophic investigation, but also for the great variety of the solutions it offers of philosophical problems.

Another feature of early Indian religion equally remarkable is furnished by the conception of *ṛta* which finds a conspicuous place in the Mantras.[4] Expressions like 'guardians of *ṛta*' (*gopā ṛtasya*) and 'practisers of *ṛta*' (*ṛtāyu*) occur frequently in the description of the gods. This word, which is pre-Indian in origin, originally meant uniformity of nature or the ordered course of things such as is indicated by the regular alternation of day and night, while in the Mantras it not only bears this significance but also the additional one of 'moral order.' The Vedic gods are accordingly to be viewed not only as the maintainers of cosmic order but also as upholders of moral law. They are friendly to the good and inimical to the evil-minded, so that, if man is not to incur their displeasure, he should strive to be righteous. This equal responsibility of divinity for the maintenance of cosmos as well as moral order is particularly clear in the conception of Varuṇa. He represents the sky and is the god of heavenly light. He is described as having fixed the laws of the physical universe which no one can violate. Through his power for instance, it is said, the rivers flow into the ocean without overfilling it. But his sway is not restricted to the physical sphere; it extends beyond to the moral, where his laws are equally eternal and inviolable. He is omniscient so that the least sin even will not escape detection by him. To indicate the all-searching nature of his vigilant sight, the Sun is sometimes poetically described as his eye. The conception of Varuṇa was soon superseded in Vedic mythology by that of Indra who, as we have stated above, is a god of battles rather than of righteousness. This has led some modern scholars to the conclusion that there was a corresponding lapse in the moral standards of the Indian.[5] But they forget the peculiar circumstances in which the conception of Indra came into prominence. The immigrant Aryans had to subdue the numerous indigenous tribes; and it was in the process of this subjugation in which Varuṇa—essentially a god of peace—could not well be invoked that the idea of this warrior-god as known to the *Ṛgveda* was developed. 'Nations are never coarser,' it has been said,[6] 'than when they put their own nationality into antagonism against another nation.' We may grant that during the period of Indra's supremacy the self-assertion and violence which distinguish him were reflected in the character of his worshippers. But it was only a passing phase. Indra did not finally become the supreme God of the Indians, but had to yield place to others ethically more lofty so it is not justifiable to conclude that in the Indian view might replaced right. Besides, Indra is not altogether bereft of moral traits; nor is Varuṇa the only support of ṛta, all the sun-gods of whom he is one being regarded as equally so.[7] Further, Varuṇa stands only for a certain type of theistic conception—the Hebraic, as it has been said. But the development of religious thought in Vedic India, as we shall presently see, proceeded on altogether different lines rendering the idea of divinity generally speaking more and more impersonal. The neglect into which the Varuṇa ideal fell in the course of the period may therefore be taken as indicating the gradual rejection then of that idea of godhead and it need not necessarily mean a fading away from the Aryan mind of the moral idea itself. That question has to be settled on independent considerations. Without entering into the details of this discussion, we may cite the opinion of Rudolph Roth, one of the deepest Vedic scholars of modern times, who in considering this question,[8] reviews the fundamental conceptions of the Veda such as those touching the relation of man to god and the future state of departed souls, and concludes that it is impossible not to allow a positive moral value to them and 'esteem a literature in which such ideas are expressed.'

II

Early Vedic ritual was quite simple in its form as well as in the motive which inspired it. The gods worshipped were the familiar powers of nature, and the material offered to them was such as milk, grain and ghee. The motive was to secure the objects of ordinary desire—children, cattle, etc., or to get one's enemy out of the way. Occasionally the sacrifice seems to have served as thanksgiving to the gods for favours already won from them. The idea of sacrament also was perhaps present in some measure, the worshipper believing that he was under a sacred influence or in communion with the divine when he partook of the sacrificial meal. This simplicity soon disappeared; and, even in some of the early Mantras, we find instead of this childlike worship an organized sacrificial cult which is already hieratic. Yet the ritual in the early Vedic period cannot be said to have outgrown its due proportions. But it did so and became highly wrought in the age of the later Mantras and the Brāhmaṇas. Since, however, the direct bearing of this development on Indian philosophy is not great, a detailed consideration of it is not called for here. It will suffice to indicate only some of its general features: One such feature is the great change that takes place in the character of the gods to whom offerings are made. In addition to the old ones, drawn chiefly from some sphere or other of natural phenomena, we now see honoured at the sacrifice several artificial deities. Thus the clay-pot used in a certain rite is made 'the object of fervid adoration as though it were a veritable deity of well-nigh paramount power (Śat.Br.Vol.V) (SBE).' The poet-priest, we sometimes find, chooses to glorify any insignificant thing, if it only happens to be connected in some way with a sacrifice. There is for example an entire poem devoted to the sacrificial post (ṚV.III.VIII), and we have another which seriously institutes a comparison between the ornamental paint on it and the splendour of Uṣas or the Goddess of dawn (Ṛ.V.I.92.5). Symbolism also comes to prevail on a large scale. According to an old myth, Agni was the offspring of water. So a lotus leaf, betokening water, is placed at the bottom of the sacrificial altar on which fire is installed.[9] More striking still is the change which comes over the spirit with which offerings are made. In the place of conciliation and communion as the motive, we now have the view that the sacrifice is the means not of persuading the gods, but of compelling them to grant to the sacrificer what he wants. Not only can the gods be compelled by the sacrificer to do what he likes; the gods themselves, it is thought, are gods and are able to discharge their function of maintaining the world-order by virtue of the offerings presented to them. In other words, the sacrifice is now exalted above the gods—a position the logical consequence of which is their total denial later in the Pūrva-mīmāṁsā system. It is now commonly held that in this new turn in the efforts of the Vedic Indian to accomplish his desire, we discover a distinctly magical element introduced into the ritual; and that priest and prayer, henceforward, become transformed into magician and spell. The relation of religion to magic and the extent to which magical elements enter into the Vedic ritual are matters of controversy; but we need not stop to discuss them as they are of little consequence to us here.

It should not be thought that ritualism in this extreme form was in any sense the creed of the people at large. The Mantras of the *Ṛgveda* and the Brāhmaṇas which have so far been the basis of our conclusions were the compositions of poet-priests who had developed a cult of their own, and unfold but an aristocratic religion.[10] Even in the aristocratic circles, we may remark in passing, the excessive development of ritualism does not seem to have wholly superseded the older idea of sacrifice as what man owes to the gods, for we find that idea also persisting along with the other in later Vedic literature. Thus sacrifice is sometimes pictured in the Brāhmaṇas as a *ṛṇa* or 'debt' due to the gods (Tai.5.iii.10.5). The creed of the common people continued to be simple and consisted, in addition to the more primitive forms of nature-worship alluded to above, in various practices such as incantations and charms intended to ward off evil and appease the dark spirits of the air and of the earth. We get an idea of these folk-practices from the *Atharvaveda*, which, though somewhat later than the *Ṛgveda*, records in certain respects a more ancient phase of religious belief.

III

The emphasis on rites which appears in the literature that has come down to us from this ancient period is due in part to its selective character, to which we have already referred, and, therefore, indicates more of the spirit of the age in which the selection was made than of the one in which that literature was produced. Yet there is no doubt that ritualism, with its implications of excess and symbolism, marks one characteristic development of the early Vedic religion. There are other developments of it as well which also are attested by the same literature, though their features appear there rather faintly. We cannot, with the records at our disposal, describe them as anything more than tendencies of thought showing themselves in the period in question. It is difficult to trace these tendencies to their proper source, because they appear in very close association with the sacrifice with the spirit of which they seem to be essentially in conflict. They may be due to speculative activity outside the circle of priests, or more probably[11] they are the result of a reaction among the priests themselves against ritual which had become artificial and over-elaborate. Whatever be their origin, they are of that great importance to the student of philosophy, for in them are to be found the germs of much of the later thought of India. We shall now give a brief description of them.

(i) Monotheism*: The belief in a plurality of gods, which was a characteristic feature of early Vedic religion, loses its

* Monotheism is a belief in any one god only; it does not accept other's superiority like Vaiṣṇavism, Buddhism, Jainism, etc. *Mono* means single; *theism* means the belief.

attraction gradually; and the Vedic Indian, dissatisfied with the old mythology and impelled by that longing for simplicity of explanation so natural to man, starts upon seeking after not the causes of natural phenomena, but their first or ultimate cause. He is no longer content to refer observed phenomena to a multiplicity of gods, but strives to discover the one God that controls and rules over them all. The conception of a unitary godhead which becomes explicit now may be said to lie implicit already in the thought of the earlier period. For, owing to the incomplete individualization of deities and the innate connection or mutual resemblance of one natural phenomenon with another (e.g. the Sun, Fire and Dawn), there is in Vedic mythology what may be described as an overlapping of divinities. One god is very much like another. Different deities thus come to be portrayed in the same manner; and, but for the name in it, it would often be difficult to determine which god is intended to be praised in a hymn. There is also to be mentioned in this connection the well-known habit of the Vedic seers of magnifying the importance of the particular deity they are praising and representing it as supreme, ignoring for the time being the other deities altogether. To this phase of religious belief Max Müller gave the name of 'henotheism,' i.e. belief in one God as distinguished from monotheism or belief in one only God; and, regarding it as the instinct for unity asserting itself unconsciously, he represented it as a definite stage in the advance from polytheistic to monotheistic belief.[12] This view has not commended itself to many. Such overdrawing, it is thought, is natural to all religious poetry and does not consequently involve any necessary implication of progress from the thought of the many to the thought of the one. But yet this 'opportunist monotheism,' as the henotheistic tendency has been called, may be taken to have on the whole conduced to the formulation of a belief in a single God in place of the multiple deities of an earlier time.

To reduce the many gods of early mythology to one, the easiest course, we might suppose, is to elevate the most imposing of them to the rank of the Supreme. That was not the course followed in Vedic India. Varuṇa indeed at one time and Indra at another were on the point of fulfilling the conditions of a monotheistic creed in this sense; but neither did in fact become the supreme God conceived definitely as a personality. So we may say that monotheism in the ordinary sense of the term proved abortive in the Vedic period. The unity of godhead came to be sought after in a different manner then, and attempts were made to discover not one god above other gods but rather the comon power that works behind them all. The basis of even this 'philosophic monotheism,' as it may be termed, can be noticed in the early Mantras, for the Vedic poets couple the names of two deities like Mitra and Varuṇa for example—sometimes of even more—and address them as if they were one. It is the outcome of this tendency that we find expressed in passages of a relatively later date like the following: 'What is but one, wise people call by different names—as Agni, Yama and Matariśvan (ṚV.I.164.46).' The same is the significance also, no doubt, of the refrain of another hymn of the *Ṛgveda: mahat devānām asuratvam ekam*: 'The worshipful divinity of the gods is one (III.55).' Though thus convinced that there is but one ultimate cause which accounts for the diverse phenomena of nature, the Vedic Indian felt perplexed for long as regards what its exact nature might be. He tried one solution after another, but could not rest content with any. One of the earliest ways of arriving at a unitary conception of divinity was by taking a collective view of the gods, designating them 'Viśvedevas'—an expression equivalent to 'all-gods.' Such a mode of unity may appear to be quite mechanical; but it is not really so, for it implies a conscious-ness of the harmony of purpose underlying the workings of nature. A more abstract way of arriving at unity was to select some one distinguishing feature of divinity—'a predicate of several gods'—to personify it and regard it as the supreme God. Thus the word *viśvakarman*, which means 'maker of everything,' originally appears as a descriptive epithet of Indra and the Sun. But later it ceases to be used as an adjective and becomes installed as God above all gods (ṚV.X.81.82). A mere logical abstraction thus grows into a concrete god. The same thing happens in the case of several other predicative epithets. What is remarkable about these supreme gods is that none of them retains his supremacy long. 'The god that takes hold of the sceptre lays it down soon.' One conception is felt as inadequate and there quickly springs up another in its place, so that Vedic monotheism even of the philosophic type may be described as unstable and as continually shifting its ground. It is with the broken idols of this period, some one has observed, that in later times the temple of Purāṇic mythology was adorned.

There is no need to mention here all the gods that successively became pre-eminent during this long period. It will suffice to refer to only one of them—Prajāpati, 'Father god,' the most important of them all, who is the personification of the creative power of nature. The origin of this god is similar to that of Viśvakarman. His name signifies 'lord of living beings' and is first applied as an epithet to gods like Savitṛ, 'the vivifier.' But later it assumes the character of an independent deity which is responsible for the creation and governance of the universe. This god occupies the first place in the Brāhmaṇas. There are, one Brāhmaṇa says, thirty-three gods and Prajāpati is the thirty-fourth including them all (Śat.Br.V.i.2.10-13) (SBE). Even in the *Ṛgveda* (X.121), where the references to him are not many, there is quite a sublime description. One feels that such a deity should have satisfied the yearning of any people after a supreme God, and that Prajāpati might well have constituted the goal in the Indian search after unity in godhead. But even he ceases to appeal to the philosophically fastidious Vedic Aryan and yields place in course of time to other principles like Prāṇa (AV.XI.IV) or 'deified breath,' the cosmic counterpart of individual life and Time (AV.XIX.1 iii), the maker and destroyer of all. To some of them we shall come back later.

(ii) Monism: The conceptions thus far described as monotheistic are often found mixed with monistic ones; and it is difficult to separate them. But yet in particular passages, the one or the other view is seen to prevail. That is our justification for speaking of them as two tendencies. Of them, the monotheistic conception, regarded purely as such, is bound to involve dualism. What it aims at is only unity of godhead—the reduction of the many gods to one who is above and apart from the world which he makes and guides. It regards nature as set over against God and can, therefore, satisfy the longing for unity only in a qualified sense. There is a higher conception of unity, viz. monism, which traces the whole of existence to a single source. It is fully worked out in the Upaniṣads, but is foreshadowed more than once in the literature of the period we are now considering. There are in it at least two distinct shades of such monistic thought. To begin with, there is the pantheistic view which identifies nature with God. One of its most notable expressions is found in a passage of the *Ṛgveda* (I.89.10) where goddess Aditi (the 'Boundless') is identified with all gods and all men, with the sky and air—in fact with 'whatever has been or whatever shall be.' The central point of the pantheistic doctrine is to deny the difference between God and nature which as we have shown is the necessary implication of monotheism. God is conceived here not as transcending nature but as immanent in it. The world does not proceed from God, but is itself God. Although the object of this view is to postulate unity, it retains, somewhat inconsistently as it seems, both the notions of God and nature and so far fails to satisfy the mind in its search after true unity. Such a consideration may be regarded as having been at the root of another conception of unity which we come across in the literature of the period—for example, in the 'Song of creation' (ṚV.X.129) which has been extolled as containing 'the flower of Indian thought.' It is in parts obscure and almost baffles translation. Yet there are several renderings of it into English and the following metrical one by J. Muir is one of the best:[13]

'Then there was neither Aught nor Nought, no air nor sky beyond.
What covered all? Where rested all? In watery gulf profound?

Nor death was then, nor deathlessness, nor change of night and day.
That One breathed calmly, self-sustained; nought else beyond it lay.
Gloom hid in gloom existed first—one sea, eluding view.
That One, a void in chaos wrapt, by inward fervour grew.
Within it first arose desire, the primal germ of mind.
Which nothing with existence links, as sages searching find.
The kindling ray that shot across the dark and drear abyss—
Was it beneath? or high aloft? What bard can answer this?
There fecundating powers were found, and mighty forces strove—
A self-supporting mass beneath, and energy above.
Who knows, who ever told, from whence this vast creation rose?
No gods had then been born—who then can e'er the truth disclose?
Whence sprang this world, and whether framed by hand divine or no—
Its Lord in heaven alone can tell, if even he can show.'

In this hymn, which may be said to have passed over into world literature, we have the quintessence of monistic thought. Here the poet-philosopher recognizing, unlike the pantheist, the principle of causality, not only traces the whole universe to a single source but also tackles the problem of what its nature may be. All opposites like being and non-being, death and life, good and evil, are viewed as developing within and, therefore, as ultimately reconciliable in this fundamental principle. In regard to the origin of the universe, we have here, instead of the view of creation by an external agency, the view that the sensible world is the spontaneous unfolding of the supra-sensible First Cause. The conception is wholly impersonal and free from all mythological elements. Even the theistic colouring discernible in pantheism is absent here. It is denoted in this song by two most cautiously chosen epithets—'That One' (*tad ekam*), which suggest nothing beyond the positive and unitary character of the ultimate principle. We are here on the threshold of Upaniṣadic monism.

IV

Yet another tendency has to be noted which may comprehensively be described as 'Vedic free-thinking.' But it must be remembered that it does not form part of the teaching of the Veda. There are only allusions to it there which, though occasional, are quite clear. Those that indulged in it are denounced as 'haters of the Veda' (*brahmadviṣ*), 'maligners of gods' (*devanid*), 'men of no principle' (*apavrata*). That such heterodox views were not unknown in ancient India may also be gathered from the tradition of Jainism. It reckons several prophets who preceded Mahāvīra. Of them at least one, Pārśvanātha, is now generally taken to have been an historical personage and assigned to the eighth century B.C., which according to the accepted chronology takes us back to the period[14] when the Brāhmaṇas were composed. This tendency manifests itself sometimes as doubt and sometimes as disbelief. But under whatever form it may appear, it sets itself against the orthodox teaching of the Veda. There is a whole hymn in the *Ṛgveda* (X.151) addressed to the faith which concludes with the prayer: 'O Faith, make us faithful.' Such an invocation, as Deussen has observed,[15] would be unintelligible if we did not assume a certain lack of faith as prevalent in the age in which the hymn was composed. As other instances of unbelief we may mention two hymns, also found in the *Ṛgveda*—one (II.12) which pointedly refers to current disbelief in the existence and supremacy of Indra and endeavours by recounting his great deeds to convince the unbelievers of his majesty and power, and the other (X.82) which ridicules the votaries of the Veda by describing them as 'selfish prattling priests that go about self-deluded.' It was this tendency that in course of time gave rise to the heretical schools whose importance in the history of Indian philosophy has already been noticed.

V

We shall conclude this chapter with a brief description of the general outlook on life and things in the period. Nature and man alike form the subject-matter of speculation. The external world, whose reality is never questioned, is looked upon as an ordered whole, divided into the three realms of earth, the atmospheric region and heaven, each guided and illumined by its own specific deities. In fact, it is to account for its cosmic character that the several nature-gods are invented. The gods may be many, but the world they govern is one. This idea of unity naturally comes to be emphasized with the growth of monotheistic and monistic beliefs. Notions of creation and evolution both appear. Where the universe is spoken of as created, only one creation is mentioned; and the belief, so well known to a later age, in a series of creations, each being followed by dissolution, is absent (ṚV.X.190.3). Various accounts of the order of creation are found—one of the commonest being that water was first created and that everything else sprang from it afterwards. Sometimes we meet with the idea that the world was built by the gods, much in the manner of building a house. One poet who pictures Varuṇa as the cosmic architect describes the moving sun as his measuring-rod (ṚV.V.85.5). Another expresses wonder as to wherefrom the material might have come: 'What indeed was the wood? What too that tree from which they fashioned heaven and earth? (ṚV.X.31.7)' Sometimes the world is stated to have been generated, Heaven and Earth being its parents. There is still another view which, under the influence of ritualism, traces the world to a sacrificial act. This conceit occurs in more than one place in the Veda and particularly in the hymn known as the *Puruṣasūkta*, where the cosmic man, who is himself described as emerging from a transcendental being, is taken to have furnished, when sacrificed, the material for the entire variety of the universe. 'The moon was born from his mind; from his eye, the sun; from his mouth, Indra and Agni; and from his breath, Vāyu. From his navel came into being the mid-region; from his head, the sky; from his feet, the earth; from his ear, the quarters.' It is really the breaking up of the seen whole into its parts—a process which is the reverse of the one we sometimes find in the Upaniṣads (Ch.Up.V.XI-XVIII), viz. reconstructing the whole out of its several parts as given in common experience. We have already spoken of the more philosophical view of evolution in connection with the Song of Creation.

Naturally a prominent place is given in the plan of life to the performance of sacrifices whose efficacy in securing for man what he wants is never doubted. Indeed sacrifice, as we have seen, is sometimes regarded as a *ṛna*. It is the first of what is described as the 'triad of obligations' (*ṛnatraya*)—a description which implies a clear conception of duty. The second is indebtedness to the sages of old for the heritage of culture which they have left behind. It is to be discharged by receiving that tradition and handing it on to the coming generation. The last obligation is what is due to the race, which is to be met by becoming a householder and begetting sons. The ideal thus does not stop with the performance of sacrifices but comprehends the preservation of the race and the conservation of the culture for which it stands. It also includes the practice of virtues like adherence to truth, self-restraint and kindness to fellow-beings. Benevolence to neighbour and friend is particularly praised and niggardliness censured in the *Ṛgveda* (X.117.6), which for instance states: *kevalāgho bhavati kevalādī*: 'He that eats by himself will keep his sin to himself.' The tendency to asceticism also appears in the period, the *Ṛgveda* (X.136.2) alluding to the Muni with long hair and coloured garments. We have already considered the place of morality in the earlier part of the period. As regards the later, some are of opinion that the excessive importance attached to the sacrifice in it led to a neglect of ethical ideas and gave rise to the practice of judging goodness by the standard of ritualistic correctness. But in view of the fact to which attention has been drawn that ritualism was only one of the lines of development of early Vedic thought, it would be more correct to hold that, though in circles where the sacrifice was dominant it might have caused some confusion between ethical and ritualistic values, the idea of morality itself did not disappear. Thus Prajāpati, the principal deity of the Brāhmaṇa period, is represented not merely as the lord of creation, but also as an ethical authority reminding us of the still earlier view that the gods were responsible for upholding moral as well as cosmic order.

This ancient belief is more than a system of rewards and punishments on this side of death. Both the pious and the impious are believed to be born in another world; but except perhaps in a single passage in a Brāhmaṇa,[16] there is no allusion to transmigration. The reward of virtue and piety is enjoyment of happiness in heaven in the company of the gods. Later this blessed existence is represented as being led in the company of the virtuous dead and under the control of Yama, who appears as the ruler of heaven and not yet of the dreaded abode of hell. The punishment for sin and vice is eternal damnation. The reference to hell is not explicit in the *Ṛgveda*, but is clear in the *Atharvaveda* and the Brāhmaṇas. It is described as a place of eternal darkness below, in contrast to heaven, which is one of light above; and those that go there, it is stated, can never escape from it. All this points to a belief in the immortality of the soul. Death does not mean destruction, but only the continuance of existence elsewhere where happiness or misery results according to one's deserts.

References

1. *Rel. V.* p. 16.
2. *Rel. V.* p. 82.
3. ibid pp. 85, 151.
4. ibid p. 12.
5. See e.g. *Cambridge History of India,* vol. i. pp. 103, 108.
6. Rel. V. p. 175.
7. See Macdonell: *Vedic Mythology,* pp. 18, 65.
8. JAOS, vol. iii, pp. 331-47. See also EI. pp. 44, 61-62.
9. See Eggeling: *op. cit.* Part IV. pp. xix-xxi.
10. Cf. Rel. V. pp. 22,210.
11. Cf. Rel. V. pp. 35, 212-220.
12. SV. p. 40.
13. OST. vol. v. p. 356.
14. See *Cambridge History of India,* Vol. i. p. 153.
15. *Indian Antiquary* for 1900. p. 367.
16. See Macdonell: *Vedic Mythology*, p. 166.

Religion and Spirituality

The task of religion and spirituality is to mediate between God and man, between the eternal and infinite and this transient, yet persistent finite, between a luminous truth-consciousness not expressed or not yet expressed here and the mind's ignorance. But nothing is more difficult than to bring home the greatness and uplifting power of the spiritual consciousness to the natural man forming the vast majority of the race; for his mind and senses, are turned outward towards the external calls of life and its objects and never inwards to the truth which lies behind them. This external vision and attraction are the essence of the universal blinding force which is designated in Indian philosophy as the ignorance. Ancient Indian spirituality recognized that man lives in the ignorance and has to be led through its imperfect indications to a highest inmost knowledge. Our life moves between two worlds, the depths upon depths of our inward being and the surface field of our outward nature. The majority of men put the whole emphasis of life on the outward and live very strongly in their surface consciousness and very little in the inward existence. Even the choice spirits raised from the grossness of the common vital and physical mould by the stress of thought and culture do not usually get farther than a strong dwelling on the things of the mind. The highest flight they reach—and it is this that the West persistently mistakes for spirituality—is a preference for living in the mind and emotions more than in the gross outward life or else an attempt to subject this rebellious life-stuff to the law of intellectual truth or ethical reason and will or aesthetic beauty or of all three together. But spiritual knowledge perceives that there is a greater thing in us; our inmost self, our real being is not the intellect, not the aesthetic, ethical or thinking mind, but the divinity within, the spirit, and these other things are only the instruments of the spirit. A mere intellectual, ethical and aesthetic culture does not go back to the inmost truth of the spirit; it is still an ignorance, an incomplete, outward and superficial knowledge. To have made the discovery of our deepest being and hidden spiritual nature is the first necessity and to have erected the living of an inmost spiritual life into the aim of existence is the characteristic sign of a spiritual culture.

This endeavour takes in certain religions the form of a spiritual exclusiveness which revolts from the outward existence rather than seeks to transform it. The main tendency of the Christian discipline was not only to despise the physical and vital way of living, but to disparage and imprison the intellectual and distrust and discourage the aesthetic thirsts of our nature. It emphasized against them a limited spiritual emotionalism and its intense experiences as the one thing needful; the development of the ethical sense was the sole mental necessity, its translation into act the sole indispensable condition or result of the spiritual life. Indian spirituality reposed on too wide and many-sided a culture to admit as its base this narrow movement; but on its more solitary summits, at least in its later period, it tended to a spiritual exclusiveness loftier in vision, but even more imperative and excessive. A spirituality of this intolerant high-pointed kind, to whatever elevation it may rise, however, it may help to purify life or lead to a certain kind of individual salvation, cannot be a complete thing. For its exclusiveness imposes on it a certain importance to deal effectively with the problems of human existence; it cannot lead it to its integral perfection or combine its highest heights with its broadest broadness. A wider spiritual culture must recognise that the spirit is not only the highest and inmost thing, but all is manifestation and creation of the spirit. It must have a wider outlook, a more embracing range of applicability and, even, a more aspiring and ambitious aim of its endeavour. Its aim must be not only to raise to inaccessible heights the few elect, but to draw all men and all life and the whole human being upward, to spiritualise life and in the end to divinise human nature. Not only must it be able to lay hold on his deepest individual being but to inspire too his communal existence. It must turn, by a spiritual change, all the members of his ignorance into members of the knowledge; it must transmute all the instruments of the human into instruments of a divine living. The total movement of Indian spirituality is towards this aim; in spite of all the difficulties, imperfections and fluctuations of its evolution, it had this character. But like other cultures it was not at all times and in all its parts and movements consciously aware of its own total significance. This large sense sometimes emerged into something like a conscious synthetic clarity, but was more often kept in the depths and on the surface dispersed in a multitude of subordinate and special standpoints. Still, it is only by an intelligence of the total drift that its manifold sides and rich variations of effort and teaching and discipline can receive their full reconciling unity and be understood in the light of its own most intrinsic purpose.

Now the spirit of Indian religion and spiritual culture has been persistently and immovably the same throughout the long time of its vigour, but its form has undergone remarkable changes. Yet if we look into them from the right centre it will be apparent that these changes are the results of a logical and inevitable evolution inherent in the very process of man's growth towards the heights. In its earliest form, its first Vedic system, it took its outward foundation on the mind of the physical man whose natural faith is in things physical, in the sensible and visible objects, presences, representations and the external pursuits and aims of the material world. The means, symbols, rites, figures, by which it sought to mediate between the spirit and the normal human mentality were drawn from these most external physical things. Man's first and primitive idea of the divine can only come through his vision of external nature and the sense of a superior power or powers concealed behind her phenomena veiled in the heaven and earth, father and mother of our being, in the Sun and moon and stars, its lights and regulators, in dawn and day and night and rain and wind and storm, the oceans and the rivers and the forests, all the circumstances and forces of her scene of action, all that vast and mysterious surrounding life of which we are a part and in which the natural heart and mind of the human creature feel instinctively through whatever bright or dark or confused figures that there is here some divine multitude or else mighty infinite, one, manifold and mysterious, which takes these forms and manifests itself in these motions. The Vedic religion took this natural sense and feeling of the physical man; it used the conceptions to which they gave birth, and it sought to lead him through them to the psychic and spiritual truths of his own being and the being of the cosmos. It recognized that he was right when he saw behind the manifestations of nature great living powers and godheads, even though he knew not their inner truth, and right too in offering to them worship and propitiation and atonement. For that inevitably must be the initial way in which his active physical, vital and mental nature is allowed to approach the Godhead. He approaches it through its visible outward manifestations as something greater than his own natural self, something single or multiple that guides, sustains and directs his life, and he calls to it for help and support in the desires and difficulties and distresses and struggles of his human existence. The Vedic religion accepted also the form in which early man everywhere expressed his sense of the relation between himself and the godheads of nature; it adopted as its central symbol the act and ritual of a physical sacrifice. However crude the notions attached to it, this idea of the necessity of sacrifice did express obscurely a first law of being. For it was founded on that secret of constant interchange between the individual and the universal powers of the cosmos which covertly supports all the process of life and develops the action of nature.

But even in its external and exoteric side the Vedic religion did not limit itself to this acceptance and regulation of the first religious notions of the natural physical mind of man. The Vedic Ṛṣis gave a psychic function to the godheads worshipped by the people; they spoke to them of a higher truth, right, law of which the gods were the guardians, of the necessity of a truer knowledge and a larger inner living according to this truth and right, and of a home of immortality to which the soul of man could ascend by the power of truth and of right doing. The people no doubt took these ideas in their most external sense; but they were trained by them to develop their ethical nature, to turn towards some initial development of their psychic being, to conceive the idea of a knowledge and truth other than that of the physical life and to admit even a first conception of some greater spiritual reality which was the ultimate object of human worship or aspiration. This religious and moral force was the highest reach of the external cult and the most that could be understood or followed by the mass of the people.

The deeper truth of these things was reserved for the initiates, for those who were ready to understand and practise the inner sense, the esoteric meaning hidden in the Vedic scripture. For the Veda is full of words which, as the Ṛṣis themselves express it, are secret words that give their inner meaning only to the seer, *kavaye nivacanāni ninyāni vacāṁsi*. This is a feature of the ancient sacred hymns which grew obscure to later ages; it became a dead tradition and has been entirely ignored by modern scholarship in its laborious attempt to read the hieroglyph of the Vedic symbols. Yet its recognition is essential to a right understanding of almost all the ancient religions; for mostly they started on their upward curve through an esoteric element of which the key was not given to all. In all or most there was a surface cult for the common physical man who was held yet unfit for the psychic and spiritual life and an inner secret of the mysteries carefully disguised by symbols whose sense was opened only to the initiates. This was the origin of the later distinction between the Śūdra, the undeveloped physical-minded man and the twice-born, those who were capable of entering into the second birth by initiation and to whom alone the Vedic education could be given without danger. This too actuated the later prohibition of any reading or teaching of the Veda by the Śūdra. It was this inner meaning, it was the higher psychic and spiritual truths concealed by the outer sense, that gave to these hymns the name by which they are still known, the Veda, the book of knowledge. Only by penetrating into the esoteric sense of this worship can we understand the full flowering of the Vedic religion in the Upaniṣads and in the long later evolution of Indian spiritual seeking and experience. For it is all there in its luminous seed, preshadowed or even prefigured in the verses of the early seers. The persistent notion which through every change ascribed the foundation of all our culture to the Ṛṣis, whatever its fabulous forms and mythical ascriptions, contains a real truth and veils a sound historic tradition. It reflects the fact of a true initiation and an unbroken continuity between this great primitive past and the riper but hardly greater spiritual development of our historic culture.

This inner Vedic religion started with an extension of the psychic significance of the godheads in the cosmos. Its primary notion was that of a hierarchy of worlds, an ascending stair of planes of being in the universe. It saw a mounting scale of the worlds corresponding to a similar mounting scale of planes or degrees or levels of consciousness in the nature of man. A truth, right and law sustains and governs all these levels of nature; one in essence, it takes in them different but cognate forms. There is for instance the series of the outer physical light, another higher and inner light which is the vehicle of the mental, vital and psychic consciousness and a highest inmost light of spiritual illumination. Sūrya, the Sun-God, was the lord of the physical Sun; but he is at the same time to the Vedic seer-poet the giver of the rays of knowledge which illumine the mind and he is too the soul and energy and body of the spiritual illumination. And in all these powers he is a luminous form of the one and infinite Godhead. All the Vedic godheads have this outer and this inner and inmost function, their known and their secret names. All are in their external character powers of physical nature; all have in their inner meaning a psychic function and psychological ascriptions; all too are various powers of some one highest reality, *ekaṁ sat*, the one infinite existence. This hardly knowable Supreme is called often in the Veda 'That Truth' or 'That One', *tat satyaṁ, tad ekaṁ*. This complex character of the Vedic godheads assumes forms which have been wholly misunderstood by those who ascribe to them only their outward physical significance. Each of these gods is in himself a complete and separate cosmic personality of the one existence and in their combination of powers they form the complete universal power, the cosmic whole, *vaiśvadevyaṁ*. Each again, apart from his special function, is one godhead with the others; each holds in himself the universal divinity, each god is all the other gods. This is the aspect of the Vedic teaching and worship to which a European scholar, mistaking entirely its significance because he read it in the dim and poor light of European religious experience, has given the sounding misnomer, henotheism. Beyond, in the triple infinite, these godheads put on their highest nature and are names of the one nameless Ineffable.

But the greatest power of the Vedic teaching, that which made it the source of all later Indian philosophies, religions, the systems of Yoga, lay in its application to the inner life of man. Man lives in the physical cosmos subject to death and the 'much falsehood' of the mortal existence. To rise beyond this death, to become one of the immortals, he has to turn from the falsehood to the truth; he has to turn to the light and to battle with and to conquer the powers of the darkness. This he does by communion with the divine powers and their aid; the way to call down this aid was the secret of the Vedic mystics. The symbols of the outer sacrifice are given for this purpose in the manner of the mysteries all over the world an inner meaning; they represent a calling of the gods into the human being, a connecting sacrifice, an intimate interchange, a mutual aid, a communion. There is a building of the powers of the godheads within man and a formation in him of the universality of the divine nature. For the gods are the guardians and increasers of the truth, the powers of the immortal, the sons of the infinite Mother; the way to immortality is the upward way of the gods, the way of the truth, a journey, an ascent by which there is a growth into the law of the truth, *ṛtasya panthā*. Man arrives at immortality by breaking beyond the limitations not only of his physical self, but of his mental and his ordinary psychic nature into the highest plane and supreme ether of the truth: for there is the foundation of immortality and the native seat of the triple infinite. On these ideas the Vedic sages built up a profound psychological and psychic discipline which led beyond itself to a highest spirituality and contained the nucleus of later Indian Yoga. Already we find in their seed, though not in their full expansion, the most characteristic ideas of Indian spirituality. There is the one existence, *ekaṁ sat*, supracosmic beyond the individual and the universe. There is the one God who presents to us the many forms, names, powers, personalities of his Godhead. There is the distinction between the knowledge and the ignorance, the greater truth of an immortal life opposed to the much falsehood or mixed truth and falsehood of mortal existence. There is the discipline of an inward growth of man from the physical through the psychic to the spiritual existence. There is the conquest of death, the secret of immortality, the perception of a realisable divinity of the human spirit. In an age to which in the insolence of our external knowledge we are accustomed to look back as the childhood of humanity or at best a period of vigorous barbarism, this was the inspired and intuitive psychic and spiritual teaching by which the ancient human fathers: *pūrve pitaraḥ manuṣyāḥ*, founded a great and profound civilization in India.

This high beginning was secured in its results by a larger sublime efflorescence. The Upaniṣads have always been recognized in India as the crown and end of the Veda; that is indicated in their general name, Vedānta. And they are in fact a large crowning outcome of the Vedic discipline and experience. The time in which the Vedāntic truth was wholly seen and the Upaniṣads took shape, was, as we can discern from such records as the *Chāndogya* and *Bṛhadāraṇyaka*, an epoch of immense and strenuous seeking, an intense and ardent seed-time of the spirit. In the stress of that seeking the truths held by the initiates but kept back from ordinary men broke their barriers, swept through the higher mind of the nation and fertilised the soil of Indian culture for a constant and ever-increasing growth of spiritual consciousness and spiritual experience. This turn was not as yet universal; it was chiefly men of the higher classes, Kṣatriyas and Brāhmaṇas trained in the Vedic system of education, no longer content with an external truth and the works of the outer sacrifice, who began everywhere to seek for the highest word of revealing experience from the sages who possessed the knowledge of the One. But we find too among those who attained to the knowledge and became great teachers men of inferior or doubtful birth like Janaśruti, the wealthy Śūdra, or Satyakāma Jābali, son of a servant-girl who knew not who was his father. The work that was done in this period became the firm bedrock of Indian spirituality in later ages and from it gush still the life-giving waters of a perennial never-failing inspiration. This period, this activity, this grand achievement created the whole difference between the evolution of Indian civilisation and the quite different curve of other cultures.

For a time had come when the original Vedic symbols must lose their significance and pass into an obscurity that became impenetrable, as did the inner teaching of the mysteries in other countries. The old poise of culture between two extremes with a bridge of religious cult and symbolism to unite them, the crude or half-trained naturalness of the outer physical man on one side of the line, and on the other an inner and secret psychic and spiritual life for the initiates could no longer suffice as the basis of our spiritual progress. The human race in its cycle of civilisation needed a large-lined advance; it called for a more and more generalized intellectual, ethical and aesthetic evolution to help it to grow into the light. This turn had to come in India as in other lands. But the danger was that the greater spiritual truth already gained might be lost in the lesser confident half-light of the acute but unillumined intellect or stifled within the narrow limits of the self-sufficient logical reason. That was what actually happened in the West, Greece leading the way. The old knowledge was prolonged in a less inspired, less dynamic and more intellectual form by the Pythagoreans, by the Stoics, by Plato and the Neo-Platonists; but still in spite of them and in spite of the only half-illumined spiritual wave which swept over Europe from Asia in an ill-understood Christianity, the whole real trend of Western civilization has been intellectual, rational, secular and even materialistic, and it keeps this character to the present day. Its general aim has been a strong or a fine culture of the vital and physical man by the power of an intellectualized ethics, aesthetic and reason, not the leading up of our lower members into the supreme light and power of the spirit. The ancient spiritual knowledge and the spiritual tendency it had created were saved in India from this collapse by the immense effort of the age of the Upaniṣads. The Vedāntic seers renewed the Vedic truth by extricating it from its cryptic symbols and casting it into a highest and most direct and powerful language of intuition and inner experience. It was not the language of the intellect. but still it wore a form which the intellect could take hold of, translate into its own more abstract terms and convert into a starting-point for an ever-widening and deepening philosophic speculation and the reason's long search after a truth original, supreme and ultimate. There was in India as in the West a great upbuilding of a high, wide and complex intellectual, aesthetic, ethical and social culture. But left in Europe to its own resources, combated rather than helped by an obscure religious emotion and dogma, here it was guided, uplifted and more and more penetrated and suffused by a great saving power of spirituality and a vast stimulating and tolerant light of wisdom from a highest ether of knowledge.

The second or post-Vedic age of Indian civilization was distinguished by the rise of the great philosophies, by a copious, vivid, many-thoughted, many-sided epic literature, by the beginnings of art and science, by the evolution of vigorous and complex society, by the formation of large kingdoms and empires, by manifold formative activities of all kinds and great systems of living and thinking. Here as elsewhere, in Greece, Rome, Persia, China, this was the age of a high outburst of the intelligence working upon life and the things of the mind to discover their reason and their right way and bring out a broad and noble fullness of human existence. But in India this effort never lost sight of the spiritual motive, never missed the touch of the religious sense. It was a birth time and youth of the seeking intellect and, as in Greece, philosophy was the main instrument by which it laboured to solve the problems of life and the world. Science too developed but it came second only as an auxiliary power. It was through profound and subtle philosophies that the intellect of India attempted to analyse by the reason and logical faculty what had formerly been approached with a much more living force through intuition and the soul's experience. But the philosophic mind started from the data these mightier powers had discovered and was faithful to its parent light; it went back always in one form or another to the profound truths of the Upaniṣads which kept their place as the highest authority in these matters. There was a constant admission that spiritual experience is a greater thing and its light a truer if more incalculable guide than the clarities of the reasoning intelligence.

The same governing force kept its hold on all the other activities of the Indian mind and Indian life. The epic literature is full almost to excess of a strong and free intellectual and ethical thinking; there is an incessant criticism of life by the intelligence and the ethical reason, an arresting curiosity and desire to fix the norm of truth in all possible fields. But in the background and coming constantly to the front there is too a constant religious sense and an implicit or avowed assent to the spiritual truths which remained the unshakeable basis of the culture. These truths suffused with their higher light secular thought and action or stood above to remind them that they were only steps towards a goal. Art in India, contrary to a common idea, dwelt much upon life; but still its highest achievement was always in the field of the interpretation of the religio-philosophical mind and its whole tone was coloured by a suggestion of the spiritual and the infinite. Indian society developed with an unsurpassed organising ability, stable effectiveness, practical insight in its communal coordination of the mundane life of interest and desire, *kāma, artha*; it governed always its action by a reference at every point to the moral and religious law, the *dharma*: but it never lost sight of spiritual liberation as our highest point and the ultimate aim of the effort of life. In later times when there was a still stronger secular tendency of intellectual culture, there came in an immense development of the mundane intelligence, an opulent political and social evolution, an emphatic stressing of aesthetic, sensuous and hedonistic experience. But this effort too always strove to keep itself within the ancient frame and not to lose the special stamp of the Indian cultural idea. The enlarged secular turn was compensated by a deepening of the intensities of psycho-religious experience. New religions or mystic forms and disciplines attempted to seize not only the soul and the intellect, but the emotions, the senses, the vital and the aesthetic nature of man and turn them into stuff of the spiritual life. And every excess of emphasis on the splendour and richness and power and pleasures of life had its recoil and was balanced by a corresponding potent stress on spiritual asceticism as the higher way. The two trends, on one side an extreme of the richness of life experience, on the other an extreme and pure rigorous intensity of the spiritual life, accompanied each other; their interaction, whatever loss there might be of the earlier deep harmony and large synthesis, yet by their double pull preserved something still of the balance of Indian culture.

Indian religion followed this line of evolution and kept its inner continuity with its Vedic and Vedāntic origins; but it changed entirely its mental contents and colour and its outward basis. It did not effectuate this change through any protestant revolt or revolution, or with any idea of an iconoclastic reformation. A continuous development of its organic life took place, a natural transformation brought out latent motives or else gave to already established motive ideas a more predominant place or effective form. At one time indeed it seemed as if a discontinuity and a sharp new beginning were needed and would take place. Buddhism seemed to reject all spiritual continuity with the Vedic religion. But this was after all less in reality than in appearance. The Buddhist ideal of *Nirvāṇa* was no more than a sharply negative and exclusive statement of the highest Vedāntic spiritual experience. The ethical system of the eightfold path taken as the way to release was an austere sublimation of the Vedic notion of the right, truth and law followed as the way to immorality, *ṛtasya panthā*. The strongest note of the Mahāyāna Buddhism, its stress on universal compassion and fellow-feeling was an ethical application of the spiritual unity which is the essential idea of Vedānta. The most characteristic tenets of the new discipline, *Nirvāṇa* and *karman*, could have been supported from the utterances of the Brāhmaṇas and Upaniṣads. Buddhism could easily have claimed for itself a Vedic origin and the claim would have been no less valid than the Vedic ascription of the Sāṇkhya philosophy and discipline with which it had some points of intimate alliance. But what hurt Buddhism and determined in the end its rejection, was not its denial of a Vedic origin or authority, but the exclusive trenchancy of its intellectual, ethical and spiritual positions. A result of an intense stress of the union of logical reason with the spiritualized mind,—for it was by an intense spiritual seeking supported on a clear and hard rational thinking that it was born as a separate religion,—its trenchant affirmations and still more exclusive negations could not be made sufficiently compatible with the native flexibility, many sided susceptibility and rich synthetic turn of the Indian religious consciousness; it was a high creed but not plastic enough to hold the heart of the people. Indian religion absorbed all that it could of Buddhism, but rejected its exclusive positions and preserved the full line of its own continuity, casting back to the ancient Vedānta.

This lasting line of change moved forward not by any destruction of principle, but by a gradual fading out of the prominent Vedic forms and the substitution of others. There was a transformation of symbol and ritual and ceremony or a substitution of new kindred figures, an emergence of things that are only hints in the original system, a development of novel idea-forms from the seed of the original thinking. And especially there was a farther widening and fathoming of psychic and spiritual experience. The Vedic gods rapidly lost their deep original significance. At first they kept their hold by their outer cosmic sense but were overshadowed by the great trinity, Brahmā-Viṣṇu-Śiva and afterwards faded altogether. A new pantheon appeared which in its outward symbolic aspects expressed a deeper truth and larger range of religious experience, an intenser feeling, a vaster idea. The Vedic sacrifice persisted only in broken and lessening fragments. The house of fire was replaced by the temple; the kārmic ritual of sacrifice was transformed into the devotional temple ritual; the vague and shifting mental images of the Vedic gods figured in the *mantras* yielded to more precise conceptual forms of the two great deities, Viṣṇu and Śiva and of their Śaktis and their offshoots. These new concepts stabilised in physical images were made the basis both for internal adoration and for the external worship which replaced sacrifice. The psychic and spiritual mystic endeavour which was the inner sense of the Vedic hymns, disappeared into the less intensely luminous but more wide and rich and complex psycho-spiritual inner life of the Purāṇic and Tāntric religion and Yoga.

The Purāṇo-Tāntric stage of the religion was once decried by European critics and Indian reformers as a base and ignorant degradation of an earlier and purer religion. It was rather an effort, successful in a great measure, to open the general mind of the people to a higher and deeper range of inner truth and experience and feeling. Much of the adverse criticism once heard proceeded from a total ignorance of the sense and intention of this worship. Much of this criticism has been uselessly concentrated on side-paths and aberrations which could hardly be avoided in this immensely audacious experimental widening of the basis of the culture. For there was a catholic attempt to draw towards the spiritual truth minds of all qualities and people of all classes. Much was lost of the profound psychic knowledge of the Vedic seers, but much also of new knowledge was developed, untrodden ways were opened and a hundred gates discovered into the Infinite. If we try to see the essential sense and aim of this development and the intrinsic value of its forms and means and symbols, we shall find that this evolution followed upon the early Vedic form very much for the same reason as Catholic Christianity replaced the mysteries and sacrifices of the early Pagan religions. For in both cases the outward basis of the early religion spoke to the outward physical mind of the people and took that as the starting-point of its appeal. But the new evolution tried to awaken a more inner mind even in the common man, to lay hold on his inner vital and emotional nature, to support all by an awakening of the soul and to lead him through these things towards a highest spiritual truth. It attempted in fact to bring the mass into the temple of the spirit rather than leave them in the outer precincts. The outward physical sense was satisfied through its aesthetic turn by a picturesque temple worship, by numerous ceremonies, by the use of physical images; but these were given a psychic-emotional sense and direction that was open to the heart and imagination of the ordinary man and not reserved for the deeper sight of the elect or the strenuous *tapasyā* of the initiates. The secret initiation remained but was now a condition for the passage from the surface psycho-emotional and religious to a profounder psychic-spiritual truth and experience.

Nothing essential was touched in its core by this new orientation; but the instruments, atmosphere, field of religious experience underwent a considerable change. The Vedic godheads were to the mass of their worshippers divine powers who presided over the workings of the outward life of the physical cosmos; the Purāṇic trinity had even for the multitude a predominant psycho-religious and spiritual significance. Its more external significance, for instance, the functions of cosmic creation, preservation and destruction, were only a dependent fringe of these profundities that alone touched the heart of its mystery. The central spiritual truth remained in both systems the same, the truth of the One in many aspects. The trinity is a triple form of the one supreme Godhead and the Brahman; the Śaktis are energies of the one energy of the highest divine being. But this greatest religious truth was no longer reserved for the initiated few; it was now more and more brought powerfully, widely and intensely home to the general mind and feeling of the people. Even the so-called henotheism of the Vedic idea was prolonged and heightened in the larger and simpler worship of Viṣṇu or Śiva as the one universal and highest Godhead of whom all others are living forms and powers. The idea of the divinity in man was popularised to an extraordinary extent, not only the occasional manifestation of the divine in humanity which founded the worship of the *avatāras*, but the presence discoverable in the heart of every creature. The systems of Yoga developed themselves on the same common basis. All led or hoped to lead through many kinds of psycho-physical, inner vital, inner mental and psycho-spiritual methods to the common aim of all Indian spirituality, a greater consciousness and a more or less complete union with the one and divine or else an immergence of the individual soul in the absolute. The Purāṇo-Tāntric system was a wide, assured and many-sided endeavour, unparalleled in its power, insight, amplitude, to provide the race with a basis of generalized psycho-religious experience from which man could rise through knowledge, works or love or through any other fundamental power of his nature to some established supreme experience and highest absolute status.

This great effort and achievement which covered all the time between the Vedic age and the decline of Buddhism, was still not the last possibility of religious evolution open to Indian culture. The Vedic training of the physically-minded man made the development possible. But in its turn this raising of the basis of religion to the inner mind and life and psychic nature, this training and bringing out of the psychic man ought to make possible a still larger development and support a greater spiritual movement as the leading power of life. The first stage makes possible the preparation of the natural external man for spirituality; the second takes up his outward life into a deeper mental and psychical living and brings him more directly into contact with the spirit and divinity within him; the third should render him capable of taking up his whole mental, psychical, physical living into a first beginning at least of a generalized spiritual life. This endeavour has manifested itself in the evolution of Indian spirituality and is the significance of the latest philosophies, the great spiritual movements of the saints and *Bhaktas* and an increasing resort to various paths of Yoga. But unhappily it synchronized with a decline of Indian culture and an increasing collapse of its general power and knowledge, and in these surroundings, it could not bear its natural fruit; but at the same time it has done much to prepare such a possibility in the future. If Indian culture is to survive and keep its spiritual basis and innate character, it is in this direction, and not in a mere revival or a prolongation of the Purāṇic system, that its evolution must turn, rising so towards the fulfilment of that which the Vedic seers saw as the aim of man and his life thousands of years ago and the Vedāntic sages cast into the clear and immortal forms of their luminous revelation. Even the psychic-emotional part of man's nature is not the inmost door to religious feeling nor is his inner mind the highest witness to spiritual experience. There is behind the first the inmost soul of man, in that deepest secret heart, *hṛdaya guhāyāṁ*, in which the ancient seers saw the very tabernacle of the indwelling Godhead, and there is above the second a luminous highest mind directly open to a truth of the spirit to which man's normal nature has as yet only an occasional and momentary access. Religious evolution, spiritual experience can find their true native road only when they open to these hidden powers and make them their support for a lasting change, a divinization of human life and nature. An effort of this kind was the very force behind the most luminous and vivid of the later movements of India's vast religious cycles. It is the secret of the most powerful forms of Vaiṣṇavism and Tantra and Yoga. The labour of ascent from our half-animal human nature into the fresh purity of the spiritual consciousness needed to be followed and supplemented by a descent of the light and force of the spirit into man's members and the attempt to transform human into divine nature.

But it could not find its complete way or its fruit because it synchronized with a decline of the life-force in India and a lowering of power and knowledge in her general civilization and culture. Nevertheless here lies the destined force of her survival and renewal, this is the dynamic meaning of her future. A widest and highest spiritualizing of life on earth is the last vision of all that vast and unexampled seeking and experiment in a thousand ways of the soul's outermost and innermost experience which is the unique character of her past; this in the end is the mission for which she was born and the meaning of her existence.

The Sanātana Dharma

The Sanātana Dharma was most appropriately so named for various reasons. The first word *sanātana* is easy enough to translate; and it means eternal; but the second word *dharma* is difficult to translate into English, because there is absolutely no word which can correctly convey, in English, what the word *dharma* means to us in Sanskrit and all the various languages of India. It may be roughly translated as "religion"; but this is really a very unsatisfactory rendering thereof, because the very conception which the Western mind has of religion is something very narrow and restricted in its nature and scope. It is not all comprehending as our Sanātana Dharma is, in the sense that it pervades and permeates every activity of ours in every branch and department of life, not merely from our birth to our death but commencing long before our birth and continuing its rule over us for long ages after our death.

Thus, as regards the various departments of life and knowledge coming under the jurisdiction of *dharma* according to the scriptures, the very conception thereof is absolutely foreign, nay, apparently even impossible, to the followers of these other religions. To them, *dharma* is something of an intensely narrow, cramped, cabined, restricted and circumscribed character; and this is why there is no word in English for correctly translating all that the word *dharma* means to us. Our Sanātana Dharma defines *dharma* thus:—धारणाद् धर्म उच्यते ॥

(i.e., *dharma* is that which prevents us from going down, ruining ourselves in any manner or respect whatsoever, and makes for our welfare, progress and uplift all-round). It is not something very small and circumscribed (like 'Religion' in the Western sense of the word) but really and thoroughly all-comprehending, as it knows no limitations of any kind whatsoever.

For example, besides the fact that our Vedas themselves deal not merely with the means required for the attainment of happiness and joy in a future world, but also prescribe the necessary means for securing of happiness on the physical, material and other so-called purely 'secular' planes of life (during this life itself), there is also the eloquent fact that the very names of our four Upavedas: i.e. Āyurveda (which includes Anatomy, Physiology, Medical and Sanitary Science and Surgery), Dhanurveda (including Archery and other Military Sciences), Gandharvaveda (including the Science and Art of Music) and Sthāpatyaveda (Architecture, Engineering, Sculpture, Drawing and Painting) will suffice to show how wide is the range of Sanātana Dharma's jurisdiction. Similarly, the inclusion—within the Vedāṅgas—of व्याकरणम् (Grammar), छन्दः (Prosody), निरुक्तम् (Lexicography), ज्योतिषम् (Astrology based on Astronomy) and other such departments of what the modern western world would call purely 'secular' knowledge, will also clearly show and conclusively prove this very same unique feature of Sanātana Dharma.

Thus, for instance, we find the *Manusmṛti* and other sacred scriptures of Sanātana Dharma telling us:

नाप्सु मूत्रपुरीषे कुर्यात् ॥

'Thou shalt not pass urine and stools in reservoirs of water.' If and when a Westerner reads the English translation of a passage like this, he jumps up at once and says: 'This is a matter of purely Sanitary Science; what has this got to do with religion?' And our reply is, that, just because it has to do with our welfare and happiness (in any plane of life), therefore, it is *ipso facto* a part of our *dharma*. And, similarly, it needs no elaborate pointing out that it seems almost impossible even to conceive of the western world ever recognising the study of Grammar, Prosody, Lexicography, Astronomy and other such 'purely secular' departments of knowledge as necessary and inherent parts of religious study.

But our Sanātana Vaidika Dharma includes, within its all-comprehending jurisdiction, all departments of knowledge (including all branches of what, in modern terminology, we speak of as the Positive Sciences). It is, therefore, in the fitness of things, that our Sanātana Dharma, which has not merely existed from the time of creation, but has to and does cater for all kinds of Adhikārins, has naturally made all the necessary provision for all the different activities of life, by going into detailed disquisitions on all the varied requirements thereof, and setting forth an all-embracing and thorough-going system of injunctions and prohibitions, correct and faithful adhesion whereto is not only intensely and extremely useful but also positively and absolutely necessary for the attainment by us of all-round health, strength, peace, happiness and joy (of body, mind and spirit).

Undoubtedly, it is this very fact that is responsible for the intensely wonderful and immensely gratifying confirmation which the precepts of our Sanātana Dharma have been systematically receiving of late—on intrinsic merits—from Modern Science in all its multifarious branches. It is clear, therefore, that the Sanātana Vaidika system was based, not merely in its general plan and outlook but also in every one of its details, on a thorough-going and scientific basis of the most unexceptionable and far-reaching character which took into account all the various phases and aspects of life (physical, material, mental, intellectual, moral, political, industrial, economic, psychic, spiritual and so forth).

Under these circumstances, it is naturally impossible for us to translate the Sanskrit word *dharma* into English (or any other western language, for that matter) by means of a word which can fully convey all that the word *dharma* means to us. However, for practical purposes we may use the word 'religion' as a rough equivalent therefor and ask our listeners and readers always to be careful to remember the differences of outlook, scope and jurisdiction just explained. Now then, *sanātana* means Eternal; and *dharma* means religion. And the compound word, according to the rules of Sanskrit grammar, as we shall presently proceed to show, carries with it four beautiful and splendid meanings which throw light on the wonderful nature and unique greatness of Sanātana Dharma and prove it to have been most appropriately and felicitously named.

The First Meaning

Taking the first meaning of the word Sanātana Dharma, we explain it grammatically as a षष्ठीतत्पुरुषसमास: i.e. सनातनस्य धर्मः—सनातनधर्मः (in other words, Sanātana's Dharma) and the meaning of the षष्ठी विभक्तिः (genitive case) therein as स्थाप्य-स्थापकभावसंबंध: In other words, just as Christ's, Mahomed's, Zoroaster's and Buddha's *dharmas* mean the religion founded by Christ, Mahomed, Zoroaster and Buddha respectively, so Sanātana's Dharma means the religion of (i.e., the religion founded by) the Eternal One, namely God Himself and not by any person born subsequently.

In other words, we have this fact to take into account that, with the exception of Sanātana Dharma alone, all the other religions of the world—both past and present—can be brought under one of two headings:

(1) Religions which were but are not and

(2) Religions which are but were not. But Sanātana Dharma does not come under either category, for Sanātana Dharma alone existed before the birth of all these Religions and it alone continues to exist to the present day.

But what about the future? In connection with this point, we have, willy-nilly, to reckon with the inexorable Law of Nature यज्जन्यं तदनित्यम्। (i.e. whatever is born, must necessarily die). This is a Law to which there never has been any exception and to which there never can be any exception.

For instance, when, for the purely philanthropic purpose of the protection, the welfare and the uplift of the world in any respect and from any point of view, Śrī Bhagavān Himself comes into the world in the shape of an *Avatāra* (i.e. an Incarnation) like Śrīrāma, Śrīkṛṣṇa and so forth, we find that when He has finished His work and fulfilled the purpose for which He came and it is time for Him to go away, even He abandons the physical body which He took up for the purposes of that particular incarnation. In other words, even the physical body assumed by God for the nonce of a particular purpose—even that is not eternal. Thus, there is no exception to this Law of Nature viz: that whatever comes into existence (i.e. is born) must necessarily go out of it (i.e. die).

The Second Meaning

And this means, that, if there be any religion which can hope to remain for ever, it can and must be the one and only religion, which was at the very beginning of things and which continues to exist to the present day, to wit, our own beloved Sanātana Vaidika Dharma. It, on this account of being अनादिः (i.e. beginningless) and अनंतः (i.e. endless), inasmuch as it began with the world, continues to exist and can only end with the world itself. Sanātana Dharma is not merely the *dharma* established by the Sanātana (i.e. Eternal One) Himself viz: God, but is also itself सनातनः i.e. Eternal. It is bound to exist and will alone exist till the final extinction of the world itself. And even then, it will not really die but will only remain latent (i.e. temporarily out of sight) for the simple reason that there will be no one left to make use of it and benefit by it. And as soon as the next Kalpa is created, Sanātana Dharma must—and will, therefore,—automatically reappear and resume its function of protecting and uplifting humanity, nay, all creation. This second meaning of the word Sanātana Dharma is justified and proved by its grammatical analysis as a कर्मधारयसमासः i.e., सनातनश्चासौ धर्मश्च (the eternally-existing religion).

Relative Utility: All The Same

By this, we do not mean, however, to suggest—even remotely—that all the other religions are false and so on. On the contrary, we have already—at great length—pointed out that all religions, sincerely followed, ultimately lead to God. So, there should be no misunderstanding on this matter of our attitude towards other religions. Our point is merely that, while all the other faiths are good in their own way as far as they go and as long as they last, they too—like the Roman, Greek, Norse and Druidical religions—will, however, have to disappear from the world in due course; but, in the case of Sanātana Dharma, it is the world that will first go out of existence and then Sanātana Dharma will become latent thereafter, to re-appear when the world re-appears in a new Kalpa.

The Third Meaning

For the third meaning of the word Sanātana Dharma, we take it as a कर्मधारयसमासः, i.e., सनातनश्चासौ धर्मश्च but the adjective 'Sanātana' is itself to be derived in a slightly different way thus:

सदा भवः सनातनः (as usual) सनातनं करोति सनातनयति। सनातनयतीति सनातनः। सनातनश्चासौ धर्मश्च सनातनधर्मः॥ (as before). According to this third grammatical analysis and interpretation of the word, Sanātana Dharma has not merely been established by the eternal one (i.e., God) and is not merely (in itself) Eternal; this explanation goes one step still further and answers the question: "What is the use or the value of Sanātana Dharma?" by pointing out that Sanātana Dharma makes and keeps eternal those who believe in it and act according to it.

Other Ancient Empires

Let us now, in this connection, take up and make a comparative and analytical study of the history of all the great

Empires of the ancient world—the Greek, the Roman, the Syrian, the Assyrian, the Persian, the Babylonian, the Chaldaean, the Phoenician, the Egyptian, the Ninevah, the Carthaginian and other such ancient Empires whose very names inspired terror in the hearts not merely of their neighbours but also of all kingdoms even in the farthest nooks and corners of the world. Well, all of them by turns, achieved tremendous greatness, reached the highest pinnacle of national, nay, imperialistic glory, kept it up and stood there for two or three centuries, and then toppled down, down, until at last they not only reached the lowest point in active national existence but even went out of existence altogether and were wiped off the face of the map. None of them survives today. Why? Is this great, grim and awful fact in the world's history to be accounted for by any such explanation as, for example, that they did nothing to think over, devise and adopt all the requisite and humanly possible means and measures for keeping themselves eternal? No, not at all. On the contrary, each one of them did everything possible and conceivable not only to live but also to rule for ever as the Suzerain Power of the whole Universe. They did everything practicable for the creation, preservation and conservation of all possible human strength all-round i.e. physical, military, political, economic, financial and so on. And yet, what was the result of all these grand efforts and fond endeavours of them all? What has become of all these glorious empires of the past? They have all gone off and been exterminated altogether.

The Secret of Greece's Greatness

Now, let us dive deeper down and try to find out what made these ancient Empires so great; and let us begin with the case of Greece. The great historians of the world are all agreed—and not a single scholar is there who doubts or disputes their verdict—that the secret of Greece's ancient greatness is to be found in what we, with our study and experience of modern Indian history, may aptly describe as Lord Curzon's Cult of Efficiency (all-round—physical, intellectual and so forth). Greece paid concentrated attention to and worshipped at the shrine of Efficiency and believed that if and when the State devoted and dedicated itself to the correctly organised development and the absolutely unimpaired maintenance of Efficiency in all aspects, phases, branches and departments of life, as its National Ideal, then there could be no possibility of Greece going down in any respect whatsoever from its high level of intense, unquestioned and omnilateral superiority to all the nations of the world. The Cult of Efficiency, therefore it was, in which Greece in general and Sparta in particular sought to excel and did actually surpass all, during the halcyon days of their history.

Physical Efficiency

On the physical side, this ultra-idealized idolising of Efficiency in the daily life and practice of the Spartan people manifested itself in the shape of the Spartan Law and Practice, whereby, as soon as a new child—whether boy or girl—was ushered into the world, its parents took it immediately and straight-away over to the top of Mount Taygetus and mercilessly abandoned it there absolutely unprotected from rain and sun, from wind and frost and from the ravages of the wild beasts, to return after three or four days to see how the infant was faring. If, perchance, the babe had not merely survived all the inclemencies of the forest weather and the tender mercies of the prowling denizens of the wilderness and was still alive but was also found to be in the happy enjoyment of sound and even robust health and strength, then declared they—proudly and triumphantly—to themselves and to others: "This child is fit to become in due course a worthy citizen of Sparta, capable of routing invaders from abroad and quelling insurgents from within." They would then carry the child home and give it the splendid training which was carefully designed for the sole purpose of the successful evolution of perfect Spartan citizenship.

Intellectual Efficiency

And, then, on the intellectual side too, ancient Sparta had its own special outlook and angle of vision and its own unique devices for bringing about, in its citizens, the perfect fruition of splendid efficiency. Into details hereof, we need not enter just now; but we must refer to one point of great moment herein, as it was typical and characteristic. It was this. Like the penal codes of all countries in the history of the world, the Spartan Penal Code, too, had its own graded scale of punishments for various criminal offences (e.g. theft, murder and so forth); but the motive underlying the punishments was a peculiar one, absolutely unknown to, nay, even undreamt of by, the whole race of human legislators in the pages of history. Theft, for example, was punished not because it was religiously or morally held to be a sin to thieve and such sins ought to be punished, nor even on the juridical ground that the suffering caused by such acts to the owner of the property stolen ought to be prevented by the State and statutory provision for the severe punishment of such offences was the best deterrent against a tendency to commit them, but solely because the Spartan legislators held that if and when a man was found thieving and was hauled up, tried, convicted and punished, it meant, in reality, that, while thieving, he had bungled so badly as to get caught and punished and this was regarded as the worst sin, the greatest offence and the most heinous crime conceivable against Sparta's Cult of Efficiency.

How it Worked in Practice

The natural result of such a conception and outlook and the detailed and elaborate provisions based thereon was that the procedure followed in some cases by the criminal courts of Sparta was diametrically opposed to the one with which the world at the present day is familiar. Now, you all know that, when a person is hauled up before the criminal courts and charged with a theft or murder or any other such offence, it is the police and the prosecution witnesses on whom the onus rests for proving him guilty, while the accused and his witnesses try their best and utmost (by alibi pleas and in various other ways) to prove him innocent. In Sparta, however, it often happened that a man who had gone on undetected for a decade and more, thieving and murdering and so forth, went before a Magistrate, proudly narrated his crime and sought (by means of as detailed and circumstantial evidence as possible) to substantiate his allegations against himself; whereupon, as his proving them to be true would mean not merely his great intellectual efficiency from the standpoint of the Spartan ideal of efficiency but also the corresponding inefficiency of the Police in not detecting him. The Police would move heaven and earth to demonstrate to and satisfy the trying Magistrate, by means of convincing evidence, that the man had never committed any such crimes but was dishonestly seeking to achieve false allegations about his own criminal exploits. If and when, at the termination of these topsyturvy proceedings, it was proved to the satisfaction of the court that the man had really committed all the crimes in question and the Police had not detected and arrested him for a decade or more, the State hailed him as a great "Intellectual Efficient" of Sparta and voted grand honours to him (e.g. historic festivities and special processions wherein he was taken round in palanquins borne on the shoulders of the highest officials and other grandees of Sparta). In cases of extraordinary skill having been evinced by the criminal in the undetected committing of the most diabolical crimes, marble statues (and not mere festive processions of a few hours' or even a few days' duration) were regarded as the only fitting acknowledgment and recognition of such a glorious level of Ideal Intellectual Efficiency and as the only sufficient means for keeping the memory of such a great personage eternally green in the history of Sparta, so as to serve as a perennial source of eternal inspiration to future generations of the sons and daughters of Sparta.

The Consequence

But what was the resultant benefit, to Greece in general and to Sparta in particular, of all these grand plans and superhuman efforts for the achievement of Physical and Intellectual Efficiency? Did Sparta—or even Greece—achieve the expected result of becoming the Suzerain Power of the world? Nay, rather, have they even survived as an empire on the face of the earth? No, not at all. On the contrary, the Greek Empire itself is nowhere. And, beyond the memory left behind by Greece of her ideal of artistic finish and her cult of perfect physical, intellectual, cultural and other departmental efficiency as its legacy to the modern world, which even the most modern of modern artists and culturists feel bound to and do therefore actually pay their hearty tribute and reverential homage to in their lectures, their magazine-articles and so forth, the great Greek Empire of ancient European history has left practically no mark on the history of the world, nay, even of the Greeks of the present day.

Rome's Cult of Law and Order

Turn we now to the case of Rome and analyse her story. If the secret of Greek's ancient greatness is to be found in Lord Curzon's Cult of Efficiency, it may be said with equal historical truth and accuracy that the secret of Rome's ancient greatness is to be found in what, from our experience of modern Indian history, we may similarly describe as Lord Curzon's Successors' Cult of Law and Order; and that Rome paid one-pointed attention to and performed *Pūjā* at the shrine of Law and Order and fondly believed that, if and when the State carried out all things in the strictest possible accordance with a carefully planned, thoroughly organised and correctly codified system of Law and Order governing all conceivable aspects of life as its national ideal, then there could be absolutely no possibility of any confusion or weakness ever creeping into Rome's national life in any respect whatsoever and dragging it down, even to an infinitesimally small extent, from its lofty level of absolutely uncontroverted and all round superiority to all the other nations of the world. The Cult of Law and Order, therefore, it was, which Rome sought to and did actually beat all others in, throughout the mighty days of her ancient history.

The Consequence

But with what ultimate consequence? Has the Roman Empire remained the ruling power of the world, nay, even survived as an empire in the history and on the map thereof? Once again, a clear and emphatic 'no, not at all' is the only possible answer; for, beyond the single fact that Rome's legacy to us of Law and Order has left such a prominent mark on the history of the world that, even today and even in India, students of Law in our Law-colleges are called upon to begin their course with a study of Roman Jurisprudence, it is no exaggeration to say that the Roman Empire has left no mark worth mentioning on the history of the world. The fact that the Vatican (the Holy seat of the Pope, the Ecclesiastical Pontiff of Roman Catholic Christianity) is geographically located at Rome is a matter of history of later-day Italy and has absolutely nothing to do with the ancient Roman Empire and its Cult of Law and Order.

Other Empires

Let us now turn to the history of the other Empires, namely, the Syrian, the Assyrian, the Persian, the Babylonian, the Chaldean, the Phoenician, the Egyptian, the Nineveh, the Carthaginian and so on, of the ancient world. The honest historian has no option but to admit that their cases are, alas, much worse than even those of Greece and Rome. We know from the pages of history something about the daily life, the religious beliefs, the national practices, the social customs, the legal usages, the cultural ideals, and so on, of Greece and Rome; but we know nothing—or next to nothing—about the corresponding facts regarding the lives of the people of these other Empires which we have just named. And, what little we do know of them, e.g., with regard to Hasdrubal, Hamilcar, Hannibal of Carthage and so forth, has not come down to us from the historical literature of these peoples themselves but only from the pages of books written about them by enemy historians, like the Romans.

Oblivion

Doubtless there was (as there must necessarily have been) some secret, some particular factor, some special feature, which made each of them great and tremendous in its own way and in its own time; but whatever that factor, feature or secret was, it could only keep that particular empire alive and predominant for a short while, but was not sufficient to keep it in life and in predominance for ever. They all had their own separate religions which they believed in and followed; but, obviously, as testified by history, none of these religions had the necessary vitality and capacity to maintain themselves, let alone hold and enable their adherents to live on for ever. They have all gone into absolute oblivion.

The Case of India

Let us now turn our attention—over against the history of Greece, Rome and other empires as a whole—to a study of the picture of India's history, compare and contrast the two, observe the salient points of difference in the actual history thereof and trace therefrom and determine for ourselves the inevitable differences in outlook, ideal, cult, principles and mode of life which must necessarily have accounted for the serious differences thus observed in the actual history. Have we, in India, from ages past, paid similar attention to any such Cult of Efficiency, Law and Order and so forth which made Greece, Rome and other empires great in the past? The answer to this question is 'Yes' and 'No'. It is 'Yes' to some extent but not to the same extent as in Greece, Rome and so forth and, therefore, it is, to some extent, 'No'. Let us go into this a little deeper and analyse things clearly for ourselves.

India and Efficiency

The Spartan ideal of efficiency was certainly given a high place in India's Sanātanic scriptures too. In fact, the great value, the tremendous importance and the absolute necessity of Brahmacarya for achieving perfect physical and intellectual efficiency have been insisted on in our scriptures as in no other scriptures of the world. The perfection of the individual, physically and intellectually, in order to make his body and his intellect absolutely perfect instruments in his hands for achieving his goal—this was and has always been our Hindu ideal. But, in spite of all this emphasis and insistence on perfect and all-round efficiency, it must be carefully noted that this seeming ideal of efficiency is, according to our scriptures, really not an ideal for and by itself, but really a means to the realising of another and a higher ideal which is the real objective of the Sanātanic scriptures. What this real, higher and ultimate goal was, we shall presently see.

India and Law and Order

As regards law and order too, it may be truly said that no nation, no race and no religion in the history of the world has ever emphasised law and order in the way that India, the Hindus and Sanātana Dharma have done, the tremendous stress laid on discipline, i.e., on absolute and implicit obedience on the part of the son towards the father, the younger towards the elder brother, the servant towards the master, the disciple towards the Guru, the *Prajā* towards the *Rājan* and so forth, is a characteristic and unique feature of Sanātana Dharma which is well-known. And yet, even here, as we shall presently see, the seeming ideal of law and order, of discipline and of obedience is not an ultimate and real ideal by itself but only subordinate to a higher ideal which is the real objective. In fact, one might correctly sum up the whole position herein by saying that whatever contributing factor towards national greatness be taken into consideration—be it individual physical efficiency, military powers, financial strength, intellectual acumen, power of organization, self-forgetting service of the country or any other whatsoever—every one of these items was taken into account and actually enjoined too by our scriptures but not a single one of them was the actual ideal; each of them was there only as a means towards a specific end; and each such means was carefully considered with a due and vigilantly balanced sense of proportion and perspective and ordered to be made use of and acted upon in accordance with the requirements of a perfectly coordinated plan into which all the several means fitted to perfection.

The Real Objective

And what was this real objective? The only method by which we can rightly understand this is to study the attitude of Sanātana Dharma towards the hitherto-mentioned ideals and cults of other nations and the exact place given thereto in the Sanātanic scheme of national life.

(1) As regards efficiency, the Upaniṣadic text:

नायमात्मा बलहीनेन लभ्यः ॥

shows clearly that, according to the Sanātanic conception of life, not merely worldly success but even Spiritual Self-realization is impossible except on the basis of all-round strength. The examples of Śrīhanumān, Bhīṣma and other great Brahmacārins of ancient Indian history will go to show how in ancient India the ideals of perfect physical efficiency and intellectual efficiency were always put together and found to go together as contributory factors to success. But they were not desired for their own sake but merely as contributory factors towards the achievements of *dharma* and spiritual efficiency. The passage in the *Bhagavadgītā* which says:

बलं बलवतां चाहं कामरागविवर्जितम् ॥

(i.e., that strength alone which is free from the influence of the passions at its source and from tyrannical tendencies in its effect is of the divine nature) makes this clear, namely that the

Sanātanic cult of efficiency is not of the Spartan type which places a premium on physical powers and intellectual 'cuteness' achieved at the expense of all spiritual and even moral considerations but of one which brings them all together and keeps them under the control of and in subjugation to *dharma*.

(2) Similarly, with regard to law and order, it will be noticed that the striking and unforgettable instances of Prahlāda v. Hiraṇyakaśipu, Vibhīṣaṇa v. Rāvaṇa, Bhīṣma v. Paraṣurāma and so on, throw light on the fact that even the law of discipline and obedience was one which came under the Higher Law of subordination to Dharma. And this is why we have Śrīkṛṣṇa saying in the *Bhagavadgītā*:

धर्माविरुद्धो भूतेषु कामोऽस्मि भरतर्षभ ॥

i.e. (all desires not inconsistent with *dharma* are of the divine nature).

(3) In the same manner, it can be seen that all the other desirable factors in life which can possibly make for individual or national prosperity, progress and success are all permissible to us; but, at the same time, even the best and the loftiest amongst them has to be under the control of *dharma*, which ought to be our predominating consideration at all times, in all places and under all circumstances.

Our Dharmaśāstras tell us that, when two persons, both on horseback, are fighting with each other and one of them unhorses the other by killing the latter's horse, the former is religiously prohibited from continuing on horseback and fighting the man whose horse has been knocked down. And he is called upon to get down from his horse and fight with his opponent on terms of equal vantage. The most surprising thing about this is that this kind of most exacting *dharma* was scrupulously followed in actual daily practice, not merely by the great Dhārmic souls whom we all venerate but even by those whom our scriptures describe as Asuras (demons). For example, in the third and sixth Skandhas of the *Śrīmadbhāgavata*, we have the incidents narrated to us wherein Bhagavān Śrīvarāhāvatāra and Devendra had their weapons knocked off from their hands by the Asuras Hiraṇyākṣa and Vṛtra respectively and both the Asuras stopped fighting. Similarly, in the 10th Skandha of *Śrīmadbhāgavata*, there is the episode in which, on being called to mortal combat with Bhīma (who goes as a guest and is unarmed) Jarāsandha brings out of his stock his own best and favourite Gadā (mace), hands it over to Bhīma (in obedience to the Sanātanic law of the *Atithisatkara*, (hospitality) and fights with him with the second best mace in his possession. And, as soon as each evening's battle is ended, he again faithfully follows the law of hospitality by waiting upon Bhīma and serving him at his supper, and so forth. We do not find even such an oppressor, tyrant and monster like Jarāsandha seeking to poison or otherwise surreptitiously injure his foe who is thre as his guest.

In spite of all the disadvantages and handicaps which are the natural and inevitable consequences of foreign invasions and foreign rule, not merely political but even cultural, which India has been subjected to for several centuries past—in fact, for more than one thousand years—in spite of all these disadvantages and handicaps, we are still alive as a nation. What is this vitality of India due to?

The Saṁskāras

1. Introductory

An investigation into the real purpose and significance of ancient institutions like the Hindu *Saṁskāras* is beset with many difficulties. First of all, the peculiar circumstances under which they arose are buried deep under thick crusts of ages, and around them have clustered a mass of popular superstitions. So, at such a distance of time, it requires a well-trained imagination coupled with a thorough knowledge of facts to probe into the problem. The second difficulty is that of national sentiment, which looks only at the bright side of the past and clouds the critical vision so essential for any research work. But a more stubborn difficulty is presented by the *a priori* tendencies of the modern mind. It is apt to assume that any thing ancient must be superstitious; it is suspicious of spiritual values of life; and it is impatient of understanding strict discipline, which is a great characteristic of ancient religions. A student of ancient culture has to guard himself against credulity on the one hand and the ultrascepticism on the other. He should study the *Saṁskāras* with due reverence to the past and full sympathy with human nature through its various stages of development.

2. Two-fold Purpose

We can broadly divide the purpose of the *Saṁskāras* into two classes. The first class is popular and superstitious, which is motivated by unquestioned faith and naive simplicity of the unsophisticated mind. The second class is priestly and cultural. Its origin is due to conscious forces governing the development and evolution of society, when human beings try to improve upon nature. The priest, though not beyond the common run of people, was above the ordinary man in the street, and he introduced considerable refinment and culture into social customs and rites in a variety of ways. *Saṁskāras* of both the types have continued to figure in society from the very beginning, they have reacted on each other and they are still represented in Hinduism.

3. The Popular Purpose

To begin with the popular purpose, the ancient Hindus, like other nations of the world, believed that they were surrounded by superhuman influences which were potent enough for good or evil consequences. They thought that these influences could interfere in every important occasion in man's life. Therefore, they tried to remove hostile influences and attract beneficial ones, so that man may grow and prosper without external hindrances and receive timely directions and help from gods and spirits. Many items and ramifications of the *Saṁskāras* arose out of these beliefs.

(i) The Removal of Hostile Influences:

For removing the unfavourable influences the Hindus adopted several means in their *Saṁskāras*. The first of them was propitiation. Goblins, demons and other uncanny spirits were offered praise, oblations and food, so that they may return satisfied with offerings, without causing injury to the individual. The householder was anxious to protect the life of his wife and children and regarded it his duty to deal with them. During the pregnancy of a woman, at the birth of a child, during childhood etc., such propitiation took place. In the birth ceremonies "if the disease-bringing demon, Kumāra attacks the child, the father murmurs......." *Kurkura*, *Sukurkura*, who holds fast children, Chet! Chet! doggy let him loose. Reverence be to thee, the Sisara, a barkar, a bender."[1] The second method was that of deception. Sometimes propitiation was thought unnecessary or purposely avoided. For example, at the time of tonsure, the severed hair was mixed with cowdung and buried in a cowstall or thrown into a river, so that none could play magic upon it.[2] Deception is also evident in the funeral ceremonies. At the approach of death the image of a man was burnt before his death to deceive it.[3] The motive underlying this act was that death while haunting the proper body of its victim would mistake him for an already dead person. But when propitiation and deception both proved inefficient, a third drastic step was taken. Mischievous spirits were plainly asked to go away, threatened and directly attacked. During the birth ceremonies the father pronounces, 'May Śuṇḍa and Marka, Upavīra and Śauṇḍikeya, Ulūkhala and Malimlucha, Droṇāsa and Cyavana, vanish hence. Svāhā"[4]! The householder also invoked the help of gods and deities to drive away foul influences. While performing the Caturthīkarman (the fourth day after marriage) the husband invites Agni, Vāyu, Sūrya, Candra and Gandharva to remove the injurious elements from the newly married wife.[5] But sometimes, he himself, by means of water and fire, frightened and drove them off.

Other devices were also used for this purpose. Water was invariably used in every *Saṁskāra*. It washed away physical impurities and warded off demons and goblins. Noise was made at the time of burial to scare away lurking spirits. Sometimes the man himself asserted his boldness. He equipped himself with weapons to face any odds that might come in his way. For instance, the student was given a staff.[6] He was forbidden to part with it and asked always to keep it close to his body. When this staff was thrown away at the end of studentship, he was provided with a stronger bamboo-staff at the time of Samāvartana.[7] It is clearly stated that it was used not merely for protection against animals and human foes but also against Rākṣasas and Piśācas.[8] Shaking was also a means to remove evil influences. Combing the hair at the time of the *Sīmantonnayana* (Hair-parting) was done for the same purpose.[9] Selfishness of man sometimes compelled him to transfer bad influences from his side to that of others. The marriage costume worn by the bride was given to a Brahmā, as it was thought injurious to her. In this case, however, the Brahmā was thought too powerful to be attacked by evil influences. The nuptial clothes were also put in a cowpen or hung on a tree.[10]

(ii) Attraction of Favourable Influences:

Just as untoward influences were tried to be got rid of, so the favourable influences were invited and attracted for the benefit of the recipient of a particular *Saṁskāra*. The Hindus believed that every period of life was presided over by a deity. Therefore, on every occasion, that deity was invoked to confer boons and blessings on the man. At the time of the *Garbhādhāna* (conception) Viṣṇu was the chief deity, at the time of the Vivāha Prajāpati, and at the time of the Upanayana Bṛhaspati and so on. But there was no entire dependence on gods only. Men helped themselves also by various means. Suggestion and reference to analogous phenomena played a great part. Touch exercised a magic power. By touching things that were beneficial in themselves one expected good influences to follow. In the *Sīmantonnayana* ceremonies a branch of the *Udumbara* tree was applied to the neck of the wife.[11] Here touch was believed to bring about fertility. Mounting a stone brought about firmness and was, therefore, prescribed for a student and a bride. Touching the heart was thought to be a sure means of union and producing harmony between student and teacher or husband and wife. As breath was a symbol of life, the father breathed thrice on the new-born child to strengthen its breaths. For securing a male child the expectant mother was required to eat a barley corn with two beans and curd attached to it.[12] The reason is obvious. The things which the expectant mother took were symbolical of the male sex and were expected to impart it to the embryo. To produce offsprings the juice of a many-rooted and luxuriant banyan-tree branch was inserted into the right nostril of the wife.[13] Anointment produced love and affection. In the marriage ceremonies the bride's father anointed the couple while the bridegroom pronounced, "May all gods, may water unite our hearts.......[14] Avoidance of ugly and inauspicious sights, and giving up contact with impure persons preserved the purity of an individual. The Snātaka was forbidden even to pronounce a word beginning with an unlucky letter, or containing a repugnant idea.[15] Sometimes dramatic utterances were also requisitioned to bring about the desired thing. In the *Sīmantonnayana* ceremonies the wife was asked to look at a mess of rice whereupon the husband inquired whether she was seeing into its offsprings, cattle, prosperity and long life for him.[16]

(iii) The Material Aim of the Saṁskārs:

The material aims of the *Saṁskāras* were the gain of cattle, progeny, long life, wealth, prosperity, strength and intellect. The *Saṁskāras* were domestic rites and naturally during their performance things essential for domestic felicity were asked from gods. It was a belief of the Hindus that by prayer and appeal their desire and wishes were communicated to the deities who responded to them in form of animals, children, corn, a good physique and a sharp intellect.[17] These material aims of the *Saṁskāras* are very persistent and they are found uppermost, even now, in the minds of common people. The priest has always welcomed and blessed the material aspirations of people. He has tried to sanctify and thereby make them legitimate for a householder.

(iv) Saṁskāras as Self-expression:

The householder was not only an ever terror-stricken man, nor was he a professional beggar of gods. He performed the Saṁskāras also to express his own joys, felicitations and even sorrows at the various events of life. The possession of a child was a coveted thing, so on its birth the joy of the father knew no bounds. Marriage was the most festive occasion in the life of a man. Every land-mark in the progressive life of a child brought satisfaction and gladness in the household. Death was a tragic scene which brought forth much pathos. The householder expressed his happy feelings in the shape of decoration, music, feast and presents, his sorrows were manifested in the funeral ceremonies.

4. The Cultural Purpose

While fully recognizing the popular purpose of the *Saṁskāras*, the great writers and law-givers have attempted to introduce higher religion and sanctity of life into them. Manu (II.27) says: "By performing the *Saṁskāras*, conception, birth-rites, tonsure and *Upanayana*, seminal and uterine impurities are washed away." He (II.26) again adds: "The bodily *Saṁskāras* of the twice-born sanctify this life as well as the other." Yājñavalkya (I.16) also endorses the same view. Some kind of impurity was attached to the physical side of procreation and lying in the womb. Therefore, it was thought necessary to remove that impurity from the body by performing various Saṁskāras. The idea of sin (*enas*) associated with the physical process of birth as mentioned in the *Manusmṛti* (II. 27) is differently interpreted by different commentators. In the opinion of Medhātithi here 'sin' means mere imparity. According to Kullūka blemishes of seed are those arising from intercourse in a prohibited manner and the blemish of womb in that which arises from staying in the womb of an impure mother. The *Mitākṣarā* commenting on the *Yājñavalkyasmṛti* (I. 13) explain that the Saṁskāras are calculated to remove the bodily defects transmitted from the parents but they are not intended to remove the tint of sin arising from immoral parents. The whole body was also consecrated to make it a fit dwelling place for the soul. According to Manu (II.28): "The body is made Brāhmī by studies, observing vows, offering oblations, performing sacrifices, procreating children and undergoing the Pañca-mahāyajñas."

Hārīta as quoted in the *Saṁskāratattva* (p. 857) maintains that 'when a person has an intercourse according to the procedure of the Garbhādhāna he establishes in the wife a foetus that becomes fit for the reception of the Veda. The theory was also current that every man is born a Śūdra, who requires refinement and polish before he becomes a full-fledged Aryan: "By birth every one is a Śūdra, by performing the *Upanayana* he is called a twice-born, by reading the Vedas he becomes a Vipra and by realizing the Brahman he attains the status of a Brāhmaṇa."[18]

Social privileges and rights were also connected with the *Saṁskāras*. The *Upanayana* was a passport for admission into the Aryan community and its sacred literature. It was also a special privilege to the twice born and denied to the Śūdras.[19] To mark the end of education and for entering the married life one had to perform the *Samāvartanasaṁskāra*. The *Upanayana* and the *Vivāha-saṁskarās* with Vedic hymns entitled a person to perform all kinds of sacrifices befitting an Aryan and increasing his status in the society.

Another purpose of the *Saṁskāras* was the attainment of heaven and even *mokṣa* or liberation. When great sacrifices ceased to be mere propitiation of gods and became a means for securing heaven, the *Saṁskāras*, which were domestic sacrifices, also rose in their efficacy. Hārīta[20] speaks about the fruits of the Saṁskāras: "One who is consecrated with the Brāhma-saṁskāras attains the status of Ṛṣis, becomes their equal, goes to their world and lives in their close vicinity. One who is consecrated with the Daiva-saṁskāras attains the status of gods, etc." As the heaven was regarded the ultimate goal of life by common people in ancient times, the *Saṁskāras* naturally became instrumental in the attainment of that coveted state of existence. Śaṅkhalikhita remarks: "Purified by the *Saṁskāras* and always practising the eight virtues of the soul, one gets, merits and heaven, he goes to the world of Brahmā and reaches the state of Brahmanhood from where he never falls.[21]"

5. The Moral Purpose

In course of time a moralizing feature emerged from the material body of the *Saṁskāras*. Gautama (G.D.S.VIII.24) after enumerating forty *Saṁskāras* gives 'eight good qualities of the soul," viz., mercy, forbearance, freedom from envy, purity, calmness, right behaviour, and freedom from greed and covetousness. He (G.D.S.VIII.25) further says: "He that has performed forty sacraments but has not the eight good qualities enters not into union with Brahmā. But he that has performed only a part of the forty *Saṁskāras* and has eight good qualities enters into union with Brahmā and into the heaven of Brahmā."

The *Saṁskāras* were never regarded as ends in themselves. They were expected to grow and ripen into moral virtues. For every stage of life rules of conduct were prescribed in the *Saṁskāras*. No doubt, in them there is much that is religious and superstitious, but ethical attempt for the moral uplift of an individual is also visible. This stage of the *Saṁskāras* marks a great advance over the individual benefits that were solicited in them.

6. The Formation and Development of Personality

The cultural purpose that evolved from the ancient rites and ceremonies of the Hindus was the formation and development of personality. Aṅgiras[22] giving the analogy of a painting says, "Just as a picture is painted with various colours, so the character of an individual is formed by undergoing various *Saṁskāras* properly." The Hindu sages realized the necessity of consciously moulding the character of individuals instead of letting them grow in a haphazard way. They utilized the *Saṁskāras*, already prevalent in the society, for this purpose.

The *Saṁskāras* cover the full span of life, and they even try to influence and impress the individual after his death through the cult of soul. They were arranged in such a way that they may produce suitable impressions from the very beginning of one's life. The *Saṁskāras* were a guide that directed the life of an individual according to his growth. So a Hindu was required to live a full life of discipline and his energies flowed into a well-guarded and purposive channel. The *Garbhādhāna Saṁskāra* was performed at the proper time when the couple were physically fit and in a healthy condition, when they knew each other's heart and had intense desire for possessing a child. Their whole thought was concentrated towards the act of procreation and a pure and congenial atmosphere was produced by means of sacrifices and recital of apt hymns.

Throughout her pregnancy the wife was guarded and protected against evil influences physical and superphysical and her conduct was regulated to influence the growing child in the womb. At the time of birth, *Āyuṣya* (for long life) and *Prajñājanana* (for talent) ceremonies were performed when the new-born was blessed to become firm like a stone, strong and crushing like an axe and grow into an intellectual man.[23] On every occasion during the childhood joys and felicitations of an optimistic life were thrown into atmosphere which was breathed in by the budding child. After the *Cūḍākaraṇa* or tonsure when the child grew into a boy, his duties were prescribed and his responsibilities explained before him without encumbering his mind and body with book-knowledge and school discipline. The *Upanayana* and other educational *Saṁskāras* formed the great cultural furnace where the emotions, desires and will of the boy were melted and shaped and he was prepared for an austere but a rich and cultured life. The *Samāvartana* was an entrance and probation for the life of a married householder. The marriage arrangement was a developed code of eugenics and the nuptial ceremony a homily on the life of a married couple. The various sacrifices and vows prescribed for a householder were introduced to remove selfishness clinging to one's individuality and make him realize that he was the part and parcel of the whole community.

The death of a man was made easy by previous arrangement and his soul was given solace and help in its journey to the other side of life. No doubt, there are many items in the *Saṁskāras* that may be called a matter of faith. But none can deny the operation of the cultural motive underlying the *Saṁskāras*, though one may not concede them a place for a perfect scientific scheme.

By making the Saṁskāras compulsory, the Hindu sociologists aimed at evolving a type of humanity uniform in culture and character and having the same ideal in life. They were successful to a great extent in their attempt. The Hindus form a peculiar race with a wide cultural background. They influenced and assimilated the people who came in contact with them by their cultural scheme, and they are still living as a nation.

7. Spiritual Significance

Spiritualism is the chief feature of Hinduism and every phase of Hindu religion is tinctured with it. This general outlook of the Hindus transformed the *Saṁskāras* into a spiritual *Sādhanā*. The spiritual purpose and significance of the *Saṁskāras* cannot be given an open demonstration nor can it be evidenced with paper documents. It is the experience of those who have received the sacraments. To a Hindu the *Saṁskāras* conveyed more than their constituents. They were 'an outward visible sign of an inward spiritual grace.' He looked beyond the ceremonial performances and felt something invisible which sanctified his whole personality. So, for the Hindus the *Saṁskāras* were a living religious experience and not a dead formalism.

The *Saṁskāras* served a mean between the ascetic and the materialistic conception of the body. The advocates of the first school try to worship the spirit while discarding the body – an absurd procedure in the world of elements (Man.II.16). The upholders of the second view do not go beyond the body and deny the spiritual aspect of man's life, and therefore they are deprived of that peace and joy that are nestled in the calm recesses of the spirit (ṚV.X.14.16). It was the business of the *Saṁskāras* to make the body a valuable possession, a thing not to be discarded, but made holy, a thing to be sanctified, so that it might be a fitting instrument of the spiritual intelligence embodied in it.

The *Saṁskāras* were a gradual training in spiritualism. Through them the recipient realized that all life, properly understood, is a sacrament and every physical action should be referred to, and connected with, the spiritual reality. It was the way in which an active life of the world was reconciled with spiritual realization. In this system of living the body and its functions ceased to be hindrances, and became helpers in attaining perfection. By performing these *Saṁskāras* the life of an ordinary Hindu, with whom the world would have been too much but for timely intervention of spiritual discipline, was made a grand sacrament. Thus, duly celebrating the rites and ceremonies, the Hindus believed that they escaped the physical bondage and crossed the ocean of death.

8. Different Stages

Such was the purpose of the Hindu *Saṁskāras*, when they formed the part and parcel of the life of the Hindus, who felt and acted accordingly. The *Saṁskāras* in their creative period were true to life, a flexible and living institution and not a fixed rigid ritualism. They were adapted to different localities and different times. Every Vedic family performed the ceremonies in its own way. Then set in the intellectual classification of the *Saṁskāras*, when they were codified. At this time the creative period was drawing to its close and an attempt was made to settle every thing finally. There are numerous discussions and options about the various details of the *Saṁskāras*. Minutest details were recorded and no departure from them was desired. But change was still possible. The Hindu mind was not stagnant as yet. Then came a third period in the religious life of the Hindus. They thought that their energy was exhausted, they could not create any thing new and their only business was to collect and preserve. They regarded even a slight variation from the fixed course of the *Saṁskāras* a sin and they felt that they could not turn even a pebble, or utter a single word without the prescription of the ancient Ṛṣis. To make the matter worse, the language of the procedure and *mantras* became unintelligible in course of time. This was the stage when the true spirit of the *Saṁskāras* departed and their sepulchures were left behind to be worshipped by their blind followers. The *Saṁskāras* ceased to be refined, elevated and adapted to the specific needs of the time. Therefore, they became, more or less, a defunct institution not serving their real purpose. In modern times reformist religious movements have tried to simplify and unify the *Saṁskāras* to serve the Hindu society as a whole. There have been also attempts at their rationalization.

References

1. P.G.S. i 16. 20; A.G.S. i. 15; G.G.S. ii. 7. 17.
2. P.G.S. II. 1. 20.
3. K.S. xlviii. 54 ff; 39 ff.
4. P.G.S. i. 16. 19; AP. G.S. i. 15.
5. P.G.S. i. ii. 2. 1-5.
6. A.G.S. i. 19. 10; P.G.S. ii. 5. 16.
7. G.G.S. II. 6. 26.
8. P.G.S. ii. 6. 26.
9. Āp. G.S. xiv; H.G.S. ii. 2.
10. A.V. xiv. 2. 48-50; K.S. lxxvi. 1; lxxix. 24.
11. P.G.S. i. 15. 4. 6; G.G.S. ii. 7.1.
12. H.G.S. ii. 2. 23; A.G.S. i. 13. 2.
13. P.G.S. i. 14. 3.
14. P.G.S. i. 4. 15; G.G.S. ii. 1. 18.
15. P.G.S. ii. 7. 11-13. A.G.S. iii. 9. 6.
16. The Sāmavedamantrabrāhmaṇa i. 5. 1-5.
17. A.G.S. i. 7. 19.
18. Atri, 141-142.
19. Āp. D.S. i. 1. 16.
20. Quoted in V.M.S. vol. I. p. 139.
21. V.M.S. vil. i. p. 142.
22. Cf. Parāśara, VIII. 19.
23. Āp. G.S. xiv; P.G.S. i. 16; J.G.S. i. 8. F. 5.

The Marriage

1. The Nature of Hindu Marriage

In Hindu law, that is to say in the Dharmaśāstra or 'orthodox' juridical theory of India, marriage (*vivāha*) was one of the ten *saṁskāras* necessary for men of the twice born classes and the only Vedic sacrament for women. As in canon law and moral theology matrimonium is treated under sacraments, so in Hindu law *vivāha* is not treated under *vyavahāra* (litigation) but under *saṁskāra*. A *saṁskāra* is a sacrament or a purificatory act. Marriage is considered sacred because it is said to be complete only on the performance of the sacred rites attended with sacred procedure. This *saṁskāra* gives rise to the status of wifehood and its performance cannot be annulled by the fact that the husband or wife lapses from virtue, i.e., by committing adultery.[1]

It is almost impossible to define marriage in legal terms but the *śastric* concept of marriage would seem to be as a union between a man and a woman which arises at the time when the ceremony of marriage (i.e., *saṁskāra*) has been completed, the bridegroom having the requisite qualifications for taking a girl in marriage and the bride the qualifications for being given in marriage, and this procedure having been completed before the nuptial fire.[2] Marriage is a sacramental rite, which is performed for the girl for the purpose of making her a wife and is marked by the holding of hands, along with its entire procedure and subsidiary details.[3] It gives the status of husband and wife to the married couple. The *mantras* used in the ceremony of wedding create a wife. The sacrament becomes complete by the use of those *mantras*. As regards the marriage of a Śudra, there are no *mantras* but other rites apply excluding the *mantras*.[4]

2. The Purpose of the Saṁskāras

The exact purpose of *saṁskāras* was left rather vague in our authorities. A critical look at the list of *saṁskāras* will reveal that their purposes were manifold. According to ancient Hindu religious belief man was surrounded by superhuman influences which were powerful for good or evil consequences. These influences could interfere in every important occasion in man's life. Therefore, the Hindus tried to remove hostile influences and attract beneficial ones, so that man might grow and prosper without external hindrances and receive timely directions and help from gods and spirits. Another purpose of the *saṁskāras* was the attainment of heaven. It had also a psychological value, impressing on the mind of the person concerned that he had assumed a new role and must strive to observe its rules.[5] The *Vivāha-saṁskāra* consists essentially in an acceptance, which produces the mental impression that this girl is the man's wife, and wifehood arises from her having undergone the *saṁskāra*, which *saṁskāra* itself could not occur but for the marriage.[6]

During the *saṁskāra* of marriage a bridegroom is said to be an active receiver of the bride, who is taken by him and given by her father or guardian. From the *śāstric* point of view the religious aspect of marriage was so highly rated that a father was supposed to be under a sacred duty to give his daughter in marriage at the appropriate age, neglect of which duty was regarded as a sin.[7] A critical look at the concept of Hindu *śāstric* marriage will show that it underwent changes from time to time.

3. Marriage in the Vedic Period

It was a simple religious ceremony consisting of grasping the hand of the bride by the bridegroom. The *Ṛgveda* enjoins:

"I take thy hand for good fortune, that thou mayest attain old age with me as thy husband; the gods have given thee to me that I may be the master of the household."

4. Marriage in the Sūtra Period

The procedure of marriage became complex during the *Sūtra* period. The bridegroom was to lead the bride three times round the nuptial fire, and the ceremony was completed on taking the seven steps by the couple, The wife was shown the Pole Star, which was symbolic of the fact of her stability in her husband's home.

5. Marriage in the Smṛti Period

During this period we meet with various forms of marriage, eight of which will be briefly dealt with below.

(i) *The Brāhma*

The gift of a daughter, after decking her with costly garments and honouring her by presents of jewels, to a man learned in the Vedas and of good conduct, whom the father himself invites, is called the Brāhma rite. Medhātithi on Man. XXVII comments that there is nothing to indicate the connection of special dressing with either the bride only or with the bridegroom only; hence they should be taken as relating to both. This seems to be the correct view, because in practice even today both the bride and the bridegroom are specially dressed and adorned for the wedding.

(ii) *The Daiva*

This was a gift of a daughter whom her father had beautifully clothed when the sacrifice had already begun, to the officiating priest, who performed that act of religion.

(iii) *The Ārṣa*

When the father gave away his daughter according to the rule, after receiving from the bridegroom, for the fulfilment of the sacred law, a cow and a bull or two pairs, that marriage was termed the Ārṣa. On the face of this text it appears that the taking of the consideration from the bridegroom rendered this form inferior to the above two and the Prājāpatya below. But this is doubtful, for Medhātithi on Man. III, 29 comments that such receiving of the cattle by the father was done in obedience to law, and not with the idea of receiving it in exchange for the price of the girl.

(iv) ***The Prājāpatya***

When the father gave away his daughter with honour saying distinctly: "May both of you perform together your civil and religious duties." Again Medhātithi comments that the formula implies the condition that the daughter is to be given to the bridegroom only if he fulfills his duty, property and pleasure along with her. Therefore, this form was regarded as inferior by reason of this condition. Ludwick Sternbach,[8] whose study is based on the Dharmaśāstra, Arthaśāstra, Kāmasūtra, Gṛhyasūtras and the *Mahābhārata*, concludes that when the forms of marriage are closely examined there existed in ancient India not eight but eleven forms of marriage. The difference between the Prājāpatya and the Brāhma is that the bridegroom in the former is the suitor, i.e., he has solicited the girl, and is not invited by the father of the bride. He is an applicant for the bride's hand, and this makes it inferior to the Brāhma form, where the bridegroom is voluntarily and respectfully invited by the father of the bride to accept his daughter. A Hindu marriage, being a gift of the bride, loses a part of its merit if it is not voluntary or wilful, but has to be applied for.

The Prājāpatya was probably used only for a monogamic marriage and the husband could not renounce his wife and take to the order of Sanāyasa or Vānaprastha without her consent or her company. In fact the Brāhma was originally identical with the Prājāpatya, because Āpastamba and Vasiṣṭha do not mention Prājāpatya at all. The Prājāpatya was added later, therefore, the Smṛti writers fail to bring out the difference between the two. The Prājāpatya is the second best and approved form. As in the Brāhma form so in the

Prājāpatya one the bridegroom is invited and honourably received by the father of the bride.

(v) *The Āsura*

The bridegroom having given as much wealth as he could afford to the father, paternal kinsman and to the girl herself took her as his bride. This being a sale of the bride was regarded as a base form of marriage and was prohibited by Manu. This form was recognized by the Hindu Law during the British period. In the *Kailāsanātha* v. *Parāśakti* it was held that the distinctive feature of the Āsura form of marriage is the giving of money or money's worth to the bride's father for his benefit or as consideration for his giving the girl in marriage. However, a courtesy or complimentary present given to the bride or her family has to be distinguished from bride-price. Money paid by the bridegroom for the specific purpose of making jewellery for the bride is not bride-price and does not make the marriage an Āsura one. Now after Indian Independence the whole situation was reviewed by the Supreme Court, which held that the Āsura is an unapproved form of marriage and the test of it is that there shall be not only benefit to the bride's father, but that benefit shall form a consideration for the sale of the bride.

(vi) *The Gāndharva*

This was a marriage arising out of mutual desire of a man and a woman, and can be compared with the modern love marriage. It was enjoined by the Śastra that a Brāhmaṇa could contract a marriage legitimately in one of the first four forms. However, in practice at least according to the Mithilā School of Law, the Gāndharva was recognised amongst Brāhmaṇas.

In the *Bhaoni* v. *Maharaj*[9] the Gāndharva was equated with concubinage. It was held that this form had become obsolete as a form of marriage giving the status of wife and making the issue legitimate. This case is unlikely to be followed in view of the Hindu Marriage Act, 1955 and changing public opinion, which tends to encourage grown up persons to make their own decision in the choice of their life partners.

(vii) *The Rākṣasa*

This was a marriage by seizure of a girl by force from her house while she wept and called for assistance, after her kinsmen and friends had been slain in battle or wounded and their houses broken open.

(viii) *The Paiśāca*

Where the suitor secretly seduced the girl while she was asleep or drunk or disordered in intellect that sinful marriage was called the Paiśāca. This is the eighth and the basest.

The first four marriages are regarded as "approved" marriages. It was a Hindu religious belief that sons born of these marriages were radiant with knowledge of the Vedas and were honoured by good men. Having these qualities of beauty and goodness, possessing wealth and fame, obtaining as many enjoyments as they desire and being most righteous, they would live a hundred years. The remaining four are regarded as blameworthy, from which spring sons who are cruel and liars, who hate the Vedas and the sacred law. Rākṣasa and Paiśāca, which were condemned by Manu as base and sinful, however, did not legalise force or fraud as the marriage ceremony had in theory to be performed with sacred rites,[10] without which the marital relationship did not arise. Their recognition can be justified on the ground that they existed in order to validate the circumstances of which the unfortunate woman was the victim. The jurists were concerned with the results flowing from the circumstances preceding the marriage and classified those circumstances accordingly.

According to the Śāstra inferior forms of marriage, namely, Āsura, Gāndharva, Rākṣasa and Paiśāca do not involve a change of the *gotra* of the bride, which is an essential part of the ceremony of the Vedic marriage, because in such forms there is no voluntary gift of the bride by her father to the bridegroom. Approved forms were meant for Brāhmaṇa who were an important caste. According to Manu the first six forms of marriage were lawful for a Brāhmaṇa, the four last for a Kṣatriya, and the same four, excepting the Rākṣasa, for a

Vaiśya and a Śūdra. The significance of the approved and unapproved forms of marriage was that it determined the devolution of a woman's property on her death. In the former the husband and his family, while in the latter the father and his family succeed to her *strīdhana*. Where a woman was married in the unapproved forms, her death ceremonies were to be performed by a member of the *gotra* of her father, whereas in case of the approved marriage, they might be performed either by her husband's *gotra* or her father's. The reason for this distinction seems to be that approved marriages were authorized by the families of the couple concerned, while the unapproved were contracted against the wish of family of the woman concerned, if we reserve the case of the Āsura marriage, which originally did not imply a sacramental transfer but only a sale—spiritually (so the Śāstra seems to imply) she remained a member of her natal *gotra*. That is why she retained the *gotra* of her father.

If we look critically at the above mentioned eight forms of marriage, it will be evident that they were a mere elaboration of the concept of marriage (*vivāha*). They took account of local custom and usage, which were developing alongside the Śāstra. A survey of the Dharmaśāstras, Smṛtis, Nibandhas and the commentaries will prove that Hindu law was never static, but was modified by the practice of the time to suit the just demands of the people. With the advent of the British rule, the ancient sources of the Hindu Law began to be modified by judicial decisions and legislative enactments, while Hindu society assumed a new character because of its contact with Western education, civilization, economic and scientific progress. In fact the Hindu Marriage Act, 1955 is the result of the influence which had started in the British period. Thus the Dharmaśāstra's contact with actual usage, though sometimes difficult to trace, has been, in practice, continuous.

According to Kauṭilya, whose *Arthaśāstra* (a predominantly secular book), reflects practical usages, there can be no divorce in case the marriage is contracted in one of the approved forms. But if the marriage is in an unapproved form, then it can be dissolved by mutual consent, if both have come to hate each other. There can be no release at the instance of only one party to the marriage who has begun to feel aversion to the other party in whatever form the marriage may have been performed. Kauṭilya actually says: *amokṣo dharma-vivāhānāṁ*—"The law does not allow the dissolution of marriage between spouses who have undergone a Dhārmika-vivāha." The first four marriages are *dharmya*, i.e., connected with righteousness, because they are brought about under the authority of the father. Such marriages do not admit divorce.

6. Nuptial Ceremonies

According to the plain Smṛti texts marriages in the unapproved forms do not require the performance of the religious ceremony, but the Śāstric Law as applied by the courts during the British period in India held that such a ceremony was essential for the validity of the marriage. This is so even in modern Hindu Law. It was held in the *Deivani* v. *Chidambaram* that there are two essential elements to constitute a valid marriage, viz., a secular element, which is the gift of the bride in the four forms, the transference of dominion for consideration in the Āsura form, and mutual consent of the spouses in the Gāndharva form. These must be supplemented by the actual performance of marriage by going through the forms prescribed by the Gṛhyasūtras, of which the essential elements are 'Pāṇigrahaṇa' (joining of hands of the bride and the bridegrooms) and '*saptapadi*' (taking of seven steps by the bridal couple). In the case of *Rākṣasa* and *Paiśāca* forms also (should these be capable of validity in modern times), there should be a marriage ceremony prescribed by the Śāstras. In the *Bhaurao* v. *State of Maharashtra* it was laid down that solemnisation of the marriage with proper rites and ceremonies was essential in the Gāndharva 'form'. Similarly it was recently held by the Supreme Court in a case of bigamy that in order to prove the validity of the second marriage it is necessary to prove that the essential nuptial ceremonies were performed.

The performance of rites and ceremonies according to religious beliefs (e.g., *saptapadī*) or according to custom and usage has been preserved by the Hindu Marriage Act. 1955. The modern law has been developed in such a way as to show that the ceremony though vital to the religious purpose is no longer vital to the working of the secular rights. Thus where a man and woman live as husband and wife and have children who are recognised as such by their community by the custom the rights of the spouses and their children will not be destroyed merely by someone's attempting to bring forth evidence that no ceremonies of marriage were performed on the couple.

Whether or not such ceremonies are essential, their non performance or wrong performance can be excused under certain circumstances by the doctrine of *factum valet,* e.g., where the *saptapadi* (taking of seven steps) is not completed because of an accidental fire or some other mishaps, the validity of such a marriage cannot be upset subsequently. Where a marriage takes place under a custom according to which *saptapadi* is not an essential ceremony, the non-performance of *saptapadi* does not invalidate the marriage. In considering the validity of a marriage it is necessary to distinguish between the essentials and non-essentials of the custom. The presumption that a valid marriage took place can be raised where it is established that the marriage was duly solemnised but some unessential ceremony was not performed or there was some defect in the completion of the rite. Thus the sacramental and Śāstric characteristic of the Hindu marriage so far as the performance of the religious ceremonies is concerned is still in existence.

According to the Śāstric view the spiritual aspect of marriage was so important that the husband was said to have received his wife from the gods and not wedded her according to his own will, for he was doing what was agreeable to gods. The consequence of marriage was that man and woman became one person, as the Veda expresses: "Her bones become identified with his bones, flesh with flesh, skin with skin." From the time of the marriage, they are united in body and mind as well as in religious ceremonies. As a river loses its identity by merging itself into the ocean, so a wife was supposed to merge her individuality with that of her husband. In the revealed texts of the Veda, in the traditional laws of the Smṛti, and in the popular usage, the wife is declared to be half the body of her husband, equally sharing the outcome of good and evil acts. So a Hindu marriage was a sacred union of two personalities into one for the purpose of the continuance of the society and for the uplift of the two by self-restraint, self-sacrifice and mutual cooperation for the performance of holy rites. This is a central concept of Hindu ethics and law.

7. The Object of Marriage

It was threefold, namely *dharma* (the performance of religious and righteous dutis), *prajā* (progeny) and *rati* (pleasure). Where the Hindu lawgivers regarded *dharma* as the first and the highest aim of marriage, and procreation as the second, *dharma,* according to the Śāstra, dominated marriage. Marriage was a means not merely for satisfying sexual desire or to obtain progeny, but to secure a partner for the performance of religious duties. It enabled a man, by becoming a householder to perform religious sacrifices to the gods and to procreate sons. It was the duty of the husband to require and the right of the wife to give cooperation in all religious acts. Manu on the authority of the Veda declares that religious rites must be performed by the husband and wife together. Women were not allowed to perform any sacrifice, vow or fast apart from their husbands. They could obtain heaven merely by being obedient to their husbands.

It was a Hindu belief that a Hindu from his birth is born with three debts, i.e., he owes the Brahmacarya (study of the Vedas) to the sages, sacrifice to the gods, and progeny to *pitṛs* (ancestors). The second purpose of the marriage was to procreate sons, who were supposed to save a man from hell. A son is called *putra* because he delivers his father from the hell called *Put*. So much importance was attached to the birth of a son that a man was said to have conquered the spiritual worlds and obtained immortality and heaven by having a son. Immediately upon the birth of his first-born son a man was freed from his debt to the ancestors. Legitimate progeny being the objective, marriage was a religious necessity.[11]

The purpose of the marriage is further evidenced by the procedure of the marriage ceremony, when the bridegroom addresses the bride as: "I am heaven, you are earth, Come! Let us join together so that we may generate a male child, a son, for the sake of the increase of wealth, a blessed offspring of strength." Marriage enabled a man to make himself complete by the association of his wife and his son. His sacred obligations, i.e., the proper performance of his religious duties, faithful service to gods, his offspring, highest conjugal happiness, heavenly bliss for himself and his ancestors, depended on his wife alone, as he was incompetent to perform the above mentioned acts without the help and presence of the latter.

8. The Dissolution of Hindu Śāstric Marriage

It has been seen that a Hindu marriage, being a sacrament, once performed before the nuptial fire with the sacred texts, becomes irrevocable on the completion of the ceremony of taking seven steps by the couple. There is no evidence as to the practice of divorce as such during the Vedic and post Vedic periods. It was a holy union of mind, body and soul of the spouses and, it was believed, that even death did not put an end to it, for the wife remained linked with her husband in soul after death in the next world. It was the highest duty of husband and wife to remain united in marriage and be utterly faithful to each other. It was ordained by the Creator that a husband could not release his wife by sale or repudiation. The wife was required to be obedient to her husband under all circumstances. She was expected to worship him as God even if he was lacking in good qualities and virtue.

According to Āpastamba (II.10.27.5) if the solemn vow of marriage is transgressed both husband and wife certainly go to hell. Hindu marriage was regarded as an eternal and sacred bond which united the husband and wife for the performance of their religious sacrifices. Dissolution of marriage was thus not contemplated by the Śāstra, for it was Non-dhārmic, unrighteous and sinful.

References

1. P.V. Kane, *H.D.*, Poona, 1941, vol. II, part I, p. 620; Dwarka Nath Mitter, *The Position of Women in Hindu Law,* Calcutta, 1913, p. 195.
2. J.D.M. Derrett, *Hindu Law Past and Present,* Calcutta, 1957, p. 86.
3. Medhatithi on Man. XX, the *Manusmṛti* translated by G. Jha, vol. II, part I, Calcutta, 1921, p. 45.
4. Medhatithi on Man., *The Principles of Hindu Law—The Commentaries* translated by J.C. Ghose, vol. II, Calcutta, 1917, p. 46.
5. P.V. Kane, *H.D.,* vol. II, part I, p. 193.
6. J.D.M. Derrett, "*The Discussion of Marriage by Gadadhara*", The Adyar Library Bulletin, 1963, vol. XXVII, at p. 180.
7. G.D.S. XVIII, 21-23.
8. Ludwick Sternbach, *Juridical Studies in Ancient Indian Law*, Delhi 1965, part I, pp. 347-348, 375-376.
9. *Bhaoni* v. *Maharaj* (1881) 3 All. 738; see also M.L. Jain, "*Validity of Hindu Marriage Solemnised without performing any Customary Ritual or Ceremony*" A.I.R. 1961, Journal, p. 84.
10. Vṣṭ.D.S., P.N. Sen, *The General Principles of Hindu Jurisprudence,* Calcutta, 1918, pp. 269-270.

The Stages of Life

While the individual and the social sides of *karman* are inseparably intertwined, the theory of *varṇa* or caste emphasizes the social aspect, and that of *āśrama* or stages in the life of the individual aspect. The four stages of Brahmacarya or the period of training, Gārhasthya or the period of work for the world as householder, *vānaprastha* or the period of retreat for the loosening of the social bonds, and Sannyāsa or the period of renunciation and expectant awaiting of freedom indicate that life is a pilgrimage to the eternal life through different stages.

The first period is that of training and discipline of body and mind. Plastic youth is moulded to a life of duty. The student is required to live for a fixed period in the house of his teacher, where he is taught the arts and sciences which would be useful to him in after-life. Women were also entitled to Brahmacarya. They were given the training of their classes, and thus enabled to take up the functions of the caste in the emergencies of life. Restrictions regarding Vedic study were introduced when women of other racial stocks with different customs were accepted in marriage.

The second stage is that of the householder or the Gṛahastha. A human being is not ordinarily self-sufficing. The God of Aristotle may enjoy his solitary existence, but not the men and women of the world. These are as a rule encouraged to enter the married life. India has known for centuries what Freud is popularizing in Europe, that repressed desires are more corrupting in their effects than those exercised openly and freely. Monastic tendencies were discouraged until one had a normal expression of natural impulses. He who runs back from marriage is in the same boat with one who runs away from battle. Only failures in life avoid occasions for virtue. Marriage is regarded as sacred. The very gods are married. When the Hindu descends from the adoration of the Absolute and takes to the worship of a personal god, his god has always a consort. He does not worship a bachelor or a virgin. Śiva is an Ardhanārīśvara, and his image signifies the cooperative, interdependent, separately incomplete but jointly complete masculine and feminine functions of the supreme being. There is nothing unwholesome or guilty about the sex life. Through the institution of marriage it is made the basis of intellectual and moral intimacies. Marriage is not so much a concession to human weakness as a means of spiritual growth. It is prescribed for the sake of the development of personality as well as the continuance of the family ideal. Marriage has this social side. Every family is a partnership between the living and the dead. The Śrāddha ceremony is intended to impress the idea of the family solidarity on the members. At the end of the ceremony the performer asks: "Let me, O fathers! have a hero for a son."

The Hindu ideal emphasizes the individual and the social aspects of the institution of marriage. Man is not a tyrant nor is woman a slave, but both are servants of a higher ideal to which their individual inclinations are to be subordinated. Sensual love is sublimated into self-forgetful devotion. Marriage for the Hindu is a problem and not a datum. Except in the pages of fiction we do not have a pair agreeing with each other in everything, tastes and temper, ideals and interests. Irreducible peculiarities there will always be, and the task of the institution of marriage is to use these differences to promote a harmonious life. Instincts and passions are the raw material which are to be worked up into an ideal whole. Though there is some choice with regard to our mates, there is a large element of chance in the best of marriages. Carve as we will that mysterious block of which our life is made, the black vein of destiny or chance, whatever we may call it, appears again and again in it. That marriage is successful which transforms a chance mate into a life companion. Marriage is not the end of the struggle, it is but the beginning of a strenuous life where we attempt to realize a larger ideal by subordinating our private interests and inclinations. Service of a common ideal can bind together the most unlike individuals. Love demands its sacrifices. By restraint and endurance, we raise love to the likeness of the divine.

In an ideal marriage the genuine interests of the two members are perfectly reconciled. The perfectly ethical marriage is the monogamous one. The relation of Rāma and Sītā, or Sāvitrī and Satyavān, where the two stand by each other against the whole world, is idealized in the Hindu scriptures. In the absence of absolute perfection we have to be content with approximations. We need not, however, confound the higher with the lower. Eight different kinds of marriages are recognized in the Hindu law books. Manu did not shut his eyes to the practices of his contemporaries. He arranges the different kinds of marriages in an order. While marriages in which personal inclination is subordinated rank high, those by mutual choice (Gāndharva), force (Rākṣasa), purchase (Āsura) come lower. The lowest is Paiśāca. When the lover ravishes the maiden without her consent, when she is asleep, or intoxicated or deranged in mind, we have a case of Paiśāca marriage (Man.III.34). It is a very low kind of marriage, but admitted as valid with the laudable motives of giving the injured women the status of wives and their offspring legitimacy.

Insistence on the interests of the family led to a compromise of the monogamous ideal. While the monogamous ideal is held up as the best, polygamy was also tolerated. When you have no male offspring, or when, by mistake or chance, you seduce a woman when you are married, it is your duty to protect her from desertion and from public scorn, save her from a life of infamy and degradation, and protect her children who are in no way responsible for the ways of their parents; in such cases polygamy is permissible. The story of the epic *Rāmāyaṇa* has for one of its chief lessons the evils of polygamy. The palace of Daśaratha was a centre of intrigue, and Rāmā, the hero of the story, stands up for the monogamous ideal.

A system which looks upon marriage as compulsory for all has its own weaknesses, though it does not develop large numbers of unmarried women who see no meaning in life. It is obliged to discountenance the remarriage of widows (ṚV.X.18.8). It unconsciously tends to lower the marriageable age of girls. It is necessary for the leaders to remember the Hindu ideals and bring about a more satisfactory state of affairs.

The recognition of the spiritual ideal of marriage requires us to regard the marriage relation as an indissoluble one. So long as we take a small view of life and adopt for our guide the fancy or feeling of the moment, marriage relation cannot be regarded as permanent. In the first moments of infatuation we look upon our partners as angels from heaven, but soon the wonder wears away, and if we persist in our passion for perfection, we become agitated and often bitter. The unrest is the effect of a false ideal. The perfect relation is to be created and not found. The existence of incompatibility is a challenge to a more vigorous effort. To resort to divorce is to confess defeat. The misfits and the maladjustments are but failures.

Modern conditions are responsible for the large numbers of divorces and separations. Life has become too hurried. We have no time to understand one another. To justify our conduct, we are setting up exaggerated claims on behalf of the individual will and are strongly protesting against discipline. We are confusing self-expression and self-development with a life of instincts and passions. We tend to look upon ourselves as healthy animals and not spiritual beings. We have had sin with us from the beginning of our history, but we have recently begun to worship it. It is not very modern for a man or woman who is sick of his or her partner to take to another, but what is really modern is the new philosophy in justification of it. Disguised feeling is masquerading as advanced thought. The woman who gives up her husband for another is idealized as a heroine who has had the courage to give up the hypocritical moral codes and false sentiments, while she who clings to her husband through good report and bad is a cowardly victim of conventions. Sex irregularities are becoming less shocking and more popular.

Though we have had our share of exaggerating the wickedness of women, and though we have some texts which regard the woman as the eternal temptress of the man Adam, a snare of perdition, as Donaldson expressed it: "a fireship continually striving to get alongside the male man-of-war and blow him up into pieces", the general Hindu view of woman is an exalted one. It regards the woman as the helpmate of man in all his work, Sahadharmiṇī (ṚV.X.61.8). The Hindu believes in the speciality of the contribution which woman makes to the world. She has special responsibilities and special duties. Even such an advanced thinker as Mr. Bertrand Russell allows that "each class and sex has that to give to the common stock of achievement, knowledge and thought which it alone can give, and robs itself and the community by inferior imitation." So long as children cannot be shaken from heaven, but have to be built within their mothers' bodies, so long will there be a specific function for women. As the bearing and rearing of children take a good deal of their time and attention, women were relieved of the economic responsibilities for the family. While man is expected to take to the worldly pursuits (*yajñapradhānya*), woman is capable of great heights of self-control and self-denial (*tapaḥpradhānya*). The stricter code of morality applied to women is really a compliment to them, for it accepts the natural superiority of the women. But the modern woman, if I may say so, is losing her self-respect. She does not respect her own individuality and uniqueness, but is paying an unconscious tribute to man by trying to imitate him. She is fast becoming masculine and mechanical. Adventurous pursuits are leading her into conflict with her own inner nature.

The third stage arises when the responsibilities of home are given up. The wife accompanies the husband to the forest, if she shares his spiritual aims. According to Manu, one must enter the third stage when one becomes a grandfather, or one's skin begins to show wrinkles or one's hair turns grey. When one's bodily powers wane, it is time to depart to the forest and prepare oneself for the true life of the spirit. The main objective of this stage is to escape from the bustle of life into the solitude of the forest to meditate on the higher problems.

The stature of man is not to be reduced to the requirements of the society. Man is much more than the custodian of its culture or protector of his country or producer of its wealth. His social efficiency is not the measure of his spiritual manhood. The soul which is our spiritual life contains our infinity within it. What shall it profit a man if he gains the whole world but loses his own soul? A Sanskrit verse reads: "For the family sacrifice the individual; for the community the family; for the country the community, and for the soul the whole world." Family and country, nation and the world cannot satisfy the soul in man. Each individual is called upon at a certain stage of his life to give up his wife and children and his caste and work. The last part of life's road has to be walked in single file.

The aim of the Sannyāsin is not to free himself from the cares of outward life, but to attain a state of spiritual freedom when he is not tempted by riches or honour, and is not elated by success or depressed by failure. He develops a spirit of equanimity and so 'bears patiently improper words and does not insult anyone; he does not hate anyone for the sake of his physical body (Man.VI.47).' These free men are solitary souls who have not any personal attachments or private ambitions, but embody in their own spirit the freedom of the world. They take on the wideness of the whole earth, dwell in love and walk in righteousness. The social order regards the

Sannyāsin as a parasite since he does not contribute to it materially and does not care for its forms. The state looks on him with suspicion as he does not profess any loyalty to any family or church, race or nation. He does not function in any industrial factory, social system or political machine. These Sannyāsins do not serve our policies that make the world unsafe for human life, do not promote our industries that mechanize persons, and do not support our national egoisms that provoke wars. Patriotism is not enough for these fine souls. Life, and not India's life or England's life, demands their devotion. They look upon all men and all groups as equal (*samatā sarvasmin*).

While some forms of Christianity and Buddhism judge the life of the world to be inferior to the life of the monk, and would have loved to place the whole of mankind at one swoop in the cloister, Hinduism, while appreciating the life of the Sannyāsin refrained from condemning the state of the householder. Every state is necessary, and in so far as it is necessary it is good. The blossom does not deny the leaf and the leaf does not deny the stalk nor the stalk the root. The general rule is that we should pass from stage to stage gradually.

The liberated soul is not indifferent to the welfare of the world. Renunciation is the surrendering of the notions of I and mine, and not the giving up of the work enjoined by the scriptures. It is related of the Buddha that when he was on the threshold of Nirvāṇa he turned away and took the vow never to cross it so long as a single being remained subject to sorrow and suffering. The same idea comes out in the sublime verse of the *Bhāgavata*: "I desire not the supreme state (of bliss) with its eight perfections, nor the cessation of rebirth. May I take up the sorrow of all creatures who suffer and enter into them so that they may be made free from grief." Mahādeva, the prince of ascetics, drank poison for the sake of the world. Freedom on the highest level of existence expresses itself on the lower as courage to suffer, sacrifice, and die.

This fourfold plan of life yet dominates the Hindu mind. The general character of a society is not always best expressed by the mass of its members. There exists in every community a natural elite, which better than all the rest represents the soul of the entire people, its great ideals, its strong emotions and its essential tendency. The whole community looks to them as their example. When the wick is ablaze at its tip, the whole lamp is said to be burning.

The System of the Āśramas

The Hindu Śāstrakāras (i.e., those who have written the *śāstras*, the scientific treatises) have taken man into account as a social being with reference to four broad factors that influence his life and its conduct. He is considered in relation to: (i) *deśa*, (place, region) which may be said to be the regional approach to the study of society; (ii) *kāla* (time) which, we may say, constitutes the historical approach to the study of society, (iii) *śrama* (effort) which takes into account man with reference to his nurture and development in the contemporary environment; and (iv) *guṇa* (natural traits), which refers to the natural inherent psycho-biological equipment of man.

The importance and significance of 'place' and 'time' or geography and history in the activities and behaviour of man has been acutely recognized by the Hindu thinkers; and the Royal Sage (*Rājarṣi*) Bhīṣma (*Śantiparvan*.78.32) teaches us, indeed, that according to the conditions, demands and exigencies of the time-and-place (*deśa-kāla*), what is otherwise *dharma* may become *adharma*, and what is *adharma* may become *dharma*, for the time being. Evidently, however, it is not possible to visualize and anticipate all the probable variations of the locale (*deśa*) and the times (*kāla*) which human beings are likely to be confronted with, and hence, it may be said, no generalizations have been attempted by the Dharmaśāstrakāras regarding men's conduct under conditions such as may be peculiar to these two. Indeed, the recognition of *deśa* and *kāla* as significant factors affecting *dharma* itself is a tacit acceptance by the Śāstrakāras of the fact that despite their attempts at canalizing and regulating man's conduct of life and behaviour through *dharma,* this is not to be taken as a rigid, static principle but has to be allowed a certain flexibility, a modifiability, a dynamic potentiality for its operation to suit the conditions dictated by the locale and the times. And, moreover, to speak of *dharma* itself becoming *adharma* and *vice versa* according to the times and the locale is really to speak of much more than just allowing the possibility of modifications in *dharma*; it is to ask men to be prepared for such complete and radical changes in *dharma* which may even be contradictory to the generally sanctioned *dharma* practices in order to suit the exigencies of the times and the conditions, if the latter necessitate such changes. It is in view of the impossibility of visualizing the emergencies of the locale and the times that the Śāstrakāras have not attempted to dwell on the *dharmas* of *deśa* and *kāla*, while the *dharmas* of *śrama* and *guṇa* have been discussed in such details by them.

And so, in the present work, we have attempted to make an investigation into the Hindu social thought under the last two headings, i.e. on man as a social being in connection with his nurtural development (*śrama*), and in connection with his natural endowments (*guṇa*). Here we may note that in substance, all the Hindu sages agree that any plan or scheme of social organization which aims at the best functioning of every human being as a social unit, must, in the first instance, take him into account from these two aspects: First, it must consider man as a social being with reference to his training and development in the natural and social environment in order to enable him to fulfil the final aim of his existence; and secondly, this has to be coordinated with another scheme which studies man with reference to his natural endowments, dispositions and attitudes. The first of these is the problem undertaken in the scheme of the *āśramas*; the second is thought out in the scheme of the *varṇas*.

The two organizations of the *āśrama* and the *varṇa* (the *varṇāśrama-vyavasthā*), which, to put it briefly, refer to the problems of the nurture and the nature of man, rightly serve as the cornerstones of the Hindu theory of social organization. And, we may also note here that the scheme of the *āśramas* as thought out and devised by the Hindu is a unique contribution in the whole history of the social thought of the world, without even a parallel to it in any other thought-system, excepting, perhaps, to some extent, in Plato's *Republic*. The same may be said to be true to a great extent of the *varṇa*-organization also.

Now, both the schemes of the *āśrama* as well as the *varṇa* presuppose, and are fundamentally based upon, a certain point of view in regard to the problem of life and its conduct, upon a certain basic outlook, a certain philosophy of life; this fundamental philosophy of life was the topic of our first chapter. There we have discussed the ways in which the problem of existence and human destiny was conceived by the Hindu, and how attempts were made to arrive at a basis for the solution of that problem. In this chapter, we shall attempt to find out how, on such basis, the whole superstructure of the Hindu social institutions has been planned and erected so as to give effect to the principles enunciated in the first chapter, within the orbit of the practical day-to-day life of the Hindu. In other words, in the first chapter, we dealt with the theory of the problem of life and its solution, while in this chapter and in the chapters that follow, we are going to consider the practices based on that theory, by following which the ideals preached by the theory could be realized.

And here lies, broadly speaking, what appears to be one of the main distinctions between the Hindu way of understanding, tackling and solving social problems and the Western way. In the West, generally speaking, the social sciences, as such, of today are mainly built up straight in terms of the relations between man and man, and between man and his environment. Rarely, if at all, would the social scientist take into consideration the more fundamental questions of the ultimate human values, of the ultimate aim and fulfilment of man's existence, of the basic social philosophy which does and should govern the super-structure of social practices, conduct and institutions and take such basic ideas and concepts as the starting points in his discussion. This is particularly true of the social scientists who are working in the field of economics and politics; and it is also true to a considerable extent of even those who are working in the field of general sociology barring very rare exceptions like P. Sorokin, who is now considered to be "out of fashion" in sociological circles in his country by some of his colleagues just because he is interested in such problems. Of course, some sort of a social philosophy will always be found implicitly underlying any sociological discussion, but it is not given a conscious and deliberative consideration, it is not explicitly discussed and taken as the basic starting point in the modern treatises on social organization. Modern social scientists, *qua* social scientists in general, are on the contrary inclined to consider such questions of ultimate values as of more or less "speculative" nature, of "meta-physical" interest; on the other hand, they concern themselves directly with the "actual" and "factual" interactions between man and man and between man and his environment. These are their starting points, and also the main themes of discussion.

A pointed attack against the "philosophical" approach to social studies on the bases of ethical values was made by Ēmile Durkheim, Lucien Lévy-Bruhl and their school in France at the end of the last century and in the beginning of this century, among others. These writers vigorously advocated the "scientific" approach of studying "social facts" in the social sciences, which seems to have meant, for them, exclusion of any consideration of the ultimate and higher values of human life. We do not propose to enter here into the controversy of "social philosophy vs. social science", but the interested reader may profitably peruse the relevant writings of Durkheim and Lévy-Bruhl, and the spirited attack on their position by Simon Deploige who himself quotes a large number of relevant excerpts from them.

In sharp contrast with such attitude, the Hindu, in his *śāstric* discussions of social life and practices, first raises the fundamental question of the significance of man's existence on earth, gives consideration to basic questions of the relation between man and the possible ultimate purpose and fulfilment of his existence, and, upon such bases, seeks to define and formulate his relations with every other thing, person, event and circumstance in the world. Thus, for the Hindu, the individual's relations with the Ultimate Principle or the Universal or Primal Cause defines his relations with other men, with his family, with the group or society in which he lives or with which he comes in contact, with his village and his country,—and, indeed, with the entire animate and inanimate creation!

And this general statement of the case applies on the *Āśrama* theory which we propose to discuss in this chapter. The whole of the life of an individual is, for the Hindu, a kind of schooling and self-discipline. Now, during the course of this schooling, he has to pass through four stages,—four grades of training, as it were,—called the *Āśramas*. And, in regard to the *āśramas*, too, every item and stage and phase has to be defined in terms of the already defined relations between man and God. Here, therefore, practically we start with supernatural basis; upon this, we erect the superstructure of man's earthly career. The earthly existence has thus to be defined primarily in terms of *dharma*; and *dharma* has to be interpreted in the concrete in terms of *karman*. The *āśrama* scheme, therefore, defines our *dharma* in and through a life of worldliness, of *samsāra*, before it, and beyond its pale; and, in practice, it seeks to delineate the implications of *dharma* in terms of *karman*.

In order to understand the psycho-moral basis of the *āśramas* proper, it is advisable that we should look into the theory of the *puruṣārthas* which concern themselves with the understanding, justification, management and conduct of affairs of the individual's life in relation to the group, in and through the *āśramas*. The *puruṣārthas* are four, viz., *dharma, artha, kāma* and *mokṣa*. We speak of these *puruṣārthas* as the 'psycho-moral' bases of the *āśrama* theory, because, on the one hand, the individual receives a psychological training through the *āśramas* in terms of lessons in the use and management of the *puruṣārthas*; while, on the other hand, in actual practice, he has to deal with the society in accordance with these lessons. It is in the light of the understanding of the meaning and place of the *puruṣārthas* in the *āśrama* scheme that we shall be able to comprehend the right method, way and outlook for the management of each of the *āśramas*.

It is usual to translate these terms *dharma, artha, kāma* and *mokṣa* in English by such words as morality, wealth, desires or passion, and salvation respectively. But the Sanskrit terms are potent with deeper meanings than these English words singly convey. Thus, the word *dharma* is derived from the Sanskrit root '*dhṛ*' meaning 'to hold together, to preserve'.[1] The social implications and meaning of *dharma* as a principle for maintaining the stability of society is brought out by Śrī-kṛṣṇa in three verses in the *Mahābhārata*: In advising Arjuna as to what is *dharma* he explains that "*dharma* is created for the well-being of all creation" (*Karṇaparvan*.69.57), and further that "all that is free from doing harm to any created being is certainly *dharma*; for, indeed, *dharma* is created to keep all creation free from any harm." Śrīkṛṣṇa proceeds, next, to give a still more comprehensive view of *dharma*: "*Dharma* is so called because it protects (*dhāraṇāt*) all; *dharma* preserves all that is created. *Dharma*, then, is surely that principle which is capable of preserving the universe." *Artha*, on the other hand, is to be understood as referring to all the means necessary for acquiring worldly prosperity, such as wealth or power. And *kāma* refers to all the desires in man for enjoyment and satisfaction of the life of the senses, including the sex drive to which the word *kāma* more prominently refers.[2] The term refers to the native impulses, instincts and desires of man, his natural mental tendencies, and finds its equivalent, we may say, in the use of the English terms "desires", "needs", "basic or primary motives", "urges", or "drives" and the collective use of the term "*kāma*" would refer to the totality of the innate desires and drives of man.[3] The term is also often used in a broader sense to include socially acquired motivation too. *Dharma, artha* and *kāma*, therefore, refer respectively to the moral, material and mental resources, accessories and energies available to man.

Of these three, *artha* and *kāma* refer to two of man's earthly belongings, while *dharma* stands on a higher level. At its lowest level of manifestation, *kāma* is understood in the sense of pure sex drive, and is said to be one of the six 'enemies' of human beings. But it is equally true that a human being cannot conduct his life without *artha* which constitutes the material means of living, and *kāma* which helps the propagation of the species. Therefore, it is needed that the correct quality and quantity, the place, and the time of *artha* and *kāma,* be determined and laid down by the wise sages. This is done in terms of *dharma*, which defines, for man, the proper quantum, place and season, for the right functioning of *artha* and *kāma*. By attending to his *dharma*, therefore, a person is able to live a proper life even though it may be lived in terms of *artha* and *kāma*. As Vidura says: "It is by the help of *dharma* that the sages have been able to cross the world. The stability of the universe depends upon *dharma*: *artha* and *kāma*, too, depend for their proper management upon *dharma*. *Dharma* is the foremost of all; *artha* is said to be middling: and *kāma*, it is said by the wise, is the lowest of the three. Therefore, we should conduct our lives with self-control, paying major attention to *dharma* (*Śantiparvan*.167.6-9)."

In the opinion of Manu, the good of humanity lies in a harmonious management or coordination of the three (*trivarga*), viz., *dharma, artha* and *kāma*. Says he: "Some declare that the good of man consists in *dharma,* and *artha*;

others opine that it is to be found in *kāma* and *artha*; some say that *dharma* alone will give it; while the rest assert that *artha* alone is the chief good of man here below (on earth). But the correct position is that the good of man consists in the harmonious coordination of the three." Now this advice, the commentator Kullūka explains, is meant for those who weigh the issue from the viewpoint of the immediate and worldly objectives of life. But, from the point of view of the final purpose and meaning of life, *mokṣa* alone would prove to be the best guide. With reference to the supreme end of *mokṣa*, therefore, the other three immediate objectives of life become but the means for the attainment of that end.

Now, as we shall see in our discussion of the *Gṛhasthāśrama* (Ch. VI), *artha* and *kāma* have to be practised by the individual with reference to one or more individuals. So also, the practice of *dharma* cannot be possibly conceived as existing apart from the relation between the individual and the group,—except when the *dharma* directed is entirely in the interest of the *mokṣa* of the individual, as in the case of the Sannyāsin (the recluse), in whose case *artha* and *kāma* become transformed and get merged into *mokṣa*. Thus, on the whole, the *puruṣārthas* are concerned both with the individual as well as the group. They enunciate and justify the kinds of relation between the individual and the group; they define the just relations between activities of the individual and those of the group; they also state explicitly and by implication, the improper relations between the individual and the group with a view to enabling the individual to avoid them. Thus, the *puruṣārthas* control both the individual and the group, and also their inter-relations.

Here, it is to be remembered that when we refer to *artha* and *kāma* as *puruṣārthas*, we refer to them in their proper proportions, that is to say, only in the best sense of these words. *Artha* refers to the problem and activities connected with the finding, making, gathering, conserving and organizing of the material necessities of life and all that accompanies the same. Similarly, *kāma* refers to the sex and the reproductive aspect, its understanding, its right functions, its functioning, its organization and management both with reference to the individual and the group. As we have pointed out above, *Kāma* in the wider sense refers to all the innate desires and urges of man. *Dharma* seems to be the arbiter, the conscience keeper, the director, the interpreter, of the properties that govern the right functioning and management of the relations between the inner man and the outer man, and between the individual and the group. *Dharma* is, therefore, the holder of the balance in terms of which *artha* and *kāma* have to be dealt with, weighed, practised and apportioned. *Mokṣa,* on the other hand, seems to be concerned mainly with the individual. It refers, perhaps, to the appeal of the inner man to the individual, unaffected by the group. It is perhaps too personal an outlook that defines the struggle and hope and justification within the individual for *mokṣa*. But, from the Hindu's point of view, we must also remember, that the inner personality of the individual, at its best, is identified by him not only with the group, nor only with the society, nor with the nation, nor the race, not even with the entire human race, but with the whole creation, animate and inanimate, seen and unseen, which includes all these and is still much more than all these! This will be amply evident from our discussion on the problem of *mokṣa* in the previous chapter. In the light of these considerations, the goal of *mokṣa* does not possess the narrow individual outlook, for the Hindu. Nor is it to be pursued exclusively and directly by an individual unless and until he has duly satisfied all his society debts (*ṛṇa*) or obligations.

And now let us turn to the theory and practice of the *āśramas* proper. The word *āśrama* is originally derived from the Sanskrit root *śrama* 'to exert oneself'; therefore, it may mean, by derivation (i) a place where exertions are performed, and (ii) the action of performing such exertions.[4] Literally, an *āśrama* is a 'halting or resting place.' The word therefore signifies a halt, a stoppage, or a stage in the journey of life just for the sake of rest, in a sense, in order to prepare oneself for further journey. The *āśramas*, then, are to be regarded as resting places during one's journey on the way to final liberation which is the final aim of life. The four stages of life, says Vyāsa in the *Mahābhārata* (*Śantiparvan*.242.15), form a ladder or flight of four steps. That flight attaches to the Brahman. By ascending that flight one reaches the region of Brahmā. Whichever of the above be the original meaning of the word, the historical development of the *āśrama* scheme as an institution and the social implications within it include all the interpretations given above. Each of the *āśramas* is a stage of life in which the individual has to train himself for a certain period, and exert himself within the circuit of the same in order to qualify himself for the next.

The *āśramas* are four in number: (1) the *brahmacarya*—that of a student, (2) the *gṛhastha*—that of a married man, the house-holder, (3) the *vānaprastha*—that of retired life in the forest, after abandoning the home, preparatory to complete renouncement of worldly relations, and (4) the *sannyāsa*—the life of complete renunciation of worldly relations and attachments.

Attempts have been made to show that in the beginning there were only three *āśramas*, that originally the *vānaprastha* and the *sannyāsa āśramas* formed only one order, and that these came to be distinguished from one another in later times. Thus the *Chāndogya Upaniṣad* mentions three orders of life according to *dharma* (*trayo dharmaskandhāḥ*): (1) the householder's order, where one is expected to perform sacrifices (*yajñaḥ*), study (*adhyayana*) and charity (*dāna*); (2) the order of the recluse, wherein one is expected to perform penances (*tapas*); and (3) the order of a perpetual or life-long (*atyanta*) student residing permanently in the house of a teacher (*ācārya-kula-vāsīn*). All these three (*sarve ete*) reach the worlds of bliss (*puṇyaloka*) after death; but any of these three who is established in Brahman (*brahma-samstham*) attains immortality (*amṛtatva*). Dr. Modi also refers to two other passages from the *Manusmṛti* where a positive assertion that the scheme of *āśramas* consists of three *āśramas* is made.

Now, even though in early literature we find, as in the *Chāndogya Upaniṣad* quoted above, a mention of the three phases of life viz., the student, the householder, and the hermit, yet it was not enjoined that these must be followed compulsorily one after the other. A man, it seems, could become a householder after he finished his student's life, or he could live the life both of a student and a householder together, or he could turn to the hermit's life after he finishes his student's career, without marrying. This means that the Sannyāsin's stage need not necessarily be preceded by the *grihastha* phase. The four stages come to us in sequential form from later Upaniṣads like the *Jābāla*, according to which the order of the student must precede that of the householder, and that of the householder must be followed by the order of the hermit (*vānaprastha*), while the order of the wandering or begging ascetic (*parivrājaka* or *bhikṣu*) must be preceded by those of the householder and the hermit.

In trying to identify the three *āśramas* mentioned in the *Chāndogya Upaniṣad* with the four traditional ones, one can say that a system of three *āśramas* rather than four could find justification from another point of view also. There is a view according to which the *sannyāsa* state was not regarded as an *āśrama* proper; it was rather considered as outside the meaning, and therefore beyond the limits, of an *āśrama* as in the *Śvetāśvatara Upaniṣad*, wherein the *sannyāsin* is said to be above all the *āśramas* (*atyāśramin*); as such, he is no longer a "social personality"; he is devoid of any family bond; he is a homeless wanderer, begging, without any belongings or property of his own; and such a one bears the name of Sannyāsin, that is, a person who has made complete (*saṁ*) renunciation (*nyāsa*) of everything. And, we may also point out that even in the later development of the *āśramas* into a scheme of four stages, the personal identity of the man who ends with the *vānaprastha* stage and enters into the *sannyāsa* stage ceases to exist altogether both for himself and for the rest of the world in a formal way too. In fact, such a person is actually supposed to have been dead, the usual death ceremonies (*antyeṣṭi*) being actually performed by his kinsmen; and the Sannyāsin is said to have been born out of the ashes and the flames of the funeral pyre of the dead person. Such a person, in fact, even abandons his personal name and the family surname by which he was known before he took up *sannyāsa*, and actually adopts a new name by which he comes to be known thereafter. And, since the man is supposed to be dead, and his body is taken to have been already burnt away and the death ceremonies performed, his actual death after the *sannyāsa* is accepted by him has to be by the special rites of what is known as *samādhi*, and not by the *antyeṣṭi* death rites meant for the ordinary man.

Now, according to the Hindu Dharmaśāstra, each individual should normally pass through these four phases of life, one after the other, (*kramaśaḥ*), and live in them in accordance with the *śāstras* if he desires to obtain salvation (*mokṣa*). After passing from *āśrama* to *āśrama*, and after offering the sacrifices with senses under control (*jitendriyaḥ*), comprehending and realizing the limitations and futility of a life dependent upon alms and offerings (*bhikṣābali-pariśrāntaḥ*), if one goes forth as a wandering mendicant (*parivrajan*) and dies thereafter, he becomes blessed; that is, as explained by Kullūkabhaṭṭa, such a person attains *mokṣa*. However, before entering the last phase viz., the *sannyāsa*, he has to pass through the three previous phases of life in their proper order; besides, he has to satisfy himself that he has carried out the duties and obligations laid down for each of the *āśramas*; and he has also to see that he has duly given his dues in connection with the social obligations or the three "debts" (*ṛṇas*). These three *ṛṇas* are: (1) the debt to the *ṛṣis* (*ṛṣi-ṛṇa*), (2) the debt to the ancestors (*pitṛ-ṛṇa*) and (3) the debt to the Gods (*deva-ṛṇa*). Now these three debts could be vicariously satisfied, respectively, (1) by studying the Vedas in accordance with the rules laid down for the study (*vidhivad*), that is to say, by passing through the *brahmacaryāśrama*, (2) by begetting sons in accordance with the *dharma* (*darmataḥ*), i.e. by going through the *gṛhasthāśrama* and (3) by offering sacrifices according to one's capacity (*śaktitaḥ*), i.e. by performing the duties of the *vānaprasthāśrama*. After carrying out these duties in the first three *āśramas,* one should apply one's mind exclusively towards the attainment of *mokṣa*. It is opined that the man who fails to carry out any of these obligations due to him during the first three *āśramas* is not entitled even to try to attain *mokṣa*; and Manu says that he who seeks *mokṣa* without fulfilling his duties in the first three *āśramas* will sink low to damnation (*vrajatyadhaḥ*).

There are differences of opinion among different authorities concerned as regards the particular age at which one is expected to enter each of the *āśramas,* and the period of life he is expected to spend in it. Different ages at which a man is expected to enter the *gṛhasthāśrama* have been prescribed by different authorities; and, moreover, for different *varṇas*, again, different ages at which an individual may enter the *brahmacarya* stage i.e. the first *āśrama*, of education and studies, are given. After the prescribed course of education is completed, the young man enters the *gṛhasthāśrama*; this is bound to be obviously in the maturity of youth, when he has completed all the requirements of *brahmacaryāśrama*, and is fit to marry. And, he is expected to retire from the *gṛhasthāśrama* after playing his part as a member of the *āśrama* in the proper manner (*vidhivat*); this happens when his skin gets wrinkled, when his hair turns white, and when he sees the sons of his sons; he has now to take to a life in the forest; he may leave his wife to the care of his sons, or he may take her with him. In the forest he has to live the simplest life: receiving alms, performing sacrifices, and studying the Vedas and the *Upaniṣads*. After having thus spent the third part of (a man's natural term of) life in the forest, he may live as an ascetic during the fourth part of his existence, abandoning all attachment to worldly objects and relations (*tyaktvā saṅgaṁ*).

The Kāmasūtras of Vātsyāyana point out, in this connection, that as the natural span of the life of a human being is supposed to be a hundred years (*śatāyur vai puruṣaḥ*), one should divide this period into childhood (*bālya*), youth (*yauvana*) and old age (*sthāvira*). In childhood, the individual should acquire education (*vidyā-grahaṇa*); in youth he should seek to satisfy his natural craving for enjoyment and pleasure (*kāma*); while in his old age he should seek *dharma* and *mokṣa*.[5] But, Vātsyāyana adds, that owing to the uncertainty of life (*anityatva*), one should follow these viz., *vidyā, kāma, dharma* and *mokṣa* as they come to him at any period of life (*yathopapādam seveta*)[6]; this is to say, one has to pursue each of these, not to the exclusion of the rest, but whenever he gets opportunities to practise any of these, he should properly avail himself of the same, in whatever *āśrama* he may be. According to Vātsyāyana, in fact, one should pursue all the three *puruṣ ārthas* (*trivarga*) viz. *dharma, artha* and *kāma*, together in proper adjustment with each other, without any one of these coming in the way of the other. This is also the tone in which Manu has advised that the real good of man consists in the harmony or aggregate of the three *puruṣārthas* (*trivarga*).

Of the four *āśramas*, the first two will be treated here only in brief, as they will be described in details in the chapters that follow; on the other hand, we propose to discuss the *vānaprastha* and the *sannyāsa āśramas* rather more fully in this chapter, so as to give us an idea of the kind of discipline and training which the individual is expected to undergo in these *āśramas*.

The *upanayana* ceremony introduces the young boy into the *Brahmacaryāśrama*. After the course of studies is over in accordance with the *dharmas* laid down for the Brahmacārin, he takes a bath, symbolic of his completion of that *āśrama* course; so he now becomes a *snātaka* i.e. (one who has taken the bath). He now becomes fit to enter the next *āśrama* viz., the *gṛhasthāśrama*. The ceremony of returning back home from the teacher is called the *samāvartana*. In the *gṛhasthāśrama*, the individual has to fulfil his obligations (*ṛṇas*) to the members of his family, to his deceased ancestors, to strangers and to gods, in order to become fit to enter the next *āśrama* of *vānaprastha*.

Now, in the *vānaprasthāśrama*, as the name itself suggests the individual has to leave the shelter not only of the family (*kula*) and of the home (*gṛha*), but of the village (*grāma*) too; he must go to the forest (*vana*) and live there, all the while striving to bring under control his senses of enjoyment (*niyatendriyaḥ*) in the following manner: He has to eat vegetables and fruits only; he is not to touch sweet things or meat, he must never accept fruits or roots grown in the village even when he is sorrowful (*ārto'pi*). For his clothing he has to use the deerskin or the bark of a tree. He should make no deliberate attempts to obtain comforts; and, he has to lead a celibate life, sleeping on the floor, residing under a tree, without any attachment to where he happens to reside. Yet, he has to continue the performance of the five great sacrifices (*mahāyajña*) which he used to perform in the *gṛhasthāśrama*, in the proper manner, and has to offer to the fullest for sacrifices; and out of whatever he collects for eating, he has to offer to the guests who may visit him, according to his might. Besides, he should utilize his time in studying the Upaniṣads and the Śrutis, and practise penances (*tapas*) for the purging of his body, as also in order to elevate his soul up to higher and higher levels. Thus, he must devote himself heart and soul to his studies and meditation; at the same time, he has to lead a life of self-control and friendliness and charity to others—a life wherein though he never accepts charity from others (*nityam anādātṛ*), he bears a compassionate attitude towards all creatures (*śarvabhūtānukampakaḥ*). If the individual dies while he is pursuing his life in the *vānaprasthāśrama* in this manner, he is expected to reach the region of Brahmā—that is, he attains *mokṣa*, as the commentator Kullūkabhaṭṭa, on the *Manusmṛti*, explains.

But if he survives the *vānaprasthāśrama*,[7] the individual has to enter the last *āśrama* of *sannyāsa*, casting off all attachment (*saṅgaḥ*) with the world. Manu also permits the individual to enter this *āśrama* immediately after the *gṛhasthāśrama*. Commenting on this *śloka* of Manu, Kullūkabhaṭṭa quotes from the *Jābālaśruti*: "One should complete *brahmacarya* and enter *gṛhastha's* order, after that he should enter *vānaprastha*, and thence he should take to *sannyāsa*: or else, he may take to *sannyāsa* directly after *brahmacarya*, or after the *gṛhastha* stage is completed." Yājñavalkya, too, takes the same view by allowing a person to take up the *sannyāsāśrama* either after the *vānaprasthāśrama*, or directly after he has done with the *gṛhasthāśrama*. The man who has entered the *sannyāsārama* should possess nothing; he must always move about all alone without being dependent upon any one for help or support; he could beg alms only once in a day; and he should not feel dispirited when he fails to procure alms nor should he feel elated when he is able to procure it. Indeed, he should care neither for living nor death. By restraining his senses, by casting away the love and hatred within himself, and by living a life of harmlessness to living beings, the Sannyāsin becomes fit to achieve immortality—that is, as Kullūka explains, to attain *mokṣa*. All the sins of the man who passes through the *sannyāsāśrama* in this manner are washed off and destroyed, and thus he attains the ultimate end or goal of existence (*paramāṁ gatiṁ*)—which end is again explained by Kullūka as the same as '*mokṣa*.'

The *Mahābhārata* describes the duties and obligations of the *āśramas* in almost similar terms. And Kauṭilya too, summarizes them in his *Arthaśāstra* in a like manner. Kauṭilya further adds that it is the duty of the King to see that his subjects abide by the rules made obligatory for persons following each of the four *āśramas*. He asserts that the violation of the codes of behaviour for the *āśramas* as well as for the *varṇas* would lead to a confusion of the *varṇas* and *āśramas* and thence to a chaotic state of the society (*saṅkara*) such that the world (*lokaḥ*) would thereby come to an end. On the other hand, he adds, if all people follow these regulations, the world would certainly progress. The *āśrama* and the *varṇa* schemes are thus conceived as means not merely towards furthering the best ends of social organization, stability and equipoise, but also of social progress.

Apart from the special duties concerned with the life of the individual in each of the *āśramas*, there are certain obligations of a general or universal nature; these are considered as part of the duties of every human being without reference to the *āśrama* to which he belongs. Thus, according to the *Smṛtis*, to whatever *āśrama* a man may belong, he should with diligence and assiduity (*prayatnataḥ*) practice the following ten characteristic features of a proper life of *dharma* (Man. VI.91):[8] Steadiness, forgiveness, self-control, abstention from appropriating anything belonging to others, purity, control of the sense organs, correct discernment, knowledge, truthfulness, and absence from anger. Kauṭilya, (A.S.I.iii.8) too, has said that harmlessness, truthfulness, purity, absence of spite, abstinence from cruelty and forgiveness are the duties common to all human beings.

Of all the *āśramas*, however, the *gṛhasthāśrama* is given a very high place of honour. The *Mahābhārata* is quite emphatic in this connection. Thus we are told in the *Śāntiparvan*, that once Yudhiṣṭhira became so disgusted with the ways and affairs of the world that he proposed to take to the *sannyāsin* mode of life; but eventually he was pursuaded to remain in the *gṛhasthāśrama* by the wise counsels of his brothers, wife, and the wise Dvaipāyana Vyāsa himself. The story was narrated to him of how "certain little-witted, well-born Brāhmaṇa youths, before attaining manhood, forsook their homes and came to the woods for leading a forest life." Indra felt pity for them, and taught them that "Asceticism is attainable by leading the life of a householder (*kuṭumbavidhinā*) upon which the proper management of everything depends (*yasmin sarvaṁ pratiṣṭhitaṁ*). In fact, says Indra, "the life of a householder itself only (*ayam eva*) is very superior and sacred, and gives scope for fulfilment (of life's mission)." We are told that on hearing these beneficial words full of *dharma*, those "ascetics" abandoned the idea of Renunciation saying—'This is not meant for us now,'—and started living like householders. After all his relatives did their utmost to dissuade Yudhiṣṭhira from taking up *sannyāsa*, the

Dvaipāyana Vyāsa himself advised him to follow the counsel of his brothers and wife of not abandoning his post as a member of the *gṛhasthāśrama*. For, in the opinion of that sage, the highest *dharma*, as sanctioned by the *śāstras*, consists in a training through the duties and living the full life of a householder. The householder is the support of birds, animals and various other creatures; "he, therefore, who belongs to that mode of life, is superior to all." In this *āśrama*, moreover, can the three *puruṣārthas*, *dharma, artha* and *kāma*, exist together and can be used towards the end of *mokṣa*. In fact this mode of life is considered as the very basis of all the bothers. The other three *āśramas* "derive from this *āśrama* the means they live upon, the offerings they make to the departed manes and the gods, and, in short, their entire support." All the obligations of life, the individual and social, all the three 'debts' (*ṛṇas*)—the debt to the gods (*devaṛṇa*), the debt to the manes or ancestors (*pitṛṛṇa*) and the debt to the sages (*riṣīṛṇa*)—could be satisfied by a person living a full life in the *gṛhasthāśrama*. So also, the trust vested in us by the Creator could be executed in this *āśrama* by the proper begetting of offsprings in the family.

And the Smṛtis, too, bestow the highest praise upon the *gṛhasthāśrama*. Just as all living creatures subsist by receiving support from air, so all the *āśramas* subsist by receiving support from the *grihastha*; and since men in the three other *āśramas* are daily supported by the householder with sacred knowledge and food, the householder's is the leading *āśrama*. As rivers, great and small, find a resting place in the ocean, even so men of all *āśramas* gather their stability and support at the hands of the householder. "And, in accordance with the precepts of the Veda and the Smṛti, the householder is declared to be superior (*śreṣṭha*) to all of them; for he supports the three." He who desires imperish-able bliss in heaven and permanent happiness here, must strive through this *āśrama* with great care and effort; for it is difficult to be practised by men with weak faculties.

Now, this special eulogy bestowed upon the *gṛhasthāśrama* should not be misunderstood; we must try to comprehend its meaning in its proper perspective. The *gṛhasthāśrama* is glorified, not in terms of absolute superiority of the *āśrama* over all the others, but from a particular angle of vision and with reference to the particular position which that *āśrama* occupies in the scheme of life. The Śāstrakāra's praise for the *gṛhastha* as the best *āśrama* emanates, we must not fail to notice, from the point of view of the "social values" of the *āśramas*. Otherwise, in general, since each *āśrama* is regarded as an essential stage for the development of the individual, it is the best in its own place, and any comparison of merits between them on absolute grounds would be surely beside the point. But, from the point of view of a particular aspect, viz. the aspect of social valuation, the *gṛhastha* is exalted on the grounds of its lending support to the other three *āśramas*, the scope it affords for the practice and cultivation of all the three *puruṣārthas*, viz., *dharma*, *artha* and *kāma*, as well as of its direct contact with the society and the consequent direct contributions made by it to the society. On the other hand, from the point of view of the acquisition of knowledge by the individual, the *brahmacaryāśrama* would evoke the highest praise; while from the point of view of individual salvation, the *sannyāsāśrama* would take the place of honour.

It is quite possible to maintain, on the other hand, on the strength of the foregoing high compliments paid to the *gṛhasthāśrama*, that of all values, social values were regarded as of supreme importance by Hindu Śāstrakaras, the Hindu writers on social life like the *Smṛti*-writers and the Epic-writers. This interpretation is further confirmed by one or two statements already quoted above, which specifically compare the *gṛhasthāśrama* with the next two *āśramas* by asserting that in this *āśrama* could be achieved the merits that are achievable in the other two *āśramas* too! Thus, it is said that in the *gṛhasthāśrama* alone can the three *puruṣārthas* be practised together, and the three *ṛṇas* could all be discharged satisfactorily. May we say that such a view of the *gṛhasthāśrama* was due to the fact that the Hindu Śāstrakāras perhaps found that it was, in practice, not always possible, or was exceedingly difficult, for the average individual to follow the course of all the four *āśramas* one after the other, considering the actual average lifespan of man,—which would be in most cases much less than one hundred years,—and that therefore, they wisely suggested that one can hope for salvation even if he continued in the *gṛhasthāśrama* till the end of his life, provided that he discharged in that *aśrama* the three *ṛṇas* and practised the three *puruṣārthas* in the manner prescribed.

In the light of our description of the theory and practice of the *āśramas* given above, let us try to find out the significance and position of the *puruṣārthas* as envisaged in the *āśrama*-scheme: In the *brahmacaryāśrama, dharma* is the predominating *puruṣārtha; dharma* has to be learnt up in all its aspects and ramifications; and it has to be practised particularly as a check upon *kāma* and *artha*, because these latter two are far from the objectives of the young trainee; besides, the ultimate value of *mokṣa* has to be learnt during this *āśrama*.

In the *gṛhasthāśrama*, both *artha* and *kāma* become the fields of the personality of the individual who has already acquired a knowledge and practice of *dharma*, and who has studied the value and place of *mokṣa* for his own self-realization. Here, let it be admitted that *kāma* and *artha* are part of the essential heritage of both the human individual and races. In this sense, *artha* and *kāma* form what may be called part of the natural, physical and psycho-physiological apparatus for the functioning of both the group and the individual. We must observe, however, that this apparatus may be, and as a natural history of facts, has been and is being misused and misfunctioned by individuals and races. Now instead of demanding a total repression of this apparatus by damning them as merely base and worthless, the Hindu seers have taught that *artha* and *kāma* shall, on the one hand, be wisely directed into proper life-functions, as prescribed by *dharma,* and shall, on the other hand, be controlled from misfunctioning or disfunctioning as prescribed and proscribed also by *dharma.* In this way, *artha* and *kāma* have been so placed in the *āśrama* scheme, each in terms of *dharma,* that both of them may, by right functioning, contribute their necessary quota for the upkeep, stability, growth and development of the human race consistent with the personality of each of the individuals whose conscious self-control and self-direction carry the seeds of the race and its cultural heritage through history.

Thereafter, in the *vānaprasthāśrama, dharma* and *mokṣa* become the main concern of life, *dharma* occupying the primary position. And, in the *sannyāsāśrama, mokṣa* occupies the supreme position in the *sannyāsin's* mind; in fact, his *dharma* now becomes identified with *mokṣa.* Of course, throughout the *āśrama* scheme and throughout life in every and any phase, *mokṣa* always lurks as the ultimate aim, permeating sometimes explicitly, sometimes implicitly, underneath and defining the course of the other three, viz. *dharma, artha* and *kāma* also.

Like the tradition of *dharma* (*dharma-paramparā*), the tradition of *yajña* (*yajña-paramparā*) also persists and permeates through the Hindu scheme of life, through the *āśramas.* In terms of *yajña*, all the four *āśramas* must be considered as four kinds of *yajña.* The nature, practices and the forms of the *yajña* in each of the *āśramas* are obvious. It is, in fact, a part of the theory of the *āśramas*; as such, *yajña* must of necessity be the spirit that hovers over every stage of the life of a person in any of the *āśramas.*

Thus, in the *brahmacaryāśrama,* the individual has to surrender his life of sense (*indriya*), mind (*manas*) and intellect (*buddhi*), that is to say, all the intellectual and emotional apparatus,—to the handling of and moulding by the adept (*guru*). Therefore, in this *āśrama*, on the one hand, a sort of a *yajña* of the lower self has to be practised, in the sense that the student (Brahmacārin) has to undergo all sorts of lessons in self-control imposed upon him by his preceptor (*guru*); and on the other hand, as he has also to acquire knowledge from his *guru, jnāna-yajña,* i.e. *yajña* or 'sacrifice' in terms of devotion to and practice of learning has also to be increasingly practised by him.

The *gṛhasthāśrama* proves another kind of field for a life of *yajña*. At its best, it is, in a sense, the fully dedicated life. Here it is one's duty to practise *artha* and *kāma* in terms of *karmans* in strict accordance with the *dharmas*, the meaning and value and the justification of which he has learnt in the first *āśrama*. He can partake of *artha* and *kāma*, of the material and the physical pleasures available on earth, but without any feelings of covetousness, greed or lust, taking only his due share in these pleasures in strict accordance with the *dharmas* of this *āśrama*. The Gṛhastha's life has also to be a continuous stream of giving (*dāna*)—a life of selfless service and dedication of his best and utmost for his elders, children, wife (who also is his sharer in his service to others) and other members of his family (*kula*), his dependents and strangers (*atithi*), through his acts of fulfilling his social obligations (*ṛṇas*). Here in the home, he has to bear in mind and practise the parting advice given by his *guru* in the preceding *āśrama* that he has to give his dues to the mother, to the father, to the teacher and to the strangers (*mātṛ-devo bhava, pitṛ-devo bhava, ācārya-devo bhava, atithi-devo bhava*). The devoted service of and for these is considered the same as the service of God. Here, therefore, a *karma-yajña* consistent with and in accordance with *dharma* has to be practised as fully as possible by the individual.

In the third *āśrama*, the beginnings (*ārambha*) are made for the yielding of the self for the final *yajña* which is expected to be performed in the last *āśrama*. The individual now gives up his fields of *artha* and *kāma* by leaving his near and dear ones, his family (*kula*), his village (*grāma*), and by abandoning his belongings and possessions; he now goes out into the forest (*vana, araṇya*), where by meditation and service of others, he trains himself up for the execution of the final *yajña* that awaits his soul-pouring in the *sannyāsāśrama*, the last *āśrama*.

And, this last *āśrama* provides the fullest opportunities for the self-expression and self-expansion of the individual in terms of the final *yajña*. This consists of a complete offering of the self (*ātmāhuti*) wherein the self, out of a will and purpose to be perfect, surrenders all that was nearest and dearest to his lower ego, in order that thereby and thereafter he may be enabled to be one with the real self, the *ātmā*. In both these last *āśramas* a kind of *bhakti-yajña* has to be practised in that the dedication to God is complete, the entire self of the individual having been now surrendered to God (*sarvārpaṇa*). Again, the individual becomes, in a sense, a Jnānī-bhakta when he takes to *sannyāsa*, for he has undergone the schooling and discipline from stage to stage, *āśrama* to *āśrama*, realizing more and more that he belonged not to this *samsāra* nor that this *samsāra* belonged to him; thus, now fully realizing the place and meaning of the self in the midst of *samsāra* he brings himself face to face with the final aim of all existence, viz., *mokṣa*, in this last *āśrama*.

The *āśramas*, then, as we have already said, are regarded as schools of life at several stages of human existence, devised and organized towards the best likelihood for the individual to attain the end of *mokṣa*, in accordance with the theory of the ultimate nature of things, or in accordance with the conception of existence and its relation to the Ultimate. During these different stages of life, the functions of the group and the individual are both different and definite with regard to each other. Thus, during the first *āśrama*, the function of the group is to look after the individual. On the other hand, as far as the individual is concerned, this may be said to be natural, neutral phase. In the second *āśrama* the individual has to look after the group; he is the trustee and manager of the social estate, of the social mores, and of the three *ṛṇas*. The group here is interested in giving him and taking from him the fullest opportunities, social, economic, physical and spiritual, so that the individual may and should best satisfy these obligations.

The third *āśrama* is, once more, a largely neutral phase from the point of view of the individual, as well as of the group. Here, on the part of the individual, efforts have to be made to yield up his responsibilities in the midst of power and pelf, and thus, by and by, to take to a life in accordance with the best lessons acquired in the *brahmacaryāśrama,* viz., of going into one's self and finding the truth out for oneself. The feeling of separation from the Ultimate or God begins to make itself felt at this stage. Even then, however, the individual is pledged to the young and the junior that he shall serve them, the family and the group, as a counsel occasionally advising them, rather than as a manager of their estate which position he had to undertake in the second *āśrama*. In this third *āśrama* and in the fourth, the function of the individual is to deal with the supernatural, with the life within; and the function of the group becomes gradually thinned out till in the fourth, it becomes almost nil. And in the last stage, the individual who is now completely free from all social obligations, has to help himself in the search of the self (*ātma-cintana, ātma-jnāna*).

And the justification of such a scheme of the functions and interdependence of the group and the individual in the first three *āśramas* and their independence from each other in the fourth *āśrama* is to be taught during the first stage of life, the *brahmacarya*; and the management of the whole scheme is to be organized, supported and established by the group as well as the individual in the second stage, the *gṛhasthāśrama*. In the first stage, the group rears, protects and gives the best of its heritage to the individual. In the second stage, the individual yields his best and most for the efficient and harmonious functioning of group life, consistent with the dictates of his own conscience; here, the individual seeks to make the group the chief medium and instrument for the upkeep and growth of his personality. In the third stage, the individual, giving up the close attention formerly required of him to manage the affairs of group life, starts on a preliminary journey of self-search. While, in the fourth stage, the individual retires altogether from group activities and seeks to know and find and realize the self that hides within the core of his being.

References

1. For the several stages of meaning through which the word has passed from the Ṛgvedic period onwards, see P.V. Kane: "*H.D.*", *Section* I, pp. 1-4.
2. "*The Vaiṣṇavas of Gujarāt*", pp. 44-45.
3. T.M. Newcomb : *Social Psychology*, pp. 80-83.
4. Hastings : "*Encyclopaedia of Religion and Ethics*"—Art. on "*Āśrama*" by P. Deussen.
5. *K.S.*, i, ii, 1-6.
6. *ibid.*
7. On *Man.* vi, 32; *Mokṣamāpnoti ityarthaḥ.*
8. *Man.* vi, 91.

Caste

The institution of caste occupies the most important place in the social organization of India. It has come to be bound up with the Hindu religion and has pervaded many of the social conceptions of the Hindus and the codes of the Hindu law-givers. It has largely coloured their outlook on life. European and Indian scholars alike have described it as a unique institution peculiar to the soil of India. It is a vast and complicated subject which has given rise to a mass of speculation, ancient and modern. It excited the curiosity of the ancient sages and law-givers, travellers from foreign countries in the middle ages, European observers in modern times, the authors of our periodical census reports and European and Indian scholars interested in historical and sociological investigations. Let us, however, try and form a clear idea of caste. We are living in the midst of a caste organization which is all around us. We feel it and we have a conception of it. There is, however, considerable difficulty in formulating a scientifically precise definition of caste which will apply to all the groups which now consider themselves as separate groups with caste characteristics. We are concerned not so much with the sentiments or convictions or practices of individual members of the caste, but with the body of beliefs, sentiments and practices entertained or observed by the generality of the people belonging to the caste. The fissiparous tendency of the institution has manifested itself in the formation of a large number of sub-divisions, sects or groups bearing resemblance to each other in many respects, but separated by differences of language, residential areas and occupations. From a scientific point of view it might be useful to reserve the term 'caste' to indicate the main fundamental divisions and use other terms to denote the sects and sub-divisions. But no scientific terminology has been adopted in the vernaculars and by the people at large and the word commonly used by the people at the present time to indicate even the minor sub-divisions or groups is the word '*jāti*'. As applied to some of the smallest sub-divisions and groups, the ideas connoted by the common term '*jāti*' do not necessarily hold good in their entirety or with rigour. For instance, among the sub-divisions of Tamil Brāhmaṇas known as Vaṭamas there is a distinction between the northern and the southern Vaṭamas. They were not generally in the habit, till recently, of inter-marrying with each other.

Prof. Rapson has adopted the definition of caste given in the Indian census report of 1911 as "an endogamous group or collection of such groups bearing a common name and having the same traditional occupation, who are so linked together by these and other ties, such as the tradition of a common origin and the possession of the same tutelary deity, and the same social status, ceremonial observances and family priests, that they regard themselves, and are regarded by others, as forming a single homogeneous community."[1] This definition is obviously loose and faulty. A common tutelary deity or a common set of family priests is not necessary for a common caste. The essential incidents of caste are the restrictions imposed by it upon inter-marriage, inter-dining and occupations. Numerous problems have been raised in connection with this subject and we shall refer to some of them to indicate the complexity of the subject. It is often said that caste is of Brāhmaṇical origin. Is this correct, and if so, in what sense and to what extent? Was caste based in its origin upon racial differences? Was there any caste among the Aryan invaders of India before they came to India, or did it come into existence for the first time after the invasion and settlement of the Aryans in India amongst the peoples of a different race or races? Was the institution the result of the development of certain universal instincts of human nature under specially favourable conditions in the new environment in which the Aryan invaders found themselves, or was it entirely the result of certain poisonous germs indigenous to the social atmosphere of India? Was caste the invention of a cunning priesthood deliberately planned to secure their own selfish purposes and imposed upon the rest of the population? If caste had its origin in a difference of colour or *varṇa*, were the Dvijas or twice-born classes of the same colour or racial stock? If they were all members of the same Aryan stock, when were the Brāhmaṇas, Kṣatriyas and Vaiśyas divided into the three separate *varṇas*? Who were the Śūdras and was there any caste besides the Dvijas and the Śūdras? Were there any people who were not members of any caste at all, or who were literally outcastes, or did the outcastes themselves form a class? Were the social barriers and restrictions between the different castes rigid or flexible? If they were originally flexible, when did they become rigid? Has there been any large inter-mixture between the different castes and how far has it been recognised by law and custom? It is not possible to furnish any precise answer to all the questions I have indicated above and I do not propose to embark upon so extensive an inquiry.

We have already observed that the origin of caste engaged the speculations even of the ancient sages. The explanations given by them are mostly of a mythical or mystical character and sometimes rationalistic. The popular belief among Hindus is that the main divisions of castes are of immemorial antiquity and in fact coeval with creation. It is supported by the account in the *Puruṣasūkta* of the origin of the four castes from the mouth, arms, thighs and feet of Puruṣa, the Supreme Being. Obviously it is an allegorical account of the functions or occupations of the four castes and is clearly mythical. As pointed out by Sir W. Muir, no uniform or consistent account of the origin of the castes can be gathered from the Hindu sacred books.[2] According to some accounts the four castes were derived from four different progenitors; according to others they were all descendants of Manu, the common ancestor of humanity. According to some, the castes were naturally distinguished by different *guṇas* involving varieties of moral character; and according to others, mankind was originally endowed with the same uniform moral qualities, there being no distinction of classes, and the existing distribution has arisen out of differences of character and occupation. While it is true that the inter-mixture of castes has given rise to new castes, it is not possible to accept the theory contained in the *Manusmṛti* which seeks to account for the origin not merely of castes, but of the racial divisions of mankind, like Yavanas (or Greeks), Śakas (or Scythians), Pahlavas and the Chinese, by supposing that they were Kṣatriya tribes who had gradually sunk to the condition of Śūdras as the result of their omission of their sacred rites and of their not consulting the Brāhmaṇas.[3] It is obvious that no weight can be attached to ethnological statements based upon such wild and fanciful conjectures. While the theories of origin embodied in such speculations cannot furnish any basis for rational conclusions, the Smṛtis furnish indirect indications with regard to the history of caste at different epochs. Valuable use has been made of the data contained in the Vedas, the epics and the Smṛtis by modern scholars, European and Indian. I will briefly refer to the conclusions which seem to emerge from their researches. Whether the caste system had been developed during the age of the *Ṛgveda* has been a subject of controversy and it has been said that the *Puruṣasūkta* was a later composition than the bulk of the *Ṛgveda* and cannot therefore prove the state of things which existed when the bulk of that Veda was composed. The *Puruṣasūkta* is obviously a speculation on a system which was flourishing at the time and the origin of which must have been lost in antiquity. It is difficult to accept the opinion of Prof. Rapson that the institution of caste is essentially of Brāhmaṇical origin and that it is based on the religious unity of the family symbolized by offerings to deceased ancestors and the doctrine of *svakarman*.[4] (This word is used by Rapson. But '*svadharma*' is the more appropriate and commonly used term.) The Brāhmaṇical theories were either allegorical representations or speculative explanations of a pre-existing institution and the institution was not the consequence of the theory. The religious unity of the family and offerings to deceased ancestors were not confined to the Hindus or to India. They were to be found among the Romans and other nations also and the doctrine of *svakarman* (or *svadharma*) as a religious doctrine was rather the offspring than the parent of the institution of caste. According to Prof. Keith, there is no actual proof in the *Ṛgveda* that the priesthood was not then a closed hereditary class. There are traces of the division of the Aryan tribe into the "holy power (the Brahman), the kingly power (Kṣatra) and the commonalty (Viś), and though the caste system was only in process of development in the *Ṛgveda*, it seems impossible to deny that much of the groundwork upon which th later elaborate structure was based was already in existence."[5] The kingship was normally hereditary and there is no trace that the King was developed from the priest. According to E. Senart,[6] there is a distinction between *varṇa* and *jāti*, the former corresponding to class and the latter to caste. But the two words are generally used by Sanskrit writers in one and the same sense. Etymologically *varṇa* indicated colour which depended on race, but as the Dvijas were in all probability of the same racial stock and divided only by occupation, they could not have formed three separate *varṇas* or colours. The original divisions of *varṇas* could have been only two, the fair-skinned Aryans and the dark-skinned Śūdras or Dasyus. When divisions of occupation led to separate groups and racial and occupational differences combined to help the formation of separate new groups, there must have grown up a tendency to use the words '*varṇa*' and '*jāti*' in the same sense of exclusive groups or castes. The notion of exclusive groups permeated even the Aryan Dvijas and the occupational divisions among them were also designated as *varṇas*.

According to Mr. C. V. Vaidya, the Indian Aryans had already developed caste before the beginning of the epic period which he places at 3000 B.C., and the germs of caste were probably brought by the Indo-Aryans from their original home or developed during the Vedic period. Mr. Vaidya relies upon the facts admitted by Sir H. Risley that "among the Iranians there were four divisions of society, *viz.*, priests, warriors, agriculturists and artisans, and that the priests or the Atharvans did not generally give their daughters in marriage to the men of the lower classes."[7] The tendency to restrict marriages to the same class can be discovered among other communities belonging to the Aryan race, as for instance, among the Romans.[8] When the Aryans invaded India and settled in the Punjab, they were divided into three classes composed of the priest, the warrior and the agriculturist. The Śūdras or Dāsas were entirely of a different race and colour and they had to labour in the fields and do other menial work. The upper three classes were of the same race and colour and had marriage relations with one another. During this period which was anterior to the time of the *Manusmṛti*, a son born of a Brāhmaṇa from a wife belonging to any of the first three castes was a Brāhmaṇa. There were only four castes and a fifth did not exist.[9] At first the Aryans did not allow marriage relations with the fourth caste, *i.e.*, the Śūdras. There were exceptions to this rule, especially among the Vaiśyas or agriculturists who were in constant contact with the Śūdra or labouring class. Śūdra wives were taken rarely by the Brāhmaṇas, often by Kṣatriyas and more frequently by Vaiśyas. The practice which previously obtained among the Indo-Aryans *inter se* was for the progeny to follow the caste of the father. There was a repugnance to the application of this rule to the offspring of Śūdra wives. Brāhmaṇas assigned a separate caste to such progeny and strongly interdicted such marriages. The next step was for Kṣatriyas following the example of Brāhmaṇas to prevent the son born of a Śūdra wife taking equal rank with sons of Kṣatriya wives. No separate name was assigned to the son of a Vaiśya by a Śūdra woman, probably because such inter-mixture of race was more pronounced in this case. The next step was to place a further restriction upon the marriage of a Brāhmaṇa with a Vaiśya woman owing to the fact that the Vaiśya blood had lost its purity by inter-mixture. The son of a Brāhmaṇa by a Vaiśya wife was treated as a Vaiśya. The son of a Brāhmaṇa by women of the first two castes was a Brāhmaṇa. But when more than one caste intervened between the Brāhmaṇa and his wife, the progeny was regarded as belonging to the caste of the mother. In the time of Manu probably and certainly in the days of Yājñavalkya the restrictions on marriage had made further progress and a separate caste was assigned to the son of a Brāhmaṇa by a Kṣatriya wife also. Mr. Vaidya's theory is supported by the passages to be found in *Manusmṛti* and other Smṛtis regarding the status of sons born of *Anuloman* marriages with wives of different castes. Originally the property of a deceased Brāhmaṇa had to be divided into ten shares, four were to go to the share of a son by a Brāhmaṇa wife, three to the son by a Kṣatriya wife, two to the son by a Vaiśya wife and one to the son by a Śūdra wife. *Pratiloman* marriages were condemned and the progeny was generally despised as half-caste. The further development of caste grew apace with the spread of the Aryans in the country and the larger opportunities for contact between the Aryans and the Śūdras and aborigines.

Starting originally in difference of occupations the conception of caste was modified by contact with people of alien races and colour after the invasion of India by the Aryans. Its further development was determined by considerations of racial purity or admixture. These factors and community of creed seem to me sufficient to account for the four main divisions of caste. The numerous fantastic ramifications of caste were determined by other considerations, such as residence in the same place, community of language, growing differences in occupations and the like. Brāhmaṇas could not possibly have created the institution of caste, though they indulged in speculations and theories about the origin of caste and, like the priestly class in other countries, endeavoured to exalt the status of the priest and the warrior. It is also probable that when some of the non-Aryan races invaded India and were sufficiently assimilated to the people of the country in language, manners and customs, the Brāhmaṇas helped to discover pedigrees establishing the genealogical connection of the ruling families with the ancient Aryan chiefs of India.

It is pointed out by Mr. Vaidya that in King Harṣa's days a Kṣatriya could marry a Vaiśya woman and a Brāhmaṇa could marry a Śūdra woman. Bāṇa, the famous Sanskrit author, had two Pāraśava brothers, *i.e.*, born of a Brāhmaṇa father by a Śūdra wife. But at the time of Alberuni's visit (about 1030 A.D.) the practice of a Brāhmaṇa marrying outside his own caste had fallen into disuse.

It has been suggested by some social reformers that caste had originally nothing to do with birth and was merely a distinction based upon qualities, character and occupation. They rely upon a passage in the *Bhagavadgītā* and certain passages occurring in the *Mahābhārata* (IV.13). The verse in the *Bhagavadgītā* merely states that the division into four castes was made by the Creator himself with reference to the functional occupations of society and the innate qualities and dispositions of men befitting them for one or other of the functions. This verse must be regarded as a speculative account of the origin of the four main castes and contains a considerable measure of truth. But there can be no doubt that whatever the reasons for the origin of the system, castes soon became hereditary and more or less rigid. Fictions might have been occasionally adopted for the purpose of absorbing new tribes into a caste, but the theory has throughout been that the caste of an individual is determined by birth, *i.e.*, parentage. The considerations which furnished the historical origin of caste or which often led to the multiplication of castes have never affected, during the course of ages, the popular belief in the hereditary character of the institution. A person may of course lose caste by misconduct. There are also instances in the old legends of persons being exalted to a higher caste by virtue of their austerities. It is also stated in some of the Smṛtis that by inter-marriages in successive generations an exaltation or degradation of caste may be brought about (Man.X.42). The passages in the *Mahābhārata* which are relied upon contain a discussion between Nahuṣa (transformed into a python) and Yudhiṣṭhira as to how caste was to be determined. The answer given by Yudhiṣṭhira might at first sight seem to support the view that it was to be determined by character and conduct, but reading the passages as a whole, the proper interpretation seems to be that a Śūdra possessing the qualities and virtues of a Brāhmaṇa should be treated as a Brāhmaṇa and *vice versa*. There is a well-known maxim in Sanskrit that a fact cannot be altered by a hundred texts. The fact of parentage in a certain caste could not possibly be altered. But the social esteem of the individual would depend upon his character. If Yudhiṣṭhira meant to suggest that caste was determined simply by character and not by birth, the view is opposed to the facts of history. The verses dealing with this point start with the assumption that the individuals whose social position was considered were Śūdras and Brāhmaṇas. Another conclusion which might be fairly drawn from the later verses in the same chapter is that where on account of the admixture of castes and irregular connections between them the paternity of an individual was not ascertainable, it should be inferred from his character and conduct and that membership of the twice-born classes was dependent not merely upon birth, but also upon the performance of the sacraments prescribed for the twice-born. While we may deplore the evil effects of the institution, it is not possible to entertain the view that social classifications were determined merely by character.

There were no serious restrictions upon inter-dining among the twice-born classes. According to the Smṛti of Vyāsa (III.52), Dvijas can take meals with each other, and all that is necessary is that the person whose food one takes must be a member of a known family. The Smṛtis allowed the taking of food by Dvijas with certain classes of Śūdras also.[10] According to Gautama, a Brāhmaṇa may eat the food given by twice-born men who are praised for the faithful performance of their duties. He may also take food from a herdsman, a husbandman, an acquaintance of the family, a barber and a servant. If the means of sustaining life cannot be otherwise procured, they may be accepted from a Śūdra. Food brought unsolicited, small fish, venison, and roasted grain, if offered spontaneously by a man of any caste, must not be refused. According to Āpastamba, pure men of the first three castes could prepare the food of the householder which is used at the Vaiśvadeva offering; or Śūdras may prepare the food under the superintendence of a man of the *ārya* (*i.e.*, any of the first three) caste. If the food has been prepared by a Śūdra cook without supervision, it should be placed on the fire and sprinkled with water and it is then fit for the gods. According to Manu, the members of the Śūdra caste from whom a Brāhmaṇa may take food are a man's own cultivator, his family friend, his cowherd, his slave, his barber and a poor man who has taken service under him (*Vanaparvan*.207.18). In the *Dharmavyādha* episode of the *Mahābhārata* a Brāhmaṇa was advised by a Brāhmaṇa lady to seek knowledge of *dharma* from a butcher and he accepted water at the hands of the butcher. Udayanācārya, the author of the *Nyāyakusumāñjali*, who lived about the tenth century, complained that in his time there had been a degeneracy of the Brāhmaṇas in the matter of sexual relations and procreation, in the restriction of their studies to one Śākhā only of the Veda and in regard to their occupation and livelihood, and he stated that Brāhmaṇas had begun to take food even from Śūdras. The restrictions in the matter of inter-dining must have become more stringent in subsequent times.

According to Manu, the three means of livelihood open to a Brāhmaṇa were teaching, officiating at sacrifices for others and accepting gifts from pure men. These were forbidden to a Kṣatriya and a Vaiśya. The profession of arms was a legitimate one for a Kṣatriya; and trade, agriculture and cattle-breeding were the prescribed occupations of a Vaiśya. But if a Brāhmaṇa was unable to procure subsistence by his own special occupations, he could adopt any of the occupations of a Kṣatriya or a Vaiśya. It is very curious that even in cases where a Brāhmaṇa is reduced to the necessity of adopting these occupations, he is prohibited from the pursuit of agriculture, the reason being that it causes injury to many beings and requires external aid like bulls, implements, etc.; the ploughshare injures the earth and the beings living in the earth. There is a very long and most curious list of exceptions. A Kṣatriya is also permitted in distress to adopt the occupations open to a Vaiśya and a Vaiśya may subsist by following the occupations of a Śūdra. But neither a Kṣatriya nor a Vaiśya is allowed to adopt any of the occupations of a higher caste, the penalty for a breach being deprivation of property and banishment. A Śūdra who is unable to find service under the twice-born classes may in distress maintain himself by handicraft and may follow those mechanical occupations by following which the twice-born are best served. It will be seen from a perusal of these rules and restrictions that they could not possibly have been strictly followed at any time and that they must have been more honoured in the breach than in the observance. In case of necessity a Brāhmaṇa may study even under a non-Brāhmaṇa. Considerable laxity seems to have grown up with regard to the pursuit of the prescribed occupations owing to the influence of Buddhism and economic necessity. The picture furnished by the *Jātaka Tales* of social and economic conditions shows many instances of such laxity.[11]

Outcastes seem to have always existed in society and to have been regarded as untouchable. According to Āpastamba it was sinful to touch, speak to or look at a Caṇḍāla, and penances were prescribed for this. Yājñavalkya (Yaj.II.234) provided for the punishment of a Caṇḍāla who touched a man of the higher castes. The Chinese Traveller Hieun-Tsang noticed the segregation of the outcastes outside towns and villages. The same thing was also noticed by Fa-Hian who states that the

Caṇḍālas "live away from other people and when they approach a city or a market, they beat a piece of wood in order to distinguish themselves. Then people know who they are and avoid coming into contact with them."[12]

To understand the attitude of the Smṛti-writers with regard to the treatment of Śūdras, it is necessary to bear in mind that the Śūdras were different in colour and race from the Aryan settlers and had been conquered by the Aryans and reduced to servitude. The term 'Dāsa' or 'Dasyu' which was applied to them originally meant a foe. They were therefore treated as slaves or as members of a servile class and their primary duty was to serve the twice-born classes. Just as the Negroes were considered by the European settlers in America as the descendants of Ham meant under the curse pronounced by Noah to be kept in slavery, the Aryan settlers in India also set up the theory that the Śūdras were created to serve the twice-born classes.[13] The Śūdras were forbidden to study the Vedas and could acquire a knowledge of *dharma* from the Purāṇas and other sources. According to the *Aitareya Brāhmaṇa* (VII.XXI.4), a Śūdra is the servant of another liable to be expelled at will and to be slain at pleasure. The Śūdra was created to be the slave of the Brāhmaṇa, and even if he is emancipated by his master, he is not released from his servile status. A twice-born man is directed by Manu (VIII.413-14) not to give advice to a Śūdra on secular or religious matters. According to Gautama (G.D.S.XVIII.24), to defray the expenses of a wedding, a man may take money by fraud or force from a Śūdra: "If a sacrifice offered by a twice-born man and especially by a Brāhmaṇa cannot be completed for want of any requisite, the article required for completion may be taken forcibly from the house of any Vaiśya who owns a large number of cattle, but does not perform the Soma or minor sacrifices. Brāhmaṇa is also allowed to take at his pleasure two or three articles required for a sacrifice from the house of a Śūdra, since a Śūdra has no business with sacrifices. If a Dvija possessing a hundred cows does not kindle the sacred fire, or one possessing a thousand cows does not perform the

Soma sacrifice, a Dvija who performs the sacrifice may unhesitatingly take the two or three articles from their houses, even though they be Brāhmaṇas or Kṣatriyas; or he may take by force or fraud from a Brāhmaṇa who always accepts and never gives and who refuses to give them. Thus the fame of the taker will spread and his merit increase." Likewise he who has famished for three days may on the fourth day take what he requires for a day's subsistence either from a man who neglects his sacred duties or from the threshing floor or from a house or wherever he finds it. But if the owner should ask him, he must confess his deed and its causes. But on such occasions a Kṣatriya must never take the property of a virtuous Brāhmaṇa. If he is starving, he may appropriate things from a Śūdra or from a twice-born who neglects his duties. And finally it is stated that "he who takes what is permitted by the texts on such occasions and bestows it on the virtuous becomes a raft enabling the owner to tide over the effects of his sin and the taker over his distress." These extraordinary rules are deduced from the sacredotal theory that "whatever exists in the world is the property of Brāhmaṇa; on account of the excellence of his origin, Brāhmaṇa is entitled to it all." It is of course obvious that the object of this and other verses of a like character is merely laudatory and intended to indicate the exalted status of Brāhmaṇa in the social order. The principle of exaggeration is often resorted to in the sacred books for the purpose of emphasising the merit or demerit of a person or an action, a virtue or a vice. Texts of this sort are intended to convey praise or censure and are treated as Arthavāda statements which have no obligatory force. They could only be invoked in favour of the ideal Brāhmaṇa who conducts himself according to the letter and the spirit of the sacred ordinances, and such Brāhmaṇas must, from the very necessities of the case, have been exceptionally few. It is further obvious that such rules could not possibly have been practically enforced at any time. But it cannot be denied that the differences in social status led to inequalities in the treatment of the different classes.

References

1. *C.H.I.*, Vol. I, p. 53.
2. For a summary of the accounts of the ancient Hindu writers, see Sir W. Muir: *Sanskrit Texts* (3rd edition), Vol. I, p. 159.
3. *Man.* X, 43-44.
4. *C.H.I.*, Vol. I, p. 53.
5. *C.H.I.*, Vol. I, pp. 93-94.
6. E. Senart: *Caste in India*, p. 128.
7. C.V. Vaidya: *Epic India*, p. 53.
8. E. Westermarck: *The Origin and Development of the Moral Ideas,* Vol. I, p. 714.
9. *Anuśāsanaparvan,* 47, 17-18.
10. C.V. Vaidya: *H.M.I.* Vol. II, p. 186.
11. *C.H.I.*, Vol. I, pp. 209-210.
12. *Travels of Fa-Hian* (399-414 A.D.), re-translated by H.A. Giles, p. 21.
13. E. Westermarck: *The Origin and Development of the Moral Ideals,* Vol. I, pp. 370-371 and 712-714.

The Life after Death

A people's view of life after death is intimately connected with their cosmology and cosmography. But their view of the human personality may not be so connected, though their acceptance of the idea of a spiritual and imperishable element as its constituent or non-acceptance of it appears to have such a relation. The Buddhists alone, it appears to me, with their indifference about the probability of the human soul, could and can think of complete annihilation called *Nirvāṇa* as the final condition of human beings in their endeavour of living their lives well and usefully! In the case of the Hindus whose views on human personality are conditioned by their cosmology both sets are very intimately connected with, nay may be said to determine in a large measure, the people's view of life after death.

In the earliest stage of Hinduism, as far as it can be judged from the scattered references in the hymns of the *Ṛgveda*, which must be dated between 1800 to 1200 B.C., we are aware of the people having belief in a spiritual or non-material element as a constituent of human personality. This element could wander away from the material body and could return to it under certain circumstances. Though it is designated as 'manas', mind, it is generally considered to be the same as 'soul' of later terminology. There is a whole hymn concerning it (*ṚV.* X. 58). There are a number of hymns which either are concerned with describing in some part what happens at death or refer to the conditions after death. Perhaps, the most important one from our view-point and for the subject of discussion in this chapter, is the 14th hymn of the Xth book of the *Rgveda*. The spirit or the soul of the dead is asked to proceed by the paths made by seers of old to the realm of the fathers, where both Yama, the deified Lord of dead and Varuṇa, the Law-giver, dwell. It is asked to meet Yama and the fathers as well as the merit of the acts, ordained or/and voluntary, performed by the person while living, there in the highest heaven. In the Ṛgvedic universe three heavens, lowest, middle and highest, are postulated (*ṚV.* I, 35, 6; VIII. 5, 8; VIII. 41, 9; IX. 113, 9). The soul is conjured to leave sin and evil down below and seek its new dwelling, the highest heaven, the world of the fathers and of Yama, their Lord, and of Varuṇa, the Law-giver. Perhaps this clearance from sin and evil was to be accomplished through the agency of the rays of the sun and the passage of the soul through the realm of eternal light. The fathers are said to be connected with the rays of the sun or are united with or are said to guard the sun; and their abode is described as the highest point of the sun, or they are connected with the highest step of Viṣṇu (*RV.* I. 109, 7; etc.).

In the abode of the fathers, the world of Yama where Varuṇa too is present, in the highest heaven, the spirit of the deceased unites with a glorious or refulgent body. The resurrected dead becomes dear and welcome to gods and enters upon a delectable life. For the Lord of the dead and the blessed sits under a tree with fine eternal foliage (*ṚV.* X. 135, 1; *AV.* V. 4, 3) drinking with the gods in the company of Varuṇa, in a world where there is 'pasturage', which nobody can rob the dead of. There old age and other frailties and imperfections of mundane life do not exist. There the strong cannot subject the weak. In immortal life the dead, when they reach there, join Yama to delight themselves at his banquet, which is evidently imperishable and continuous. The strength of the body acquired in the resurrected form in the realm of Yama is said to vary with the faithfulness with which the rules are observed in life. With the resurrected form the dead person is believed to be able to go on without food for "thirteen days, and later four, six or twelve months or even a hundred years." Finally "they are able altogether to dispense with it." Deussen summarized the conditions of living in the world of Yama as described in this early literature, in the following felicitous verses, more than half a century ago: "The kingdom of inexhaustible light,... Among the holiest of the heavenly world,.... Where the third loftiest heaven spreads its vault,... Where resides bliss and felicity.... Where the craving of desire is stilled, There suffer me to dwell immortal."[1] The last line expressing the desire of a dying person pinpoints the state of the dead in the realm of the hereafter.

In more particulars, the life in the realm of the pious dead is full of music and singing, of the elevating drink 'soma', of ghee, of milk and of honey. One meets one's parents and children too, as the *Atharvaveda* states: The joys are said to be hundredfold higher and deeper than those of the earth, as the two or three centuries later work, the *Śatapathabrāhmaṇa* (XIV. 7, 1, 32-33), has it.[2]

It should be carefully noted that the body is said to be acquired in the hereafter, and that the soul is described more or less clearly as leaving the body without carrying anything with it. It is said to be united with the merit of good mundane work, no doubt; but there is no indication of any subtle vehicle like the later subtle, or *liṅga* body, enveloped in which the soul is conceived of as departing in the later theory. Secondly, the existence in the hereafter is very much like that of the gods, more or less independent of any needs of the kind we mortals know of and suffer from. Thirdly, the living in the company of gods, and particularly that of Yama and Varuṇa, indicates that though the possibility of weighing the merits and the demerits of the dead is there, such a test, if any, is to be supposed to have been passed. And it must be with the help of one's merit, and of prayers either offered by oneself or by others on one's behalf to such gods as Agni, Pūṣan, the path-finding deities of the Vedic age.

Pūṣan is prayed to conduct the dead to the fathers and he sees that they go safely to their destined place (*ṚV.* VI. 55 and 58; X. 17, 4). Both Agni and Savitṛ lead the dead to the abode of the righteous (X. 16, 1-4; X. 17, 3). In order to reach the world of Yama, the soul had to pass by the two spotted four-eyed dogs of Yama that guard the entrance to it.[3]

The dead on entry into the realm of Yama meet and become one with the fathers, '*pitṛs*' or '*pitaraḥ*'. The fathers are said to be of three classes, the highest, middling and the lowest. They are conceived as sorts of gods; they partake of '*soma*' and are said to deserve a share of such an offering. Agni is invoked and invited to come along with them. They are primeval God-adorers, Eaters and drinkers of oblations and travel with the deities and Indra. They are known to Agni. They are prayed to for aid and blessings. In short, as Deussen stated more than half a century ago, the fathers in the *Ṛgveda* figure on a footing of equality with the gods. There are more than half a dozen groups of them mentioned by name as Agniṣvāttas, Aṅgirasas, Atharvans, Bhṛgus, Kāvyas, Navagvas, Virūpas, Vasiṣṭhas, etc.[4]

One direction or request made in *ṚV.* IX. 90, 13, though it occurs in a different context, is noteworthy as indicating the speculative source of the cardinal ideas of the origin of the human being and his personality. And that is the direction given to the eyes and breath of a dead person to depart to the sun and the wind or air respectively. It has been stated in the previous chapter how, in one of the Upaniṣad texts (*Br. Up.* III. 2, 13) describing what happens at the death of person, it is asserted that the eyes go to the sun, the breath to the air or wind and the other organs to various other deities. What is expressed as a desire, a wish, a request or a direction in the Ṛgvedic text became in the next three or four centuries, with the speculative development of the current ideas, a fact to be accepted as such and a basis for a whole theory. As S.V. Ketkar pointed out more than forty years ago, no doubt the idea is intimately connected with that cosmology of the Ṛgvedic age which was based on the sacrifice of the

Primordial Being described in the famous *Puruṣasūkta*, the hymn of Puruṣa (the Primordial Being). It is said therein (*ṚV.* X. 90) that when the Primordial Being was cut up His eyes formed or became the sun and His breath, the wind or air. The direction for the eyes and the breath of a dead person occurs therein too. It is clear that the idea is more or less directly suggested, as Ketkar says, by the cosmological theory.

However it may be, it must be admitted that with this direction for the eyes and the breath of a deceased person, the latter's soul cannot be presumed to be enveloped in or ccompanied by any of the organs of the deceased person in a subtle form as its subtle or *liṅga* body. The notion of the subtle body could have only one of its aspects originating in this idea and had to wait till the more general theory of a subtle state of all natural elements was developed. Even then, in all probability, an intermediate stage of theoretical development, which, I believe, is preserved in the notions of the subtle body mentioned in the *Manusmṛti* (I. 56; XII. 16-22), had to be passed before the full theory could be formulated. Of this development, however, I shall speak later.

At this juncture there is another important point arising out of the description of the fathers and their world which deserves our special attention. The fathers appear in the role of some kind of Divinities and not merely as manes. There are a number of different groups of them, bearing specific names, whatever might have been the principle of naming. In the next period of the development of religious thought we find the groups to be many more. Those that are named, and we are assured that they are only some of the very many such groups evidently known but not specifically mentioned by name in the time of the *Manusmṛti*, which may be ascribed to a time not later than the 2nd century A.D., are: Agnidagdhas, Agniṣvāttas, Anagnidagdhas, Ājyapas, Aṅgiras' (Haviṣmantas), Barhiṣadas (Atrijas), Kāvyas (Somapās), Mārācas, Saumyas, Somapās, Vairāṭas (Somasadas), Vasiṣṭhas (Sukālins) (the *Manusmṛti*, III. 195-200). It is further stated that the fathers (*pitaraḥ* or *pitṛgaṇas*) are the sons of the ten sages, who are asserted to have been the sons of Manu himself, the grandson of Hiraṇyagarbha, the Golden Embryo that began the creation of the cosmos.

In the early Vedic literature the fathers are not represented as part of the original creation. They are, however, not only declared to be immortal (*AV*, VI. 41, 3) but are described as Gods (*ṚV*. X. 56, 4). In a number of texts they are said to be worshipped and prayed for both protection and succour as also for compassion and favour. They are further ascribed some work of the cosmic order.[5] In the *Bh.G*, about the 2nd century B.C., they figure in the company of multifarious gods as another variety of gods. And Lord Kṛṣṇa (IX. 25) tells Arjuna that the worshippers of the fathers—an expression which testifies to the god-hood of fathers and to their regular worship and devotion as an established practice—go after death to them. Thus the world of the fathers, which as is amply clear from an earlier chapter, the one on cosmology, was a well-known unit in the cosmological and cosmographical notions of the later period, one which antedates the age of the *Bh.G* by about three to five centuries and thus is separated from and later than the Vedic age by about five to seven centuries.

The fathers are further mentioned as seen among many Vedic gods like Aśvins, Maruts, Rudras, Ādityas, Vasus and Sādhyas, though under a name, *uṣmapā*, which is a peculiarity of the manes (*Bh.G* XI. 22). The *Manusmṛti*, too, mentions them in one place (XII. 49) along with gods, Sādhyas, sages, luminaries and some other categories as the breed which is the consequence of the Sattvaguṇa, the pure quality, while in another place (III. 195) it declares that one of the above-mentioned groups of the fathers is the manes of the Sādhyas and another of the gods. Again in another mood, the same work states (III. 201) that the fathers were born from the sages and in turn created gods and men. Further, it declares the fathers to be even primordial deities that are celibate, pure and un-angered (III. 192). More specifically the *Manusmṛti* (III. 284) identifies the first generation of the fathers, the

Pitṛs, with Vasus; the second, the 'Pitāmahas' (grand-fathers), with Rudras; and the third, the Prapitāmahas (great-grand-fathers), with Ādityas. These are the three main deity-categories that are mentioned along with the Sādhyas and the fathers in the above quoted text of the *Bh.G* (XI. 22) together as seen in the open mouth of the Great Being.

The early Vedic literature makes the fathers immortal like gods and denizens of the highest heaven in perpetuity.

It becomes necessary to know what kind of a place heaven was considered to be apart from its abounding in perpetual, inexhaustible and varied joys. Was it desired as the goal to which souls of deceased should repair or not, even if we have no reference to the fathers dwelling there or their nature? Was it looked upon as a place of sojourn from which the soul had to go after a fixed or varying period? If heaven was looked upon as a temporary resort, one cannot expect references to it as the goal of the soul after death as if it was the final resort to aspire for, which was the most cherished idea in the pursuit of which all manner of prescribed good living, however trying it may be, was to be attempted through mundane existence.

We have seen in an earlier chapter how some of the Upaniṣadic (cf. the *Kena Upaniṣad*, IV. 9) thought represented heaven, *svarga*, as if it was the final resort of the pious and righteous dead. This view carries forward the early Vedic belief in heaven as the be-all and end-all of life after death for the pious and the righteous. The impious and the unrighteous evidently were relegated to the dark world, the nether world, called *naraka*, the hell. We have studied, too, the emergence and the almost full-fledged development of the other view, best and earliest represented in the speculations of the Upaniṣadic sages, that even heaven (*svarga*) and its joys are perishable. Leaving the further advance of thought and belief in that line for later consideration, I shall have to state in brief the continuities or the vestiges as the case may be of the early Vedic belief in the finality and permanence of heaven and its joys, as the condition of life after death for the pious, a future reward for good life led on this earth.

No testimony in favour of the finality and permanence of heaven and life in it as the future reward of pious and righteous living on earth can be as authoritative and compelling as the persistence of the view that heaven is the final goal of hereafter. Buddha himself always brushed aside any query about it.[6] So much is this the case that D. C. Sircar[7], finding Emperor Aśoka, the first mighty Buddhist follower, speaking of the attainment of *svarga*, heaven, and the importance of safeguarding one's living there after death as the other world to be inhabited, suggests without any authority, and therefore hesitatingly, that "a school of early Buddhists may have believed that the attainment of Svarga by lay worshippers ultimately led them to *Nirvāṇa*."

Emperor Aśoka in his inscriptions has left to posterity not only his views of what is good, pious and righteous living on earth but also his mental processes which proceeding from and working on them dictated to him his goals, both 'mundane' and 'other-worldly'. The last two expressions, 'mundane' and 'other-worldly', are straight translations of the ones used by the extraordinary Emperor himself in three or four different Prākṛtic and Sanskritic versions. For the mundane world he has the following expressions as rendered by D. C. Sircar, evidently following the standard experts on the subject: '*ihaloka*', '*aihika*', '*aihatya*', '*aihalaukika*', '*iha*', '*ihatya*'.[8] For the objective, the goal after death, the other world par excellence, he uses words whose Sanskrit equivalents are: '*paraloka*', '*paratra*', '*pāralaukika*', '*pāratrika*'.[9]

The gist of Aśoka's pronouncements on his endeavour of living righteously, expressed in the passges referred to here, is that he was convinced that the pattern of activity and living adopted by him and prescribed by him to his subjects was calculated not only to procure earthly fame and happiness but was competent to secure bliss in the hereafter, that world being nothing different from *svarga*, the heaven. Actually more than once in these texts he either specifies the wooing of heaven (*svarga*) as the goal to be aimed at or asserts that his prescription if followed would grant that reward, which evidently must have been to him and his society a coveted one. Once or twice he even asserts that the bargain for the practitioner of his pattern of living and activity of heaven or *svarga*, is relatively a very favourable one, *vipula* (vast) in comparison with the endeavour of living involved. In view of this, D. C. Sircar's suggestion, whatever its plausibility in regard to the early Buddhism, that *svarga* or heaven in Aśoka's inscriptional exhortations is to be taken to imply only an intermediate stage and not a final one of bliss, cannot apply to Aśoka and his teaching as preserved in his inscriptions. To Emperor Aśoka, in spite of his enthusiasm for his new faith, *svarga* or heaven remained the goal of earthly living to be attained on one's death, the final blissful condition of life after death.

The ten centuries of belief in heaven as the final and blissful condition of life after death, attained by the pious and the righteous, which the Ṛgvedic poet-sages represented as the world of the fathers, whom, because of it, they portrayed as gods of a kind, had fixed the fathers and their varied groups or 'houses' as immortal denizens of heaven (*svarga*), so that in spite of the onslaught of the Upaniṣadic school and of the post-Upaniṣadic Buddhist sect on the impermanence of heavenly bliss and the promise and speculative substantiation of an eternally blissful condition is the ideal goal for attainment in the hereafter, the view of heaven (*svarga*) as the final abode held sway for a long time.

The view peeps out as a vestige from time to time in many later speculations and deliberations on the subject of life after deth. Suffice it here, in order to clinch the issue about *svarga* and its nature, as they figure in about the 3rd century B. C. in Aśoka's thoughts, to state that the *Manusmṛti* (III. 89), which may be a century or even four centuries later than Aśoka's time, specifically asserts the possibility of life in *svarga* or heaven being eternal (*akṣayya*, inexhaustible). Anticipating a little, I may further mention as evidence of the continuity of this view the fact that on the eve of resurgence of Hinduism in A.D.279 an inscription from a place near Bhopal, written in

Sanskrit, asserts that the utility work, the tank, got executed by the donor was intended to procure for him not only pleasure, happiness and prosperity in this world but also to secure for him hereafter the attainment of eternal *svarga* happiness (*akṣaya svarga*).[10]

That the fathers were offered some worship or oblation or libation without any reference to one's manes is a practice recorded in a side-reference in Kālidāsa's dynastic semi-epic *Raghuvaṁśa* (V. 8). And Mallinātha, the thirteenth-century learned commentator of the work, names the age-old groups or 'houses' of fathers, i.e., 'Agniṣvāttas' and others, as the recipients of such attention. We may infer that Kālidāsa's reference was specifically to them and take it as evidence of their currency till his time.

In the *Rāmāyaṇā*, whose compilation may be dated between the 2nd century B. C. and the fourth century A. D., though the groups or 'houses' of the fathers are not named, the fathers figure in a number of important legends and incidents. In the potent incantation called *ādityahṛdaya*, sun-heart, the recitation of which on the battlefield was calculated to secure victory to its reciter, imparted by the hoary miracle-working sage Agastya to Rāma (VI. 105, 2-21), among the various names under which the sun is invoked occurs the fathers (*pitraḥ*) along with Vasus, Sādhyas, Aśvins and other deities as in the earlier texts quoted or referred to above. In a legend, in which a fanciful account of the loss of Indra's testicles and of his having later grafted on him those of a ram is given, it is the fathers who were importuned by all the gods, they being called not merely *pitṛs* but *pitṛdevas*, father-gods, to do the skilful operation (I, 49, 1-10).

At least four of the Purāṇas, dated about the 5th century to about the 9th or the 10th, mention a varying number of these groups. In three of them seven of these occurring in the list of the *Manusmṛti* figure. In one, their number is stated to be thirtyone! The relation between gods and these fathers is curiously stated to be that of father and son as well as that of son and father. They are stated to be of two kinds, either as embodied and disembodied or as divine and human or as *deva-deva* and *sāntānika* or again as express-framed and subtle-framed. The seven groups are traced to the seven great sages, created with the primordial cosmos. It is also asserted that the human manes became through their own good work the divine fathers.[11]

The notion that by good and pious living human beings and other similar creatures or their advanced representatives could attain divinity and that the first-stage divine beings could progress into a higher class of divinities, evidently by similar means is a belief implicit in the distinction between Ājāna-devas, born-gods, and Karmadevas, work-gods, i.e., those gods who attained their divinity through good living, stated in the oldest Upaniṣad, *Bṛhadāraṇyaka* (IV. 3, 32), and referred to in an earlier chapter. In A.B. Keith's opinion the notion that the gods earned their divinity is implicit in the Ṛgvedic mythology.[12] The *Manusmṛti* (I, 22) describing the creation of the cosmos by Brahmā mentions Sādhyas and Karmadeva, 'Karmātman deva', is the expression used.

Jñāneśvara, in the fourth quarter of the thirteenth century, in his comment (XV. 195-6) on *Bh.G.*, XV. 2, elaborating in detail the picture of the cosmic scene in the imagery of a vast banyan tree, mentions the fathers along with sages, and Vidyādharas, another mysterious race of beings, and also the sun and the moon as side-branches of it.

Fathers, who were thus originally manes, who had attained godhood and dwelt in heaven in perpetual, ample, and varied bliss, and were in no need of being supplied with food and drink by their descendants living on earth, continued to figure in the imagination and belief of the people ages afterwards as more or less such, even when the development of another set of beliefs about the future condition of the human soul and all life had made such a situation impossible and incompatible with the fully developed theory of life and death!

I shall now review the situation as regards their erstwhile permanent abode heaven (*svarga*), and the means for its attainment and the changes, if any, in it, before examining briefly the rise and progress of the theory of life and death which turned the fathers and their permanent bliss into a temporary and transitory phenomenon.

The *Ṛgveda* (X. 154, 1-3) promised heaven after death to doers of certain actions; and that attainment must have guaranteed immortality to them for that is what was desired by the Ṛgvedic poets and their patrons (*ṚV.* V. 55, 4; V. 63, 2). The *Bhagavadgītā* (IX. 20-21) in the same tune as that of the much earlier philosophical work, the *Chāndogya Upaniṣad* (VIII. 1, 6), asserts the impermanence of the broad and pleasant heavenly world, mentioning that pious people have in the past worked zealously through various sacrifices for its attainment. The heavenly world, blessed and divine, providing enjoyments fit for gods, is called the world of Indra or the Lord of gods.

However, in the epic and other literature and in the doings and aspirations of the heroes of both, there is very clear and outstandingly prominent evidence showing that heaven, *svarga*, or the world of Indra, had continued to be looked upon as the be-all and end-all of life, the goal that was so covetable that no effort for it was considered too heavy or costly. And whether in imitation of or out of inspiration from that assurance of salvation while still living on earth (*jīvanmukti*) through a particular system of living or from the recorded examples of such individuals as Vāmadeva and some others, we have in that literature a record of the efforts at the endeavour of walking into or being transported into heaven (*svarga*) with the mundane body as either a feat attempted and achieved in green old age, on the eve of the call for death, or in healthy middle age. The notion itself finds mention in the later Vedas where it is stated that by performing certain sacrifices a man could go to heaven in person.[13]

Nahuṣa, one of the far-famed legendary kings, is the most outstanding example of such men, and perhaps the earliest recorded one in traditional history. In his own person he had actually held sway over the whole of Indra's heavenly domains and was being served by all the divine damsels and even perhaps by the consorts of some of the gods. He figures in the literature from about the 3rd century B.C. onwards as having lost his heavenly acquisition and possession through misconduct while he had the sovereign command over them.[14] The famous tale of a remote ancestor of Rāma in his pursuit of this feat of going to heaven in his bodily form, that of Triśaṅku, who has remained almost a laughing stock of the people[15] as the standard example of a person who gets to neither end of an enterprise but has to be hanging in between, is told at length in the *Rāmāyaṇa* (II. 57-60), as the greatest exploit of the sage Viśvāmitra.

Indra, the natural and constitutional ruler of heaven, himself appears in literature owing to his alternate name of Śatakratu (one who has performed one hundred horse-sacrifices) as being jealous of kings bent on performing one hundred horse-sacrifices and of sages practising severe austerities and thus jeopardizing his heavenly rule. Kālidāsa, the mirror of the national mind of ancient India, whose passing reference to Triśaṅku is already attended to, gives us a full description of the obstacle that Indra created in the performance of the hundredth horse-sacrifice of Dilīpa, the fourth ancestor of Rāma, and of the circumstances which procured for Dilīpa a place in heaven in spite of the non-performance of the hundredth sacrifice, as a special case (see the *Raghuvaṁśa*, III. 50-69).

The idea of walking to heaven in person as equivalent to preparing for one's death, *mahāyātrā* or *mahāprasthāna*, the great pilgrimage or the great journey, as it came to be significantly called, is implicit in the description of Rāma's last days as described in the *Rāmāyaṇa*, though in the end Rāma, being by then looked upon as an incarnation of Viṣṇu, is shown as having disappeared into His original form. In the *Mahābhārata* there is a whole book (*parvan*) entitled the *Svargārohaṇa* (XVIII), meaning ascending to the heaven, in which the progress of the Pāṇḍavas on their way to heaven is described, Yudhiṣṭhira, the eldest of them, alone being shown as reaching his destination.

In the *Rāmāyana* it is stated that Rāma having assumed His original Viṣṇu form asked Brahmā to assign his associates an appropriately deserving but evidently unending world (VII. 110). Thereupon Brahmā assured Rāma that all of them should be admitted to the world known as Santāna or Santānaka, which is only next lower than or next previous to the final abode, the most perfect world of Brahmā.

The later version of the happenings and the assignments of worlds to Rāma and his associates bear testimony to the changing notions regarding *svarga*, the final goal, and to the rise of new conceptions of salvaging activity.

Kālidāsa's version must be considered to be only a little later than that of the *Rāmāyaṇa*, though its being more or less contemporary with it is not impossible. When Rāma was admonished about his time for departure from the earth, he, with the household fire being carried before him started northwards with all his associates. At a particular spot on the bank of the river Śarayū, known as Gopratarana, which is considered by the Hindus as a holy place of pilgrimage, he received the divine air-vehicle for him to take to His abode. Boarding it he arranged that all those bathing in the river at that spot would go to heaven (*svarga*). For his intimate followers like the monkey-king Sugrīva, he had another *svarga* made; for they were, as Mallinātha gives us the reason, only 'new gods'. *Svarga* in this account could not have been a place from which its denizens would have to return to earth but must have been looked upon and conceived as a permanent abode of final release (*Raghuvaṁśa*, XVI. 92-102). From Tulasīdāsa's version[16] of about twelve centuries later we learn that Rāma arranged with Brahmā the entrance to the city of gods for people touching the waters of the river Śarayū in one particular month. There is no reference therein to another special world for Rāma's associates; but there is an assurance of Rāma given to Vibhīṣana, the demon-devotee of Rāma and the ruler of Laṅkā, that after he had ruled over Laṅkā for a whole *kalpa*-period he would go to the world of gods (*svarga*).

Rāma's injunction to Brahmā to create a special *svarga* for his close associates and his assurance that people bathing in the Śarayū shall attain heaven, *svarga*, which were only whittled down in Tulasīdāsa's version of the story owing to the development of new thought and practice regarding life after death, must raise the presumption that not only till Kālidāsa's time but till even much later, *svarga*, the perfect and blissful world of the Ṛgvedic and the Atharvavedic poets, continued to figure and therefore to be looked upon as such, and did not get completely eclipsed as the final goal to be achieved through pious and righteous living on earth!

For ages, *svarga* has been the reward for heroes who die on the battlefield fighting without turning their backs to their opponents. Thus Lord Kṛṣna's worldly retort to Arjuna on his declaration that he will not fight is that he would thereby be throwing away the golden opportunity of open gates to heaven (*svarga*). Arguing the matter he points out that fight at that stage was doubly advantageous to Arjuna. For if he was killed in battle he would attain heaven (*svarga*) and if he succeeded he would gain sovereignty over the world (*Bh.G.* II. 32-33 and 37).

Perhaps this sentiment is much older than the 5th century B.C. In the *Kauṣītakībrāhmaṇa Upaniṣad* (III. 1) we are told that Pratardana, the son of Divodāsa, attained the favourite abode of Indra, i.e., heaven, through fight and manly courage. This should naturally mean that Pratardana died while fighting bravely in some cause and thereby attained heaven.

Anyway the belief and the sentiment are very well represented in the national poet's, Kālidāsa's work, and also in the still later popular text of hortatory nature, *Pañcatantra*. In his *Raghuvaṁśa* (VII. 53) Kālidāsa makes a reference, which is quite definitive not only to show that the attainment of heaven for death in a battle was sure but also that it was instantaneous. That is why Kālidāsa represents two opponents of Aja, who succumbed to his arrows simultaneously, as quarrelling over beautiful Apsaras, one of a class of charmingly enticing damsels who attend on persons in heaven. And the tabloid expression *amartyabhāve'pi* (even though they had become immortals or gods), almost as an aside remark, vouchsafes to us the significant information that going to heaven, *svarga*, meant even so late as Kālidāsa's time attainment of immortality.

In the *Pañcatantra* the belief and the sentiment that a hero dying in a battle goes to heaven without any ado are repeated more than once (I. after verse 227; I. vv. 332, 335; IV. v. 69). In three other contexts at least *svarga* (heaven) as the goal of meritorious living in this world is emphasized and recommended as an objective which is rather difficult to achieve (I. v. 276; II. v. 115, IV. vv. 2-5). There is one context, the most important one for our present purpose, as it widens our knowledge of the extent to which the attainment of heaven as a great prize after death and of its view as near-eternity had reached. We are told that a woman on immolating herself on her husband's funeral pyre wins the right to live in heaven (*svarga*) for thirty-five million years, thirty-five million being the number of hair on woman's body (II. V. 179).

Though the gods like Agni and Pūṣan are prayed to take the soul of the deceased to the world of the fathers, yet it was described as the world of the pious only, implying, and, as mentioned earlier, even stating it in so many words sometimes, that the non-pious had no access to it (*ṚV*. X. 15; X. 154, 3). It is also mentioned that severe austerities, death in a battle on the battlefield or liberal gifts and charities in sacrifices earn the persons concerned as a reward a place in *svarga* (heaven) (*ṚV*. I. 125, 5; X. 107, 2; X. 154, 2-5).[17]

It is to be presumed, though explicit mention of the belief comes later, that the impious ones and perpetrators of evil, including of course non-performers of sacrifices and non-donors, were relegated to the dark nether world known as *naraka*.[18] This world evidently of Yama, had received a specific name some time later, as Bādarāyṇa in his *Brahmasūtras* (III. 1, 13) calls it *Saṁyamana*, the place where appropriate torments had to be suffered by its inmates. In later literature, however, the name does not figure. Instead the specific names of many hells, as already noted in an earlier chapter, take its place.

But a priori, the nature of *svarga* and its provisions for its denizens, including the ancient fathers and the new ones admitted to it, leave no need for any food or drink being provided to the fathers, except perhaps what might have been thought to be necessary during the transit of the soul from this world to that of the fathers. Accordingly we do not find any specific mention of funeral worship and oblations to the manes in the early literature, except a stray mention of fathers-worship in its later name of Pitṛyajna (*ṚV*. X. 16, 10). And P.V. Kane[19] has not discovered any earlier reference to the later and the standard form of oblationary worship of the manes, *śrāddha*, than the one in the late-looking and late-breathing epilogue of the *Kaṭha Upaniṣad* which appears at the end of the chapter (I, 3, 17), though he sees an implied reference to such a rite in *ṚV.* VIII. 30, 3 and VIII. 63, 1.

In this connection the tradition that is recorded in the *Āpastambadharmasūtra* (II. 7, 16, 1-3) is significant. It is stated there that gods and men were living together on earth. Gods went to heaven having acquired it as a reward for their sacrifice. To enable men to acquire heaven Manu promulgated the rite known as *śrāddha*. In it, the fathers, *pitaraḥa*, are the deities, invited to dinner serving the role which Agni does in a sacrifice, i.e., of the conveyer of the offerings. The rites known as *śrāddha*, whose chief function was to provide for the animal needs of the manes by offering them to Brāhmaṇas—had they come to be looked upon as gods on earth even if no such express statement is attested for that early date?—thus providing the priestly class with an additional, or rather, as becomes probable in the light of the religio-social condition of the time between Janamejaya's death and the resurgence of Brāhmaṇic Hinduism about the 3rd century B. C., a substitute source of livelihood.

References

1. Deussen, *Philosophy of the Upaniṣads*. pp. 319-21.
2. S.V. Ketkar, *Mahārāṣṭriya Jñānakośa*, 11. pp. 390-1.
3. Deussen, op. cit., p. 309.
4. A.A. Macdonell, *Vedic Mythology*. p. 170.
5. S.V. Ketkar, op. cit., PP. 393-4.
6. Elliot, *Hinduism and Buddhism*, I, pp. 233-4.
7. D.C. Sircar *Select Inscriptions*. p. 30. fn.
8. Op. cit., PP. 26, 30, 33, 40.
9. *ibid*. PP. 26, 31.
10. D.C. Sircar, op. cit., p. 181.
11. Saiddheśvaraśāstrī, *Prācīnacariitrakośa*, pp. 327-8.
12. A.B. Keith, *Religion and Philosophy of the Veda*, pp. 71, 82.
13. *Prācīnacaritrakośa*. pp. 3, 294-5.
14. S.V. Ketkar, op. cit., p. 392.
15. *Śākuntalā*, II, Vidūṣaka's remark before verse 17.
16. Jwala Prasad Miśra's edition of Tulasīdāsa's *Rāmāyaṇa*, pp. 1263-6.
17. S.V. Ketkar, op. cit., p. 391.
18. *ibid*., pp. 235, 292.
19. Kane, H.D. IV. pp. 349-52.

The Funeral Rites

Funeral Rites (*antyeṣṭi*) are a *saṁskāra*. *Antyeṣṭi* is one of the 16 (or more) *saṁskāras* of a twice-born person performed with Vedic *mantras* according to *Man*. II. 16, *Yāj*. I. 10, Jātūkarṇya. These *saṁskāras* were formerly performed for women also (Āśv. G.S. I. 15.12, I. 16.6, I. 17-11, *Man*. II. 66) but without Vedic mantras (except in marriage) and for śūdras also (*Man*. X. 127, *Yāj*. I. 10) but without Vedic mantras. The *Bdh*. P.S. III. 1.4 states that there are two *saṁskāras* of every human being and they are like a debt i.e. they must be performed, just as a debt must be discharged viz. the *saṁskāra* on birth and the one on death (*mṛtasaṁskāra*). Funeral rites and rites after death varied according as the deceased was an Āhitāgni (one who had consecrated the *śrauta* fires) or one who had only kindled the smārta fire, or one who had neither the *śrauta* fires nor the *smārta* fire, or a woman, a child, an ascetic (*parivrājaka*), or one dying in a distant land or one dying by accident or committing suicide etc. The Śrauta and Gṛhyasūtras differ among themselves in many details even on the same topic and the procedure becomes more elaborate in medieval and later times. It would be impossible to state all the differences on each topic in this section. A separate volume would have to be written for the purpose of setting out all the variations and additions from ancient times to modern times, to discuss why and how they arose or were made, to compare the various *sūtras* and to compare these again with the Purāṇas and medieval digests, and to appraise their worth or usefulness. All that can be attempted here is to give the bare outlines of the procedure in different sūtras, Smṛtis and digests by way of sample in a chronological order. The Nirṇayasindhu expressly says that the last rites differ in each *śākhā*, though certain things are common to all. Chronological conclusions have been drawn about the relative ages of the sūtras, of the smṛtis, purāṇas and nibandhas from the presence or absence of this or that detail or the elaboration of this or that ritual. But with all respect to the industrious scholars of the West such conclusions are often tentative or misleading and are purely subjective in many cases and are often due to ignorance or loss of ancient works.

Before setting out the rites of cremation contained in the Śrautasūtras, Gṛhyasūtras and later works, it would be best to give here a translation of the five hymns from the *ṚV.* (X.14-18). The verses in these hymns are employed by most of the sūtras and are used even now in the cremation rites and most of them occur in the other Vedic Saṁhitās. Varying interpretations have been given of some of these stanzas by Indian and Western commentators and critics. Only a few of these have been mentioned in the notes. Besides some stanzas are employed for different details of the cremation rites by the different *sūtras*. All such differences cannot be set out for want of space. The five hymns are so placed that they follow the order of the stages in which the funeral ritual proceeded in fact and is performed even now to a great extent.

ṚV. 14.1 (O! sacrificer!) worship with an offering Yama, King (of *pitṛs*), son of Vivasvat, the gatherer of men (that are dead), who sought out the way for many (men who do meritorious acts) and who passed along great (non-terrestrial) heights. 2. Yama was the first to know (find out) the path for us men; that is a pasture (abode) that cannot be taken away (by anybody), that is (an abode) where our ancient ancestors went, each knowing his own way thereto. 3. Mātali (Indra's charioteer or Indra himself) with the (*pitṛs*) called *kaiya*, Yama with the Aṅgirases and Bṛhaspati with the Ṛkvans become prosperous (or increase in strength); whom (the *pitṛs*) the gods support and who support the gods; some of them (the gods, Indra and others) are delighted by *svāhā* (by offerings given after uttering that word) and others (*pitṛs*) are delighted by *svadhā*. 4. O! Yama! Being of one mind with the pitṛs called Aṅgirases come to this (sacrifice) and sit down on the seat (of Kuśas). May the *mantras* recited by the wise (priests) bring you (here). May you (O King) delight yourself with this offering! 5. O Yama! (come with the adorable) Aṅgirases and Vairūpas and delight (or exhilarate) yourself. I invoke Vivasvat, your father; (May he delight himself) after sitting on the kuśa grass (spread) in this sacrifice. 6. The Aṅgirases, the Navagvas, the Atharvans, the Bhṛgus are our pitṛs and love soma (drink). May we secure the good will of those adorable ones! May we be in their gracious favour also! 7. Hasten, hasten by the ancient paths (to that place) where our forefathers that went before us passed. May you (the departed) see the two kings Yama and god Varuṇa rejoicing as they will. 8. (O departed one!) be united in the highest heaven with the *pitṛs*, with Yama and with your *iśṭāpūrta*; leaving here blamable acts (sins), come back to your home! Being endowed with bright lustre, be united with a (new) body! 9. (Ye evil spirits!) Go away, depart, move aside from this place (the cemetery); the pitṛs made (or assigned) for him (the departed person) this abode. Yama gives to him (this) resting place characterized by waters, days and nights. 10. (O departed!) proceeding by a good path, hurry on past the two dappled dogs (of Yama), offspring of Saramā, each having four eyes. Thus approach the *pitṛs* who will recognize you and who enjoy delight in the company of Yama. 11. O King Yama! Give him (the departed one) in charge of those two dogs of yours, who are guards, having four eyes each, who guard the path (to *pitṛ-loka*) and who watch men. May you bestow on him happiness and health! 12. The two messengers of Yama, that have wide nostrils, that are very strong, that are satisfied with difficulty, move among the people. May those two (messengers) restore to us to-day auspicious life in order that we may see the Sun! 13. Extract Soma juice for Yama (O priests!), offer oblation to

Yama. Sacrifice, in which Agni is messenger (carrier) to the gods and which is well prepared reaches Yama. 14. (O priests) offer oblation sprinkled with ghee to Yama and then start. May he keep us (tied) to the worship of gods, so that we may live a long life! 15. Offer to King Yama an oblation which is extremely sweet. Here is salutation to the sages who were born before us and who made the path for us. 16. The one great (Bṛhat-sāman) passes in three sacrifices (called *Jyotir-gaur-āyuḥ*) to the six wide expanses. Triṣṭubh, Gāyatrī and the metres are all centered in Yama.

ṚV. 15. 1. May the Soma-loving *pitṛs*, whether of the lower, middling or higher grade, come forward, those pitṛs that attained life (an eternal life or a life of spirit) being kind-hearted and knowing *ṛta* (the rule of right)! May those pitṛs protect us when invoked! 2. Today may this be our salutation to the *pitṛs* who went (died) before (the birth of this departed one) or who went after (the birth of the departed), also (those *pitṛs*) that are seated in this world or those who have places among the powerful people. 3. I have known the *pitṛs* as those who will recognize (me, their descendant) and I have known the stride of Viṣṇu and the child (viz. Agni), the *pitṛs* who sit on *kuśa* grass and partake of food and Soma offering at their will, repeatedly come here. 4. O pitṛs, that occupy kuśa grass! (come) down towards us with your protection; we have prepared for you these offerings; accept them. May you come with very blissful protection and then may grant us happiness that is free from trouble (or evil)! 5. May the Soma-loving pitṛs invited by us to the dear treasures (offerings) placed on the kuśa grass come! May they hear (our prayers) here! May they speak in favour of us and may they protect us! 6. O Father! May you all, bending your knee and sitting to the right side (of the offering) commend our sacrifice; whatever fault we may commit in reference to you through our being (erring) men, do not injure us for the sake of that. 7. O Fathers! sitting in front of (in the lap of) brilliant (flames) may you bestow wealth on (me) the mortal sacrificer! May you give wealth to the sons (of the deceased mortal) and may you impart vigour (to them)! 8. May Yama desiring offerings and enjoying the company of our ancient and rich pitṛs, who came to (or valued) Soma drinks one after another, who were glorious and in whose company Yama (the King of pitṛs) found great delight, partake of (eat) the offerings (given by us) according to his liking. 9. O Agni! come down towards us with the pitṛs that were thirsting and gaping (to reach the world of the gods), that knew about sacrifice and that were authors of *stomas* by means of prayers (that they offered), that know us well, that are unfailing (in responding to our call), that partake of the *kavya* offering and that sit round the heated milk. 10. O Agni! come with the *pitṛs* earlier and later (in time) that are unfailing, that partake of the offerings (presented to them), that drink the offerings, that are seated in the same chariot with Indra and the gods, that make obeisances to the gods in their thousands, that sit round the hot milk. 11. O *pitṛs* called Agniṣvātta , that are good guides! Come (to this rite) and sit down each on his proper seat. Eat (partake of) the pure offerings (offered) on the sacred *kuśa* grass and then bestow wealth (or prosperity) together with all heroic sons. 12. O Agni Jātavedas! when praised (by us) you, having made the oblations savoury, have carried them and presented (them to the pitṛs). May they eat them as is their wont (or as they are offered with the word *svadhā*)! O God! May you eat (partake of) the pure offerings! 13. O Jātavedas! you know how many (*pitṛs*) are there, viz. those who are here (near us), those who are not here, those whom we know and those whom we do not know (because they are remote ancestors). Be gracious to accept as is your habit this sacrifice which is well prepared. 14. (O Agni) Resplendent (or self-ruling) along with those (*pitṛs*) who (whose bodies) were burnt by fire and also whose bodies were not burnt and who enjoy delight (on account of offerings made) with *svadhā* (or as is their wont) in the midst of the heavens. May you arrange a body as (the deceased) desires that will inspire him to a (new) life (in heaven)!

ṚV. 16. 1. O Agni! Do not burn out this (departed person?), do not singe him all round, do not throw here and there (parts of) of his skin or his body; O Jātavedas (fire)! when you burn him completely, may you send him (the deceased) on to the *pitṛs*! 2. O Jātavedas! When you thoroughly burn this (departed person), then may you hand him over to the pitṛs! When he (the dead person) follows this (path) that leads on to a (new) life, may he become one that carries out the wishes of the gods! 3. May your eye (of the deceased) go to the sun, your breath to the wind, may you go to Heaven and earth by your merit or you may go to the waters if you find pleasure there (or if that be your lot)! May you rest (stand) with all your limbs in the herbs! 4. O Jātavedas! May you burn by your heat the goat that is your share! May your flame, may your bright light burn that goat; carry this (departed) to the world of those who do good deeds by means of your beneficent bodies (flames). 5. O Agni! discharge again towards the pitṛs (this deceased) who being offered on to you moves about (or wanders) as is his habit. O Jātavedas! may he take on (a new) life and increase his offerings and be united with a new (ethereal) body. 6. (O dead man!) May Agni who consumes all make free from blemish that limb of yours which the dark bird (crow) has pierced or an ant or a snake or a wild beast struck at and may Soma that entered into Brāhmaṇas do the same. 7. (O deceased) put on (yourself) with cows an armour (i.e. against fire flames) of Agni (i.e. with the skin of the cow) and surround yourself with the thick fat (of the cow), so that (Agni) that overwhelms with his lustre, that takes delight (in destroying things), that is bold and seeks to burn completely may not scatter (all your parts). 8. O Agni! do not destroy this cup that is dear to the gods and the Soma-loving (*pitṛs*). In this cup from which the gods drink, the immortal gods take delight . 9. I send far away the fire that eats raw flesh: may Agni that carries evil (or sins) go (to regions) where Yama reigns! The other Agni (Jātavedas), knowing everything, may take even here the offering to the gods. 10. I, observing the other Agni (Jātavedas) for the purpose of offering a sacrifice to the *pitṛs*, leave aside the fire that devours raw flesh and that entered your house; may he (the other fire) urge on to the highest world the *gharma* (heated milk or sacrifice). 11. May that fire which carries the *kravya* offerings offer them to the pitṛs that prosper according to *ṛta*! May he offer the oblations to the gods and *pitṛs*! 12. (O Agni!) we who love you have established you and have kindled you. May you loving (the *pitṛs*) bring here the pitṛs that love us in order that they may partake of the offering! 13. O Agni! May you extinguish (with water) that spot which you burnt (at the) time of cremation! May Kiyāmbu (plant) arise here and may *dūrvā* creeper spreading its tendrils grow here! 14. O Śitikā (cool plant), O herb full of cooling effect, O Hlādikā (freshening herb) causing delight, may you be well associated with a she frog! May you gladden this fire!

ṚV. 17. The verses of this hymn, except 3-6, have hardly any bearing on funeral rites. Therefore, only those four verses are translated here. The first two verses refer to the marriage of Vivasvat with the daughter of Tvaṣṭṛ and to the legend of the birth of Yama and Yamī from Vivasvat. Both are explained at length in Nir. XII. 10-11. Verses 7-9 which contain prayers to Sarasvatī are almost the same as AV. 18. 1. 41-43 and are employed by the *Kauśikasūtra* (81.39) in the cremation rite along with A.V. 7.68. 1-2 and 18.3.25.

3. May the all-knowing Pūṣan, who does not allow cattle to perish and who protects the world, discharge (despatch) you from this (world to the next)! May he (Pūṣan) hand you over to these pitṛs and may Agni hand you over to the gods that know you well. 4. May Puṣan, who is the life of the Universe and who is himself life, protect you! May he who is ahead of you guard you on the way (to heaven)! May God Savitṛ place you in that place where the doers of good deeds went and dwell. 5. Pūṣan knows all these quarters in order; may he take us by (a path) most free from danger! He is the bestower of happiness, full of refulgence, he has all heroes with him; may he (Pūṣan) the wise one go in front of us without committing a mistake! 6. Pūṣan exists (stands) in the forefront of the paths (leading to the world of *pitṛs*), of the paths leading to heaven and of the paths on the earth. He stands facing both the worlds

that are very dear (to all) and he, the knowing one, travels towards and away from both.

RV. 18.1. O Death! Move aside along another path that is your own and different from the Devayāna path. I address you who have eyes and ears. Do not injure our children, do not harm our heroic sons. 2. (O relatives) that are sacrificers! Since you have come obliterating the foot-prints of Death and firmly establishing long life for yourselves, prospering with progeny and wealth, may you be pure and holy! 3. These living (relatives) have turned back separated from the dead; this day our invocation (sacrifice to) of the gods became auspicious. We then went forward for dancing, for laughter (with our children) firmly establishing our long life. 4. I place (here) this barrier (stone) for the (protection of) the living (relatives, son and the like) so that none of them may go this goal (that the departed went). May they live for a hundred prosperous autumns! May they keep off Death by means of the mountain (the stone). 5. O Dhātṛ! Arrange the lives of these (the survivors) in the same way as the days come one after another in proper order, as the seasons follow each other in a proper order, as a younger one does not abandon an elder (a relative) . 6. May you (the survivors) accepting old age attain (long) life, striving in order (of age) whatever your numbers may be; may Tvaṣṭṛ of noble birth and gracious give you here (in this world) a long life to live! 7. Let these women whose husbands are worthy and are living enter the house with ghee (applied) as collyrium (to their eyes). Let these wives first step into house, tearless, without any affliction, and well adorned. 8. O wife (of the dead)! Raise yourself up towards the world of the living (your sons and other relatives); you lie down near one (your husband) who is now lifeless; come! You have kept true to this your wifehood of the husband who held your hand (formerly in marriage) and who loved you passionately . 9. (I) Take the bow from the hand of the departed (Kṣatriya) in order that there may be in us martial vigour, brilliance and strength . May thou (the departed) there and may we here be endowed with heroic sons and conquer here all competing and aggressive enemies! 10. (O departed) approach this mother Earth which is spread wide and is pleasant. May this young one (the Earth) as soft as (wool) to you who have bestowed gifts save you from the lap of Death . 11. O Earth! heave yourself up, do not crush it, be of easy approach and of easy resort to him, and O Earth! cover him (the dead person represented by his bones) just as a mother would cover her son with the fringe (of her garment) . 12. Let the Earth heave itself up and remain firm. Let the pillars in their thousands stand up supporting this house. May these homes (the clods of earth) drop him nourishment! May they become here for all days the shelter for him (the departed represented by bones)! 13. I prop up the earth around you for your sake. May I placing this lump of clay receive no harm! May the pitṛs support (make steady) this post! May Yama provide here seats (or resting places) for you. 14. (The gods) have placed me in the day that will come back (tomorrow) like the feather of an arrow; (therefore,) I restrain backwards (stop) my speech as a person restrains a horse with a bridle.

It should be noted that the word *pitṛ-yajña* actually occurs in *ṚV*. X. 16.10. What does it mean? It has to be remembered that the hymns *ṚV*. X. 15-18 refer to rites immediately on the death of a single person. They are not concerned with rites performed for deceased male ancestors long after their deaths. The anxiety (in X. 15-18) seems to be to make the ancient *pitṛs* (styled Barhiṣadaḥ and Agniṣvāttāḥ in *ṚV.* X. 15. 3-4, 11) favourably disposed to the recently departed spirit. *Havis* (sacrifical food such as boiled rice) was offered to the ancient *pitṛs* (*ṚV*. X.15.11) who were supposed to have partaken of the food offered (X.15.12). The purpose of these Ṛgvedic hymns is entirely different from the purpose of the *mantras* in Tai. S.I. 8.5 (which refer to the *pitṛyajña* performed in Sākamedha). As a matter of fact, three of the *mantras* in Tai. S.I. 8.5 do occur in *ṚV*. X.57. 3-5 and are employed in the *piṇḍapitṛyajña*. There is hardly any reason to suppose that the pitṛyajña in *ṚV.* X. 15. 10 is more ancient than the *piṇḍapitṛyajña*. It is quite possible that both referring as they do to different matters were coeval.

It would be interesting to see how the ceremonies on the death of an Āahitāgni are described in the Śrauta and Gṛhya-sūtras. The *Āśv. Śr. S.* VI. 10 describes what is to be done in case one that has undergone a *dīkṣā* (initiation) for a Soma sacrifice or a *sattra* dies before the sacrifice is finished. It states: "When the Dīkṣita is dead, they take out the body by the *tīrtha*, place it on the spot where it was intended that *avabhṛtha* (bath at the end of a soma or *sattra* sacrifice) was to be taken and deck the body with the decorations that ordinarily are placed on a dead body. They cut the hair (on the head) of the corpse, the hair on the lips, the hair on the body and also pare the nails. They apply paste of *Nalada* (Indian spikenard) to the corpse and throw on it a garland of *naladas*. Some (having cut open the entrails) take out the fecal matter from them and fill them with *pṛṣadājya* (when clarified butter is mixed with curds it is so called). They cut off a portion as wide as the foot of the corpse from a new (unworn) garment and cover the dead body with it in such a way that the fringe is towards the west (the head being placed towards the east) and the feet of the corpse are exposed to view. The portion cut off from the piece of cloth is taken by the sons and the like. The deceased man's *śrauta* fires are placed on the churning sticks (the two *araṇis*), the dead body is taken outside the *vedi* (fire altar) towards its south, fire is produced by attrition and then the body is burnt therewith. After returning from the cremation, they should finish the work of the day. On the next morning, the recitation of the śāstras, the singing of the stotras and the *saṁstavas* (reciting hymns in chorus) should be without repetition and the uttering of the *hiṁ* sound. On the same day before taking up the *grahas* (cups), the priests come out by the *tīrtha*, go round the place of cremation with the right hand turned away (from the place) and sit round it in the following manner viz. the Hotṛ priest sits to the west (of the place of cremation), the *Adhvaryu* to the north, and the sāma priests to the west of the *Adhvaryu* (and the Brahmā priest to the south). Then the sāma priests sing in a low voice the verse beginning with *āyaṁ gauḥa pṛśnirakramīti*. When the singing is finished the hotṛ walks round the place of cremation thrice with his left turned towards the place of cremation and without uttering the syllable *om* recites immediately after the song of the sāma priests the *Stotriya* in a low voice and also the following verses attributed to Yama and Yāmyāyanas (as seers or authors) viz. *ṚV.* X. 14. 7-8, 10-11, X. 16. 1-6, X. 17. 3-6, X. 18. 10-13, X. 154. 1-5. They should finish with *ṚV*. X. 14.12, then collect the charred bones in a jar, take the jar by the way of the *tīrtha* and place it on the seat that was occupied by the deceased scrificer.

Ancestor Worship

Śrāddha is a form of 'ancestor worship', which reflects the gratitude of the living descendants to dead forbears, or the awe and fear inspired by belief in such ancestor's occupying a position, after their death, in which they can confer benefits or cause harm. Blessings and curses from the spirits of departed ancestors are universally held to be potent. Both ideas are reflected in verses on *śrāddha-phala* cited in digests. The idea that doing a *śrāddha* to a particular dead person is a duty imposed by *dharma*, irrespective of its result, is on a higher plane than that which encourages the discharge of the duty by holding out hopes of good as a result. Duty has to be discharged, in the real spirit of *dharma*, without expectation of benefit (*niṣkāmya*). In this sense, one class of *śrāddha*, *viz.*, *kāmya-śrāddha* is an inferior type, and is almost like an incantation. Another type, *viz.*, *vṛddhi-śrāddha or nāndīmukha-śrāddha* does not have this feature. In moments of approaching festivities or joyful occasions, like marriages, or after incidents like the birth of a son, it is right to recall one's obligations to ancestors and conceive them as sharing one's joys as well as sorrows. The prayer that is repeated by every one who does a *śrāddha* for benefits is not to be deemed a *quid pro quo* for doing what one is duty-bound to do, but a recognition of the interest of gods and the departed ancestors in the good (material prosperity) of their living representatives. It is only on the occasion of a *śrāddha* that they are invoked and conceived as *actually* present. Dr. Rajkumar

Sarvadhikari rationalizes ancestor worship, as reflected in the *śrāddha*. "The love we feel for our father and grandfather, the gratitude we owe to them, and the respect we entertain for them, prompt us to honor their memory, when dead; and the act of remembrance takes the form of a solemn offering to the manes of our ancestors. The idea that the spirit of our parents hovers around us, and is gratified by our acts of devotion, takes strong possession of the human mind, when unenlightened by the spirit of philosophy. Both love and devotion bear no analysis as to their nature, and spurn the hard realities which would dissolve the charm. We long to show to the spirits of our ancestors that they live in our memory; we realize their embodied existence by the mind's eye, and forgetful of the surrounding world, we become conscious for a moment of their actual presence, and in the exuberance of our feelings we offer them food and water to allay their hunger and thirst. This is *śrāddha*, the tribute of respect paid to the memory of our ancestors, the food offered to the manes, the solemn feast of the dead."[1]

Like rationalization of idol worship (*arcā-pūjā*,), this explanation misses the chief element in the conception of *śrāddha*, the intense conviction (*śrāddha*) in its actuality and obligatory character. *Śrāddha* is derived from *śrad,* 'truth' 'reality' and *dha* 'to hold'. "It signifies, accordingly, the holding of, or belief in truth." He who does a *śrāddha* must, in propriety, be filled with the conviction of every part of the rite being *real, i.e.* true. Over and over again in the rules for the performance of the different elements of the ritual, this need for implicit belief is stressed. A *śrāddha* is not to be conceived, as is done by Dr. Sarvadhikari, as "emblematic," any more than the worship of an idol is worship, not of a present (but invisible) power, but emblematic worship. Dr. Sarvadhikari's other statement that the idea is unleavened by the spirit of philosophy will also not meet the facts. Among the numerous mediaeval writers on *śrāddha* are some of the acutest Vedāntins and logicians of India. They cannot be held to have had a double personality, a rational and an irrational one, and their acceptance of the practice and theory of *śrāddha* as indicative of a lower personality based on habit and not on reason. The *śrāddha* rite is founded on beliefs in the nature and constitution of the world, such as are exhibited in the great law-books of Manu and Yājñavalkya. The cosmology which it presupposes is also reconciliable with basic concepts of Indian philosophy., *e.g.* the ideas of the nature and relation of the individual soul to the Universal Soul, of *ātman* to Paramātman, of the cosmic law of *karman* and of transmigration and rebirth under the impact of *karman* and of the nature of existence, as well as the doctrine of the puruṣārthas. The ultimate end of all effort is to stop the cycle re-birth by overcoming the drag of *karman*. One who is 'in debt' (*ṛṇī*) is handicapped in the ascent to emancipation (*mokṣa*). Failure to perform appointed or enjoined duties (*karman*) implies being 'in debt'. The debt to one's ancestors is discharged only partially by marrying and having a son to carry on the line, which itself is to ensure the due performance of rites to ancestors in the form of *pitṛ-tarpaṇa* and *śrāddha*. Further, the immanence of the Supreme Being makes homage to any being in effect worship of the Supreme Being. He who worships the *śrāddha-devatāḥ* and the Manes does in reality worship only the Supreme Being. That this might not be forgotten in the formal expressions in use in the *śrāddha,* this idea is explicitly stated, as in the *pariṣecana mantra,* instead of "*oṁ prāṇāya svāhā*" the expression "*oṁ prāṇāya nārāyṇāya svāhā*" is used. In every *śrāddha* its being equivalent to a *śrāddha* done at Gayā, and of the consumer of the offerings being Viṣṇu as Gadādhara is recited. This is done specially by Vaiṣṇavas of South India.

The same idea is expressed in the Purāṇas and the *Mahābhārata*. Mitramiśra cites a verse from the great epic in which Viṣṇu says: "Know that I am the father, the grandfather and the great-grandfather, to whom the ball (*piṇḍa*) is offered, and I am also in the *piṇḍa* so offered."[2] The *Nandīpurāṇa* has a verse identifying each of the three ancestors with one of the triple forms (*trimūrti*) of the Supreme Being. The four *vyūhas* of Viṣṇu, *viz*. Aniruddha, Pradyumna, Samkarṣaṇa and Vāsudeva are each identified with the performer of the *śrāddha* (*kartṛ*) the mane representing his father, that representing his grandfather and the mane representing his great-grandfather. Every householder has to perform the five *yajñas* daily, and one of them is the Vaiśvadeva which the performer of the *śrāddha* cannot omit even on the *śrāddha* day, though he must do it only after the *śrāddha* is finished and before he takes his food. The offerings in this rite consist of the food prepared for his own consumption, and after a part is thrown into the fire as offerings to the gods etc., the remnants (of the *pañcayajñas*) have to be given, according to Āpastamba (II.9.5) to animals, and even to *caṇḍālas* and dogs. "The injunction in the *pañcayajña* to give water to the manes, *bali* to the elementals, offerings to gods, food to guests and the remnants of Viśvedeva to dogs, birds and outcastes, involves two implications, *viz*., permeation of all beings, both in this life and beyond it by the Universal Spirit, and the duty of those to whom hearths and homes have been given to recognize in the common bond a debt to be discharged by daily offerings which commemorate the obligation."[3]

Classes of Śrāddha (II)

Twelve classes of *śrāddha* are named by Viśvāmitra and described by the *Bhaviṣyapurāṇa*. *śrāddhas* to be done daily, and even with oblations of water in case of inability to do them in the normal way, are termed *nityaśrāddhas*. It is one of the five daily sacraments (*pañcayajña*). It is to be offered to the Manes (*pitaraḥ*) in general, and the three immediate ancestors and their wives receive offerings also in them. The type is described as one without Viśvedevas (*Vaiśvedeva-vihīna*). *Naimittika* or occasional types are those for one ancestor alone (*ekoddiṣṭha*) the term applied to the annual *śrāddha* for an ancestor. It is to be done without oblations to gods (*adaivika*), and an odd number of persons should be fed in it. The *Kāmya* or voluntary class is for the attainment of a desired end (*kāmya*), and it should follow the method of the *pārvaṇaśrāddha* or the ordinary ancestral type, in which oblations are offered to maternal as well as to paternal ancestors. The *vṛddhiśrāddha* is offered on occasions of rejoicing, like the birth of a son (*putra-janmādi*). In this type the rite should be in the forenoon, and all movement should be from the left to the right (*pradakṣiṇa*) and the sacred thread should be worn on the left shoulder (*upavīti*) by performer. The *sapiṇḍanaśrāddha* should have four separate vessels (*pātra*) for the three Manes (*pitaraḥ*) and the deceased person (*preta*) respectively, and the last should be dipped into the vessels of the Manes, and for the remainder of the rite the procedure (with *mantras*) of the normal *pārvana* type should be followed. The *pārvaṇa* or 'ancestral' *śrāddha* is done on new-moon days and the two *saṅkrāntis*. It is the commonest form and its performance is enjoined on many special occasions, and is done for both lines of ancestors. When a number of persons, who have to perform a *śrāddha* individually, elect to do it together (*goṣṭhī*), because a number of suitable learned men are gathered together, whose services can be utilized by doing the rite together, the performers can save separate expenditure on the articles needed. This view of Śaṅkhadhara in regard to the purpose and advantage of the *goṣṭhīśrāddha* is accepted by Lakṣmīdhara. The advantage is to the performers. But according to a view cited by Rajkumar Sarvadhikari the combined performance is for the convenience of the assembly of learned Brāhmaṇas gathered together on an occasion, when they have all to do a *śrāddha* with separate cooking of food and gathering of necessary utensils and materials. When a number of Brāhmaṇas are fed in a rite of purification (*śuddhi*) and a *śrāddha* is then done, it is termed *śuddhiśrāddha*. The *karmāṅgaśrāddha* is that done in the preliminary part of an important ceremony like nuptials (*niṣeka*), birth etc. The description "*niṣekakāle some ca*" is interpreted by Lakṣmīdhara as implying both Vedic and Smṛti rites (*śrauta-smārta*). The *daivikaśrāddha* is that done in honor of gods, with special *havis*. The *śrāddha* done when one starts on a pilgrimage to holy places (*tīrtha-yātrā*) or again on re-entering the house on return from the pilgrimage is termed *yātrā-śrāddha*. The last type, known as *puṣṭi-śrāddha* is done when for restoration of health in disease, and before taking medicines or preparing medicine (*rasāyanādi kartavye*), and the Manes are propitiated.

It is noteworthy that Lakṣmīdhara's citations and commentary are reproduced or summarized by later writers like Divākara[4] and Nandapaṇḍita.[5]

Vijñāneśvara (*Yāj.*, I, 218) offers a classification of *śrāddhas*, which is simpler; first into *pārvaṇa* (*i.e.* that done for three ancestors in the line of ascent) and into *ekoddiṣṭa* (*i.e.* that done for only one deceased person); secondly, into three classes, *nitya* (ordinary), *naimittika* (occasional) and *kāmya* (for a special object). The first of these three is to be performed on the happening of a fixed and determinable event, like the New Moon (*amāvāsyā*); the second, *naimittika* is that which has to be done on the occurrence of an uncertain event, like the birth of a son, or an eclipse; and the third, *kāmya* is to be done to attain a desired object or realize a wish. Some of the twelve kinds can be regrouped under this classification, but some will be on the border line, or can go into one class or another.

Time for Śrāddhas (Śrāddhakālāḥ)

One of the tests of a proper *śrāddha* is that it should be performed at a prescribed time or occasion. These are carefully detailed. Even the performance of a *śrāddha*, "when the desire to do it," outside the named times, occurs (*śrāddhaṁ prati ruciḥ*). Gautama (XV.5) declares that the pres-cription of an obligation to do a *śrāddha* at a particular moment, is conditional on the availability of materials, holy Brāhmaṇas and the accessibility, of a holy spot, and that if these are readily available, the performer need not wait for a prescribed occasion to do the *śrāddha* but may do it at once. Lakṣmīdhara interprets the exemption as implying that the performance of the *śrāddha* rite on New Moon days etc., is conditional on the person on whom the duty is laid being able (*śakta*) to do it, by being free from disease (*aroginā*) and commanding the ingredients necessary for the rite (*dravyādiyogin*). If a person is really unable to do the rite, as for example in the absence of these conditions (*asāmarthye*) he does not incur blame or face misfortune (*pratyavāya*) by the involuntary omission.

Certain general rules regarding time are laid down. *śrāddhas*, except those done on the anniversary of a parent or ancestor, must be done during the dark fortnight (*apara-pakṣa*). All *śrāddhas* should be done after mid-day is past (*aparāhṇa*). Where there is freedom to choose the day, the odd (*ayugma*) lunar day (*tithi*) must be chosen. *Śrāddhas*, except when lunar eclipses occur (*uparāga rāhu-darśana*), should not be done at the evening twilight (*sandhyayorubhayoḥ*) or at night because, as Manu warns (III. 280) nights belong to the demons (*rākṣasāḥ*) or when the sun has newly risen (*surye acirodite*). The condition that a *śrāddha* should not be done at the approach of the night will be violated by the *Piṇḍapitṛ-yajña* rule that it should be done when the rays of the setting sun are just visible over the trees Āp.D.S. I. 7.2). As this rite is done on New Moon days, authorities like Karka have considered it to be a subordinate part (*aṅga*) of that rite, while Jaimini declares it to be an independent rite (the *Jaiminisūtra*, IV. 4.19-21) and that it is not a subordinate part of the *darśa* (New Moon) sacrifice. This rite is intended for both the gods and the Manes (*pitaraḥ*) and balls of rice (*piṇḍāḥ*) are offered along with a *yajña* to both. Its nature has given room for much scholastic discussion on the definition of *śrāddha* and the determination of its essential features.

The classical text enumerating the normal occasions on which *śrāddhas* have to be performed is that of Yājñavalkya (I. 217-218), with which Lakṣmīdhara begins his *parva* on *śrāddha-kāla*. These verses enjoin *śrāddha* on *amāvāsyā* (New-Moon days), the eighth (*aṣṭakā*) day of the dark fortnights of two seasons, *hemanta or śiśira* (*i.e.* from the middle of December to the middle of April), the dark fortnight (in the months of Bhādrapada-Āśvina *i.e.* September-October) known as *Mahālaya* or *Pitṛpakṣa*, the two solstices (*ayanadvaya, i.e. dakṣiṇāyana* and *uttarāyaṇa*), the two equinoxes (*viṣuvat i.e.* about the third week of March and September), and the entry of the sun on a sign of the zodiac (*sūryasaṅkramaḥ*), when the moon in the course of the month reaches the seventeenth division of its path known as *vyatīpāta,* and when it is in the asterism Magha while the sun is in the asterism Hasta, (*Gajacchāyā,*) and eclipses of the sun and the moon. The *aṣṭakas* are reckoned by Vijñāneśvara, following Āśvalāyana, as four, whereas Raghunandana, takes them as only three. Lakṣmīdhara cites the *Viṣṇusmṛti* to show that the *aṣṭakas* are only three (*tisro aṣṭakāḥ*). He also adds, on the same authority, three *anvaṣṭakāḥ* and the thirteenth in Proṣṭapada month, and in Māghi, which Lakṣmīdhara interprets as Full-Moon day, and the two seasons of *vasanta* and *śarat* (*i.e.* middle of April to middle of June, and the middle of October to the middle of December). Yājñavalkya enjoins the performance of *śrāddha* during *vṛddhi*, which Aparārka illustrates by the Vedic rites in marriage (*vivāha* etc.) and the birth of a son. He also enjoins the performance, when the mood comes on one to do it (*pratiruciḥ*), and the necessary, Brāhmaṇas and materials for the rite become available. The *Viṣṇusmṛti* describes *vṛddhi* as *abhyudaya*, and adds the natal asterisms of the performer, his son and wife to the occasions when *śrāddha must* be done, for in the words of Prajāpati, "they are the constant (*nityān*) days for the performance of *śrāddhas*." Lakṣmīdhara cites Manu for the duty of doing every month, in the evening following the performance of the New Moon (*amāvāsyā*) *śrāddha,* the *piṇḍapitṛ-yajña* and proceeds to describe the rite itself in detail.

While the performance of *śrāddhas* on all such occasions is an obligation to be discharged without any expectation of a reward, special merit and consequential goods attached to the doing of *śrāddhas* in special periods (e.g. *Mahālaya* or

Pitṛpakṣa), on specified asterisms and *tithis*, and in places like Gaya, and (according to Lakṣmīdhara) Vārāṇasī similar benefits are held to spring from offering of honey, and flesh of certain animals during *śrāddha*. Gayā is pre-eminently the place for the performance of *śrāddha*, and even in the ritual followed for the annual *śrāddhaṣ*, the rite is called "*gayāśrāddha*" and the performer walks in the direction of Gayā. Daily *śrāddha* (*aharahaḥ*) should not be done, according to Nandapaṇḍita, during the *pitṛpakṣa*. Unlike Nandapaṇḍita and later writers, who disapprove of the offering of flesh in *śrāddhas*, and explain the numerous *smṛti* dicta enjoining the offering of flesh of various animals as specially acceptable to the Manes, by declaring that they relate to other cycles of Time and are interdicted in Kaliyuga (ct. the *Śrāddhakalpalatā*, p. 56), Lakṣmīdhara makes no such qualification to the dicta that he cites enjoining the use of meat in *śrāddha*.

Kāmyaśrāddhakālāḥ

The optional nature of *kāmyaśrāddha* makes for selection of an appropriate time for its celebration, as it is not fixed as in the case of the *nitya* and *naimittika* rites. To aid in the selection of the proper time in relation to the benefit aimed at, the results that follow performance on each of the days of the moon's transit (tithi) and asterism are given in the Smṛtis. They are collected in the fourth *parvan* of the *Śrāddhakāṇḍa*. A comparison of the citations will show that different results are indicated by different authorities for doing the rite on the same *tithi* or *nakṣatra*. Thus by doing the *śrāddha* on the first day after full moon (as *śrāddhas* must be done in the dark fortnight only), the benefit according to Kātyāyana is obtaining women (*striyaḥ*), while according to Manu it is male progeny, and according to Āpastamba it is daughters, and wealth according to the *Brahmapurāṇa*. Similarly if it is done on the twelfth lunar day (*dvādaśi*) the results according to Kātyāyana, Manu, Āpastamba, Hārīta, Viṣṇu and Paithīnasi are wealth and grain (*dhana-dhānya*), gold (*jātarūpa*), cattle, prosperity (*śrī*), gold and silver and land respectively. The differences should be treated as indicating any one of the results foreshadowed, and should not be treated as inconsistencies.

Śrāddhadeśaḥ

The efficacy of a *śrāddha* is enhanced by its being done in places of special sanctity. This leads to a collection of dicta-indicating sacred rivers, sands, hills, hermitages etc., numbering about two hundred. The list is illustrative and the number can be increased from the Purāṇas. A *śrāddha* done in such a holy spot is said to be millions of times more efficacious than if done at home. Lakṣmīdhara observes that the catalogue of such sacred spots is to direct the inhabitants of any area to perform *śrāddhas* at the holy place nearest their residence. But in regard to certain sacred streams like Gaṅgā, Yamunā, Sarasvatī and Narmadā, sacred lakes like that at Puṣkara, famous spots like Kāśi, Kurukṣetra and Gayā, the merit in doing śrāddhas in those spots is so transcendent that they must be regarded as specially recommended to all. Gayā and the *akṣaya-vaṭa* (the undying tree) near it are specially recommended for the performance of *śrāddhas*. In fact its value as a *tīrtha* rests almost solely on this aspect. The indication of places of special sanctity for doing *śrāddhas* at, is coupled with a general and specific recommendation to reject certain areas. First, *śrāddhas* should not be done in any area in which the system of *varṇāśrama* has disappeared (*pranaṣṭāśramavarṇa*). Such areas are treated as *mlecchadeśa*, unfit for Aryan occupation. The kingdom of Triśaṅku (to the north of the Mahānadī and south of Kīkaṭa), Kāraskara, Kaliṅga, and the countries to the north of the Sindhu (Indus) river are specifically banned. The warning of Nandapaṇḍita should be noted; the indication of holy *tīrthas* does not necessitate one's doing *śrāddhas* only in those places; they have special sanctity but those who are unable to journey to them can still obtain full merit (*puṇya*) by performing *śrāddhas* in their own places.

Śrāddha Oblations (Havīṁṣi)

The efficacy of a sacrifice is dependent among other things on the use of proper substances as oblations (*havis*). According to Gobhila the chief *havis* is barley (*yava*), and rice if barley is unavailable, and if both are not available, curds, milk, milkgruel (*yavāgu*) and even water may be poured into the fire. There is a specific prohibition against the use of certain cereals like *māṣa* (black-gram), *kodrava* and *gaura*. A verse quoted by Nārāyaṇa, the commentator on the *Āśvalāyana Gṛhyasūtra* (I. 9, 6) mentions ten substances as fit for *havis*, *viz*. milk, curds, gruel (*yavāgu*) clarified butter (*sarpis*), cooked rice and husked rice (*odana-taṇḍula*), flesh (*māṁsa*), sesame oil and water. Manu mentions as a *havis*, (II. 272) the food of hermits (*munyannāni*), which is interpreted by Lakṣmīdhara as forest rice (*nīvāra*). He also mentions *pāyasa*, a liquid preparation of milk and sugar as a *havis*.

In *śrāddhas* there is a *homa* (fire-rite) in which oblations to gods and the Manes are offered in the fire. There is a general prohibition against the use of flesh as a fire oblation. The gods receive their offerings through the fire; and they as well as the Mane through the "mouth of Brāhmaṇas" (*Brahmaṇā-mukha*). The Brāhmaṇa is, according to a Vedic dictum, Fire (Agni-Vaiśvānara), and one should, therefore, sacrifice in Brāhmaṇas's right hand (*Tai. Br.* III. 7, 3). The description by Manu (IV. 117) that the hand of the Brāhmaṇa is his mouth as pointed out by Medhātithi, makes the feeding of a Brāhmaṇa and giving him a *dakṣiṇā* on that account equal.

Accordingly, the term *haviṣyāṇī* in *śrāddha*-ritul includes not only the ordinary oblations to the Fire like clarified butter and cooked barley or rice, but all edible substances that are specially recommended or not interdicted.

Flesh of many kinds seems to have been in use in *śrāddhas* and they are held in *nibandhas* as interdicted in Kaliyuga. In the section on *havis,* Lakṣmidhara has collected many texts to show the relative value as *śrāddha* food (or "oblation" metaphorically) of many kinds of meat, fish and fowl. It is noteworthy that the use of meat is not obligatory. In indicating the relative periods of satisfaction to the Manes by different kinds of food, Manu states that articles used by hermit (*munyannāni*) afford "endless satisfaction" (*ānantya*). This is consistent with Manu's position in regard to flesh-eating.

Madhu (honey) and sesame seed (*tila*) the latter in heaps— are specially recommended for *śrāddha.*

Lakṣmīdhara concludes this section (*parvan*) with the following pointed remarks:

> "Wherever the specification of a special good result (*phalaviseṣa*) is made in regard to a substance to be used as *havis* (food) in a *śrāddha*, it is a recommendation only to those who seek that good result (*guṇa-phalārthinaḥ*). Where no special benefits are specified to a substance, it is to be regarded as a constant factor in *śrāddha* performance and the rite will be regarded as incomplete without its use. Ordinarily the lineaments of a *srāddh*a are completed by the use in it of substances that are commonly recommended, as far as obtainable. If articles so recommended are unobtainable, substances that are not prescribed and at the same time, are not forbidden, may be treated as equal to substances that are prescribed for use. The substitute (*pratinidhi*) of any forbidden substance is equally interdicted, and cannot be used. Where a special benefit *phalaviśeṣa* is attached to a substance, that special benefit is in addition to the completion of the features of a *śrāddha*, and substances like the flesh of cows and buffaloes which are recommended only for special advantage (*phalaviśeṣārthaṁ*), can be used only by those who desire those *special* results and by no others, who only desire to complete a *śrāddha* in

the ordinary way. The meat of buffaloes and the like, which are neither recommended nor rejected, may still be used in the absence of articles that are prescribed for use. The satisfaction of Manes for short or long periods by the use as *haviṣya* of certain substances is great or small according to the nature of the articles prescribed." *Śrāddha* is an enjoined rite and to do it is a duty, to be done irrespective or without the expectation of any reward (*niṣkāmya-karman*), in the true spirit of *dharma*. It is needless, therefore, to go in for such special *havis*. It may be noted that the passages dealing with periods of satisfaction following the use of flesh of many animals, like the rhinoceros, (*khaḍga-māṁsa*), are all brought by Lakṣmīdhara in the *parvan* on *Kāmya-karman*. In the true spirit of *dharma*, a *Kāmya-śrāddha* is an inferior act; *kāmya-śrāddha* follows the ritual but not the spirit of true *śrāddha*.

Things to be Rejected (Varjyāni)

Lakṣmīdhara cites verses to show that black gram, wheat and barley among grains, liquorice (*madhuka*), asafoetida (*rāmaṭa*), camphor, (*karpūra*), jaggery (*guḍa*), rock-salt (*saindhava*) and pepper (*marīca*) are specially valuable for *śrāddha*. Clarified butter should be so served that it overflows the vessels of the Brāhmaṇas who are guests. It may be noted that while buffalo milk is interdicted, buffalo ghee is commended. *Pāyasa*, a preparation of cow's milk, sugared and loaded with cooked wheat or rice, is said by the *Devīpurāṇa* to be equal to all eatables (*sarvānnadaḥ saca proktaḥ yena dattaṁ tu pāyasaṁ*). The passage of the *Mahābhārata* which condemns *hingu* or asafoetida among resinous substance is explained, in relation to its sanction for use in *śrāddha* in other works thus: "It cannot be given in its natural state but is allowable if it forms part of the preparation (in cooking) of something else." Divākara reconciles the prescription and rejection of asafoetida as giving a discretion (*vikalpa*) to the user. He also states that certain authorities construe the interdiction to apply only to white asafoetida (*śvetahiṅgu*). Whatever food substances are ordinarily unallowed are also disallowed for *śrāddhas*. In a *śloka* cited by Aparārka such articles are divided into four classes: *viz.* those which are bad by nature (*jātiduṣṭa*) *e.g.* garlic (*griñjanam*), those which are bad by lapse of time (*kāladuṣṭa*), such as stale food, those which are bad by undesirable or impure contact (*saṁsargaduṣṭa*) and those which cause disgust (*sahṛllekha*). Food substances that emit a foul smell (*durgandha*) or are foamy (*phenila*) like those with hair in them, are forbidden even for ordinary consumption, and much more so in *śrāddha*. Water in tanks dug by outcastes is forbidden for use in *śrāddha*. Food covered with a cloth after cooking cannot be served also. Articles begged specially for the sake of Manes should not be used (p. 54). The wood-apple (*kapittha*) cannot be used for the Manes. Cooked food on which salt is sprinkled after cooking is rejected. Among articles normally allowed which are rejected for *śrāddha* may be mentioned cummin seed (*jīraka*), artificial salt, brinjals (*vārtāka*) and the grey gourd (*kūṣmāṇḍa*). Any article, like a vegetable, of which part has already been used (*upabhukta*) cannot be used in *śrāddha*.

Śrāddha Guests

The devotion (*śraddhā*) which is the essential mental attitude of the person doing a *śrāddha* rite should be reflected in the care with which those asked to preside over the rite, and those who after it is over are treated as guests (*atithayaḥ*). The qualities which are most desirable in persons to be treated as Brāhamaṇas officiating in the ceremony itself, as representing the Manes and Viśvedevas, and the features which should lead to their summary rejection are dealt with in the next four *parvans* (7 to 10). To begin with a close examination of the fitness of the Brāhmaṇa to be invited is enjoined before a *śrāddha* invitee is approached. In the same way persons possessed of the requisite noble ancestry, learning and character are regarded as priceless. As the oficiating Brāhmaṇas the former if of the highest quality are termed "the wealth of the *śrāddha*" (*śrāddha-sampat*). while the presence of even one or two such persons in a row of guests is held to purify the whole line of diners (*paṅkti*), and they are accordingly described as *paṅktipāvānāḥ* (purifiers of guest-rows). When a person claiming to be a Brāhmaṇa presents himself for food or at a sacred place of pilgrimage, to officiate in a rite there the scrutiny of his qualifications (*parīkṣā*) is forbidden, but such scrutiny is specially enjoined in selecting a Brāhmaṇa for a *śrāddha*, by Manu himself (III. 149). Such an examination is necessary, as the merit of the rite is proportional to the learning and sanctity of the invitees who are to represent in it the gods and the Manes. Even in regard to the persons so selected, the competence is not equal for representing the *deva* and *pitṛ-varṇas*. Thus, while a young man, who possesses the qualification is eligible, he should not be put to a *pitṛ-varṇa*. Gautama cites the view of "some" (*eke*) "the age of the guest shall be proportionate to that of the Manes." The commentator on Gautama explains the dictum thus: in honor of the father a young man is to be invited, in honor of the grand-father an old man, and in honor of the great-grandfather a very old man." Lakṣmīdhara gives this explanation of the rule: when the father etc., died in old age, and a representative as guest has to be chosen, he should be equal in age to the deceased. Maskarin, however, limits the rule only to the rite of *sapiṇḍī-karaṇa*. Among persons of equal qualifications the older, and among persons of equal age the poorer are to be preferred for a *śrāddha*, according to Āpastamba. Between persons of equal good birth (*kula*) and learning (*śruta*), he who is uncovetous should be preferred, or he who has stayed longest in the house of his teacher (*ciravāsī*).

The scrutiny should be not merely of the personal equipment of the person but of his ancestry for at least three generations (*dūrādeva parīkṣeta*). Manu forbids invitations to relations or friends, when other qualified persons are available, as that would be making use of a *śrāddha* to gain friendship or strengthen it (III. 138-142). Learning and birth are neutralized by the practice of astrology, according to a verse of Yama cited by Lakṣmīdhara. Like the rejection of the Vedic expert, who makes a living by teaching the Veda for money, this is a rejection of a professional element.

A *śrotriya* explained by Kullūka as one who has studied the *Sāmaveda* alone, is most eligible. A good choice benefits the giver, the guest, the gods and the Manes. Those who have mastered the first three Vedas are the most eligible. Such terms indicating qualifications as *trisauparṇaḥ, Jyeṣṭ-hasāmagāḥ* and *pañcāgniḥ* are explained by Lakṣmīdhara in less exacting terms than by Hemādri. A verse of Bṛhaspati (which is an *arthavāda*) states that the three immediate ancestors are respectively placated by persons having qualifications in the three Vedas respectively. Śātātapa makes a special plea for the master of the fourth Veda also, which is significant, as it deals with spells and incantations and is usually looked down on. Gautama lays stress on personal appearance also (*rūpasampanna*). Good disposition (*sādhu*) is emphasized by Vasiṣṭha. One under pupillage cannot be invited to officiate. Ascetics (*yati*) and one who is an expert in Yoga (*yoga-vit*) are suggested by Vasiṣṭha and the *Matsyapurāṇa*. If all others fail, even close relations like the grandson, father-in-law, the maternal uncle and the son-in-law (*viṭpati*) and a teacher may be invited. Ordinarily they are not to be invited.

Exceptionally Qualified Guests

Persons of exceptional learning, good birth or personal sanctity and strictness in adherence to the enjoined duties are deemed to radiate all round them a purifying influence, which extends to all fellow guests sitting with them in a row (*paṅkti*). One who is so designated is thus the exceptionally superior Brāhmaṇa. Naturally such a person will be an admirable asset for a *śrāddha*, if he does not come under one of the excluded categories, in spite of his personal merit. Thus among those excluded from *śrāddha* participation are persons of the same *gotra* such as being of the same *gotra* or near relations. But they can be in the wider category of guests. Conversely, if no others are available with the high qualities described to preside over the *śrāddha*, one with less qualification can be invited rather than allow the *śrāddha* to fail. But such persons are not of the class of *paṇktipāvanas*. Lakṣmīdhara's devoting a long *parvan* to the high qualities of this class of Brāhmaṇa is following the great smṛtis. It is indirectly of value as showing the exalted ideals kept before the Brāhmaṇa, who is not to depend only on his birth, and not personal merit, to find casual feeding, and become a social parasite.

Some of the qualities that are indicated may be noted : a householder to be of this class should scrupulously follow the regimen of his *āśrama*. Thus he should not fail to approach his wife in her fertile period (*ṛtu*) (*ṛtukālābhigāmin*). His mother must have been married when she was a *gaurī, i.e.* not over eight years of age at marriage. Erudition includes the Nītiśāstra. As a householder he should not care for gifts (*pratigraha-nisneha*). The Sannyāsin and the Yogin are exalted above those of equal qualifications. Moral qualities are not less vital than birth, learning and the performance of sacrifices and enjoined ritual to complete one's qualification for being counted in this exalted class.

Persons to be Excluded from Śrāddha, Varjyāḥ

Certain persons must be excluded from invitation to officiate as Brāhmaṇas in *śrāddhas*. They are termed *varjyāḥ*. Certain persons are regarded as so bad that their presence in a line of guests pollutes the line, (*paṅktidūṣakāḥ*) and they are styled persons unfit to sit in the line (*apāṅkteyāḥ*). There is a small element of difference between the two. Certain persons, who are otherwise eligible, if their birth, learning and character are considered, may have to be rejected ordinarily from invitation to officiate in *śrāddha*. Thus, Manu prohibits the feeding (*i.e.* as Brāhmaṇa) of the friend and the foe and explains that their presence will make the ceremony futile. So are near relations, like the maternal uncle, the son-in-law and others, as well as persons of the same *gotra* and *pravara*, according to a verse of the *Kūrmapurāṇa* cited in the *śrāddha-candrikā,* for according to Gārgya (cited in Hemādri) "*śrāddha* oblation (*havis*) is like a virgin (*kanyā*)" *i.e.* not to be given to one of the same *gotra* or *pravara* (*yathā kānyā tathā haviḥ*). One otherwise excellent, whose wife is pregnant (*garbhiṇī*) cannot be invited to officiate. A person regarded as a *paṅktidūṣaka* or *apāṅkteya* is of course unfit to officiate as a chief guest in a *śrāddha*. Thus, one whose wife is in menstruation, (*raktāmbarā*) is among the latter according to Lakṣmīdhara; this follows the rule that for a religious rite or sacrifice husband and wife must officiate together, and if one is disqualified (as a menstruous wife will be) the other cannot officiate. But in a *śrāddha*, the ceremony, must go on, even if the wife of the officiant is impure.

This is the practice. Not only does a *paṅktidūṣaka* pollute a line of guests by sitting with them but even if he sees them eating they become polluted and must stop eating. (Man., III. 176, p. 96). Every *paṅktidūṣaka* is ineligible for a *śrāddha*; but every person who is excluded (*varjya*) from a *śrāddha* is not a *paṅktidūṣaka*. Some of those excluded from *śrāddha* guestship may be named. The Brāhmaṇa who does not study the Veda (*anadhīyānaḥ*), who follows a low occupation (*hīnavṛtti*) *e.g.* living by snaring fowl, beasts or by fishing, who is the servant of a Śūdra or a king' or is the village beggar (*grāmayācaka*), who "sells the Veda" (*i.e.* teaches it for a fee), who teaches the Veda to those whose *upanayana* has not been done, who does not perform the prescribed fire rites or who makes a living by practising jugglery or "magic" (*indra-jāla*). One who suffers from any of the eight sin-caused diseases" (*aṣṭa-pāparogāḥ*) must be dropped. The eight are stated as insanity (*unmāda*), skin-disease (leucoderma and leprosy), consumption (*rājayakṣman*), asthma (*śvāsa*), diabetes (*madhu-prameha*), *bhagandara* (dropsy and *aśmari*).

The idea is that they result from evil action in a past birth. Like birth in a low *varṇa* or in animal or vegetable form, such diseases reflect past bad *karman* or deeds. It is regarded as best to avoid contact with the persons so suffering. They are objects of compassion but not thereby entitled to be admitted to *śrāddha* or *śrāddha-paṅkti*. The dumb, the congenitally blind person, the deformed, the cripple, the person who has more or fewer *aṅgas* (limbs) are also excluded. Such persons are helpless. Those who are moral derelicts stand in a different footing; their rejection is demanded by their bad conduct. The adulterer, the person who profits by his wife's adultery, he who marries before his older brethren (*parivetṛ*) the unchaste acolyte (*avakīrṇi*), the drunkard (*madyapa*), the husband of a Śūdra wife (*śūdrāpati*), the usurer (including in it the black-marketer), the miser, the habitual slanderer, the betrayer of friends (*mitradruḥ*), the Brāhmaṇa who deserts his parents, wife and children and preceptor, the thief, the *vrātya* one who has passed the maximum age without *upanayana* and the open athiest (*nāstika*). The six types of sex impotents (*klībāḥ*) are excluded on the same ground as the persons suffering from "diseases caused by past sins." The person who sails over the sea, and the sorcerer are also to be rejected.

The Unfit for Commensality

The list of persons declared unfit to sit in a dinner row overlaps that of the excluded persons. It is more extensive in one sense. Among this class are, for instance, persons who aim at kingship (*rāṣṭrakāmāḥ*), because a Brāhmaṇa cannot be a king, the cattle dealer (*paśuvikrayin*), the gambler, the perjured witness (*kūṭasākṣī*) the anchorite who has renounced the monastic life (*pravrajyāvasitaḥ*) the reviler of parents and wife, the person whose teacher is his own son (*sutācāryaḥ*) the exasoboteur (*parasvānāṁ nāśakaḥ*), the hater of the Veda and of Brāhmaṇa (*brahmadviṣ*), the son who carries on a dispute with his father (*pitrā-vivadamānaḥ*), the astrologer and the carrier of corpses for money (*pretaniryātakaḥ*). Among these condemned persons are the professional temple priest (*devalaka*), the *purohita* (domestic priest, who works for money, the seller of men (*i.e.* slave dealer), the outcaste (*patita*) and the person who acts as priest to outcastes (*patita-purohita*) and the astrologer (*jyotiṣaka*). Persons of questionable origin like the son of an unmarried girl (*anūḍhāputra*), and the son of a remarried woman (*paunarbhavaḥ*). The lascivious husband is condemned equally with the husband who does not approach his wife during *ṛtu*. The Brāhmaṇa who has taken as an additional wife a Śūdra woman, and begets a son from her, while neglecting his caste-consort, is rejected along with persons whose ancestry is unknown (*avijñātapūrvāḥ*). Among those who are condemned as unworthy of commensality is he who cooks for himself alone (*i.e.* who does not entertain guests or makes food to be offered to the gods and Manes) and who forgets the Veda he has learned by neglecting it (*adhītavismṛta*). A Brāhmaṇa who lives a whole year depending for water on a well in the village is to be rejected as slipping from his *varṇa*. The Brāhmaṇa profiteer is also rejected. The catalogue is not exhaustive and digests add to the number of persons who are undesirable as guests. For example, the *Karmanvipākasamgraha* is quoted in the *śrāddhakalpalatā* for excluding from *śrāddha* repasts the person who corresponds to the modern elementary school teacher (*akṣarapāṭakaḥ*), the person suffering from elephantiasis (*sthūlacaraṇaḥ, sthūlapādin*) and the person whose ears have not been bored (*aviddhakarṇaḥ*), while Sumantu excludes *paustika*, the seller of books (*pustaka vikretā*) *i.e.* the professional bookseller. He who obstructs a gift (*pradāna-nivārakaḥ*) is among those excluded by Yama, and it must be taken more as a warning to persons not to hinder acts of munificence than as technical exclusion from *śrāddha*. Learning from books has been looked down upon in ancient India, and the sale of books encourages book learning.

Nimantraṇa, Nimantraṇaniyamāśca

The Brāhmaṇas who are to officiate in a *śrāddha* should be invited to do so in a due form. After they accept the invitation they have to observe certain inhibitions. The formal invitation is termed *nimantraṇa*, and the term is popularly used as a synonym for *śrāddha*, showing the importance attached to it as an essential feature of the rite. The invitation proper is preceded by an intimation of the approaching rite, *nivedana*. The invitation has to be made the preceding day, but if that is not possible, it should be given on the morning of the *śrāddha* itself. It has to be made with due solemnity, after personal purification by baths etc. (*śuciḥ*), in a spirit of devotion and with a controlled and calm mind. The invitees should have the necessary birth, bodily, personal and ethical qualifications. The number to be invited depends on one's ability to feed a number, but it should be an uneven number (*ayugmān*). Normally the invited persons should not be of the same *gotra* and *pravara* as that of the performer of the *śrāddha* (*śrāddha-kṛt*). Ascetics, who come unexpectedly in search of cooked food as alms (*bhikṣārthaṁ*), about the time, may be "fed", *i.e.* utilized in the *śrāddha* ceremony. A dual number of persons should be invited to take the place of the "gods" (Viśvedevas and an odd number to take the place of the Manes; *i.e.*, if the number invited is only three, one will be set apart for the Manes, and two for the "gods". In South Indian practice, one of the latter is set apart for the Viśvedevas and the other for Viṣṇu, who is styled "*śrāddha-saṁrakṣaka*," the protector of the *śrāddha*. The invitees should be given branches for cleaning their teeth. The house in which the ceremony is to be done should be washed and daubed with cowdung. Āpastamba rules that there should be three invitations to the same person, the first on the day previous, the second on the morning of the day of the rite, and the third when the invitees are to be called to sit for food; for, "in *śrāddhas* everything should be done thrice (*triḥprāya*)." The invitee's right knee should be clasped by the inviter, who should say "You are invited by me" and then he must make the invitee hear the rules he must observe (*niyamān śrāvayet*): "You should observe and so should I personal purity scrupulously and we should be continent during the night." The Manes hear the invitation and in aerial form eat the food along and then return to their illustrious world unseen by mortals. The performer should starve till the ceremony is finished (Āp.Śr.S. on p. 106). The invitees, after accepting the invitation, should "eat with restraint" (*niyatāhāra*), observe sex resraint (even if their wives are "in season"), be truthful, avoid any travelling or physical exertion, abstain from conjugality (even embracing their wives), and conversing gaily and, suspend Vedic study, and not accept food from any one but the inviter till the rite is over, for, the moment the invitation is accepted, the Manes enter the bodies of the invitees (*pītaraḥ-samviśanti*). One who has accepted an invitation cannot, at the peril of losing his merit acquired in a year, accept another invitation. A host who fails to honor an invitee is reborn as an animal. The invitee should not delay his attendance (*na cirakārin*).

Among the Manes, different sets are to be honored or invoked (*āḥvāna*) by members of the different *varṇas*. Thus the *Somapa* group (*gaṇa*) are those for Brahmaṇas, the *Havirbhuj* for Kṣatriyas, the *Ājyapa* for Vaiśyas and the *Sukalins* for Śūdras. They are respectively the children of Bhṛgu (*Kavi*), the Havirbhujs of Aṅgiras, the Ājyapas of Pulastya, and the Sukalins of Vasiṣṭha, four of the ten primeval sages created by Manu (the *Manusmṛti*, I. 35). Other groups of the Manes, *viz.*, the Agnidagdha, the Anagnidagdha, the Kāvya, the Barhiṣads, the Agniṣvātta, and the Saumya are to be invoked for *śrāddhas* by Brāhmaṇas alone (*Man*. III. 199). A different enumeration by Hārīta is also given by Lakṣmīdhara. He concludes the parva with the remark that at the time of invocation the deceased ancestors are to be mentally contemplated in the forms of the Manes appropriate to the *varṇa* of the performer of the *śrāddha*.

Preliminary Rites on Śrāddha day

A *śrāddha* must be done only in the afternoon of the day on which its performance is due, and must begin at *kutapa-kāla*, *i.e.* the 8th *muhūrta* of the day, the duration of a *muhūrta* being 48 minutes, or two *nāḍis*. This and the next four *muhūrtas* are best for doing the *śrāddha*. *Kutapa* is explained etymologically by the *Mitākṣarā* (I. 226) as sin (*kum*) killer (*tapati*).

The invited Brāhmaṇas must arrive in the morning, with their nails pared and hair shaved, and must be received ceremoniously by the performer of the rite. They must be made to stand on *maṇḍalas,* smeared with cowdung, and offered a welcome with the words *svāgata* have their feet well washed with cowdung, ghee and water, and be given *arghya*. After the reception, they must be given oil (*añjana*) for their bath. The reception should take place outside the house in which the *śrāddha* is to be done. When the guests return after their oil-bath they must again be received in the same manner and let into the house, where the ceremonies will begin. A third formal reception of the kind must take place before the guests are taken inside to sit for their food. In common practice nowadays, the three are combined into one, and made to come on the occasion last specified. The guests, it may be noted should have finished their morning *kriyās* before arriving at the performer's house. Meantime, the performer should have got ready for the ceremony, by bathing, wearing pure and white clothing, purifying himself with *ācamana* etc., and finish the morning rites before the fire, along with his wife. The place where the *śrāddha* has to be done must be swept, cleaned and well-rubbed down with cowdung and white clay (*śveta-mṛt*). According to the *Viṣṇusmṛti* the guests must be first received in the forenoon if the ceremony falls in the white fortnight (*śuklapakṣa*) and in the afternoon if it is in the dark fortnight (*kṛṣṇapakṣa*). Sesame seed should be scattered all over the places used, as it is credited with the power to drive away demons (*asura*).

Much space is devoted in special treatises on *śrāddha* to such matters as the selection of a suitable place for doing the rite, the kinds of *darbha* or *kuśa* grass to be collected and their form, the other ingredients or instruments for the rite, the materials of which the cooking vessels must be made, as also the vessels in which the food should be served (*pariveṣaṇa-pātrāṇi*), or eaten (*bhojanapātrāṇi*), the sorts of flowers, incense, scents, unguents, the timber of which the planks on which the guests are to be seated may or may not be made, their proper covering (*āsanāni*) the kinds of cloth for presentation, the type of umbrellas to be given, etc. The rules in regard to these will apply to all sacred rites, and are accordingly omitted by Lakṣmīdhara. What is so collected (*sampādita*) for a *śrāddha* is *śrāddha-sampat*. Manu catalogues these as the afternoon, sesame seed, *darbha* grass, a proper place for celebration (*vastu*) and its being made fit, a spirit of liberality in dispensing food etc. (*sṛṣṭiḥ*), the proper cooking of tasty food (*mṛṣṭiḥ*) and eminent Brāhmaṇas are the real 'riches' (*sampadaḥ*) of *śrāddha*. As regards the place in which the rite should be done, Lakṣmīdhara cites texts to condemn the performance in places not owned by the performer, as the Manes of the owner of such a place get the merit of the rite. Forests, mountains, rivers and similar places that are in individual ownership are commended as fittest, where one's own house is unavailable. The supply of seats to the invitees should be accompanied by gifts of the skin of the black antelope (*ajina*) for covering the seats. Those invited to officiate as 'gods' should be seated facing north, and be supplied with *darbhas* in pairs, while those who represent the Manes should be seated facing south and be given single *darbha*. They should be so seated as not to touch one another. For the representation of the gods, the selected invitees should be in pairs, and in odd numbers for those that represent the Manes, as they have to represent three generations of ancestors. They should observe silence, when seated, for breach of the rule will mean the loss of the *śrāddha*. Haradatta lays down that only Brāhmaṇas should be fed at *śrāddha*, not even learned Kṣatriyas possessing the requisite learning, purity, etc. Hārīta justifies the placing of the representative of the gods (*viśvedevāḥ*) facing north on the ground that they are the protectors of the *śrāddha* (*rakṣakāḥ*) and so should face the Manes whom they are to guard. If only one Brāhmaṇa is available, he should be made to represent the Manes, and the place of the gods should be occupied by *darbha* and the food (*naivedya*) should be placed in front of it.

Hospitality in Śrāddha

Casual hospitality in a *śrāddha* should be extended to Brāhmaṇas who come as guests, and particularly to ascetics accompanied by acolytes (*bramacāriṇaḥ*). They are regarded as 'Lords' (*i.e.* owner) of all cooked food' (*pakvānna svāminau*), for neither stage (*āśrama*) permits its members to cook food for themselves but compels them to seek it from householders. Such casual guests whether ascetics or householders should be fed with the permission of the invited *śrāddha* guests, according to Manu.

Those to be Kept Away from Śrāddha

The purity of the preparations and the ritual of the *śrāddha* are held to be ruined by contact or even being seen or touched by certain animals and persons, and they are accordingly to be kept away (*dūrataḥ parivarjayet*). Among human beings those who are not to be allowed to touch, or see the food being prepared, served or eaten or witness, even from a distance of the fire rite of the ceremony, are outcastes, eunuchs, persons suffering from 'sinful disease' (*pāparoga*), the husband of a *vṛṣalī* (an elastic term which includes many types of women), the Śūdra, the atheist (*nāstika*), and the *nāgna* (a term interpreted as meaning 'those who have abandoned the Vedas (*vedaparityāginaḥ*), like Jainas and the like, an adulteress (*puṁścalī*) and a woman in her courses (*rajasvalā*). Certain animals are also not to see or in any way contact the *śrāddha* food, ingredients, guests, etc., *e.g.*, village swine, cocks, dogs, cats, and crows. The list is to caution the performer of a *śrāddha* to have the ceremony done in a place in which such animals or persons will not come near.

Some Śrāddha Technique

A short chapter is devoted to the indication of some important rules (*vidhi*) to be observed in different types of *śrāddha*. This is preliminary to the consideration of such types later. First, as to the inclusion of the *Viśvedevas* in the invocation and worship. The daily *śrāddha,* the *ekoddiṣṭa* (for one person) at the eleventh day after death should be done without the Viśvedevas; all other *śrāddhas* should include the gods, as without the 'gods' the demons rob the *śrāddha*. In a *śrāddha* of the gods (*daiva-śrāddha*), nothing should be used without first having water sprinkled on it with due mantras and articles should be taken from the north side of the sacrificial enclosure and thrown to the south of it. To the twice-born the rite in honor of the Manes is more important than that in honor of the gods but offerings made first to the gods are not indicative of the relative importance of the two, but show that it is to fortify the *śrāddha* by obtaining the protection of the gods, (Manu) for the demons will 'devour' the *śrāddha* which is without such protection (Manu). Brāhmaṇas who are to represent the Viśvedevas must be invited, received and fed first but dismissed after those who represent the Manes (Medhātithi). In rites to the Manes, the sacred thread (*yajñopavīta*) should be over the right shoulder, and the circling must be from the right to the left (*apasavya*). In homage to the Viśvedevas, the right knee should be bent, and in that to the Manes the left knee.

Bṛhaspati enumerates the Viśvedevas as ten. Though addressed collectively, they are individually approached for certain types of *śrāddha*. Thus, Kratu and Dakṣa are invoked in *Iṣṭi,* Satya in *Nāndi,* Vasu in *Naimittika,* and in the annual *Naimittika,* in which the *śrāddha* is in honor of one ancestor (*ekoddiṣṭa*) but is done with the Fire rite as in *Pārvaṇa-śrāddha,* both Kāla and Kāma, in *Kāmyaśrāddha* Dhuri and Rocana and in the *Pārvaṇaśrāddha,* Purūravaḥ and Mārdrava. They may all be invoked with the words: Let the great ones come, the grantors of wishes, the Viśvedevas! They who are brought to this *śrāddha* may they be attentive *sāvadhānā.*

Invocation and Incidental Rites

The gods and the Manes have to be invoked after the guests have arrived and been ceremoniously received, seated and decorated. The procedure of these preliminary acts is next described, with appropriate citations from Smṛtis, Sūtras and Purāṇas. The object of quoting nearly the same rules from different Sūtras is to meet the rule that every performer should follow the rules laid down in the *sūtra* of his own branch (*śākhā*) of the Veda. The guests are made to stand on a *maṇḍala* (circles drawn on the ground) with powdered grain, white earth, ashes or stones. *Arghya* and water for washing the feet (*pādya*) are to be offered to the standing guests, who are then to be taken to the place of performance of *srāddha* and given seats on which barley or sesame seed have been sprinkled after they have sipped water (*ācamanīya*). The *Mitākṣarā* (I. 229) notes the procedure, which Lakṣmīdhara also cites, of the seats of both the *devas* and the Manes being covered with *kuśa.* The performer should then mutter the *gāyatrī mantra*, after obtaining permission to do so from the guests (*tadanujñayā*). He must also repeat the *mantra* beginning with the words 'To the gods and to the Manes,' which was framed by Brahmā, the repetition of which thrice at the beginning and the end of the *śrāddha* and in the placing of the rice-ball (*piṇḍa*) is efficacious. The Viśvedevas should be first invoked, after seeking and receiving from the guest or guests, who represent them, the permission to do so. This invocation is to be through prescribed *mantras.* As a preliminary rite, sesame seed should be scattered all round with a *mantra* calling on the demons, who may disturb the *śrāddha* to flee. The *mantra* used for this purpose is held to drive them away.

After the Brāhmaṇas are seated, the performer should ask first for permission to invoke the Viśvedevas. This is granted in a set form of words. He should then invoke the gods with the *ṛk* beginning *Viśvedevāḥ āgata* and the Smṛti hymn beginning *āgacchantu mahābhāgāḥ*. This should be done with the sacred thread on the left shoulder (*upavīti*). He should then offer *arghya* to the gods (through their representative) or representatives, by pouring water on their palms, the water coming from a vessel in which a *pavitra* or ring of *darbha* had been placed with barley in the water. The *ṛk* beginning *śanno devīrabhiṣṭaye* (*ṚV.* X. 9.4) should be recited when this is being done, and when barley (*yava*) is put in, with the *mantra* beginning *yavo'si*. He should repeat the *mantra* (the *Taittirīya Brāhmaṇa* II. vii. 15) beginning *yā divyā āpaḥ* when pouring water for the *arghya*. The gods, during worship, are given sandal paste, scents, (*gandha*), flowers (*mālya*), incense (*dhūpa*) and a lamp which is lit is waved before them (*dīpa*). Each of these acts is preceded by an appropriate *mantra*. The Brāhmaṇas representing Viśvedevas should be shown these honours also.

Only certain perfumes, flowers and incense can be used in *śrāddha*. Sandal, saffron, camphor and also heart-wood (*agaru*) are alone allowed by the *Viṣṇusmṛti*, cited in the *Mitākṣarā* (I. 232). Red flowers should not be used nor flowers with bad smell. Certain flowers like those of the *arka* plant must not be used. For the *dhūpa* incense animal perfume should not be used. Lamps filled with clarified butter or sesame oil are to be used for *dīpa*. The representative of the Viśvedevas should be given *darbha pavitra* or *darbhas* for making the ring. A similar procedure is to be followed in regard to the representatives of the Manes, but the sacred thread must be worn on the right shoulder and all movements must be *apradakṣiṇa, i.e.* from the right to the left, and the left hand should be used instead of the right for the *camasa*, and the water in the vessel should be poured into the palm of the *pitṛ-varga* through the *pitṛ-tīrtha* gap of the right palm into the outstretched palm of the invitee. Each generation of the Manes is to be called by designation, and *arghya, pādya,* etc., should be offered to each individually, even if only one representative officiates for all three generations of Manes. Sesame seed should be put into the water thus used, instead of barley, as for Viśvedevas. The Manes are to be invoked with the *ṛk* beginning *uśantastvā*. The vessel in which the water is kept should be turned down, after the pouring of water in both cases. The vessel so turned face down should not be lifted up, because according to Śaunaka the Manes stay within the vessel, and the food of the *śrāddha* is rendered unfit for being eaten by the Manes, if the water vessel is lifted back into position.

The presentation of unbleached (*ahata*) pairs of cloth to all the guests is recommended as necessary.

In regard to the vessels, broken vessels should not be used. Likewise for cooking the *śrāddha* food, earthen vessels are prohibited. Silver and gold vessels among metals are commended, especially the former, as well as vessels made of specified kinds of wood. Gifts of kind to the Manes are held in high esteem. The sacred string (*yajño-pavīta*) is one of them. A water vessel (*kamaṇḍalu*), pairs of wooden sandals (*pāduka*) fans (*vyajana*), umbrellas (*chatra*), etc. A long list of other gifts is given on pp. 158-9, but the gift of apparel is regarded as the best, because without clothing one cannot do any rite to gods or Manes. He who fails to present clothes to the guests at *śrāddha*, will become a *piśāca* (demon) after death, according to a verse cited by the *Śrāddhakalpalatā*. The cloth presented should not be torn, dirty, previously bleached, or colored. If gold or silver vessels are not possible, vessels of copper or brass (*taijasa*) may be presented. Earthen pots can on no account be presented.

Cooking Utensils

Mitramiśra deals with the vessels that may or may not be used for cooking food for *śrāddha*. He permits vessels of baked earth to be used, if they are new and strong, *i.e.* will not get broken during cooking. All broken vessels are barred, and so are all made of iron (*kālāyasa*). Wooden plates are commended for keeping cooked rice. Iron is held to be specially bad for rites to Manes. Iron knives used for cutting up fruit and vegetables must be kept in the kitchen only (*mahānasa*) and not be brought within sight of the Brāhmaṇas. The use of vessels of copper for cooking in *śrāddhas* is commended.

The Burnt Offering

Making burnt offerings in the fire, with the permission of the Brāhmaṇas invited, and before they are fed is an essential part of the *śrāddha*, and may be regarded as important as the feeding of the Brāhmaṇas. The ritual is directed to be that of the *Piṇḍapitṛyajña* which is towards sunset on New Moon days, after the *śrāddha* of the day is finished. This rite is described as sacrifice to the Manes (*pitṛ-yajña*). As part of the *pārvaṇa* or annual *śrāddha* it precedes the feeding. The oblation (*haviṣya*) should be of resh cooked food (rice or barley) soaked in clarified butter. The fire-sticks to be used should be of *palāśa* wood, and their tips should be dipped in *ghee* before they are thrown into the fire. In works on *śrāddha-prayoga* the Fire in which the oblations should be thrown is stated to be the *gṛhyāgni*, the fire kindled on marriage (which is also known as *aupāsanāgni*, *aupasada, āvasathya, vaivāhik, śālāgni and smārtāgni*), according to Aparārka. The three *śrauta* fires are the *āhavanīya,* the *gārhapatya*, and the *dakṣiṇāgni*. He who has kindled the *śrauta* fire (*āhitāgni*) alone should do it in *dakṣiṇāgni*, and not every one as laid down in the passage from the *Brāhmapurāṇa*. They should do it in the *gṛhyāgni* (the nuptial fire). The *Vāyupurāṇa* (p. 168) even allows it to be done in the *laukikāgni* or ordinary cooking fire. The *Matsyapurāṇa* gives the option to do the rite either in *dakṣiṇāgni* or in the *āvasathya* (or *gṛhyāgni*) which has been specially kindled for the purpose (*praṇīte, i.e. pṛthak-kṛte*). The cooked mess to be used as oblation should be free of *salt* and condiments (*vyañajana*). According to Āśvalāyana the performer should wear the sacred thread on the right shoulder (*apasvya*) or *prācīnāvīti*. Kātyāyana states that the fire offering should be made with the thread on the left shoulder (*upavīta*) facing east, if it is for the gods, and it may also be done with the thread on the right shoulder, facing south. Lakṣmīdhara explains that the option given means that one must follow whatever is laid down in regard to this in his own *Gṛhyasūtra*.

If a fire is absent (*agnyabhāve*) the oblation of food may be put into the palm of the Brāhmaṇa, with the same mantras as used in the fire oblation. The learned Brāhmaṇa is the fire. The "absence of the fire" (*agnyabhāva*) is explained by Lakṣmīdhara as the performer not having either the *śrauta* or *smārta* fire prescribed for the rite. Āparārka construes the expression as meaning that the *kartṛ* has no wife *i.e.* is a widower or bachelor. Alternatives to placing the *havis* on the right palm of the Brāhmaṇa are given. They include throwing the oblation into water. The unused portion of the *havis* should be kept covered in a vessel, and is to be used later for being mixed with the food served to the Brāhmaṇas. The Brāhmaṇa in whose palm the oblation is placed is not to eat it!

The fire having been got ready with the prescribed rites for that ceremony, (*idhmamādhāya*) the *kartṛ* offers successive oblations with the words To Yama and Aṅgiras alone with the father, *svāhā*, to Agni who carries the oblation (*kavyavāhanā*), *svāhā*, and to Soma along with the father, *svāhā*. The offering should be coupled with the specification of the ancestor to whom it is being offered also, namely the father, the grandfather and the great-grandfather. It has already been stated that among the Manes, the Somapas are for Brāhmaṇas as also the Kāvyas, Barhiṣadas and the Agniṣvāttas. Hārīta states that an offering to Soma along with the father pleases the *Somapa* Manes. The offering to Yama and Aṅgiras pleases the elders of Yama, the Barhiṣads, and the Agniṣvāttas.

The *Viṣṇusmṛti* prescribes the recitation of the first five, the second five and third *ṛks* of the *rākṣoghna-mantras* given in the *Kāṭhaka* for *nāndīśrāddha, kāmyaśrāddha* and terminal *sapiṇḍīkaraṇaśrāddha* respectively.

Baudhāyana directs that the giving away of the *piṇḍas* (balls of rice) should be done immediately after the fire rite, and what remains after the *piṇḍas* have been made should be given to birds, because of the vedic statement that Manes move about in the form of birds. The fire rite should be done with the sacred thread worn on the left shoulder, according to Kātyāyana. Gobhila directs the oblations to the Manes to be done *prācīnāvīti*. The *havis* (material for oblation) should be made of the same cooked rice that is to be served to the Brāhmaṇas. Govindānanda states that the option must be exercised according to one's own *Gṛhyasūtra*.

The Serving of Food

The feeding of Brāhmaṇas who represent the gods and the Manes is the chief rite in a *śrāddha*, and all others lead to it. The devotion of devout and pious mind which is indicative of *śrāddha* is to be shown in the serving of the food. The *kartṛ* should be calm, free from anger, serve without haste, neither laugh nor weep when the food is being served, nor ask if the food is relished or whether any food may be brought, nor speak any falsehood when the food is being served. If crows or kites (*śyena*) come in, they are not to be driven out, as the Manes may have taken their form. But as crows cannot see the food being served, the rule of serving the food and doing the *śrāddha* in an enclosed (*samvṛta*) place is intelligible. The thumb of the Brāhmaṇa should be grasped by the *kartṛ* and it should be taken round and made to touch all the food that is served already on the plate, beginning with ghee. Ghee should not be put into the hand of the eater; cold rice should not be served. Food should not be served in iron ladles. No discrimination should be made between one *bhoktṛ* and another.

When the eater is introduced to the food, *i.e.* when the food is being offered to him, after being placed on the plates, the *kartṛ* should repeat, according to Baudhāyana three *mantras,* one each for the food served to the Manes of father, one of the grandfather and one of the great grandfather. If the presiding Brāhmaṇas are three for the Manes, each *mantra* is repeated separately before the appropriate person; if there is only one *bhoktṛ*, all the three are recited in sequence. The *mantra* for the father is: "fire, sees thee, who art coextensive with the *earth* (*pṛthvisaman*) the ṛk-verses are thy greatness, lest the gift be in vain; the earth is the vessel for thee, the sky is the cover; I offer thee in the mouth of the Brāhmaṇa, I offer thee in the *prāṇa* and the *apāna* of the learned Brāhmaṇas; thou art imperishable, mayest thou never fail to the Manes who are our fathers yonder in the other world." To the food for the grandfather, the *mantra* is altered by substitution of 'air' for 'fire', 'the middle sphere (*antarikṣa*)' for the 'earth' "hears thee" for "sees thee", the 'Yajus formulae' for '*ṛk*' and "grandfathers'" for fathers. The third address is to the food for the great-grandfather with the changes "Sun" for Agni and Vāyu "and" Sāmans), *antarikṣa* for the "earth" and the "middle sphere" in the two other *ṛks*. The omission of this "*mantra*" in offering the food, as well as the omission of the *praṇava,* when beginning to eat ruins the food offered (*i.e.* makes it go to the demons).

Rules for Eating

The Brāhmaṇas who are guests at a *śrāddha* should not speak of the quality of the food they have consumed. They should not speak also of the quality of the *havis* (*i.e.* the food), offered in their palms. They should not praise one another. They should not indicate the insufficiency of the food or drink offered by speech but they may make signs with their hands. They should not eat with their sandals on, or touching their seats with their feet, (*i.e.* the feet must rest on the ground) nor with their heads covered. They should all begin to eat simultaneously.

Lakṣmīdhara's sanction of the old rule of flesh eating in *śrāddha* is indicated by his citing the dictum of Vasiṣṭha condemning an ascetic, who when eating at a *śrādddha* declines to eat the meat served, for detention in Hell for "as many years as the slaughted beast has hairs." The leavings of the *śrāddhas* should not be given away to women, (other than those of the family), Śūdras and uninitiated boys.

Before the guests begin to eat, the *kartṛ* should recite *rakṣoghna* (demon-expelling) *mantras*, and meditate on the Manes and the gods being present in the bodies of the Brāhmaṇas. He should place *piṇḍaṣ* on the ground, and say that the Manes of the father, the grandfather and the great-grandfather may be propitiated by the *piṇḍa* so placed. The guests also should repeat certain *mantras*. When eating they must be made to hear (*śrāvayet*) Vedic hymns, the Purāṇās and the Dharmaśāstra, and the music of the Vīṇā and the flute. In expelling demons the presence of Viṣṇu (Hari) as the consumer of the offerings (*havya-kavya*) should be assumed at the *śrāddha*.

According to Śaṅkha the *śrāddha* guests should not touch one another. Food served with only one hand should not be eaten.

Concluding Rites in Śrāddha

When the guests have finished eating, the *kartṛ* should take a plate with food and a vessel of water, and ask: "Lords, any more food and water?" (*svāminaḥ tīrthamprasādam?*). When they reply "All full" (*sakalam sampūrṇam*), he asks again: "Are you satisfied?" (*ṭraptāsthaḥ*), they reply: "We are satisfied" (*tṛptā'smaḥ*). He then asks: "What should be done with the food that remains?" (*annaśeṣaḥa kim kriyatām*) and they reply: "Let it be eaten by you along with friends" (*iṣṭaiḥ saha upabhujyatām*). Then taking some of the food, he draws a line of the length of six inches and places the *piṇḍa* (ball of rice) on the line. The *piṇḍa* should be of the size of an husked coconut. Then having sprinkled water over the line, he should spread food on the line in front of the guests. The *mantra* for the *piṇḍas* should be: "Let those women of my family who have been cremated or not cremated because they have been cast off, may they obtain satisfaction by the *piṇḍa* placed on the ground." The food scattered (*vikirānnam*) should be scattered over the line in front of the Brāhmaṇas representing the gods (Viśvedevas) and say: "To the gods who do not drink Soma, and who are excluded from a share in sacrifices to them I offer food in the form of scattering Viśvedeva offering." To the Manes, he offers the scatterings: "To the women of my family who have died without undergoing *saṁskāras*, or who have been abandoned, to them I give scattered food from the share of the Manes." Then after the guests have risen and washed their mouths and hands and feet and received *ācamana* water, and been seated, he should offer them *dakṣiṇā*, and request them to say *Svadhā*. When they have said it, he must pray, "May the Viśvedevas be satisfied" he should add the prayer: "May liberal donors increase in family, and also the Vedas and progeny. May faith (*śrāddha*) never forsake us. May we have plenty to give away." The guests give a benediction in the same words. Then he repeats the Vedic parting *mantra* (*ṚV.* VII. 38. 8): "Deeply skilled in law, eternal, deathless, Singers, oh Vajins help us in each fray for booty. Drink of this mead, be satisfied, be joyful. They go on paths which gods tread" and then he makes a circumambulation of the standing guests (who have been asked to get up) and sees them off. He is then free to eat the remnants, and feed Brāhmaṇas with them. The *piṇḍa* should then be taken out and given to crows.

Besides the *piṇḍa* placed on the ground as above, the Manes of three generations should be invoked and separate *piṇḍas* should be offered to each of them and their wives, specifying each, and water should be taken round the six *piṇḍas*, from the right to the left. The water vessel should at last be turned down. The *piṇḍas* should be taken, pair by pair, and blended, and the middle *piṇḍa* may be given to a chaste wife, who desires male progeny.

The remnants on the plates of the guests should be buried, or thrown into water, and should not be eaten by others.

This finishes the *śrāddha*. The Kartṛ may then proceed, before taking his food, to do the daily Vaiśvadeva with food separately cooked. On the night of the *śrāddha*, he should remain without eating, and also avoid conjugal intercourse. He should also avoid Vedic study that day.

Praise of Śrāddha

The value of *śrāddha* is indicated by the blessings which accrue to one who does it and the evils that fall on one who neglects it. In a *śrāddha* the Manes, the gods and the Brāhmaṇas are sacrificed to. If they are so dealt with, they bestow wealth, food, male progeny and longevity, by the blessing of the Manes. They also bestow on the doer of a *śrāddha* fame, strength and joy, following health and affluence. Even reading of the rules of *śrāddha* confer blessings on the reader. In the family of one who neglects his duty to perform *śrāddhas*, heroic and healthy sons are not born nor does fame accrue to them. So, let the *śrāddha* be done even with water, or roots or fruits, and on no account let the doing of a *śrāddha* be omitted for want of means.

Mitramiśra offers other citations in praise of *śrāddha* to show its importance. Sumantu holds that there is nothing more important than doing *śrāddha*. The *Brahmavaivartapurāṇa* (which Lakṣmīdhara never quotes) holds that the rites for the Manes are even more important than those for the Gods, and the propitiation of the Manes (*pitrāpyāyana*) is prescribed as a prologue to all rites to gods. In a *śrāddha* those who are worshipped are the Manes, the Gods, the Brāhmaṇas and fire; when these are worshipped, it is Viṣṇu who is worshipped, declares Yama. In a *śrāddha* nothing is wasted, claims another Purāṇa, because even the leavings are used up, and accordingly, whatever be the difficulty in the way, it must be overcome and the rite of *śrāddha must* be done, according to the prescribed ritual (*yathāvidhi*).

Nature of the Manes (Pitrādisvarūpa)

The dead are not Manes; they become so when *sapiṇḍīkaraṇa* has been done at the end of the eleven days of obsequies following death. By the expression, however, it is not meant that obsequial offerings should not be offered to the dead, who have not become Manes. Each generation of the Manes is represented by specific gods (*devatā*), the Vasus represent the fathers, the eleven Rudras represent the grandfathers and the twelve Ādityas represent the great grandfathers. What is implied is that the fathers, grandfathers and great grandfathers are to be meditated on as the appropriate gods, and their wives as the females of the gods. The position is clarified thus by the *Mitākṣarā* (I. 269): "As a mother during pregnancy gets satisfaction herself from food etc. given to herself from food etc. given to her as *dohada* and also nourishes the foetus and also give satisfaction to the giver of *dohada*, so also the Vasus, Rudras and Ādityas are the real *pitṛs*, and they receive the *śrāddha* offerings. When they are satisfied, they in turn satisfy the *pitṛs*, and also grant many blessings to the *śrāddha* performer. This is also the view of Viśvarūpa.

Āmaśrāddha

Āma is uncooked food. A *śrāddha* has to be performed with cooked food (*anna*) and it has to be offered to the fire and to the Manes through the fire and Brāhmaṇas. Lakṣmīdhara corrects the common error of assuming that he who has not been initiated into Vedic study (*anupanīta*) is not entitled to have a fire (*anagnikaḥ*) like a widower though a *dvija* or a *dvija* boy. The person who is not entitled to have a sacramental fire can still have a cooking fire (*pākāgni*). The *anagnika* is interpreted by Lakṣmīdhara as one who does not even have a cooking fire. That is to say in an emergency, when no fire is available even to a *sāgnika* he may perform the *āmaśrāddha* in lieu of the regular *śrāddha*. Vaidyanātha regards an eclipse as one of such occasions. The Śūdra may always perform *śrāddha* in this form, without *mantra*, as he is not entitled to utter it, and with *namaskāra* (homage) to the recipient Brāhmaṇa instead of the other rites, including feeding and *homa*.

Mitramiśra quotes Kātyāyana for the occasions in which *āmaśrāddha* may be done. They are when one is bereft of a fire, as in a misfortune (*āpadi*), when one is away from his home, or in a place of pilgrimage *tīrtha*. Baudhāyana is cited by him to show that during the commencement of the equinoxes (*saṁkramaṇa*) or commencement of solar months, when cooked food and Brāhmaṇas are unavailable, or during exile or when a son is born (and a pollution comes to the *kartṛ*) instead of dry or uncooked grain (*āma*) gold (*hema*), *i.e.* money may be used as a substitute. But it should be four times the value of grain (*āma*) used in this substitute *śrāddha*. It is a device to get over non-performance of a *śrāddha* when it is due to be done, and there is no other way of doing it.

Vaidyanātha cites Hārīta for the rule that *āmaśrāddha* should not be done as a substitute for the monthly (*māsika*) and annual (*ābdika*) *śrāddhas*. Both these are devices, of which there are simpler ones like giving grass to cows, or making a *śrāddha* with libations of water mixed with sesame seed, rather than drop so obligatory a rite altogether.

Śrāddha by One With Father Alive

The rule in regard to one with a father who is alive is that he should not perform a *śrāddha*. An exception to the rule will arise if a son, whose father is alive has kindled the sacred fire (*sāgnikahā*), and thereby acquires the obligation to perform the *piṇḍapitṛyajña*, and later on the *pārvaṇa-śrāddha*. Another is the *abhyudaya-śrāddha*, which one may have to perform on an auspicious occasion like a marriage, even when the father is alive. In such a case, the *piṇḍa* is offered to the three generations of ancestors to whom the father will offer it, if these are not alive. If a grandfather is also alive, the next three generations must be offered *piṇḍas*. If a father is dead, the son has to perform his *śrāddha*; and if in such a case the father's father is alive, then he is omitted in *piṇḍa-dāna* and the next two ancestors are invoked and given *piṇḍas*. Manu rules that the grandfather who is alive (though his son, *i.e.*, the *kartṛ's* father is dead) may, at his option eat at the *śrāddha* as a guest. Only three ancestors are to be given *piṇḍa*, no fourth. If one's father and grandfather are both alive, the *piṇḍa* should be offered to the three ancestors to whom the grandfather usually offers them. If both the father and grandfather are dead, but the great grandfather is alive, the *piṇḍa* must be offered to the two dead and to the father of the great grandfather. If the father, grandfather and great grandfather are all alive he should offer no *śrāddha* at all. The dictum that *piṇḍa* should not be offered overlooking a living father is an indication of the general rule that one whose father is alive does not perform an ordinary *śrāddha*. It will not apply to *vṛddhi-śrāddha* and other ceremonies which have to be done in connection with other rites (*karmāṅga*) as omitting them is wrong. Govindānanda holds that if the father is disqualified for performing *śrāddha* by becoming an outcaste (*patita*) or an ascetic (*pravrajita*) or by incurable disease or excessive debility due to age, the son has competence (*adhikāra*) to do a *śrāddha* even if the father is alive. The *Kātyāyana-śrautasūtra* considers three alternatives open to one whose father is alive, and has yet to do the *piṇḍa-pitṛ-yajña*: (1) he may pass over the father and offer *piṇḍas* to the three ancestors above the father; (2) he may stop short of the offering of *piṇḍas* and perform only the *homa*; or (3) he may omit the rite altogether, which is the view favored by Jātūkarṇya on the ground that when the main rite, *piṇḍadāna* is prohibited by such a person, it is best for him not to begin the *piṇḍapitṛyajña*.

Śrāddha by One With Two Fathers

A person who may be said to have two fathers is an adopted son (*dattaka*), but it is confined to one type of adoptee, *viz.* *dvyāmuṣyāyaṇa*. When a man gives his only son away in adoption but with an undertaking that he should be deemed the son of both fathers, he is called even now a *dvyāmuṣyāyaṇa* and he inherits to both his natural and adoptive father. According to the *Pravarādhyāya*, if an agnate (*pitṛvya*) makes an agnate of his, his son by a ceremony (*vaikāryena*) the son belongs to the adopter. If either father has no issue by his wife, the adoptee inherits to him also. He has to do the *śrāddha* to both and offer *piṇḍas* to both the natural and the adopting father. The *śrāddha* may be done separately for each father, or it may be done together, the two being invoked together for one *piṇḍa* but the ancestors are counted from the adopter (*parigṛhītā*). The son of a *dattaka* inherits to his adoptive grandfather.

Lakṣmīdhara considers, however, a son of two fathers, created by *niyoga* (levirate) on a sonless widow. The owner of the "field" (the wife) is the putative husband; the giver of the seed (*bījin*) is the impregnator. Without seed there will be no plant; without soil also there will be no plant, as the soil is necessary for the reception of the seed. The giver of the seed (*utpādayitṛ*) is the more important of the two, according to Hārīta (p. 241) and his *pravara* takes precedence in the son so produced. Two *piṇḍas* may be offered by him to both fathers or they may be both offered as one together, and so with the *piṇḍas* to the grandfathers and great-grandfathers. Ordinarily, *niyoga* is done by one of the same *gotra* and an agnate. But it may happen that a widow gets a son by a father, who is either appointed (*niyukta*) or unappointed (*i.e.* in adultery). In both cases, the son should first offer water and *piṇḍas* to the dead husband (nominal father), and then offer them to the bestower of the seed (*bījin*). The first to be offered them is the real father, and then the nominal.

Nārada deals with a different class of sons, who might be deemed to have two fathers. If a loose woman (*svairiṇī*) has sons by several men (other than the real husband), the offspring belongs to the real fathers, and should offer *piṇḍas* only to them. But if the mother has been obtained from the nominal husband by payment of a price (*śulka*) by the procreator, the *piṇḍas* should go only to the latter; but if the procreation is clandestine or without payment to the nominal husband, then the *piṇḍas* should go only to the husband.

The types had become obsolete long ago, and *niyoga* had been condemned even by Manu. Lakṣmīdhara merely repeats old authorities for a practice which had gone out of use. It also indicates that he did not know, or accept the *kalivarjya* list of practices (like *niyoga*) interdicted in *Kaliyuga*.

Putrikāputra

A man with an only daughter may make an agreement with her husband that she will be treated as a son and that her offspring will belong to him as well. The son of an "appointed daughter" (*putrikā*) should offer water and *piṇḍa* in *śrāddha* to both his paternal and maternal grandfathers. If he loses his natural father, he should offer *piṇḍas* in three generations on both lines, *i.e.* mother's and father's.

Ekoddiṣṭa

Ekoddiṣṭa is, as explained by the *Mitākṣarā* (I. 251) that intended (*uddiṣṭaḥ*) for "one" (*ekaḥ*). The ceremonies done for one recently dead are designated *ekoddiṣṭa*, as they are held in honor of only one individual, *viz*; the dead person. "The first sixteen funeral repasts taking place after the ten days immediately succeeding the day of death, as well as that on the anniversary of such day, are *ekoddiṣṭas*. It is a *naimittika* rite. The ritual for *śrāddhas* are the same, except for the alterations indicated for specific forms. Thus, Yājñavalkya notes that *ekoddiṣṭa* is done without invoking the gods (*i.e.* Viśvedevas), with *one arghya* only, one *pavitraka*, without invocation *āvāhana* and the fire oblations (*agnau karaṇa*). It should be done *apasavya*, from the right to the left, and with sacred thread on the right shoulder. Different forms of words are to be used at the time of bidding farewell to the guests (*visarjana*). It should be performed at mid-day, as noted by Devala. A single *piṇḍa* is to be offered.

Rajkumar Sarvadhikari holds that *ekoddiṣṭa* was the form in which the *śrāddha* was first instituted, and that the *Pārvaṇa śrāddha*, in which three generations of ancestors are worshipped, is a later improvement. According to the *Varāhapurāṇa* the first *śrāddha* was done for a son, not for an ancestor. "The deceased parents, or dear kinsmen, whose loss was deeply deplored, must have been the first objects of the *śrāddha* rite and it must have been long after the institution of this ceremony that the *pārvaṇaśrāddha* was developed."

The citations made by Lakṣmīdhara deal with the modifications of the ritual of *pārvaṇaśrāddha* in *ekoddiṣṭa*. The question about being satisfied (*tṛpti-praśna*) should be in the form *svadita*. The libation with *tila* (*tilodaka*) is one only. The word "*anu*" (in the formula *ye ca tvāmanu*) is not to be used. The dead person is not to be addressed or referred to as *pitṛ* (Mane): he becomes one of the Manes only after the rite of *sapiṇḍīkaraṇa*. The feeding should be on a sumptuous scale and presents should be given to the guests. The first *ekoddiṣṭa* which is the one properly so called must be done on the eleventh day after the death of the person commemorated by it. The presiding Brāhmaṇa should be invited the evening previous to the ceremony. The host and the guest should be ritually pure the next morning after bath etc. The guest should be received with *arghya, pādya,* etc., be seated ceremoniously and presented with white flowers, incense, perfumes, clothes etc., shoes and umbrella, etc. The remnant of the food served may be given only to agnatic relations. The *kartṛ* should dig three trenches after the Brāhmaṇas have left, four *aṅgulas* long and deep, light three fires close to the trenches, and make in them three oblations of cooked rice to Soma accompanied by the Manes," "To Agni who carries oblations to the Manes", and "Reverence to Yama Aṅgiras."

These rules are laid down by the *Viṣṇusmṛti*.

The ceremony should be repeated every month on the day of the death of the person commemorated. The twelve monthly *śrāddhas* (*māsīka*), follow the *ekoddiṣṭa* on the dates of death, with the first *ekoddiṣṭa* and the three adjunct *śrāddhas* (*anyūna māsika*) make the sixteen *śrāddhas* in first year of death. It is only after a year of the *sapiṇḍīkaraṇa* that the dead spirit gets peace (*āpyāyana*) and becomes one of the Manes. A water vessel should be given to the presiding Brāhmaṇa, in the *māsika* ceremonies and just before the *sapiṇḍīkaraṇa*, and the ceremony in which this is done is termed *sodakumbha*.

The fear that if the person who is bound to do the funeral rites dies within the twelve months following the death of the person commemorated, the dead spirit might remain a *preta*, is responsible for a common practice. On the twelfth day following death, and the day after *ekoddiṣṭa*, the sixteen monthly *śrāddhas* are performed *in advance,* commonly in the form of *āamaśrāaddha*, and on the thirteenth day, the *sapiṇḍīkaraṇa* (which can be done only after the sixteen monthly *śrāddhas* have been performed) is done. The extract from the *Viṣṇusmṛti* given by Lakṣmīdhara apparently assumes this practice as it authorises the use of terms *pitṛmate* in the oblations on the fire, when the word *pitṛ* cannot be used till the *sapiṇḍīkaraṇa* is done. Accordingly, in common usage the monthly *śrāddhas* (though done in substitute form of *āmaśrāddha*) take the ritual of *pārvaṇa-śrāddha*, and three ancestors are invoked in them. They are not accordingly *ekoddiṣṭa*, except in the sense of being in honor of the death of one person only.

Sapiṇḍīkaraṇa

The rite of *sapiṇḍīkaraṇa* is intended for the peace of the deceased person. It unites him to the dead ancestors, and after such ritualistic introduction and union, he loses his corpse (*preta*) quality and joins the ancestors in the world of Manes (*pitṛloka*). As long as the ceremony is unperformed, the spirit of the dead person is unable to get access to the world of ancestors. The *sapiṇḍīkaraṇa* guarantees the united soul against loss of *śrāddha* benefits, even if his direct descendants fail; for, he gets a share of the offerings made by collaterals and agnates in the *śrāddhas* they perform to common ancestors. The failure referred to need not be through the death or extinction of the direct line of descendants of the dead person. The failure may arise by their becoming outcastes or cursed (*patita, abhiśaśta*).

The ceremony should be done only after the sixteen *māsika* or monthly *śrāddhas* and *ekoddiṣṭa* of the eleventh day after death are done. The practice already referred to as a precaution of performing the sixteen "monthly" *śrāddhas* on the twelfth day after death is sanctioned by the *Viṣṇusmṛti*. This practice is referred to as *ākarṣa* i.e., anticipation. The *sāgnika* (the person who has secured a fire) *must* perform *pitṛ-yajña* (or *piṇḍa-pitṛ-yajña*) on New moon days. He cannot do those rites unless he has done *sapiṇḍīkaraṇa* to his dead father etc. This is one more reason for doing *sapiṇḍīkaraṇa* on the thirteenth day after death, and not at the end of twelve months, and before the first anniversary (*pārvaṇa*) *śrāddha*. A *vṛddhi-śrāddha* cannot be done before *sapiṇḍīkaraṇa* has been done; accordingly, the rite should be done in anticipation on the thirteenth day, or before the *vṛddhi-śrāddha* is begun. When a nephew, brother or *sapiṇḍa* of a dead person has to do an *abhyudaya-śrāddha* (*vṛddhi*) he must first do the *sapiṇḍīkaraṇa* to the uncle, or brother etc. if it has not been done already.

The performance of the anniversary *śrāddha*, as long as life lasts (*yāvadjīva*) becomes a duty after the *sapiṇḍīkaraṇa*.

The ritual is symbolic. Four vessels for *arghya* water are got ready, one for the recently dead person, and one for each of his father, grandfather and great-grandfather. Similarly a ball of rice (*piṇḍa*) is made for the dead person and three balls for the next three ancestors. With prescribed *mantras* (*ye samānā, etc.*) the water of the vessel dedicated to the dead person is sprinkled into the vessels which contain water for the three higher ancestors. The ball of rice offered to the dead person is divided into three parts, and one part of each is added to the three remaining balls of the ancestors. The father and grandfather of the dead person are invoked to unite with the dead person, and the fourth is released. For the *kartṛ*, thenceforth, the three ancestors will stop short of the great-grandfather of the dead person, as he has been released.

Vaijavāpa is cited for the rule that one who has been cursed (*abhiśasta*) or has become an outcaste (*patita*) or been guilty of the comprehensive sin of *bhrūṇahati* or an adulteress, if dead, must not be sought to be thus united in a *sapiṇḍīkaraṇa* rite. It is post-mortuary and permanent excommunication for vicious persons.

As regards females who are dead : in the case of a girl who dies unmarried, the father performs the rite, and in the case of a married but sonless woman the husband. The *gotra* should be that of her father in the first case if the marriage has been *āsura* etc. and that of the husband in the second. After the *sapiṇḍīkaraṇa*, the dead wife joins her father, the husband's father etc. and the two families are united. After *sapiṇḍī-karaṇa* whatever *piṇḍa* or water is given to a mane goes also to the wife of the mane. Libations and food for dead women should be offered invoking them by the *gotra* of the husbands, since after the performance of the *homa* on the fourth day of marriage (*caturthī*) the husband is united to the bride in all organs. When a father is dead but the grandfather is alive the union should be effected of two ancestors above the grandfather. In doing a *sapiṇḍīkaraṇa* to ancestral spirits (Manes) those who have not been united (by a collateral by not doing *sapiṇḍī karaṇa, asaṁskṛtāḥ*) should be united by the one now doing the rite. The union of the mother's mane should be not with that of her mother but with that of the paternal grandmother of the performer. In the case of one who is the son of a "woman who has been made a son" (*putrikā*), he should effect the union of her spirit with that of the maternal-grandmother first, and then the maternal great-grandfather.

Śrāddhas After Sapiṇḍīkaraṇa

The dead when united with the Manes of higher ancestors become satisfied (*kṛtārthāḥ*). Accordingly, to invoke them alone and offer *piṇḍas* to them alone is wrong. The invocation of one spirit is proper only till his union by *sapiṇadīkaraṇa*. The son of the body (*aurasa*) and the son raised on the wife by another (*kṣetraja*) must do all *śrāddhas* after *sapiṇḍīakaraṇa* only by the *Pārvaṇaśrāddha* ritual, *i.e.*, by invoking all three generations of ancestors. This is the view of Jābāla. The *Matsyapurāṇa* holds that the *pārvaṇa* ritual must be followed by all who have lit their fires (*agnimataḥ*). The *Matsyapurāṇa* also condemns those who abandon the *ekoddiṣṭa* form (invoking only one ancestor) even after *sapiṇḍīkaraṇa,* in all forms of *śrāddha*. The contradictory dicta are reconciled by Lakṣmīdhara, following the author of *Mahārṇavaprakāśa* thus: the sons who are of the body (*aurasa*) or of the wife (*kṣetraja*), who have also acquired fires (*sāgni*) should do the annual *śrāddha* only by the *pārvaṇa* ritual (invoking all three ancestors); all the other ten types of sons and *aurasa* and *kṣetraja* sons, who have not lit their fires should follow the *ekoddiṣṭa* ritual only.

Who are Competent to do Śrāddhas?

Adhikāra means both competence or capacity and duty or obligation. He who has an *adhikāra* for a rite *must* do it. When different persons are stated in a serial order as having *adhikāra* the duty to do the rite devolves on them in that order.

The devolution of property of a dead person follows the line of descent of competence to do the funeral rites of the dead person. It reflects the idea that property is owned by the dead even after death, and by the unborn even before birth. It is a tie between the dead, the living and the unborn. The persistence of the claim of the dead on the living is shown by the latter having an obligation to perform the funeral rites and *śrāddhas* of the former. The custom in some parts of the world (*e.g.*, Malabar) restricting to owners of land the right of cremation within their lands, and of the conservation of groves of trees in which ancestral spirits dwell in the form of serpents are called *kāvu* in Malayalam.

A distinction has to be made in regard to the form of obsequial rites, of which the *śrāddha* is one. The *Viṣṇupurāṇa* (p. 264) divides them into three classes: the first (*pūrva*), the middle (*madhyama*) and the last (*uttara*). The first are the rites which start from cremation of the dead person and end with the period of death impurity; the second start from the rite of *ekoddiṣṭa* and go on till *sapiṇḍīkaraṇa*, and include the monthly *śrāddhas* done before *sapiṇḍīkaraṇa*; and the last are the rites which come up for performance after the dead person is united to the Manes by *sapiṇḍīkaraṇa*. The first consists of offerings of water mostly (*udakāñjali*) and even remote agnates have an equal duty with nearer to offer them (*samānodaka*). The other two are *śrāddhas* proper and involve the offering of balls of cooked food (*piṇḍa*) to the spirit of the dead person whether united with the Manes or not. This, only closer relations can do. They are *sapiṇḍas*. It is only on failure of *sapiṇḍas* on the paternal and maternal sides that the *samānodakas* come in for *śrāddha-piṇḍa* offering.

Lakṣmīdhara was a contemporary of Vijñāneśvara, whose dicta have been (in the absence of Laksmīdhara's work) the most widely accepted hitherto.

Both cite Marīci: "When the father dies, the obsequial rites should be done by the son according to rule (*vidhānataḥ*). If there are many sons, who still dwell together, whatever rites are done by the eldest son with the consent of the other sons and with the undivided family property (*avibhāgena dravyeṇa*) is held to be done by each and all of them."

Bṛhaspati states the duty of sons, in the first instance to do the *śrāddha* of the dead father, and if there are no sons, by agnates (*jñāti*), cognates (*bandhu*), friends (*suhṛt*), pupils (*śiṣyāḥ*), teacher (*ṛtvic*), servant (*bhṛtya*) and priest (*purohita*), each succeeding person taking the duty if the preceding are unavailable. A similar rule is given by Gautama:

"In the unavailability of sons, the *sapiṇḍas*, the *sapiṇḍas* on the mother's side, and the pupils (*śiṣya*) should do the *śrāddha*, and failing them the *ṛtvic* and *guru*". The *Viṣṇupurāna* makes it clear that the absence of "sons" must be taken as absence of their sons, grandsons, etc. The son, the son's son, the son's son's son (*prapautra*), and in the same way the brother and his sons, grandsons, great-grandsons etc. and the descendants of *sapiṇḍas*, and on failure of even these the *samānodakas* and their male descendants, and after them similarly the *samānodakas* of the mother's family. Paiṭhīnasi and the *Viṣṇupurāṇa* refer to a contingency now remote: *viz.* the interruption of the line within three generations (*atri-puruṣa*) by an outcaste (*patita*) or one of a lower caste, as such intrusions destroy the continuity of the family. If both the male and female lines are extinct on the male side, the rites should be done by the women of the family. Similarly, if the dead man had wives of lower castes and sons by them, then all of them should offer jointly one *piṇḍa* and not each one *piṇḍa*, though their periods of impurity will be according to the *varṇas* of their respective mothers. Such mixed marriages give rise to rules which are now obsolete, but which probably were not so in Lakṣmidhara's time, as he cites the rules relating to them. Thus, one authority declares that children by mothers of lower *varaṇas* to a dead Brahmaṇa father do the obsequial rites to him, but the father cannot in such cases do the rites to sons of non-Brahmaṇa origin; in such cases their mothers should do the rites for them, as they will have to do to their mothers. No funeral rites (and *śrāddha*) should be done to a dead ascetic by sons etc. Even the cremation is interdicted to ascetics (who have to be buried), on the model of the saintly Vidura, in whose case the cremation was prohibited on the ground that he had already been "burnt" by wisdom (*jñānāgnidagdha*) and a second "burning" was ruled out. The normal rule is that when one of the same *gotra* (among relations) is available, one of another *gotra* (*e.g. a-sapiṇḍa* of the mother) should not do the rite. The dictum of the *Mārkaṇḍeyapurāṇa* that his women (*striyaḥ*) should do, without repetition of Vedic *mantras*, the obsequial rites (including *śrāddha*) is explained by Lakṣmīdhara as referring to the dead man leaving no widow of his own *varṇa* but leaving widows of other *varṇas*; for, it is explicitly ruled that before a dead man's brother can undertake the duty there should be no *savarṇa* widow to do it in preference to him. The rites to women follow the same rules, but a sonless woman cannot have *sapiṇḍīkaraṇa* done for her.

Certain rules given by other digests may be now indicated. Śaṅkha's dictum that in the absence of sons (*putrābhāve*) the widow of the same *varṇa* as the dead man (*patnī*) should do the rites, is widened by making "sons" synonymous with all the twelve kinds of sons. But on the *Kalivarjya* rules, the only sons that are to be recognized in Kaliyuga are the son of equal *varṇa* (aurasa) and the adopted son. The *aurasa* son has competence and duty to do the *śrāddha* of his father even if he has not been 'initiated' (*anupanīta*). But the uninitiated boy must have had his *cūḍākaraṇa* done and be above three years of age. The adopted son cannot do the father's *śrāddha* without first becoming initiated (*upanīta*). If a man leaves more than one *savarṇa* widow of whom the senior is the *patnī* (the wife for religious rites) if there is a son by a co-wife (*apatnī*), he has preferential claim to do the rites (*Ibid.*, p. 15). If a man dies sonless but leaves daughters, the married daughter (*ūḍhā*) takes precedence of the unmarried (*anūḍhā*) in doing his obsequial rites (p. 15, Bharadvāja). The grandson who inherits his maternal grandfather's estate (*i.e.* a *putrikāputra*) should perform the *śrāddha* to that grandfather.

Nandapaṇḍita cites the following comprehensive rule from the *Smṛtisaṁgraha* (p. 9); each of the following succeeds to the duty of performing the obsequial rites and giving *piṇḍas*, in the absence of all those named before him; or her: "The son, the grandson, *his* son, the son of the daughter made *putrikā*, the lawfully wedded wife (*patnī*), the brother, *his* son, the father, the mother, the daughter-in-law (*snuṣā*), the sister (*bhaginī*), *her* son, (*bhāgineya*), the *sapiṇḍa* and *samānodaka*." If all fail (or are not available), the King should have the *śrāddha* and obsequial rites performed from the property of the dead man for "the King is the kinsman of his subjects, whatever *varṇa* they may belong to," (The widow who had been married in Dharmic form) according to Nandapaṇḍita is entitled to perform the funeral obsequies and *śrāddha* of the husband with Vedic *mantras*. The acolyte (Brahmacārin) does not commit a breach of his vows by doing parental obsequial rites and *śrāddha*. "An elder brother is not competent to perform the rites and *śrāddha* of a younger brother" says Baudhāyana, but the rule is explained away by Nandapaṇḍita as applicable only in cases in which a competent son is unavailable or there is no friendliness between the dead and the surviving brother. The son of a *putrikā* should do his mother's father's rites. He must do the rites of his natural father only if he has no brother, since only the eldest son of the *putrikā* belongs to the maternal grandfather. If a father is an outcaste (*patita*) the obsequial duties that would have been his, devolve on his son, *i.e.* he is treated as dead although alive.

The common rule is that a son has no competence to do a *śrāddha* during the lifetime of his father (if not an outcaste). There are six exceptions to the rule. The son can do *śrāddhas* even in the lifetime of his father in *vṛddhi-śrāddha* on his *second* marrige (for in his first marriage, the father must do the *śrāddha*) the birth of a son, the *iṣṭi* for Manes, Soma sacrifice, in pilgrimage centres (*tīrtha*) and when an honored guest arrives. Nandapaṇḍita denies the need to do a *vṛddhi-śrāddha* for a second marriage. The marriage (*udvāha*) must mean, therefore, that of a son or daughter. Mitramiśra discusses a number of matters on which authorities have differed. For example, Śūlapāṇi has upheld the view that when there are several sons, and they are all living separately and with their shares of the paternal property, every one of them should do the sixteen *śrāddhas* following *ekoddiṣṭa* (on the 11th day after the death of the father) and upto the *sapiṇḍīkaraṇa*, and must do the annual *pārvaṇa* separately. It might happen that the brothers might be in different and far-off places and the consent and contribution, which the dictum of Marīci holds as enabling the eldest brother to do the obsequial rites on behalf of all brothers, may not be given. In that case, the obsequial rites might be done by the brothers separately in different places. Otherwise the younger son becomes guilty of a grave lapse, and he becomes a *vidhighna*. The common rule is that even if a younger son, in the absence of the eldest son, does the cremation, he must continue the rites upto *ekoddiṣṭa*, and if the eldest brother comes within the period, he must also do all the rites, as on him lies the obligation to do them. Manu rules that undivided brothers should do the obsequial rites together, through the eldest, and when they have a common mess (*ekapākena vasatām*) they must do the *śrāddhas* together. Śūlapāṇi holds that this rule is only permissive in favor of the undivided younger brothers, and they obtain additional merit if they do *śrāddhas* separately, when living together." He relies on Laghu-Hārīta's rule that the sixteen *śrāddhas* upto *sapiṇḍīkaraṇa* should be done by every son separately. Mitramiśra questions the soundness of the practice of southerners (*dākṣiṇātyāḥ*) to have the eldest son re-perform all rites including *sapiṇḍīkaraṇa*, if the death has taken place when he was away, and a younger brother has had to do them. His contention is that after *sapiṇḍīkaraṇa* the dead person has ceased to be a *preta* and has become a *pitṛ*, and cannot again be invoked as a *preta*.

Another point discussed by Mitramiśra is the *adhikāra* of the daughter to do the obsequial rites to the father, if she has no brothers, on the basis of the dictum of Manu (IX. 130) "the daughter is equal to the son" (*putreṇa duhitā samā*) and on the assumption that the word *bhrātā* (brother) in the enumeration includes sister (*bhaginī*).

In the rule giving a daughter the obligation to do the funeral rite and *śrāddha* of a father, the unmarried daughter (*anūḍhā*) is preferred to the *samskṛtā i.e.* the married daughter. Why is this distinction made?

Mitramiśra explains it thus: Manu rules that the *piṇḍa* follows the *gotra* and the estate (*gotra-riktā-nu gatānugāḥ piṇḍāḥ)*, and a married daughter belongs to a different *gotra* from the deceased, and is also not entitled to a share of the father's estate (*rikta*). Accordingly he explains away the rule of Bhāradvāja: "the married daughter should give the libation and *piṇḍa* to the dead father, and do the *ekkoddiṣṭa* equally with brothers," as referring to married daughters, when there remains no daughter unmarried.

Ābhyudayika

It is natural for one to remember one's ancestors in moments of joy or seasons of prosperity, and to invoke their blessings when about to undertake any important act of an auspicious character. All these are termed *Vṛddhi* or *abhyudaya*. As the means of pleasing the Manes is by *śrāddha*, the rite performed either before or after such occasions is known as *vṛddhiśrāddha* or *ābhyudayika*. It is also called *nāndīśrāddha, nāndi* meaning *samṛddhi*, 'plenty', or 'affluence' (*nāndi samṛiddhiriti kathyate)*. The Manes are usually pictured as "tearful in visage" (*aśrumukhā*). In these rites, they assume a joyous expression, and are described as '*nāndīmukhāḥ*.' Gods (*devāḥ*) assume the form of 'joyous Manes' (*nāndīmukhāḥ*) when invoked in this rite, and eat the food offered. When the gods are satisfied by the rite, in this form, they in turn give satisfaction to the Manes.

The *śrāddha* performed in this way loses some of the features distinctive of rites to Manes. Thus, the sacred thread should be worn in the normal way, as in rites to gods, and not hang from the right shoulder. All circumambulation and movements should be from the left to the right (*pradakṣiṇa*). Sesame seed should not be used, and barley should be substituted for it (*yavaistitārthaḥ*). The balls (*piṇḍa*) should not be of cooked rice (*anna*) but curds mixed with unbroken rice (*kṣata*) and jujube fruit (*badara*). The *darbha* should be used unbent (*ṛju*). The expression *svadhā*, which is used in rites to Manes, is not to be used. The Brāhmaṇas who are guests should be in pairs (*yugma*). The ceremony should take place in the forenoon. The prayers (*ajapa*) should drop the *mantras* in honor of the Manes. The *piṇḍas* should be offered facing east (*prācīmukha*) and placed on *darbha* (grass) with the end to the east, unlike the *pārvaṇa-śrāddha* where it should be pointed to the south (*dakṣiṇāgra*).

The *ābhyudayika* proper should be prefaced by a *mātṛ-yajña* or *mātṛ-pūja*, to placate the "divine Mothers." The "Mothers" may be adored in the form of pictures drawn on paper or idols (*pratimā*). The ten "Mothers" are named thus in *Caturvimśatimata*:- Gaurī, Padmā, Sacī, Dakṣā, Savitrī, Vijayā, Jayā, Devasenā, Svadhā, and Svāhā. Śātātapa substitutes Medhā for Dakṣā in the list of ten Mothers.

The forms in which the Mothers should be imagined or represented pictorially for purposes of worship are given in detail in the *Śrāddhaprakāśa*. The *Bhaviṣyapūrāṇa* declares that if the *vṛddhiśrāddha* is begun without first doing the *Mātṛpūjā,* they in their anger will cause harm to the performer of the *śrāddha*.

The ritual prescribed is that of *pārvaṇaśrāddha*, with important changes, some of which have already been indicated. The invocation of the *nāndīmukha-pitaraḥ* is to begin from the great-grandfather, proceed next to the grandfather and come last to the father. The wives of these are to be separately invoked by name and *gotra* on their paternal line, and they are included in the invocation of the maternal grandfather, maternal great-grandfather and the father of the first. Nine are thus to be invoked and placated with food etc. The prayers and recitations during the feeding of the guests should not be those described for ordinary *śrāddhas* but different ones which are specified.

The *nāndīśrāddha* should be done by a father for his son till the latter completes his *snāna* and *samāvartana*, after which the son should do such rites himself. In counting ancestors those who are alive should be dropped, and the next in ascent invoked. Eight Brāhmaṇas are to be fed at this *śrāddha*.

The occasions for doing the *nāndīśrāddha* are many. Lakṣ-mīdhara's two citations are not exhaustive, but illustrative.

About eighteen occasions are given in other digests. They too are not exhaustive. It may be assumed that no important event should pass without the performance of *nāndīśrāddha* as a preliminary rite.

If the required number of Brāhmaṇas cannot be secured, eight married women, who have husbands and children alive (*suvāsinī*), are to be worshipped and fed.

This is analogous to two practices which are authorized and described in the *Śrāddhkalpalatā*. If a mother died in the lifetime of the father (*mātā mṛtā maṅgalasūtreṇa*), women with husbands and children (*suvāsinī*) are to be fed along with the *Śrāddha-Brāhmaṇas* and given presents of clothes, ornaments and toilet requisites. If a woman has become a *sati* or predeceased her husband, the same procedure should be followed, and they should be invited along (*niyuñjīta*) and fed along with the Brāhmaṇas (*dvijaiḥsaha*).

Śrāddha to One Alive

The concluding chapter of the *Śrāddhakāṇḍa* is devoted to an account of the *śrāddha* that may be done to one in his own lifetime. Such a *śrāddha* involves a contradiction, as the definitions of *śrāddha* make it a rite in honor of the dead, whether they are *preta* or have been united to the Manes by *sapiṇḍīkaraṇa*. In the *śrāddha* to a living person the rites stop with *ekoddiṣṭa*, and do not include *sapiṇḍīkaraṇa* (Baudhāyana). The underlying idea seems to be that the whole is animated by a conviction of the instability (*anityatva*) of all life, of the transcendence and immanence of the Supreme Being (conceived as Viṣṇu), and of the confident hope that on his own death he merges in the Supreme Being and has no existence in the *Pitṛloka* "the world of Manes." To such a person, as to an ascetic, no *śrāddha* need be done after his physical death. After the conclusion of *ātmaśrāddha* (a *śrāddha* to oneself) one is released from all obligations of life, including the performance of *śrāddha* to ancestors. He is ritually unalive. He does not contravene the rule that the *śrāddha* should be done as long as life lasts. A *śrāddha* done at Gayā is held to give eternal satisfaction (*akṣaya-tṛpti*) to the Manes. One who does the *śrāddha* at Gayā is assured that he needs do no more *śrāddha*. He who wishes to do his own *śrāddha* is accordingly told that he must first do the *śrāddha* at Gayā. In a sense the person who has done his own *śrāddha* is like a *jīvanmukta*.

The ritual is given in a passage of Baudhāyana, and in the two Purāṇas, viz. the *Brahmapurāṇa* and the *Liṅgapurāṇa*. Lakṣamīdhara relies on the first and Mitramiśra on the second.

The doer of a *śrāddha* (*kartṛ*) is reminded always that he must possess *śrāddhā*, *i.e.* devotion and belief. In *jīvacchrāddha* there must, in addition, be a conviction of a philosophical and Vedāntic nature. This is why the *kartṛ* has to spend the first night in repeating the eight-letter (*aṣṭākṣara*) homage formula to Viṣṇu. The ceremony begins on the thirteenth day of the dark fortnight, and its main feature is the cremation of a bundle of *darbhā* made to resemble, and represent the *kartṛ*. The post-cremation rites are done for it. The performer is now ritually dead. He is one without a fire (*niragni*) as his fire has been used up in the cremation.

The rites on the second day stimulate those of sañcayanam following death. The form it takes is to fill three vessels with pulse, mixed with sesame seed and rice, and throw the contents as offerings to the Earth, the god of death (Yama) and to Rudra, as the Lord of the crematoria (Smaśānapati). The ground is sprinkled with milk to assuage the heat generated by the cremation of the "corpse". The *kartṛ* then enters a river, walks into it till the water comes to his navel, and offers seven libations, ending with *svadhā* and *namaḥ*, to the Lord of Death, invoked by seven descriptive epithets. Then calling to mind Śiva as Rudra and lord of crematoria, fried rice (*lāja*) is scattered in his name. Then, ten libations of water mixed with *tila* seed are made to the three ancestors and their wives, and ten balls of rice (*piṇḍa*) are offered, nine to them and the tenth libation and *piṇḍa* being to himself. He should throw into the water ten pots (*kumbha*) of water mixed with *tila*. He should then come back to his house, sprinkling milk on *darbhā* spread near the door-step, and sleep with his head facing south. Next day, (*amāvāasyāa* or new moon) he should do the *māsika-śrāddhas* and the *sapiṇḍīkraṇ* (note—it is condemned above). The period should be observed as one of impurity (*āśauca*) by relations. The word *preta* is, however, to be avoided in every part of the ritual of this ceremony.

References

1. *H.L.I.*, pp. 60-61.
2. *Śrāddhaprakāśa*, p. 11.
3. Ayangar K.U.R., *Introduction to the Gṛhasthakāṇḍa*, p. 68.
4. *Śrāddhacandrikā*, pp. 5-7.
5. *Śrāddhakalpalatā*, pp. 6-8.

Sacrifice

The idea of 'offering sacrifices' is very familiar in India, but a student needs to understand the principle which underlies all sacrifices, so that he may realise that every one should sacrifice himself to the good of others, and that all sacrifice of other things are meant to teach a man how he ought, at last, to sacrifice himself.

The first thing to grasp is that creation is sacrifice. Īśvara confines Himself, limits Himself, in matter in order that a universe may be made manifest. Śruti and Smṛti alike proclaim this truth, as in the *Puruṣasūkta* of the *Ṛgveda* or as in the allusion by Śrīkṛṣṇa to the formal sacrifice that causes the birth of beings.[1] Immersion in matter is, in spiritual language, called 'death,' and Īśvara thus sacrificed Himself in order that he might bring into separate beings portions of Himself, the *jīvas* who might develop all His powers in matter in an infinite variety of forms. This is the primary sacrifice, and on this is based the Law. This also gives us the meaning of sacrifice: it is the pouring out of life for the benefit of others.

The Law of Sacrifice is the Law of Life of all *jīvas*. In the earlier stages of their growth they are forcibly sacrificed, and so progress involuntarily without their own consent or even knowledge, their forms being violently wrenched away from them, and they propelled into new ones, a little more developed. Thus the *jīvas* of the mineral kingdom are prepared to pass on into the vegetable, by the breaking up of their mineral bodies for the support of plants. The *jīvas* of the vegetable kingdom are prepared to pass on into the animals, by the breaking up of their vegetable bodies for the support of animal life. The *jīvas* of the animal kingdom are prepared to pass on into the human, by the breaking up of their bodies for the support of other animals, of savages, and of certain types of men. And even the *jīvas* of the human kingdom are prepared to rise into higher races by breaking up of their human bodies for the support of other human lives in cannibalism, war, etc.

In all these cases the bodies are sacrificed for the benefit of others, without the assent of the embodied consciousness. Only after untold ages does the *jīva* recognize, in the body, the universality of the law, and begin to sacrifice his own *upādhis* deliberately, for the good of those around him. This is called self-sacrifice, and is the showing forth of the divinity of the *Jīva*, the proof that he is of the nature of Īśvara.

A wonderful story of uttermost self-sacrifice is told in the *Mahābhārata*.

Indra, the King of the Devas, was sore beset by the Asura Vṛttra, born of the wrath of a Ṛṣi, whom Indra had offended by an unrighteous act. Vṛttra heading the Daityas defeated Indra and his armies in battle, drove him away from his capital, Amarāvatī and took away his sovereignty. For long the Devas wandered with their King in exile, and repeatedly they made endeavour to regain their capital, but were vanquished again and again. Finally they learnt that the righteous wrath of a Ṛṣi could not be allayed, except by the voluntary self-sacrifice and pity of another Ṛṣi; and that Vṛttra could be slain by no other weapon than the thunderbolt made with the self-given bones of a holy one. And they went eagerly to the Ṛṣi Dadhīci and told their woeful tale to him. And he was filled with a great pity and said: 'I give to you my body willingly to make what use of it you like.' And when their artificer Viśvakarman shrank from laying a rude and painful hand upon that shining body of purity and *tapas*, Dadhīci smiled and said: 'Cover this body up with salt; bring here a herd of cows; they shall lick off the salt and flesh together;

and yet shall take the bones which only ye require; and so naught of this body shall be wasted.' And this was done and Vṛttra fell before the might born of that wondrous sacrifice.[2]

The *jīva* is led up to this point by the teachings of the Ṛṣis, who bid him make sacrifices of his possessions for a good that he does not receive immediately: they show him that when a man sacrifices to others, his gifts return to him increased in the future. A man is to sacrifice some of his goods, which may be looked on as outlying pieces of himself, and he is promised that this act of self-denial shall bring him increased possessions. Next he was aught to make similar sacrifices and to deny himself present enjoyments, in order that he might lay up for himself increased happiness on the other side of death in *svarga*. Thus the practice of sacrificing was made habitual, and man, by sacrificing his possessions in the hope of reward, prepared to learn that it was his duty to sacrifice himself in the service of others, and to find in the joy of that service his reward.

Another lesson taught in these sacrifices was the relation man bears to all the beings round him; that he is not a solitary, isolated life, but that all lives are inter-dependent, and can only prosper permanently as they recognize this inter-dependence. The Ṛṣis taught him to sacrifice daily to the Devas, to Ṛṣis, to ancestors, to men and animals, and showed him that as all these made sacrifices to enrich his life, he had incurred to them a debt, a duty, which he must pay by sacrifice. As he lives on others, he must, in common honesty, live for others. Sacrifice is right, a thing that ought to be done, that is owed.

Finally, as the *jīva* recognizes his parentage, his identity in nature with Īśvara, sacrifice becomes happiness, a delight, and the pouring out of life for others is felt as a joyous exercise of innate divine powers. Instead of seeing how much he can take and how little he can give, he tries to see how little he can take and how much he can give. He begins to look very carefully into what he takes for the support of his own *upādhis*, and seeks to reduce to the lowest point the suffering inflicted by the breaking up of lower forms for his support. He abandons the foods and the amusements which inflict pain on sentient beings and tries to become 'the friend of all creatures.' He realises that while the preying of animals on animals, of men on men, and the slaughter of animals by men for food or sport, are necessary at certain stages of evolution for the development of needed faculties and powers, men should gradually evolve from these, and cultivate the faculties of gentleness, sympathy and tenderness, regarding the weaker as younger Selves to be helped, instead of as victims to be immolated.

As a man lives in such thoughts of his non-separateness from younger Selves, he begins to feel more, really his non-separateness from elder Selves and from the Universal Parent, Īśvara. Slowly he realises that his true function is to live for others, as Īśvara lives for all, and that his true happiness lies in becoming a channel in which the life of Īśvara is flowing, a willing instrument to do the will of Īśvara. Then every action becomes a sacrifice to Īśvara, and actions no longer bind him. Thus the law of sacrifice becomes also the law of liberation.

सहयज्ञाः प्रजाः सृष्ट्वा पुरोवाच प्रजापतिः ।
अनेन प्रसविष्यध्वमेष वोऽस्त्विष्टकामधुक् ॥
देवान्भावयतानेन ते देवा भावयन्तु वः ।
परस्परं भावयन्तः श्रेयः परमवाप्स्यथ ॥
इष्टान्भोगान्हि वो देवा दास्यन्ते यज्ञभाविताः ।
तैर्दत्तानप्रदायैभ्यो भुङ्क्ते स्तेन एव सः ॥
यज्ञशिष्टाशिनः सन्तो मुच्यन्ते सर्वकिल्बिषैः ।
भुञ्जते ते त्वघं पापा ये पचन्त्यात्मकारणात् ॥
अन्नाद्भवन्ति भूतानि पर्जन्यादन्नसंभवः ।
यज्ञाद्भवति पर्जन्यो यज्ञः कर्मसमुद्भवः ॥
कर्म ब्रह्मोद्भवं विद्धि ब्रह्माक्षरसमुद्भवम् ।
तस्मात्सर्वगतं ब्रह्म नित्यं यज्ञे प्रतिष्ठितम् ॥[3]

"Having in ancient times emanated mankind together with sacrifice, Prajāpati declared: 'By this shall ye propagate; be this to you the Kāmaduh.

"With this nourish ye the Devas, and may the Devas nourish you; nourishing one another ye shall reap the supremost good.

"For, nourished by sacrifice, the Devas, shall bestow on you the enjoyments you desire. A thief verily is he who enjoyeth what is given by them without returning them aught.

"The righteous, who eat the remains of the sacrifice, are freed from all sins; but the impious, who dress food for their own sakes, they verily eat sin.

"From food creatures come forth; from rain is the production of food; rain proceedeth from sacrifice; sacrifice ariseth out of action.

"Know thou from Brahman (the Veda) action groweth, and Brahman (the Veda) from the Imperishable, cometh. Therefore Brahman, the all permeating, is ever present in sacrifice.' "

काङ्क्षन्तः कर्मणां सिद्धिं यजन्त इह देवताः ।
क्षिप्रं हि मानुषे लोके सिद्धिर्भवति कर्मजा ॥[4]

"They who long after success in action on earth sacrifice to the Devas; for in brief space, verily, in this world of men, success is born of action."

आ वो राजानावध्वरे ववृत्यां
हव्येभिरिन्द्रावरुणा नमोभिः ।
अस्मे इन्द्रावरुणा विश्ववारं रयिं
धत्तं वसुमन्तं पुरुक्षुम् ॥
इयमिन्द्रं वरुणमष्टमे गीः प्रावत्तोके तनये तूतुजाना ।[5]

"O Kings, Indra, Varuṇa, to this our sacrifice be
ye turned by offerings and homage,...

"O Indra, Varuṇa, plenteous wealth and food and blessing give us....

"This my song may it reach Indra, Varuṇa, and by its force bring sons and offspring."

एतेषु यश्चरते भ्राजमानेषु यथाकालं
चाहुतयो ह्याददायन् ।

तं नयन्त्येताः सूर्यस्य रश्मयो यत्र
देवानां पतिरेकोऽधिवासः ॥
एह्येहीति तमाहुतयः सुवर्चसः
सूर्यस्य रश्मिभिर्यजमानं वहन्ति ।
प्रियां वाचमभिवदन्त्योऽर्चयन्त्य
एष वः पुण्यः सुकृतो ब्रह्मलोकः ॥[6]

"Whoever works (sacrifices), pouring libations into the shining of these [the seven flames previously mentioned at the proper time, him these sun-rays lead where dwells the one Lord of the Devas. Saying to him, 'Come, come,' these resplendent libations carry the sacrificer by the sun-rays, worshipping him and saying the sweet words: 'This is your pure well-deserved Brahman-world.' "

यज्ञशिष्टामृतभुजो यान्ति ब्रह्म सनातनम् ।
नायं लोकोऽस्त्ययज्ञस्य कुतोऽन्यः कुरुसत्तम ॥[7]

"The eaters of the life-giving remains of sacrifice go to the eternal Brahman. This world is not for the non-sacrificer, much less the other, O best of the Kurus."

गतसङ्गस्य मुक्तस्य ज्ञानावस्थितचेतसः ।
यज्ञायाचरतः कर्म समग्रं प्रविलीयते ॥[8]

"From one with attachment dead, harmonious, with his thoughts established in wisdom, his works sacrifices, all *karman* melts away."

यत्करोषि यदश्नासि यज्जुहोषि ददासि यत् ।
यत्तपस्यसि कौन्तेय तत्कुरुष्व मदर्पणम् ॥
शुभाशुभफलैरेवं मोक्ष्यसे कर्मबन्धनैः ।[9]

"Whatsoever thou doest whatsoever thou eatest, whatsoever thou offerest, whatsoever thou givest, whatsoever thou doest of austerity, O Kaunteya, do thou that as an offering unto Me.

"Thus shalt thou be liberated from the bonds of action, (yielding) good and evil fruits."

References

1. *Bh.G,* viii, 3.
2. *M. Vanaparvan*, c.
3. *Bh.G,* iii, 10-15.
4. *Bh.G,* iv, 12.
5. *ṚV*, VII, lxxxiv, 1, 4, 5.
6. *Mu.Up.*, I, ii, 5, 6.
7. *Bh.G,* iv, 31.
8. *ibid.*, 23.
9. *ibid.*, ix, 27, 28.

Penances and Vows

One of the three main pillars upon which the superstructure of *dharma* (duty) rests is designated as *prāyaścitta* (penance), a highly technical term coined by the Indian sages and universally adopted everywhere in India from the earliest times. The highest perfection of man cannot be attained unless his religious and civil conduct (*ācāra* and *vyavahāra*) is refined by a proper regulation of his moral and spiritual relations. The Indian sages started with this fundamental concept, and its realization led to the formulation from very ancient times of an elaborate scheme of penances and vows, which sought to eliminate all sins and evils from society.

Literature on Penance

Any student will be struck by the vastness, antiquity, and remarkable continuity of Sanskrit literature on penance, which forms an integral part of the Dharmaśāstra. It is dealt with by all the extant Dharmasūtras, notably those of Gautama, Baudhāyana, Āpastamba, Vasiṣṭha, and Viṣṇu, as well as by most of the comprehensive Saṁhitās and Nibandhas. There are, besides, a large number of independent treatises on penance, about a hundred of which have been listed by P.V. Kane. Of the Nibandhas, the *Prāyaścitta-prakaraṇa* of Bhavadeva Bhaṭṭa is the earliest and probably the best book on the subject now available in print, and forms, together with the standard works of Śūlapāṇi and Raghunandana, the three ruling authorities on the subject in the Bengal school. One of the last works on the subject is the

Prāyaścitta-vyavasthā-saṁgraha of Kāśīnātha Tarkālaṅkāra, who lived in Calcutta and died in A.D. 1857; it was published in the life-time of the author in Śaka 1774 (A.D. 1852). Kāśīnātha was a distinguished pupil of the famous Jagannātha Tarkapañcānana and a leading Smārta of his time. From Gautama, who is supposed to be the earliest among the writers of the surviving Dharmasūtras, to Kāśīnātha there is almost an unbroken period of nearly 2,500 years, during which time the moral foundations of the Aryan culture stood like a rock against waves of hostile forces. The innumerable writers and exponents of the literature on penance played an important part in this great array. But while Gautama was hailed as a great sage in his time, Kāśīnātha had to face an aggressive modernism in the metropolis of British India.

Penance in the Vedas

There are many Vedic texts where expiation of sins by means of penances is referred to. One interesting case is cited here. Manu (Man. XI. 45) states that a penance may be performed even for an intentional act of sin on the strength of the Vedic texts. According to Medhātithi, 'the legend of Upahavya' (Upahavya-Brāhmaṇa) should be cited here as an illustration. Indra, the chief of the gods, threw some (heretic) ascetics unto wild dogs. It was obviously an intentional act, technically constituting a *brahma-hatyā* (murder of a Brāhmaṇa, the highest of sins), for which a censure confronted him. Indra ran to Prajāpati, who prescribed as a penance a single-day Vedic rite thenceforth called *upahavya*. The whole text as cited and explained by Kullūka is found in the *Tāṇdya-mahā-brāhmaṇa*, where Indra is stated to have expiated the same sin by other similar means. Viśvarūpa in his commentary (Yāj. III.212) based his arguments on the same Vedic text, more fully cited. The most striking feature of the story is the fact that Indra went through all the essentials of a penance as performed in India even today for the commitment of a sin—repentance through public censure (or the bidding of conscience, the word *aślīla* may after all mean *aśarīra*), approaching the proper authority for the prescription of a penance, and its actual performance. It only proves that a convention had already grown about the practice of penances in the age of the Brāhmaṇas.

Definition and Scope of Penances

According to Medhātithi (Man. XI.44 - Medhātithi) the word *prāyaścitta* denotes in a traditional sense (*rūḍhi*) a particular kind of 'causal' (*naimittika*) act. Bhavadeva, however, quotes a verse, ascribed to Aṅgiras by Śūlapāṇi and others, which derives the word as a compound of *prāyas* meaning austerity and *citta* meaning resolution. Raghunandana defines it on the basis of a text of Hārīta, cited and explained by him, that a penance is an act enjoined in a sacred precept as the means of only removing sins.[1] The occasion for penances is the widest possible range of offences, for, according to the well-known texts of Manu (Man. XI.44) and Yājñavalkya, (Yāj. III.219) supported by older authorities, a man who omits a prescribed act, or performs a blamable one, or cleaves to sensual enjoyments, must perform a penance. According to the interpretation of Medhātithi and Viśvarūpa, it extends to all the four castes i.e. in the language of Govindarāja, to every man. The law of penances is mainly founded on the correct interpretation of these basic texts. Medhātithi clearly states that the real incentive to the performance of an at—and in the above text of Manu the reference is to all obligatory acts whose omission is an 'offence' (*pratyavāya*)—is traceable in the *arthavāda* (exegesis) portion of the Vedas; for, the fear complex stirred up therein is, as stated in a cited text, an infinitely more powerful force than the injunctions.

In this connection a pertinent question arises that has been a matter of great controversy among the Indian philosophers and writers on the Dharmaśāstra: whether an act of penance can remove the effects of an act of sin. One opinion is, as stated pointedly by Gautama (G.D.S. XIX.4-5), the earliest among the authors of the Dharmasūtras now extant, that penances should not be done, 'because the deed does not perish.' After

Gautama onwards all the writers on *dharma* agree that penances do remove the effects of sinful acts. Medhātithi refuted an opinion (Man. XI.46 - Medhātithi) that acts cannot perish without giving effects which must be tasted, but the non-performance of penances in each case creates an extra sin. This compromise is unacceptable to the Smārtas. Śūlapāṇi, for instance, restricts the above rule beyond the pale of penances.[2] The efficacy of penances is also accepted in the Purāṇas, where sectarian views are promulgated on that basis. The *Viṣṇupurāṇa,*[3] for instance, regards the recollection of the name of Hari as the best penance for all repentant sinners, and according to the commentator Śrīdharasvāmin, other penances are nevertheless useful for those who do not believe in the name of Hari.

The institution of penances, moreover, is based on certain notions and beliefs which are confirmed articles of faith in the Aryan culture. The mythological conception of heaven and hell is one such fundamental thing, which is ingrained in the whole Indian literature from the Vedic period.

Penances and Hells

The relation between penances and hells is clearly stated in the *Yājñavalkyasaṁhitā* (III.221)—men addicted to sins without repentance and without performing penances go to hells. According to Viśvarūpa, this applies only to intentional sinners and not to those who commit sins unintentionally. Twenty-one hells are enumerated here by Yājñavalkya (Yāj. III.222.4), which fairly agree with the list given by Manu (IV. 88-90). The various Purāṇas also agree that the hells are for those who do not perform penances for sinful acts. The number and description of these zones, however, vary in the different Purāṇas considerably. It should be mentioned here that both Manu (XI.67) and Yājñavalkya (Yāj. III.236) include *nāstikya* (heresy) among minor sins (*upapātakas*), and the term primarily means, according to Medhātithi and others, disbelief in the existence of the 'other world' (of heavens and hells). The mention of hells in the very first line of the section on penances in the *Yājñavalkyasaṁhita* points to the inseparable connection between the two, which is further proved by the fact that for the words 'man must perform a penance' in the basic text of Manu (Man. XI.44) cited above, Yājñavalkya (Yāj. III. 219) substitutes the words 'man courts a hell' in the corresponding passage. Viśvarūpa curiously interprets the phrase 'addiction to sensual enjoyments' both in the texts of Manu and Yājñavalkya as equivalent to 'non-performance of penances.'

Karmavipāka

Another fundamental article of faith established in the Dharmaśāstra literature is the theory of *karmavipāka* or the ripening of antenatal acts. This is essentially based on the connected theory of the transmigration of souls, and according to it all diseases of the human body are the result of sinful acts committed in previous lives. In some cases, according to Manu (Man. XI. 48), they are the result of misdeeds committed in the present life as well. Manu (Man. XI. 49-53) and Yājñavalkya (Yāj. III. 207-15) cite a few interesting instances of the working of the theory e.g. a stealer of food (in a former life) suffers from dyspepsia (in the present life). These are in consequence of a remnant of former misdeeds, subsisting after the inescapable hell-life fated to the unrepentant. Another consequence of such misdeeds is a rebirth among the lower animals, and Yājñavalkya (Yāj. III. 207-8) has specified them by way of example for the mortal sinners. Penances prescribed for the repentant are considered to have the power of removing all the three successive horrors of hells, animal lives and human afflictions.

The theory so briefly sketched by Manu, Yājñavalkya, and other ancient sages was later on elaborated into a regular scheme, and an important section of the Dharmaśāstra named *karmavipāka* grew up on the subject. The well-known manual ascribed to the ancient sage Śātātapa and long available in print is a comparatively late work—the reading of the *Harivaṁśa* (II. 30) is a penance prescribed in it. Many famous authors composed separate books on the subject. We mention only the *Mahārṇava* in forty chapters, a sister work of the famous *Madanapārijāta*. It appears that no specific penances for antenatal misdeeds inferred from the present bodily ailments were known to Medhātithi (Man. XI. 47-Medhātithi), who applies the rule of Gautama in the matter—'the *kṛcchra* and *atikṛcchra* and the lunar penance' for all unspecified sins, though he also cites a text of Vasiṣṭha, recommending a partial observance of the penance suitable for each supposed original sin. At present, however, almost every disease is taken by the above theory to be caused by a particular sin of the previous birth, and an appropriate penance is prescribed and duly performed before death by a good number of the believing public.

Classification of Sins

All ancient sages from Gautama downwards have divided sins into two broad classes, viz. *mahāpātakas* (mortal sins) and *upapātakas* (minor sins). There is practically no difference of opinion in the enumeration of the former; they are: killing a Brāhmaṇa, drinking wine, stealing, and adultery with a guru's wife. They unmistakably point to the four corner-stones of Aryan criminology, and their bracketing together lends colour in a peculiar manner to the Indian standard of morality. The murder of a Brāhmaṇa as the greatest of all crimes is already an admitted fact in Vedic times. One such Vedic text is cited by Viśvarūpa (Yāj. III. 221). Association with the four above mortal sinners is regarded as the fifth great sin, after which both Manu (Man. XI. 56-9) and Yājñavalkya (Yāj. III. 228) enumerate a number of sins which are equal to the four great sins. Falsely accusing one's teacher, for instance, is regarded as 'equal' to *brahmahatyā* (killing a Brāhmaṇa). A long list of the minor sins (*upapātakas*) follows in the works of Manu (Man. XI. 60-71) and Yājñavalkya (Yāj. III. 234-41). These lists differ considerably in the different texts and are not, as pointed out by Viśvarūpa, exhaustive in any way. Cow-killing tops the list of the minor sins.

Bhavadeva arranges all sins in a more scientific way under five categories, viz. murder, taking forbidden food, theft, adultery and association with the wicked. They are dealt with in five successive chapters of his *Prāyaścitta-prakaraṇa*,[4] which ends with a small chapter, the sixth and last on the nature of the 'hard' penances. The book opens with a brilliant dialectic on the term 'murder'; according to his analysis, a murderer is of seven kinds, or of fourteen with intention as an additional factor.

Śūlapāṇi in the *Dīpakalikā* (Yāj. III. 259) and the *Prāyaścittaviveka* adopts a better and more detailed classification on the authority of *Viṣṇudharmasūtra* and *Saṁvarta*. The deadliest sins called *atipātakas* are adultery with one's mother, daughter and daughter-in-law. If intentional, no sort of penance, not even suicide, can expiate them. Next come the well-known *mahāpātakas*, while their equals are placed in a separate class, next in order, named *anupātakas*. A miscellaneous class is added at the end. The *Śabdakalpadruma* (under the word *prāyaścitta*) adopts a nine-fold classification, adding four minor classes after the longest list of *upapātakas*.

Penances and Other Means of Expiation

There is wide divergence among the sages in the matter of formulating the exact means of expiation of the various sins. The great task before the authors of the Nibandhas is to reconcile the ancient texts and evolve out of them a uniform law of penances. Viśvarūpa's commentary on the section of *prāyaścitta* in Yājñavalkya's work, which can well pass for a separate book, is the first attempt to bring together the conflicting views on the subject to a harmony. The ever expanding literature on the subject that grew up subsequently succeeded in evolving a regular code of penances applicable in all parts of India. The word *prāyaścitta* in a wide sense covers all the various means of expiation, only a few typical specimens of which are touched below:

1. In the earlier Vedic period, 'Vedic rites and recitals'

were largely prescribed and performed as penance. Gautama in his *Dharmasūtra* (G.D.S. XIX. 12) mentions twenty-one purificatory texts which include nine *sāmans*. In the typical section on Brāhmaṇa-killing, Manu (Man. XI. 75) prescribes among numerous alternatives the horse sacrifice and six (or four, according to Medhātithi) other Vedic rites as well as thrice reciting a whole Veda (Man. XI. 77). But these privileges of kings and others of higher caste were never open to the lower classes, and they fell away in the course of time. Bhavadeva altogether omits them, and under cow-killing makes the interesting remark that the conflicting views of ancient sages about the penances of cow-killing evidently refer to various holy sacrificial milch-cows. These sacrifices were not in vogue in his time.

2. The hardest penance prescribed and largely practised in ancient and mediaeval India was 'suicide' in various spectacular manners. According to Viṣṇu (V.S. XXXIV.1-2), followed among others by Śūlapāṇi, all guilty of *atipātakas* (incest with mother, daughter and daughter-in-law) should enter a burning fire, and no other penance exists for them. According to Manu (Man. XI. 74), a Brāhmaṇa-killer should willingly become the target of archers or throw himself thrice headlong into a blazing fire. Yājñavalkya (Yāj. III. 247) prescribes the alternative that he should offer the vital parts of his body as oblations into the fire with appropriate incantations—till he is dead, according to Bhavadeva;[5] Viśvarūpa, however, comments that it is not a death-penance. Various other death-penances are prescribed for the remaining three *mahāpātakas*. Their scope and function have been regularized by Bhavadeva, Śūlapāṇi, and other authors.

3. The hardest penance, next to suicide, is the twelve years long vow prescribed by Manu (Man. XI. 73) and Yājñavalkya (Yāj. III. 243) for Brāhmaṇa-killers. This

requires the (unintentional) homicide to dwell in a hut in the forest, subsisting on alms and making the dead man's skull his badge. Bhavadeva[6] makes here an important statement that an age-old irreproachable convention had grown in his time to equate this very hard twelve years' forest-life of exacting duties to an easier one of domestic penance named *prājāpatya* to continue for the same length of time. It is, moreover, converted to a life-long penance when the victims are the parents and other near relatives. Many lesser penances are calculated on the basis of this twelve years' vow.

4. The penances proper that pass by the well-known term *kṛcchra* (hard) are described already in the *Sāmavidhānabrāhmaṇa* (I. 2), from which Gautama (G.D.S. XXVI) and all later sages and authors have borrowed and amplified. These are mainly the *sāntapana* (subsisting on the five products of cows for a day followed by a day's fast), the five-day *parṇa-kṛcchra* (drinking only water boiled with five kinds of leaves), the four-day *tapta-kṛcchra* with hot water, milk, clarified butter and air; the twelve-day *prājāpatya* (a combination of three morning meals, three evening meals, three unasked for meals, and three fasts successively); the twelve-day *parāka* fast, and the lunar penance *cāndrāyaṇa* with food regulated by the phases of the moon. Their observance in many more intricate forms has not yet completely vanished from the austere section of the Aryans.
5. Among other means of expiation 'the gift of cows' is prominently mentioned by sages like Āpastamba (Āp.D.S. I. 9.24.1), Manu (Man. XI. 128), and Yājñavalkya (Yāj. III. 266-7). In one case Manu (Man. XI. 140) prescribes a *kṛcchra,* which normally means the *prājāpatya*, when one is unable to make the proper gift. This suggests an equation of a twelve days' vow with the gift of a single milch cow, as actually stated in

a text of Mārkaṇḍeya cited by Bhavadeva.[7] Accordingly, all the hard penances have long been converted by a convenient convention to such gifts, for the benefit of the rich who are unable to observe the former. A twelve years' vow, for instance, is equal to a gift of three hundred and sixty milch cows. By one more subsequent convention, elaborately worked out by Śūlapāṇi, the latter again is convertible to its money value, the traditional price of a cow accepted for calculation being only three copper coins. Such gifts of money as penance are still largely practised in India.

All penances are practised subject to certain common rules. They are doubled when the sins are committed intentionally, and are reduced to half for minor, old, invalid, and women sinners. They are performed openly when the sins are known to the public, but secretly otherwise. These secret penances, somewhat different from the public ones, are specially noted by Bhavadeva and other authors on the basis of ancient texts. The two well-known classes of virtues *yama* and *niyama* (self-control) are enumerated by Yājñavalkya under penance (Yāj. III. 313-4). On the other hand, the main aim of a penance is the purification of the soul (*ātmaśuddhi*). This moral and spiritual appeal runs through the whole literature on penance, imparting an elevating character to it.

Those who do not perform penances out of heresy are in the first instance dealt with by the people of their respective communities, who must ostracize them in the Indian style. For, the effect of a penance is the fitness for social fellowship (*saṁvyava-hāryatā*). Secondly, they come under the provisions of the *daṇḍa* (criminal law) and are inflicted as corporal punishment and fines. If, however, they perform the due penances fines alone are to be imposed on them.

The law of penances is to be administered by an assembly (*pariṣad*) consisting of three members learned in the Vedas, according to Manu (Man. XI. 86), though by a text of Yama (cited by Raghunandana in the *Prāyaścittatattva*) one or two members also would suffice. They must be well read in the

Mīmāṁsā and the Dharmaśāstra. Such a competent person must not refuse to state the proper penance to a penitent, who again must approach him with due respect and ceremoniously ask him for a ruling in the open assembly. Auspicious moments are observed for the purpose. The Brāhmaṇa administering the law should be properly remunerated. Formerly, it was the gift of a milch cow and a bull or garments. At present a written ruling duly signed is obtained by a penitent with some money, and in matters of controversy, healthy disputes arise among scholars over it.

The law of penances, we conclude, comes under and forms only a part of the great law of castes and orders universally established among the Aryans in India from very ancient times. This explains why Gautama in his *Dharmasūtra* commences the chapter on penances with the head-line 'Laws of castes and orders.' To shut our eyes under the blinding forces of modernism against the achievements of these ancient institutions subsisting through millenniums, is in a sense denying the first lesson of Indian history that she possesses an undying culture and a glorious past.

References

1. *Prāyaścitta-tattva*, p. 5.
2. *Dīpakalikā* (Gharpure's Ed., p. 94): *Nābhuktaṁ kṣīyate karmetyādi prāyaścittetaraviṣayam.*
3. II. 6. 36.
4. Rajshahi Ed., 1927, pp. 127-32.
5. *Prāyaścitta-prakaraṇa*, p. 8.
6. *Prāyaścitta-prakaraṇa*, p. 11.
7. *Prāyaścitta-prakaraṇa*, p. 11.

Śrāvakācāra

The Jain way of life is chiefly divided into two forms, namely Śrāvaka and Śramaṇa. The Śrāvakas are householders whereas the Śramaṇas are monks and there is a great difference between the two ways of life. The Śramaṇas observe five kinds of *mahāvratas* or great vows, namely *sarvaprāṇātipātavira-maṇa, sarvamṛṣāvādaviramaṇa, sarvāadattā dattaviramaṇa, sarvamaithunaviramaṇa* and *sarvaparigrahaviramaṇa*. In these *vratas*, total refrain from all kinds of violence, falsity, stealing, cohabitation and possession over material things is strictly maintained. On the contrary, the Śrāvakas are found to have discharged a great deal of faithful duties which are divided into three sections based on two different viewpoints. From the *vrata* point of view the Śrāvakas undertake twelve kinds of *vratas* whereas from the *pratimā* point of view they are advised to follow eleven categories of *pratimā*. In this way the *ācāra* of the Śrāvakas is maintained through both *vrata* and *pratimā*. In the first half of life the Śrāvaka has to undertake the *pratimās* gradually. In this paper an attempt has been made to make a critical analysis of *śrāvakācāra* concentrating upon the *anuvratas* and their resemblance in the householder's duties prescribed in Dharmaśastras. The first-hand sources of this paper are: The *Upāsakadaśāṅga*, the *Tattvārthasūtra* and the *Ratnakaraṇḍaka-śrāvakācāra*; the secondary sources are the *Caritrapravṛtta* of Kundkundācārya. The *Anuprekṣā* of Svami Kartikeya, the *Śrāvakācāra* of Vasunandi and the *Jainācāra*—Ch.iv by Mohanalal Mehta (Varanasi: The Parshvanath Vidyashrama Sodha Sansthan, 1966).

The twelve kinds of *vratas* prescribed for Śrāvakas are grouped under three heads, namely *anuvrata, guṇavrata* and *śikṣāvrata*. Of these, the *anuvratas* are five in number whereas the *guṇavratas* and *śikṣāvratas* are three and four respectively. In the *Upāsakadaśāṅga* both the *guṇavratas* and the *śikṣāvratas* are termed the *śikṣāvratas*. These twelve kinds of *vratas* are part and parcel of the Jaina householders life.

Mention may be made here that the *anuvratas* are of lesser importance for the Śrāvakas in comparison with the *mahāvratas* followed by the Śramaṇas. *Anuvratas* are of five categories. They are *sthūlaprāṇātipātaviramaṇa, sthūlamṛṣāvādaviramaṇa, sthūlaadattādānaviramaṇa, svadārasantoṣa* and *icchāparimāṇa*. In the *mahāvratas* of the Śramaṇas complete withdrawal from violence is included for which the Śramaṇa is called *sarvavirata*. But the *aṇuvratī-śrāvaka* gives up only the gross violence (*sthūla-hiṁsā*). Since the Śrāvakas are householders and the householders are required to maintain their life with the help of some sort of subtle violences, complete withdrawal from violence in a Śrāvaka's life is not possible. Therefore, withdrawal from violence in *śrāvakācāra* takes place partly. This is termed *deśavirati*. In *śrāvakācāra*, it is held that, occurrence of violence to a smaller extent is pardonable if it occurs in spite of due attention to non-violence. This sort of violence does not bear the testimony of *aticāra* of *aṇuvrata* in *śrāvakācāra*. The *aṇuvrati*-śrāvakas are found to have committed five types of *aticāras*: deviation from non-violence: restraining (*bandha*), killing (*vadha*), cutting of limbs (*chaviccheda*), imposition of unnecessary burden (*atibhāra*) and obstructing food and drink (*annapānanirodha*). The Śrāvakas are advised to remain aloof from these *aticāras*.

Complete withdrawal from telling the lie (*sthūla-mṛṣāvādaviramaṇa*) is the second element of *anuvrata*. For maintenance of non-violence withdrawal from telling a lie is inevitable. During life time, it is impossible on the part of a man to completely give up violence. One has to commit violence in course of eating, breathing and travelling, etc. But this is not applicable for *asatya* (untruth). One cannot give up untruth into to. But he can give up gross untruth. Gross untruths, for example, are those which are committed

(a) at the time of negotiation with the parties for finalising a marriage of one's own child by praising him in his presence which he (the party) does not deserve;

(b) telling a lie at the time of purchase and sale of goods;

(c) telling untruth for getting a job;

(d) being unfaithful to a deposit;

(e) telling a lie by giving false evidence;

(f) telling a lie for taking bribe, etc.

The Jainas also do not forget to record four forms of deviation (*aticāra*) from *sthūla-mṛṣāvādaviramaṇa* viz., *sahasā-abhyākhyāna* (sudden expression), *rahasya-abhyākhyāna* (divulging secret), *svadāramantrabheda* / *svapatimantrabheda* (breach of confidence of one's wife / husband) *mṛṣā upadesa* (false advice) and *kūṭalekhakaraṇa*. (delivering sudden decision without getting proper information, study of the subject and knowledge of the end and means of the topic) is considered to be *sahasā-abhyākhyāna*.

Rahasya-abhyākhyāna is different from this: it is disclosure of the secret matters of an individual before others. A chaste woman does not disclose the secrecy of her husband before the public and *vice versa*. Deviation from this is known to be *svapatimantrabheda* or *svadāra mantrabheda*. False advice is called *mṛṣā-upadeśa*. Preparation and submission of false document, according to the Jainas, is *kūṭalekhyakaraṇa*. A Śrāvaka is advised to get rid of these four *aticāaras*.

The third *anuvrata* is *sthūla-adattādānaviramaṇa*. In it non-acceptance of non-given articles is materialized. This is as good as untruth (*asatya*). According to *śrāvakācāra*, collection or saving of anything without requirement comes under this category. The Śrāvaka is advised to keep himself away from this sort of dealing. Misutilization of any article, also, is considered to be stealing. Therefore, a Śrāvaka is required to undertake this vow, i.e. *sthūla-adattādānaviramaṇa* during his lifetime. According to the *Tattvārthasūtra* deviation from this vow is of five kinds, viz. acceptance of an article from a thief (*stenāhṛta*). Any kind of acceptance of non-required article out of temptation is considered to be *stenāhṛta*. This is one of the five deviations (*aticāra*) of this vow. A Śrāvaka is required to keep himself untouched with this sort of act.

Purchase of stolen articles is termed *taskaraprayoga*. This is the second category of *aticāra* under *adattādanaviramaṇa* kind of *anuvrata*. The Śrāvaka is advised not to encourage stealing, not to make himself a cause of stealing and not to be involved in stealing. Activities like inspiration for stealing, assistance to stealing, giving shelter to a person who is involved in stealing, providing weapons to the dacoits for stealing and supporting the persons who are connected with stealing are included in *taskaraprayoga* class of *aticāra* of this vow.

The third category of *aticāra* is *rājyādiviruddhakarman*. Infringement of national laws, which are laid down for the welfare of the people, is construed to be an *aticāra* termed as *rājyādiviruddhakarman*. The Jainas include a number of objectionable activities in this *aticāra* like business without license, non-payment of tax, intrusion into the border of other countries without permission, transportation of prohibited articles, negligence of duty and infringement of rules for sake of self-gain, etc. A Śrāvaka is advised to restrain himself from this sort of *aticāra*.

The fourth category of *aticāra* is *kūṭamāna* i.e. cheating in measurement, counting and weighing of articles, etc. Showing unfaithfulness to a recognized gentleman is also considered to be an activity relating to this kind of *aticāra*. The Śrāvaka is advised to get rid of this *aticāra*.

The fifth category of *aticāra* is *tatpratirūpakavyavahāra* i.e. adulteration. Admixture of impure with pure, low grade articles with high grade articles and non-edible stuff with edible things are considered to belong to this class of *aticāra*. The Śrāvaka has to remain detached from these *aticāras*. It is observed that the purpose of this vow : *adattādānaviramaṇa* is more associated with public than individual interest.

The fourth *aṇuvrata* is *svadārasantoṣa* i.e. satisfaction with one's own spouse. Cohabitation with women other than own spouse is forsaken in body, mind and speech in this vrata. Similarly cohabitation with men other than husband is given up in body, mind and speech. Mention may be made here that for the Śramaṇa and Śramaṇī cohabitation is completely prohibited whereas for the Śrāvaka and Śrāvikā it is permitted under certain provisions. A Śrāvaka is not a fulltime celebate. He is partly celebate and partly householder. Cohabitation in Śrāvaka*cāra* is maintained under accepted social provision and marriage-law according to which limit of cohabitation is confined to one's own spouse only; their relation with others' wife, prostitutes and unmarried girls is automatically forbidden. This *vrata* like other *anuvratas*, has five categories of *aticāras*. They are: (i) *itvarikaparigṛhitāgamana*, (ii) *aparigṛhītāgamana*, (iii) *anaṅgakrīḍā*, (iv) *paravivāhakaraṇa* and *kāmabhogatīvrābhilāṣa*.

(i) *Itvarikaparigṛhītāgamana* is that where cohabitating relation is held with a woman who is not supposed to be the wife of anybody. This relation is kept only for a certain time. That is termed as *itvarika*.

(ii) *Parigṛhītāgamana* is a type of deviation from this *vrata* where cohabitation is held with a woman who is not accepted as own. This category includes women with whom betrothal has been made but marriage has not been solemnised, unmarried women, widows, professional prostitutes, divorced women or wives abandoned by their lawful husbands, wives of mad-men, one's own maid-servant, etc.

(iii) *Anaṅgakrīḍā* is one kind of activity where one embraces his counter-sex out of sexual excitment. This is also a contravention of *anuvrata*.

(iv) Holding of negotiation for marriage between a male and a female is taken into account as *paravivāhakaraṇa*. By this sort of activity one's vow for *anurvrata* is deviated.

(v) The fifth deviation is committed by *kāmabhogatīvrābhilāṣa*. Making cohabitation with own wife even can be marked as an *aticāra* if it is held deviating the conjugal law. This implies sort of activity which the husband may have on the wife which has a painful infliction. That is why it is considered to be a deviation from *anuvrata*. A Śrāvaka has to maintain the continuity of his *ācāra* by keeping himself unassociated with these five kinds of *aticāra*.

The last but not the least is the fifth *anuvrata* termed *icchāparimāṇa*, i.e. confinement of ambition. It is almost impossible on the part of a householder to relinquish all kinds of ambitions in tote. But those ambitions should be confined to a certain extent. This is called *icchāparimāṇa* or *icchamaryādā* or *icchāniyantraṇa*. When ambition is confined, then attachment to anything out of ownness becomes limited, as a result of which non-possessional attitude evolves. The Śrāvaka has to keep ambition for earning something, but that ambition is only made for meeting the necessity. This is, in other words, called *sthūlaparigrahaviramaṇa*. This vow is practised where the Śrāvaka utilises his capacity of earning to meet his necessity.

The Jaina Śāstrakāras have computed nine kinds of *parigrahas*. They are *kṣetra* (lands), *vāstu* (house), *hiraṇya* (articles made of metals other than gold), *suvarṇa* (golden pots and ornaments), *dhana* (wealth), *dhānya* (food or paddy) *dvipada* (servants, birds, etc.), *catuṣpad* (cow, house, buffalo, etc.) and *kupya* (any kind of article other than silver and gold). *Icchāparimāṇa* is to be confined to the possession of those nine categories of articles.

Deviation from this *vrata* can be marked when the above listed objects are kept in possession without necessity. The Śrāvaka is required to be reached from this *aticāra*.

In the four-fold *āśrama* system of vedic *smārtadharma* prescribed by the Dharmaśāstrakāras it is pointed out that in maintaining the house-holder life (*gṛhasthāśrama*), a house holder has to commit violence to others in five places which are termed as *sūnā* (slaughter house). They are: the hearth (*culli*), the grinding stone (*peṣaṇī*), the broom (*upaskara*), the pestle and mortar (*kaṇḍanī*) and the water vessel (*udakuṁbha*). By using these he is bound with the fetters of sin (*Man*. III. 68). In order to successively expiate for all these five, the great sages have prescribed for householders the daily performance of five great sacrifices, i.e. *mahāyajñas*. They are the *brahmayajña* (teaching and studying of the Vedas), *pitṛtarpaṇa* (offering of water to the manes), *devayajña* (burnt oblation offered to the gods), *bhūtayajña* (offering of *bali* to the creatures) and *nṛyajña* (hospitable reception of guests). Manu says that he who does not neglect these five *mahāyajñas* while he is able to perform them, is not tainted by the sins committed in the five places of slaughter, though he constantly lives in the order of householders. (III. 71). In the *śrāvakācāra* of the Jainas the purport of *sthūlaprāṇātipātaviramaṇa* has similarity with that of the five mahāyajñas.

In the second *aṇuvrata, sthūlamṛṣāvāda* is pointed out. It has some similarity with four kinds of evil verbal action counted by Manu in his Dharmaśāstra (XII. 6). They are *pāruṣya* (abusing others), *anṛta* (speaking untruth), *paiśunya* (detracting from the merits of all men) and *asaṁbaddha-pralāpa* (talking idly).

In the third *aṇuvrata, sthūla-adattādāna* is taken into account. This has been included in the three kinds of wicked bodily action, i.e. what has not been given: *adattānāmu-pādānam* (*Man*.XII. 7).

In the fourth *anuvrata, svadārasantoṣa*, i.e. satisfaction with one's one spouse, Dharmaśāstrakāras point out that deviation from this *vrata* is called *paradāropasevā*, i.e. holding criminal intercourse with another man's wife. They have recorded those sins in ten heads which are under five heads in *aṇuvrata* category of *śrāvakācāra*.

It is submitted that whereas the Dharmaśāstrakāras give emphasis upon expiation of sins, the Jainas lay stress on *viramaṇa*, i.e. cessation from sinful acts. They prescribe prevention of sin in lieu of exoneration after commitment of sin.

Indian Pilgrim Tradition

Millions of people visit holy places every year in India. The recent Kumbhamelā in Allahabad is said to be the greatest religious festival of the century, where it is reported, more than two and a half crore people bathed at the *saṅgama* (confluence) at an auspicious time.

In almost every part of India one can find *tīrthayātrā* or going on a pilgrimage as an important part of the local religious tradition. People from every part of the country make pilgrimages to *tīrthas* of national importance such as Banaras. In the South, devotees make pilgrimage of a cluster of places devoted to a single deity or personality such as visiting the five *bhūtaliṅgas* of Śiva. In the North, pilgrimage practice involves a holy circuit within the area of the centre. A pilgrimage in the Garhwal Himalayas includes the *tīrthas* of Hardwar, Badrinath, Kedarnath, the river sources Gaṅgotrī and Yamunotrī, the famous rivers of Bhāgīrathī, Alakanandā and Mandākinī.[1]

Pilgrimage among the Hindus has become more popular these days. The religiosity of the people may not be the sole reason for this phenomenon. The advanced modes of travel and communication and the improved economic conditions of the people have definitely changed the situation.[2] Most professions today have better working conditions with many holidays for leisure. The government and voluntary employer in addition to granting leave facilities provide financial concessions to their employees to take up tours to different parts of the country and abroad. And incidently most *tīrthasthānas* in India are centres of scenic beauty that provide solace and delight to the weary. Consequently, at least a small percentage of the crowd at *tīrthasthānas* are tourist pilgrims. There are also people who crowd the pilgrim centres for trade and business. Political leaders and film stars with their supporters and fans sometimes bring in big crowds at *tīrthasthānas* and turn them into arenas of fame and popularity. Despite all these inexpedient factors it must be admitted that the number of people who make pilgrimages with purely spiritual reasons are not totally in the decrease.

The sacred geography of India has made it a great *tīrtha*. In its sacred landscape North, South, East and West have been interconnected, thus making it a single unit of *tīrtha*. Pilgrims have circumambulated the whole of India, visiting hundreds of *tīrthas* along the way bringing Gaṅgā water from the North and pouring it over the liṅga to Rameswaram and taking sand from the sea-coasts of the South and mixing it with the lands of the river bed of Gaṅgā.[3]

Meaning and Origin of Tīrthayātrā

The great epic *Mahābhārata* (c.a. 300 B.C.) is believed to contain the earliest reference to the Indian pilgrim tradition which considers going on pilgrimage superior to sacrifice.[4] The first major treatment of *tīrthayātrā* is found in the *Tīrthayātrāparvan* of the *Mahābhārata* where the Pāṇḍavas take a circulatory tour of all *tīrthas* around the country. A great number of them are described as bestowing the benefits of the particular sacrifices, Aśvamedha, Rājasūya or Agnihotra. Later literatures, the Purāṇas and Nibandhakāras also extol the greatness of *tīrthayātra*.

The great epic *Mahābhārata* remains a great source of information about sacred places. A great number of names of sacred places are given there, though most of them are not identified till now. But wealth of place names and the location of places give an esteemed source of geography of pilgrimage. It also accounts the relative merits obtainable from each sacred place, and their relative sanctity. The *Āraṇyaka-*

paravan (book of the forests) gives a detailed description of the pilgrim places and the merits attributed to the devotees who make pilgrimages to these places. In the first part a topographical description of *tīrthas* is given. In the second part these *tīrthas* are found distributed in the four major parts of India: East, West, South and North.

The tradition of pilgrimage went through many phases of development up to the modern time. Inference from the study of the Purāṇas reveal that pilgrimages were undertaken for a wide variety of reasons. The study also indicates that the whole of India became one sacred place much before the beginning of the Christian era. Uttarakhand (Garhwal Himalayas) with its natural charm and geographic features of mountains, snow peaks, rivers and hot springs at the foot of the icy mountains took the prime of place among pilgrim centres of the Hindus.[5]

Pilgrimage is a tradition that evolved and progressed as a result of Hindu renewal in India. Bharati is of the opinion that medieval and modern pilgrimage is the development of "ruralization" of Hindu religion.[6] It is also believed that in the higher forms of Hinduism, pilgrimage is the result of an attempt to replace the animal sacrifice.[7] Vedic reference to the institution of pilgrimage is meagre and subtle though rivers and fords were considered sacred.

The earliest reference of pilgrimage could be located in the *Taittirīyabrāhmaṇa* of the *Ṛgveda*:

"Flower like the heels of the wanderer,
His body growth and is fruitful;
All his sins disappear,
Slain by the toil of his journing." (VII. 15)

The study of the places of pilgrimage and the notion of pilgrimage are of the following sources: (1) Epic and Purāṇic works, (2) Medieval works based on Purāṇic materials, (3) Travel Literatures largely from Christian missionaries, and (4) Specific studies on pilgrimage by the scholars of twentieth century. They include descriptive studies on the places of pilgrimages, analytic and problem oriented studies, pilgrims' travel guides and related literatures, gazeteers and reports; pilgrim reports and records maintained in pilgrim centres by the priests.

1. Concept of Tīrthayātrā

The reverence for rivers, and the merits of journeying was continuous from Vedic times, which later Hinduism developed as the institution of pilgrimage. The concept of *tīrthayātrā* can be traced back to the reverence Aryans had for rivers as it is clear from the famous river hymns (*nadistuti*) of the *Ṛgveda*. Later on, i.e., during the period of Epics and Puranas and in the religious life of the emerging Indian tradition *tīrtha* as the spiritual ford began to be the destination of the pilgrims. Journey made to the *tīrtha* began to be known as *tīrthayātrā* always in the context of the symbolic language of a river, a ford or a crossing.

Many pilgrim centres were connected with water fords. Water as cleaning physical impurities was taken symbolically as removing sins. Some such water fords are associated with legendary figures like Rāma and Lakṣmaṇa. There is a water ford known after Rāma where he is believed to have washed his sins away for killing Rāvaṇa. Lakṣmaṇadhārā is a water spring in Rishikesh near Lakshmanjhula bridge. It is believed that Lord Lakṣmaṇa developed white patches on his body after he had slain the Rākṣasa Rāvaṇa. So he washed his body and drank this water. He got cured of his skin disease. Lepers flock to this area today believing that the water of Lakṣmaṇadhārā would cure them. Commenting on the understanding of *tīrthayātrā* of the believer Morinis notes:

> The conceptual gulf between the all pervasive unconcerned absolute and the teaming, suffering, sentient masses who live and die requires a philosophical bridge. It is the latter group that seeks an understanding of the cosmic order from religion, and is little satisfied with a doctrine which states with finality, All is All. It is phenomenologically clear that 'All' is in some sense divisible.

A deeper understanding of Indian pilgrim tradition (*tīrthayātrā*) requires a careful analysis of the terms *tīrtha* and *yātrā*.

Tīrtha - The Etymology

In a wider sense all places of geographical importance, a river, its source, its confluence, a mountain, a tree, a cave, boundaries of a place, a person and organs of the body, all came to be known as *tīrtha*. The literal meaning of *tīrtha* is a crossing over or a ford-crossing over to the other side of a river or lake. A natural place where a symbolic crossing over from *saṁsāra* to *mokṣa* takes place was also called *tīrtha*—a place of *pilgrimage*. This devotion to *tīrtha* and the journey made to such *tīrthas* is called *tīrthayātrā*. In India, this tradition of *tīrthayātrā* is older than the myths and deities to which it is often attached.

The Vedic word *tīrtha* was known in Pali and *Prākṛta* as *tittha*.[8] This is said to have come from the root √tṝ (*tarati*) meaning, to get through, to cross over. Hence, its noun *tīrtha* meant the following: (1) a passage, road, way, ford; (2) a descent into the river, the stairs of a landing place; (3) remedy, means; (4) place of water; (5) a holy place, place of pilgrimage, a shrine dedicated to some holy object or near the bank of a sacred river; (6) a sacred or holy personage; (7) a sacred preceptor; a teacher; (8) a source, origin; (9) sacrifice; (10) minister; (11) advice, instruction; (12) right place or moment.[9]

The noun *tīrtha* means a bathing place or a ford. It also means a passage or a path. The root √tṝ has other meanings too—to master, to subordinate, to be saved, to fulfill and hence, the noun *tāraka* means a boat, a ferry, a pilot or a saviour. With its varied meanings the word *tīrtha* stands for a passage, path or way of a traveller, not the goal.

The meaning of *tīrtha* today is associated with a place of pilgrimage which may or may not be in the vicinity of a river or lake. A *tīrtha* in depth is a consecrated spot as a crossing over to heaven, it could be a temple, shrine, river, mountain, cave, tree or a person. Eck epitomizes: "No place is too small to be counted a *tīrtha* by its local visitors. In a sense each temple is a *tīrtha*, especially, consecrated as a crossing place between heaven and earth."

Tarati: The Act of Crossing

Tarati, the verb has a number of subsidiary meanings such as to conquer, to subdue, and to surpass. All its uses in the Saṃhitās, the Brāhmaṇas and the Upaniṣads are in a ritual or spiritual sense. The wind is said to cross (*tarati*) the whole universe like a runner carrying the offerings to gods. *Tarati*, the verb of passage is used with sacrifices. The hymns of sacrifices are called ships that carry the sacrifices to the other shore. The sacrifices (*taranti*) cross over the year just as one crosses over the river.

Gods make frequent crossings from heaven to earth. Agni and Soma make their descent and ascent manifesting their divine presence on earth and in heaven. Agni, the fire of heaven, descends on the sacrifice on earth as sacrificial fire. Uṣas, the threshold between the night and the day, is a crosser reaching out with its own rays of radiance, crossing the waters and reaching the hills. Sūrya (sun) crosses over the sea of space between heaven and earth and this crossing is known as *sētu* (bridge). The notion of *avatāra*, or divine descent, is also an act of crossing over (*ava*+$\sqrt{\text{tṛ}}$ = to cross downwards).

Tirtha as Crossing Places

The Sanskrit root $\sqrt{\text{tṛ}}$ recurs in places related to pilgrimages. Tārā, Tārāpīṭh and Tārakeśvara are pilgrim centres in Bengal. Vaitaraṇī, the mythological river separating earth and Yama's nether world is also a word originating from the root $\sqrt{\text{tṛ}}$ meaning crossing over or passage. One of the derivations of *tīrtha* is closely related to river, it is the crossing place, a landing place on the river bank (*tīra*). It is associated with good water for drinking and bathing—pure running water.

Tīrtha as Pure Running Water

The rivers of India great and small remind us of *tīrtha* waters, on the bank of which are some of India's famous *tīrthas*, Prayaga and Varanasi on the Gaṅgā, Amarkantaka and Tryambaka at the head waters of Narmada and Godavari respectively, and Srirangam on the island of Kaveri, to mention a few. *Tīrtha* is so closely related to pure running waters of these rivers that in the South *tīrtha* has come to mean sacred water given at the temple as *prasāda*. *Tīrtha* is translated also as 'holy water' and '*tīrthasthāna*' as a holy water place.[10]

Tīrtha, as drinking water was considered purifying and nourishing. It was identified with nourishing milk and intoxicating and purifying *soma*. The *tīrtha* waters are called "strength and sap". All the sacredness attributed to Gaṅgā myths comes from this notion of *tīrtha*. Gaṅgā is said to flow with milk and *amṛta*, the nectar of immortality.

Tīrtha as the Place of Bathing

Bathing in a *tīrtha* is an act of penance and purification. It is also a preparation for some ritual act. The priest in a *soma* sacrifice is to bathe in a *tīrtha*. The pilgrim tradition of bathing has its foundation here. One who bathes and is purified becomes a *tīrtha,* a crossing place for others.

Tīrtha as A Boundary Line

The liminal nature of *tīrtha* is clear from its other meanings—a 'threshold' or a 'betwixt'—a link between this world and the other. The best time for *Aqnihotra* are the two twilights—Uṣas and Sandhyā—called the *tīrthas,* because night and day take away everything as if by flood. The introductory and concluding parts of *soma* sacrifice also are known *tīrthas* since they are the threshold of time and space. It is at *tīrthas* that the journey between heaven and earth is launched.

Tīrthas as Sacrifice

Tīrtha was also used to mean sacrifice. *Yajña* is *tīrtha*.

Sacrifices were meant to link this world with the other. A real communication between God and man is made at sacrifice. The path at which both Gods and the priests drink the *soma* was known as *tīrtha*. Having approached the sacrifice by this *tīrtha* they obtain all desires. By performing a sacrifice one transcends this world to the world of heaven. This crossing is the crossing of the sacrifice.

The Upaniṣads also use the word *tarati* to mean a spiritual transition or transformation into the Brahman illumined by knowledge. The knower of the Brahman becomes the Brahman: "He crosses over (*tarati*) sorrow. He crosses over (*tarati*) sin. Liberated from the knots of the heart, he becomes immortal. The Upaniṣadic notion of the verb √tṝ is the crossing over of birth and death to immortality, from darkness to light and from ignorance to knowledge. The Vedic meaning of crossing over is transcending old age and death and the troubles of this world. The *Ṛgvedic* prayer is that we may cross over all troubles to a place of glory where there is no sorrow. Pointing to another prayer in the *Taittirīya Brāhmana* Eck mentions that the purified man crossing over (*tarati*) sins prays that we may likewise cross over (*tarema*) sins. The sacrificer also prays that we may cross over (*tarāmi*) death.

The word *tīrtvā* is also used for an interior crossing in the yogic discipline. Eck quotes an Upaniṣadic passage (*Maitri Up. 6. 28*): "Having slain the door keeper called egoism and after having crossed over (*tīrtva*) with the raft of the syllable 'OM' one enters the other side of the space of heart and enters the hall of Brahman. One who has united with the Brahman is not followed by good or evil, he has passed beyond (*tīrṇo*) all sorrows of the heart. One who knows *ātman* crosses beyond (*tarati*) this world of quality.

Kāla Tīrthas

Time becomes a *tīrtha* when such time is auspicious, known as *kālatīrtha*; the day and time of worship, such as *Kartikeya* in the month of Kārtikā, the time for the study of the Purāṇas, months such as Māgha and Vaiśākha.

A *tīrtha* may be a sacred place, a sacred river, a sacred mountain, or a sacred forest. Sometimes not just one spot, but a large space, region or centre is considered sacred, then *Kṣētra* or *Maṇḍala*[11] is used in place of *tīrtha*. The Buddhist scriptures use *kṣētra* (Pali, *khetta*) very frequently. Though all *tīrthās* are not *kṣhētras* the word *kṣētra* is sometimes used to denote a *tīrthā*. In the Brāhmaṇic scriptures some of the *tīrthās* are described as *Siddha-kṣētras*, the place of supreme attainment.

Kṣētras are sacred dwellings of all principal Hindu pantheons like *Brahma-kṣētra, Viṣṇu-kṣētra, Śiva-kṣētra* and *Śakti-kṣētra*. Similarly there are many gods associated with *kṣētra*: such as *Gaṇapati-kṣētra* of Kumbakonam, *Sūrya-kṣētra* of Konarka and *Bhṛugu-kṣētra* of Narmada.

The study of *tīrtha* in the light of the above discussions may be summarized in the words of Morinis:

> A *tīrtha* is an institution which may be analysed on several levels. It is a geographical location which draws people to it from a wide area. It is thus a 'central place' with many central place functions. It is an important node in the religious life of the people, often a centre for the propagation of the orthodox faith of the cult. It thus has functions within the religious community of the region. The *tīrtha* is also an institutional system in its own right, with a temple, priests, service of worship etc. Fourthly, it is a focus of symbolic behaviour, and particularly of symbolic behaviour appropriate to the specific character of the different deities who reside in the pilgrimage shrines. The ritual activities of the pilgrims are largely indistinguishable from those of ordinary worshippers except for the necessity of the pilgrims journeying. This will be an important and in fact defining, symbolic activity of the pilgrims. None of the above is a pre-eminent characteristic of the place of pilgrimage. All are different aspects of its institutional character and all exist simultaneously in every place of pilgrimage.

Tīrthasthāna

The sacredness of a *tīrtha* is extended to the whole area of an object or site and not just to the shrine built upon the *tīrtha*, that is why even after the destruction of the shrine at Kāśī by the Mughals the sanctity of the *tīrtha* remained. Every inch of Kāśī, even the dust particle is said to be sacred. The *maṇḍala* or *kṣētra* concepts are important here. Perpetuating a *tīrtha* by building a shrine or a temple in a large walled campus is a South Indian tradition. The sacredness of *tīrtha* is confined to the *maryādā* (outer walls) of the temple complex.

Pilgrims usually attribute the cause of their attraction to a certain place of pilgrimage to *sthāna-māhātmyā*, the greatness of the location. Thus it is not the rituals performed at a *tīrtha* that are important—"it is going there and being there. *Tīrthayātrā* is the rite, the place is the power." So it is said in Varanasi even sleep is *yoga* and causal conversation is the repetition of *mantra*. But on close observation it may be seen that it is the belief about the power of the sanctity of the sight taken together with its geographical location, its well-endured temple or the sanctity of its founder that makes a place sacred or a place of pilgrimage, rather than its mere location or importance of its saintly founder.

Tīrthaṅkaras and Tīrthas

Tīrthaṅkara is a Jain patriarch of the highest order, the word *tīrthaṅkara* means ford maker, (*tīrtha* + $\sqrt{}$*kṛ*) ford finder, because he is supposed to show men a path in the dark waters of life. He is also known as Jīna—'conqueror', because he has overcome the problems of life and attained perfect knowledge. This terminology *tīrthaṅkara* is also found in Buddhist literature.

Tīrtha is a title of an order of Sannyāsins of the Śaṅkarācārya School, like Svamī Rāma Tīrtha (1873-1906) and Mahātmā Pūrṇānanda Tīrtha (1875-1947). The term *tīrtha* is used for any learned man. A teacher, father, a chaste wife, are all *tīrthas*. *Tīrtha* is also the 650th name of Śiva.

2. Yātrā as Spiritual Journey

The word *yātrā* (*ya*+ $\sqrt{tṛ}$) means an act of going. Hence, it meant a journey, and later a journey to a sacred place—pilgrimage. In all Indian languges *yātrā* stands for pilgrimage. The word *yātrā* did not seem to have this infused meaning in the ancient past. *Yātrā* in the Vedas meant only a journey or a travel and pilgrimage to holy places did not enjoy a meritorius treatment. The English equivalent for *yātrā* or *tīrthayātrā* is pilgrimage.

The exile of Sītā and Rāma is seen as *yātrā*. The rejection of Sītā by Rāma—"the ideal to which she was married" doubled her sufferings, Yet she kept her commitment to Rāma. Fire (*agni*) proved her purity and the ideals he stood for and she was proved faithful by Rāma too. Endurance and persistence in our individual spiritual journey alone can give us lasting joy and satisfaction and a sense of belonging.

Eligibility for Pilgrimage

The eligibility (*adhikāra*) for pilgrimage is for both men and women of any age or caste. A bath in Kāśī (*avimukta*) is believed to wash away the sins of all *varnas*, Candālas and persons whose bodies are full of dreaded skin diseases and aggrevated sins.

Persons of all *āśramas* or stages of life are eligible for pilgrimage. But Dharmaśāstras prescribe that a Brahma-cārin only with the guidance of his guru, a householder with his wife, a woman with the permission of her care-takers, may go for pilgrimage. Before going on a *tīrthayātrā* one has to pay off all the debts.

One may not undertake a *yātrā* leaving aside the duties of one's life. Such people will not reap the fruits of *tīrtha-yātrā* in this world as well as in the next. Anyone going for a *yātrā* has to see to the maintenance of his dependants till his return.

References

1. Jagdish Kaur. 1979. *Traditions of Himalayan Pilgrimage in Garhwal : A Historico-Geographical Enquiry.* Srinagar, 1979, p. 58.
2. S.M. Bharadwaj. *Hindu Places of Pilgrimage in India.* Berkeley: University of California Press, 1973, p. 5.
3. Diana L. Eck "India's Tirthas: Crossing in Sacred Geography", *History of Religions* 20; 4 (1981), 336.
4. Bharadwaj. 1973 : 29.
5. Jagdish Kaur. 1979 : 58-60; Bharadwaj 1973 : 33.
6. Agehananda Bharati, "Pilgrimage in the Indian Tradition," *History of Religion* 3 (1963), 137.
7. James Hasting. (ed.) 1918. "Pilgrimages", *Encyclopaedia of Religion and Ethics*, X, 24.
8. Baidyanath Saraswati, *Traditions of Tīrthās in India : Anthropology of Hindu Pilgrimage.* Varanasi : N.K. Bose Foundation, 2. 1983.
9. V.S. Apte. 1958. "Tirtha". *Sanskrit - English Dictionary.* Poona : Prasad Publication, 1958, 775.
10. Savitri V. Kumar. 1983. *Purāṇic Lore of Holy Water Places.* New Delhi : Munshiram Manoharlal Publishers.
11. *Ibid.* 8-10; Mircea Eliade. 1954. *Yoga, Immortality and Freedom.* Trask Williard (trans), London : Routledge & Kegan, 219-20; 1954.
12. Benjamine Walker, 1968 *Hindu World : E.S.H.* 2 vol. London : Allen & Unwin, 1968, 505. Jain religion is said to have derived its name from this word.
13. Caroline McKenzie. n.d. "Sita as Yātrika : A Meditation on Deepavali", *Yātrika : A Women's News Letter.* Caroline and Vishram. (ed.) Bangalore : Silvepura Turbanhalli, 4 & 5.
14. P.V. Kane. 1953. *H.D.*, IV. Poona : Bhandarkar Oriental Institute, 1953, 568-70.

Women and Religion

Let us consider in this chapter the status and privileges which Hindu religion accorded to women. In the present age when religion is gradually losing its hold on popular mind, the subject may appear as of no great importance to some of our readers. The case, however, was quite different in the past. Religious rights and privileges were valued most highly; even political and proprietary rights faded before them in importance. The social status of an individual was vitally connected with the place which religion accorded to him in its rites and rituals. Privileges accorded or denied to women by religion will, therefore, throw valuable light on their position in society.

In his early history man is seen excluding women from religious service almost everywhere because he regarded her as unclean, mainly on account of her periodical menstruation. During this period the woman was the object of the greatest dread. The case is on record of an Australian aborigine going stark mad because he had unknowingly touched the blanket used by his wife during her period, and then killing first his wife and then himself under the influence of his frenzy. The dread which this Australian felt was shared by the average man in early history, when he did not know the physiological causes of the mysterious phenomenon, which he feared so much.

The Aryans also regarded the woman as untouchable during her monthly period. This was the case as early as the Indo-

Iranian age. Like the Hindus, the Iranians also used to segregate women during this period and regard them as religiously impure (Vendidad, 16). The Vedic age assigned this temporary impurity of women to their taking over from Indra one third the sin of Brāhmaṇa murder, which he incurred when he had killed Vṛtra (the *Taittirīya Samhitā,* II, 5, 1, 5-7). During this period, therefore, Hindu society has been regarding women as extremely impure and temporarily untouchable. Even the sight of their person and the sound of their voice were to be avoided. Hygienic rules often appear in the form of religious taboos in Hindu culture, and there can be no doubt that the complete isolation of women that was insisted upon during this period was partly due to the desire of ensuring complete rest which is so desirable for them during this period.

Child-bearing was regarded as the special function of women, and evil spirits were believed to be very anxious to visit them during their periods to prevent conception. In the Vedic age brides were grown up in marriage and its consummation took place usually on the fourth day. One Vedic stanza in the marriage hymn prays that the bride should have no evil eye, and hopes that she would not be the cause of the sudden death of her husband (ṚV. X. 85. 44). We can understand this strange prayer only if we note the belief of the early times that evil spirits, haunting the period of the bride, render her touch and sight very dangerous to her husband. One stanza of the marriage hymn expressly refers to a female spirit taking possession of the bride and attempting to do harm to her husband through her person (ṚV. X. 85. 29). The prayer, above referred to, praying that the bride may not be the cause of her husband's death is a magical formula intended to immunise the husband from the possible consequences of his contact with the evil spirits, haunting his bride at the time of the menstruation and consummation.

From the Vedic time downwards women have been regarded as impure during the time of confinement also. The phenomenon of menstruation is repeated at child-birth.

Besides it was apprehended that evil spirits would be haunting the mother during her confinement on account of their eagerness to kill new-born babies.

Apart from the periods of menstruation and confinement women were not regarded as impure by religion. It is true that a ceremony to purify the wife before her participation in sacrifices has been enjoined (*Śat. Br.,* V, 2, 1, 8-10); we cannot however, attach much importance to it, for a similar purification has been prescribed for men also (*Tai. Br.*, 1, 3, 7). In the Vedic age women enjoyed all the religious rights and privileges, which men possessed. In Chapter I we have seen that women used to receive Vedic education. Some of them were even the authors of Vedic hymns (*ante*, p. 10). They, therefore, could recite the Vedic *mantras* as a matter of course. Some women, especially unmarried ones, are seen offering Vedic sacrifices all by themselves. In one place we find a maiden taking a shoot of the *soma* shrub while returning from her bath, and straightway offering it in sacrifice to Indra, when she reached home (Tai. Br. VIII. 91.1). In another place we find a lady, named Viśvavārā, getting up early in the morning and starting the sacrifice all by herself (Ṛ̣V. V. 28. 1). In the Vedic age there were no images to worship or temples to visit. The Bhakti school, advocating simple prayer to God by mere songs of devotion, was yet to come into prominence, as also the Jñāna theory recommending merely the contemplation of Brahman or Ātman. So the offering of sacrifice was the only popular and well-established method of worshipping divine powers. Naturally, therefore, it could not be interdicted to women, especially because they were all initiated into Vedic studies after their *upanayana*. All of them therefore could offer sacrifices after their initiation.

Marriage, and not renunciation, was the ideal recommended to society by Vedic religion. The woman therefore was not an impediment in the path of religion; her presence and cooperation were absolutely necessary in religious rites and ceremonies. This naturally increased her religious value. Man could not become a spiritual whole, unless he was accompanied by his wife (Ai. Br. I. 2.5); gods do not accept the oblations offered by a bachelor (Śat. Br. V. I. 6. 10). The husband alone cannot go to heaven; in the symbolical ascent to heaven in the sacrifice, he has to call his wife to accompany him on the occasion (*Śat. Br.*, V. 2, 1, 8). A son was indispensable for spiritual well-being in the life to come, and he could be had only through the wife. She was thus indispensable from the spiritual and religious points of view. This circumstance was responsible for ensuring her a religious status as high as that of her husband.

Normally, religious prayers and sacrifices were offered jointly by the husband and the wife. There are several references to couples waxing old in their joint worship of gods (ṚV. V. 53-15). The wife used to take an active and real part in family sacrifices. Like the husband, she too had to perform a special *upanayana* on the occasion of some sacrifices. She had her own hut in the sacrificial compound, and also her own cow to provide her with sacred milk during the sacrifice (*Śat. Br.*, X. 2, 3, 1; XIV. 3, 1, 35). In the early Vedic period, the duty of chanting musically the Sāma songs seems to have been usually performed by the wife; later on it came to be entrusted to special class of male priests called Udgātṛs. The wife used to pound the sacrificial rice, give bath to the animal that was to be immolated and lay in bricks, when altar was to be built (*Śat. Br.*, VI. 5, 3, 1; III. 8, 2, 1-6). She participated with her husband in the preparation of the offering, the consecration of the fire, the offering of the oblations and the concluding ceremonies. She herself had to recite some formulae. It is true that sometimes these had to be dictated to her; but the case was probably the same with her husband also with reference to the prayers in many of the sacrifices. Women's participation in Vedic sacrifices was thus a real and not a formal one; they enjoyed the same religious privileges as their husbands.

If the husband was away on a journey, the wife alone performed the various sacrifices, which the couple had to offer jointly. This was the case in the Indo-Iranian period as well (Erpatistan, Fargard 1). This practice continued down to the Sūtra period (*c.* 500 B.C.).

Indrāṇī in one place proudly claims that she had started some rites and rituals (ṚV. X. 86.10). Gods and goddesses are usually fashioned after the human model. We may therefore well infer that a few lady theologians may have made some contributions to the development of the Vedic ritual. What Indrāṇī did might well have been possible for some of the cultured ladies of the Vedic age, whose songs have been honoured by their inclusion in the Vedic *saṁhitā*. We have, however, no direct evidence on the point.

There were some sacrifices which could be offered by women alone down to 500 B.C. Sītā sacrifice, intended to promote a rich harvest was one of them. Rudrabali was another; it was intended to ensure prosperity and fecundity among the cattle (*P.G.S.*, II. 17; III. 8, 10). Rudrayāga, intended to secure goodluck to maidens in marriage, was a third one. The last mentioned sacrifice could of course be performed by women alone; in the case of the earlier two, it is possible that the exclusive association of women with them was due to the theory that since they are intended to promote rich harvest and fertility, they should be performed by women alone, who are their visible symbols.

If the cooperation of the husband was unavailable for any reason, the wife could offer the sacrifices all alone. On the morning of Rāma's installation as the crown prince, Kauśalyā is seen performing all alone the Svastiyāga to ensure felicity to her son; she was the neglected wife, and probably she felt that it would be too much to expect her husband to come to participate in the sacrifice. At that time he was as a matter of fact engaged in assuaging the wrath of his favourite wife Kaikeyī. Similarly Tārā is represented by Vālmīki as performing alone the Svasti sacrifice, when her husband Vālin was about to issue out to fight with Sugrīva. This was probably because Vālin was then too busily engaged in equipping himself to find time to participate in his wife's sacrifice. These instances show that in the early period women's participation in sacrifices was a real one; nay, very often husbands used to leave the whole affair to the exclusive charge of their wives, when they were otherwise very busy. The normal practice, however, was that the couple would jointly perform the various sacrifices.

Intercaste *anuloman* marriages were permitted during this period. What then was the religious status of a wife who belonged to a lower caste? Could she participate in sacrifices? Later writers like Manu no doubt ordain that only the wife of the same caste could be associated with the husband in the sacrifices. The view of the earlier age was different; it allowed a *dvija* wife of the lower caste also full religious privileges, if she were the only wife of the husband.[1] A Śūdra wife, or a wife for whom a bride-price had been paid was, however, not entitled to any religious rights and privileges.

The participation in sacrifices presupposed Vedic study, and girls used to devote themselves to it during their maidenhood (*ante*, p. 10-11). The Initiation Ceremony (*upanayna*) of girls used to take place as regularly as that of boys at the normal time. This was the case as early as the Indo-Iranian age. The Parsis have still preserved this custom; Naojot ritual, which corresponds to Hindu *upanayana*, is even now performed by them regularly in the case of girls as well. In India, the initiation of girls used to take place regularly down to the beginning of the Christian era. The Vedic age held that *brahmacarya* discipline and training was as much necessary for girls as it was for boys. It was apprehended that if the most important religious *saṁskāra* of *upanayana* was not performed in the case of girls, women would be automatically reduced to the status of Śūdras; how then could Brāhmaṇas, Kṣatriyas and Vaiśyas be born of them? *Upanayana* of women was absolutely indispensable, if the cultural tradition of the different Aryan classes was to be preserved.

After their *upanayana* girls used to follow a discipline more or less similar to that of boys. They were, however, shown certain concessions. They were not to grow matted hair. Like boys, they were not to go out to beg their daily food. As far as possible, they were to be taught by their near relations like the father, the uncle or the brother. They were permitted to discontinue their course, when their marriages were settled at about the age of 16 or 17. A few, however, continued their studies for a much longer time and were known as Brahma-vādinīs. It is a great pity that most of the above rules about the *upanayana* of girls should have to be gathered from works written at a time when the custom was rapidly going out of vogue, or had already ceased to be followed. We therefore get only very scrappy and insufficient information on the subject.

We have seen already (*ante*, pp. 12-13) how after their *upanayana* women used to specialise in Vedic theology and philosophy. Nay, some of them figure among the authors of Vedic hymns, the very reading of which was going to be prohibited to their sex by a later age. Women held that they were inherently entitled to study the Vedas; we find a sweetheart flatly declining to marry her lover, when she suspected that he was disinclined to reveal to her some of his Vedic dogmas and theories (*Tai. Br.*, II. 3, 10). When *upanayana* of girls was common, it is needless to add that women used to offer morning and evening prayers as regularly as men; the *Rāmāyaṇa* twice discloses Sītā discharging this religious duty (II. 87. 19; V. 14. 48).

During the age of the Brāhamaṇas (1500 to 1000 B.C.), the volume of Vedic studies became very extensive, as a number of subsidiary sciences were developed and lengthy commentaries were written on Vedic texts. The spoken dialect of the age had begun to differ considerably from the language of the Vedic hymns, and the theory had found universal acceptance that to commit a single and even a most minor mistake in the recitation of a Vedic Mantra would produce disastrous consequences to the reciter.[2] As a natural consequence, society began to insist that those who wanted to undertake Vedic studies must be prepared to devote a fairly long period, of about 12 to 16 years to the task. We have seen that at this time women used to be married at about the age of 16 or 17, and could thus give only 7 or 8 years to their Vedic studies. So short a period was quite insufficient for an efficient grounding in the Vedic lore in the age of the Brāhmaṇas. Society was not prepared to tolerate dilettante Vedic studies, and as a consequence, lady Vedic scholars began to become rarer and rarer.

Vedic sacrifices also became very complicate at this time; they could be properly performed only by those who had studied their minute intricacies very carefully. As a consequence, the participation of women in sacrifices gradually became a mere matter of formality. For some time wives continued to perform the duties that were formerly allotted to them in sacrifices, but gradually a tendency arose to allot most of the sacrificial work to males. Many sacrificial duties that could be once discharged by the wife alone, came to be assigned to male substitutes in the age of the Brāhmaṇas.[3] In some rituals like the *srastarārohaṇa*, women continued to take a prominent part and recite the Vedic *mantras* down to 500 B.C. (*P.G.S.*, III. 2), but the practice became gradually unpopular. The wife was originally entitled to offer oblations in the Gṛhya fire in the absence of the husband; now a son, or a brother-in-law began to act in her place (*Śan. G.S.*, II. 17, 13). She continued to perform the evening sacrifice down to the beginning of the Christian era, but the recitation of the Vedic mantras was prohibited to her on the occasion.[4]

As amateur Vedic studies could not be encouraged, and as women had now to take a purely formal part in sacrifices, the *upanayana* of girls began to become a mere formality in course of time. At 500 B.C., as we learn from Hārīta, only a few Brahmavādinīs used to devote themselves seriously to Vedic studies after their *upanayana*; in the case of the vast majority of girls the formality of the sacrament was somehow gone through just before their marriage. A few centuries rolled on in this way and then writers like Manu began to advocate that girls' *upanayana* may be performed, but no

Vedic *mantras* should be recited on the occasion (Man. III. 66). This development may be placed at about the beginning of the Christian era. *Upanayana* without Vedic *mantras* being recited in and taught after the ritual was a contradiction in terms, and so later authors like Yājñavalkya began to advocate the more honest and straightforward course of prohibiting the ceremony altogether in the case of girls (I. 13). A theory was started that the marriage ritual in the case of girls really served the entire purpose of *upanayana*; service of the husband corresponded to the service of the preceptor, and household duties were a fit substitute for the service of the sacrificial fire (Man. II. 67). *Upanayana,* therefore, was unnecessary for girls. It may have been prescribed for them in a former age, but that rule was a dead letter in the present one. It is interesting to see how later writers like Medhātithi proceed to explain away clear passages in earlier texts permitting women's *upanayana* (on Man., V. 155). Eventually medieval digest writers like Mitramiśra made wonderful discoveries of stray passages from lost Purāṇas, which boldly declared that women have the same status as that of the Śūdras and are, therefore, altogether ineligible for *upanayana*.

Minor religious rituals like the *jātakarman*, *nāmakaraṇa*, *cūḍā*, etc. were originally performed just as regularly in the case of girls as they were in that of boys. When *upanayana* was discontinued in the case of girls, it began to be advocated that other rituals also should be permitted to them, only if they were performed without the recitation of the Vedic *mantras*. This position has been taken up by almost all the Smṛti writers.

The prohibition of *upanayana* amounted to spiritual disenfranchisement of women and produced a disastrous effect upon their general position in society. It reduced them to the status of Śūdras. We have seen how in the earlier age women could, if necessary, perform sacrifices all by themselves. But now Manu came forward to declare that a pious Brāhmaṇa should not attend a sacrifice, which is performed by women (IV. 205). There were many Śruti texts which clearly declared that the husband and the wife were to perform the Vedic sacrifices jointly. When the *upanayana* of women became a mere formality at about 200 B.C., there arose a school which advocated that wives should not be associated with their husbands even formally in the performance of Vedic sacrifices. It argued quite seriously that the references in sacred texts to the sacrifices in the dual number did not refer to the husband and the wife, but to the sacrificer and the priest (*P.M.*, 1, 1, 2, 2)!

This new theory was opposed by the orthodox tradition, as it was all along accustomed to see sacrifices being jointly performed by the husband and the wife. The wife's participation had no doubt become a formal one, but society was not prepared to stop it altogether. Jaimini was the spokesman of the orthodox school, and he has explained very clearly how the references to the sacrificers in the dual number can denote only the husband and the wife. While doing so, however, he emphatically declares that a woman alone is quite ineligible to perform any sacrifice. 'The woman can stand no comparison with man. The sacrificer is learned, his wife is ignorant.' The new theory took some time to popularise. In Jaimini's own time queen Nayanikā of the Deccan performed a number of Vedic sacrifices during her widowhood, and there was no dearth of learned Brāhmaṇas to accept her handsome gifts on the occasion. The practice of women performing sacrifices by themselves, however, died down by the beginning of the Christian era. As pointed out already, Manu (Man. IV. 205) is seen condemning it sternly in his code. The Smṛti school on the whole was inclined to curtail the earlier religious rights and privileges of women, mainly because *upanayana* was no longer performed in their case. Those, who had not undergone this Vedic *saṁskāra* were naturally held to be incompetent to offer Vedic sacrifices.

The prohibition of Vedic sacrifices to women did not, however, produce any long standing hardship; for these sacrifices themselves soon went out of vogue. Neither men nor women were eager to perform them from about the beginning of the Christian era. What, however, did infinite harm to women was the theory that they were ineligible for them because they were of the status of the Śūdras. Henceforward, they began to be bracketed with Śūdras and other backward classes in society. This we find to be the case even in the *Bhagavadgītā* (IX. 32).

It must be here pointed out that the exclusion of women from Vedic studies and sacrifices was not due to any deliberate plan to lower their status. Custodians of the Vedic lore honestly believed that no one should be allowed to recite and use the Vedic *mantras* who had not studied them properly. Women found it impossible to devote the necessary time for this purpose on account of their early marriages. It was, therefore, but fair that they should not be allowed to invite on themselves and their relations those dreadful calamities, which were honestly believed to result from an incorrect recitation of the Vedic stanzas. The desire was not to humiliate women, but rather to save them from dire consequences.

When the Vedic *karmamārga* gradually went into background, its place was taken by the new *bhakti* and Pauranic schools, which rose into prominence at 500 A.D. The leaders of these movements had a catholic outlook and threw open their doors to all, irrespective of sex and caste. This was a welcome development for women. Their religious disenfranchisement had created a vaccum; it was filled by the Bhakti-Pauranic religion. In fact they became its *de facto* custodians.

Women are by nature more religious and devotional than men. They can visit temples with greater regularity, perform sacred rites with higher faith and submit to religious fasts with more alacrity than men. The Pauranic religion which came into prominence by 500 A.D., made ample provisions, for the religious requirements of women. As early as the 3rd century B.C., women were already accustomed to perform a number of vows and fasts (*vratas*), which were unknown to Śrutis and Smṛtis. They are referred to by Aśoka in his Rock Edict No.

IX. and the *Vimānavatthukathā* in the *Dhaṁmapada* refers to a lady, who being anxious to devote herself to some *vrata* without being disturbed by her gay husband, paid him some money out of her own *strīdhana*, so that he may get his pleasure elsewhere (I. 15). Vratas, therefore, were quite common even before the beginning of the Christian era. The reorganisers of the Pauranic religion increased their number, spread them evenly over the whole year and invested them with a moral fervour by associating a number of ethical and edifying stories with them. Hinduism, as it is known to and practised by the masses today, is not the Hinduism of the Śrutis or Smṛtis, but the Hinduism of the Purāṇas, and women have been its most devoted followers and patrons. Most of the women in society at this time were uneducated and, therefore, incapable of understanding or appreciating subtle intellectual arguments like those advanced by the Vedānta school. The new religion, however, mostly relied on an appeal to faith and devotion. It, therefore, appealed to women immensely. Being certain that the sections of society, which were its devoted followers, had an inexhaustible fund of credulity, the writers of the Purāṇas, did not take much care to offer a reasonable or rational explanation in every case. Very often virtues were so much exaggerated that they assumed the garb of vice. Vices were sometimes condoned because they were associated with some heroes or demi-gods. Hindu women, who went on performing the *vratas* and listening to the stories contained in the Purāṇas, became by temper and training very credulous and devotional. Most of them became strangers to rationalism based upon discriminative reason under the influence of the new religion. The same, however, was the case with men at this time, if perhaps to a slightly less extent. It, however, cannot be denied that the continuance of the old religious vein, moral fervour and spiritual tradition is largely due to the zeal, sincerity and devotion of women. Thus those very women, whom religion had once regarded as outcastes, eventually enabled it to tide over most difficult times. They were the most faithful custodians of its spirit and traditions.[5]

Buddhism and Jainism

Let us now see what place and position was assigned to women in Buddhism and Jainism. Both these were ascetic religions, and they have not devoted much attention to the duties and ideals of lay women. The founders and leaders of both these movements shared the indifference to, or contempt of women, which is almost universal among the advocates of the ascetic ideal. The Buddha was reluctant to admit women to his Church, and the Digambara Jains hold that women can never get salvation except by first being reborn as men. It may be added here that Buddhism did not subscribe to this dogma.

Owing to the pressing entreaties of his foster mother, the Buddha eventually decided with great reluctance to admit nuns into his Church. Mahāvīra is not known to have raised any objection in the matter. But both Buddhism and Jainism placed nuns under a more rigorous discipline than monks. Some of the restrictions placed upon the nuns were no doubt reasonable ones; thus it was laid down that they should not stay alone without the protection of monks; that they should avoid the company of men of doubtful character; that only monks of unquestioned purity and integrity should be allowed to preach before nuns; that they should always live together in groups of twos and threes, etc. Some other rules, however, betray a lack of confidence in the character and judgment of women. Thus the admission of a new nun was to be sanctioned by a joint meeting of the monks and nuns; new monks, however, could be admitted without consulting the nuns at all. Nuns were to go out to beg only when led by an experienced matron. The climax is, however, reached by the rule which lays down that a nun, though 100 years old, must stand in reverence before a monk, though he may have been just initiated in the Church. The reader will not now be surprised to learn that a nun could never preach before a congregation of monks, though the selected ones among the latter could preach before a congregation of nuns.[6] It may be here added that early Christian Fathers shared similar views; they held that it was contrary to nature that women should be allowed to career preach. The Council of Laodicea closed the doors of the preaching career to women in 365 A.D., and not all the feminist agitation has succeeded even now (1956 A.D.), in getting them reopened for them. Islam permits women to read the Koran, but not to preach from it.[7]

The above rules betray that inherent air of superiority, which man usually finds it difficult to renounce with reference to women. Not all of them were, however, followed in practice; thus the theory that nuns could under no circumstances preach to monks did not stand in the way of Rājīmatī, the wife of Neminātha, in delivering a stirring sermon to her brother-in-law Rathanemi, when the latter had lost self-control under the influence of tempting circumstances (the *Uttarādhyayanasūtra*, No. 22).

In spite of some discriminative rules, referred to above, the permission that was given to women to join the Church by Jainism and Buddhism raised a new and respectable career before them. In Brāhmaṇical religion also there were some nuns like Sulabhā and Gārgī Vācaknavī; their number, however, seems to have been much larger in Buddhist and Jain circles. Buddhism declared that womanhood was no bar to salvation,[8] and Śvetāmbara Jains concurred with the view. Marriage was not necessary for women; nay, it was a fetter which women were advised to avoid. They were, therefore, urged to become nuns without entering into matrimony. Among the nuns of the *Therigāthā* the majority consists of women, who had renounced the world during their maidenhood. The career of preaching and evangelising that was thus opened before women by Jainism and Buddhism attracted a large number of talented ladies, who distinguished themselves as teachers and preachers. Several inscriptions show that senior nuns had their own female disciples and novices and used to possess influence sufficient to collect funds necessary for the maintenance of their establishments. We find rich heiresses, refusing tempting marriage offers and joining the preaching army of the new religions. Such, for instance, was the case of Guttā, Anopamā and Sumedhā, who eventually became very famous preachers (The *Therigāthā*, 54, 56, 73). Similar was the case of Saṅghamitrā, the daughter of Aśoka, who went to far off Ceylon, to spread the gospel of the Buddha. Jayantī, a daughter of King Sahasrānīka of Kausāmbī, doffed her royal robe and became a devout nun, the moment her questions about the nature of the individual soul, the ideal of life, etc., were satisfactorily answered by Mahāvīra. Some ladies like Abhirūpā Nandā and Sumaṅgalā no doubt joined the Church as a welcome escape from household tyranny, but their number does not seem to have been large.

When discipline became slack and unworthy persons began to be admitted into monasteries and nunneries, the tone of moral life deteriorated. It hastened the process of the downfall of Buddhism. Later Hinduism took a lesson from what it saw in Buddhist monasteries and nunneries and declared women to be ineligible for renunciation (*sannyāsa*). It maintained that not renunciation but due discharge of family responsibilities was the most sacred duty of women.[9] Nuns, therefore, have disappeared from Hinduism during the last 1500 years.

The reader has already noted the main religious disabilities of women. In the modern feminist movement in India, we hardly notice any effort made to get them redressed. This is natural. When men themselves have given up Vedic sacrifices, women naturally feel no inclination to agitate for the right to perform them. The Aryasamaj, which has revived these sacrifices, has extended the right to perform them to women as well. In the modern materialistic world, the average woman feels no grievance for being deprived of the right to become a nun. She looks with a contemptuous smile on a dogma, which would declare that she is ineligible for spiritual salvation because of her sex. *Upanayana* has become a meaningless formality even in the case of boys; women naturally feel that they have nothing to gain by becoming re-eligible for it. It is true that the religious disenfranchisement that resulted from the ineligibility for *upanayana* produced a disastrous consequence upon the general status of women in society; but women have realized that improvement in this direction in modern days depends mainly upon the spread of education and the acquisition of economic rights and independence. They, therefore, naturally feel no inclination for initiating an agitation for the restoration of their old religious rights and privileges.

It would be, however, in the interest of Hindu society if it remains constantly alive to the full implications of the Vedic theory that the husband and the wife are equal and necessary partners in divine worship. The principle implies that men and women have equal rights and responsibilities in matters temporal as well. Since the spiritual disenfranchisement of women, men have become accustomed to regard them as their inferiors in all the spheres of life. This outlook must disappear. We must remember that women have done greater service to religion than men by preserving the old religious tradition, moral fervour and spiritual vein in Hindu society. These constitute a priceless heritage, and men ought to be greatful to women for preserving it. If an effort is made to spread a rational knowledge of the fundamental principles of Hinduism among women, they would undoubtedly become much better representatives of our culture and religion than what men are today.

References

1. *V.S., Ch. Up* XXIV; see also *Man*, IX. 87; *V.D.S.* XVIII. 17.
2. *Pāṅiniśikshā*, 52.
3. *Śat. Br.*, I. 1, 4, 13.
4. *Man*, III. 121.
5. *Āp. D. S.*, II. 29. 16.
6. The *Vinaya*, Chullavagga, X. i, 4; *Mūlācāra* of Vaṭṭakera, pp. 177-97.
7. J. L. Davies, *A Short History*, p. 238.
8. The *Therīgāthā*, 61.
9. Yama in *SCV.*, p. 596.

Hierarchy

A. Proposition

In this chapter we propose to look into the nature of the social hierarchy and consider its implications. We want to put side by side the natural social hierarchy (as the basis of the theory of *varṇa*) and the artificial social hierarchy, in particular as it has been built up in the Indian caste system. We shall point out that the word hierarchy has become rather unpopular in modern times on account of its 'power associations' (and on account of the ideals of equality which we shall consider in the next chapter), and also that the sense of *varṇa* has been largely lost by modern man, and that it would be to the advantage of society if it came forward again out of the social-subconscious to the light of day, the natural phenomenon of hierarchy being again realized and appreciated.

In these pages we take the word 'hierarchy' not in its older sense as 'a reign of priests', but in its more modern and wider sense as the whole of the different ranks of groups and individuals in society. If one would preserve also the meaning of 'a reign of' (like in monarchy, oligarchy, etc.), it could be given as implying a co-management of social affairs by the different social ranks in proportion to their social function and sociality.

B. Hierarchic Composition and Hierarchic Constitution

As the commentator on the 8th verse of the 189th Adhyāya of the *Śāntiparvan* of the *Mahābhārata* remarks: "righteousness, and not birth, is the cause of the division into *varṇas*." This fundamental idea of *varṇa* we have treated elsewhere.

The *varṇas* do not correspond to the four social classes of general sociology:

1. the social, as represented by the natural aristocracy;
2. the non-social, as represented by those who cling to narrow individualism, and only ask to be left alone, to lead their own life;
3. the pseudo-social, as represented by the congenital and habitual paupers; and
4. the anti-social, as represented by the instinctual and habitual criminals. The second class, the non-social, is considered to be the original, the primordial class, out of which the other three classes generated.[1]

The *varṇa* theory takes the lower three classes into one, and considers the anti-social to be the extreme form of the non-social, the non-social a modified anti-social class. And it is indeed impossible to draw a hard and fast line between them, if one considers them well and remembers that certain acts which are not criminal in the ordinary sense of the word may be incomparably more anti-social than a single act of manslaughter even with malice afore-thought. Let us mention as an example the moral crimes of the placing on the market of arms of war (not even to speak of the manufacture of poison gas), and the mere possession of shares of such manufacturing companies.

In contradistinction to the conception that the different social classes evolved from the non-social, the Hindu theory holds that they evolved from the highest class. The Śāstras speak of the existence of only one *varṇa* in the original Golden Age of man. This may, like golden age legends and paradise myths all over the world, point to the vague remembrance of the anthropogenic stage in the evolution of man, when human society still possessed the natural sociality (like that manifested by animal herds) which was pictured by Wilhelm Wundt and other scholars.

The four *varṇas* represent four degrees of sociality from the most highly social to the extreme non-social (incl. pseudo-social and anti-social) in addition to the functional principle which is inextricably interwoven with the principle of sociality.

Yet the definitely anti-social was at times felt by the Hindus to be an unnatural and abnormal phenomenon of the social constitution, and as such not really in its place in the fourth *varṇa* (since *varṇa* concerns the social composition). From this we may perhaps explain the fact that at times the scriptures mention a fifth class, to which all criminal and socially impure elements were consigned.[2] If not in its place in the theory of natural class as applying to a society which is still relatively natural, the positing of this 'fifth *varṇa*' may perhaps be justified for the constitution of modern society. The analogy of the human body is illuminating. For the normal physical body the different organs may be put into several categories, the function of some organs being more important than that of others which might perhaps even be missed. Some organ may perhaps be less healthy than others, and perform imperfectly its function in the organic whole, yet the body may yet be relatively healthy. But when the body develops some cancerous tumour, it can no more be classed among the cases of normal health, neither can the tumour be classed among the organs of the body, though it has the appearance of an organ. Another class of organs has then to be recognized, of anti-organic, anti-social tendency.

To revert to society people belonging to this class—and they will not be many—will not ordinarily fall into the fourth social class as mentioned above, the anti-social class. Such people will be cases for the psycho-analyst rather than for the judge, they will be found rather in the upper than in the lower classes. But when the ancient Indian sociologists posited this fifth class, they meant no such anti-social class, but one somewhat more in the usual sense of a class comprising criminals and irresponsible primitives.

In the natural hierarchy everyone indicates his own place by his social conduct, by the degree or kind of his sociality. The natural hierarchy is not a dream and a mere ideal, neither is it only a theory, the natural hierarchy is a fact in society, it is always there, but at times in history it may not be consciously realized. *varṇas* exist, but man has largely lost the capacity to recognize them, because the population classes of the social constitution: in India the castes, in the West the economic classes, obsess the social mind.

Yet here and there we find indications that the sense of *varṇa* has not been entirely lost by the public. India is always ready to recognize and bow to the 'holy man'. The West is always ready to respect the 'true gentleman'. The conception and ideal of the 'born leader' which is coming to the foreground more and more, is also significant. We do not mean to say that there have not always been individuals who had the sense of *varṇa*; of course there were many at all times who were conscious of standards of *varṇa* to a certain degree of clarity.

In a healthy and harmonious society the population classes correspond to the *varṇas*. In early Ṛgvedic India this may have been approximated, and the *varṇas* may have corresponded to some extent to the four classes of Brāhmaṇas, Rājanyas, Viś and Śūdras.

If in the natural hierarchy people determine and betray their place in the scale according to their degree of sociality and function, in the artificial hierarchy of the social constitution of the modern state, either in the East or in the West, not the degree of sociality but the amount of power wielded by the individual decides his place in relation to that of others in the scale. The art of the power may differ widely between different groups. In the West the power is largely economical (money is crystallized power), predominating even over the power of the Church. In India it is the power of caste, largely the product of the power of Brāhmaṇas and of the ruling classes.

In the West the social mind is obsessed by the idea of economical power, and in India by the idea of caste power. The orthodox Brāhmaṇas are afraid of nothing but an attack on their position in relation to the lower castes and untouchables, on their social and religious privileges.

If the social mind did not attach its seal to the economic power in Western society, and to the power of caste in India, these different kinds of power could never tyrannize society as they do by obstructing the freedom of the individuals. A reviving sense of *varṇa* only may free the social mind of its obsession, then the natural hierarchy must again emerge out of the social subconscious into the light of recognition, and in proportion to this the tyranny of power will be weakened.

If a hierarchy be founded upon some principle of force, it is not a natural hierarchy. If some individual or group of individuals (a priest, a ruler, a family father, a meeting) or an abstract power (a law, a state, a Church, a caste, a society, public opinion) irreversably decides a person's profession, behaviour or *dharma*, it denotes an unnatural constitution of the social group in question. In the social constitution corresponding to the natural hierarchy there can only be freedom of choice. This does not mean that even if the hierarchies correspond, force will not be applied to the definitely anti-social elements by the proper *varṇa* of ruling and regulating people. As to the other rules of law, if the two hierarchies correspond, the *varṇas* will naturally obey the laws of the *varṇa* of rulers, even as they will naturally follow and respect the highest *varṇa*.

The yoke of power of one or more population classes or groups, when the two hierarchies did not correspond, has been the main source of suffering to other population classes or groups. History provides us with a profusion of examples up to the present day.

Largely because of the power association the word hierarchy has become rather unpopular. The unpopularity grew by the propagation of the ideals of equality and brotherhood (which were a reaction to it) which we shall consider in the next chapter.

Desire for power together with jealousy of the power of others were the main factors in the development of caste: caste privilege, caste separatism. But for the desire of power caste could never have become as it is.

Yet it will not do to condemn a caste system a prior as something anti-social. Caste has more than once served its purpose in history. To give an example here which has interest in connection with the conception of an organic hierarchy, Megasthenes writes: "If the Indians are at war with one another, it is not customary for them to touch those who are tilling the land, but the one group may be engaged in battle,....the other is peacefully engaged in plowing, or reaping, or pruning, or mowing nearby."[3] Dr. Timmer, who compares this statement carefully with the rules and information given by the Hindu Scriptures comes to the conclusion that this has probably indeed been customary.[4]

To return to natural hierarchy. In natural hierarchy there cannot be one moral standard for all. As we saw in Chapter III the exigencies of social life are the greater, the higher the *varṇa*. The normal standard of one high up in the natural hierarchy will be the ideal for a person lower in the scale, and will be entirely unintelligible to a person at the bottom. It is illogical to require and expect the same conduct from these three people, to preach to them the same moral law and to put before them the same ideal. The Christian Church has tended to do this with the positing of 'the Christian duty'. The Church pointed to the goal but did not show the steps. In this respect it failed to show sense of reality and a sense of proportion. One standard of good and evil cannot be upheld in accordance with natural hierarchy. What may be unintelligible and seem stupid to the man low in the hierarchy may be deemed good by the man in the middle and be just perfectly natural and evident to the man at the top. The unintelligible and seemingly stupid maxim will be of no use to the man at the bottom, whereas a simpler, less exalted rule might be appreciated and followed by him, and in the course of time lead him on, to understand and follow more exacting and nobler rules, and rise accordingly in the natural scale.

The Indian scriptures provide a profusion of instances to illustrate this in application. They will be found in many places in this book. We want to mention here only the eight different grades of marriage for the four *varṇas*.[5] They are:

1. The Brāhma Rite: the gift of a daughter after decking her with costly garments and honouring her (by presenting jewels), to a man learned in the Veda and of good conduct.
2. The Daiva Rite: the gift of a daughter who has been decked with ornaments to a priest who is officiating at a sacrifice.
3. The Prājāpatya Rite: the gift of a daughter after the father has addressed the couple with the text: "May both of you perform together your duties" and has shown honour to the bridegroom. (Yājñavalkya calls this marriage Kāya).
4. The Ārṣa Rite: the gift of a daughter, after that the father received from the bridegroom for the fulfilment of the sacred law (i.e. not with the intention of selling his child) a cow or a bull or two pairs.
5. The Gāndharva Rite is the voluntary union of maiden and lover which springs from desire.
6. The Rākṣasa Rite is the forcible abduction of a maiden against her will, after a fight with her relatives.
7. The Āsura Rite: the bridegroom gives as much wealth as he can afford to the kinsmen and to the bride herself, according to his own will.
8. The Paiśāca Rite is the seducing of a girl who is sleeping, intoxicated or disordered in intellect.

The first four are for Brāhmaṇas, the 5th and 6th are for Kṣatriyas, the 5th, 7th and 8th are for Vaiśyas and Śūdras. The Śāstras discourage the 7th and the 8th altogether, as immoral, and the last four for Brāhmaṇas.

If we read the Gospels we cannot escape from the conclusion that Christ also distinguished grades of morality and sociality, organs with different social functions and had a clear sense of distinguishing between reality and the ideal. Especially St. Matthew and St. Luke contain significant matter on this point. It would lead us too far to go into this in detail, we refer to the source, giving the main points in a footnote.[6]

The tendency to weave all pieces on the same loom has also appeared in criminal law. Law in Western countries, under the influence of the above mentioned tendency of the Church, and perhaps psychologically strengthened by modern ideas of quality, has been generally until very recently to hold all people (except children, idiots and the mentally weak) to be equally responsible for their actions. That this is really illogical, is clear. That for practical reasons, however, the principle of equality has been generally adhered to is quite understandable.

The scale of natural hierarchy is kept in internal equilibrium by the general principle, which everybody may easily verify for himself, that on the whole the higher a person's place in the natural scale, the more severely he will judge himself and the less severely others, and that on the whole the lower a person's place, the more severely he will judge others and the less severely himself.[7]

If the class-consciousness in the modern sense tends to separate people, the sense of *varṇa*, the realization of the natural hierarchy, tends to unite people into a whole.

If the population classes and the castes predominate in the social mind and do no more correspond to the *varṇas*, we get what the Śāstras so often warn against, the 'mixture of *varṇas*', to which we shall devote a special chapter.

If we protract the conception of organs with special functions in the whole from any delimited group of men, be it a tribe or a state or a continent, to the world as a whole, we see that the conception of autarchy is entirely anti-social in the wider sense. No organ in a body can be self-sufficient; if it desires and tends to grow out into an independent organ, or rather body, it becomes a cancerous tumour.[8] Free-trade, not necessarily coupled with an entirely free production and competition ('Śūdras' and 'Vaiśyas') but controlled to some extent by some international body ('Kṣatriyas') is thus a natural and scientific consequence of the organic and hierarchic theory. The present day super-nationalism and policy of protection is from a sociological standpoint unscientific up to the degree of stupidity. Surely not the realization that it is wrong or immoral (which so many know) but the realization that it is unscientific and stupid and that in the end it will not pay, will eventually lead to the policy of co-operation and internationalism. For after all we are living in a mental age, and the mind will bring succour where the emotions fail and where the spirit is yet relatively helpless.

Also the hierarchical graduation applies to the world at large. The constitutional hierarchy is the fundament of what is commonly called civilization, the natural is the basis of culture. Nobody will contradict that Africa falls into a lower place in the natural as well as in the constitutional hierarchy. In what organic and hierarchic relation the Great Powers stand to one another nobody will be able to decide. Continuing our line of thought we might say that the highest in the constitutional hierarchy is the nation that has the most powerful army, the most poisonous gases at its disposal, and has the most powerful financial position. And the highest in the natural hierarchy that nation will prove itself to be which most strongly manifests the spirit of internationalism, which most convincingly takes the initiative to disarmament, to the abolishment of the unnatural economic measures of protection, to a revision of the Treaty of Versailles etc. Whether the two hierarchies cover each other or not, only history can prove. As in the case of the individual man: does his class and position correspond to his *varṇa*? His conduct indicates it.

As it is, Europe has no cause to look down upon the Indian caste system which is in spite of all its shortcomings still organic, since Europe has developed separative nation-castes which for the moment tend to grow away more and more from the organic basis.

Internationalism is nothing but (speaking mystically) the sense of social unity plus the urge to the expression of unity, or (speaking sociologically) the sense of sociality plus the urge towards integration.

To conclude with a few words about the religious and occult doctrines of hierarchy. They do not fall within the scope of this book, yet we may not pass on without just mentioning them. Many of the ancient religious and philosophical systems pictured the world and the cosmos on the basis of some great organic Being or Man, the Cosmic Christ of the Gnostics and the Puruṣa of India being the best known instances. And all the ancient (as well as many modern) theological and theosophical doctrines and mythologies have mentioned, taught or proclaimed their hierarchy of devas, angels or nature-powers. Lucifer appears under different names as a symbol of the anti-social element of power and privilege which developed the hierarchy of power from the natural hierarchy.

As a recent book on the spiritual aspect of Hierarchy expresses it: "Hierarchy is not coercion—it is the law of the world-structures. It is not a threat—but the call of the heart and a fiery admonition directing towards the General Good."[9]

Conclusions

We have distinguished between the natural hierarchy (which is the basis of *varṇa*) and the constitutional hierarchy, and seen that the characteristics of the natural hierarchy are:

1. If the actual social hierarchy corresponds to the natural hierarchy, every individual naturally falls into his proper place. If not, he yet betrays his hierarchical degree to those persons who have the sense of *varṇa*.
2. There is not one moral standard but there are grades of sociality.

3. In connection with this there are organic groups each with a specific function, differing in social usefulness (e.g. *varṇas*).
4. There is a tendency towards social integration, it is the manifestation of that socializing element of human nature which is called either the consciousness of kind, fellow-feeling, or just: love.
5. The natural hierarchy is based upon individual responsibility, and thus always tending towards equilibrium.

On the other hand the characteristics of the constitutional hierarchy, that so far do not correspond to the natural, are:

1. Every individual comes into his place by the application of some amount of power, either by himself or by his group.
2. Not his degree of sociality, but his trade or profession, his wealth or his social power count in the social estimation.
3. The groups (of every conceivable kind) may or may not be organic, may tend to be social, unsocial, or anti-social. The Indian caste system is largely organic, the groups of the Western society seen as a whole are dangerously tending towards the anti-social, both if considering the nation-castes of the world, and the different population classes which more or less agree in the different countries.
4. There is a tendency towards a class-struggle, it is the manifestation of the desire for power and privilege.
5. There is a tendency of individuals to strive towards the summit, this tends to upset equilibrium. That equilibrium is yet maintained in society is due to the psychological influence of natural hierarchy. Which force will prove the strongest in this present period?

We have seen that due to the confusion of the two hierarchies the word has become unpopular, and that the realization of hierarchy or sense of *varṇa* has been largely lost by modern man. Insight into the nature of hierarchy has to be won again, this knowledge has to come forward again out of the social unconscious into the light of day. Only then the socializing forces of man may be liberated more profusely and the internal harmony of society improved.

Thus there are three distinct happenings: (i) the mental act of realization; (ii) the awakening of the sense of social unity and sociality, followed by (iii) the urge towards integration.

Hierarchy has some more implications which do not fall within the scope of this book, we may mention only that in the natural hierarchy there is a passing on of power and knowledge downwards, whereas in the constitutional hierarchy power and knowledge extend through the upward movement of the individual.[10]

References

1. F.H. Giddings, *Principles of Socioogy*, p. 126-127.
2. *Bh.Pu.* XI : 17 : 20; etc.
3. *Arr. Ind.* 11 : 9; quoted from B.C. J. Timmer, *Megasthenes en de Indische Maatschappij*, p. 114.
4. *Op. cit.* pp. 118-120.
5. *Man* III : 27-34; *V.S.* XXIV : 17-25; *Yāj.* I : 58-61; *A.S.* III : 2 : 2-9.
6. *St. Matthew* : 7 : 1-2.
7. Cf. *St. Luke* 6 : 41-42; *St. Matthew* 5 : 22 and 7 : 1-5.
8. Cf. G. Simmel, *Sociologie*, p. 429.
9. *Hierarchy, 1931* (*Signs of Agni Yoga*) p. 5.
10. H. Spencer, *Social Organism, Essays* I.

The Rājadharma

We shall now analyze the concept of Rājadharma—the *dharma* of the King, as referred to in the Dharmasūtras, the *Mahābhārata* and the *Manusmṛti*. Although these books were written in different historical periods, we have deliberately chosen to treat them together for the sake of coordination and for two more reasons. Firstly, these books were definitely influenced by the Brāhmaṇical worldview. By Brāhmaṇical I do not necessarily mean the view of the Brāhmaṇa caste, but the view propounded in the Vedas and the Brāhmaṇas as distinguished from the Upaniṣadic idealism and Buddhism. Secondly, these books treat the functions and duties of the King under the terms Rājadharma. Common theological and philosophical presuppositions and the common concept of *dharma*, which comprehends the facts and phenomena of individual, social and political life, impart a great similarity to the views set forth in these books and, therefore, we are justified in treating them together.

The Dharmasūtras are the products of the period from the seventh to the third century, B.C. and even later.[1] Out of these Dharmasūtras developed the later Dharmaśāstras.[2] The chief Dharmasūtra works are those of Gautama, Baudhāyana, Vasiṣṭha and Āpastamba. These books outline the canons of social conduct and also deal with royal duties, civil and criminal law. The books also contain references to the social customs of that period, but they are didactic and normative in their standpoint and any writer who constructs out of them a picture of the historical institutions and politics of those times will be mistaken. These books only supply some general hints and notions but no exact reference to what was actually taking place in the society of those times.

The notion of social duty is central in the Dharmasūtras. According to Gautama, the Vedas are the source of *dharma*.[3] He also mentions the traditions and practices of those who know the Vedas and act in accordance with the Vedic injunctions as another source. Āpastamba (Āp.D.S.I.1.2.3) holds the consensus of those who know the *dharma* and the Vedic literature to be authoritative about *dharma*. Baudhāyana regards the Vedas to be the primary source of *dharma*; the second source is the Smṛti. In the absence of these books, the properly initiated and disciplined persons are the authority on *dharma*. Vasiṣṭha hails the views of the Brāhmaṇas knowledge of the Vedas, in matters of *dharma*.

The *Mahābhārata* glorified the notions of non-violence and compassion in its view of *dharma*. "He who is the friend of all, is devoted to the good of all, through actions, mind and speech, knows *dharma*."[4] "The true and eternal *dharma* is non-maliciousness towards all creatures, in action, mind and speech, as well as compassion and gifts."[5] The *Mahābhārata* refers to a period of human existence when there was no coercion and no king. People were guided by *dharma* and the prevalence of *dharma* led to a completely stable existence.

Manu (Man.I.108) exalts *dharma* to the status of the supreme principle of human life. If *dharma* is maintained it preserves the person who maintains it, but if it is violated it ruins the violator. According to Manu there are four sources through which *dharma* can be known. The first is the Veda, the second, the Smṛtis, the third, the ways of life and conduct of good people and the fourth, what pleases the soul or self of a man. This latter source of *dharma* postulates the possibility of a situation involving a conflict between the institutionalized structure of political power and the dictates of human conscience. Manu, however, does not raise the question in this Lutheran and Kantian form and hence does not answer it. According to Manu, *daṇḍa* or the royal power of punishment in its double aspects of coercion and protection is equated with *dharma*. This is important because it shows the great importance which Manu attaches to punishment in social life. Judicial conflict should be settled with reference to *dharma* in Manu's opinion. According to Manu, the King shall establish a law that may have been practised by the virtuous, by such twice born men as are devoted to *dharma* provided it is not opposed to the customs of countries, families and castes. He says that *dharma* has to be protected because if *dharma* is allowed to be defeated by non-*dharma* it means that the councillors are as good as dead.

This analysis of the sources and functions of *dharma* leads us to the question of the meaning of *rājadharma*. The word Rājā means a king. It is a very common word in Hindu political literature and is found from the Vedas onwards. The Dharmasūtras prescribed a number of duties for the King and these were supposed to have a Vedic sanction. The King was to wield the sceptre of punishment and if there was any miscarriage of justice or if the culprit excaped, the King had to not only compensate for the loss but also had to perform penance. This involved the notion of extra-political sanctions on the King for the violation of his duties.

There is a great emphasis in *Rājadharma* on the idea of the protection of the fourfold social order. But in spite of this emphasis we do not find any support to the theory that the concept of *dharma* implied some notion of the "balancing of the principles of authority and responsibility." We can only speak of the moral responsibility of the King and that also in a vague sense of "debt" to the people as found in the Aśokan inscriptions. But we should not read into the ancient texts highly technical and legal-constitutional notions. The *Mahābhārata* speaks interchangeably of *daṇḍanīti* and *rājadharma* but it gives primacy to the latter because it groups the chapters dealing with political matters under the heading of *rājadharma*. According to the *Mahābhārata*, the security and expansion of the Vedic sacrificial system depends on the King's performance of his duty. It conceives of the personification of *dharma* as a god and identifies the King with that. It also speaks of the *dharma* of the Kṣatriya and comprehends under it self-abnegation, universal compassion, insight into the affairs of the world, security and social betterment by curing the diseased and afflicted. It says that the King who practices *dharma* approximates to the position of a god while he who does the reverse goes to hell.

Manu (Vii.10) advocates the supremacy of *dharma*. He says that if the King transgresses the injunctions of *dharma*, he is smitten to death by the *daṇḍa* which is full of divine lustre. The King, according to Manu (VIII.41), should also take into cognisance *dharmas* of castes, countries, guilds and families in settling the peculiar *dharma* of each section. Manu is a strong advocate of the moral roots of political power. He says that through want of discipline and humility (*vinaya*) many kings have perished. Vena, Nahuṣa, Sudāsa—the sons of Pijavana, Sumedha and Nemi perished because they neglected the concept of Vinaya. On the other hand, by virtue of Vinay, Pṛthu and Manu (the first King) gained political power, Kubera acquired immense wealth and Viśvāmitra obtained the status of a Brāhmaṇa. Manu is an outspoken champion of the moralisation of the concept of *dharma* to which he ascribes a tenfold content— contentment, forgiveness, self-control, non-stealing, purification, self-restraint, intellectual firmness (*dhī*), knowledge, truthfulness and abstention from anger. This tenfold *dharma* was to be adhered to constantly by all the four Āśramas (The *Manusmṛti* V. I. 91-92).

The *rājadharma* is definitely monarchical in its orientation. The attempt to comprehend all political things under the *dharma* of the King shows that *dharma* is to be equated with the totality of all social, political as well as individual duties, obligations and functions of the King. The *Arthaśāstra* of Kauṭilya also had a monarchical orientation since it only devotes one chapter to the republican states. But as we have seen, the definition of the *Arthaśāstra* conceives of it as the science of the acquisition and protection of territories. Contrasted with the *Arthaśāstra*, the *rājadharma* chapters of the

Dharmasūtras, the *Mahābhārata* and the *Manusmṛti* are less emphatic in their conception of politics as an independent branch of knowledge. Kauṭilya writes a systematic treatise on things political. The *rājadharma* tradition produces no independent work. The Dharmasūtras devote only a very small section to political issues. The *Mahābhārata* is a great epic and only in one book of it do we find political discussions. Manu has only one chapter on Rājadharma.

Dharma and Political Ethics

The discussion of *rājadharma* would be incomplete without a discussion of the relation between the notions of *dharma* and political ethics. It is often asserted that some Hindu writers distinguish the science of ethics from the science of politics because they prescribe the use of assassination, espionage, etc. Before we discuss the problems I would like to refer to a few of such views held by Hindu writers. Kauṭilya refers to various means by which the enemy should be assassinated. He advocates espionage and battle of intrigues, gives a long list of drugs and black magic to ensure the destruction of the enemy and even goes to the length of asserting that money should be made by royal agents by playing upon the religious credulity of the people.[6] Hence, some scholars feel that according to Kauṭilya the end justified the means. In the *Mahābhārata*, Bharadvāja says that a king desirous of prosperity should slay the individual who thwarts his purpose, be this person even his son, brother, father or friend. With reference to the behaviour of a king, he says: "When wishing to smite he should speak gently, after smiting he should speak gentler still, after striking off the head with his sword, he should grieve and shed tears."[7] The remnants of debt, fire and enemies increase over and over again, and hence the King should not tolerate the remnant. According to Bhīṣma, the King should learn both the path of *dharma* and that of non-*dharma*.[8] Bhīṣma advocated the seizure of the property of all except Brāhmaṇas and ascetics in times of crisis. He justified his view on grounds of the value of self-preservation. He further says that this policy is in accordance with the nature of *dharma* of a Kṣatriya. These views have occasioned the following comments by two modern Hindu writers. Ghosal writes with reference to Kauṭilya:

> "When we turn..... to consider..... the author's attitude towards religion and morality, we find him following, as might be expected, in the footsteps of the early masters. We find him, in other words, frequently inculcating rules of a grossly unscrupulous nature on the plea of public interest and without the least pretence of moral disapproval. Thus Politics, distinguished as it is in the system of the *Arthaśāstra* as a separate science is, as before, further separated from the science of Ethics."[9]

With reference to certain views of the writers mentioned in the *Mahābhārata,* Bandyopadhyaya states:

> "......the further importance of the *rājadharma* chapters lies in the fact that they show a decided tendency towards the separation of ethics from the sacerdotal canon and in some chapters we find even a tendency towards the separation of politics from the traditional lines of ethical enquiry.[10]

Before we analyze this problem of the relation between politics and ethics, we would like to say a few words about the Hindu view of ethics. Since the post-Vedic days great stress was laid on truth as a cardinal moral virtue.[11] The Vedic poets pray for attaining truth by rejecting the untruth. In the Upaniṣads there are examples of kings who follow a moral life of philosophic detachment and inword contemplation. In Buddhism is found the concept of *śīla* which is the generic name for five cardinal moral virtues. The Yoga philosophy refers to the universal "great vows" of truth, non-violence, non-stealing, non-accumulation and non-adultery. But notwithstanding the distinction between truth and untruth in the Vedic literature and the Buddhistic notions of Vinaya, discipline and *śīla*, Hindu writers do not speak of social versus ethical or political versus ethical. The notion of *varṇāśrama*—the four castes and the four orders, all with their assigned specific tasks and duties—makes the problem of the extent to which a good citizen can be a good man meaningless. There is no conflict between the pursuance of political life and the contemplation of Brahman. According to the Greek thinkers, the citizen was to participate in civic and political activities and was to mould his life according to the ideals and patterns of the constitution. This implied that the virtues of the citizen were to be formulated in relation to the spirit of the constitution. A good citizen in oligarchy will mould himself according to the oligarchic spirit and a good citizen in democracy will mould himself according to the spirit of democracy. Thus relativism is characteristic of the virtues required from a good citizen. But the virtues of the good man were regarded as absolute and not relative to any specific constitution. Hence, the virtues of the good man and those of the good citizen did not coincide in imperfect states. Only in the perfect state will the good citizen also be a good man. This distinction between the virtue of the good man and the good citizen is a very important point in Aristotle's Politics. But the sociology of the *varṇāśrama* is oriented not to the political and constitutional differences but to the notion of *svadharma*. The performance of one's own duties is the uppermost consideration. A good Kṣatriya is one who faithfully adheres to the duties of the Kṣatriya. A good Śūdra is one who is faithful in the performance of his own specific *svadharma*. There is no implication of superiority or inferiority of status. According to the *Bhagavadgītā* whosoever performs his *svadharma*, finally gains by virtue of that the realization of Brahman. Hence, there is no conflict between the political, the social or the ethical. Adherence to *svadharma* will be a social task, it will also serve the good of the kingdom, it will be an ethical imperative and if performed with a spirit of disinterestedness it will also lead to divine realization. As a matter of fact, I would say that according to the Vedic view, which was given a philosophic basis in the Mīmāṁsā system, there is no conflict even between the temporal and the spiritual. A man has to perform his own *dharma* and this will result in the attainment both of mundane prosperity and spiritual good. The notion of the conflict between this world and a divine world is further obliterated by the metaphysics of Vedānta according to which each human being is in essence the absolute. Due to ignorance he is bound by the limitations of empirical particulars and relative phenomena. He can attain the ultimate knowledge and realize his eternal spiritual essence. There is really no qualitative transition from the terrestrial to the divine status. A man does not pass from the earthly city to the divine city after death. There is no conception of two distinct cities or two different kingdoms—it is only one homogeneous reality. Only because of the blinding power of ignorance man does not know his inmost self which is spiritual. If the separatist particularizing action of egoistic ignorance ceases, man comes to realize the supreme spirit. There is no existence of any worldly phenomena or ignorance for him. He is aware only of the eternal spiritual presence. Hence, there is a fundamental difference between this philosophical outlook and the view of those thinkers who maintained a basic qualitative difference between God and human beings. It is the virtual difference between spiritual monism and religious monotheism. Thus the idea of *varṇāśrama* and the metaphysical views of the Vedānta warn us against reading Aristotelian[12] and Augustinian[13] ideas into Hindu social philosophy.

According to the *varṇāśrama* theory each man is to pursue the task assigned to him in accordance with his particular caste and particular order in life. A king has his own duties. He has to carry on the duties of the Kṣatriya householder. So long as he is true to his duties which have been prescribed by the Vedas and elaborated by the Smṛtis he is a good man and is a good citizen. So long as he is a householder he is caring for his mundane prosperity. When the time comes for retirement, he can give up political duties and concentrate on austerities, meditation and God-realization. From this type of synthetic world-view Kauṭilya and the other writers discuss the duties or *dharmas* of the King. If Kauṭilya (III.1) prescribed a dynamic game of power, he is not conscious of doing something intellectually shocking. If he would have been conscious of saying something against *dharma*, he would not have said: "The King who administers (the kingdom) according to *dharma*, evidence, history and institutional practices (caritra) and royal edicts, will be able to conquer the whole world bound by the four quarters."

Kauṭilya prescribes four ways of conquering the earth and after having given the details of each he says that having conquered the earth the King should enjoy it according to his own *dharma*. He refers to three types of conquerors— whether they are satisfied with mere submission or with submission and monetary gains or with destruction of the enemy. He calls the third by the name of Asuras—demons, perhaps implying thereby his disapproval of the ways of ruthless power-seekers. According to the traditional Hindu view which is fully subscribed to by Kauṭilya it is the duty of a Kṣatriya king to expand his territories and conquer the enemies. Rāma and Kṛṣṇa, who are regarded as incarna-tions of God, take recourse to some actions which can be considered against *dharma*, but those actions have been regarded as necessary for the maintenance of *dharma* itself. Kauṭilya, it is true, catalogues the ways of poisoning and drug-making, but it is only necessary for the pursuit of warfare which it is the duty of a king to undertake. Hence, from the theoretical standpoint of the philosophical implications of social *dharma* we do not see how Kauṭilya discards ethical and moral considerations. Ethics can be divided into two sections—personal ethics and socio-political ethics. So far as personal ethics is concerned, Kauṭilya is an emphatic and determined exponent of the moral philosophy of kingship. He is remarkable in his insistence on the conquest of the senses. In the *Arthaśāstra*, IX. 7, he says that intensity of lust and other appetites provokes one's own peopie while lack of policy creates enemies. Hence, according to him sensuality and impolicy are species of demonic actions. In his remarkable stress on the conquest of passion Kauṭilya appears, to me, to be a sage and seer and not a mere political thinker. But according to the framework and method of argumentation of conquest during his age, even relentless and ruthless conquest, was a part of the socio-political ethics of the King. Kauṭilya prescribed techniques of imperialism. It is true, however, that he tends to become an unscrupulous imperialist. But he would not prescribe that a Vedic student or an ascetic should give up studies or asceticism and take to warfare because to do so would amount to transgressing *dharma*. Every person has his own *dharma* and if he tries to pursue it efficiently he is not committing any sin. As has been already pointed out, Kauṭilya never repudiates the transcendental goal accepted in contemporary society. It cannot be said that Kauṭilya separates politics from ethics in view of his acceptance of the traditional theological goal of the attainment of heaven, as well as of ethical virtues like self-restraint and discipline. He has his own ideas of professional ethics which are in consonance with the concept of *dharma* which is a generic term and comprehends political, social, ethical and religious considerations.

We have tried to analyse the concept of the *dharma* of the King according to Kauṭilya. If we take up an idealistic or intuitional-ethical approach we can say that he is unmindful of moral considerations. Suppose we adhere to the code of morality of the New Testament or of Buddhism or of Leo Tolstoy, then we can criticize Kauṭilya. But so long as we want to discuss what ethical and moral considerations Kauṭilya had in mind and how far did he remain faithful to them, we should confine ourselves to studying the problem as to whether he was conscious of deliberately presenting any goal or code of action and behaviour which would be unethical and immoral. We have no evidence to show that Kauṭilya knew he was saying something against *dharma*. It is quite a different matter if his view of *dharma* may strike us to be morally shocking or at least morally neutral to a critic trained in different notions of social ethics. But notwithstanding this theoretical defence of the conceptual structure of Kauṭilya's politics, we can say that from a normal moral standpoint, his political ideals and methods appear ruthless and relentless.

Passing now to an analysis of the views of Bhāradvāja who has been regarded as the advocate of cold, calculating treachery and heartless cruelty, we find that some scholars have been busy condemning him rather than understanding his philosophical presuppositions and sociological conclusions. Of course what Bhāradvāja says is indeed shocking if divorced from its context. But the context of the discourse should be remembered. Yudhiṣṭhira asks Bhīṣma in the *Mahābhārata* how a king should act when *dharma* and people have declined and ceased to function and robbers and evil-mongers are infesting the country. Bhīṣma narrates to him the dialogue of Bhāradvāja which inculcates a policy for times of crisis. The Sanskrit word *āpaddharma* or the *dharma* to be followed in time of trouble and crisis has its use and operation when normal activities are not performed due to the appearance of abnormal difficulties. According to a Hindu notion, this "*dharma* of crisis" can allow a man to transgress some of the injunctions of the *dharma* of ordinary normal life. But this "*dharma* of crisis" is certainly never a part of the routine action. More than that, Bhīṣma quotes Bhāradvāja's statements to the effect that these so-called base and cruel measures should never be used, except to counteract the machinations of enemies. "A person (or a king) should never act in accordance with these rules. These measures laid down by me should be taken recourse to only in times of extremes of distress. Inspired by the motive of doing good to you, I have said this for instructing you in counteracting the use of these measures by the enemy."[14] Hence, in view of these presuppositions and conclusions of Bhāradvāja we are doing an injustice to him if we say that he negates all moral and ethical considerations. He is not formulating a complete political philosophy but is trying to prescribe some measures which could be used only in extreme cases and only to foil their use by the enemies.

So far as the immorality in the statecraft of Bhīṣma is concerned, it should be borne in mind that his prescription of the policy of unjust financial extortion from subjects occurs in the last chapter of the *rājadharma* section of the *Śāntiparvan*, which marks the transition to the *āpaddharma* chapters of the book. Bhīṣma refers to those techniques of extortion only when Yudhiṣṭhira asks the former's views about how a king should act when the treasury is empty, the army is small, and he has no friends and allies and is troubled by enemies. Hence, here also is present the same situation of the "*dharma* of distress." Bhīṣma is emphatic in his statement that nothing can equal the *dharma* of a king but the situation is complicated in times of distress and requires a different policy. He definitely indicates his disapprobation from the standpoint of normal times, of the techniques used in times of distress. He is still careful to assert his settled and ultimate political view that in times of peace, one should not desire treasury or heaven or any covetable object by transgressing the canons of *dharma*. But he says that when people are put to extreme troubles then they can maintain themselves by taking recourse even to unrighteous means. Thus we find that the problems of Kauṭilya, Bhīṣma and Bhāradvāja were different from the modern juxtaposition of politics and ethics. They have to be understood in terms of *dharma* and "*dharma* of distress."[15]

References

1. P.V. Kane in his *H.D.*, Vol. II, p. 965.
2. Julius Jolly: *Hindu Law and Custom* (Calcutta, 1928), p. 2.
3. Kane : *H.D.* (Poona, 1930), I, 4.
4. The *Śāntiparvan*, cclxi, 9.
5. *ibid.*, lxii, 21.
6. Cf., M. Winternitz : *Some Problems of Indian Literature* (Calcutta, 1925), p. 106.
7. The *Śāntiparvan*, cxl.

8. *ibid.*, lxxx, 5.
9. Ghoshal, U.N., *History of Indian Political Ideas*, p. 148.
10. Bandyopadhyaya, p. 271; also cf., Benoy Kumara Sarkar *The Positive Background of Hindu Sociology* (Allahabad, 1921), II. 30-31.
11. Radhakrishnan, *Indian Philosophy* I., chapters "*The Hymns of the Ṛgveda*" and "*The Transition to the Upaniṣads.*"
12. Aristotle: *Politica*, iii, 1176 b; *Nicomachean Ethics,* 1130 b.
13. St. Augustine's theory of the transmutation of the terrestrial social consciousness into the illuminated divine consciousness. *De Magistro, Retractations, Confessions* and *The City of God* discuss Augustine's substitution of Plato's dialectic by the theory of illumination.
14. The *Śāntiparvan*, cxl. 70.
15. D. Mackenzie Brown, *The White Umbrella*, p. 23.

Sources of Hindu Law

The three main sources of Hindu *dharma* or law are (1) the Śruti, (2) the Smṛti and (3) Custom.

A practical division of the sources of Hindu law would be (1) Original texts of the Dharmaṣāstras: (2) Commentaries and Digests and (3) Custom. Hindu law at the present day is the result of many ingredients. To these main sources must be added for all practical purposes the auxiliary indice, justice, equity and good conscience: Judicial decisions: and legislative enactments modifying or abrogating previously existing law.

The sources of Hindu law have been considered in the Introduction added to this work.

Commentaries as a source of law—The law of the Smṛtis was empiric and progressive and in course of time several Commentaries and Digests (*nibandhas*) were written on it. The authority of the several commentators varied in different districts, and thus arose the schools of law which are operative in different parts of India.

Judicial decision as a source of law—Judicial decisions on Hindu law are sometimes spoken of as a source of law.[1] Almost all the important points of Hindu law are now to be found in the law reports, and to this extent it may be said that the decisions on Hindu law have superseded the commentaries. The decisions of the Privy Council and the Supreme Court are binding on all the Courts of India including the High Courts; but the decisions of any one High Court are not binding on any other High Court, though they are binding on the Courts subordinate thereto.

The Hindu law was at first administered by the English Judges with the assistance of Hindu pandits. The institution of pandits, as official referees of the Courts was abolished in the year 1868.

Mitākṣara and Dāyabhāga School—(1) "The remoter sources of the Hindu law [that is, Smṛtis] are common to all the different schools. The process by which those schools have been developed seems to have been of this kind. Works universally or very generally received became the subject of subsequent commentaries. The commentator put his own gloss on the ancient text; and his authority having been received in one and rejected in another part of India, schools with conflicting doctrines arose."

(2) There are two schools of law, namely, the Mitākṣarā school and the Dāyabhāga school. The Dāyabhāga school prevails in Bengal; the Mitākṣarā school prevails in other parts of India.

(2a) As to the Marumakkattāyam, Eḷayasantāna and Nampūtiri systems of law see Mulla p. 49.

(3) The Mitākṣarā is a running commentary on the Code of Yajñavalkya. It was written by Vijñāneśvara in the latter part of the eleventh century.[2] The Dāyabhāga is not a commentary on any particular Code, but purports to be a digest of all the Codes. It was written by Jīmūtavāhana who flourished in about the beginning of the twelfth century.[3]

(4) The *Mitākṣarā* is of supreme authority throughout India except in Bengal. The Dāyabhāga is of supreme authority in Bengal. But even in Bengal the *Mitākṣarā* is still regarded as a very high authority on all questions in respect of which there is no express conflict between it and the Dāyabhāga and the other works prevalent there. The Dāyabhāga may also be referred to in a *Mitākṣarā* case on points on which the latter treatise is silent.

(5) It is said that the *Mitākṣarā* school is the orthodox school, and the Dāyabhāga school is the reformed school, of Hindu law. The Dāyabhāga school is also called the Bengal school of Hindu law.

(6) The Bengal school differs from the *Mitākṣarā* school in two main particulars, namely, the law of inheritance and the joint family system.

Sub-divisions of Mitākṣarā School—(1) The *Mitākṣarā* school is sub-divided into four minor schools; these differ between themselves in some matters of detail relating particularly to adoption and inheritance. All these schools acknowledge the supreme authority of the *Mitākṣarā*, but they give preference to certain treatises and to commentaries which control certain passages of the *Mitākṣarā*. This accounts for the differences between those schools.

The sub-schools and the principal works which supplement the *Mitākṣarā* in each sub-school are mentioned below:—

Benares school	:	*Vīramitrodaya* *Nirṇayasindhu*
Mithilā school	:	*Vivādacintāmaṇi* *Vivādaratnākara* *Madanapārijāta*
Maharashtra or Bombay school [Western India]	:	*Vyavahāramayūkha* *Vīramitrodaya* *Nirṇayasindhu*
Dravida or Madras school [Southern India]	:	*Smṛticandrikā* *Parāśara-Mādhavīya* *Sarasvatīvilāsa* *Vyavahāranirṇaya*

(2) As regards authorities in Western India the *Mitākṣarā* ranks first and paramount in the Maharashtra, Northern Kanara and the Ratnagiri District. In Gujarat, the Island of Bombay and the North Konkan, the *Mayūkha* is considered as the overruling authority where there is a difference of opinion between it and the *Mitākṣarā*.

The principle, however, adopted by the High Court of Bombay, and sanctioned by the Privy Council, is to construe the two works so as to harmonize them with each other wherever and so far as that is reasonably possible (*w*). In Poona, Ahmednagar, and Khandesh the Mayūkha is considered to be of equal authority with the *Mitākṣarā*, but not capable of overruling it as in Gujarat, the Island of Bombay and the North Konkan.

Works on Adoption—The two special works on adoption are the *Dattakamīmāṁsā* and the *Dattakacandrikā*. Generally speaking they are equally respected throughout India, but where they differ the *Dattakamīmāṁsā* is preferred in Mithila and Benares, and the *Dattakamīmāṁsā* in Bengal.

As to these two works their Lordships of the Privy Council said in *Balusu* v. *Balusu*:[4] "Both works have had a high place in the estimation of Hindu lawyers in all parts of India, and having had the advantage of being translated into English at a comparatively early period, have increased their authority during the British rule.

As to the *Dattakamīmāṁsā* it may be said that in Bengal there is a tradition that it is a literary forgery by Raghumaṇi Vidyabhūṣaṇa who was the Pundit of Colebrooke, the celebrated English translator of numerous Sanskrit works on Hindu law. It is said that it was written to help a claim set up by an adopted son to a King in Bengal.

In *Abhiraj Kuer* v. *Debendra Singh*[5] the Supreme Court examined the text of Nandapaṇḍita in the *Dattakamīmāṁsā*: "*viruddhasambaddhaḥ putro varjanīyaḥ*" and held that it was merely recommendatory. Reference may be made to § 480(3).

Personal law: Rule of Presumption—A Hindu family residing in a particular state of India is presumed to be governed by the law of the place in which it resides. The mere transfer, however, of a district to another presidency or state for administrative purposes is not sufficient to affect the personal law of the residents in that district, unless and until it is shown in the case of any resident there that he had intended to change and has in fact changed his personal law.

The rule that a Hindu family residing in a particular state is *prima facie* governed by the law of that place is not founded on any doctrine affecting *lex loci*. The rule rests on personal law and status. In general it may be said that in matters of status there is no *lex loci* in India and every person is governed by the law of his personal status.

Migration and School of Law—(1) Where a Hindu family migrates from one state to another, the presumption is that it carries with it its personal law, that is, the laws and customs as to succession and family relations prevailing in the state from which it came. But this presumption may be rebutted by showing that the family has adopted the law and usages of the province to which it has migrated.

(2) It is the law existing at the time of migration which continues to govern the migrated members until it is renounced. It is the law in force in the state at the time of their leaving it which continues to govern persons who have migrated to another state. Thus they are affected by decisions of the Courts of their state of origin which declare the correct law of the state up to the time of their leaving it, but not by customs incorporated in its law after they have left it.

Illustrations

(1) A Hindu family migrates from the North-Western Provinces where the *Mitākṣarā* law prevails to Bengal where the Dāyabhāga law prevails. The presumption is that it continues to be governed by the *Mitākṣarā* law, and this presumption may be supported by previous instances of succession in the family according to the *Mitākṣarā* law after its migration and by evidence relating to ceremonies performed in the family at marriages, births and *srāddhas*, showing that the family continued to be governed by the *Mitākṣarā* law after its migration: *Parbati* v. *Jagadis* (1902) 29 Cal. 433, 452, 29 I.A. 82. If the migration is proved, and it is also proved that the family followed the customs of the *Mitākṣarā* school, it is not necessary to prove also that the family immigrated to Bengal after the establishment of the Dāyabhāga System of Law.

(2) A joint Hindu family, consisting of two brothers *A* and *B*, migrates from the N.W.P. to Bengal. *A* dies leaving a

widow *C*. The presumption being that this family continues to be governed by the *Mitākṣarā* law, the joint property will, on *A*'s death, pass to his surviving brother *B*; *C* will be entitled to maintenance only. But if the family had renounced the *Mitākṣarā* law, and adopted the Dāyabhāga Law, *A*'s share would pass to his widow *C*: *Parbati* v. *Jagadis* (1902) 29 Cal. 433, 29 I.A. 82.

A Maharashtrian family residing in Chhatisgarh, in Central Provinces, is presumed to have come as immigrant and if it retains its individuality as Maharashtrian, is governed by the Bombay interpretation of the Mitākṣarā: *Keshao Rao* v. *Sadasheorao* (1938) Nag. 469, ('38) A.N. 163. Similarly, a Rajput family which had migrated to Berar, and were proved to have retained its old manners and customs were held to be governed by the Benares and not the Bombay School of Hindu Law.

In *Abdurahim* v. *Halimabai*[6], their Lordships of the Privy Council said: "Where a Hindu family migrates from one part of India to another *prima facie* they carry with them their personal law, and, if they are alleged to have become subject to a new local custom, this new custom must be affirmatively proved to have been adopted, but when such a family emigrate [from India] to another country [East Africa], and, being themselves Mahomedans [*e.g.*, Memons], settle among Mahomedans, the presumption that they have accepted the law of the people whom they have joined seems to their Lordships to be one that should be much more readily made... The analogy is that of a change of domicile on settling in a new country rather than the analogy of a change of custom on migration within India." Of course, if nothing is known about a man except that he lived in a certain place, it will be assumed that his personal law is the law which prevails in that place. In that sense only his domicile is of importance.

Clause (2).—The law must be the family law as it was when they left. A judgment declaratory of law as having always been would bind: but it would be a different thing if subsequent customs became incorporated in the law.

Raghuvaṁśins of Nandurbar.—These migrated from Oudh and settled in Khandesh and they are governed by the Benares School of Hindu Law.

Hindus of North Canara—They are governed by the Bombay and not the Madras School of Hindu Law. Komtis of Chanda District are governed by the Mitākṣarā and not the Madras School of Law.

Yelmis of Berar are governed by the Madras School of Law.

Custom as a Source of Law—Custom is one of the three sources of the Hindu Law. When there is a conflict between a custom and a text of the Smṛtis, the custom overrides the text: "Under the Hindu System of Law, clear proof of usage will outweigh the written text of the law."[7]

Rattigan's Digest of Customary Law is regarded as authoritative on the subject of customs in the Punjab.[8]

Three Kinds of Customs—The Hindu customs recognized by the Courts are—(1) local, (2) class and (3) family customs.

Essentials of a Valid Custom—(1) A custom is a rule which in a particular family or a particular class or community or in a particular district, has from long usage obtained the force of law. It must be ancient, certain and reasonable, and being in derogation of the general rules of law, must be construed strictly. It is further essential that it should be established to be so by clear and unambiguous evidence, for it is only by means of such evidence that the Courts can be assured of its existence and of the fact that it possesses the conditions of antiquity and certainty on which alone its legal title to recognition depends. It must not be opposed to morality or public policy and it must not be expressly forbidden by the legislature. It must not be in derogation of the fundamental rights of a citizen to hold and dispose of property by absolutely prohibiting alienation of property even after actual division. Where the evidence shows that the custom alleged was not followed in numerous instances, the custom could not be held to be proved. A custom derives its force from the fact that it has, from long usage, obtained the force of law. It must be ancient; but it is not of the essence of this rule that its antiquity must in every case be carried back to a period beyond the memory of man. All that is necessary to prove is that the usage has been acted upon in practice for such a long period and with such invariability as to show that it has, by common consent, been submitted to as the established governing rule of a particular locality.

(2) It is incumbent on a party setting up a custom to allege and prove the custom on which he relies. Custom cannot be extended by analogy. It must be established inductively and not by *a priori* methods. Custom cannot be a matter of mere theory but must always be a matter of fact and one custom cannot be deduced from another. It is well established law that custom cannot be enlarged by parity of reasoning since it is the usage that makes the law and not the reason of the thing.

In *Saligram* v. *Munshi Ram* the Supreme Court was considering a case of custom under Section V. of the Punjab Laws Act.

(3) Where the proof of a custom rests upon a limited number of instances of a comparatively recent date, the Court may hold the custom proved so as to bind the parties to the suit and those claiming through and under them; but the decision would not in that case be a satisfactory precedent if in any future suit between other parties fuller evidence with regard to the alleged custom should be forthcoming. A judgment relating to the existence of a custom is admissible to corroborate the evidence adduced to prove such custom in another case. Where, however, a custom is repeatedly brought to the notice of the Courts, the Courts, may hold that the custom was introduced into the law without the necessity of proof in each individual case.

Family Custom—In respect of family custom, the same principles are applicable, though, of course, in the case of a family custom instances in support of the custom may not be as many or as frequent as in case of customs pertaining to a territory or to the community or to the character of any estate. In dealing with family customs the consensus of opinion among members of the family, the traditional belief entertained by them and acted upon by them, their statements and their conduct would all be relevant and it is only where the relevant evidence of such a character appears to the court to be sufficient that a specific family custom pleaded in a particular case can be held to be proved. Custom binding inheritance in a particular family has long been recognized in India.

References

1. Mulla, D.F., *Principles of Hindu Law*. pp. 70-71.
2. Mulla p. 51.
3. *ibid*. 62.
4. (1899) 22, Mad. 398, 411-412, 26 I.A. 113, 131-132.
5. (62) A.S.C. 351. Also see *Vallabhalalji* v. *Mahalaxmi Bahuji* ('62) A.S.C. 356, 64 *Bom. L.T.* 433.
6. (1916) 43 I.A. 35, 41, 18 Bom. L.R. 635, 32 I.C. 413, ('15) A.P.C. 86.
7. *Collector of Madura* v. *Moottoo Ramalinga* (1868) 12, M.I.A. 397, 436.
8. *Daya Singh* v. *Dhan Kaur* (74) A.S.C. 665.

The Sacred Laws of the Hindus

The study of the sacred languages of India, which has given to the world the modern science of Philology and the modern theory of Race, began virtually in the study of sacred Indian law. Sir William Jones, who, though he was not absolutely the earliest of Anglo-Indian Sanskritists, was the first to teach the West that there was in the East such a language as Sanskrit, and a literature preserved in it, does not appear during his Oriental studies in England to have suspected the existence of the treasure he was destined to disinter. He seems rather to have sought the key to Eastern knowledge in two spoken and highly-cultivated languages—Arabic and Persian. But he accepted a Judgeship in a Court of Justice newly established in Bengal, under an Act of Parliament which reserved to native litigants the application of their own laws and usages in all questions of inheritance and contract; and, from a much earlier period, it had been the practice of all the Indian Courts to attach to themselves Moolvies and Pandits—that is, native professors of Mahommedan and Hindu Law—for the purpose of advising them on the legal rules, of which these experts represented themselves to be the depositaries. The correspondence of Sir William Jones repeatedly expresses his suspicions (perhaps not always quite just) of the fidelity and honesty of the native advisers of the tribunals: "I can no longer bear," he writes in September 1785: "to be at the mercy of our Pandits, who deal out Hindu Law as they please, and make it at reasonable rates when they cannot find it ready-made." He therefore, formed a determination to acquaint himself personally with the sources of the law from which they pretended to draw their opinions. With Arabic he was already familiar, and he therefore required no assistance in his studies of the Mahommedan Law; but for the purpose of mastering the virtually unknown language in which the Hindu Law was contained, he found it necessary to visit during his vacations several of the decaying and decayed seats of learning in which knowledge of it was still professed, and he organized a staff of Hindu scholars to aid him in his Sanskrit studies, and to record their results. The plan for improving the administration of Anglo-Indian justice which finally commended itself to him was one for the preparation of a Digest in English of the Hindu and Mahommedan Law, which should need no pandits or Moolvies for its interpretation. Much to their honour, the Indian Government of the day, formed of Lord Cornwallis and his Council, accepted his offer to preside over the undertaking, and his staff of native experts, considerably increased, was taken into the Government service. On his monument by Flaxman, in the chapel of the University College at Oxford, he sits surrounded by his company of native literates, amid conventional Indian foliage, bareheaded, in the open air.

It was in fact from these native Hindu teachers that Sir William Jones learned, and the learned and curious all over the West were gradually informed, that in a part of the world just coming under the British sceptre there exists an ancient language, the elder sister of the classical languages so honoured in the West, a series of poems which might not unjustly be compared to the Homeric epics and the Attic drama, and laws twice as old as the legislation of Solon and the Twelve Tables of Rome. It is impossible now—now that India has become more commonplace as she has got nearer; now that, here at all events, she is associated with frontier wars, budgets, opium, and grey shirtings—to reproduce the keen throb of intellectual interest which the literary portion of these discoveries sent through Europe. But Sir William Jones was even more of a jurist than a scholar, and nothing seems to have surprised and interested him more than the assurance of his teachers that, in the ancient language he was learning, there survived legal writings asserted to be of sacred origin, of vast antiquity, and of universal obligation among the Hindus. The oldest of them was said to have been dictated by Manu, a divine being who had been mysteriously associated with the creation of all things; and it was described as the acknowledged basis of all the Hindu Law and Hindu institutions, the fountain of all civil obligation to more than a hundred millions of men. The book was actually extant, and the translation of it which he gave to the world, with the title 'Institutes of Hindu Law, or the Ordinances of Menu, according to the Gloss of Cullúca,' was the first fruit of his labours on the Digest which he had planned. He seems, in fact, to have regarded it as standing to this projected Digest much in the same relation as the Roman Institutes to the celebrated Digest of the Emperor Justinian.

It does not seem to me possible to doubt that the account which Sir William Jones gave of the Book of Manu in his Preface to his translation was a rationalized version of the statements made to him by his native teachers, who seem all to have belonged to one particular school of Hindu learning, accustomed to hold Manu in especial honour. Sir William Jones considered this personage, who, in the treatise called after him, sits 'reclining on his arm, with his attention fixed on one object, the supreme God,' as a real individual human being, and the personal author of the legislation attributed to him. Sir William Jones compares him to the Cretan Minos and the Egyptian Men, partly on account of the consonance of names. As I have just stated, he sees an analogy in this law-book to the Institutes of the Roman Justinian, but he assigns to it the prodigious date of 1,280 years before Christ. In the light of newer knowledge, which nevertheless might not have existed but for Jones, we can see that these statements of his require correction. There is no doubt that, if Manu is to be compared to a book known to Englishmen, it should have been to a book a good deal more familiar to them than the Roman

Institutes, the book of Leviticus. For Manu, though it contains a good deal of law, is essentially a book of ritual, of priestly duty and religious observance; and to this combination of law with religion the whole family of Hindu writings, to which the book of Manu belongs, owe some remarkable characteristics on which I am desirous of dwelling. It is not at the same time to be supposed that the combination is peculiar to the Hindus. There is no system of recorded law, literally from China to Peru, which, when it first emerges into notice, is not seen to be entangled with religious ritual and observance. The law of the Romans has been thought to be that in which the civil and Pontifical jurisprudence were earliest and most completely disentangled. Yet the meagre extant fragments of the Twelve Tables of Rome contain rules which are plainly religious or ritualistic:

> Thou shalt not square a funeral pile with an adze.
> Let not women tear their cheeks at a funeral.
> Thou shalt not put gold on a corpse.

We are told by Cicero ('De Legibus,' 2, 25, 64) that several of these rules contained in the Tenth of the Roman Tables were taken from Greek originals. He attributes the Greek rules to Solon, and explains that they limited the costliness of the ancient ritual of funerals.

The opinions of Sir William Jones produced great effects both in the East and in the West. One result which followed from them I must pass by with notice very unequal to its practical importance. The Anglo-Indian Courts accepted from the school of Sanskritists which he founded on the advise of his Brāhmaṇical advisers, that the sacred laws beginning in the extant book of Manu were acknowledged by all Hindus to be binding on them. The impression in the mind of the English judicial officers—an impression shared, I infer from its language, by the English Parliament—manifested that the sacerdotal Hindu Law corresponded nearly to the English Common Law, and was at least the substructure of all the rules of life followed by Hindus. It is only just beginning to be perceived that this opinion had a very slender foundation, for it is probable that at the end of the last century large masses of the Hindu population had not so much as heard of Manu, and knew little or nothing of the legal rules supposed to rest ultimately on his authority. The original range of operation which it is possible to allow to the sacerdotal laws has been much narrowed by very recent investigation. Some years ago, on my return from India, I stated in a book on 'Village Communities in the East and West' (pp. 52, 53) the opinion which I had formed after personal inquiry among Indian judicial officers. "The conclusion," I said: "arrived at by the persons who seem to me of highest authority is, first, that the codified law—Manu and his glossators—embraced originally a much smaller body of usage than had been imagined; and next, that the customary rules, reduced to writing, have been very greatly altered by Brāhmaṇical expositors, constantly in spirit, sometimes in tenor. Indian law may in fact be affirmed to consist of a very great number of local bodies of usage, and of one set of customs, reduced to writing, pretending to a diviner authority than the rest, exercising consequently a great influence over them, and tending, if not checked, to absorb them." Since then, my conclusion has been greatly fortified by more systematic examination of the phenomena. There is in India a province, the Punjab, the country of the Five Rivers, which was the earliest seat of the Aryan Hindus on their descent from their original home into the Indian plains. The laws and institutions of this province have quite lately been the subject of an exhaustive official inquiry ('Punjab Customary Law,' edited by C.L. Tupper, Calcutta, 1881). Among several results of great interest which seem to me to have been reached, one is that we have in the Punjab the Hindu institutions very much in the state in which they were before the Brāhmaṇical expositors took them in hand. The traces of the religious ideas which profoundly influenced the development of what is known as the Hindu Law are here extremely slight; and few things can be more instructive to the legal archaeologist than the comparison of the Punjab rules with those worked out in Brāhmaṇical schools far to the south-east. This Punjab Hindu Law exhibits in fact some singularly close resemblances to the most ancient Roman Law. There is also evidence that the stream of Hinduism which at some time or another flowed over the southern peninsula of India was extremely superficial. The southern Hindu has always been regarded as a lax Hindu; but the truth seems to be, not that he negligently violates the Hindu sacerdotal Law, but that neither he nor his forefathers ever knew it in anything like its integrity.

Some other views, which are not now accepted by the most learned Sanskritists, had their origin in the theories first propounded in Sir William Jones's preface. The probable antiquity of Manu's law-book was much exaggerated. Its true date is unknown: in Indian literary history there are almost no trustworthy dates: but it is now believed to be relatively modern—almost the most modern of a large family of Sanskrit writings more or less treating of law. This opinion is the result of a test first applied by Professor Max Müller, and now universally accepted by Sanskritists as conclusive. The law-book of Manu is in verse, and verse is one of the expedients for lessening the burden which the memory has to bear when writing is unknown or very little used. But there is another expedient which serves the same object. This is Aphorism or Proverb. Even now, in our own country, much of popular wisdom is preserved either in old rhymes or in old proverbs; and it is well ascertained that during the Middle Ages much of law and not a little of medicine was preserved among professions, not necessarily clerkly, by these two agencies. A great deal of the old German Law compressed into maxims has been preserved, and it is probable that the Latin legal maxims well known to English lawyers, and sometimes spoken of as the quintessence of wisdom, were really aids to recollection. As to verse, the ordinary medical practitioner once carried his professional knowledge with him in the versified Latin rules of the school of Salerno—that curious body of medical precepts which begins with the grim warning:

"*contra vim mortis non est medicamen in hortis.*" In Sir William Jones's day, an abridgment of Lord Coke's 'Reports' in verse was in existence; and he gravely remarks that, if the verse had been smoother and the law more accurate, every student might have been advised to use it. Now, the Sanskrit law-books are sometimes in aphoristic prose, sometimes in verse, sometimes in a mixture of both; and the canon established by Max Müller is that, in India at all events, books of aphorisms are older than books of verse; and the clue being once found, many more proofs disclose themselves that Manu, which is wholly in verse, is much more recent than the Hindu law-books (such as Āpastamba and Gautama, which are wholly in aphoristic prose), and even more modern than books (like Viṣṇu and Vasiṣṭha) which are partly in prose and partly in verse. 'In the whole of Vedic (that is Hindu scriptural) literature,' says Max Müller, 'there is no work written, like Manu, in the regular epic *śloka*, and the continuous employment of this metre is a characteristic mark of post-Vedic writings.' Manu, therefore, in spite of its great modern reputation, belongs to the Hindu Apocrypha. Nor is it believed that we have the book in its original form. Dr. Jolly (preface to Viṣṇu) speaks of the 'abundant evidence' for its having undergone modifications and entire transformations in successive periods.

The result of all this literary investigation and discussion is, that no book has had so many dates attributed to it as the book of Manu. Sir W. Jones placed its age at 1280 B.C., Schlegel at 1000 B.C., Elphinstone at 900 B.C., Monier Williams at about the fifth century B.C., Max Müller at not earlier than 200 B.C. But the high authority of the late Dr. Burnell is now cited for so late an age of the original book as 400 A.D., and it has even been attributed in its present form either to the eleventh or the fourteenth century of our era. (See Nelson, *Scientific Study of Hindu Law*, p. 37). It is as though it were thought doubtful whether a particular work were composed at the fabulous date of the Taking of Troy, or at the historical date of the Battle of Bannockburn. The book itself, however, purports to be coeval with the creation of the world, and I suppose that a Hindu holding the opinions now considered orthodox would be bound to claim for it an indefinitely high antiquity. At the same time, its audacious pretension to be of divine origin is out-done in some of the writings now shown to be older, for the so-called Code of Viṣṇu professes to have been dictated by one of the Persons of the Hindu Trinity to the Goddess of the Earth.

When this sacred legal literature of the Hindus is surveyed in its entirety, it is impossible not to recognise the plausibility of the modern theories of its origin. No one treatise, and still less the aggregate of treatises, is the production of an individual man or of an individual mind. The literature is the gradual growth of schools of learned Brāhmaṇas, which are still found in India. They are companies or corporations of men devoted to sacred learning. Perhaps the nearest analogy to their work is to be found in the labours of the Benedictines. But the comparison must not be pushed too far. The conception of a celibate order appears to have been unknown to the early Hindus. Each school was either in its beginning an actual family, or, if originally it was a mere collection of voluntary pupils sitting at the feet of a teacher, it tended to shape itself upon the model of the family, as the only known form of permanent association. The distinction between one school and another probably consisted in the particular set of authorities (as it would now be, the particular standard books) which it followed; and, as it went on from generation to generation, it was recruited partly by voluntary adherence and partly by hereditary descent. The double process is clearly reflected in the text of one of our oldest authorities, Āpastamba. The student desirous of being initiated into sacred learning is to go to a man 'in whose family it is hereditary, who himself possesses it, and who is devout in following the law' (Āpastamba, I, i. 1. 11). On the other hand, the pupil is directed to consider the teachers of his teacher as his ancestors (Āpastamba, I, i. 7. 12). This view of the relation of teacher and pupil has by no means died out in India. The Hindus still regard 'a school consisting of a succession of teachers and pupils as a spiritual family' (Dr. Bühler, *loc, cit.*) And according to the letter of the law recognised by the Indian Courts, though not perhaps according to the actual practice, teacher and pupil still inherit from one another, just as they did in the remote days of Āpastamba, who lays down that, on failure of the nearer kinsmen: "the spiritual teacher inherits, and in failure of the spiritual teacher a pupil shall take the deceased's wealth, and use it for religious works for the deceased's benefit, or he may himself enjoy it." (II. vi. 14. 3).

There are analogies to this sacredness and strictness of literary relations in the literary history of two societies with little or no intellectual likeness to the Hindus. Mr. Grote's theory of the Homeric poetry, taken in a mass (ii. 176-178), is that it was the aggregate production, not of one man, but of a *gens* or clan of Homeridæ, of whom Homer was the name-giving ancestor, real or supposed, the 'divine or semi-divine eponymus or progenitor, in whose name and glory the individuality of every member of the *gens* was merged.' 'Homer is no individual, but the divine or heroic father of the Homerids, the ideas of worship and ancestry, coalescing, as they constantly did, in the Grecian mind.' A still nearer analogy is one which, like many others, occurs in the ancient legal literature of the Irish. "Literary foster-age," I wrote in a former work (the *Early History of Institutions*, p. 242), "was an institution nearly connected with the existence of the Brehon law schools, and it consisted of the various relations established between the Brehon teacher and the pupils he received into his house for instruction in the Brehon lore. However, it may surprise us that the connection between Schoolmaster and Pupil was regarded as peculiarly sacred by the ancient Irish and as closely resembling natural fatherhood, the Brehon tracts leave no room for doubt on the point. It is expressly laid down that it created the same *Patria Potestas* as actual paternity; and the literary foster-father, though he teaches gratuitously, has a claim through life upon portions of the property of the literary foster-son. Thus the Brehon with his pupils constituted, not a school in our sense, but a true family. While the ordinary foster-father was bound by the law to give education of some kind to his foster-children—to the sons of Chiefs instruction in riding, shooting with the bow, swimming and chess-playing and instruction to their daughters in sewing, cutting out and embroidery—the Brehon trained his foster-sons in learning of the highest dignity, the lore of the chief literary profession. He took payment, but it was the law which settled it for him. It was part of his status, and not the result of a bargain."

On the whole, few literary theories of modern mintage have more to recommend them than that which Professor Max Müller first gave of the large extant body of Hindu sacerdotal legal writings. They were gradually evolved by Brāhmaṇic families, real or artificial. 'The great number of these writings,' he says in his letter, first printed in Morley's Digest, 'is to be accounted for by the fact that there was not one body of the Kalpasūtras binding on all Brāhmaṇic families, but that different old families had their own Kalpasūtras. These works are still very frequent in our libraries, yet there is no doubt that many of them have been lost. Sutras are quoted which do not exist in Europe, and the loss of some is acknowledged by the Brāhmaṇas themselves.' As regards the *Mānavadharma-śāstra*, the *Manusmṛti* translated by Sir William Jones and asserted by his native teachers to be the basis of all sacred Hindu Law, it is a late redaction of the legal doctrine of the Mānavas, a *gens* or clan called after a Manu frequently mentioned in Sanskrit literature, but mentioned by the writer of the extant book as somebody different from himself. If the old Manu ever composed a law-book (which is doubtful), it would certainly not have been composed in the metre of the extant code.

The theory upon which these schools of learned men worked, from the ancient, perhaps very ancient, Āpastamba and Gautama to the late Manu and the still later Nārada, is perhaps still held by some persons of earnest religious convictions, but in time now buried it affected every walk of thought. The fundamental assumption is, that a sacred or inspired literature being once believed to exist, all knowledge is contained in it. The Hindu way of putting it was, and is, not simply that the scripture is true, but that everything which is true is contained in the scripture. From very early times, the Hindu doctors appear to have been conscious of difficulties in the interpretation or application of their theory. Sometimes books of authority contradicted one another. Sometimes they failed to supply a basis for received doctrines or for immemorial religious practice. One of the earliest of expedients was to suppose the loss of passages in the most ancient portion of the scriptures. "If you ask," says Āpastamba, "why the decision of the Aryas presupposes the existence of a Vedic passage" then I answer: All precepts were originally taught in the Brāhmaṇas, but these texts have been lost. Their former existence may, however, be inferred from usage. It is not, however, permissible to infer the former existence of a Vedic passage where pleasure is obtained by following the custom: "he who follows such usage becomes fit for the Hell" (I. iv. 12. 10). With the aid of such expedients, of which several are still in use among learned Hindus, the theory has survived; and it is to be observed that such a theory, firmly held during the infancy of systematic thought, tends to work itself into fact. As the human mind advances, accumulating observation and accumulating reflection, nascent philosophy and dawning science are read into the sacred literature, while they are at the same time limited by the ruling ideas of its priestly authors. But as the mass of this literature grows through the additions made to it by successive expositors, it gradually specializes itself, and subjects, at first mixed together under vague general conceptions, become separated from one another and isolated. In the history of law the most important early specialization is that which separates what a man ought to do from what he ought to know. A great part of the religious literature, including the creation of the Universe, the structure of Heaven, Hell, and the World or Worlds and the nature of the Gods, falls under the last head, what a man ought to know. The law-books first appear as a subdivision of the first branch, what a man should do. Thus the most ancient books of this class are short manuals of conduct for an Aryan Hindu who would lead a perfect life. They contain much more ritual than law, a great deal more about the impurity caused by touching impure things than about crime, a great deal more about penances than about punishments. They are intended to guide the faithful Hindu of the three higher castes from birth to death, and give him full directions for living first as a student of holy books, next as a householder (or, as we should say, a citizen), and finally—for that is assumed to be the proper lot of every man in old age—as a religious ascetic or a hermit.

This remarkable distribution of life runs through the whole series of sacred legal writings, and only disappears when they become mere law-books. The Brāhmaṇa alone teaches, but the entire youth of the three higher castes, Brāhmaṇas, Kṣatriyas and Vaiśyas, come and sit at his feet to be instructed in sacred learning; it is not even certain from some passages whether the lowest and most despised of castes, the Śūdras, are always excluded. This is the period of studentship. When it comes to an end, the instructed hindu returns to his family and to civil affairs. He is then the Householder. But, when old age is beginning, it is assumed in these books (whatever may have been the actual practice) that he withdraws from active life and closes his days as a hermit or ascetic, following a code of self-denial which is prescribed for him in full detail. It is of course to the second of these periods, that of life as a householder, that we must look for whatever light the sacred laws of the Hindus may throw upon the ancient history of law. The first of them, studentship, is remarkable, as disclosing the true secret of the hold of the sacred literature on large portions of the Hindu race, and of the respect paid by it to the teachers of the race, the Brāhmaṇas. For the education of the young Hindu is not merely an education in the holy texts and doctrines; it is a training in reverence, almost amounting to abject servility, bestowed on the literature and its professors in about equal proportions and inculcated by a system of rules adapted with extreme skill to immature minds. The third period, however, that of Asceticism, is the one which on the whole seems most unintelligible to the modern reader of these books, and it merits some special attention before this chapter is closed. The duty of adopting the ascetic life, and the rules for following it, referred to in all the law tracts, are discussed at much length by Manu in the sixth chapter. 'Having thus remained,' it is written, 'in the order of householders, let the twice-born man ("twice-born," that is, through the study of the Vedas), who has before completed his studentship, dwell in a forest, his faith being firm and his organs wholly subdued. When the father of a family perceives his muscles become feeble and his hair grey, and sees the child of his child, let him then take refuge in a forest. Abandoning all food eaten in towns, and all his household utensils, let him repair to the lonely wood, committing the care of his wife to his sons, or accompanied by her, if she choose to attend him... Let him to his sons, or accompanied by her, if she choose to attend him... Let him be constantly engaged in reading the Vedas, patient of all extremities... Let him bear a reproachful speech with patience; let him not, on account of this frail and feverish body, engage in hostility with any one living. With an angry man let him not in his turn be angry; abused, let him speak mildly; nor let him utter a word referring to vain illusory things... Delighted with meditating on the supreme spirit, sitting fixed in such meditation, without needing anything earthly, without any companion but his own soul, let him live in this world, seeking the bliss of the next... A gourd, a wooden bowl, an earthen dish, or a basket made of reeds, has Manu, the Svāyaṁbhuva, son of the Self-existent, declared fit vessels to receive the food of men devoted to God.'

It is still a comparatively common practice in India for the aged Hindu to retire into 'religion,' and the law, as administered by the British tribunals, makes provision in many places for the case of a Hindu who has embraced a religious life, and ceased to participate in any kind of secular business. There is nothing by itself surprising in the custom, considering the tremendous series of experiences which the devout believer in Hinduism is led to expect as awaiting him at the moment of his death. Nevertheless, there is reason for thinking that the withdrawal of the aged from activity is more ancient than the Hindu theological system, and has existed independently of it, as a secular practice, in many early societies. The Patria Potestas, which is witnessed to by the ancient law or custom of so many communities, was found on power quite as much as on parentage; and when the power fails, there are many signs that the patriarchal authority departs. In the Hindu Law of Succession, death is not by any means necessarily the occasion of inheritance; the contingency quite as commonly contemplated is withdrawal from secular life; the householder quitting his family and dividing his substance among his children—nay, being even liable (though this is a violently disputed point) to be forced into retirement by his sons. There is some evidence, moreover, that, when the larger associations of Hindu kindred, the Joint Families, were in a more ancient state than that in which we see them, they recognized three classes of persons as entirely helpless and, therefore, dependent on the group at large; the children, the unmarried daughters and widows, and the old men. The 'seniors' not infrequently mentioned in the Irish Brehon Law, and stated to be persons for whom the sept must make provision, are no doubt aged men.

There is reason, in fact, to believe that at some period of human history a revolution took place in the status of aged men, not perhaps unlike that which is still proceeding in the case of women. There is abundant testimony that tribes, long pressed hard by enemies or generally in straits for subsistence, systematically put their members to death when too old for labour or arms. The place from which a wild Slavonic race compelled their old men to leap into the sea is still shown. And the fiercer savage has often in many parts of the world made food of them. Nevertheless, the ancient records of many communities, especially those of Aryan speech, show us old age invested with the highest authority and dignity. Mr. Freeman (in his *Comparative Politics*, pp. 72, 73) has given a long list of honorific names belonging to classes or institutions, which indicate the value once set by advancing societies on the judgment of the old. Among them are, Senate, γερονσια (the Spartan Senate), δημογέρονες (its Homeric equivalent), πρέσβεις (Ambassadors), Ealdorman, Elder, Presbyter, Monseigneur, Seigneur, Sire, Sir, and Sheikh; and Mr. Freeman closes with the Old Man of the mountain. So great a number of titles, civil and ecclesiastical, are evidence of a very strong sentiment, and suggest that this exaltation of old age was a definite stage in the ascent to civilization.

There is a story of a New Zealand chief who, questioned as to the fortunes of a fellow-tribesman long ago well known to the enquirer, answered: "He gave us so much good advice that we put him mercifully to death." The reply, if it was ever given, combines the two views which barbarous men appear to have taken at different times of the aged. At first they are useless, burdensome and importunate, and they fare accordingly. But at a later period a new sense of the value of wisdom and counsel raises them to the highest honour. Their long life comes to be recognized as one way of preserving experience. The faculty of speech, which separates man from the brute, and the art of writing, by which the society capable of civilization is distinguished from the society condemned to permanent barbarism, are simply methods by which experience is enlarged, compared and transmitted, and by which mankind is enabled to have more of it than is contained in single separate lives. Yet the individual life is always the original source of experience, and at some time or other it must have been perceived that the more the individual life was prolonged, the larger was its contribution to the general stock. This seems the best explanation of the vast authority which, in the infancy of civilisation, was assigned to assemblies of aged men, independently of their physical power or military prowess. It probably sprang up among communities which had no writings to learn from, and who were conscious that the importance of the arts which were necessary for their very existence was out of all proportion to the average shortness of life. Almost everywhere in the advancing portions of the ancient world we find that the old, generally organized in assemblies, had a large share of the public powers, and there is a survival of these ideas in the minimum limit of age which has been made the condition of a seat in the artificial Second Chambers which have been constructed over most of the civilised West as supposed counterparts of the English House of Lords. But these modern Second Chambers reverse to a great extent the functions of the ancient assemblies, known, from their names and otherwise, to have originally consisted of old men. The Second Chamber is nowadays assumed to have a veto in the legislation of the Chamber which has the initiative; but the ancient Senates, in their primitive condition at all events, decided beforehand what measures should be submitted to the Popular Assembly, and if they legislated themselves, their enactments had reference to special departments of State, such as religion and finance. On the whole, they were rather administrative than the legislative bodies. The nearest analogy to the very important control over the law-making power which they once possessed, must be sought in the indefinite but most real and effective authority which an English Cabinet enjoys through its virtual monopoly of the initiative in the legislation.

Custom and Law in Ancient India

On the *śāstra's* provision for recognition of custom, misconceptions abound. The relationship between positive law with its scriptural origin and the unwritten laws which we call 'custom' is subtle and complicated. Although the British and French appreciated the distinction between these two sources of law, and recognized the traditional as well as legal priorities to be observed between them in courts of law, no full juridical discussion of the relationship has been published. We need to examine a theory of the relative importance of sources of law, which obviously existed in ancient India, but which, when once consigned to written form, failed as it stood to satisfy authors of the Smṛti material which is virtually unexplored.

The original maxim seems to have been:

dharmaścā vyavahāraśca caritraṁ rājaśāsanam /
catuṣpād vyavahāro'yam uttaraḥ pūrvabādhakaḥ //

or something very similar, the meaning of which will have been that (all) litigation rests on four feet (or moves on four feet), as it were, namely *dharma* (righteousness), *vyavahāra* (practice), *caritra* (actual usage in the sense of custom) and *rājaśāsana* ('royal decree'), and that each later one in this series overruled or put out of court the earlier; so that, for example, one who relied on a previous 'royal decree' would have nothing to fear from an opponent who relied on customary usage. But was this exactly what was implied?

Let us start immediately with the very full text of Kātyāyana (c. A.D.300), who is comprehensive if not perspicuous.[1] When this has been mastered we may look at the work of the other Smṛtikāras and test the validity of their contributions.

Kātyāyana says:

> "In dispute where the person guilty of wrongdoing accepts his responsibility for it and where the real owner of the money secures his wealth by the admission of the defendant the decision is by *dharma* itself."

This tells us that the discussion we are bout to embark upon presented itself to the Smṛtikāras as an analysis of the method of deciding lawsuits. The ambiguous word 'method' is used deliberately, for on this it is unfortunately possible to differ from M. Robert Lingat and numerous Indian writers, who have filed to observe that here we have a self-conscious and tendentious debate amongst the Smṛti writers themselves as to the meaning of an ancient formula which listed the 'methods'. Our present author continues:

> That is said to be *vyavahāra* where, for the purpose of deciding causes, those who are to execute the law rely upon principles derived from the Smṛti.
>
> Whatever a person practises, whether it be in accord with *dharma* or not, is declared to be *caritra* because it is the invariable usage of the country.

This explains what the word *caritra* means in the formula to which we shall return. A lot of emphasis is placed on this verse:

> "What a king establishes as *dharma* which is not in conflict with reason (or equity?) and the *śāstra* or with the outlook of the country is a lawful *rāja-śāsana* (royal decree).
>
> "Where a cause is tried by reference to inference and ordeals are excluded, appeal to *dharma* is overruled by *vyavahāra*, but not in other cases."

This warns us that *dharma* as a method of decision had at least two meanings in Kātyāyana's own mind, the first being that noticed in the first of the verses quoted above, where the word means 'righteousness', and the second, where it means 'unseen justice, divine intervention'. To continue:

> "He (the King) should not disregard the rules of conduct amongst those who belong to *pratiloman* castes and amongst inhabitants of forts (? including criminal tribes), even if they are repugnant (to Smṛti).
>
> "When the King gives a decision in accordance with that *dharma* (here; 'rule of conduct'), then *vyavahāra* is overruled by *caritra*."

For, as we shall see, the formula is concerned with the relative appropriateness of the various methods of decision *inter se*:

> "Where kings consider a custom is repugnant to equity (or 'law', 'justice') there the custom is overruled (or 'repealed'?) by the King's command (or the 'royal order').
>
> "Each succeeding one, when possessed of these characteristics, overrules (the preceding); any other method of exclusion (or overruling) leads to a destruction of *dharma*."

Here, then, we have the 'relative appropriateness' point, in Kātyāyana's formulation. He continues:

> "If a king decides by his own fiat where there is a text (or maxim) on the point it leads him away from heaven, causes ruin to the public, brings danger from the army of the enemy and strikes at the essence of his own longevity.
>
> "Therefore, a king should decide causes according to the *śāstra*, but in the absence of texts (or maxims) he should administer justice according to the outlook (or 'customs') of the country.
>
> "Whatever course of conduct is in use in a country, is of long duration, and is not repugnant to *śruti*

> (Veda) and Smṛti, is said to be 'outlook' (or 'custom') of the country.
>
> Between residents of the same country or the same capital or the same hamlet of cowherds and of the same town or village, decision must be by their own conventions, but in disputes between these and others it must be in accord with the Dharmaśāstra.
>
> Conventions settled with the consent of the country, committed to writing and sealed with the royal seal should always be upheld. They should be sedulously preserved as if they were *śāstra*, and the King should decide cases only after consulting them. Conventions arrived at by merchants and reduced to writing must be given effect to and the King should not initiate anything contrary to them.
>
> Whatever had once been decided upon as authorized by the outlook (or 'custom') of the country, and whatever, though not formerly in use, has been laid down in deference to Śruti and Smṛti, shall not be departed from subsequently: and what is inconsistent with equity (or 'law', 'justice') must be avoided.
>
> That is called family usage which has come down hereditarily in family as their rule by way of *dharma*. The King shall preserve it.

These verses sum up, as we may suppose, the correct śāstric position relative to the King's duty to observe and enforce custom. Now we must see what was the background to these statements and how other writers' opinions fit in with them.

The Object of the Investigation

Very extensive investigations of the written law exist—though they are too little exploited in our time—and there is no dearth of records of customary law in many parts of India. The necessity to examine the customary law in order to form a balanced picture of the written law was apparent to Joseph Köhler, whose efforts in that direction ought to be better known than they are. Attempts to place the written texts in a periodical order upon the assumption that customs developed, and that the development is reflected in the texts, have been undertaken from the beginning of this century. Yet what precise part custom played in the development of the written law, what relationships actually prevailed between them in practice, and what processes needed to occur before the law might influence custom, custom might overrule law, and both might be varied by legislation are questions which have been tackled satisfactorily by no one. It is the purpose of this paper to show that the jurists of ancient and mediaeval India were alive to problems that occurred elsewhere amongst their contemporaries, but produced a solution which is in many respects peculiar. The scope of this study does not include the period of European administration, though the question ought not to be studied without reference to work done on the topic after 1800. The period prior to 1800 is treated as 'ancient' since the jurisprudential techniques were traditional and indistinguishable from those in use a millennium earlier.

The doctrine which this paper sets out incidentally to destroy is that law in India was immutable, immemorial custom was transcendent law, and the customs and usages that bound the public were neither open to be influenced by the classical jurists (whose theories were thought to be largely academic) nor amenable to alteration at the option of a political superior. All that is false. There appears to have been no stage at which law was immutable, at which custom was not open to influence from jurists, or to modification or even abrogation at the hands of the ruler. At first sight this seems to be contrary to Indian legal doctrine; an inspection of the facts puts the matter into perspective. Details of the actual customs, and their complex relation with the *śāstra* needs a separate treatment.

History and Vocabulary

In the Vedic period (c. 1500-800 B.C.) the invading Āryans conquered and intermingled with native Dravidians, Kolarians and other peoples. Out of their ancestral cults and the needs of their new environments sprung the literature (Śruti) attributable to the period and the need to systematize and record it. We now believe that numerous pre-Aryan customs, such as fraternal polyandry, and institutions of law which would have no meaning to nomads, were adopted as a result of intermarriage and a gradual process of colonization and settlement. In the period of the Dharmasūtras, or earlier mnemonic texts dealing with *dharma*, the essentials of religious and secular duty and many details of legal institutions were recorded. The variations between the prescriptions laid down are supposed to reflect the changed habits of tribes or peoples in different areas, more or less influenced by the indigenous usages or the peculiar exigencies of the political or economic situation. The Dharmasūtras are believed to have been compiled between about 800 and 500/400B.C. Between that period and about A.D.200 additional works were written to summarize *dharma*, including secular law, which aimed at an educated and adult public, and consequently went into some detail, though with a high degree of subtlety and compression. These were called Dharmaśāstras or Smṛtis: they purported to be the remembered wisdom of the race.[2] The extent to which they bound the non-Aryan peoples, such as the Dravidians of the extreme South, is a matter for debate. It appears that orthodox Hindu rulers would have wished to regard the Dharmaśāstras as binding in an ideal sense, and indeed they had no other system of jurisprudence open to them. Upon the *sūtras* and the *śāstras* or the Smṛtis commentaries began to be written as early as A.D.600, and perhaps earlier. All the while 'spurious' editions of early lost juridical writers were being produced, attempting to give in verse the up-to-date and complete law which the commentators were attempting to provide by way of commentary on the 'genuine' texts. The two processes were not completely mutually exclusive, for we find some commentators citing from and relying upon such 'spurious' works as if they were 'genuine'. The period of the commentators was also the period of the great digest-compilers. The *nibandha*, 'digest', has in vogue, especially with those who wanted authentic texts, and were content to supply applications of their own. Commenting upon Smṛtis or editing numerous Smṛtis together in the form of a digest were activities which continued until the period of foreign administration, and were even encouraged by European administrators.

The question: 'what is *dharma*?', was the question to be asked with reference to practical problems. The authors of the Smṛtis and also their followers, the commentators, were in no doubt but that *dharma* was to be found out from the Dharmaśāstra ('science of righteousness'), which meant consulting written law, as expounded with the current learning of Śāstrins.[3] The authority of the ancient texts could not be replaced by rules of any individual's invention. Yet the texts themselves, in particular the text of Kātyāyana set out above, stated categorically that when one looked for the *dharma* appropriate to a given problem one must often look outside the texts. As we, following Nārada,[4] have already seen, *vyavahāra* ('litigation') stands upon four feet: *dharma* (some would say this means the *śāstra* itself), *vyavahāra* ('business', 'practice'—see below), *caritra* ('custom'), and *rājaśāsana* ('royal decree'). Each of these derogated from or excluded the prior-mentioned. The view strongly argued for by M. Lingat[5] is that the four 'feet' of *vyavahāra* are means of proof, or of arrival at a decision. He is supported by certain textual material. The opposite view, which happily has the support of the fresh mind of the late Louis Renou, brought to bear upon the problem in the course of an investigation of Bṛhaspati, is that these four are not means of proof of a litigant's case, but sources of law. This is the view which in our opinion was the original, but which, for a reason as yet withheld from us, later jurists found less than satisfactory. Thus, in any litigation, the pleas must rely upon a source of law, but the practical needs of the context will exclude principles of written law which are stated in general terms and which must, according to the general precept, be administered in conformity with *nyāya* or *yukti*, 'natural reason', 'equity'. The usages of business and the course of legal practice, the *summum ius* or *apices iuris*, may have to be set aside where a custom can be proved to be contrary to or inconsistent with the Dharmaśāstra. Custom itself could not be relied upon where a royal proclamation, or legislation, or administrative order excluded such a plea.

Such would appear to be the effect of the following verses from Bṛhaspati, who is generally supposed to be older than Nārada or Kātyāyana, though this is far from certain:

> "By *dharma*, by *vyavahāra*, by *caritra*, by the royal order: the decision of a disputed matter is declared to be of four (possible) kinds.
>
> "Where the decision is made by resorting solely to the *śāstra* that is characterized as a *vyavahāra*. By this method alone *dharma* increases.
>
> "Where the decision is made by means of the settled practice of the district, applied with logical reasoning, and by virtue of the approval of the citizens (or 'merchants'), *vyavahāra* is excluded.
>
> "However, where the King makes the decision by disregarding the accustomed usage this is the 'royal decree'. Through it *caritra* is excluded.
>
> "Royal decree is that decision which is devoid of authority (i.e. has no text or custom behind it, or is not based upon the evidence or any evidence); another of this kind is well known as that which occurs in a conflict between *śāstras* or among the councillors (or between the *śāstra* and the members of the court)."

It is evident that even at so early a period the maxim of the four feet of litigation was so well established that there might be some vagueness as to its meaning, for the three authorities differ uncomfortably and unconvincingly. Probably the variations experienced in practice made too rigid a scheme undesirable. Yet we are clear that only royal injunctions, general or particular, could overrule *caritra*, 'custom'.

What sort of custom would qualify as *caritra*? There are long discussions over this question. From the earliest periods *sadācāra*, 'the usages of the good', 'good custom', or *śiṣṭācāra*, which is more or less synonymous, was of prime importance.[6] *Śiṣṭācāra* was, subject to some qualification, even a source of *dharma* itself where Smṛti failed. If one followed one's ancestral usages one was more or less certain to be exempt from punishment: but there could be exceptions, to which we refer below. In order that an *ācāra* should be capable of being pleaded in court it must be old, related to a social group or locality (when it may be called *kula*, *jāti*, or *deśadharma*), followed as a matter of obligation and not repudiated or abandoned by the party relying upon it. Naturally it could not be relied upon if the opposite party was not assumed to have knowledge of it. Consequently traders, and other communities with special skills and traditions had their own occupational customs, and as often as not their own tribunals before which the customs need not be specially pleaded. Lastly an *ācāra* must not be repugnant to the *śāstra*. This seems like an argument in a circle. The *śāstra* refers in proper circumstances to customs for the solution of disputes, and yet must the customs not be inconsistent with the *śāstra*? The meaning was that the custom should not of its very nature be hostile to the fundamental tenets of the Hindu socio-religious system as expounded in the *śāstra*: thus a custom to allow the younger brother to have intercourse indiscriminately with the elder brother's wife, and a custom allowing the marriage of a girl of a higher caste with a boy of a lower caste would almost certainly be void in kingdoms accepting the authority of the Dharmaśāstra, i.e. the greater part of historical India, though it is certain that both customs did exist amongst some Indians in different time periods. The claim that an ancient family custom is more authoritative than all the *śāstras* is late, needlessly frank, and perhaps not properly representative of the position. Uneradicable immoral customs of Kerala, for example, are exceptions that prove the rule.

Ācāra and the Śāstra: Custom within and beyond the Written Law

The *śāstra* incorporated numerous customs, inevitably, since it was itself the fruit of customs systematized, compared and summarily set down. As early as Āpastamba (I. i, 1, with Haradatta's commentary) *dharmas* were *sāmayācārika*; *dharma* was that which was approved by Āryas (i.e. Śiṣṭas). Since the *śāstra* is based on usage, in particular in its practical (*vyavahāra*) chapters, usage may be cited to explain the written law. The customs of Brāhmaṇas living in a particular region of northern India were taken as the norm, but numbers of alternative usages, and in particular usages amongst lower castes, were included. The exact method of selection must remain unknown, as numerous customs of early times have disappeared, and others have survived either in attenuated forms, or amongst classes different from those amongst whom they were prevalent when the Smṛtis were compiled. The *śāstra* admitted that all, or even most, customs in relation to the ceremony of marriage could not be treated, and only general rules would be given. The *śāstra* made very little attempt to record or to standardize commercial customs, though examples of general commercial usage are to be found. The peculiar customs of specialized trades and communities are referred to, as having a well-known existence, without being represented in detail. The main principles of partnership, for example, are present (very much as are the *pro forma* provisions on the subjects of fines and tolls), but the detailed application to different manifestations of partnership (as to local conditions) is left to individual custom or to juridical development ad hoc. That documents must conform to local usage is asserted, but questions of draftsmanship are not entered into beyond generalities. Customs relating to land tenure, to tenancies, and the like are given very little space. There is evidence that spurious Smṛtis and Purāṇas were written in an attempt to make the *śāstra* complete: but there is also evidence that the texts in question became out of date or repugnant to the general concept of the *śāstra*, and were evicted. The *śāstra* attempted to offer an umbrella, under which various juridical forms could shelter, and in this sense the relation between *ācāra* and the *śāstra* was similar to the one between the *jus commune* and the *jus scriptum* of the Romano-canonical system. Customs relating to marriage (the celebrated eight 'forms') were incorporated to a limited degree:[7] but the *śāstra* developed tendencies destroying the legal peculiarity of disapproved customary forms, recognizing a public desire for assimilation towards Brāhmaṇical norms. Similarly it is well known that in Adoption the customary usages which are reflected in the earliest texts were kept as a matter of form, but the validity of transactions of a customary character was subjected to principles which tended to unify and to reform. The complicated law of succession applied by usage only in the minority of cases. Proof of custom would (in the ultimate view) override the written law, and, therefore, the jurists' task was to perfect the latter and not to expatiate on customary deviations. We may take as a further example the law of usury, and the law of prescription. In both contexts customary rules prevailed. A few found their way into the śāstric texts over the centuries—as an embarrassment to the jurists when they became out of date or appeared to be contrary to justice: we have seen that the result was that they were emasculated by interpretation. The law of pre-emption is a further example. Early texts must have retained evidence of rights in favour of relations and neighbours. In the late mediaeval period texts were 'discovered' which explained the institution. A very late text, of very peculiar origin gives various new details, deriving from custom and the author's notion of what was proper. Whether the important institution was finally rehabilitated as a śāstric, as opposed to a customary, institution is still open to doubt: probably it was not. Some customs undoubtedly remained outside the *śāstra* and the question would not, therefore, arise when it should be pleaded in derogation from the caronical law.

Custom versus *the Śāstra*

In the inferior courts, such as a family or caste tribunal or in a trade or mercantile tribunal, no doubt custom was sufficiently well-known to render its comparison with śāstric principles (where appropriate) unnecessary, and reference to the *śāstra* can seldom have been employed. But where a dispute involved persons or communities whose affairs could not be determined so simply, as for example where there was a dispute between persons of different castes and different occupations, or between bodies or institutions in different kingdoms, reference to the *śāstra* would be made in the first instance, and to custom if it were pleaded that custom ruled out the book law, or rendered it superfluous.

We may take one actual instance. The *Vaiśyavaṁśa-sudhākara* records[8] the reference to a committee presided over by the celebrated scholar and writer, Mallinātha, of a dispute between castes claiming to be Vaiśyas, and so entitled to privileges accorded to merchants, and other castes which had those privileges and denied that the former were so entitled. This occurred between 1422 and 1466. In effect, the committee was to reopen a question that had already been dealt with in a *śāsana* some time before. The final solution to that important caste-dispute was arrived at, apparently, after consideration of actual usage and precedent: but the decisive learning was obtained from the *śāstra* and the literary and other ancillary material explaining the meaning of the Smṛti texts in question. The castes were found to be Vaiśyas, their status was indistinguishable from that of their opponents and they were held to be entitled to the privileges they had claimed. Here custom and the *śāstra* were viewed together in a remarkably modern manner, and we have no reason to suppose that similar techniques were not in use much earlier.

The King was traditionally the custodian and also the censor of customs. It was his responsibility (as Kātyāyana has told us) to determine if any were repugnant to the *śāstra* and to cancel or modify customs of proved repugnancy. When it was established that the *ācāra* was valid, and not repugnant, a problem often arose as to the manner in which to apply it. There are traces that in ancient times efforts were made to record customs, and to use the records as means of checking upon the correctness of the plaintiff's plea, and the effect of the custom upon his case. The proof of custom therefore lay in written records, either provided for the purpose by royal inquest, or by special muniments, called *śāsanas*, which set out what the custom was, or provided what it should be. Vijñāneśvara is particular to distinguish (in his commentary on Yāj. II, 187) conventions (*samaya*), which are as a rule arrived at by corporations or corporate units (*samūha*), and those which the King himself validates or makes law. But that was by no means enough. The implications in the actual case would seldom be covered entirely by any such written records, and the same difficulty would arise when the custom was established by the evidence of witnesses, such as caste-elders, and so forth. Here the skill of the trained jurist came in; and here the *śāstra* took over.

A proved custom would control the topic so far as reason and analogy would allow, and as long as abuses did not undermine the validity of the custom. Where custom failed the principles of the *śāstra* must be resorted to. By what authority? The King decided whether his kingdom was to be governed upon orthodox Hindu principles or not. His decision was guided by the temper and inclination of his people or peoples, who would support a rival claimant to the throne if he offended them in this regard. In nothing were the public so tenacious as of their ancient customs and the social system which they upheld. One who accepted the *śāstra*, either as a hereditary possession, or as a novel import, accepted with it the facility to enforce customs, and also the duty to guide them and to apply them in a manner consistent with the basic principles of the *śāstra*. The authority for using the *śāstra* as the residual system lay, therefore, in the Hinduism or Hinduizing tendencies of the ruler, and ultimately, of the ruled.

What was the authority behind the *ācarā* itself? Inertia. The maxim *Nil innovandum* could well have been Indian. An ancient custom might be disapproved by Brāhmaṇas, and might be confined to small sections of the public. But it was a valid custom and those who practised it could not normally be forced to abandon it. When a conqueror came into conquered land he had the authority to alter customs or laws which he regarded as repugnant to *dharma*, but this merely set up in the new territory a position which existed *ex facie* in his old dominions. The failure of the *śāstra* to embrace and document in detail all current customs was due partly to the impossibility of achieving this; it was also partly due to the missionary and didactic character of the *śāstra* which, while it educated jurists who could function in any area ruled by a Hindu monarch, recognized the possibility of great divergence from its own prescriptions, and of great scope for supplementation in particular chapters. It was thus free to concentrate on the religious and ritual aspects of *dharma*, where it was perfectly possible to be dogmatic without fear of violent economic and social upheavals.

Thus, to sum up, a custom was valid if accepted according to the śāstric principles: in derogation from the *śāstra* a valid custom was binding by śāstric authority; but the source of the *śāstra's* authority was the public's acceptance of the postulates of Hinduism, and the source of the custom's factual content and applicability was the public desire not to move from the ways of ancestors. Yet in practice custom was not static, neither was the umbrella provided by the *śāstra* inelastic.

Variation of Customary Law

It might well be argued that just as the *śāstra*, being derived from the teachings of primeval sages who were in communication with the Self-existent one, is essentially immune from amendment, as for example by legislation, so the *ācāra,* though by no means so sacred, was, if it was valid, immutable. We know that Smṛti rules were far from being static. We have seen that Smṛtikāras themselves rearranged and adjusted their material, and previously it was explained how they and their commentators treated the Smṛti rules as obsolete or inapplicable. Rules which were apparently imperative were treated as merely moral injunctions. The ingenuity of commentators was immense, and alterations were made in the law without varying the text: and if that was not adequate they did not scruple to alter the text itself. There are occasional references to variant readings. Yet the writings of the commentators did not necessarily bind the court. In practice the Smṛti itself would be relied upon. The various opinions of commentators would be canvassed in a committee of Brāhmaṇas convened to settle knotty points of law, which would not happen often unless a good deal of money was at stake. On the other hand customary law would effectively vary by properly constituted legislative bodies.

This is a delicate issue, about which feeling runs somewhat high. Indian scholars have been wedded to the view that the rulers were subject to the law, and when asked to whom law was subject they are forced to reply 'God'. One my assume this is wishful thinking, and unconsciously entertained for the purpose of making unflattering comparisons with the legal systems of the West, which was the motive that sent this doctrine on its way. It is true that the śāstric texts, fables, and fantasy sometimes support this notion: it is nice to think that the oriental despot is not a tyrant; but the *śāstra* bound him only in conscience, unless his subjects' discontent with him encouraged invasions from abroad (as Kātyāyana hints). The cause of the difficulty is the failure on the part of scholars adequately to distinguish between the *śāstra* and the law of the courts. We may see some details in another connection, but the theory may be conveniently explored here. We saw that the *rājaśāsana* overrode all other sources of law in a judicial dispute. This did not mean that the *śāstra* was changed, even *pro tanto*, by royal decree. It must go its own way entirely in the hands of competent Śāstrins who were alone responsible for it.

The Smṛtis do not throw light directly specifically on the question how the King shall make his *śāsana* or decree. What sources should he consult and in what order? Kauṭilya appropriately solves this (III. 1. 43-4): he should consult *dharma* (righteousness), practice, custom (*saṁsthā*) and reason (*nyāya*). He should dispose of the question by reference to custom or usage, by the Dharmaśāstra, or, in cases where the science of litigation (practical jurisprudence, *vyāvahārikaṁ śāstraṁ*) would be frustrated or obstructed thereby, by reference to righteousness alone. Mere textual law must take second place to a rule of reason where the science (an academic consideration) is contradicted by a rational principle in a point of righteousness (*V.* 45). This is the reason why a properly-founded *rājaśāsana* takes precedence over *dharma*, etc., when it comes to actual litigation. What happened when a royal order came directly in confrontation with (*a*) a śāstric rule, or (*b*) an established custom? Instances will clarify the position for us. A front-rank jurist, points out that if the King orders Brāhmaṇas to present themselves at his palace at the very time when they must be performing their *sandhyā-vandana* ('evening worship') the order is void and may be ignored. If the King were to order that gifts should not be given in charity, or that people should not proceed on pilgrimage to holy places, or that priests when performing rituals should or should not use certain formulas or certain implements, his orders would be void. Orders in the two other fields open to him, namely in conformity with the *śāstra*, as for example an order that cattle should not be slaughtered—a class of legislation for which Aśoka is deservedly famous—and in cases when no one could cite an injunction in the *śāstra* one way or another, as for example what should be the extent of pasture in a new settlement, were not open to challenge and therefore must be obeyed subject to royal punishment for disobedience. Where a custom apparently held the field, and it was desired to change it, and the order would come within either of the permitted fields, the custom went down before the royal order: about this there could be no question. An instance would be the late mediaeval instrument whereby a religious institution known as a *maṭha* was converted from being subject to a celibate (or nominally celibate) incumbent to one in which the incumbent was permitted to marry. The competent authority not only passed the necessary orders but, most interestingly, cites as his reasons passages from various scriptures which support the existence of *maṭhas* of which the head was a married man. Whether married men should be heads of *maṭhas* was a moot point; the ancient *maṭhas* were ruled by Sannyāsins who were naturally unmarried, (whatever their sexual behaviour). But abuses must be remedied, textual authority was available for the line taken, and, supported by this and by considerations which are tactfully withheld from us, the patron of the *maṭha* passed the necessary order.

A *śāsana* embodying a new law, or declaring an old one which had been doubted, was often inscribed on a stone pillar erected at the most important and relevant spot. As to the procedure whereby the *śāsana* was arrived at, there is no evidence that there was any difference between a decision in a dispute which had reached the ruler's court and a decision of a question of policy, as for example whether a grant should be made, whether custom should be changed, or whether a fair should be set up.

Thus, though it could not be argued that royal decrees could in any way affect the course of development of the *śāstra*, a decision in a dispute could turn upon a royal decree given in some other context, whether in regard to indifferent matters, matters in which the *śāstra* was silent, or in aid of the purposes recognized by the *śāstra*. Not only could custom derogate from the written law, but even when custom was about to be pleaded the opposite party could rely upon a royal decree abrogating or varying custom. Thus for purposes of litigation *śāstra* and *ācāra* were equally vulnerable to modification by royal determination; but apart from litigation the *śāstra* maintained a life of its own, with its appeal to conscience which no royal mandate, no legislation could diminish.

This is important, for, though years have elapsed since the last Hindu kingdom pursued independent rule—the Hindus retain an ambivalent attitude to legislation which their Muslim compatriots may, or at any rate should not. In 1955-6 the personal laws of the Hindus in India were radically changed, at a time when many vocal opponents of the Hindu Code Bill claimed that the then subsisting law represented the *śāstra* (though it hardly did). The vast project of legislation went through, as many equally radical changes had gone through before. The judicial legislation of the Anglo-Indian period had been tolerated without resentment: and the constitutional parliamentary legislation came to partner and correct it. Both operated on the citizen in the context of litigation. There the Hindus admitted it without undue animosity or resentment: indeed the signs are that it was welcomed and is being worked like the systems before it. But the *śāstra* and its spirit no one purports to touch. What Parliament does cannot bind the conscience where the religious elements of law are confronted. And this dichotomy is nothing new: it was built into the Hindu outlook on law and government since antiquity. The *śāstra* (not altogether blindly) prepared the way for its own relegation to the background of business and practical life, without forfeiting a claim the more securely to bind the private and personal aspects of the individual, which (as we shall see) were always its primary target.

References

1. P.V. Kane, ed. and trans., *Kātyāyna* Smṛti *sāroddhāra or Kātyāyana* Smṛti *on Vyavahāra* (Bombay, 1933), *vv.* 35-53, 85.
2. R.C. Hazra at *Our Heritage*, 3 (1955), pp. 221-38.
3. Kane, *H.D.*, II, p. 969.
4. Medhātithi on Man. III. 6 (Jha's trans., I. 1, 204-5).
5. *Journal Asiatique*, 1962, pp. 489-503.
6. Man. I. 108.
7. By L. Sternbach, *The Juridical Studies in Ancient Indian Law, Part I.* (Delhi, Motilal Banarsidass, 1965), chapter 11. pp. 347 ff.
8. V. Raghavan, "The *Vaiśyavaṁśasudhākara*...', in *A Volume presented to Sir Denison Ross* (Bombay, 1939), pp. 234-40.

The Family—Economic Institution

Over and over again we find in the *śāstras* statements affirming the supreme value attached to the household life, as we shall see presently. In this Hinduism differs somewhat from Christianity, as held by the great majority of its adherents. Among the Roman Catholic and the Greek Christians celibacy, following the dictum of St. Paul, is regarded as a higher state than that of marriage, since the celibate can devote himself, or herself, wholly to religious matters, while the married man, or woman, must needs mix much in the matters of the world. This division between the sacred and the secular is alien to the spirit of Hinduism, which sees God immanent in everything, and teaches that He can be as truly served in the home as in the jungle.... This difference in the view of religious life is largely due to the fact that Christianity has lost sight of the fact of reincarnation: the Christian thinks that he has but one life, the present one between cradle and grave, and that on this life his ever-lasting fate depends.

Dharma, duty, certainly comes first and is to rule the whole life; but pleasure not contrary to *dharma*, profit not contrary to *dharma*, these also are recognised as rightful parts of human life. And this is the maxim of the life of the householder. It is to be full of duty, duty faithfully discharged; but it is redolent of pleasure—pleasure in conjugal love, pleasure in parentage, pleasure in the little ones that fill the household ways with laughter. This natural happiness is as much God-given as strenuous labour and heroic death, and this should fill with its glow and beauty the righteous household life.

But the householder may be said to play the part of each caste in his household: for as a priest of the household, he is a Brāhmaṇa; as protector of the household, he is as a Kṣatriya; as provider of the household, he is as a Vaiśya; as servant of the household, he is as a Śūdra. Everywhere in noble human life we see service; and the householder incarnates service.

He must have a strong character, otherwise he will not be an ideal Gṛhastha. There is too much tendency in modern India to lay stress on the softer virtues and to ignore the sterner, but the presence of the sterner virtues is vital for the national welfare... Justice, strength, vigour, defence of the right—these are equally needed.[1]

Education over, the individual moves on to the second stage of his life, that of the householder. He is equipped with the necessary knowledge and he knows the real purpose of life. Education has fitted him in all respects for his new task. The second stage is intended to give him an opportunity of satisfying another side of his nature. Desire for satisfaction of biological needs, for building a family, and for property has to be given its due share, but with an eye to the development of his higher Self.

This chapter is devoted to a discussion of the family institution, *gṛhasthāśrama*, and the economic group, vaiśya *varṇa*. The psychological basis of both is desire. Under the former come marriage and family. Marriage is a legal institution, its basis is biological, though, according to Manu, it should be governed by ethical considerations. But family comes into being as soon as a child is born. The presence of a child starts a series of new relationships and involves new responsibilities for the married couple.

Desire manifests itself in many ways: sex is one form of it, property is another. The basis of the economic institution is also desire. Through desire, the Īśvara projected Himself into the universe and made that universe a part of Himself. Desire is not to be curbed; it has to be accepted and given its due share of attention. It forms the basis of both the family and the economic institutions. To each of these are attached certain ethical values. This chapter falls, then, into the following outline:

1. *Āśrama,* Gṛhastha.
   i. Marriage—biological and ethical aspects.
   ii. Family—educational and ethical aspects.
2. *Varṇa,* Vaiśya. Economic group.
   i. The occupations.
   ii. Their ethical basis.

I. Marriage

Nature and Place of Woman

Woman, according to Manu (Man.IX.4-5), should be protected and honoured at all stages of her life. Her father should protect her in her childhood, her husband in her youth, and her son in her old age. Woman should not be left unguarded. The father who does not give his daughter in marriage at the proper time, the husband who does not approach her in due season, and the son who does not protect her when her husband is dead, should all be reprehended (Man.V.147-49).

But this is not intended to suggest that she should be closetted in the house by compulsion. She has certain duties; she should keep the household accounts, keep the vessels clean, attend to the religious duties of the family and prepare food for the members (Man.IX.10-11). The performance of these duties ensures her safety and progress. No extraneous protection can be of much use if she neglects her duties. Woman guarded in the house by trustworthy and obedient servants cannot be said to be well-guarded; she who is self-protected is best protected (Man.IX.12).

Women should be honoured and adorned by fathers and brothers, by husbands, and also by brothers-in-law. Where women are honoured, the gods rejoice; but when they are neglected, all rites and ceremonies are fruitless. Where women grieve, that family quickly perishes. But where women do not grieve, it ever prospers. Houses on which unhonoured women pronounce a curse perish as if by magic (Man.III.55-58). Woman is the instrument of prosperity, a source of joy to the gods, and she deserves honour from all.

But she can work her own ruin. Manu (Man.IX.13) gives the circumstances under which she is likely to go astray. Drinking, associating with men of easy morals, separating from her husband, roaming around, sleeping late and dwelling with other men: these are the six causes of her ruin. She may neglect her appearance, succumb to artificial stimulation, become heartless, disloyal to her husband, given to excessive love of bed and ornaments, may harbour impure desires, be wrathful, dishonest, or malicious (Man.IX.14-17). In the company of such women no sacramental rites should be performed. That is the law. For those who are destitute of moral strength, know not the Vedas, and are impure and false, there are no rites (Man.IX.18).

Woman should consider her marriage a sacrament, and should discharge the duties befitting her life. Her residence in her husband's house after she is married is equal to the boy's residence with the teacher; and the discharge of the household duties constitutes her daily worship (Man.II.67). Her husband should be everything to her. Through devotion to and love for him, she fulfils her duty and develops her highest possibilities. Whatever be the qualities of the husband with whom she is lawfully united, such qualities she assumes, like a river united with the sea. Akṣamālā, a woman of low birth, united with the sage Vasiṣtha and Sāraṅgī, united with the sage Mandapāla, became worthy of honour. These and other women of humble parentage attained eminence by following their husbands' good qualities (Man.IX.21-24). When a woman observes the sanctity of her marriage, serves her husband, and attends to the household duties, she is entitled to equality in study and worship with her husband. Without her no sacrament is valid. If a wife obeys her husband, she will, for that reason, be exalted in heaven (Man.V.155).

Woman occupies an exalted place in the social order. The arduous task of motherhood, which is her natural function, awaits her. To be mothers were women created, and to be fathers men. Sacred ritual is therefore ordained in the Vedas to be performed by the husband with the wife (Man.IX.96). To deny her that right is to deny her the legitimate joy of creation. If she seeks her self-fulfilment, she will find it only through recognition of her duties of loyalty, service, comradeship in study and worship and motherhood. This is her path of progress.

Biological Aspects of Marriage

A human being is endowed with biological needs which will brook no suppression. A social order that does not provide for the natural needs of its members is doomed to failure. The life of spiritual pursuits, which is yet to come in the last stage of life, requires by way of preparation a sublimation of desire in the earlier stages. The life of an ascetic, given to serious meditation and contemplation, is an arduous task, and its success depends upon the consistency of the individual's early life. A life of balked desires is not in conformity with Manu's ideal; a suppression of legitimate desires of sex and wealth distorts and cripples the soul. The individual should, therefore, be given an opportunity for the satisfaction of his desires. Marriage, family and wealth, if properly used, are not antagonistic to the development of the highest personality. Our candidate for spiritual enlightenment has to pass through this phase of life.

Forms of Marriage

There are eight forms of marriage. The Brāhma and Prājāpatya marriages are more or less similar. The bridegroom is selected by the parents. He is a man of learning. The daughter, duly dressed, is offered by the parents and the bridegroom takes the vow to associate her closely with all his activities. In Daiva marriage, the bride is offered by the parents to the priest and the marriage is decided upon during the course of the sacrament. The Ārṣa marriage is celebrated by the bride's father on receiving an assurance from the bridegroom that he and his daughter will live together in conformity with *dharma*. The Gāndharva marriage is based on mutual consent. The bridegroom selects the bride. Romance, outraged parents, absence of ceremonial solemnisation characterise this type. In Āsura marriage, the bridegroom purchases the bride for a price. In Rākṣasa marriage, the bride is a prize of war, while, the last, the Paiśaca, is of the lowest type. The bride is overpowered, made helpless through drugs or drink, is unconscious, off her mental balance (Man.III.27-34). The first four forms of marriage are "blameless"; there is nothing unbecoming or immoral about them. But the second four are "blameworthy" and should be avoided.

The first four, in which the element of desire is controlled and which are based on the intellectual and moral competence of the parties concerned, help not only the progress of the couple but also of their ancestors and descendants. The children born within such sacred wedlock will be great souls (Man.III.37-39). But from the second four marriages will be born children who will be cruel, will speak untruth, and will hate the Vedas and the sacred law (Man.III.41).

Manu would thus try to eliminate all that goes by the name of "romance". He would put marriage on a mental and moral plane. The sex urge there certainly is, but it should be brought under control of intelligence. Marriage should be arranged by parents. One should marry first and then learn to love, and not "fall in love" and then marry. That would not be real love, it would be desire, and desire should be brought under control as much as possible. In a marriage, based on a law higher than mere lust, one develops virtues which otherwise would not find a place in his life (Man.IX.89).

Eugenics

Manu advises endogamy, that is marriage in one's own group.

Such marriages will attract souls of similar nature, and there need be no fear of confusion of castes. There is a law according to which a soul takes birth in a family that can supply the necessary psychic elements and environment that will aid his evolution. A child of harmonious nature, *sāttvika*, for instance, is born in a family of Brāhmaṇas, and so on. A child born of parents of the same group will inherit their biological, mental and moral traits. But when there is a difference, between the temperaments or the groups of the parents, the child will be like one parent or the other.[2]

Manu (Man.III.15) is averse to indiscriminate amalgamation of different ethnic stocks. Men of the upper three groups who marry women of the Śūdra group in their folly soon degrade their families and their children to the state of a Śūdra. A Brāhmaṇa who takes a Śūdra wife to bed lowers his mental and spiritual status: if he begets a child, it will not be of the Brāhmaṇa type. Gods and ancestors will accept no offerings and guests no hospitality from a man married to a Śūdra wife. There is no expiation for the man who kisses a Śūdra woman, is tainted by her breath, and begets a son by her (Man.III.17-19).

Manu (Man.III.12), however, seems to have realized that in any region more than one race of people live at any time, and their members cannot live wholly apart from each other. There is bound to be some amount of race-mixture. This, he permits, with certain reservations. The first marriage of members of the twice-born groups must always be with a woman of their own group. But those who, through desire, wish to marry again, must follow a certain fixed order.

Manu (Man.III.7-10) gives detailed instructions with regard to the selection of a wife. A girl coming from a family where there is no male child, and where the Vedas are not studied, should not be accepted in marriage. Nor should one marry a red-haired girl, or with too much hair, a quarrelsome, sickly woman, or one that bears inauspicious names. One should marry a girl who is free from physical defects, who has an agreeable name, is graceful of gait like a swan or an elephant, has a moderate quantity of hair on the body and on her head, small teeth and soft limbs.

These are Manu's views on eugenics. They combine physical, ethical and metaphysical considerations. The element of desire in marriage should be controlled. Marriage should take place in families of the same social, cultural and spiritual status. Racial amalgamation, unless based on evidence of moral and mental attainments on the part of the outsider, should be avoided. Precautions should be taken with regard to the physical health of the marrying couple.

Ethical Basis of Marriage

The whole subject of marriage is put on an ethical plane. Marriage should be treated as a sacrament. In it, two complementary halves are brought together to make a complete whole. It is more of a psychic bond rather than the merely physical. The husband is born of the wife in his child. The three become psychically intertwined.

This psychic union cannot be easily repudiated. There is no way of escaping its sanctity, barring a few exceptional circumstances, once the bond has been forged. Neither by sale nor by repudiation is a wife released from her husband. Such is the law. Once is the partition of inherited property made; once is a maiden given in marriage; once does a man say, "I will give." These three acts are done once only. Mutual-idelity should continue until death; this may be considered the sum and substance of the highest law for the husband and wife. A man receives his wife from the gods, he is linked with her from the past, and he must honour her and protect her. This is his duty.

Love for each other and acceptance of mutual obligations of service is real loyalty. Such comrades will not be rent asunder either in life or in death. They will help each other's spiritual progress in or out of the body. Though destitute of virtue, pleasure-seeking, devoid of good qualities, yet a husband must be worshipped by a faithful wife as a god. No sacrifice, no vow, no fast can be performed by a woman without her husband. If she obeys him, she fulfils her part, she will be exalted in heaven. A wife that wants to be with her husband even in death should never displease him; she who controls her thoughts, words and deeds, does not disgrace her husband, will live with him even in death.

Widowhood

In the case of her husband's death, the wife should keep her fidelity by a pure life, by meditation and prayer for his onward progress into the realm of the Beyond. Until her death, she should be patient, self-controlled, chaste, and fulfil the duties prescribed for her as though her husband were living. Thousands of individuals lived celibate lives from their youth and went to heaven without marriage or offspring. A wife who remains pure after the death of her husband will join him in heaven, even if she has no children. A widow should honour the memory of her husband by a pure life. She should not have illicit relations with another man. That is yielding to desire. Fidelity is the main virtue of widowhood as of married life. A woman who, from desire to have offspring, violates her duty towards her deceased husband brings disgrace on herself. Offspring begotten of another man, or of another man's wife, is unlawful. Nor is a second husband necessary for a virtuous woman. She who forsakes her husband because he belongs to a lower group, and has relations with a man of a higher group, is a contemptible woman. By violating her duty towards her husband she lowers herself to the animal stage.

However, should a childless widow desire to have a child, she should be allowed to beget one from a relative of her husband by special permission. A brother-in-law or another relative of her dead husband should be selected to approach her. He should come clean, remain silent, give her only one child. One child is enough, according to law, though some sages are prepared to allow two. But when the purpose of the meeting such as this is over, these two should behave towards each other as a father and daughter-in-law. If they deviate from this rule and act under the impulse of carnal desire, they should both be considered dishonourable people, as persons who defile the bed of a daughter-in-law or of a teacher.

Divorce

After considering marriage as a highly ethical institution, Manu states, at great length, the grounds on which a legal dissolution is allowed. These grounds are summarised in Manu's (Man.IX.77-80) words here: A husband should live with his wife for one year even if she hates him. After that they must part. She who disrespects her husband, is passionate, drinks, is of bad conduct, rebellious, diseased, mischievous, should be superseded by another wife. On the other hand, a woman should not be compelled to live with a mad husband, a mentally defective man, an eunuch, one destitute of manly strength, or one afflicted with diseases. She should be allowed to separate from such a husband after receiving her share of property.

Further, a husband should live with a barren wife or with one whose children die, for ten or eleven years, but must separate from a quarrelsome wife immediately. A sick wife, kind to her husband and virtuous in conduct, may separate if she desires. She should never be disgraced.

Thus, three facts stand out quite prominently in the whole discussion of marriage, widowhood, and child-begetting. First, we should accept the presence of desire. It is a part of human nature. But it must be transmuted. Secondly, marriage should be based on intelligence, not on impulse. A man equipped with the wisdom of the spirit is best entitled to marry. When married, he must exercise self-control. He should not allow passion to dominate him. Thirdly, when the wife is dead, the husband should live like a bachelor. If desire persists, he should marry from a lower group. In the case of the woman, she should remain pure and controlled. But if desire persists, she should be allowed to beget a child or two in the manner indicated above, and nothing more.

II. Family

Family, the First Primary Group

As Manu (Man.IX.45) presents it, the family is the most significant of all social groups. Marriage should culminate in a family. The child is the central figure of this institution. Both parents see a summation of themselves in a child. He only is a perfect man who consists of three persons—his wife, himself, and his child. The constituent unit of social life, therefore, is not the individual, but the trinity of the father, the mother, and the child. The family is not merely a legal institution but has its basis in human nature itself.

The family forms the earliest environment of the child, his first training ground in life; it is the first primary group. It moulds the behaviour of the growing child and sets its stamp on him permanently. Whether the child shall grow up to be a social menace or a well-adjusted individual, looking forward with joy to the adventure of a full, wholesome life, with all his faculties functioning at their best, is determined by the family.

The family is the support of all other groups, the student, the teacher, the hermit, the political group and the forest dweller.

Besides, one can discharge his duties to the entire social order only through the medium of the family. Each individual takes certain obligations before he enters the family stage. As a student, he is supported by other families when he goes round begging food for himself and his teacher. Later, as a hermit, and still later as a forest-dweller, he will have to be supported by the group. In these last two stages, he will be of no material use to the community. He will be concerned with his own spiritual pursuits. Thus the family-stage of his life is the only one in which he can pay back what he has taken from the group and accumulate what he has yet to take in the later part of his life. This is the ethical significance of the family. These two aspects of the institution, the educational and the ethical, will be discussed separately.

Educational Significance of the Family

The birth of the first-born child is the fulfilment of obligations to the race. That child should inherit the property. He is the child of duty. The subsequent children are born of desire. The bearing of children, their nurture, the daily life of man, the performance of the sacred duties, conjugal happiness, the spiritual evolution of the ancestors and of oneself, all these depend on the family. The prolonged infancy of the child, with the necessity of continued parental care, is one basis of the family. Father, mother and child are nature's "practical syllogism".

Further the family is the chief agency of transmission of social heritage. The child watches and imitates his parents in his early years, and this moulds his life for ever. It is here that he develops social attitudes of love, friendship and altruism. The noblest virtues of the human race grow in the hot-house of the family. The educative influence of the mother during the early years is incalculable. She is the first teacher of the child. The teacher of the Vedas is ten times more venerable than an ordinary teacher, a father a hundred times more than the teacher, but a mother a thousand times more than the father.

The father and the mother transmit to the child the social ideals and values. The process of transmission of social heritage and the formation of the growing personality of the child are only continued further in the educational institution under the guidance of the teacher.

Ethical Significance of the Family

But there is also an ethical significance of the family. It should be useful in promoting the spiritual progress of the living members as well as of the dead. It should help the former to realise their highest possibilities and the latter to move forward in their upward journey of the spirit, on the other side of life.

With these values in view, Manu (Man.III.63) devises five sacred duties or sacrifices. A family has five sacrificial-houses, as it were, in its household. These are the hearth, the grinding stone, the broom, the pestle and mortar, and the water-vessel. By using these five objects, human beings sacrifice the lower forms of life for their own and incur "sin". Some small invisible creatures are burnt in the fire when it is lighted for cooking food; some are killed in grinding things; others in sweeping the floor; and others still in drinking water. To all these human beings owe debts.

Five Debts

Thus, the householder does not live unto himself. He has duties to all beings whom he uses for his own existence, and these must be discharged properly. It is a sign of human culture and compassion to acknowledge these obligations and make amends in the following manner:

(1) By studying and teaching the Vedas, which is an offering to Brahmā, the Creator.

(2) By giving food and water, which is an offering to the ancestors.

(3) By pouring oblations in the fire, which is an offering to the Gods.

(4) By giving food to animals, the sick, and the needy, which is an offering to nature's elements.

(5) And, finally, by offering hospitality to guests and alms to students, which is an offering to humanity. He who discharges these five duties, while he is able to perform them, is not affected by the above mentioned "five sins," even though he lives the life of the householder. But if he neglects them, he incurs the burden of undischarged duties (Man.III.69-72).

A family should daily keep in touch with the Vedas, the source of illumination, and perform the ceremonies due to the Gods. This is owning kinship with both the moveable and the immoveable creation. The sages, the gods, the ancestors, the elements, and humanity, all expect service from the family. Hence, a family that knows the *dharma* should fulfil its obligations to them all. The sages are worshipped by the study of the Vedas, the gods by oblations in fire, the ancestors by post-mortem ceremonies, the elements by food given to the bird, the beast, the sick and the needy, and humanity by hospitality. The family institution is the focal point of cosmic symbiosis.

Thus the family is something more than a casual meeting-ground of its members. They are linked to each other by ties of the past, and will be linked in the endless future. Fulfilment of mutual duties is the unifying bond of the family.

Significance of the Five Duties

Let us look a little closer at the rationale of the duties imposed on the family. The first duty is to the sages who gave the Vedas and have left behind them a rich heritage of spiritual wisdom. It is incumbent on the family to keep in touch with their teachings and pass them on to the rising generation. The family must keep up the level of culture so laboriously acquired, and at the same time transmit it to the safe keeping of the next generation. This is the family's duty to Brahmā, the Creator, to the sages, and to the human race. By attending to this first duty it is possible for each member to insulate himself from the Socio-cultural pressures of his little cosmos of empirical experience and line within the aura of inner Self, develop his highest personality.

The second duty of the family is to the Gods, the Devas, the invisible agencies that evolve alongside the man. They are fellow-travellers; to them, the family must offer oblations of clarified butter in the fire. This is their food. It is the Homa sacrifice performed for their sake.

The third duty is to the ancestors, the pitṛs. Those to whom we owe the physical heredity and who gave the early nurture deserve our grateful remembrance. They should not be forgotten because they are dead. Their memory should be kept alive and sacred by ceremonies at regular intervals, and they should be helped by meditation and prayer. These ceremonies should be conducted with the help of the priests who know the laws of the super-physical worlds. These ceremonies should be performed for the mother and the father—if they are dead—the grandfather and the great-grandfather of the family. Manu goes into the subject of these ceremonies at great length and devotes a major part of the third chapter to its discussion.

The fourth duty is to Nature's elements, the *bhūtas*, those other invisible agencies that help the lower forms of life to grow. These lower forms are consumed by man, as food; his gratitude to these agencies should take the form of food-offering placed on the ground in all directions, intended for the bird and the beast, the sick and the poor.

And finally, comes the duty to humanity. This is discharged by offering hospitality to guests, to the houseless, and to the begging student.

These are the five sacred duties by means of which the family becomes a highly significant institution in the social order to all forms of life, above, around and below. The members learn here to realise the oneness of all life and to do their share to keep the wheel of life moving. Thus alone can they prepare a better future for themselves and insulate the institution from forces of disruption and disorganization. In the discharge of duties lies the strength and solidarity of the family.

III. The Economic Group

The chief characteristic of the economic group is desire. Desire is the unifying factor between the family and the economic group. There are no hair-splitting arguments concerning property in the *Manu Dharmaśāstra*. The possessive instinct is a manifestation of desire. A human being can never remain contented if his desire is thwarted in any form. Moreover, the maintenance of the family institution is not possible without some economic resources. If the family is as significant as it is made out to be, its economic security has to be scrupulously ensured. The whole social order is dependent on the family. All the other groups derive their support from this institution. The student, the householder, the hermit and the ascetic, these constitute four separate groups. But they all depend on the householder for their support (Man.VI.87). As all living creatures subsist by absorbing cosmic energy, *prāṇa*, even so the four social groups subsist on the support of the householder. According to the Vedas, the householder is superior of all the four groups, for he supports the other three. As all rivers flow into the sea, so men of all other groups find protection with the householder.

It is, therefore, essential that there should be some earning members in the family. Economic pursuits serve a two-fold purpose: they satisfy the desire aspect of the individual, and they help to consolidate the family institution.

Professions Allowed

The male member of the family is enjoined to take up some occupation and become an 'economic personality,' a member of the Vaiśya *varṇa*. The Vaiśya should study the Vedas, discharge the sacred duties, give in charity, carry on commerce, banking, agriculture or tend cattle (Man.VI.89-90). He should know the respective values of gems, pearls, coral, metal, cloth made from thread, of perfumes and condiments. He should be acquainted with the manner of sowing seeds, the comparative merits of soils, and know all the weights and measures. He should know how to discriminate between good and bad commodities, calculate profit and loss on products of various countries, wages of servants, different languages, methods of preserving goods and the rules of bargaining.

Business Ethics

Competition should be eliminated from social life as far as possible. Competition is a law of the jungle, not of human society. The possessive instinct need not be so blind as to make one callous in the mad lust for wealth. Occupations should be socially useful, morally uplifting. One need not take up a task that militates against personal and social welfare, nor should the body be abused. Desire for wealth must not be allowed to become a mania and defeat its own purpose.

Values cannot be divorced from economic pursuits. A Vaiśya should not, for the sake of his subsistence, follow evil ways. He should live a pure, straightforward, honest life of a Brāhmaṇa type (Man.IX.329-32). A person who lives unrighteously, acquires wealth by underhand methods and by harming others will never be happy. Unrighteousness may not show its effects immediately but it grinds slowly and cuts off the man from the ground of his being. The offender may even escape the evil consequences of his actions, but they shall be visited upon his children and grand-children. *Karman* overtakes all. Therefore, one should never turn his heart to unrighteousness even when he continues to suffer by adopting a righteous course of action. The unrighteous are easily overthrown (Man.IV.67-68).

The Vaiśya should seek a means of livelihood that causes as little pain to others as possible. He should employ means that are beyond reproach, are socially approved and physically unfatiguing (Man.IV.II).

A Vaiśya engaged in agriculture should be kind to animals; they are a part of his equipment, a means of his livelihood. They too have life and should be used kindly. He should not use untamed, hungry, diseased, injured animals, not those whose tails have been twisted. He should use broken-in, swift, beautiful beasts and not urge them with a goad.

Duties

Study of the sacred scriptures, self-purification, meditation, non-injury to living beings, are the best means of his happiness (Man.IV.2-3). A Vaiśya should not neglect his study. A constant reminder of the ultimate goal through daily study of and meditation on the sacred word is his best protection. It will help to orient him to the ideal daily. Nor should the five-fold family duties be ever neglected, however, pressing the demands of daily life may be. He should devote time to the study of those subjects that elevate his mind, give him a fresh accession of strength and efficiency in earning a livelihood, promote his interests in every walk of life and deepen and heighten his capacity for understanding the Vedas.

Finally, the individual engaged in the task of earning his daily bread, should learn to be content. Neither jealousy of other's riches, nor competition with them in amassing wealth, but generosity of heart in giving, right charity, fair play and fulfilment of the tasks appropriate to his temperament are the best means of his self-fulfilment. Contentment is doubly necessary for a man of desire and he must strive hard to cultivate it; for happiness has contentment for its root, and the root of unhappiness lies in discontent.

And, finally, he should receive, according to his means, every guest that comes to his house. He should offer him a seat, food, couch, water, roots and fruits.

In this manner, it is possible for one, engaged in the hustle and bustle of worldly life, to make spiritual progress and develop his highest Self. One should not be lost in mad pursuit of things that do not matter much and have no relevance to the ultimate purpose of human existence. If he is his own friend, he should guard his own interests, keep a watch over his company, not associate with heretics, people who follow forbidden paths, who live like cats and herons, rogues and logic-choppers, arguing endlessly against eternal verities.

Principles Underlying Charity

It is gracious to give when one has the means. Charity is one of the major duties of the Vaiśya. But he must guard against indiscriminate philanthropy. Wealth, earned with hard work, is not to be thrown away. He must judge the merits of each appeal made to him for succour, and not allow himself to be carried away by high sounding claims made by hypocrites and pretenders to high spiritual calling. A discerning person should not even give water to a Brāhmaṇa if he acts like a cat or a heron and is ignorant of the deeper truths of life. Wealth earned by hard work and rightful means should not be wasted.

Both an ignorant giver and receiver sink like a boat full of stones. A covetous man who displays the flag of virtue is a hypocrite, a deceiver, a detractor of others' merits, is very much like a cat; and one who has a cruel disposition, is bent only on gaining his own ends, is dishonest and pretends to be gentle, is like a heron (Man.IV.29).

Summary

This is a broad outline of the second institution of Manu. It is so planned as to help the householder to fulfil his allotted tasks and develop the best in him. There should be no balked desires, no repressions. A sane society must provide for satisfaction of desire, one of the basic urges of human nature. Wife, children, home, means of livelihood and a modicum of security conduce to the emotional and spiritual contentment of man. It is only then that he can fulfil satisfactorily the obligations that his status in the group imposes on him. The happiness and contentment of the individual and social harmony are obverse and reverse of the same coin.

But this *varṇāśrama* is also only a means, and not an end in itself. It is intended to help the man on his way in this life. Earthly existence is brief, short-lived. The relentless wheel of births and deaths keeps moving. The individual can only get out of life what he puts into it. A life of virtue and self-sacrifice ensures happiness and freedom. Inflicting no pain on any living creature, a man may accumulate spiritual merit like an ant that ultimately makes the hill. Harmlessness and compassion accompany him to the next world. Thither, nobody keeps him company: neither father, mother, wife, relations nor friends. Alone is each person born and alone does he die. Alone does he reap the effects of the causes he has set in motion. He moves in single file on this path; only an increasing awareness of the unity of life above, below and around abides. When one dies, his relatives leave him like a log of wood or a clod of earth. Only the quintessence of his earthly toil and self-direction and ascent into the life of the Spirit remain. Every effort put forth by him will illumine his path in that Land of Gloom that is difficult to traverse alone (Man.IV.192-96).

When the "five debts" have been paid, when grey hairs begin to make their appearance and when grand children are born, the second stage of life should be considered as coming to a close. It is time to prepare for the return journey. The householder should now hand over everything to his son and live in the house in a completely detached manner. Alone he may meditate in the sanctuary of his heart. This has to be the mode of his life from now on and, relieved of the daily distractions, he will move faster in the direction of freedom and self-fulfilment (Man.IV.257-60).

References

1. Besant, Annie, *Hindu Ideals*, Annual Convention Lectures, Theosophical Society, 1907.
2. X. 5-6. It will be recalled that Manu's classification of human personalities is based on psychological differences. The brāhmaṇa is a man of harmonious and intellectual nature (*jñāna*), the warrior is the active type of individual (*kriya*) and the Vaiśya is a man of desire (*icchā*). It is in the light of these psychological differences that the above statement concerning endogamous marriage is to be taken.

The Administration of Justice

In the small kingdoms to which the early Dharmasūtras refer the King might be the sole source of justice and indeed his own executioner, striking down condemned thieves with his mace; but in general the administration of justice was delegated, the King's court being reserved for appeals and serious crime against the state. In medieval kingdoms, the councillor called Prāḍvivāka, the King's chief legal adviser, was responsible for justice and might also himself act as a judge.

The composition of the courts varied with time and place, but the evidence indicates that ancient India preferred a bench of magistrates to a single judge. A Jātaka story tells of a bench of five magistrates, all of whom, incidentally, are corrupt, while the *Arthaśāstra* advises that a court with a bench of three magistrates be set up for every ten villages, with higher courts in districts and provinces. Manu suggests a bench consisting of the Prāḍvivāka and three lesser judges, while the drama called "The Little Clay Cart" (p. 443) contains a scene in a court of justice, presided over by a chief judge, here called *adhikaraṇika*, a wealthy merchant (Śreṣṭhin), and a representative of the caste of scribes (Kāyastha). The title given to the chief judge is derived from *adhikaraṇa*, "a government office", and suggests that he was an official who combined judicial and administrative functions, the two other magistrates were evidently leading citizens, who served on the bench as do our justices of the peace.

Though judicial corruption is often referred to, the standards set for judges and magistrates are very high; they are to be learned, religious, devoid of anger and as impartial as humanly possible. To prevent bribery it is suggested that no private interviews should be allowed between judges and litigants until cases are settled. The *Arthaśāstra* advises that the honesty of judges should be periodically tested by agents provocateurs, while the *Viṣṇusmṛti* prescribes banishment and forfeiture of all property for a judge found guilty of corruption or injustice—the most severe penalty a Brāhmaṇa could incur under the Sacred Law.

False witness was generally looked on with great abhorrence, and, besides various temporal penalties, it incurred a hundred unhappy rebirths in future lives. In serious criminal cases evidence might be accepted from all sources, but in civil law only certain witnesses were qualified; generally women, learned Brāhmaṇas, government servants, minors, debtors, persons with criminal records and persons suffering from physical defects could not be called on to give evidence, while the evidence of low-caste people was not valid against persons of higher caste. Several tests, some very sound psychologically, are laid down to assess the veracity of witnesses.

Where the accused was open to grave suspicion not amounting to certainty he might be tortured to elicit confession. The tortures enumerated for this purpose are generally not of the most extreme type, and include various forms of whipping. Brāhmaṇas, children, the aged, the sick, lunatics and pregnant women were theoretically exempt from torture, while only light torture was prescribed for women.

Another means of ascertaining guilt was the ordeal, which could be used in both civil and criminal cases, and in certain forms is still sometimes resorted to to settle disputes out of court. Ordeals are little mentioned in early texts, but they seem to have grown more popular in later times. The Smṛti writers apparently distrusted ordeals, and generally limited their application to cases in which there was no concrete evidence on either side. Several ordeals are mentioned, however, including ordeals by fire and immersion similar to those known in medieval Europe, and possibly having a common Indo-European origin in the remote past. Specially interesting is the ordeal of the ploughshare, in which the accused man had to touch a red-hot iron ploughshare with his tongue; if he was not burned he was deemed innocent—psychologically a fairly sound test of his own confidence in the result, since if he had a guilty conscience his salivary glands would not function properly, and his tongue would be burnt.

Megasthenes remarked that the Indian was not inclined to litigation, and he may have been correct, though the same could not be said of India of more recent times. In any case, though there were many Brāhmaṇas learned in law they never constituted a class of professional pleaders, and those who did not serve on the bench presumably used their knowledge to settle cases out of court. There is evidence, however, that by the end of our period a class of lawyers, in the modern sense, was beginning to develop, for some late text-books allow litigants to employ proxies, who are to be rewarded with a share of the money involved, while one source grants to any learned Brāhmaṇa the right to give his views on a case from the body of the court.

Punishment

The penalties imposed for criminal offences developed from two very ancient customs, the wergeld and the religious penance imposed for ritual offences. The influence of both can be clearly traced in the system of punishment followed in later times.

The early Sūtras laid down fines for the punishment of murder—1,000 cows for killing a Kṣatriya, 100 for a Vaiśya, and 10 for a Śūdra or a woman of any class; the killing of a Brāhmaṇa could not be expiated by a fine. The cattle were handed to the King, who passed them on to the relatives of the slain man, a bull being added as the King's perquisite. Later sources lose sight of the true nature of the fines as means of buying off the vengeance of the family of the dead man, and lay down that the cattle are expiatory gifts, to be given to the Brāhmaṇas. But the wergeld left its mark on the legal system in the form of the fines, which, with or without other punishment, are a special feature of ancient Indian justice. Fines ranging from a small copper coin to the confiscation of all property were levied, and could atone for all but the most serious crime. They were an appreciable source of income to the state, and many medieval charters, giving revenue rights over a village or district, specifically include the right to receive the fines levied at the local court. A condemned person who could not pay his fine was reduced to bondage until it was paid by his labour.

The Smṛti writers rarely mention imprisonment, but all other sources show that it was common. Aśoka was proud of the many gaol-deliveries which he had ordered in the course of his reign; according to a later tradition he is said to have maintained in his unreformed early years a prison in which the most fiendish tortures were inflicted, and from which no prisoner came out alive. Hsüan Tsang mentions imprisonment as the usual form of punishment under Harṣa. Forced labour in the state mines and elsewhere is mentioned as a punishment in the *Arthaśāstra*, and no doubt amounted to imprisonment of a very severe type. Mutilation and torture were common penalties for many crimes, and numerous forms are described by legal writers. Such punishments were often looked on rather as penances, and the idea of religious penance was never completely absent from the thought of the pious authors of the Smṛtis, in considering the punishment of crime. It was generally believed that by undergoing punishment in this life the criminal escaped the evil consequences of his crime in the next.

The death penalty is laid down in many forms and for many crimes. Unlike the early Sūtras the *Arthaśāstra* prescribes it for murder, even as a result of a duel or quarrel, if the injured man dies within seven days. Hanging is the penalty for spreading false rumours, house-breaking and stealing the King's elephants and horses. Those who plot against the King, force entry into the King's harem, aid his enemies, create disaffection in the army, murder father, mother, son, brother or an ascetic, or commit serious arson, are to be burnt alive. Beheading is the penalty laid down by the *Arthaśāstra* for wilful murder or stealing a herd of cattle. The man who deliberately breaks a dam is to be drowned in the same dam. Women murdering their husbands or children, killing others by poison, or committing arson are to be torn apart by oxen. Civilians stealing military supplies are to be shot to death with arrows. These are some of the many forms of execution suggested by the *Arthaśāstra*. This text is comparatively lenient towards sexual crime, but Manu also prescribes death in various unpleasant forms for most types of adultery and sexual assault. Even the benevolent Aśoka, for all his distaste for the taking of life, did not abolish the death penalty. The usual form of execution, little mentioned in the textbooks on law but often referred to in general literature, was impalement.

Nevertheless, it is evident that some opinion definitely opposed the death penalty, and the question is considered from both sides in a remarkable passage in the *Mahābhārata*. Here the argument against capital punishment and heavy penalties in general is not based, as might be expected, on the doctrine of non-violence, which in no way forbade either capital punishment or war, but rests wholly on humanitarian considerations. In most cases mutilation, long imprisonment and execution result in untold suffering for many innocent people, especially for the wife and family of the criminal. The argument is quickly refuted—in this dark age the innocent must suffer with the guilty, in order that society may be protected, anarchy avoided, and men enabled to pursue the Sacred Law in peace.

Humanitarian ideas, probably encouraged by Buddhism, were effective in Gupta times in moderating the fierce punishments of earlier days. Fa-hsien records that the death penalty was not imposed in Northern India, but most crime was punished by fines, and only serious revolt by the amputation of one hand. The Chinese traveller may have exaggerated, but his testimony at least suggests that executions were rare. Hsüan Tsang 200 years later, reported that prisoners were not executed under Harṣa, but were left to rot in dungeons. In later times there is good evidence that capital punishment was inflicted, and criminals often became the victims of human sacrifice, but in the medieval period we read of sentences which, even by modern standards, seem surprisingly mild. Thus a Cōḷa inscription records the gift of ninety-six sheep to endow a perpetual lamp in a temple, the donor being a man who had stabbed an army officer to death; this was apparently the only penalty he suffered. Other South Indian instances can be found of murderers being let off with comparatively small penances of this nature. It would seem that here the blood feud had by no means disappeared, and if a murderer could appease the enmity of his victim's family the court would let him off lightly. Killing in self-defence was justified in law, as was the stealing of small quantities of food to stave off starvation.

In later times the lives of many animals were protected by law, especially that of the cow. The story of the Cōḷa King who ordered the execution of his own son for the accidental killing of a calf is certainly a legend, and we need not believe that Kumārapāla (c. 1143 – 1172), the Jaina King of the Caulukya dynasty of Gujarāt, so strictly enforced non-violence that heavy fines were inflicted on people who killed fleas, but these stories show the climate of opinion in medieval India. In the later period the wanton killing of a cow was among the most serious of crimes.

The legal system envisaged by the Smṛtis would impose graduated punishment according to class. Thus a Brāhmaṇa slandering a Kṣatriya should, according to Manu, pay a fine of fifty *paṇas*, but for slandering a Vaiśya or a Śūdra the fines are only twenty-five and twelve *paṇas* respectively. For members of the lower orders who slander their betters the penalties are much more severe. Similar gradations of penalty according to the class of the offender are laid down for many crimes, and the equality of all before the law was never admitted in ancient India, and was quite contrary to most Indian thought. If the *samatā*, which Aśoka instructed his officials to employ in their judicial dealings, means equality the case is unique; it is probable that the word implies no more than consistency, or perhaps mildness. It is hardly likely that even Aśoka was bold enough to introduce so drastic a change in the administration of justice—one which no other ancient lawgiver, Indian or otherwise, would have agreed to.

In the later Vedic period some Brāhmaṇas claimed to be above the law altogether. At the proclamation of the King at the end of the royal consecration ceremony the chief officiating Brāhmaṇa turned to the assembled multitude and cried "Here is your King, O Kurus—for us, our King is [the god] Soma". At all times the priestly class demanded many privileges in law. According to most orthodox sources the Brāhmaṇas were exempt from execution, torture and corporal punishment, the worst penalty that could be imposed on them being the humiliation of losing their topknot (p. 161), followed by confiscation of property and banishment. But the Smṛti of Kātyāyana allows the execution of a Brāhmaṇa for procuring abortion, the murder of a respectable woman, and the theft of gold, while the *Arthaśāstra* admits it for sedition, and also sanctions the branding of Brāhmaṇas. In "The Little Clay Cart" the hero, though a Brāhmaṇa, is threatened with torture and sentenced to death, and there is much other evidence that the Brāhmaṇas did not always obtain the privileges which they claimed.

In fairness to the Hindu legal system, we must note that it did not always work in favour of the Brāhmaṇa. Manu lays down that as the penalty for theft the Śūdra should pay a fine equal to eight times the value of the stolen goods, while the Vaiśya, Kṣatriya and Brāhmaṇa should pay sixteen, thirty-two and sixty-four times the value respectively. The upper classes were expected to follow higher standards of conduct than the lower, and their thefts were correspondingly more heinous.

As well as the royal courts there were other tribunals which could arbitrate in disputes and deal with minor crime. These were the councils of villages, castes and guilds, whose validity as judicial bodies for their members was fully recognized in the legal literature. They could punish offenders by fines and excommunication, the latter a very serious penalty indeed, and they probably played as important a part in the life of the community as did the King's courts. Unfortunately we have little knowledge of their procedure.

The Secret Service

Perhaps the least pleasant feature of political life in ancient Indi was the espionage system. The most detailed picture of the working of this secret service is given in the *Arthaśāstra*, the author of which devotes two chapters to its organization, and refers to it throughout his treatise. The text visualizes a country riddled from top to bottom with secret agents or spies. They were organized through "institutes of espionage" to which they delivered information, sometimes in cipher, and from which they received their orders. These institutes were not responsible for the whole organization of espionage, however, for there were special spies, directly subordinate to the King or a high minister, and employed to spy on the ministers themselves.

The spies might be recruited from any walk of life, and might be of either sex. Brāhmaṇas unable to make a living by their learning, merchants fallen on evil days, barbers, astrologers, humble servitors, prostitutes and peasants—all might be enrolled as secret agents. A special class of spy was the *satṛ*, an orphan trained from childhood for the work, and usually mansquerading as a holy-man or a fortune-teller, two professions whose members, being specially trusted by the public, could gain access to information which others might find difficulty in obtaining. A further class was that of the desperado, recruited from professional prize-fighters; the main duty of such an agent was the assassination of those enemies of the King for whom a public trial was not expedient, but he also performed other secret deeds of daring and violence on behalf of his master.

The ancient Indian secret service has incurred much criticism, some of which is not wholly fair. Probably no government at any time has been able to function without secret agents of some sort, if only honest detectives for the suppression of crime, and every ancient civilization had its spies, though perhaps not so thoroughly organized as those envisaged in the *Arthaśāstra*. The ancient Indian spy system was not quite comparable to the secret political police of some modern states, since its function was by no means confined to the suppression of criticism and sedition, and it was looked on not as a mere machiavellian instrument for maintaining power, but as an integral part of the state machinery.

Certainly one of the spy's chief duties was protecting the King's power. He sought out sedition, whether in the brothel or in the palace of the crown-prince. He served as agent provoker, to test the loyalty of high ministers, generals and judges. In the territory of enemies, whether potential or actual, he not only obtained information on the strength and plans of the King's foes but also encouraged sedition, and plotted the assassination of the enemy King and his ministers. He also acted as a detective for the suppression of crime. For this purpose he frequented, in disguise, taverns, brothels and gambling dens, listened to the conversation of men in their cups, and carefully watched those who seemed abnormally affluent.

But he had also other duties of a more positive character. He was an important means of keeping a finger on the pulse of public opinion. In the story of Rāma it is a spy who informs the King that his subjects suspect Sītā's chastity. The secret service, in fact, kept the King in touch with his people. It was also a means of maintaining the King's popularity. One of the spy's duties was to spread stories favourable to the King, to praise him in public, to argue with those who criticized the administration, and in general to spread propaganda in the King's favour. There is no reason to believe that mild criticism of the King or his administration was normally punished. The ancient Indian secret service might no doubt, in the hands of an unjust King, be a very evil thing, but under a just administration it had positive and useful functions, and was not a mere instrument of repression.

The Theory of Adoption

"There is a singular disproportion between the space necessarily devoted to adoption in the English works on Hindu Law, and that which it occupies in the early law books. One might read through all the texts from the Sūtra writers down to the Dāyabhāga without discovering that adoption is a matter of any prominence in the Hindu system." In the *Manusmṛti* itself there are only 4 verses relating to the subject of adoption: they are 141, 142, 159 and 168 of the Chapter IX. Of these verse 168 defines the adopted son, while 159 mentions him as one of the six who are heirs, and verses 141 and 142 speak of his leaving the natural family and of his inheriting in the adoptive family, and performing ceremonies to the adoptive parents. In all the other treatises the subject does not occupy larger space, even down to the very recent time when the *Dattakamīmāṁsā* and the *Dattakacandrikā*, the two special treatises on adoption, were written. Hence, the question naturally suggests itself to all thinking minds, as to what is the origin and nature of this institution of adoption and what is the reason for its gradual development. The theories that have been started with regard to this subject, of course, basing them generally on the authoritative statements of the Smṛti writers, may be mentioned as being two-fold. The first theory is what has been denominated the religious theory of adoption, which says that on account of the great importance of the son in the performance of ceremonies for satisfying the ancestors, even in the very early days of the history of the Hindus, a son was considered to be indispensable for every man, and hence, when a man had no sons, he satisfied his religious craving for a son, by affiliating a stranger to his own family. This may be characterized as the orthodox view. The second theory says that even in the case of Hindus religion was not the chief motive for the craving for a son, and that it is a vanity of human nature to see that his line is continued, while the origin of the institution itself is traced to a remote period when the existence of a son was a material help in swelling the number of male members in a family, and thus adding to its strength and power in withstanding attacks from outside. We have to examine what is the correct theory that can be deduced from the Smṛti texts.

In the *Manusmṛti* the adopted son is described as follows: "He whom his father or mother gives, with water, in distress, equal, affectionate, he is known as the given son" (V. 168). Now it is admitted by all people that in the later times, the law of adoption was developed by the introduction of the religious theory, and that, therefore, at the present day adoption like marriage is essentially a religious act, and that it is purely and solely for motives of religion, the existence of property not being a condition precedent for the validity of adoption. Hence, it becomes necessary for us to examine whether in the earliest times of our Smṛtis, the religious or the secular notion prevailed. It cannot be denied that every society must, previous to the development of religion and Godhead, have passed through stages of comparative simplicity and absence of intellectuality, and of irreligion and thoughtlessness about God and the future. And in those remote and semi-barbarian stages of society, any idea of religious merit is absolutely out of the question. In such cases if a family comes to the verge of extinction by the last male, he being an old and decrepit man, it may perhaps be that he would try to get hold of somebody to look after him during his old age, and consequently for the trouble of having done that allowed him to take whatever property the man would leave behind. But there would absolutely be no motive, apart from the probability or otherwise of the acceptability of such a fiction as sonship, for the old man to consider that the youngster whom he has secured is his son and will continue his lineage. Even if by the mere continuous contact and living together of the persons, a certain amount of attachment and affection grows between them, which must be naturally the case, there is no reason whatever for supposing that the deception of considering him his son and calling him like that, should also have taken place. The one can exist without the other. Hence, it seems to me, that the view advanced by some jurists that the affiliation of sons is to a large extent based upon the original necessity of every family to be well-fortified and equipped with young men who not only support the older ones, but also protect them by preventing external attacks natural and perhaps common too in the early stages of society, does not fully explain the fiction of sonship that is at the base of the whole law of adoption. It, therefore, still becomes necessary to examine why even in those early stages of Hindu society at any rate, when adoption was in vogue, though not perhaps to the extent to which it has been subsequently or is at present, there was the fiction of sonship introduced. Some answer the question by saying that the vanity that is inherent in and characteristic of every man in the world, makes each wish and desire that his name should ever be known and spoken of in this world by his line being continued, but even this answer does not strike me as fully explaining the reason for the introduction of the fiction of sonship, inasmuch as, I cannot conceive of human nature restricting itself to this of all methods of satisfying its vanity, when there are numerous ways for such satisfaction. Hence, arguing from the possibility of the case, it seems to me that much more potent and powerful influences than those should have been at work in compelling men to accept the fiction of sonship in even such early stages of society, and to lavish upon those who are utter strangers, completely known to be so, that family affection which is proverbially strong among us Hindus, and that influence I shall try to trace in the Hindu society with the aid of the materials furnished to us by the Smṛtis and other works.

In the first place, it is very necessary to exactly comprehend in what view and estimation a son was held even in the remote antiquity of Hindu society when the Vedas were written. In the *Ṛgveda* it is said: "The wealth of the debtless suffices. May we be the possessors of such offspring," etc. These statements perhaps are not so clear as they ought to be, but I would draw attention to one more fact discovered by the aid of Philology, and that is the ancestral abode of the Aryans and their habits and manners. From the known and observed habits and customs of the Hindus and of the Greeks and the Romans, certain conclusions have been drawn, and a very remarkable one amongst them is that on account of the existence of he custom of ancestor-worship both in the Eastern and Western Aryans, ancestor-worship was a common feature of the original stock before separation. That ancestor-worship consisted in the propitiation of the manes of the ancestors by offerings and ceremonies at periodical intervals, and the idea had arisen that every man owed a debt to his ancestors and had to satisfy it by performing these duties for him. In the light of this view, the passage from the *Ṛgveda* becomes clear. Possession of offspring is considered to be possession of great wealth, much more valuable than that of real wealth itself. Hence, it is clear that in the Vedic society, the son was viewed as the most valuable possession in satisfying the debts due to their ancestors. This view is made still clearer by illustrations of events in the Vedas themselves. To take one for example: Viśvāmitra was possessed of many sons, but they having been degraded on account of some act, he adopts a son Śunaḥśepa. Now it may very well be asked, on what ground could it be said that Viśvāmitra affiliated him as a son, when he already had so many sons, who are sufficient in number for the celebrity of the name, although by the fact of degradation they rather make it a notoriety. And the irresistible answer seems to be that Viśvāmitra affiliated that son, because the others having become degraded and polluted, were unfit to fulfil and discharge the duties of a son. From the Vedic period, where we find ample evidence of affiliation for purposes other than merely secular, we may next come to the period of the earliest of law compilations extant, the *Manusmṛti*. It has been roughly placed by European scholars three or four centuries before Christ and refers to a period of antiquity. If we turn to the 9th chapter of this Smṛti we find that the subjects of marriage, sonship, inheritance, etc., are treated therein. In this chapter, there are various and undeniable indications of the religious efficacy and of liability to ancestors Verses 137 and 138 describe a son:

पुत्रेण लोकान् जयति पौत्रेणानन्तमश्नुते।
अथ पुत्रस्य पौत्रेण ब्रध्नस्याप्नोति विष्टपम्॥

"By a son he gets the worlds (heavenly), by a son's son he stays there endlessly, by the son's grandson he obtains the pleasure of the solar world." (V. 137).

पुन्नाम्नो नरकाद् यस्मात् त्रायते पितरं सुतः।
तस्मात् पुत्र इति प्रोक्तो स्वयमेव स्वयंभुवा॥

"Because the son saves the father from the hell called *put*, so he is termed Putra by Brahmā himself." (V. 138).

These two verses place the matter of the son's efficacy in saving their ancestors from hell, beyond doubt. But to show that it was a matter of supreme importance religiously even at the time of the *Manusmṛti*, we will quote some more verses.

V. 107. यस्मिन् ऋणं न श्रयति येन चान्नं तमश्नुते।
स एव धर्मजः पुत्रः कामजानितरान् विदुः॥

"By whom the debt leaves, by whom the endless is got, he is the son born by a sense of duty, all the rest are known as children of love." (V. 107).

V. 106. ज्येष्ठेन जातमात्रेण पुत्रीभवति मानवः।
पितृणामनृणश्चैव तस्मात् सर्वस्वमर्हति॥

"By the eldest son, as soon as born, a man becomes a father; he makes the father debtless, and he, therefore, deserves the whole (V. 106)."

It is not necessary to multiply instances, but I may refer to a Śruti quoted in the commentary on the above verse to the same effect.

[पुत्रेण जातमात्रेण पितॄणामनृणश्च सः]

Having thus seen the religious necessity of a son in satisfying the debts to the ancestors of the father, we have next to notice the twelve kinds of sons and their characteristics. After describing the twelve kinds of sons in verses 159 and 160, he says in verse 161:

यादृशं फलमाप्नोति कुप्लवैः संतरं जलम्।
तादृशं फलमाप्नोति कुपुत्रैः संतरं तमः॥

"What kind of fruit he obtains who wishes to cross the sea by the bad boat, that kind of fruit he obtains who wishes to cross the darkness by means of bad sons." This is an advice to every father to provide himself with sons of good qualities, who will consequently save the father from the darkness of hell. I need not quote in extenso the verses which speak of the different kinds of sons as being bound to offer oblations to their ancestors. I will only give the reference to a few of them by way of illustration, V. 132 and 140, as regards a daughter's son, verses 136, 139, etc. By far the most important verse is 180 which is as follows:

क्षेत्रजादीन् सुतानेतानेकादश यथोदितान्।
पुत्रप्रतिनिधीनाहुः क्रियालोपात् मनीषिणः॥

"These eleven kinds of sons the Kṣetraja, etc., are said by the learned to be the substitutes of sons, as they make up the loss of religious acts." This is a clear pronouncement that these eleven kinds of sons are called substituted sons, not because they will simply celebrate the name of their supposed father, but because they make up the loss of religious acts due to the absence of a son, by their performing them: and it is quite certain that according to Manu that was the object for which these sons were allowed. In the face of this verse it seems to me that it is absolutely impossible, to contend that the fiction of sonship by substitution was based on any principle other than the religious. Of course, in the case of the Kṣetraja, Gūḍhaja, Kānīna, etc., there seems to be no reason why the supposed father should be compelled to keep to himself a child who is not his, and I cannot pretend to bring myself to the view that with a full knowledge of the fact of illegitimacy, which is the same as the above kinds, a father would allow the boy to be in his family or to be called his son. Now as regards the adopted son in the age of Manu.

"The Datrima son should never take the *gotra*, or the wealth of the natural father, the *piṇḍa* follows the *gotra* and the wealth, and the religious ceremony of the giver ceases." (V. 142).

This verse points out what material change is effected by the adoption of a boy from one family to another. The *piṇḍa* ceases in the one, and commences in the other, and there is a complete change of paternity. In this connection it is also important to notice a verse that is ascribed by some to Atri and by some to Manu.

अपुत्रेण सुतः कार्यो यादृक् तादृक् प्रयत्नतः ।
पिंडोदकक्रियाहेतोर्नामसंकीर्तनाय च ॥

"By a sonless man should a son be made by one way or other with every effort, for the purpose of the *piṇḍa*, the water and other ceremonies, and for the celebrity of the name."

This verse brings most prominently to our view the very purpose for which a son is taken in adoption, and such a clear and unmistakable expression can but lead to one conclusion. Now it may be asked what is the purpose for which the celebrity of the name is mentioned. Is it merely the pleasure of having one's name celebrated or has it any religious significance? It seems to me that the religious necessity for the existence of a son for the payment of the debts to the ancestors having been established by independent verses, the fiction of sonship is made allowable on that ground, so that whatever strangeness might be found in the relationship with the new comer, it is entirely counterbalanced by that religious frame of mind which makes one think that it is absolutely necessary somehow to discharge the debts of one's ancestors, and that, therefore, for such purpose the person is to be accepted as a son; and being such he, by performing the ceremonies of the adoptive father's ancestors, celebrates their name, and by the fiction continues their lineage. The effect of celebration of name is not, to my mind, an independent effect produced by motives and causes outside the religious view of the matter, but is a proximate and direct result of the religious view and the consequent fiction of sonship. To view otherwise would be to invert what, in the natural course of things, is the relation of cause and effect. We next come to Vasiṣṭha and Baudhāyana, who give the formalities of adoption after first laying down that a father or mother can give, that an only son can not be so given, and that a woman cannot give except with the consent of her husband. Vasiṣṭha says: "He who means to adopt a son must assemble his kinsmen, give humble notice to the King, and then having made an oblation to fire with words from the Vedas, in the midst of his dwelling-house, he may receive, as his son of adoption, a boy nearly allied to him, or (on failure of such) even one remotely allied. But if doubt arise, let him treat the remote kinsman as a Śūdra. The class ought to be known, for through one son the adopter rescues many ancestors." The key to the whole passage is the underlined sentence, and it goes fully to support our view of the question deduced from Manu. Then in Baudhāyaṇa the passage is similar except that the adopter receives the child with the words: "I take thee for the fulfilment of religious duties. I take thee to continue the line of my ancestors." Strongly enough Mayne in his celebrated treatise quotes this passage for the position that the religious motive never excluded the secular, and he depends upon the last clause that was a secular motive. Such we have already explained was not probable on the true view of the things, and that even that clause in question is but a result of the act based upon the original religious theory.

It is not deemed necessary to mention Śaunaka's *kārikās* at greater length than pointing out that the phrase *putracchāyāvahaṁ sutam* has been made the origin of a number of restrictions which have grown in later days. The phrase means bearing the reflection of a son. Upon this the construction was placed by Nandapaṇḍita, that it meant that the boy should be such that he could have been begotten on his natural mother by his adoptive father through *niyoga* and so forth. Although, as translated by Dr. Bühler and as pointed out by Mayne, the phrase is not really a metaphor, but only an expression which conveys the idea that the son after having been adorned, resembles a son of the adopter's body, still Nandapaṇḍita's construction of the passage has been universally accepted, as an authoritative exposition of the true view of the law on the matter in question, and is practically beyond dispute now. But it is not a little strange to observe that Nandapaṇḍita and the latter-day writers had introduced these restrictions upon adoption, when adoption still fulfils such an important duty and is so favoured. Still on a close examination of the question, his interpretation of it is capable of simple explanation, and that is this. Here is a matter of affiliation of a son, and what sort of man is he to be? You have a number of relations, and whom are you to select? Naturally the answer is that boy who would even otherwise be in a position to do the same ceremonies to men of the same degree as the adopter. His affiliation has the effect of transferring his religious acts to another line of the same degree, instead of the line in which the adoptee was born, or to explain the matter much simpler the selection will always be in the agnatic line, and Nandapaṇḍita, well aware of the practice in daily life, propounds a rule whose effect is very nearly the same as that seen in actual practice, but which is based upon the single principle of capacity to beget by *niyoga* and so forth. We had referred to Manu that a Kṣetraja is to perform the ceremonies, and is the chief substitute, so does this son who is such a person as to be fit to be brought forth through *niyoga* and so forth, thus establishing our original theory about the matter: "If the primary object of adoption was to gratify the manes of the ancestors by annual offerings, it was necessary to delude the manes, as it were, into the idea that the offerer really was their descendant. He was to look as much like a real son as possible, and certainly not to be one who could never have been a son. Hence, arose that body of rules which were evolved out of the phrase of Śaunaka, that he must be the reflection of a son. He was to be a person whose mother might have been married by the adopter, he was to be of the same class; he was to be young that his ceremonies might all be performed in the adoptive family: he was to be absolutely severed from his natural family and to become so completely a part of his new family as to be unable to marry within its limits. His introduction into the family must be a matter of free will and love unsullied by every mercenary element." (Mayne, para. 94.) From these things it is, therefore, clear that the origin as well as the development of the law of adoption has been wholly and completely on religious lines.

Ethics and Politics in Hindu Culture

1

The contents of this article are to be discussed in the context of the importance of the Vedic conception of *ṛta* as the foundation of the Hindu moral theories. Alongwith *ṛta*, we find in the *Ṛgveda* another concept, that of *svadhā*. This means either nature or conformity to nature. *Svadhā* is implicitly present in things and is responsible for their development. Whether it is a living being, an inanimate thing or god—each has its own *svadhā*. It was from this conception that another doctrine was evolved in course of time, *viz.*, to remain in the position in which one finds himself is natural as well as appropriate. As was said in the previous paper, it is this theory which underlies the caste system.

Ṛta is unswerving and inexorable. As was said by Vamadeva, it is *ṛta* which provides various types of food that sustain; meditation on *ṛta* removes transgressions; praise of *ṛta* opens our ears and awakens us to moral consciousness. While the foundations of *ṛta* are firm it has varied and fair forms, which present themselves as duties to be performed. Thus *ṛta* is the principle which makes the world a universe and a cosmos. But it is realized in various ways—through the performance of different duties at different times.

The rules ordained for specific purposes which are variable and by which are guided the conducts of men are derived from *ṛta*. The Veda calls them *vratas* and due performance of *vrata* constitutes justice. The Veda recognized that *ṛta* has both ethico-rational and material dimensions. Thus it is both natural as well as moral law. And its off-shoot, *vrata*, is in conformity with divine reason and is meant for human welfare. When the Veda says that it is *ṛta* which makes the rivers flow for fertilizing the earth and makes the fire burn for giving warmth, the natural law is meant. On the other hand, when it is said that intelligent men can know it, that the prudent can attain it by striving and that all children are potentially containers of *ṛta*, it is moral law that is meant.

Svadhā and *vrata* represent the social aspects of *ṛta*. That which constitutes the essence of a thing and is responsible for its growth and for its becoming what it is, is *svadhā*. Thus not only individuals, but also society will have its *svadhā*. It is because of *svadhā* that societies and traditions last, for that which is not in tune with nature will not last. Even a god has to follow his *svadhā*. He cannot be arbitrary. Thus morality and law are based upon immutable divine reason and not on divine will.

From these conceptions it followed that justice is a condition in which each keeps within his appointed sphere (*Cp*. Aristotle). Hindu thinkers in general thought that the business of government is to preserve justice. This implies that a government has to see every individual remains in his sphere of duties, determined by the country, religion, caste and family, to which he naturally belongs. Hindu thinkers further believe that justice without force is impotent. Without punishment or *daṇḍa* neither justice nor security can be realized. As the *Mahābhārata* said: "It is the fear of the punishment of a King, or of hell, or of society, that keeps people away from sin." Punishment not only threatens possible offenders but purifies the sinners. Thus in Hindu ideology law becomes almost wholly punitive. The rod of punishment or *daṇḍa* is also the rod of justice. Some competent writers on comparative law opine that the concept of *ṛta* influenced especially the Romans to develop their own concepts of law and morality. In Roman thought *ṛta* became *ratum* or ratio and Augustine Christianized it as *Pax*.

We do not have any exact historical data regarding the origins of kingship in India. The *Aitareya Brāhmaṇa* says that when the Devas were defeated by Asuras, the former thought this was because they had no king. So they all agreed to elect Indra as the King of Devas, because he was the best and the most powerful of them. A Ṛgvedic passage which says that Indra's strength is derived from the Devas and his power is founded in wisdom, seems to support this. Some modern historians think that the Devas, or the shining ones, referred to here were no other than the Aryans in India, whereas the Asuras perhaps were the Sumerians. It is possible that in early Ṛgvedic times the natural military leader, he who could sack cities (*purāṁ bhettā*), became also the ruler (*goptā janasya*), the King and protector.

In the *Śatapatha Brāhmaṇa* it is mentioned that a king rules over many because he is the viceregent of Prajāpati, the Lord of beings. The *Manusmṛti*, which was perhaps developed into its present form in the Sunga period, says that a king is the deity in human form, that kings are created by God. Thus we see that in later times the law codes tried to make kingship a divine institution, but the old idea that a king is after all human was never lost. For example, Baudhāyana conceives a king almost as a salaried official.

The *Mahābhārata* puts forward two different accounts as to how government arose, reminding us of the speculations of Hobbes, Locke, Rousseau and earlier European thinkers.

1. There was at one time an age of righteousness. There was then no government and no punishment. All men then lived by *dharma* alone. Later they developed anguish and became deluded. As a result of this they lost their discrimination and destroyed the moral law. Greed, lust and desire overpowered them. Seeing this they prayed to the creator, who appointed a ruler and also gave him a code of law composed by himself.

2. At another place the *Mahābhārata* gives a different account. In the beginning men lived, governed by the law of

fishes. Power was the only law and strength the only rule. Finding life intolerable they made a covenant and agreed that transgressors should be expelled for some time. Later when they found that it was difficult for all voluntarily to follow the covenant they prayed to the creator that they might be given a ruler who would enforce the covenant and this was done.

Thus while some thinkers tried to base kingship upon the common consent of the people, there were others who tried to represent it as divine, as something which was imposed from above.

It may, however, be surmised that during the Vedic times monarchy was the usual form of government, and prior to the time when the *Aitareya Brāhmaṇa* was composed there was no hereditary kingship. Even the *Mahābhārata* admits at places that a monarch is elected. The story of the deposition of King Vena found in it and all the Purāṇas shows this. The Dharmasūtras believe it is possible for a king to be sinful, and for such kings penance is prescribed. The *Mahābhārata* quotes an ancient treatise which says that a king who is unfit must be shunned like a split boat in the sea. In another passage, an incompetent king is compared to a useless bullock and a barren cow. A king who cannot uphold virtue ceases to be a king, and an incompetent one should be slain by his subjects like a mad dog. Even the conservative Manu suggests in some passages that people have the right to rebel against an oppressive king. Thus the right to tyrannicide seems to have been granted by some Hindu thinkers.

An analysis of the coronation oaths in the Vedas and the Brāhmaṇas shows that Hindu kingship at that time was regarded as a human institution. A king, they show, was elected; by becoming a king one entered into a contract with people. Rulership was a trust placed in him. He could not be arbitrary but had to work in cooperation with a council. After the coronation and a ceremonial drive, a newly made king was enthroned and silently touched on the back with a rod—the sceptre of justice. This was to show that the King was not above law but below it and that he too was punishable (*tasmad rājā daṇḍyaḥ*). The most ancient book available on Hindu polity, Kautilya's *Arthaśāstra*, acknowledges this when it says that a king cannot be arbitrary, that he can make only regulatory laws but not substantive laws, and when it adds that a king who uses *daṇḍa* wrongly is destroyed. Kauṭilya is emphatic that the unrighteous and the foolish cannot wield *daṇḍa*. Elsewhere the *Arthaśāstra* says that for the King the good is not his personal likes, but the likes of his subjects. Even Manu admits that a king is below law and is liable to fine. The *Śukla Yajurveda*, the *Atharvaveda*, the *Taittirīya Brāhmaṇa* and the *Kṛṣṇa Yajurveda* admit that a king can be deposed, and exiled, and also reinstated by the people. A situation like that described by Herodotus in the Persia of Cambyses' time when the judges thought that the King can do whatever he liked was never found in Hindu India.

The Vedic King's power was limited by the deliberations and the expressed will of two different kinds of peoples' assemblies—the *sabhā* and the *samiti*. On the concord between the *samiti* and the King depended a realm's prosperity (*Ṛgveda*, X. 191. 3), though a powerful king could dominate it. The later Vedic King was more often an elected one. The Post-Vedic King's power was limited by that of the *pariṣad* and the *sabhā*, in which Vaiśyas and Śūdras also found places. We learn this from Pāṇini and the *Mahābhārata*. Iranian and Greek influences and the growth of Mauryan power might have contributed to the weakening of these democratic checks. But the *Śatapatha Brāhmaṇa* is quite specific regarding the task of a ruler. He is the director and the regulator of the people. He is steadily responsible for agriculture (*kṛṣi*), for economic prosperity (*raai*) and development (*poṣa*) and the general welfare of people (*ksema*). The same book insists a king must be law-abiding and law-protecting. The *Atharvaveda* makes it clear that the increase of material prosperity is the King's business. The *Jātaka* tales tell us that a king is not the master of all citizens but only of the lawbreakers. As the *Arthaśāstra* picturesquely puts it, the King has to rule by the sword, but the inner content or the embryo of the sword must be righteousness (*asinā dharma-garbheṇa pālayasva*). A king, it says, must obey a Purohita (the spiritual preceptor), as a servant obeys his master. (I. 5). Laws and conventions, says the *sukranti*, should not be changed by the King except after discussion by learned wise men, who will take into consideration the following factors: what are the present laws? What were the past laws? Which of them were taught by the scriptures and which of them are against the scriptures and against the welfare of the world at present? The *Mahābhārata* tells us that a king on assumption of his office must take the following oath and follow it: "I will govern or protect always all that belongs to the country as Brāhmaṇa itself. All the law that there is, and endorsed by ethics (*Nīti*)—that I will undoubtedly maintain by resorting to punishment (*daṇḍa*). I will never be arbitrary or self-willed". A king who during his rule transgresses this oath is liable to deposition and tyrannicide. From all this it can be concluded that the moral law is above sovereignty and that the Hindu theory of sovereignty does not give any scope for being described as oriental despotism.

As many of the Pali Buddhist books show and as Magasthenes testifies writing in the fourth century B.C., the Vedic age of monarchies was succeeded by a number of democracies. The *Aitereya Brāhmaṇa*, which may be put at 1000 B.C., suggests this when it says that at that time, except the midlands (by which was meant the country from Kurukṣetra to Allahabad, the Doab between the Gaṅgā and the Yamunā), all Aryan India was republican. But in the East there was an empire. That in the Buddha's time there were many republics as well as powerful monarchies is well known from Pali sources. Pāṇini's Sūtras refer to republics (*gaṇas*) and confederations of republics ruled by the free will (*chandas*) of all the people, the government consisting of a body of Kṣatriyas. The rules for the government of the Buddhist Saṅgha (monastic order) were adopted from the rules and conventions followed by the republics at that time. We learn from Pali sources that these republics in general followed these seven principles: 1. They held full and frequent assemblies; 2. They met in concord, rose in concord, and carried on their business in concord; 3. They always acted in accordance with ancient institutions; 4. The elders were always honoured and obeyed; 5. Force was not used towards women and girls; 6. Religious establishments were honoured and supported; 7. The wise men among them were protected and rightfully defended. In the *Digghanikāya* the Buddha is reported to have said that so long as a republic follows these principles it cannot be conquered. In the place of the above three last rules the Buddhist Saṅgha substituted for itself the following: 1. One should not become subject to craving; 2. One should take delight in solitude; 3. One should train the mind.

From the accounts left by Magasthenes and Strabo and from Buddhist books, we learn that the Licchavis at Vaiśalī, the Videhas at Mithilā and the Kathians to the east of the river Rāvī with Sankala as their capital, were the earliest republics. At a later date the Licchavis and the Videhas combined to form a mammoth republican federation—the Vajji Saṅgha which lasted from the time of the Buddha to the time of the founding of the Gupta Empire. Some of these republics were states governed by Aristocracies (*Kulas*), whereas others were governed by elected magistrates. These latter were called "*gaṇas*". As the Greek writers testify, these and other similar republics were free, autonomous, and independent. The Greek descriptions of the Kathians remind us of Sparta. Courageous and able in war, the Kathians and the Saubhūtis (another republic) practised eugenics. Children among these were reared under the direction of state medical men, while the deformed and the defective were killed in the second month. Marriages were made by choice and women immolated themselves along with their husbands. Strabo and Diodorus mention this. It is interesting to note that the great Upaniṣadic teacher Naciketas, who confronted Death and learned the secret of immortality, belonged to this republic. A portion of the *Kṛṣṇa Yajurveda*, the *Kāṭhaka Saṁhitā*, was composed by the Kathians. The basis of a Hindu Law Code, the *Viṣṇusmṛti,* was a Dharmasūtra composed by the Kathians. It is again interesting to see that the Buddha belonged to a republic ruled by an aristocracy. Two other great religious geniuses, Ariṣṭanemi of Jainism and Kṛṣṇa of the *Bhagvadgītā*, belonged to the republic of Andhaka-Vṛṣṇis or Sātvatas. The state to which the Buddha belonged was ruled by a number of Rājans, one of them being the president, whereas the state to which the Sātvatas belonged was ruled by two Rājanyas. From the *Mahābhārata*, however, we learn that the Sātvatas together with other republican peoples such as the Yādavas, the Kukuras and the Bhojas formed a confederation of which Kṛṣṇa was the federal president, though each had their own chief.

In the *Mahābhārata* we find an analysis of the reasons responsible for the destruction of republics and aristocracies. Due to greed and jealousy and absence of mutual confidence, internal dissensions slowly raise their heads. Due to the method of openly discussing all the problems of the state it becomes difficult to maintain state secrets. This gives an opportunity to foreign spies. On the other hand, when the citizens of a republic do not discuss the matters of the state openly and when they do not act in concert, they are weakened and are endangered. We can see that this problem of republican government still remains unsolved and in this respect monarchical and totalitarian states have a greater advantage over open societies. Also in the *Mahābhārata* (XII-81), in a dialogue between Nārada and Vāsudeva-Kṛṣṇa, the problem of retaining the leadership in a democracy is discussed. There it is said that the use of the soft and easy weapon will easily secure success. To play host to others, whenever possible, patience and straightforwardness, courtesy and due respect to others is that weapon. That implies that suave manners and patience along with upright conduct and hospitality preserve one in leadership. It may be commented that even today persons who are in the position of leaders in democracies fulfil these requirements. It is plain that to be able to play host to others and secure friends by gifts and sweet words, both money and tact are required. The advantage here lies with the upper classes.

Hindu literature on politics consists of the Arthaśāstras and the Nītiśāstras. The book composed by Kauṭilya, Chancellor of the founder of the Mauryan Empire, is perhaps the earliest available *Arthaśāstra*, whereas the *Nītiśāstra* attributed to a Śukra is a good example of the *Nītiśāstra* treatises in general. The principle on which these two classes of books seem to be based has been long ago summarized in the *Māgha*: Success of oneself and injury to enemies (2.30). These books seem to have been composed by scholars who were practising politicians like Kauṭilya, or by mere theoreticians. Like the Stoics, the Christian Fathers and Burckhardt in the nineteenth century, some of them regarded politics itself as evil and could not see how he who wants to practise politics can remain good. On the other hand, some of them regarded power politics as a natural phenomenon and, therefore, saw no reason why something natural should be censored. It is possible that Kauṭilya, who was responsible for the building up of a mighty empire through the uprooting of an older dynasty and the welding together of a number of small states, and who was constantly threatened by foreign invasions, should have preached the autonomy of politics from morality. It is also understandable that the Nīti writers of the middle ages, whose great desire was to see that a strong Hindu state emerged, should have preached the gospel of power. A new dynasty has to legitimize itself and win stability, and the first task of a newly formed empire would be the subjugation of the conquered peoples and the liquidation of the rebellious and the disgruntled.

Almost all conquerors, colonial powers, and founders of new dynasties have resorted to these methods. But the Hindu writers of the *Arthaśāstras* seem to be the first to theorize and validate these methods. To go into some details, Kauṭilya suggests that a prince should ingratiate himself with heretics, corporations, gods, rich widows and merchants, but at the same time should rob them either by taxation or by direct seizure of properties. Poison, spies and provocation may be used to control people who disturb peace. Through intrigue, assassination by use of poison and magic, and by setting against one's rivals and enemies their own relatives, one can get rid of inconvenient persons and groups. By claiming that gods are associated with oneself, enemies should be discouraged and friends encouraged. Any means can be used for raising money. For instance, Kauṭilya suggests that by deceit an idol can be implanted in a lonely place and it can be announced that it is self-sprung and money can be made out of it.

For a discussion regarding the justification of these methods, we have, however, to turn to the *Mahābhārata*. In that book while at most places a king is advised to follow *dharma* always and rule in accordance with the scriptures, considering himself to be the guardian of all the people, at other places it is suggested that a king cannot sometimes succeed unless he willingly practises duplicity, deceit and ruthlessness. Thus in some places it advises that a king should be soft in speech but hard at heart. He must be humble before the enemies when the time is unfavourable, but must destroy them when the opportunity comes. There must be no hesitation to kill anybody, whether a relative or a friend, for achieving one's ends. Without cruelty kings cannot attain felicity. While showing outward sympathy enemies must be mercilessly destroyed. When the odds are against, one should sacrifice self-respect and honour, but must strike back when the time is ripe.[1]

This question was also raised in the *Mahābhārata* itself, if politics in itself is immoral why should one practise it? And how does it differ from other immoral activities like robbery etc.? To this one type of answer says that a certain class of men, the Kṣatriyas, has the obligation to govern, fight and conquer. Since this duty is imposed upon them by their very birth and by scripture, it is not immoral for the Kṣatriyas to fight and conquer. Another type of answer says that the King or the state is above morality and in the discharge of his obligations a ruler whether indulging in war or suppressing rebellions cannot sin. A third type of answer is much more drastic. It says that politics must be based on empirical knowledge and the logic of facts; and scriptures have nothing to say in this matter. As life is more important than religious merit and as politics is after all acquisition of power, the weak virtuous man cannot succeed in politics, so strength must be acquired by any means. Lastly, it is also shown that the nature of existence itself is a struggle for survival and since everything in the world is desired by a number of men there is bound to be a struggle. Like everything else power must be fought for and won. In some places it is said that immoral means must be used only against immoral persons, or when it is not possible to preserve oneself in power through moral means, or when the achievement of the good necessarily requires their adoption.[2]

Nowhere in the classical Hindu books do we find the idea that evil must be tolerated, or that evil must not be resisted. The only two positions with regard to politics which we find in classical Hindu books are these: It is impossible to be wholly moral in politics, but since man cannot be without political life, at least certain men are destined to participate in politics. For such men it is not a sin to strive for power, win it, and preserve it. For securing these ends they might have to resort to means which are conventionally regarded as immoral, but because it is necessary for such men to be in politics, they beget no sin. In contrast to this we find the other view which holds that politics and morality have no connection with each other, that political ends must be obtained only by political means and that these are amoral. It is very curious that no classical Hindu thinker regarded it possible to moralize statecraft. Either one should choose to be in it and ignore ethics, or if one wholly wants to be ethical he must remain aloof from statecraft.

The *Manusmṛti*, the *Śāntiparvan* and the Arthaśāstras enjoin upon rulers the duty of entering into rivalry with neighbouring rulers. An unambitious king, a king who does not want to extend his suzerainty, a king who shuns righteous war, is to be despised. The ideal of the Hindu King was considered to be the founding of an All-India Empire. From 570 B.C., conquest leading to the unification of India and the establishment of an Indian order became the ideal for every Hindu king. Kauṭilya defined the imperial field or the *Cakravarṭa* as the country lying between the Himalayas and the Cape Comorin. Basing himself on Megasthenes, Arrian tells us that their sense of justice prevented the Indian kings from attempting to conquer beyond the limits of India. This led to the curious position that Hindu kings were encouraged to fight with each other, while they were discouraged from conquering neighbouring countries. It was because of this that in most extant books on Hindu polity the theme is often conquest. No neighbouring state should be considered as a friendly state and ultimately no state in India was considered to be the friend of any other Indian state. This dilemma could only be resolved by the founding of an all India Empire which, it was imagined, would lead to perpetual peace and harmony all over India, but this advice in actual practice led to incessant internecine fights among the Hindu kingdoms. This weakened and made them a prey to successive conquests from outside India.

In the twentieth century for the first time the teachings and activities of Mahatma Gandhi expressed an attitude which was very different from the classical Hindu attitude towards politics. Like some sages of old, he did not want to keep himself aloof from the social and political life of the country. On the other hand, he did not want to achieve his political ends through the means usually adopted. Enunciating the maxim that right ends should be won by right means and that means are as important as ends, he tried to introduce into politics a code of conduct which only strictly religious men usually practised. He wanted eschewal of all violence even for winning goals like the independence of one's country. He wished that there should be no scramble for power, and believed that this could be achieved by decentralizing power. If there is no such thing as a central government and the whole country lives in its thousands of small villages, each self-sufficient both industrially and agriculturally, and if, as far as possible, each family becomes autonomous producing its own food and other necessities, then, he thought, there will be an absence of the scope for power politics. Gandhi, however, recognized that such a system of autonomous villages cannot have modern advanced technological civilization, nor can they form a planned society on a large scale. He in fact considered material prosperity as having no value whatsoever. The simpler the life of a man, he believed, the more in tune with nature and the better it would be. In effect Gandhi's doctrine implies that the sacrifice of the central organization, military and police power and technology, will mean the end of power politics and the ushering in of an era when men will need the least government.

I have discussed the Gandhian doctrine of non-violence elsewhere in detail and do not propose to devote much space to it now. It involves the assumption that while physical force must totally be given up and while the aggressor or the political enemy must in no way be resisted physically, one can inflict suffering upon oneself so that it may move the heart of the opponent. Self-inflicted suffering may be used as an instrument to persuade rulers, aggressors, or political opponents. This theory is open to two criticisms: Not everybody in the world can be moved by another's self-inflicted suffering. Secondly, whether a man has the right to inflict upon himself suffering even though he sincerely believes his cause to be right, is questionable. Also, inasmuch as self-inflicted suffering seems to make an emotional appeal and tries to befuddle and goad the man whom one seeks to convert, its moral value cannot be higher than that of reasonable persuasion. When one believes one's cause to be just and when one fails to assert one's own right through discussion and rational persuasion, the moral and manly thing seems to be to fight for one's cause.

2

After this brief presentation of classical Hindu political and ethical thinking, I will now develop these thoughts and reformulate them to suit the present context.

Much of political life consists in influencing men to act in the way in which one likes them to act. Men are what they are, that is, they have their own ideas, prejudices, inclinations, virtues and defects. The politician must work with this material. To make men undertake common action, or to make them come to certain agreements, it would be necessary to soothe their illusions, flatter their vanity, or appeal to their superstitions. Thus empirical necessity might force a politician not to be good and straightforward. For achieving certain kinds of goodness evil may have to be allowed to manifest itself, if it appears to be the only means of bringing sluggish masses into the required form. The hard core of all political action is the selfish interest of a leader, a group, or a state. To achieve these interests in an existing situation, a certain type of action alone may become necessary. For this, certain rights and obligations may have to be set aside.

The politician does not always find his historic situation co-operating with him. He and the objective historic situation may often confront each other, and political necessity, i.e., the causal pressure necessary to align the people to a particular way of thinking and doing, may force the politician and the statesman to act in ways which are usually considered against morality. Every politician *ipso facto* logically needs power. This applies also to parties and states. But there are many persons, parties, and states planning to acquire power, so naturally there will be conflicts. In such a case when the end controls the means and when the only necessary means are adopted, it might be found that they are immoral means. The only solution of this dilemma would be either to renounce politics, or acquiesce in the victory of the other person, party, or state.

In this connection it is often said that power pursued for the sake of the common good is justified. But this does not seem to be tenable, because it is difficult for oneself or for others to know how far one is subject to pleonexia and how far one is trying to promote the common good. There is no agreement usually at any time as to what the common good is. Any amount of cool and rational deliberation can never achieve unanimity on this. In all politicians there is bound to be an elemental power urge and it is difficult to judge either introspectively or historically between idealistic and utilitarian actions in politics. Even in past cases it is difficult to decide how far state interests or personal emotions of statesmen motivated actions.

This problem of power is further complicated by another factor. A man becomes a politician or a statesman, because he has the power-drive in himself, or because he thinks he knows wherein the good of the people lies and that he ought to make them get it. The needs of the people and certain factors in a situation allow some men to become leaders or rulers; and because they receive compensations, the people allow themselves to be governed. When a politician wins power he must exercise it, if he wants to retain it. For this he has to organize power and gradually there comes a stage when power becomes an independent entity, transcends the politician himself, making him serve it. Thus in the end he who seeks and strives for power, and gets it, is compelled to become its slave. But so long as power remains purposive, obeying certain rules and adhering to certain values, it lives and grows, while blind power destroys itself sooner or later.

To recapitulate this discussion, a politician has to deal with the situation in which he finds himself. In Machiavelli's Italy or in Kauṭilya's India, when poison and assassination were customary means to achieve political ends, soft counter-measures could not have been of any avail. In a desperate situation when life has putrefied, forcible action alone can reorganize it. But here it might be argued that a man has some freedom and responsibility and that he must try to influence events and that he must not claim inability in the face of a situation. Against this it may be pointed out that all situations are a mixture of necessity and freedom. Historical reality is not shaped by the free and responsible actions of men alone, but also by the blind imperative urges of life. This means that every situation is unique and can be dealt with only on its level. General moral laws will not be universally applicable because political ends can be obtained by only political means, and politico-economical life is prior to moral life. It can be only urged that accepting the logic of politics and acting in a political manner, one must constantly strive to produce morality through this action. The useful must be transformed into the ethical and politics must become a means for the moral life. Since politics constantly creates new needs, current politics must always be transformed into a new type of politics and each successive transformation of politics may be made to achieve better forms of living, in other words, better forms of morality, because after all morality is the good life.

The supreme end of politics is the security, integrity and well-being of the state. A stateman's great mission is to secure these values. Now the essence of the state is power, for, without it the state cannot function. Protection of people and upholding of justice are dependent on power—*daṇḍa*; without it a society cannot develop and the beast in man cannot be held in check. Any institution requires power but a state needs it more than the others. There was a time when the state was not the supreme power even within its sphere; it had rivals like the church or the guilds. Then it always had the temptation to resort to immoral means; but to a very large extent the modern state today is supreme in its domestic sphere. Even now when a crisis like a revolution or a mass-strike occurs, the state's power is challenged, but through legislation the state can legalize the means by which it can suppress these movements. Still the question of the ethics of a particular legislation could be raised. But the final answer here has to be that the contemporary world is based on a system of nation-states and modern states are not mere power-states, but culture states. Without a state a people cannot realize higher life and culture, of which they are capable. Thus the state in the contemporary world becomes a supreme value and its security and integrity are a supreme moral value; and to achieve the realization and preservation of a nation-state through all the necessary means becomes a supreme duty. Each state has its own necessities, needs, and reason. A well-defined state with a history and a living reality becomes a kind of vital being, which wants to exist, assert itself, and develop freely and fully, without any restraint. For this the state needs power, and as it matures it becomes more and more a determinate being with its own, so to say, biological needs and its own concrete rights and these may often be at variance with universal moral commands. In such cases, one school of thinkers holds that the rights and needs of the state express a higher moral law and that the maintenance and development of the state is the highest duty, and this concrete vital duty cannot be sacrificed for an imagined ideal. From this follows the theory of *raison d'etat*, which lays down that for preserving the life and freedom of a state, any course of action is justifiable and, if need be, morality and law must be set aside. But most political theorists are agreed that such flouting of morality and law should be resorted to only in the public interest and only when to act otherwise would endanger the state. When particular and private motives, egoism, revenge, or self-aggrandizement are completely absent and only when the action undertaken is solely for the sake of the state, it cannot be judged at the bar of morality. Individuals' passions and impulses must not break out under the cloak of *raison d'etat*. To the question why the welfare of a state should justify actions which the welfare of an individual does not; there does not seem to be any adequate answer[3] except to lay it down axiomatically that the former is a much higher value than the latter and that for achieving this good, the only necessary means available must be resorted to, even if they chance to be immoral. One could go further and argue that in such cases the means are only evil in appearance, in reality they are not, but the assumption on which this position is based is unprovable.

The problem described above mainly concerns the politician who is at the helm of affairs, for all states act only through individual statesmen; and it is possible that a statesman acting on behalf of a state is ruthless while in private life he may be gentle and law-abiding; but so long as he sincerely believes he is following the interests of the state, though subconsciously it may only be his pleonexia or prejudices that are guiding him, he has at least a justifiable ground for his actions. On the other hand, the politician aspiring for power, or the party in opposition presents yet another problem. It is possible that sometimes the interests of certain parties and individuals may be in conflict with those of the state to which they belong. This is especially so when in certain countries modern parties tend to be quasi-state organizations. In such cases, wherein does morality lie, in following the political interests of oneself and one's party, or the interests of the state? Here also as the contemporary world order is constituted, the answer seems to be that state interests must remain paramount, for without the state a people cannot realize their higher cultural life independently and according to their own nature.

In opposition to the assumptions underlying the above way of thinking, it may be held that the security and integrity of the state do not constitute a more supreme value than moral law and justice. The state which is meant for the realization of justice cannot be allowed to disrupt it. As pointed out already, there is now no need for a modern state to resort to immoral means within the domestic sphere, for here at last it has become the supreme power, and when it seeks additional power, legislation can secure it, and in a fully democratic state all legislation can be taken to be more or less in tune with morality, as it is based on the consent of the majority and not on the whims and fancies of an individual's or a party's arbitrary will. On the other hand, in the international sphere, there is no established order, law and justice, and no power to uphold them. So here the law of the jungle still prevails. States fight with each other not only for what they believe to be their rights with all the means at their disposal, but also for augmenting their power. Much has, however, happened since the days when naked power politics were openly preached and pracised. Ethics has to a large extent moralized pcwer politics, and the discovery of more and more powerful destructive weapons and the possession of them by more than one country is operating more and more against power politics. The impulses of man are slowly working towards the foundation of an international order which will create a civilized world in which human rights everywhere will be protected and poverty and war will be eliminated. States then will become the instruments of an international order based on moral ideas. This ideal of the fully ethical state confronts the contemporary statesmen and does not allow the intelligent among them to concentrate solely on the limited needs of their own states. A challenge is thus presented to the political faith which regards each nation state as the ultimate value. The possibility that at least one state may still cling to the old faith and the old methods, and be successful when it has differences with another, keeps this great ideal far from realization.

Anyway, the contemporary situation with its unprecedented success in technology, and progress in universalistic moral ideals, has created new interests and is forcing the statesmen to rise to its level. These new ideas, stirrings and impulses confront the statesmen and await translation into agreements, treaties and laws, which will secure an international order based on peace, justice and socio-economic equality, values which have been to an extent realized in some states, but which have to be raised to the international level. Unless appropriate concepts are forged, statesmen cannot rise to this situation; and unless people all over the world adopt these new concepts, statesmen alone can do little. This calls for the forging, if necessary, and the promotion of such concepts and the formation of an appropriate ethical conscience and habits.

Elsewhere I have ventured to single out three such ideas: *homonoia*, tolerance and universal ethics.

Till this new climate of thought comes about, it makes no sense to talk of states practising morality, though in intra-state politics to practise morality successfully is not impossible even now, because in many modern states people are becoming more and more enlightened through the spread of universal education and growing political sense.

References

1. This Epic, however, also lays down that these methods may be resorted to only in desperate situations only, and that in any case the sin resulting therefrom must be atoned for in this or the next life. Through a just rule, sacrifice and charities, a ruler atones for his evil deeds.
2. It is also said: the strength of the ruler is the basis of righteousness, for he preserves it. *Tanmūlaṃ sarvadharmāṇām*. That and his *kośa* (treasury) are the foundations of the State. So the State must never languish (*avasīdana*) and to avoid this the ruler's strength must be preserved and augmented in every way. So for this *kārya* (duty), *akārya* (what ought not to be done) may be necessary sometimes. All this is about "Machiavellian" methods. Just wars, punishment of the wrong-doers, heavy taxation when necessary to build up the strength of the State,—these are entirely moral, a kṣatriya's duty. (For this and above note, see *Śāntiparvan*, Madras edition, pp. 656-9, 460-1, 467, 473).
3. The *Mahābhārata* maintained that if the state did not exist, *dharma* would cease to exist. So state interests become paramount.

Influence of the Dharmaśāstra on the Vaiṣṇavism of Orissa

So far as the information persists update, it is very clear that the Nibandhakāras of the Dharmaśāstra started their writings about the customs of the Vaiṣṇavas during 10th Century A.D. Ācārya Śatānanda (c. 1099 A.D.) is found to have written about the Vaiṣṇavite customs of Orissa in his work the *Śatānandasaṁgraha* and the *Śatānandaratnamālā*, the lines of which have invariably been quoted by the Nibandhkāras of different regions in their respective *nibandhas*. Subsequently Śaṅkhadhara, the author of the *Smṛtisamuccaya*, has followed the path of Śatānanda. His views, expressed in the *Smṛtisamuccaya*, have been referred tọ by the Nibandhakāras of eastern India. Unfortunately, the works of these two Nibandhakāras are not being discovered as yet. Nibandhakāras like Bṛhaspati, the author of the *Kṛtyakaumudī;* Vidyākara Vājapeyin, the author of *Nityācārapaddhati*; Pratāparudra (or Rāmakṛṣṇa Bhaṭṭa), the author of the *Pratāpamārtaṇḍa*, Narasiṁha Vājapeyin, the author of the *Nityācārapradīpa*; Viśvanātha Miśra, the author of the *Smṛtisārasṁgraha*; Divyasiṁha Mahāpātra, the author of the *Śrāddhadīpa*; Gadādhara Rājaguru, the author of *Kālasāra*; Gopinatha Vājapeyin, the author of the *Paṇḍitasarvasva*; M.M. Krishna Mishra, the author of the *Kālasarvasva* and others have exercised their brilliance upon the Vaiṣṇavite tradition of Orissa by recording their views in their respective Nibandhas. However, the subject matter of Vaiṣṇavite customs have been very meticulously discussed in the works like the *Nityācārapradīpa* of Narasiṁha Vājapeyin, the *Kālasāra* of Gadādhara Rājaguru and the *Kālasarvasva* of M.M. Krishna Mishra. A humble attempt has been made in this paper to evaluate the degree of influence of the Dharmaśāstra upon the Vaisnavite customs of Orissa concentrating upon those three works.

As regards the *cāturmāsyavrata*[1], both the followers of *smārta*-tradition and Vaiṣṇavite-tradition, are advised to observe the same without fail. But regarding the beginning day of *cāturmāsyavrata* of the Vaiṣṇavas, the tradition differs from that of the *smārtas*. We find three categories of this tradition in Orissa. In one category, the *cāturmāsyavrata* begins from the fullmoon day of *Āṣaḍha*. In the second category, the same *vrata* begins from the eleventh day of bright-fortnight of *Āṣāḍha*. In the third category, the beginning day of *cāturmāsyavrata* has been considered to be the *karkaṭa saṁkrānti*. Of these three categories, the followers of *smārta*-tradition resort to the first category whereas the followers of Vaiṣṇavite tradition have shown their inclination to abide by the other two categories.

In this context, Gadāḍhara Rājaguru in *Kālasāra* (p. 25)[2] tries to connect *kārtikvrata* with the *cāturmāsyavrata*. He puts forth a lot of textual evidences in support of the above said three categories. Quoting the text from the *Mahābhārata*[3], he opines that the *cāturmāsyavrata* is to be started on the very eleventh day of the bright fortnight of *Āṣāḍha*. Depending upon the authority of the *Varāhapurāṇa*[4] he says, this in support of the other two categories. Taking recourse to the views of the *Skandapurāṇa*[5] he suggests that a person who is not capable of observing the full course of *cāturmāsyavrata* takes the month of *Kārtika* as the ultimatum. However, with this kind of categorization the crux of the problem is not solved. Although the beginning day of *cāturmāsya* differs according to different traditions, still in Orissa, we find some sort of significant tradition in Vaiṣṇavic lore. In Orissa we find two categories of Vaiṣṇavas who worship Kṛṣṇa as their lord. In one category, the Vaiṣṇavas, who accept Chaitanya as Krishna, are regarded as Gauḍa Vaiṣṇavas. In the other, the Vaiṣṇavas who adore Jagannātha as Kṛṣṇa are regaded as the Uḍra Vaiṣṇavas. For the Gauḍa Vaiṣṇavas of Orissa, the *cāturmasyavrata* is to be started with effect from the eleventh day of the bright fortnight of *Āṣāḍha* and concluded on the same day of the month of *Kārtika*. In the same way the *kārtikavrata* is to be started from the eleventh day of the bright fortnight of *Āśvina* and concluded on the same day of *Kārtika* by them.

For the *Uḍra Vaiṣṇavas*, the *cāturmāsyavrata* is to be started with effect from the fullmoon day of *Kārtika*. Here both *Ekādaśī* and *Pūrṇimā* are marked to be the two factors for making difference between the traditions of Gauḍa Vaisnavas and Uḍra Vaiṣṇavas. In this connection, Gadādhara is of the view that if *cāturmāsyavrata* or *kārtikavrata* is to be concluded on *Kārtika Śukla Ekādaśi*, the person who undergoes this *vrata* has to observe *pāraṇā* on that very day. But the Vaiṣṇavas to whichever sect they may belong, have to strictly observe fasting on the very day of *Ekādaśī*. Therefore, in no way the Vaiṣṇavas are advised to conclude *cāturmāsyavrata* or *kārtikavrata* on the very eleventh day of bright fortnight of *Kārtika*. With this sort of argument and analysis of the texts, Gadādhara opines that the Vaiṣṇavas have to extend their *cāturmāsyavrata* or *kārtikavrata* upto the fullmoon day of *Kārtika* inspite of the fact that they start it on different days. This is very much customary in the Temple of Jagannath.[6]

We find a number of references in support of the observance of *cāturmāsyavrata* at Puri and Bhubaneswar. The Śāstrakāras advise that the Smārtas, Vaiṣṇavas, Śaivas, or whoever they may be should take the vow to remain at Puri or Bhubaneswar during *cāturmāsya*. The persons, who choose to reside at Puri, have to start this vrata with effect from the eleventh day of the bright fortnight of *Āṣāḍha* and conclude on the fullmoon day of *Kārtika*. But for the persons choosing to remain at Bhubaneswar, *Ekadaśī* as the beginning date of *cāturmāsya* or *kārtikavrata* is not mandatory since Bhubaneswar is a pilgrim centre of the Śaivites.

It is observed that for the Orissan Vaiṣṇavas the beginning day of *cāturmāsyavrata* or *kārtikavrata* may differ, but the concluding day must be the full-moon day of *Kārtika* i.e. *kārtikapūrṇimā*.

In Purāṇic Smārta tradition, the Vaiṣṇavas of Orissa are advised not to take the *naivedya* of deities who are different from their *iṣṭadevatā*. This has been corroborated by Krishna Mishra with reference to the text of the *Skandapurāṇa* quoted in the *Kālasarvasva* (p. 379). We find some sort of a liberal attitude in this tradition of Orissan Vaiṣṇavism. In this connection, Narasiṁha Vājapeyin and Krishna Mishra express their views differently. From the views of Narasiṁha Vājapeyin it is understood that the *naivedya* offered to any deity, can be accepted if it is offered according to the prescribed rules of any sect. But Krishna Mishra, in *Kālasarvasva* (p. 380), refutes this view of Narasiṁha Vājapeyin. He is of the opinion that this kind of *naivedya* is prohibited for the Vaiṣṇavas even though it is offered to any deity according to the rules prescribed in the Vaiṣṇavite[7] Śāstras.

In addition to the aforesaid view of Vājapeyin, attention of scholars may be drawn towards his second view. According to him, if a Vaiṣṇava, in the daily worship of his *iṣṭadevatā*, offers *naivedya* and takes it subsequently, then demerit of some sort in worship is created under the notion that anything dedicated to the deity is not to be taken back. But as Krishna Mishra in the *Kālasarvasva* (p. 380)[8] puts it the merit created in taking *viṣṇunaivedya* after its offering is greater than that created by taking the same in daily worship.

It is observed that although these two views differ from each other, still, in practice, these two views coincide under certain conditional options (*vyavasthitavikalpa*). Any Vaiṣṇava-householder belonging to any sect does not take the *naivedya* of his *iṣṭadevatā* offered in daily worship. But the Vaiṣṇava Sannyāsins and Vairāgins are in favour of taking *naivedya* as even though it is offered in honour of their own *iṣṭadevatā* i.e. Viṣṇu. This is maintained under the influence of the Dharmaśāstras upon the Vaiṣṇavism of Orissa.

It is an accepted tradition all over India that *naivedya* of Śiva is not to be taken even by the Śaivites. But we find some sort of exception in case of *naivedya* as offered in honour of Lord Liṅgarāja at Bhubaneswar as recorded in the *Kālasarvasva* of Krishna Mishra. According to him the *naivedya* offered in honour of Lord Liṅgarāja is not considered to be the *śiva-naivedya*. The Vaiṣṇavas are inclined to consider it as the *viṣṇunaivedya*. Here Liṅgarāja, although Śiva, as a matter of fact, is treated as a devotee of Lord Viṣṇu, is supposed to take the *viṣṇunaivedya*. That is why anything offered in honour of Liṅgarāja is at first, dedicated to Viṣṇu and subsequently offered to Liṅgarāja. This conception in respect of the acceptability of *naivedya* gives encouragement to the Vaiṣṇavas of Orissa to be liberal. On the basis of this the *smārta-vaiṣṇavas* show their inclination to take Liṅgarāja (Śiva) as Viṣṇu and his *naivedya* as the *viśṇunaivedya*. This peculiarity in Orissan Vaiṣṇavism has been richly corroborated by Krishna Mishra with the help of the text of the *Ekāmrapurāṇa* quoted in the *Kālasarvasva* (p. 381).[9]

It is an accepted custom in Vaiṣṇavite life in general that the Vaiṣṇavas decorate their body with the signs of Viṣṇu's *āyudhas*, i.e. the weapons—mace, conch (though, conch is not a weapon) and wheel in order to remind the life of Kṛṣṇa to the public for the reason that they can recall the very theme of Kṛṣṇa's life and name as well. It is note-worthy that *Viṣṇu smaraṇa* is a form of atonement of sins.

Just like the sacred thread being used as an insignia under Brāhmaṇism, the signs of mace, conch and wheel are decorated upon the body to signify ones adherence to Vaiṣṇavism as per prescription of each sect such decoration forms part of a Vaiṣṇava's *nityakarman*. But afer answering the call of nature one has to wash off those signs decorated upon the body and new signs of those *āyudhas* are to be posted afresh. We are told by the Nibandhakāras that the old signs of the Viṣṇu's weapons are also to be washed off and new signs along with a *tulasīmalā* are to be borne by one before *sandhyāvandana*. Therefore, the Vaiṣṇavites of Orissa decorate their bodies with the prescribed signs with the help of *gopīcandana* twice daily. Narasiṁha Vājapeyin records this Vaiṣṇavite-tradition in the *Nityācarapradīpa*[10] which has been followed by Krishna Mishra in the *Kālasarvasva*.[11] From the standpoint of the *Kālasarvasva*, it is observed that Krishna Mishra fails to corroborate this tradition of Orissan Vaiṣṇavas from the Śastric text. Moreover, he tries to vindicate this tradition from the local customs of Orissa using the very term *ata eva vṛddhāḥ* (i.e. thus established).

According to the Vedic *smārta*-tradition, while the Brāhmaṇas are entitled to enter into the *sannyāsāśrama*, other varnas are not allowed for the same. They are only allowed up to the *vānaprasthāśrama*. In the Vaiṣṇavite tradition all are allowed to follow the *sannyāsāśrama* according to the Āgamic provision irrespective of individual castes. On acceptance of the *sannyāsāśrama*, the Vaiṣṇavas, in accordance with their sect-wise *dīkṣā*, are divided into the traditional four sects namely Śrī (Ramanuja), Sanaka (Nimbārka), Brāhma (Mādhva) and Rūdra (Vallabha) sects while the Sannyāsins of the Śrī sect are worshippers of Sālagrāma Nārāyaṇa, Lakṣmī and Nārāyaṇa or Sītā and Rāma, those of the Sanaka sect are adorers of Kṛṣṇa. The Mādhva and the Vallabha sects worship Viṣṇu with Lakṣmī as consort and Rādhā-Kṛṣṇa respectively. In Orissan Vaiṣṇavite tradition the householder Vaiṣṇavas belong mostly to the Śri sect.

They are advised to take initiation from a *guru* of a particular sect who is a householder Vaiṣṇava himself. In case of a housewife, if the husband has been initiated in a Vaiṣṇava faith and the wife desires to take initiation subsequently, she has to take permission from her husband. Krishna Mishra corroborates this tradition by quoting a Purāṇic-Smṛti-text quoted in the *Kālasarvasva* (p. 369).[12]

In case of widows, the tradition develops in a separate direction. Under the rule of Śrī sect the widow can take *nārāyaṇa-mantra* through Vaiṣṇavite initiation and become eligible to worship Sālagrāma Nārāyaṇa. In Orissan Vaiṣṇavism, however, the widows initiated to Vaiṣṇavism are treated as Sannyāsins belonging to *kuṭicaka*-category. All of them including those who belong to Śrī sect are entitled to worship Kṛṣṇa along with Rādhā. But if they are initiated in Sanaka sect, they are allowed to worship Vāsudeva Kṛṣṇa, but not Gopīnātha Kṛṣṇa or Rādhākṛṣṇa. In this way the householder life for the Vaiṣṇavas in Orissa differs. For the Vaiṣṇavas of Brāhma sect, the parafernalia of Dvaita school (Mādhvas) are to be followed. Although the Nibandhkāras have taken much pains in framing rules for Vaiṣṇavas under Smṛti principles still they have taken the *Bhāgavata Mahāpurāṇa* as their chief authority.

Taking recourse to this sort of endeavour, Mitra Mishra, the celebrated author of the *Vīramitrodaya* has completed a volume devoting to this sensitive area entitled as the *Bhaktiprakāśa*. For rationalization of Vaiṣṇavite tradition of Orissa Krishna Mishra wrote the *Bhaktisarvasva* like the *Bhaktiprakāśa* incorporating all the dicta meant for Vaiṣṇavism, the lines of which are found quoted in the *Kālasarvasva*. But unfortunately the *Bhaktisarvasva* has not been discovered so far. This way many facets of Vaiṣṇavism in Orissa are traced in the Nibandhas of the Dharmaśāstra.

It is observed that:

(a) The Orissan Vaiṣṇavas accept Jagannāth as Kṛṣṇa.

(b) The Orissan Vaiṣṇavas very prominently mark the association of Hari with Hara in *dolāyātrā* as a result of which Śaivism has been amalgamated with Vaiṣṇavism and *vice-versa*.

(c) In Orissan Vaiṣṇavism worship of Durgā has also been accepted. Here Viṣṇu or Kṛṣṇa is designated as Mādhava. In this way Durgā Mādhava worship is evolved in course of time. During Dussera in the month of *Āśvina, the durgāmādhava-yātrā* is observed.

These three bear influence of the Smṛtis upon the Vaiṣṇavism of Orissa.

It is further suggested that an attempt may be taken to trace out the interrelationship of Vaiṣṇavism, Śaivism and Śāktism under the Smārta system of Orissa.

References

1. Kane, P.V., *H.D.* Vol. V. Pt.I, Poona : B.O.R.I. 1974. PP. 122-3.
2. Rājaguru, Gadādhara, the *Kālasāra*, Cuttack : Radharamana Press, 1971. P. 25.

   महाभारते -

   आषाढस्य शिते पक्षे एकादश्यामुपोषितः।
   चातुर्मास्यव्रतं कुर्याद्, यत्किञ्चिन्नियतो नरः॥

   वाराहे -

   आषाढशुक्लैकादश्यां पौर्णमास्यां विशेषतः।
   चातुर्मास्यव्रतारम्भं कुर्यात्कर्कटसंङ्क्रमे॥
   अभावेऽपि तुलार्केऽपि मन्त्रेण नियमं व्रती।
3. See Ref. No. 2.
4. See Ref. No. 2.
5. The *Kālasāra*. *Op.cit.* p. 26.
   अशक्तः कार्तिके मासि व्रतं कुर्यात् पुरोदितम्। पुरोदितं चातुर्मास्योक्तम्।
6. The *Kālasāra*. p. 25.
   चैतन्यमतानुयायिगौडवैष्णवैस्तु आश्विनशुक्लैकादशीं यावत् व्रतमाचर्यते। तत्र शुक्लैकादश्यां पारणे सम्यक् प्रमाणं न दृश्यते। इति तत्पक्षेऽपि पूर्णिमापर्यन्तं व्रताचरणं समीचीनम्। तथा चाचारस्य श्रीपुरुषोत्तमक्षेत्रे श्रीजगन्नाथप्रासादे दर्शनात्॥
7. Mishra, Krishna, The *Kālasarvasva* (ed. B.N. Swain), Puri, 1997, p. 380.
   यद्यपि वाजपेयिभिर्विधिनैवेद्यमपि द्विजभक्ष्यमुक्तं तथापि तद् वैष्णवनिषिद्धम्।
8. The *Kālasarvasva*. p. 380.
   यद्यपि स्वपूजाकृतविष्णुनैवेद्यं पूजावैगुण्याय स्वाभक्ष्यमिति वाजपेयिभिरुक्तं तदपि तद्वैगुण्याल्प-दोषो विष्णुनैवेद्याशनफलभूम्ना कूपखानकन्दायान्निरस्यत एव।
9. The *Kālasarvasva*. p. 381.
   यो मानचर्य नरो भुङ्क्ते भविता तस्य गौरवमित्येकाम्रपुराणे भुवनेश्वरनैवेद्यस्य विष्णुदेयत्वात् ''न लिङ्गं भुवनेश्वरः'' इति तस्य शिवत्वनिषेधपूर्वकविष्णुत्वातिदेशाच्च लिङ्गराजनैवेद्यं स्मार्तवैष्णव-भक्ष्यं प्रतीयते।
10. Vajapeyin, Narasiṁha, the *Nityācārapradīpa*, Vol. I, Calcutta: *A.B.*, p. 358.
11. The *Kālasarvasva*, p. 384.
    अत एव वृद्धाः - यज्ञोपवीतवद्धार्याः शङ्खचक्रादयः एव। इति स्थितेऽपि गोपीचन्दनशङ्खचक्रादिकं मलमूत्रादौ प्रोञ्छयन्ति.......इदमनुसन्धाय सिंहवाजपेयिभिरपि स्नानानन्तरं सन्ध्यातः पूर्वं तुलसीपद्माक्षादिधारणमुक्तमिति दिक्।
12. The *Kālasarvasva*. p. 369.
    स्त्रीणां विशेषतो दद्यात् पतिभक्तिसमन्विताम्। पत्यनुज्ञाकृतां दीक्षामित्यर्थः।

Interpretation of the Dharmaśāstra

The interpretation of law is an important branch of jurisprudence. The principles of interpretation help in understanding the correct meaning of a provision of law. A few important questions which arise for consideration while implementing or enforcing a provision of law are posed here.

(1) What is the real meaning that should be given to a particular word used in a particular law, when it is not defined in the law and when it has a general meaning as well as a technical meaning?

(2) If a sentence used in law is ambiguous, how should its meaning be ascertained?

(3) If two provisions in a law are seemingly contradictory, what is the course required to be adopted?

(4) If a provision is not happily worded or the construction of a sentence is defective, how should the real meaning be ascertained?

(5) Whether a particular law which stipulates a certain act being performed in a particular manner is mandatory or directory?

These problems are of everyday occurrence in courts when the parties opposing each other contend placing two differing interpretations on the same provision. The power and duty of the court is to implement the law, and for this purpose it is obliged to ascertain the real meaning of the law and apply it accordingly. The courts have no power to change the law. That power belongs to the Legislature. It is not open to the courts to usurp the function of the Legislature by giving an unwarranted interpretation to any law.[1] Therefore, they have to follow certain well recognized norms or rules to interpret the law in order to resolve the various problems regarding interpretation arising before them. Under the modern legal systems, a large number of well settled and accepted principles governing interpretation of law have been developed.

1. The Importance of Mīmāṁsā and Its Interpretation

In the ancient Indian society, the rules of *dharma* incorporated in the Vedas, the Smṛtis and the Dharmaśāstras covered every aspect of human activity. The Vedas, the primordial source of *dharma*, mostly prescribed rules and procedure for religious rituals and sacrifices. The source of the Vedas was believed to be divine and, therefore, the ritualistic rules contained in them were considered inviolable and unalterable by the society. But the provisions in the Vedas were in a cryptic and difficult language. Therefore, the possibility of divergent interpretations was always there. In order to resolve this difficulty and for the purpose of understanding their correct import, Mīmāṁsā (rules of interpretation) came to be written by those who were eminent Vedic scholars and logicians and who were well-versed both in language (*bhaṣa*) and grammar (Vyākaraṇa). Mīmāṁsā became an important branch of study of the Dharmaśāstras. Maharṣi Jaimini is the oldest renowned author of the monumental work under the title Mīmāṁsā. He laid down the principles of interpretation of the Vedic provisions regulating religious sacrifices and rituals. Though the principles so laid down were for the purpose of interpreting the Vedic provisions, many of those principles were so fundamental that they could be applied for interpreting the *vyavahāra* portions of the Smṛtis which contained civil and criminal laws. Leading Smṛti writers and commentators of the Smṛtis fully utilized the fundamental rules of Mīmāṁsā laid down by Jaimini for clarifying and expounding the several complicated provisions of law. Therefore, Mīmāṁsā, though originated in interpreting the rules governing performance of religious acts, came to occupy an important position in the ancient legal system of this country.

Mr. Colebrooke, who recognized the importance of Mīmāṁsā in the interpretation of Hindu law, observed:

> "A case is proposed either specified in Jaimini's text or supplied by his scholiasts. Upon this a doubt or question is raised, and a solution of it is suggested, which is refuted, and a right conclusion established in its stead. The disquisitions of the Mīmāṁsā bear, therefore, a certain resemblance to judicial questions; and in fact, the Hindu law being blended with the religion of the people, the same modes of reasoning are applicable, and are applied to the one as to the other. The logic of the Mīmāṁsā is the logic of the law—the rule of interpretation of civil and religious ordinances. Each case is examined and determined upon general principles; and from the cases decided, the principles may be collected. A well ordered arrangement of them would constitute the philosophy of the law, and this is, in truth, what has been attempted in the Mīmāṁsā."[2]

Sir John Edge stressed the importance of Mīmāṁsā (rules of interpretation) in the interpretation of the Hindu law as follows:

> "The question is, 'How is the text of Vasiṣṭha to be construed? It must clearly be construed according to the rules for the construction of the texts of the sacred books of the Hindu law, if authoritative rules on the subject exist. That rules for the construction of the sacred texts and laws of the Hindus do exist cannot be disputed, although those rules have been frequently overlooked or not referred to by Judges or English text writers probably because they are in Sanskrit and have, so far as I am aware, not yet been translated. That they are rules of the highest authority is obvious from the manner in which they have been referred to by Mr. Colebrooke."[3]

The above observation by eminent scholars and judges and the prescription of the knowledge of Mīmāṁsā as one of the qualifications for judges indicates the importance of Mīmāṁsā as also its relevance to the interpretation of the provisions of positive law. At this stage, it should be mentioned that Mīmāṁsā is a vast and independent subject and, therefore, in the nature of things it constitutes an independent subject for study. However, as indicated above, in view of its importance to the branch of law, legal history would be incomplete without any reference to the rules of Mīmāṁsā. Hence, the fundamental rules of Mīmāṁsā which are relevant to the interpretation of forensic law alone, are set out in this part and that too only to a very limited extent. As stated earlier, the Sūtras which are relevant for interpretation of law originated with reference to interpretation of rules regulating performance of religious ceremonies or sacrifices. Therefore, while setting out the relevant Sūtras, the reference to their origin is left out as unnecessary in many cases as it would serve no useful purpose, but only the principles laid down and their relevancy in the context of interpretation of law are given.

Dr. Thibaut, in his introduction to the translation of the *Arthasaṅgraha*, observes:

> "The Mīmāṁsā certainly deserves greater attention than it has hitherto received. It has indeed none of the attractions which the other Darśanas derive from the speculative character of their content; its scope is limited and the nature of the investigations in which it is engaged leaves no room for high flights of imagination. But it possesses counterbalancing advantages. Its subject matter is of a positive nature, its method is sound and its reasoning in most cases convincing."[4]

Ganganath Jha in his introduction to the third volume of his English translation of the *Śabarabhāṣya* which is an elaborate and authoritative commentary on Jaimini states:

> "Unfortunately, for modern Hindus, the examples that Jaimini chose for illustrating his rules of interpretation

were all from sacrificial rituals. Naturally, during his time, every Brāhmaṇa was familiar with these rituals, and, hence, they were regarded as providing most suitable illustrative examples. Latterly, however, sacrificial ritual has gradually all but disappeared from the life of the Hindus; and this has led to the neglect of the study of the Mīmāṁsā Śāstra. Even so, it continues to be recognized that the rules that Jaimini evolved are still found useful in the interpretation of law texts; and they have been so widely used that there is no important Legal Digest which does not draw upon the *Nyāyas* of Jaimini."

K.L. Sarkar, in his 'Tagore Law Lectures 1905', observes:

"Jaimini's Sūtras are quoted and discussed in the *Mitākṣarā*. They are referred to as the venerable old authorities. So, manifestly, they cannot be subsequent in date to the *Mitākṣarā*. By the Hindu tradition, Jaimini's Sūtras preceded the Vedānta Śāstra.

But whatever be the date of the Sūtras, they are decidedly the most comprehensive and prevailing authorities on the subject of interpretation. Jaimini's work, for the first time, reduces the subject of interpretation to what is called *Darśana* or Philosophy and, in effect, may well be regarded as a scientific system of interpretation."[5]

2. Knowledge of Mīmāṁsā was a Qualification for a Judge

Mīmāṁsā was declared to be a part of the knowledge of the Śruti and the Smṛtis, vide Yaj. 1-3. and consequently considered as one of the qualifications to be possessed by a person for being appointed as a judge.[6]

The prescription of Mīmāṁsā as a qualification for judges spells out its importance in the interpretation of civil and criminal laws.

3. Mīmāṁsā Scholar to be a Member of the Pariṣad (Assembly)

For the purpose of ascertaining as to what should be the law in respect of a matter not covered by the Vedas, the Smṛtis and the customary law, such a question was required to be referred to a legal assembly (*pariṣad*) consisting of ten members. One out of them was required to be a Mīmāṁsā scholar.[7]

4. Procedure for Interpretation

The procedure adopted by the Mīmāṁsākas to settle the meaning of a provision of the Vedic or Smṛti text has been to take up each issue and consider arguments both for and against, and to arrive at a final decision. All these aspects put together was called *Adhikaraṇa* (a complete theme). Kumārila explains the method as follows:

विषयो विशयश्चैव पूर्वपक्षस्तथोत्तरम्।
निर्णयश्चेति पञ्चाङ्गं शास्त्रेऽधिकरणं स्मृतम्॥

> "The text under consideration, the doubt concerning it, the first side, the other side or answer, and the conclusion, all these constitute an *Adhikaraṇa*."

The same was the method adopted by Śabara.

(i) The subject matter which requires interpretation is set out first.

(ii) The doubt which has arisen in the matter of such interpretation is explained.

(iii) *Pūrvapakṣa* (prima facie argument) is set out.

(iv) *Siddhānta* (the answer), i.e., the final view taken in the matter together with reasons indicating the pertinence or relevancy of such an interpretation along with the rules of interpretation applied is set out, which forms the concluding part of an *Adhikaraṇa*.

The principles laid down as above indicate the systematic way in which the Mīmāṁsākas proceeded to interpret any provision.

5. Rule of Three Debts – Key to Interpretation

Jaimini declared that there are three fundamental principles which serve as the key to the interpretation of the Smṛtis.

They are that every Hindu is under a duty to discharge the following three kinds of debts:

(1) *Devarṇa* — Debt due to God by performing religious sacrifices.

(2) *Ṛṣīrṇa* — Debt due to saints by the acquisition of and imparting knowledge.

(3) *Pitṛrṇa* — Debt due to parents by becoming a householder and maintaining the continuity of the family institution and tradition by begetting children.

Śabarasvāmin interprets this maxim and holds that this 'rule of three debts' is binding on all the Aryans.

K. L. Sarkar, on the importance of the three-debt formula, states:

> "Therefore, in interpreting texts relating to the duties and rights of the Hindus, these principles must always be kept in view, and it should be presumed that all texts are more or less intended to promote these three classes of duties.
>
> The three presumptions arising from the above maxim are in favour of (1) securing spiritual welfare, (2) encouraging learning and skill and (3) maintaining the family institution and traditions.
>
> Jīmūtavāhana, in treating the principles of succession, discriminates between the Śruti texts, many of which are conflicting with one another, mainly relying on the presumption in favour of spiritual welfare. This theory of spiritual benefit is identical with the principle of *svarga-kamo yajeta.*[8]
>
> In interpreting the texts about self-acquisitions, regard is tacitly paid by him to the principles in favour of encouraging *vidyā* (learning).
>
> Vijñāneśvara, in treating the subject of right by succession, guides himself by almost exclusively following the presumption in favour of the family institution.

In fact, the maxim of the three debts which Jaimini lays down forms the keynote and constitutes the nucleus of those nice and elaborate principles which were developed later.

It is interesting to observe how faithfully the Hindu nation has followed the Vedic commands regarding sacrifice, learning and the household institution. They have been trying to discharge these three debts in right earnest all through.

The debt to the gods, viz., that of sacrifice, was in former times to be satisfied by performing *yāgas* and *yajñas* at stated times and occasions. Latterly, the life of every individual, from birth to death is, at every stage, a part-payment of this debt. A Hindu must be conceived in the womb with a sacrifice, commence eating with a sacrifice, begin the student life with a sacrifice, marry with a sacrifice and his death is followed by a sacrifice.

As regards the debt to the Ṛṣis, *viz.*, acquiring knowledge, this debt was perhaps more sedulously paid in the early times than latterly. The study of the Vedas led to the study of the Vedāṅgas (branches of the Vedas), grammar, astronomy, the art of music, the art of medicine, the art of using weapons of war, etc.

The debt to the forefathers, that of perpetuating the family name and the family history, leads to various means of discharging it, availing various kinds of substituted sons, of which at present the son by adoption only is in vogue.

The civil law of the Hindus is at every step marked with the influence of the three-debt obligation. Matters of right and status are mixed up with the debt to the gods, *viz.*, that of sacrifice. Privileges are unsparingly conferred on men of learning. Gifts to them are praised as being acts of the greatest merit. In fact, some of the Smṛtis go rather too far, almost to the extent of abusing this principle relating to the debt to the Ṛṣis.

> As regards the other debt consisting of household duties, Hindu law is marked with its impress in various ways, such as the invariable duty of maintaining dependent members of the family, the requisition to make adoptions, the presumption in favour of joint family and the like.
>
> Therefore, it is clear that whenever two constructions of a text are possible, one tending to the discharge of one or other of the three debts, and the other inconsistent with such discharge, the former construction is to be adopted and not the latter."

It was the firm belief that the ultimate goal of all the provisions of the Vedas and Dharmaśāstras was to ensure the discharging of the three debts by every individual and this was possible only by following the path of *dharma* in all walks of life as prescribed, and, therefore, every provision was to be interpreted so as to be in conformity with the rule of the three debts.

The above principle was also adopted in the interpretation of the Smṛtis which constituted the basic legal texts governing Hindu society. This principle of interpreting the law in the light of the philosophy or object which inspired its making is comparable to the modern principles, namely—(i) that the preamble to any law including constitutional law which sets out the basic objectives of the law or the Constitution, as the case might be, as the key for interpretation of the provisions incorporated therein; and (ii) that whenever two constructions of a provision of law are possible, one which conforms to the constitutional law and another inconsistent with it, the former should be accepted and the latter rejected.

The Hindu jurists accepted the view of Jaimini that the provisions contained in the Smṛtis should be interpreted so as to promote and fulfil the object of satisfying the three debts. To illustrate the law of inheritance, the doctrine of pious obligation, the recognition of adoption, and the law on that topic, originated from the principle of *Pitṛṛṇa*. The making of gifts during religious sacrifices and the law governing gifts, owed its origin to the principle of *Devarṇa*. The great stress laid on acquisition of knowledge and its dissemination and the law on the question of the gains of learning, emanated from the principle of *Ṛṣīrṇa*. Further, as pointed out in the law relating to debts, the fourth debt, viz., debt towards society (*Samājarṇa*), was recognized in the great epic *Mahābhārata* and this principle also influenced considerably the interpretation of law for public good as well as the character of the people, and is evidenced by the historic records relating to gifts recognized and made for public purposes and selfless sacrifies made by innumerable persons, known and unknown, in rendering service to the nation or society in all walks of life.

6. Rule to Resolve Conflicts between Different Sources of Law

The source of law consisted of the Śruti, the Smṛtis composed by several authors and the Purāṇas as also *sadācara* (usage and custom). Naturally, the provision in one source, in some cases, could be contrary to a corresponding provision in another source. Rules to resolve such conflicts were laid down.

(1) Vyāsa: 1, *V.* 4:

श्रुतिस्मृतिपुराणानां विरोधो यत्र दृश्यते।
तत्र श्रौतं प्रमाणं तु तयोर्द्वैधे स्मृतिर्वरा॥

When there is a conflict between the Vedas, the Smṛtis and the Purāṇas, the Vedas should prevail, and as between the Smṛtis and the Purāṇas, the Smṛtis are superior.

The above rule indicates the comparative efficacy or superiority of the provisions in the various sources of *dharma*. They were placed in the following order: (i) the Vedas, (ii) the Smṛtis and (iii) the Purāṇas.

(1) Why Smṛtis should be regarded as authority?

An argument that only the Vedas (Śruti) should be considered as authority and not the Smṛtis, was considered and answered by Jaimini.

Jaimini 1-3-1:

धर्मस्य शब्दमूलत्वादशब्दमनपेक्षं स्यात् ॥

Pūrvapakṣa or prima facie view: In as much as *dharma* is based upon the Vedas, what is not in the Vedas should be disregarded.

The above statement indicates that the paramount authority of the Vedas was accepted. Therefore, if a provision in the Smṛtis was found to be in conformity with a known Vedic text, there was no dispute about its validity. The question, however, raised was why a Smṛti rule should be regarded as binding unless a Vedic text from which it emanated was known. It was argued for the Pūrvapakṣin, in support of his case, that giving credence to such a Smṛti (reminiscence) text would be meaningless on the following analogy:

या हि वन्ध्या स्मरेदिदं मे दौहित्रकृतमिति न मे दुहिताऽस्तीति
मत्वा न जातुचिदसौ प्रतीयात् सम्यगेतज्ज्ञानमिति ॥

"Remembrance under the circumstances would be just like the remembrance that a barren woman might have to the effect that 'such and such act was done by my daughter's son'; if she ever had such a remembrance, then, knowing as she does that she had no daughter, she could never believe that remembrance of the son's act to be correct.

तस्य कुतः । जात्यन्धान्तरात् । एवं जात्यन्धपरम्परायामपि सत्यां
नैव जातुचित् सम्प्रतीयुर्विद्वांसः सम्यग्दर्शनमेतदिति ।
अतो नाऽदर्तव्यमेवंजातीयकम् अनपेक्षं स्यादिति ॥

This case would resemble the case where a person born blind says, 'I remember this particular colour',—and being asked, 'How could you have had any cognition of colour?', he points to another person blind from birth; it being asked from where this latter derived his cognitíon, another person blind from birth is pointed out; so that even though there is an unbroken line of tradition of persons born blind, no sensible people can ever regard this remembrance as right cognition."

*Siddhānta J*1-3-2 *and* 3:

अपि वा कर्तृसामान्यात् प्रमाणमनुमानं स्यात् ॥२ ॥
विरोधे त्वनपेक्षं स्यादसति ह्यनुमानम् ॥ ३ ॥

(i) The Smṛti (Remembrance) is *Pramāṇa* (trustworthy), as there would be an inference (presumption) of its having a basis in the Vedas.

(ii) Provided where there is conflict (between the Vedas and a Smṛti rule) the Smṛti rule should be disregarded, because the presumption holds good only when there is no conflict.

In support of the above view the reasoning is given by Śabara:

ननु नोपलभन्त एवंजातीयकं ग्रन्थम्। अनुपलभमाना अप्यनुमिमीरन्, विस्मरणमप्युपपद्यत इति। तदुपपन्नत्वात् पूर्वविज्ञानस्य। त्रैवर्णिकानां स्मरतां विस्मरणस्य च उपपन्नत्वाद् ग्रन्थानुमानम् उपपद्यत इति प्रमाणं स्मृतिः ॥

"Says the Opponent—'But people do not find any such Vedic text as you would infer as the basis for the Smṛtis. Even if they do not actually find it, they would infer it. It is quite possible also that the text upon which the Smṛti is based was actually known to the Smṛti writer, but has since been forgotten.

Thus, in the case of the 'remembrance' of men of the three higher castes, the necessary 'previous cognition' being traceable,—and it being possible that the texts from which that cognition proceeded have been forgotten,—the inference of the text becomes justifiable; consequently the Smṛti text is trustworthy."

In the concluding portion, the validity of the Smṛti rules *inter alia* that (1) the *Aṣṭaka* rite, namely 'the worship of the divinity of night should be performed', (ii) 'the student should follow the teacher', (iii) 'tanks should be dug' and (iv) 'drinking water booths should be set up', were upheld. The conclusions read:

अष्टकालिङ्गश्च मन्त्रा वेदे दृश्यन्ते, 'यां जनाः प्रतिनन्दन्ति' इत्येवमादयः ।
तथा प्रत्युपस्थितनियमानामाचाराणां दृष्टार्थत्वादेव प्रामाण्यम् ॥

"*Aṣṭaka* is spoken of as the divinity of night eulogised as the 'consort of the year'; here we have a Vedic text speaking of *Aṣṭaka* as an object of adoration; and this is taken as indicative of the desirability of performing the rites of *Aṣṭaka.*"

गुरोरनुगमात्प्रीतो गुरुरध्यापयिष्यति, ग्रन्थग्रन्थिभेदिनश्च न्यायान् परितुष्टो वक्ष्यतीति। तथा च दर्शयति, तस्माच्छ्रेयांसं पूर्वं यन्तं पापीयान् पश्चादन्वेष्यतीति। प्रपास्तडागानि च परोपकाराय, न धर्मायेत्येवावगम्यन्ते ॥

"As regards the other instances of the Smṛti rules of conduct quoted above (relating to the 'following of the teacher', 'the digging of tanks', 'establishing drinking water booths', and so forth), their authority (reliability, trustworthiness) rests in the fact of the apparently useful purposes served by them; for instance, (a) if one follows his teacher, the teacher becomes pleased and teaches him with care, and also, being satisfied with the pupil, explains to him the reasoning that go to solve the various difficulties that present themselves in the course of the study of the texts. This rule of following the teacher derives support also from the Vedic text—'Therefore, the inferior always walks behind the superior walking ahead' (hence, indicates the propriety of the superior persons being followed by the inferior), and (b) Drinking water booths and tanks are philanthropic works conducive to the benefit of the people."

तेन ये दृष्टार्थास्ते तत एव प्रमाणम्।
ये तु अदृष्टार्थास्तेषु वैदिकशब्दानुमानमिति ॥

"Thus then, those rules (of the Smṛtis) that serve apparently useful purposes are trustworthy on that account, and in the case of those that pertain to transcendental purposes, we shall infer the Vedic texts as their basis (and on this basis will rest their trustworthy character)."

Thus the answer furnished to the question or the point raised by the Pūrvapakṣin was that when there was no conflict between a Smṛti rule and the known Śruti texts, the former should be presumed to be valid on the assumption that the Smṛti (memory) must have emanated from a Vedic text which had been forgotten on account of human failings.

(2) Smṛti rule invalid for improper motive:

Though the validity of the Smṛti provisions, in the absence of conflict with a known Śruti provision, was to be presumed, it was not an irrebuttable presumption. If it was shown that it came to be incorporated for collateral considerations, such a provision was held not binding and had to be disregarded.

Applying these principles, Śabara declared a few of these rules invalid. Though such invalidated rules were with reference to religious ceremonies, the reasoning behind their invalidation is forthright and forceful, and even now useful.

Example 1:

(i) Rule of the Smṛti—The whole of an *Audumbara* post (piece of wood from the *Audumbara* tree used in a religious ceremony) should be covered by cloth.

(ii) Rule of the Śruti with which it conflicts: One should sing a *sāman* touching the *Audumbara* post.

After a thorough argument the conclusion recorded was that the Smṛti rule was invalid on the ground of its conflict with the Śruti (because touching of the post as directed by the Śruti would be impossible if the whole of it was covered by cloth) and also on the ground that the Smṛti rule had proceeded from a selfish motive.

The conclusion reads:

प्रमाणायां स्मृतौ स्पर्शनं व्यामोहः ।
स्पर्शने प्रमाणे स्मृतिर्व्यामोहः ॥

If the Smṛti rule (regarding covering up the whole post) is right, then the touching (laid down in the Śruti) is wrong, and if the touching is right, then the Smṛti is wrong.

तस्मादुक्तं श्रुतिविरुद्धा स्मृतिरप्रमाणमिति ।
अतश्च सर्ववेष्टनादि नाऽदरणीयम् ॥

Consequently what has been said in the Smṛti regarding the 'covering of the whole post' has to be disregarded.

लोभाद्वास आदित्समाना औदुम्बरीं कृत्स्नां वेष्टितवन्तः केचित् ।
तत्स्मृतेर्बीजम् ॥

Some greedy priests being desirous of having a large piece of cloth, covered up the whole of the post at a certain performance; this was what gave rise to the Smṛti rule (that the whole post should be covered up).

Example 2:

The Smṛti rule: One should remain a Vedic student for forty-eight years.

The Śruti rule: One should install the fire when a son is born to him and when his hair is still black.

The Smṛti rule was declared bad on the ground that it came into conflict with the Śruti and was based on irrelevant considerations. The conclusion reads:

अष्टाचत्वारिंशद्वर्षाणि वेदब्रह्मचर्यचरणं 'जातपुत्रः
कृष्णकेशोऽग्नीनादधीत' इत्यनेन विरुद्धम् ॥

The Smṛti rule (one should remain a Vedic student for forty-eight years) is in conflict with the rule that 'one should install the fire when a son is born to him and his hair is still black'. (If a man is to remain a student for 48 years, he would not marry before he is 55 or 56 years old, by which time his hair would cease to be black, and so he could not install the fire before marriage).

अपुंस्त्वं प्रच्छादयन्तश्च अष्टाचत्वारिंशद्वर्षाणि वेदब्रह्मचर्यं चरितवन्तः ।
तत एषा स्मृतिरित्यवगम्यते ॥

Some people, with a view to conceal their want of virility, remained students of religion for forty-eight years; and this is what gave rise to the Smṛti rule permitting such a course. (For this reason also, no authority can attach to the Smṛti which is found to have its source in such motives).

(3) Worldly motive renders the Smṛti rule invalid:

वैसर्जनहोमीयं वासोऽध्वर्युर्गृह्णाति ॥

Example 3:

The rule of the Smṛti: The cloth used at the *Vaisarjana Homa* is to be taken by the Adhvaryu priest.

This rule, though it did not conflict with any Śruti rule, was declared invalid on the ground of the selfish motive behind it. The conclusion reads:

अप्रमाणं स्मृतिः । अत्रान्यन्मूलम् । लोभादाचरितवन्तः केचित् तत एषा स्मृतिः । उपपन्नतरं चैतत् वैदिकवचनकल्पनात् ॥

The *Siddhānta* view however is that such Smṛti rules cannot be regarded as authoritative; because, at the root of these, there is something totally different from motives of *dharma;* the fact being that some people did such an act through greed, and this gave rise to the Smṛti rule. This view (rejecting the authority of such Smṛtis) is more reasonable than the assuming of Vedic texts in their support.

(4) Provision of the *Manusmṛti* held invalid on the ground of conflict:

Vijñānesvara declared Man. IX. 106 as also Man. IX. 112, which provided for unequal distribution of shares as among sons by providing a higher share for the eldest son, invalid on two grounds:

(i) giving of an unequal share to the eldest son was invalid as it was opposed to a citation in the Śruti which supports equal distribution;

(ii) that it was disapproved by the people.

7. Validity of Sadācāra (Custom and Usage)

Naturally the Śruti and the Smṛtis could not have covered problems and situations for all time. Therefore, custom or usage which was agreeable to the convenience of the people (without bad motive), was also accepted as the source of law.

On this question Śabara considered the validity of a few Smṛti rules and opined as follows:

> अपि च शौचं दक्षिणाचारता यज्ञोपवीतित्वं चैवंजातीयका अर्था व्यवधातारो न भवन्ति। सर्वपदार्थानां शेषभूतत्वात्। तस्मादाचमनादीनां प्रामाण्यम्॥

> "The Smṛti rules dwelt upon here are such as (a) 'An act should be done after rinsing the mouth', (b) 'An act should be done by one wearing the *yajñopavīta*', (c) 'One should perform the acts with the right hand' and such others, with what then these acts be in conflict?" (....there is nothing against the authority of the Smṛti rule in question.)"

> On the above reasoning, it is concluded:

> "...Further, 'performing with the right hand', and 'wearing the sacrificial thread—constitute purity (or cleanliness), and such things are not regarded as interruptions at all; because, purity or cleanliness is a necessary adjunct to all actions."

> "From all this it follows that the Smṛti rules, relating to all these acts—rinsing, using the right hand, wearing the sacrificial thread and the like, are authoritative i.e., valid and trustworthy."

The above discussion indicates the reason for treating the Smṛtis and also *sadācāra* as sources of law in addition to the Śruti but subject to the condition that there was no conflict between the former and the latter. In fact the Smṛtis themselves laid down the rule that if there was conflict between the Smṛtis and the Śruti, the latter would prevail.

8. Test for Deciding Validity of Usage

Manu laid down that conscious satisfaction (*ātmatuṣṭi*) of those who are well informed in the Vedas was the test to decide the validity of usage. The test of *ātmatuṣṭi* was subjected to critical examination by Kumārila. He did not agree that *ātmatuṣṭi* (self-satisfaction) as the sole test for determining the validity of a custom or usage but held that it should satisfy a rational test also. In this behalf Kumārila observed:

के शिष्टाः ? ये सदाचाराः ॥

Who are well informed?
Those whose actions are sound.

सदाचाराश्च तत्कृताः ॥

Then whose actions are sound?
Of those who are well informed.

इतरेतराधीननिर्णयत्वादनिर्णयः ॥

This leaves us where we were.

Therefore he proceeded to state that *ātmatuṣṭi* alone was not a sure test. After a thorough discussion, he said:

तथाऽऽचारात्मतुष्ट्यादिधर्म्यं धर्ममयात्मनाम् ।
वेदोक्तमिति निश्चित्य ग्राह्यं धर्मबुभुत्सुभिः । इति ॥

"In order that a usage be valid it must be such that not only there must be absence of improper motives but also the desire for heavenly bliss should be its basis and a true believer in the Vedas is likely to observe it as a matter of duty."

Sharp intellect, absence of blind belief in or acceptance of the Smṛti rules, forceful ratiocination, all are at once patent in the above ruling given by Kumārila.

Colebrooke on the validity of usage states:

"Usage generally prevalent among good men and by them practised, as understanding it to be enjoined and, therefore, incumbent on them, is mediately, but not directly, evidence of duty; but it is not valid, if it be contrary to an express text.

....any usage which is inconsistent with a recorded recollection is not to be practised, so long as no express text of scripture is to support it."

The discussion so far made, illustration given and the conclusion reached disclose the following aspects:

(1) The Vedas were regarded as the first and inviolable source of *dharma*.

(2) As the Vedas were handed down from generation to generation (orally), the possibility of some of the Vedic injunctions having been missed or gone out of memory was accepted.

(3) The Smṛti writers were expected to incorporate in writing (obviously after the practice of writing came into existence) only such of the principles laid down in the Vedas and *sadācāra* which were not in conflict with the Vedas, though the actual text could not be traced or remembered. There was a presumption in favour of honesty and truthfulness of the Smṛti writers.

In this behalf Kumārila states:
"In the case of a Smṛti, corroborative text is assumed directly from the fact of its being compiled by people learned in the Vedas."

(4) Therefore, if the Smṛti writers recorded any rule, the presumption was that it was in conformity with a Vedic rule even if it be that that rule was not known i.e., was forgotten.

(5) If, however, a Smṛti rule contravened a known provision of the Vedas, that was to be treated as invalid, as the Smṛti writer could not incorporate any such rule into a Smṛti, as that would amount to remembering what did not exist, just like a born blind man cannot remember any colour. Therefore, any such rule, even if incorporated into the Smṛti, was invalid.

(6) (i) Even if a Smṛti rule did not conflict with any known provision of the Vedas, if any personal or selfish motive of anyone could be seen behind such a rule, want of *dharma* would be apparent from such a rule and, therefore, could not be deemed to have been sanctioned by the Vedas. In other words, the normal presumption in favour of a Smṛti rule, that it was in conformity with a provision of the Vedas which had gone out of memory, stands rebutted by the existence of a selfish motive.

(ii) In such a case the view rejecting the validity of a motivated rule is more reasonable than the view assuming support of a Vedic text in favour of such a rule.

(7) However, if on the other hand the rule only promotes public good or helps better implementation of a Vedic injunction, the presumption which favours its validity being more reasonable than its rejection, such a rule should be treated as valid.

The above tests were no doubt laid down to prove the validity of a Smṛti rule vis-a-vis the Śruti or the Vedas. But, in principle, we find a striking similarity to the following well accepted principles of interpretation in modern jurisprudence.

(i) Constitutional provisions are supreme.

(ii) There is always a presumption that legislators enact laws in conformity with the provisions of the Constitution or, in other words, that the legislative enactments are constitutionally valid.

(iii) However, if conflict is established, legislative enactment would be invalid.

(iv) Any order made under the law, by any authority on whom the power is conferred, is also presumed to be valid, but if it is found to contravene statutory provision, or made with bad motive, it is invalid.

Though the Smṛtis were regarded as of high authority and binding, the validity of any of their provisions was liable to be challenged. Actually, as shown above, Śabara, as also Vijñāneśvara, declared that some rules of the Smṛtis were invalid as having proceeded from bad motive or as being contrary to the Śruti.

References

1. Mangilal v. Sugan Chand, AIR 1965 SC 101.
2. Colebrooke's *Miscellanous Essays*, Vol. 1, p. 342.
3. T.L.L. 1905, pp.8-9.

4. T.L.L. 1905, p. 10.
5. T.L.L., 1905, pp. 29-30.
6. T.L.L. 1905, p. 18.
7. Man. XII - 111, p. 20.
8. *Svargakāmo yajeta* is a Vedic hymn which means those desirous of securing *Svarga* (heaven) should perform *yajña*. Though initially the word *yajña* appears to have been used to indicate a religious rite, in course of time the word acquired a very wide meaning, in that, performance of all the legitimate duties of an individual with utmost devotion, dedication and selflessness also came to be regarded as *yajña*. Thus the five fundamental duties of the King towards the kingdom were regarded as five *yajñas* to be performed by him.

The Dharmaśāstras and the Modern Age

I

Introduction

The very name of the subject, "Dharmaśāstras and the Modern Age," presupposes the doubt whether all that is said in them is applicable to life in the modern age. Dharmaśāstras are not treatises on ethics like the modern treatises on the subject; they are not philosophies of morality, analyses of moral experience, but ethical codes in which the duties of individuals and groups called castes etc., are codified. They are a mixture of ethical, social and positive laws used by judges in courts as well as by religious, political and ethical teachers. They include even laws about economic relationships like the laws of inheritance, obtaining of course at a time when economics was not yet a full-fledged discipline.

The question raised about the Dharmaśāstras of India may be raised about other ethical codes also, of the Muslims, Jews, Christians, Parsis etc. For there is a general question whether the codes of conduct given to a society some centuries ago can be and ought to be followed literally in the modern age. The opinion has become general that all ethical codes were composed to suit societies living in a certain set of circumstances, which are not now the same; and changes in conditions of life necessitate modifications in the codes. But at present we are mainly concerned with the ethical codes of India.

There are indeed orthodox people in India who do not wish to view the Dharmaśāstras in the perspective of history or social development, but as sacrosanct for ever. But such people are to be found in other communities also. Their attitude can easily be appreciated: all ethical codes are associated with certain institutionalized religions; they support the religions and are supported by them; and any change in the moral codes or even a critical attitude to them is considered to be a danger to religion, which promises redemption. But societies have been going through several kinds of transformation, economic, political and social and even religious ideas are getting more and more purified; and humanity is not going to admit that all this change is heading towards damnation. Unless the objections to reform are known to be not prompted by vested interests, they cannot have much weight.

II

Growth of Morality in Society

Anthropologists, sociologists, writers on ethics and law, and other scholars have shown that moral consciousness has a growth, that it differs from culture to culture, society to society, tribe to tribe, and then again from the less advanced to the more advanced cultures and civilizations. It is almost universally accepted that the development of moral consciousness determines the development of religious consciousness also, though it is not as commonly mentioned that the purification of religious consciousness influences the nature of moral consciousness by introducing a stronger sense of ethical relativism with regard to fixed moral laws and by strengthening tolerance in human relationships. The latter particularly holds of Indian religious consciousness as found in the Vedānta, which made the Hindu proverbially tolerant not only of other religions but also of other moral codes. It is of importance to note that originally the rules of moral conduct prescribed for the different castes and subcastes were motivated by the laudable and commendable desire to allow every group to follow its own moral traditions and forms of worship, which later on became a desire to insist upon its following them and to prevent it from changing them. The problem of caste was not merely one of fixing separate professions, but also of tribes and races and forms of cult and worship. India, which is determined to abolish caste system, has consistently to support all fight against race discriminations. And if the abolition on a world-wide scale materializes, the emergence of a new culture based upon new principles is bound to occur.

Ethics, as we find in modern works, is reflective morality. It appears in the history of man at quite a late stage. One may summarize the stages of the growth of morality in the following way:

1. First, there was only custom or tradition, which governed the conduct of primitive society. Tribal people may have their gods associated with different forms of conduct. But for an objective study, the gods are unimportant, the traditions handed down from generation to generation are important. Generally the leaders of the tribe do not question them even if no gods are associated with them.

2. Next, when a tribe comes into contact with another tribe having different customs and traditions, the idea dawns on the members of the tribe that customs and traditions can be different. Even apart from noticing the forms of conduct of another tribe, some members of the tribe may violate some traditions. Usually leaders of the tribe attribute calamities to such violations; but when they find that other tribes are prospering in spite of violating what they themselves consider to be right forms of conduct, some connivance at violations and a vague sense of ethical relativity begins to appear.

3. But these violations introduce some internal disorder. And when some tribes unite and constitute a nation or a larger society, the disorder is observed on a wider scale. Observation of different customs outside one's society introduces reflection; but the innovations and changes, which are in a

sense violations of the tradition, introduce unstability. Besides, when everything depends on tradition, and tradition is handed down from generation to generation, it depends, for exactness of detail, on the memory of individuals, which is not often reliable. Different persons may remember the same tradition in different ways, and their memories clash. It is in such situations that ethical codes are composed. They are meant, (1) to preserve the tradition in its exactness, (2) to prevent innovations and changes, (3) to offer ready guidance in detail for the administration of justice and (4) to relate the practices to the existing religion.

4. But just by the time of composition of codes reflective morality must have already entered the minds of men. Questions must have been raised not only about how an act should or should not be done, but also why it should or should not be done. Justification for every injunction is sought, and when justification is not obtained, reform is advocated. Opinions may differ about the forms of justification. It may be given in terms of some sacred scripture, social welfare, political stability or individual welfare. If it is given by appeal to some sacred scripture, it is acceptance of some authority and therefore tradition, though considered sacred. But the justification of the very tradition is now sought, and, therefore, justification of a tradition in terms of a sacred scripture is arguing in a circle. But when it is given in terms of the nature of society or the individual, no further justification is sought, because society and the individual are hard facts for ethics. But then some ideals of society and the individual are introduced, for no ethical conduct aims at merely preserving the brute in the gregarious man, but man with individual, social and spiritual ideals. It is at this juncture that fullfledged ethics, rationally articulated and discussed, appears on the human scene. Thus ethics as a distinct discipline appears after ethical codes, which are biased towards conserving particular forms of traditional conduct and opposed to complete rational investigation.[1]

III

Growth of Morality in the Individual

Ethics demands that one should control one's activity according to certain rules and laws. But no individual is born with a knowledge of these rules and laws. He learns them first from nature and society, then reflects over them and assimilates them with his experience, and afterwards is even prepared to go beyond them when convinced by his experience that he should and ought.

1. First, the child learns to control its activity from nature. When it places its finger near fire, it is burnt. Thus nature teaches the child through pains and pleasures. Even a grown-up learns what to eat and how much to eat through pains and pleasures.

2. Next, as the child grows, its parents and elder sisters and brothers teach it what to do and what not to do through rewards and punishments, and also praise and blame. So far the individual is not very reflective about conduct. He may now and then ask his elders why a certain act is performed in a certain way. But the majority of children are satisfied with the answers obtained, and care more about rewards and punishments than about the justification of prescribed forms.

3. But as the child grows, many of the rewards and punishments are discontinued; and many forms of conduct have no rewards except social praise. A stage is reached in the individual's life, when no concrete rewards are obtained for right conduct except social approval, praise and fame, and the opposite for wrong conduct. Many forms of wrong conduct are not legally or even socially punishable. At this stage, the individual follows the traditions and is eager for social praise and approval.

4. But a stage comes in the life of some individuals, who are of course very few, when they rise above social approval and praise. They think for themselves, question their own head and heart about the justification of the prescribed laws of

behaviour; and if they find that they are unjust, they are prepared to violate them and go against society. Such are ethical geniuses, leaders of mankind, some of whom become martyrs and other successful reformers. It is they who give real impetus to reflective ethics.

IV

Dawn of Reflection and Evolution of Codes

Now, we may give the causes leading to reflective ethics and the re-evaluation of codes as a summary and in an analytic manner.

1. The first is the observation of different social practices. In the contemporary age our knowledge of these differences is far greater than before. This knowledge is making us question the validity of many of our traditions, and is at the same time enabling us to see the living importance of equally many or even more.

2. Our attitude to physical nature has considerably changed. We view it as an inanimate force with specific laws by knowing which we can control it. We do not think of the natural forces as being controlled by spirits, and we are attributing natural calamities less and less to the spirits angered by violated traditions.

3. There has been a gradual change in our outlook on man also. Many modern Christians, for instance, are less prone to believing in original sin. The Hindus are believing less and less in the unreality of the world. We are less convinced now that it is a sin to enjoy the values of the world and lead a comfortable life.

4. There is progress in our understanding of human nature also. There are certain acts which a man can do and certain others which he cannot do, and still others for not doing which he commits a sin or crime. That all moral laws are divine commandments is not accepted by many, who say that they are to be based on the nature of man and not on the will of God. Even if God gave them, they should not conflict with

human nature; and if they do, they cannot be dictates of God, who created man also.

5. Hence, there arose a change in the methods of establishing the validity of moral and legal laws, and many view-points have been taken for establishing and justifying them. A few of these are following:

(a) First there is the standpoint of tradition. In the case of many customs like etiquette and formalities, which are not found to be particularly harmful, we follow them and justify them as belonging to "our culture", though we are not prepared to follow every practice handed down by our tradition. The amount of appeal to "our culture" varies from individual to individual, group to group, and locality to locality. In any case, justification by tradition is current throughout the world.

(b) Then, there is justification by appeal to religion. Practically every religious founder was a reformer of his time. But when once his reforms were established, religion acted as a conservative force and gave sanction to all the practices. When it got institutionalized, all the institutions of society became religious, and any violation was regarded as a sacrilege.

But now our conception of religion is changing. If God is one and if the relation of God to man is the same throughout the universe, then all social institutions must be good and God could not have been interested in any one particular set of social institutions and could not have damned the others. Besides, we are more often distinguishing than ever before the essentials from the non-essentials of religion, and are insisting that the essentials of all religions must be and are the same. Christian social forms, Islamic social forms, Hindu social forms etc., are externals to the essential spirit of religion. Indeed, as Radhakrishnan has often been saying, we demand that spirituality should be embodied in our social institutions; but we are at the same time not ready to accept that any particular traditionally handed down set of institutions alone embodies the spiritual. On the contrary, we are asserting that many institutions have lost the spiritual in them. Justification by religion is current throughout the world; but our conception of religion is more and more purified. On the one hand, there is a demand to separate religion from social and political life; on the other, there is demand to make our social and political life more and more spiritual. But ethics in its concrete form cannot be separated from social and political life, and it cannot be separated from religion too. Hence, there is a constant change of emphasis in our evaluation of traditional codes. Sometimes we argue against traditional ethics from the secular point of view; other times we want to make it religious.

(c) With the immense progress made by the physical and natural sciences, the sciences of man, scientific outlook dominates our thought and we want that everything should be viewed from the standpoint of science. I do not wish to raise the question whether scientific attitude to ethics is right or wrong. I only want that we should take note of its presence. Among the educated, the number of those who have more faith in science than in religion is on the increase. They demand that religion should not conflict with science; and where there is conflict, science is accepted and religion is doubted. They demand that traditional ethical codes must meet the requirements of scientific outlook. If they cannot, they should be modified. Some of those who advocate scientific outlook are extremists; they want to abolish all religion and condemn all reference to religion.

(d) Another basis taken for establishing and justifying ethical laws is the sociological. Those who adopt this attitude are indifferent to religion, even if they do not condemn it. The criterion for all ethical laws is social welfare, and not the salvation of the individual. Whichever of the traditional laws is found to be harmful to society and retarding its progress is to be discontinued and new laws are to be introduced which contribute to social progress.

(e) But this sociological justification may be so interpreted as to submerge the individual in society and ignore his welfare. Humanism, therefore, wants that all laws should be justified from its own point of view. Practically humanism is as old as man himself, every man with deep sympathies, compassion, kindness, love and respect for other human beings is essentially a humanist. But humanism with a distinct name and programme could appear only when a movement, both theoretical and practical, was started in the interests of the welfare of man and in defense of human values and boldly challenged the excesses of religion and laws of orthodox tradition. Immense good has been done to man by the humanistic movement, whatever be its ultimate defects. In the contemporary world, particularly in some communist countries, it seems to be fighting for the recognition of the dignity of man and freedom of the individual; and many seem to be becoming martyrs in the name of humanism. And humanism can act as a check on the extravagances of science also.

(f) We are not to forget that what are called ethical codes are not merely concerned with what are nowadays called ethical laws but with all laws of all kinds of social institutions including the economic and the political. They give their justification of economic and political relationships from the religious point of view. But now throughout the world there are demands for readjustment of these relationships; and the demand is made and justified from the point of view of various ideologies, socialistic, communistic, democratic, humanistic and even religious. If the readjustment is justified, then the traditional codes cannot be right. All that we can say is that the traditional laws suited certain conditions, which do not now exist. In any case, this new demand gives occasion to questioning the eternal validity claimed for the ethical codes. For if the institutions and their relationships are to be changed, then ethical codes also have to be changed.

6. We may incidentally note that in the world now there is a demand for revolutionary change, for burning everything past; and there is a demand for conserving everything past. In order to avoid conflict between the two and the agonies of revolutions, slow and steady change is advocated by wise men who do not want a complete break with the past and yet realize the inenvitability of change. This change has to be neither too quick nor too slow, as either large sections of people will be condemned to misery by quick changes or outworn laws will keep many sections in unjustifiable conditions too long. If change is to be introduced steadily and carefully, re-evaluation and modification of ethical codes becomes necessary.

V

Nature and Growth of Dharmaśāstras in India

So far have been presented only general considerations, which are fairly universally applicable. But as the paper is concerned mainly with the Dharmaśāstras of India, we may briefly review their nature and growth. Whatever be the orthodox opinion—it is strong in its own circles—scholars on the whole believe that the Dharmaśāstras have had a historical growth. There are several of them. Though not on fundamentals, they show differences of opinion, and the differences were due to changed conditions which historical life introduced. The largest amount of work done on Dharmaśāstras is by M. M. Dr. P. V. Kane. There are other important writers like M. M. Dr. Ganganatha Jha, and Dr. K. P. Jayaswal. Writers like Dr. Bhagavan Das have attempted to interpret Manu's ideas with the help of Plato's classification or rather stratification of classes. As the Dharmaśāstras are also works on jurisprudence, they interested writers like Maine. This paper is not primarily concerned with the history of the Dharmaśāstras, except to show that they had a growth. It is not interested also in the psychological justification of any of their ideas or in jurisprudence; its interest is mainly limited to their relevance to the modern age.

1. According to the orthodox tradition, the Dharmaśāstras are based on the Vedas. The former are called Śrutis, those which are heard, and the later Smṛtis, those which are remembered. Manu says that whatever he teaches about *dharma* (right action) was first told by the Vedas. But a little later he says that, if there is conflict between Śruti and Smṛti, the former is to be followed but not the latter,—which shows that Manu himself was not sure that the Smṛtis were always right.

2. The Smṛtis are therefore meant to present the laws of conduct, which are not given in a codified form in the Śruti. The Śruti, therefore, could not be a ready guide to conduct. This was the original reason fo r the composition of the Smṛtis. For this reason the Smṛtis are called subsidiaries to the Vedas (Śrutis).

3. Before the Dharmaśāstras came into existence, it is believed, there were Dharmaśūtras, some of which are now available. Here we are entering a controversial field. Max Müller and Bühler seem to think that the Hindu law originated in the Dharmasūtras of the Vedic *caraṇas* or schools. Kane says that the Dharmasūtras of Āpastamba, Baudhāyana and Gautama belong to the period between 600 and 300 B.C., and that Gautama speaks of Dharmaśāstras.[2] But none of those Dharmaśāstras is now available. It is also possible that the writers of the time were using the words *dharmasūtra* and *dharmaśāstra* indifferently for the same work, for both were meant to serve the same purpose. Jayaswal thinks that the source of Hindu law is Kauṭilya's *Arthaśāstra*,[3] that Manu's Code was written in order to assert the supremacy of the Brahmins when the Brāhmaṇa empire was destroyed by the Mauryas, and that Yājñavalkya's code was written during the time of the Satavāhana empire which combined orthodoxy

with Buddhism and made woman equal to man under Buddhist influence. But Kane points out that the *Arthaśāstra* is really a part of the Dharmaśāstra, that, according to Yājñavalkya, wherever there is conflict between the Dharmaśāstra and the *Arthaśāstra*, the former should prevail,[4] and that Kauṭilya was earlier than the extant *Manusmṛti*, though not earlier than its kernel.

It is the historians and orientalists who can pronounce judgment on these differences of opinion. In the present paper the attempt to fix the stages of growth and their dates cannot be made. But it seems to the present writer that it is the general feature of the development of Indian philosophical literature that at first there were scattered and uncoordinated expressions of experiences, then a coordination of them in the form of *sūtras*, and then elaborations and expositions of the *sūtras* in the form of commentaries, summaries and other presentations. Neither are *sūtras* always aphorisms or pithy utterances as usually defined, but also complete sentences and discussions as in some Buddhist *sūtras*. So to think that originally there was *sūtra* literature on *dharma* (right conduct), the ideas of which were later expounded in the extant Dharmasāstras is in accordance with the general nature of the development of India's philosophical literature. That some of the authors of *sūtras* refer to *sāstras* before them may or may not mean that, prior to the *sūtra* literature and as distinct from it, there existed another literature called *śāstra* literature. The *Arthaśāstra* can be treated as part of Dharmasāśtra, because the latter deals with what the kings have and ought to do for obtaining wealth and increasing their power.

However, according to Dr. P. V. Kane, there was some Dharmaśāstra literature prior to the period of 600-300B.C., to which the authors of the Dharmasūtras like Gautama, Baudhāyana and Āpasthamba belonged. The Śrautasūtras and *Gṛhyasūtras* belonged to a period even earlier than 600B.C. The *sūtras* make frequent references to the Vedas. Kauṭilya, the author of the *Arthaśāstra* is identified with Cāṇakya, the minister of Candragupta Maurya, and destroyer of the Nanda Dynasty, and is generally assigned to the period between 300B.C. and A.D.100. The present *Manusmṛti* is assigned to some time between 200B.C. and A.D.200, the *Yājñavalkya-smṛti* to A.D.100 to A.D.300, and the *Parāśarasmṛti's* date is left undecided, as the extant one seems to be re-written and the original one lost. Yājñavalkya and even Kauṭilya mention Parāśara. In any case, the Dharmaśāstra literature seems to have obtained particular importance after the *Manusmṛti*. It may be also true that different sects like Mānavas etc., were holding particular views about conduct and that the extant Dharmaśāstras brought them together and coordinated them. Such work was found necessary because of the prevalence of a large number of views which were sometimes conflicting. We may, therefore, say that one main purpose of the development of this literature was to present the different forms of right conduct as given in the Vedas in as consistent and exact a form as possible in the circumstances.

4. But the circumstances did not always remain the same. Buddhism and Jainism, which weakened the distinction between caste and caste and sex and sex, was born in 600B.C., and began to reinterpret and attack orthodoxy. There were conversions and reconversions. And some disorder entered society. Then rules and laws had to be fixed, and unrestricted freedom had to be restricted. That the authors of the Dharmaśāstras were aware of, and alive to the new conditions is shown not only by the changing views on the function of castes and status of women, but also for their concern for reconverting those who were forcibly converted by the *melecchas* and for purifying the women who were raped by them.[5] The author who devoted much thought to this question was Devala, who is supposed to be an inhabitant of Sindh. He is said to have taught on the banks of the Indus and perhaps knew the first Muslim invasion by Mohammad Kasim in the eighth century. Thus Dharmaśāstras were written again and again not only to make the Vedic ideas of right conduct consistent and exact but also to make new rules and laws

which changing conditions required in the interests of social stability and strength.

5. We may now give the social conditions and outlook in which the Dharmasūtras and Dharmaśāstras originated.

(a) The social conditions of the time were as complex for those people as the conditions of our time are for us. By the early *sūtra* period we find that the castes were more or less formed. The distinction and separation were not yet as rigid as later. Besides the castes, there were the untouchables and the *mlecchas*. There were tribes pouring into India from outside, both Aryan and non-Aryan by blood. And they were mixing up with the settled society at various levels. Some of them were accepting the orthodox religion and cult, but the others were not. So orthodoxy could not be decided by blood or race alone. Again, every tribe was bringing with it its own social and religious forms; and when the tribe was incorporated into the settled society, its social and religious forms also were to be incorporated, while at the same time the supremacy of the orthodoxy was to be asserted. Those who were called Śūdras and *mlecchas* were not necessarily non-Aryan by blood. Orthodoxy had its own definition of the word Aryan; the Aryan was one who accepted the *āryadharma* or the Aryan way of life, and it was the Way prescribed by the first two parts of the Veda, namely, the Saṁhitās and the Brāhmaṇas, or by the Vedas in general. But this conception was later contested by the Buddhists and the Jainas, who maintained that theirs was the true Aryan way.

The formation of the Indian society may briefly be delineated. It seems to the present writer that by the time the Aryans entered India, the Dravidians were the rulers of the land. They were experts in trade and commerce and fortification of cities. They subjugated the pre-Dravidian inhabitants. Some are of the opinion that the caste system originally belonged to the

Dravidians, for nowhere else in the Aryan countries is the caste system to be found. It is difficult to be exact on this point. However, when the Aryans, who had more effective methods of offensive in warfare, conquered the Dravidians, they found the caste system very useful for establishing their own superiority and at the same time peace in the country. They retained priestcraft and warcraft completely for themselves, thus retaining religious and political superiority in their own hands; they retained part of trade and commerce also for themselves and allowed part of it to be carried by the Dravidians, who were already experts in it. This seems to have enabled some of the Dravidians to enter the third caste. The fourth caste was comprised of the agriculturists, whether they owned the land completely or not, and of the slaves, labourers etc. Those who were too uncivilized and did not have a settled life were outside the four-fold caste system of society; and when some of them wished to settle down, they were allotted some of the lowest professions and were treated as the fifth caste.

But the actual formation of the Indian caste system could not have been as simple as presented. First, some of the new tribes, though Aryan by blood, would not accept the social and religious forms so far established. Those who accepted them were absorbed, but those who did not were called non-Aryan. Secondly, all the tribes which entered later were not Aryans, some of them were Hunas etc., who had Mongolian blood. Ways had to be found for absorbing them also, if they agreed. Thirdly, both Aryans and non-Aryans who chose to remain outside the orthodox society had inter-marriages and other relationships with it. Ways had to be found for recognizing them and legalising them. Fourthly, every tribe which had been inhabiting India or came from outside later had its own social traditions and religious cults. And it entered generally one of the four recognized castes. Hence, sub-castes had to be formed and different professions had to be assigned to each. In addition, professions had to be found for people born of mixed castes. In the fifth place, all the tribes had to be allowed to follow their own social traditions and forms of worship, so that they would peacefully settle down without bloodshed. For instance, each sub-caste was allowed to follow its own forms of marriage and worship its own gods and goddesses. A Brāhmaṇa usually officiated to such functions which meant an indirect recognition of the superiority of the orthodoxy. But sometimes this was not even required. In the sixth place, however, inasmuch as the authors of the Dharmaśāstras tried to prevent the castes from following each other's professions, the profession of ruling and fighting was taken up by every caste, and they would inter-marry. Wealth and power seem to have broken the caste barriers often, which was justified in the name of profession.

(b) The outlook of the Dharmaśāstras is generally that of the Mīmāṁsā or in other words of the Saṁhitās and the Brāhmaṇas, the first two parts of the Veda recognized as authoritative by the Mīmāṁsā. Jaimini in his Mīmāṁsāsūtras expounded their philosophy. The Mīmāṁsā is an exposition of *dharma* (duty, right action, conduct). But the right action which the Mīmāṁsā wishes to explain is confined only to sacrifices to gods, and is not so much concerned with worldly professions and laws. Hence, the need for later Dharmaśāstras and Dharmasūtras. Kane says that Āpastambha's Dharmasāstras contain many of the technical terms and doctrines of the Mīmāṁsā. And there are many cross-references between the commentaries of the Mimāṁsāsūtras and Dharmaśāstras. This is natural, as both aim at expounding *dharma*. The Mīmāṁsā is the main *karmayogaśāstra*, and all the Dharmaśāstras are meant to expound Karmayoga in all its detail for all the castes. Manu, though extolling knowledge or *ātmajnāna*, calls his exposition Karma-yoga. We have, therefore, to say that not only do the Dharmaśāstras make use of the Mīmāṁsā methods of interpretation, but also are they meant to be continuations and expansions of the study of right conduct. This is the view of Kumārila also, which it is important to note. The importance of this view is missed if the Dharmaśāstras are taken to be only texts of jurisprudence and codification of legal laws.

This expansion was necessitated by the fact that the Mīmāmsā was not concerned with many forms of conduct like the political and economic and that new rules and laws were required by the changing conditions. That is why the authors of the Dharma-śāstras accept not only the Vedas but also Smṛtis, the conduct of moral leaders, and one's own satisfaction as the valid sources of *dharma*. A little earlier Manu includes another, namely the character also of those learned in the Vedas as a source of *dharma*. He says that he gave the *dharmas* of the different countries (*deśadharmas*), of the castes, of the sub-castes, and of even the *pāṣaṇḍas* (those who were outside the Vedic fold).

Thus the authors of the Dharmaśāstras had to collect the various rules and laws of right action not only from the Vedas, but also from the extant Dharmaśūtras and Dharmaśāstras, the forms of conduct prescribed for the castes, the customs and traditions of the many tribes which constituted the sub-castes, and also of those tribes which did not accept the Vedic way of life and were called Mlecchas and Pāṣaṇḍas, and which lived in the outskirts of the Aryan kingdoms and sometimes within them. The study of *dharma* made by the Mīmāṁsā could not have included so much as the Smṛtis.

The Mīmāṁsā was mainly interested in the *dharma* that produced other-worldly effects. For it, human society was only a part of a wider society, the cosmos. The cosmic forces were at first conceived as animated and living, and later the distinction was drawn between the presiding deities (*adhidevatās*) and their material bodies. Thus the physical wind was controlled by the wind-spirit within. Besides these spirits, there were those of the ancestors. Thus, man was a member of a huge system of cosmic society and its worlds, and human society was only a small section. The Mīmāṁsā was interested in man's duties in this wider society in order to make his life comfortable and happy, and man could have such life only in and through action. Kumārila says that Mīmāṁsā is not interested in secular matters like agriculture,[6] though it is interested in right action, *karman*. But the Dharmaśāstras had to take interest in secular activities and expand the scope of *dharma*, without losing sight of its other-worldly reference and reference to the wider society. They do not indeed contain treatment of agriculture, but the relation of agriculturists to other professions. The emphasis of the Dharmśāstras is on *karman* (action), not on non-action, and here they follow the first two parts of the Veda and the Mīmāṁsā. The outlook of all the three, the Dharmaśāstras, the Mīmāṁsā, and the first two parts of the Veda is one and the same. But as the first had to enter more and more into the ways of life of all the sections of human society, they had to deal more and more with secular laws and became works on jurisprudence.

6. The orthodox society with the four castes was called the Aryan fold by the writers, though the fold did not include the Aryans only by race. Those outside the fold were called non-Aryans. Even the members of the fold had different customs in different localities. The authors of the codes had to observe and legalise them for purposes of law. Similarly, they had to

legalise the practices of those outside the fold. For instance, it was the practice of the Mlecchas to sell their children; but the members of the Aryan fold were not allowed to do it. So Kauṭilya did not prescribe any punishment to the Mlecchas, if they sold their children. Instances like this show that the authors of the codes observed the customs of the tribes and castes at different places, related them to the Mīṁāmsā ideal of *dharma*, and then codified them.

Then the difficulty arose about conflicts between the Vedas and the customs. It is said that the four sources of *dharma* are the Vedas, Smṛtis, customs and one's own desires. It is also said that each preceding source is more authoritative than the succeeding one. The latter is to be followed only when guidance is not obtained from the former. This means an admission that the Vedas did not cover all the cases covered by the Smṛtis, that the Smṛtis did not include all customs and traditions, and that even customs and traditions left out cases in which the individual could have his choice according to his pleasure. But whenever there was conflict between the higher and the lower, the higher alone was to prevail.

But this dictum was not accepted universally. The reason is simple. *Dharma* is both this-worldly and other-worldly. Some acts which are right other-worldly are not right this-worldly and *vice-versa*. The Smṛtis are concerned with both kinds of *dharma*, but the Veda is concerned only with the other-worldly *dharma*, which comprises the laws according to which the deities and spirits of all the worlds influence the happenings of this world and the lives of men both here and here-after. Śabara says that, when there is conflict between the Smṛti and the Veda, as the former is concerned with worldly purposes, it cannot prevail over the latter. But Kumārila sees the conflict in a different light. He seems to be in favour of the view that both are always right, and reconciliation must be made between the two by referring them to two different purposes or subject matters. All Smṛtis are authoritative when we consider the purpose they serve. The portions dealing with *mokṣa* and *dharma* (here Kumārila seems to be referring only to the other-worldly *dharma*) have their origin in the Veda and so do not conflict with it; but the portions dealing with wealth and pleasures (*artha* and *kāma*) have their source in worldly practices. Then also there can be no conflict, as the Vedas are not concerned with worldly practices. But this solution ignores the relation between the four values of life, while Śabara's solution ignores the latter two values by completely subordinating them to the first two which are accepted solely on the basis of the scripture.

Again, in the case of a conflict between Smṛtis and customs, many hold that the former should prevail. But some, like Viśvarūpa and Medhātithi, think differently, the latter even maintaining that custom also is Smṛti as it is one of the sources of right conduct. In fact, the Smṛti is itself a codification of several practices including the extant customs and traditions. Then customs and traditions are really part of Smṛti. So far there can be no conflict between a part and the whole. But there may be customs not observed by the authors of Smṛtis, or introduced by new tribes entering the country, or changed in different parts of the country in order to suit the new conditions of time and place. Then there will be conflict between the codified laws and the new customs. These differences of view apply to such situations, and some of the authors showed liberality. However, on the whole the gradation of the authoritativeness is accepted.

7. Another important point we have to note about the Dharmaśāstras is the recognition by the writers that, in interpreting, applying and following the four guides of *dharma*, namely, the Vedas, Smṛtis, custom and satisfaction, both head and heart are to be used. Manu gives the general characteristic of *dharma* as that which is followed by good and learned men, who are devoid of attachment and hatred, and who understand it through their heart. The word 'heart' is explained by the commentators as 'direct' (*sākṣāt*). But Manu might have meant more. The word should have meant sympatheic. The interpreter has to observe the customs of groups and tribes, not merely to reject them if they are not

similar to his own, but to understand sympathetically why and how they are being followed, what human and social purpose they have been serving.

Again, the interpreter has to use his head also. Bṛhaspati says that "the decision (in a cause) should not be given merely relying on Śāstras, for in the case of a decision devoid of reasoning loss of *dharma* results." The roots of a human and rational approach are found in the Dharmaśāstras, and their general principle is accepted, though within the limits prescribed by the conceptions of the time. But the general tendency was to follow the texts in all important cases, as it is done in many of the courts now.

VI

Points for Revaluation

1. We have seen that the Dharmaśāstras were the codifications of the extant customs and practices. This codification was done first, to bring together in a connected form all the ideas about conduct scattered throughout the Vedas, secondly to coordinate the views of all the interpreters of the Vedas, in the third place to legalise all the customs and practices of all the tribes and localities of both the Aryan and non-Aryan folds, in the fourth place to prevent transagressions and settle down people in their traditions, and in the fifth place to enact new laws suitable to changing and unforeseen conditions like rape and forcible conversion.

Now, apart from the injunctions of the Vedas, which cannot change, there is change faster than ever before in the customs and practices of castes and sub-castes and people outside the castes. We are finding many traditional customs and laws to be outdated, and we are introducing and importing new ones. The general tendency now is not to fix any group to any of its customs, though they are respected if the group likes to follow them. Again, the standpoint of our approach to the appreciation of customs has been at least modified. For instance, attempts are made to dissuade some hill tribes from continuing their custom of marriage by capture, polyandry, polygyny and so forth. And our reason is not that they will be prevented from entering heaven but that of equality of sexes and so forth, which is humanistic; and we have other human, humanistic and sociological considerations.[7] We want that both head and heart should be used on a far wider scale than the traditionalists allow. The tendency is to give greater importance to this-worldly *dharma* than before.

2. This brings us to the second point, which is more philosophical than the first. The Dharmasāstras call themselves *karmayogas* and say that every man will attain *mokṣa* if he performs his duties according to castes and *āsramas*. By the time of the Codes the ideas of God and *mokṣa* were already accepted by the Mīmāṁsā which, therefore, said that *mokṣa* was attainable through *karman*, sacrifices and other forms. Sacrifices to introduce bondage (*bandha*), but others do. Another distinction also was developed, namely, that of actions for visible fruit and actions for invisible fruit, and the Vedas were regarded as enjoining action with invisible fruit. Again, a third distinction, namely, between *karman* satisfying desires (*sakāma*) and *karmans* performed as duties without the idea of satisfying desires (*niṣkāma*), was also made, which was elaborated in the *Bhagavadgītā*. The former produce bondage and the latter liberation. Here come our philosophical difficulties.

(a) Can and does man perform any action without any desire and purpose? Can any action be well-done without concern for the result? If it is said that actions are to be performed without any attachment and with perfect attachment will they be done with all the care and deliberation necessary for them or will they be perfunctorily done? How can we prescribe the *karmayoga* as *niṣkāmakarman* to the general run of mankind and make it its philosophy of life and guide? Psychologists tell us that behaviour is purposive. If so, does *karmayoga* teach us unporposive action?

(b) Again, as regards the distinction between the visible fruit and the invisible, we are not as certain of the latter as we are of the former. Many of us like to reverse this Mīmāṁsā criterion and say that, when there is conflict between the two, texts advocating visible fruit must prevail. For our contention is: If both are true, then there should be no conflict between two truths; and when we are convinced of the truth of the visible, it is the invisible that should conform to it and not contradict it; if there is contradiction, we doubt the truth of the invisible. This is in line with our demand that religion should not conflict with science; and even if it does not confirm science, it should be compatible and not incompatible with it, if it is to be accepted.

This attitude of ours is due to the growing feeling that every statement of the scriptures cannot be equally true, and that every statement is not God-given and eternally true. This problem was easier for the ancient writers who accepted the scriptures as an absolute authority, and whenever they found it difficult to accept a statement at its face-value they wrestled with it grammatically and by introducing interpretative rules in order to extract new meanings. But there is a limit beyond which the passages cannot be stretched and historical scholarship is averse to artificial methods of interpretation. The modern view of the scriptures is that they are the expressions of experiences of historical individuals and seers, but not that the words of scriptures existed eternally in order to convey eternal truths.

(c) Our third difficulty on this point is about understanding how *karman* leads to a state beyond *karman*. Action presupposes the agent of action, man, ego, and also the result of action. *Mokṣa* is complete egolessness, according to all the Vedāntins. If the nature of liberation is pure egohood as the Mīmāṁsā thought, then it cannot be *mokṣa* for the Vedantins. But even according to the Mīmāṁsā, it is difficult to understand how purpose, desire etc., can cease, if the ego even as pure continues for ever.

(d) Our fourth difficulty also is philosophical. We are no longer prepared to accept the spirits (*adhidevatās*) of the natural forces. And so we find it difficult to treat as true the conception of cosmic society, in which the spirits of the natural forces, the spirits of ancestors and the spirits of men live as members with mutual obligations and cutting across the different worlds. We have been taught to understand the activities of the natural forces as unpurposive; only activities of living beings are purposive; and of the living beings, only man has duties and obligations. He has duties and obligations primarily to other living beings who have duties and obligations like him and secondarily to other living beings who have instinctive qualities having ethical significance like love, gratitude and faithfulness. He has no obligations to the material world of natural forces, which he can learn to control and utilize as it suits him. Thus human society acquires primary significance, and next the society of all living beings. But as the wolf and the jackal, for instance, can never be taught duties and obligations to man, man has no duties and obligations to them. They are outlaws from his ethical society. Destroying them or preserving them depends on other considerations. He has duties only towards those animals which have corresponding duties to him, whether they perform them by instinct or by a spark of reason. Thus when natural forces are known to be unpurposive in their activities, the duties of sacrifice to them lose all their significance.

(e) In the fifth place, we have to note that, according to the Mīmāṁsā, "that one should attain the knowledge of the Brahman" is not a *vidhi* or *codanā* like the other *codanās*, or in other words, *ātmajñāna* is not a *dharma*.

The Vedāntins hold different views about the nature of this injunction. And on the whole they treat it as a special sort of injunction. But from the Mīmāṁsā point of view, the injunction, "the Ātman has to be realized," is not a *vidhi* to act, to perform some action (*karman*), but to suspend action. Without reference to *karman*, there can be no *vidhi*. Hence, the conflict with the Mīmāṁsā idea that anything can be attained only through action. Here the conflict between the Mīmāṁsā and Vedānta is fundamental. This conflict also has to be resolved by the moderns. For if the injunctions of the Mīmāṁsā and the Dharmāśāstras are ethically binding, one who violates them is to be called unethical—even one who does not perform sacrifices is to be called unethical with reference to the comic society; but one who obeys these injunctions but refuses to have *mokṣa* cannot be called unethical. We may admit that he may be called unspiritual, and that the injunction: "the Ātman has to be realized," is meant to make man spiritual. But the difficulty lies elsewhere; the whole ethics is geared to *mokṣa* and is justified in the name of *mokṣa* by the Vedantins and the Dharmaśāstras under the influence of the Vedānta. Then why should one who does not believe in *mokṣa* or does not care for it regard the injunctions as ethical, if they are all geared to *mokṣa*? Will he be not justified in founding his ethics on something else? Even taking the word *mokṣa* in the wide sense of religion, so far as the general run of mankind goes, psychological tests have shown that religious faith is no guarantee of moral behaviour. H. E. Barnes says that studies carried out in New York show that orthodox religious training did not promote honesty and reliability: "To the contrary, children who have been exposed to progressive educational methods, based upon secular premises and psychology, appeared to have a far better record as to honesty and dependability. The complaint against religious ethics is that it "was designed to please the gods rather than serve man directly and efficiently."[8]

(f) In the sixth place, the ethical codes recognize three debts, debts to gods to be paid back by performing sacrifices, debt to ancestors to be paid back by having a son, and debt to sages to be paid back by propagating their learning. Our generation has grown sceptical about the first debt. Regarding the second debt, people now want to have children, but for more practical and secular considerations. The propagation of learning has become now as much society's responsibility as it is the individual's. The father does not train his son in the same profession as his. Every educated man is not a teacher, and the way he teaches his children is rather indirect. All this is due to the gradual changes in our social institutions.

3. Another philosophical point of interest is the traditional conception and classification of values into *artha* (wealth), *kāma* (desires, pleasures), *dharma* (duty), and *mokṣa* (salvation, redemption). As these are values, they are also 'oughts', in some sense, not necessarily in the sense of moral duty. Wealth has to be acquired; but it is meant for use in the enjoyment of pleasures and satisfaction of desires. 'Wealth for wealth's sake' can be the motto of only the miser. But desires should not be indulged in disorderly, but according to prescribed rules of *dharma* or duty. There is an urge to enjoy pleasures as well as a duty to enjoy them. When urge and duty coincide, *dharma* is satisfied. But 'duty for duty's sake' is not the ultimate criterion; duty is for *mokṣa*, by attaining which man transcends the sphere of duty. Thus each preceding value is a means for the succeeding one, and *mokṣa* is not a means to any.

Artha covers economic and political values. *Kāma* covers the psycho-physical values of the individual. *Dharma* covers partly religious and partly social, political and economic values. For instance, *artha* has to be acquired, but it has to be acquired only according to the rules of *dharma*. Similarly, *kāma* has to be satisfied, but it has to be satisfied only according to the rules of *dharma* again. Thus *dharma* has reference to both *artha* and *kāma* on the one side and *mokṣa* on the other. For all the three *karman* or action is necessary. There are no definite laws of *mokṣa*, because it is beyond description. The only kind of activity prescribed for attaining *mokṣa* is *niṣkāmakarman* or action without the appropriation of any of the three sets of values. But as mentioned earlier, this requires examination and explanation.

4. The next point for re-examination and evaluation is the sociological one, namely, the caste system. The modern age is not prepared to justify the continuation of this system. It is not prepared to accept that the son should take to the profession of the father, that the castes were created by God, that each caste has a particular nature (*guṇa*) and will have it eternally, that every caste should be confined to the profession assigned to it and should not take to any other profession, and that there should be no inter-mixing of castes. It is also not prepared to accept that the difference between the sexes is as great as Dharmaśāstras made it. It does not also believe that the outcastes were created as outcastes by God. It is discarding many of the legal conceptions. We have, therefore, to determine which of the conceptions are still important for us and which harmful.

VII

Re-evaluation

1. Does a codification once made remain authoritative for ever? The answer certainly is in the negative. The authors themselves of the Dharmaśāstras were not unanimous on every point, and some of the later writers were obliged to introduce new laws to suit new conditions.

We attach more importance therefore to the spirit behind a traditional law than to its word. That is, we want to know the reason and understand in what form and with what modifications it can be applied to our present conditions.

'Present conditions', so far as the laws go, mean the changing forms of social institutions, which determine the forms of social relationships including the political and the economic. Our conceptions of man, family and society have now changed or at least modified. So any set of codified laws which suited the social institutions of a particular time may not suit the social institutions of another.

In the past, the basis of laws was religious, though as a matter of fact the authors observed the social customs and traditional laws of people and gave them a religious sanction. But this made the customs not only inviolable but also unchangeable. But the modern authors approach the studies from the side of man as a member of society, and the viewpoints are sociological and humanistic. They do not all discredit religion, but demand that religion should not be harmful to social and individual welfare. They say, therefore, that only as much of the traditional codes as is useful for the welfare of man and society should be retained, and the rest modified or rejected. The codes certainly should be allowed to act as a conservative force, but should not be allowed to hinder progress. The Dharmasāstras, as we have noted, are peculiar combinations of ethical, social, political and legal laws; and as our conceptions of ethics, society, politics and economics change there is necessity for constant re-codification of laws.

2. (a) It is difficult, in formulating and enacting laws, not to take into consideration the purpose and motive of actions. *Niṣkāmakarman* is meant, even according to the ancient writers, for *mokṣa*, not even for *dharma*. For *dharma* all is *kāmyakarman*, though in higher interpretations of *dharma*, *karman* becomes *niṣkāma*. But for the Codes, which constitute jurisprudence, there is no *niṣkāmakarman* except in the case of children and the insane. *Niṣkāmakarman* may be interpreted as 'duty for duty's sake', without reference to the results of action. But when there is no desire for results, the carefulness and interest necessary for doing an act well will not be given to it, and the act becomes

perfunctory. Society and social relationships are natural to man; they grow out of his nature and serve his needs. So to ask him to act without reference to his needs is to ask him to do what is not natural to him. Visible fruits therefore are to be taken seriously into consideration so far as the laws of the Dharmaśāstras are concerned, even if we believe in invisible fruit. All visible fruits are connected, directly or indirectly, with man's desires and needs.

(b) So far as the codes go, the present age is not prepared to give primary importance to invisible fruit like *apūrva* in enacting our laws. Social and individual welfare is a visible fruit. There may be invisible fruits; but if they are true, they should not conflict, but be compatible with visible fruit.

(c) The relation, therefore, between *kāmyakarman, niṣkāmakarman* and *mokṣa* becomes more difficult to understand for us than for the ancients. *Karman* not backed by desire will be performed perfunctorily, whereas that backed by desire prevents salvation and strengthens bondage. This difficulty can be overcome only if ethically done *karman*, though backed by desire, has a way of leading to *mokṣa*. This is possible, so far as the present writer's understanding of the problem goes, only if *niṣkāmakarman* is interpreted as *karman* done from the universal point of view, that is, the point of view of reason or, as the ancient Greeks called it, the *Logos*. Such action can liquify the knot of egoity and identify the ego with the Universal Spirit or the Brahman. In order to achieve this, the ego has not only to identify its consciousness with the consciousness of the Universal Spirit, but also its own purposes with the purposes of the Cosmos, society and humanity. What is then attempted will be the raising of the ego from particularity to universality, which is tantamount to the negation of one's egoity through action and realising the universality involved in it with all its objectivity.

The transformation then will be a psychological and spiritual transformation of the inwardness of man. Action is the test of the objectivity and authenticity of he realized university and of the sincerity of ego in its attempts to raise itself to universality. This interpretation not only accords with the essential teachings of the *karmayoga* but also makes it understandable to the modern man. It is not possible to discuss this philosophical point further in the present paper, as the discussion will lead deep into many other intimately connected problems.

(d) The problem of cosmic society need not detain us long. We no longer believe in it, as we are not prepared to believe that the natural forces of inorganic matter are presided over by spirits (*adhidevatās*).

(e) So far as ethical duties are understood, the exhortation that the Ātman has to be realized cannot be treated as an ethical injunction. To the man who wants *mokṣa*, it may be said to be necessary; but to the man who does not want it or does not believe in it, but is satisfied with performing his duties to human and other living beings, it cannot be an ethical injunction. And he cannot be called unethical and his actions cannot be called unlawful, if he disobeys it. He can avoid *moṣka*, but he cannot avoid being a social animal with interests in his own and society's welfare, and so cannot avoid being an ethical animal.

There is a sociological side to religion. In the history of religion throughout the world, it has often affected and influenced social and political events, though in its essence it has often been regarded by philosophers as man's individual relation with the Universal Spirit. When man follows this definition strictly, his ties with society become weak. That is why religion in its psychological and spiritual aspects is often called individualistic. But when it has entered social forms and becomes institutionalised; it has become unprogressive and conservative, and has even degenerated itself and degenerated society. In such situations the revolt of man against religion becomes sociological and humanistic; the emphasis is laid on ethical and humanistic values. This is a peculiar feature of ethical laws which are obligatory on every man, while spiritual laws are not binding. Religion is man's own concern; but it is society's and even humanity's concern that he is ethical.

(f) About the three debts, we accept in practice that it is the duty of every man to be a useful member of society and to contribute to its future continuity by having children; and instead of regarding the duty as enabling the spirits of our ancestors in heaven to continue in the blessed life, we regard it as a contribution to society. Similarly, in order to be a useful member of society and contribute to its progress, it is the duty of every person to educate himself, and to educate his children so long as they are not able to educate themselves. In this way, we accept two of the debts, though interpreting and justifying them in our own way. The conception thus interpreted agrees with the sociological and humanistic approaches also. Regarding the third debt, the debt to gods, it is difficult to justify it in this scientific age. This change in our attitude is due to our conception of society as limited to man and other living beings and our disbelief in the spirits of natural forces.

We are not confident about the validity of our laws if they are based on conceptions rooted in a religion that peoples the material world with spirits. We approach our study of human relationships from the side of sociology, psychology, biology etc. The present writer does not want to be understood as rejecting the usefulness of religion for ethics. Something will be said on the topic at the end. But we have to demand that our laws should not come into conflict with our studies in these sciences. If there is conflict either must be false. But as religion is based entirely on scripture, if we are asked to accept every statement it makes, our own alternative is to ignore it, as we have now no way of knowing its validity.

3. The classification of values into *artha*, *kāma*, *dharma* and *mokṣa* is also a gradation. It has importance and value even for the modern man. The first three concern every man, whether he believes in *mokṣa* or not. If he does not believe in *mokṣa*, then *dharma* has to be reinterpreted for him. He will not accept it as the action enjoined by the Veda, but as the action required by human and social needs and welfare. He will not accept also that the ethical codes should be based on scripture. However, we have to accept the inter-relationship between the first three values.

The problem of the relation between *dharma* and *mokṣa* is very complicated, and will be presented last.

4. Caste distinctions will no longer be accepted. And no one will be treated as an outcaste. Opinion against such distinctions is now too strong for them to continue for ever, though similar distinctions are still existent outside India in the name of colour. Throughout the world including India, a new system called class system is becoming strong. Even communist countries, the aim of which is to build a classless society, are not without a class system now. In the communist and capitalist countries, the classes are of different kinds, because power and wealth are obtained in different ways in the two systems. One rather feels that the Indian caste system, which places a Brāhmaṇa with the ideals of poverty, learning and knowledge, and advice at the top of the social ladder is morally superior to the class system, which places the man with wealth and power at the top. The degeneration of the Brāhmaṇa caste, which is poor and powerless, cannot be so harmful to society as the degeneration of the wealthy and powerful class.

But there is another point that is worth considering. The caste system was not the result of a theory hatched by some leading Aryan, but the result of spontaneous growth, for which justification was improvised by the Dharmaśāstras. The great advantage of the system at the time of its formation was that it allowed all castes and sub-castes, which were generally different tribes, to coexist in a comprehensive pattern of society, each following its own social forms like marriage and its own religious forms and gods and goddesses, and contributing professionally its best to the society as a whole. Thus caste-system was an embodiment of the principle of co-existence of tribes, cultures, sets of social forms, religions, all of which the Aryan thinkers re-interpreted as forms and sub-forms of one spiritual life, and made them suit the conditions of the time. Instead of thinking that there was only one way of right living, which was theirs, and destroying all others, which was done in the history of other religions, the Aryan-leaders of India allowed all cultures, except the too barbarous and cruel, to coexist, giving each a place within the general pattern which they called the Aryan culture. The modern age can draw some inspiration from the ancients so far as the co-existence of religions and cultures goes. Of course, one should not blindly accept everything of the past.

The criticism of caste system is that it prevented the groups from changing their professions and social and religious forms. The principle which has to be evolved by modern thinkers for coexistence of differences should avoid this mistake of preventing all change and, therefore, progress of any culture or religion. This is as important as to allow each to continue in its own way.

VIII

Ethics and Mokṣa

Following he Dharmasāstras, the English word 'ethics' is used in this paper in its wide sense covering all forms of prescribed conduct, including the religious and secular. The word *dharma* in the Dharmasāstras covers all.

The question of the relation between *karmayoga* and *mokṣa* may be thought by some to lie outside the scope of this paper; then they may treat this section as an appendix. But this is a problem which the Dharmasāstras left unsolved, except saying that this *yoga* also leads to *mokṣa*. For instance, the *Yogasūtra* of Patañjali has a definite description and theory of the state of *mokṣa*, the nature of the world, and the relation between the two. On the basis of this description and theory, it tells us how *mokṣa* can be attained by following the methods prescribed. But the Dharmasāstras have given nothing of the kind. The Mīmāṁsā, from which they drew their inspiration, was not at first concerned at all about *mokṣa*; but later it said that performance of actions according to Vedic injunctions and in a spirit of non-attachment will bring *mokṣa*. But we are not given enough information about the processes that intervene between the performance of such actions and the state of *mokṣa*.

In this section only a few of the points that need consideration can be mentioned, as they are too many to permit the inclusion of all. And these points also will be mentioned in their relevance to the problem of the relation between ethics and *mokṣa*.

1. *Mokṣa* is a spiritual ideal. It is to be inwardly realized, not outwardly. It is said to be the original perfect state of the Ātman, and that is the most inward being of man.

2. Ethics is concerned with *dharma*. It is not necessary to refer to all the meanings of the word *dharma* for our purpose. They are many. Here we are concerned with the meaning in which the word is used in the Dharmasāstras, which are based on the Mīmāṁsā. For Jaimini, the author of the Mīmāṁsā-sūtras, it is action according to the injunctions of the Veda. The Dharmasāstras added actions according to the injunctions of the Smṛtis, well-established customs and one's own satisfactions. If we generalize, we may say that it is action according to some injunction, and in cases in which specific injunctions are not present, according to one's desires. In any case, it is action, which is concerned with reality outward to man.

3. Now, while *mokṣa* is concerned with the inwardness of man, *dharma* is concerned with his outwardness. Man's conscious being has two directions, inwardness and outward-

ness. *Mokṣa* is concerned with the former, and *dharma* with the latter. *Mokṣa* is the realisation of complete inwardness, which is differently understood by the schools, and which the Dharmasāstras do not explain at length. *Dharma* is the realization of perfect outwardness as embodied in social relationships.

The problem for us is to understand how perfection in the realization of outwardness can lead to perfection in the realization of inwardness. The former is attained through action, and the latter through cessation of all action. Now, we are not concerned with the answers given by the Vedāntic schools, which do not give *karmayoga* a place equal to that of *jñānayaoga* or *bhaktiyoga*. We want the answer from the Karmayogins themselves, but we do not find one which is satisfactory and adequate. If it is said that *karman* ceases to have effects after knowledge of the Ātman is attained, then it is tantamount to saying that *jñānayoga* is primary and *karmayoga* secondary. But this is not consistent with the Mīmāṁsa position. Moreover, the modern man wants to justify the necessity of ethical action for every one, and so has to take up the thread of the argument of the Mīmāṁsā and develop it further.

The development requires that (1) the perfection of outwardness is identical with the perfection of inwardness, (2) both of them have objective validity and inwardness is not merely subjective and (3) both of them have universal validity. The perfection of inwardness is not private to the individual, but is a state of existence common to all, and perfection of outwardness, which is the attainment of complete *dharma*, is identical with it and is also a state common to all. An additional requirement then follows, namely, (4) that the perfection of inwardness is best attained through action (*karman*), through which perfection of outwardness is attained.

4. From the standpoint of *mokṣa* then, ethics is to be an inwardising discipline. From the standpoint of sociology and humanism, ethics is a discipline meant for social and human welfare. Both society and the individual are objective facts,

and the criteria of social and individual welfare are objectively available. But the criterion of true inwardness, which is not merely subjective and imaginary, is not so easily available. Man's own subjective and imaginary states may be mistaken for true inwardness.

For attaining inwardness, there should be no other way than to be ethical, and go through ethical activity. Here can be the necessity for ethics in true spiritual realization. And here are two presuppositions: (1) ethics is an inwardising agency; (2) it alone confers objectivity on inwardness, and makes it true. In the words of modern existentialists, which are very apt here, the inwardness attained through activity alone can be truly 'authentic' or genuine, because it coincides with the objectivity involved in practical activity. There is only one way of testing the authenticity of man's true inwardness, and that is his activity. Otherwise, as he alone can know it, he may be mistaken. Others cannot enter his mind.

5. Thus only can the necessity of ethics for spirituality be established. But there is the necessity of religion for ethics also. Man is a reflective animal; and he reflects through and on his experience. He wants justification of ethical laws, proofs for their validity. We have seen that a stage is reached in the moral development of the individual when he is prepared to go, in the very name of ethics and justice, against established laws and flout social approval and praise. Then what can be the criterion of his activity?

Established laws are violated either secretly or boldly and openly. Those who violate laws in a cowardly fashion are the small men, who accept the law but disobey it stealthily. The other kind are the outlaws and reformers. Openly and boldly they go against the law. That is why people treat them as heroes. But in the outlaw, transgression is motivated by his ego, activated by egoistic motives. He becomes an outlaw through personal considerations. But the reformer, religious, social or political, is activated by impersonal or universal considerations. Egoism is absent in the reformer, but present in the outlaw.

It is here that religion, understood as spirituality, is necessary for ethics. Religion demands the surrender of the ego, its negation through universalization. This is what is wanted also in those men who are social, political and legal reformers. All of them should put the question to themselves: "Am I motivated in fighting for this reform by any selfish egoistic interest?" They should be able to get from their head and heart the answer: "No". It is not the success of their fight that is the criterion of their morality, but the negation of their ego behind their activity. Political reforms may be introduced for perpetuating a man or party in power; and social reforms may be introduced to legalise one's activity, which otherwise will be illegal and even immoral. All these acts are unethical. At the highest level of ethical perfection, self-surrender, negation or cancellation of the ego, is the only criterion. And again, this can be applied only by every man to himself alone. Application of this criterion is necessary whether the leader is an atheist or believes in the Universal Spirit. Here, at this juncture, one can appreciate the modern existentialist criterion that 'sincerity to oneself' is the primary criterion of morality.

This way of approaching the problem should reconcile the Mīmāṁsā with the Vedānta. For the Mīmāṁsā, realization of the Ātman is not even a *dharma*; it is not a *codanā* (injunction) to do *karman* (action), without which there can be no *dharma*. Its value is subsidiary, because one who performs *dharma* should know what he is, that he is the agent etc., of the *karman*. So this is taken for granted, just as the Vedānta takes for granted that one who attempts realisation of the Ātman is already ethically disciplined and has realised *dharma*, if not in this life, at least in the past. The basic difference between the two schools lies here: the Mīṁāmsā understands the Ātman not only as a plurality, but also as an active agent, and, therefore, as the ego; but the Vedānta understands the ego as different from the Ātman. But if ethics at its highest stages requires man to transcend his ego's particularlity, annul it, and rise to the level of universality, we have to accept the distinction, and say that his cancellation of the ego is necessary for ethics in its highest stages.

Then religion is necessary for ethics, and ethics is an agency for true and objective inwardisation of man's conscious being. Then from the spiritual standpoint, all ethical actions, not only at the highest level, but also at lower levels, are graded attempts at universalising the ego and so at inwardising man's being.

6. At the highest level therefore a great deal of self-analysis and care are needed to test the authenticity of the universality of one's ethical consciousness and sincerity of one's motives. This may be called ethical psycho-analysis, performed not on others but on oneself. It is here that anxiety has ethical value. It is anxiety not only about one's motives, but also about the authenticity of the universality of one's consciousness. About authenticity, there may be another mistake, which also is a source of anxiety. So far as one's knowledge goes, its universality may be authentic; but because of man's finitude and ignorance, it may not be truly universal and not truly authentic. The leader may sincerely think that the law he is introducing will certainly promote social welfare, like the Christian missionaries to whom McDougall refers; but he might have miscalculated. But we cannot treat him as unethical for that reason. Gandhi admitted his 'Himalyan blunders', which are sincere miscalculations. At the highest level, therefore, authenticity, sincerity and inner motives become more important than external consequences, because ethics is approaching spiritual inwardness more consciously.

7. Because of this inwardness and the negative criterion involved, religion cannot supply positive content to ethical laws. The source of ethical laws are social institutions, human relationships and nature. The positive content of laws is to be derived from their study. But for one who frames the laws and inter-relates them, and for one who applies them, the negative criterion also is necessary. There can be no syllogistic deduction of ethical laws from the nature of the Universal Spirit, which is acknowledged to be beyond all description by

almost all religions. What is beyond description, beyond the reach of mind and speech, cannot constitute the major premise of any syllogism.

References

1. My teacher in Navya-Nyāya, M.M. Sri Sankar Tarkaratna, was fond of telling us that his own teacher would challenge every scholar to argue with him on any philosophical point, giving him any position to defend, but would refuse to argue on any point of the Dharmaśāstras, the rules of which he regarded as sacrosanct and inviolable. This is real orthodoxy.
2. *H.D.*, Vol. I. p. 8.
3. *Man.* & Yaj., p. 2. (Butterworth and Co., Calcutta, 1930).
4. *H.D.*, Vol. I, p. 87.
5. *H.D.*, Vol. II, p. 399; Vol. IV, p. 117.
6. *H.D.*, Vol. III, p. 838.
7. McDougall *Social Psychology*, p. 233.
8. *Social Institutions,* p. 713. (Prentice-Hall Inc. New York, 1947).

Bibliography

1. Aiyer, P.S.S. "Caste." *Hindu Moral Ideals*, Delhi: Nag Publishers, 1976.

2. Altekar, A.S. " Woman and Religion." *Woman in Hindu Civilization*, Delhi: Motilal Banarasidas, 1962.

3. Aurobindo. "Religion and Spirituality." *Foundations of Indian Culture*, Pondicherry: Aurobindo Ashrama, 1975.

4. Basham, A.L. "The Administration of Justice." *The Wonder That was India*, Calcutta: Rupa & Co. 1989.

5. Bhattacharya, D.C. "Penances and Vows." *Cultural Heritage of India*, vol. II. Calcutta: Institute of Culture, 1962.

6. Chakkanatt, J. "Indian Pilgrim Tradition." *Tirtha-yātrā*, Bangalore: Dharamarama Publications, 1991.

7. Derrett, J.D.M. "Custom and Law in Ancient India." *Religion, Law and the State in India*, Delhi: Oxford University Press, 1999.

8. Ghurye, G.S. "Life after Death." *Religious Consciousness*, Bombay: Popular Prakashan, 1965.

9. Hiriyanna, M. "The Origin of Religion." *Outlines of Indian Philosophy*, Delhi: Motilal Banarasidas, 1993.

10. Jois, M.Rama. "Interpretation of Dharamśāstra." *Legal and Constitutional History of India*, vol. I. Bombay: N.M. Tripathi & Co. 1990.

11. Kane, P.V. "The Funeral Rites." *History of Dharma-śāstra*, vol. IV. Poona: Bhandarkar Oriental Research Institute, 1973.

12. Maine, M.S. "The Sacred Laws of the Hindus." *Early Law and Customs*, Delhi: B.R. Publishing Corporation, 1985.

13. Max Muller, F. "The Smārta Sūtras." *History of Ancient Sanskrit Literature*, Varanasi: Chow-khamba Sanskrit Series Office, 1968.

14. Mees, J.H. "Hierarchy." *Dharma and Society*, Delhi: Gian Publishing House, 1986.

15. Mulla, D.F. "Sources of Hindu Law." *Principles of Hindu Law*, Bombay: N.M. Tripathi & Co., 1982.

16. Murti, K.S. Ethics and Politics in Hindu Culture, *Indian Spirit*, Waltair: Andhra University, 1965.

17. Mutwani, Kewal. "The Family Economic Institution." *Manu Dharmaśāstra – A Sociological and Historical Study*, Madras: Ganesh & Co., 1958.

18. Pandey, R.B. "The Saṁskāras." *Hindu Samskaras*, Delhi: Motilal Banarasidas, 1976.

19. Prabhu, P.N. "The System of the Ashramas." *Hindu Social Organisation*, Bombay: Popular Prakashan, 1979.

20. Radhakrishnan, S. "The Stages of Life." *Hindu View of Life*, Delhi: Harper Collins, 1993.

21. Raja, C.K. "Manu." *Poet-Philosophers of the Ṛgveda*, Madras: Ganesh & Co., 1963.

22. Raju, P.T. "Dharmaśāstras and the Modern Age." *Journal of Gaganath Jha Resaerch Institute*, Allahabad, 1959.

23. Rangaswami Aiyanger, K.V. "Ancestor Worship." *Kṛtyakalpataru-Śrāddhakāṇḍa (ed.)—Introduction*. Baroda: Oriental Institute, 1950.

24. Shastri, D.S. "*The Theory of Adoption.*" Calcutta: University of Calcutta, 1909.

25. Swain, Brajakishore. "The Dharmaśāstra: An Introductory Analysis." *History of Dharmaśāstra in a Nutshell*, Puri: Post-Graduate Dept. of Dharmaśāstra, Sri Jagannath Sanskrit University, Puri, 2002.

26. ——. "Śrāvakācāra." *Śrī Jagannath Jyoti*, vol.VIII. Puri: Śri Jagannath Sanskrit University, 2003.

27. ——. "Influence of Dharmaśāstra on the Vaiṣṇavism of Orissa." *Sri Jagannath Jyoti*, vol.VII. Puri: Sri Jagannath Sanskrit University, 2002.

28. Tīrtha, Swami Bharati Krishan. *The Sanatana Dharma*, Bombay: Bhartiya Vidya Bhavan, 1970.

29. ——. "Sacrifice." *The Sanatana Dharma*, Bombay: Bharatiya Vidya Bhavan, 1970.

30. Verma, V.P. "The Rājadharma." *Metaphysical Background of Hindu Political Thought*, Patna: L.N. Agrawal.

31. Virdi, P.K. "The Marriage and Law of Divorce." *The Grounds for Divorce in Hindu and English Law*, Delhi: Motilal Banarasidas, 1972.

Index

☆ ☆ ☆